Major Inflations in History

The International Library
of Macroeconomic and Financial History

Series Editor: Forrest H. Capie

Professor of Economic History
and Head of the Department of Banking and Finance
The City University Business School, London

1. Major Inflations in History
    Forrest H. Capie

Future titles will include:

Financing Industrialization (Volumes I and II)
Rondo Cameron

International Banking
Geoffrey Jones

Deficits and Debts
Geoffrey E. Wood and Lakis C. Kaounides

Financial Crises
Michael Bordo

Price Controls
Hugh Rockoff

Monetary Regime Transformations
Barry Eichengreen

Major Inflations
in History

Edited by

Forrest H. Capie

Professor of Economic History
and Head of the Department of Banking and Finance
The City University Business School, London

An Elgar Reference Collection

Published by
Edward Elgar Publishing Limited
Gower House
Croft Road
Aldershot
Hants GU11 3HR
England

Edward Elgar Publishing Company
Old Post Road
Brookfield
Vermont 05036
USA

British Library Cataloguing in Publication Data
Major inflations in history.– (An Elgar reference
  collection) (The International library of macroeconomic
  and financial history v. 1)
  1. Inflation. History
  I. Capie, Forrest *1940–*
  332.41

Library of Congress Cataloguing in Publication Data
Major inflations in history/edited by Forrest H. Capie.
      p. cm. – (The International library of macroeconomics and
  financial history) (An Elgar reference collection)
    Includes bibliographical references.
    1. Inflation (Finance)–History. I. Capie, Forrest. II. Series.
  III. Series: An Elgar reference collection.
  HG229.M425 1991
  332.4′1–dc20   90–27557
                                                                        CIP

ISBN 1 85278 402 4

Printed in Great Britain by Galliard (Printers) Ltd, Great Yarmouth

Contents

Acknowledgements

The editor and publishers wish to thank the following who have kindly given permission for the use of copyright material.

American Economic Association for articles: B. Nogaro (1948), 'Hungary's Recent Monetary Crisis and its Theoretical Meaning', *American Economic Review*, **38**, pp.526–42; M. Friedman (1951), 'The Role of War in American Economic Development: Prices, Income and Monetary Changes in Three Wartime Periods', *American Economic Review*, **41** (2), pp.612–25.

Basil Blackwell Ltd. for article: J. Robinson (1938), 'Review of Bresciani-Turroni's *The Economics of Inflation*', *Economic Journal*, **48**, pp.507–13.

Cambridge University Press for articles: E.J. Hamilton (1977), 'The Role of War in Modern Inflation', *Journal of Economic History*, **37** (1), pp.13–19; G.E. Makinen (1986), 'The Greek Hyperinflation and Stabilization of 1943–1946', *Journal of Economic History*, **46** (3), pp.795–805.

Elsevier Science Publishers B.V. for article: F. Capie (1986), 'Conditions in which Very Rapid Inflation has Appeared', *Carnegie-Rochester Conference Series on Public Policy 24*, pp.115–68.

Foundation for Economic Education, Inc. for excerpt: A. Dickson White (1959), *Fiat Money Inflation in France*, pp.23–124.

John Wiley & Sons, Inc. for article: A.C. Huang (1948), 'The Inflation in China', *Quarterly Journal of Economics*, **62**, pp.562–75.

C. Maier for his own article (1978): 'The Politics of Inflation in the Twentieth Century', in F. Hirsch and J.H. Goldthorpe (eds.), *The Political Economy of Inflation*, chapter 2, pp.37–72.

Ohio State University Press for articles: R. Jacobs (1977), 'Hyperinflation and the Supply of Money', *Journal of Money, Credit and Banking*, **9** (2), pp.287–303; S. Webb (1985), 'Government Debt and Inflationary Expectations as Determinants of the Money Supply in Germany', *Journal of Money, Credit and Banking*, **17** (4), part 1, pp.479–92.

University of Chicago Press for articles and excerpts: M. Lerner (1954), 'The Monetary and Fiscal Programs of the Confederate Government 1861–65', *Journal of Political*

Economy, **62**, pp.506–22; C. Campbell and G. Tullock (1954), 'Hyperinflation in China 1937–49', *Journal of Political Economy*, **62**, pp.236–45; M. Lerner (1955), 'Money, Prices and Wages in the Confederacy 1861–65', *Journal of Political Economy*, **63**, pp.20–40; F.T. Lui (1983), 'Cagan's Hypothesis and the First Nationwide Inflation of Paper Money in World History', *Journal of Political Economy*, **91** (6), pp.1067–74; W.A. Bomberger and G.E. Makinen (1983), 'The Hungarian Hyperinflation and Stabilization of 1945–1946', *Journal of Political Economy*, **91** (5), pp.801–824; B.D. Smith (1985), 'Some Colonial Evidence on Two Theories of Money: Maryland and the Carolinas', *Journal of Political Economy*, **93** (6), pp.1178–1211; T.J. Sargent (1982), 'The Ends of Four Big Inflations', in R.H. Hall (ed.) *Inflation Causes and Effects*, pp.41–97; P. Cagan (1956), 'The Monetary Dynamics of Hyperinflation', in M. Friedman (ed.) *Studies in the Quantity Theory of Money*, pp.25–117.

Unwin Hyman Ltd. for excerpt: C. Bresciani-Turroni (1937), 'The National Finances, the Inflation and the Depreciation of the Mark', in C. Bresciani-Turroni (ed.) *The Economics of Inflation*, chapter 11, pp.42–106.

Walter de Gruyter & Co. for excerpt: C.L. Holtfrerich (1986), 'The Determinants of Monetary Expansion', in C.L. Holtfrerich (ed.) *The German Inflation 1914–1923: Causes and Effects in International Perspective*, chapter 5, pp.108–37.

Every effort has been made to trace all the copyright holders but if any have been inadvertently overlooked the publishers will be pleased to make the necessary arrangement at the first opportunity.

In addition the publishers wish to thank the Library of the London School of Economics and Political Science and the Librarian and staff at The Alfred Marshall Library, Cambridge University, for their assistance in obtaining these articles.

Introduction

As the title of this volume implies, this collection of essays shifts the emphasis from hyperinflation as commonly defined to a wider range of experience. It directs attention to all the known episodes in world history before 1950 of very rapid annual rates of inflation – something greater than 100 per cent. (I return below to the reason for choosing that round number.) The main purpose of the volume is to bring together the important articles on this subject so that the student/researcher has to hand a comprehensive historical and geographical coverage. Strangely, although the great concentration of such episodes came in the 1920s and 1940s, *relatively* little contemporary attention was given to them in the economic journals. Part of the explanation undoubtedly lies in the fact that there were other large issues competing for attention. But in the last 20 years, when the entire world has been on fiat money following the Americans' severing their link with gold, inflation has burgeoned around the world, in many instances in excess of 100 per cent per annum. These more recent experiences have led economists to return to an examination of the earlier episodes. Many of the best articles have thus appeared in the last decade or so which explains why some have been chosen for inclusion in this collection.

The emphasis in this volume is on the origins and experience of such rapid inflations rather than on how they were brought to an end. Being of great importance, this last issue is not wholly ignored. But readers are also directed to a second (and supplementary) volume in this series on the subject of monetary regime transformations. It does, of course, range further afield than extreme inflations.

A principal objective of this volume is to provide the basis for forming some view on how rapid inflations have arisen and perhaps, therefore, how they might be avoided. It may be that rapid inflation is of the same breed as ordinary inflation. Or it may be that it is quite different. The extreme cases have often been used as the basis for testing various monetary hypotheses as well as for some policy-making.

The coverage of inflation here is determined by the rate. A great many adjectives have been used to describe differing inflationary experiences including acute or chronic (not always correctly to mean persistent), galloping and hyper. Obviously all the terms are relative. The principal justification in defining rapid inflation as a rate in excess of 100 per cent per annum is that this rate has been equalled or 'bettered' in much of the 1960s, 1970s and 1980s. Therefore in seeking to understand these recent cases we should be familiar with other similar experiences. A further justification lies in Cagan's finding that when governments sought to exploit an inflation tax, the elasticity of demand for money was such that they were able to maximize revenue when inflation rates exceeded 100 per cent per annum. There are many other definitions of high inflation and it is largely a matter of taste or purpose as to which one chooses (see p.4 below).

The three essays in Part I of this volume reflect the three emphases mentioned earlier of the sources, experience and termination of rapid inflations: the first (Capie) provides an historical survey emphasizing origins; the second (Cagan) the basis of much theoretical discussion and empirical testing; and the third (Sargent) an interesting hypothesis on their termination. Thereafter the essays are grouped chronologically in three parts, dealing in turn with the pre-twentieth century experience and then the major bursts in the 1920s and 1940s.

The first section gives the basis of the discussion and needs a little fuller comment. My own essay explicitly deals with the origins of rapid inflation, ranging over most of the pre-1950 cases and providing an historical survey. Basically the article suggests that, contrary to quite widespread belief, rapid inflations are not so much the consequence of war as of civil war or serious social unrest. The reason for this is that while governments often print money recklessly in wartime, being united against the common enemy, the populace is persuaded to behave in a patriotic fashion and to abide by a variety of controls, and so inflation is restrained. However with civil disorder or the extreme case of civil war, the established government tries to placate the disaffected by printing money. It prints money because of static or declining tax revenue. There are of course many problems with this approach, particularly that of assessing when a government is weak or when the opposition to it is strong. These are relative but unquantifiable terms. Although civil strife has, historically, obtained in most cases of severe inflation, the detailed investigation of individual cases shows many contributory factors at work.

Germany is the country whose 1920s experience has probably been more intensively researched than any other. The most thorough early studies (such as Graham, 1930) laid great stress on the dreadful burden that reparations imposed on the German economy and on domestic economic policy respectively. A more recent study (Webb, 1985) has also blamed reparations for trapping the Germans in that hyperinflation experience. Against that is the work of Holtfrerich who identifies those circumstances of the early 1920s which led the monetary authorities to take the easy option – an inflation tax.

One of the principal objects of interest in early studies of such inflation was to discover whether the quantity theory stands up when conditions are extreme. Cagan's examination of the 1920s and 1940s is essentially concerned with stability of the demand for money when inflation was running at rates of more than 50 per cent per month. His test was of real money balances depending on inflationary expectations (in this case adaptive expectations). Exogenous monetary growth produces price rises and these affect expectations. The latter then induce further monetary expansion, and so on. As Cagan put it more recently, 'Extreme increases in the price level cannot occur without commensurate increases in the money stock. Governments resort to issuing money rapidly when they are unable to contain expanding budget expenditures...' (Eatwell (ed.), *Money*, p.180). A host of studies of various aspects of Cagan's original model followed, many of them concerned to establish particular econometric relationships. A great deal of effort, for instance, has gone into examining the nature of the feedback from prices to monetary growth. Other issues are the behaviour of the monetary authorities in their attempts to raise maximum revenue from the inflation tax, and the question of whether such hyperinflations become unstable.

Finally in Part I we have Sargent's hypothesis on how hyperinflation comes to an end. Sargent argues against the quantity theory by saying that monetary growth does not have to lead to inflation, illustrating this by reference to the major inflations of the twentieth century. Successful termination of these came about when a credible regime transformation was effected. In other words, when it became clear that the authorities' fiscal regime could quickly halt the need to print money, the inflation stopped. In a fiat money regime an appropriate fiscal policy can back the money stock. In spite of many difficulties with the hypothesis, it does lead to an interesting way of re-examining extreme inflations. (Some of the papers in Parts III and IV are indeed specific case re-examinations.) This view propounded by Sargent conflicts with that of Cagan and of firm-line monetarists who insist that rapid inflation can only be halted when monetary support for it is withdrawn.

Part II provides a wide historical and geographic survey of pre-twentieth century rapid inflationary experiences. These range from brief treatments of important episodes to lengthy expositions of particular instances. We know that some very serious inflationary episodes have occurred in the distant past, but data deficiencies have precluded serious investigation. We also know that some periods of so-called catastrophic inflation have in fact not been as serious as often painted. For example, inflation is often said to be disastrous and a major cause of decline in the last century of the Roman Empire. However, scholarly qualitative accounts of the data available all point to annual inflation rates of no more than 3 per cent or so over the century as a whole. (There would of course have been fluctuations around that trend.) The same applies to the great Tudor inflation – a long period of what by current standards were low inflation rates, again no more than 5 per cent or so.

On the other hand, twelfth and thirteenth-century China does seem to have experienced very rapid inflation, described in a short paper by Lui. Smith then deals with two aspects that are central to the topic, arguing that great monetary expansion occurred in the eighteenth century without the accompanying inflation that quantity theorists insist on. Several studies of similar instances of monetary expansion have appeared in recent years and gained some acceptance. However other studies have strongly refuted this possibility.

In spite of serious data deficiencies, particularly on specie, McCallum has recently (1990) set out to resolve the controversy. Describing the dispute as between classical and anti-classical positions, he claims that it is not primarily about the response of prices to money changes, but rather about 'whether or not there were substantial money stock changes associated with measured changes that pertain to paper currency alone' (p.24). McCallum shows that by estimating normal real balances the large majority of episodes studied provide support for the classical or quantity theory position.

Hamilton explicitly takes up the issue of war and shows that war in itself did not always bring inflation. Indeed, where a commodity standard was adhered to, a successful war could be waged with the price level held constant. There are many examples. The long study by White on France in the years of revolution is remarkable. White was an historian, diplomat and professor of history at the University of Michigan when aged only 25. The essay on inflation in France, written in 1876 and revised several times, is a classic and could hardly be faulted even by a contemporary quantity theorist. As the foreword to the 1959 edition states:

> The arguments of the inflationists then and now are essentially the same. The inflation... was to pay off a debt and finance a budgetary deficit.... Inflation was to be the 'short road to prosperity'. The great want of the country was thought to be a 'shortage' of the circulatory medium.

White demonstrates with great lucidity that the issue of paper money following deficit finance can have only one consequence, and that is inflation at least as great as the excess issue.

The papers by Friedman and Lerner describe the difficulties of trying to finance expenditure in the American civil war – with and without a decent tax base – by examining the experiences in the North and the Confederacy in the 1860s.

Turning to the twentieth century in Part III, the emphasis is on Germany. (As already indicated, other inflations are extensively treated in Cagan and Sargent.) The German experience has certainly received most intensive researching. The classic study of Bresciani-Turroni appeared in 1937 and no survey of hyperinflation is complete without reference to it. Bresciani-Turroni rejected the view current in the 1920s that reparation payments caused the mark to collapse which in turn led to inflation. He shifted attention to the monetization of the huge budget deficit. Joan Robinson's review of Bresciani-Turroni is interesting for its complete rejection of the quantity theory and its insistence that rising money wages cause inflation. Nor is she alone in disputing this view.

Holtfrerich is the modern authority on German inflation and his work refocuses attention, not on reparations, but on the inflation tax. Holtfrerich ranges over the political, social and economic spheres in a highly eclectic consideration of causes and effects. In his view money supply is not a direct determinant, but rather variations in the demand for money. But going beyond proximate determinants, it was deficit financing that flowed from political instability, military defeat and revolution. Yet currency stabilization in 1919 would have brought about gains to the rentier class that could hardly have been tolerated in the conditions of the time. Maier ranges more widely geographically and temporally and brings out various political aspects. His is a timely reminder that not nearly enough attention has been given to the political economy of hyperinflation. There are gainers from inflation (debtors) and if they are a group possessing political clout (leaving aside the fact that the biggest debtors are usually governments), then we should expect to see inflation result from the use of this political clout.

Finally in Part IV we consider the 1940s when several geographically scattered countries – Hungary, Greece and China – experienced rapid inflation. The studies by Nogaro, Huang, and Campbell and Tulloch on Hungary and China were written almost contemporaneously, while those of Makinen and Bomberger are more recent attempts to examine new hypotheses and use more recently developed techniques. They specifically analyse the hypothesis of Sargent and conclude that, in the worst of all inflations (Hungary 1946), price stabilization was achieved by fiscal rather than monetary measures.

It is salutory to recognize that in the late twentieth century inflation is more endemic around the world than at any time previously. Moreover, the rates of inflation in many countries approach those of some of the worst experiences of the past. Hazlett's summing up in his foreword to White is worth repeating:

> Perhaps the study of other great inflations — of John Law's experiments with credit in France between 1716 and 1720; of the history of our own Continental currency between 1775 and 1780; of the Greenbacks of our Civil War; of the great German inflation which culminated in 1923 – would help to underscore and impress that lesson. Must we from this appalling and repeated lesson draw once more the despairing conclusion that the only thing man learns from history is that man learns nothing from history? Or have we still time enough, and sense enough, and courage enough, to be guided by these dreadful lessons from the past.

That was written in 1959. Since then there have been more cases of rapid inflation than in the entire history of the world prior to that date.

References
Constantine Bresciani-Turroni (1937), *The Economics of Inflation: A Study of Currency Depreciation in Post War Germany*, London.
Phillip Cagan (1987, 1989), 'Hyperinflation' in John Eatwell, Murray Milgate, Peter Newman (eds.), *Money* (from The New Palgrave, Macmillan).
Frank D. Graham (1930), *Exchange, Prices and Production in Hyperinflation: Germany, 1920–23*, New York.
Bennett T. McCallum (1990), 'Money and Prices in Colonial America: A New Test of Competing Theories', Carnegie Mellon Mimeo.

Part I
The Sources, Development and Ending of Major Inflations

[1]

Carnegie-Rochester Conference Series on Public Policy 24 (1986) 115-168
North-Holland

CONDITIONS IN WHICH VERY RAPID
INFLATION HAS APPEARED*

FORREST CAPIE

City University, London

In what circumstances has hyperinflation or very rapid inflation occurred? That is the central question of this paper. The guiding investi-
gative line is that government deficits and consequent monetary expansion
are the likely conditions. Most studies of hyperinflation have concentrated on the course of the inflation or on how it was brought to an end or
on other aspects. This paper shifts the focus to the source of the inflation. The limited and fragile annual data available are suggestive of
the basic hypothesis being vindicated, but there are scores of examples of
such conditions and relatively few cases of hyperinflation. What is the
missing essential element in the story? This historical account presents
the suggestion that severe civil disorder (or perhaps weak government) has
been the critical element. Grave social unrest or actual disorder provokes
large-scale spending by the established authority in an attempt either to
suppress or placate the rebellious element. At the same time the division
in society results in a sharp fall in revenue. As Keynes (1923) put it,
inflation "is the form of taxation which the public find hardest to evade
and even the weakest government can enforce when it can enforce nothing
else." The printing press is then brought into action. The data are of
course only suggestive and do not lend themselves to rigorous analysis, and
a more complete investigation of these episodes is obviously required by
specialists in the respective countries concerned.

The organization of this paper is first to provide a definition and
outline briefly the price history of the world. This is followed by consideration of the nature of the data and some short qualitative accounts of
the hyperinflations; an attempt is then made at pulling together the common
elements to see what, if any, common explanation runs throughout. Finally

*I should like to thank Michael Bordo, Ghila Rodrik-Bali, and Geoffrey Wood for comments
on an earlier version.

a brief look at recent experience is set against the historical narrative and analysis.

DEFINITION

The first requirement is a definition of the terms hyperinflation and very rapid inflation. To some extent they are terms which inevitably "will mean what we say they mean." For example, in his now famous study written in 1956, Phillip Cagan wrote, "I shall define hyperinflation as beginning in the month the rise in prices exceeds 50 percent and as ending in the month before the monthly rise in prices drops below that amount and stays below for at least a year". Cagan's definition is now widely accepted by a recently published dictionary of economics suggests that hyperinflation means prices rising at the rate of at least 1000 per cent per month (and the rises might be as fast as 100,000 per cent per month), though this source does not say how many months the rises should last in order to qualify (Pearce, 1981).

If this latter definition were taken to mean average rate of price rise over the period, then of the seven hyperinflations Cagan examined, only one would remain - that of Hungary in 1945-46 where the average monthly rate of price rise was 19,800 per cent. The German episode of 1923 would not qualify since the average rate was only 322 per cent per month. In other words there would be only one hyperinflation in the history of the world. A slightly different definition could dispose of the problem altogether. However, if the definition were relaxed to mean a rise of 1000 per cent in any one month, then the German episode would be included, as would Greece at the end of the Second World War.

If Cagan's precise numerical definition is adhered to, then only the cases of the 1920s and 1940s remain, and as far as can be established no other hyperinflation has occurred anywhere at any time. The recent experience in Latin America and in a handful of other countries in Africa and the Middle East fades into insignificance. However, since one purpose of this paper is to view several of these experiences in relation to the more striking historical cases, Cagan's definition could be relaxed. Staying with his idea of accelerating price increases, what might be called "very rapid inflation" could occur when price rises reach an annual rate of say 100 per cent in any one year. Some justification for the round figure can be found in Cagan, who argues that note issuers seek to maximize revenue.

The elasticity of the demand curve meant that for the seven hyperinflations he examined, the maximum constant revenue was reached when the rates were over 100 per cent per annum[1] (Cagan, 1972, p. 14).

Perhaps no one will ever be entirely satisfied with the choice of definition as a recent attempt that runs into difficulty shows: "...price increases so large that erosion of normal claims is significant in a short period of time if no compensation is forthcoming through cost-of-living linkage." This approach decided on a rate of 20 per cent (Spechler, 1984).

PRICE HISTORY

A brief survey of world price history may be useful in illustrating just how rare the experience of very rapid inflation has been. In the whole course of human history the number of bursts turns out to be very few. Indeed there are only three outside the twentieth century - those of the American War of Independence in the late 1700s, the French Revolution of the 1790s, and the Confederacy in the 1860s. There are accounts in history books of fearful episodes of price rises in ancient times but the inflation rates appear to be low by modern standards. For example the declining Roman Empire was said to be beset with inflation; it was supposedly the major ill of the third century AD.[2] But the price data available suggest a rise from a base of 100 in 200 AD to 5000 by the end of the century - in other words a rate of between 3 and 4 per cent per annum compound.[3] There were undoubtedly other similar experiences around the world. Braudel (1981) for example refers to periods of "catastrophic" inflation under conditions of primitive money but there is a touch of hyperbole here. While the quantity theory is invoked on most occasions, the idea of producing sufficient cows (or observing their increasing velocity of circulation!) or tobacco or even cowrie shells is not consistent

---

[1]There are in fact disagreements about what this figure would be, and Cagan has since pointed out that to measure the maximum revenue requires estimating a money-demand function. But they money supply is not exogenous and so the estimates are unreliable.

[2]Several causes of the inflation has been advanced but chief among them are weak government, civil wars, riots, and general uncertainty (Kent, 1920).

[3]There is nothing in the qualitative accounts to suggest that the price rises were concentrated in any part of the century.

with what is meant by hyperinflation. In any event there are seldom reliable data to peruse let alone to examine these experiences. Indeed, as we
shall note shortly, even for the twentieth century the data are less than
robust and should be treated with extreme caution.

The fact is that from medieval times to the present day, examples of
accelerating and very rapid inflation are few. In the Middle Ages in
Europe, prices moved rather slowly up and down with occasional faster
movements. The measures of prices that are available are far from ideal,
and it is probably the case that some of the apparent inflation observed is
in fact a relative price change - say, in grain as a result of a bad
harvest or even a series of bad harvests. Grain prices were well-recorded
and while grain would also have been important in any price index of the
time, it is doubtful that it is always a good proxy for the general price
level. In any case, the thirteenth to the fifteenth centuries appear to
have been a period of long-term stability.

Sixteenth-century Europe is well-known as a period of high inflation,
when gold flowed in from the New World. Once again, though, by modern
standards the inflation was small. The price level did rise but was fairly
steady over long periods. The rate of increase was most common in the
region of three per cent per annum. In England in the course of 150 years
(1510-1660) the price index rose 350 per cent - an annual average rate of
between two and three per cent. In France the experience was similar.
Spain was the country in Europe through which the precious metals flowed to
the rest of the Continent and prices there rose faster, though only
slightly faster. In Andalusia, the actual point of entry for the bullion,
price rises were the most rapid. In the half century 1550-1600 prices rose
at their fastest rate - by 500 per cent in all; but this is an annual rate
of around 8 per cent.[4]

From around the middle of the seventeenth century until late in the
eighteenth, the world at large was in a period of fairly flat prices.
There were two quite striking examples of rapid inflation, however, towards
the end of the eighteenth century. We return to a fuller account of this
later. One was in the American War of Independence. In the space of under
six or seven years prices rose (in Philadelphia) by 2000 per cent, the time

---

[4]The reason for this particular price behavior is an interesting question. For example,
an initial injection should have raised the price level once and for all and a steady inflow
should have led to a steady state of inflation.

when the phrase "not worth a continental" was coined. The other was the well-known experience of France in the 1790s when assignats were issued.

The nineteenth century opened with the Napoleonic Wars at their height in Europe and America. Although there was undoubtedly inflation, nowhere was it severe by current standards. It was seldom even prolonged. In Philadelphia prices rose by 50 per cent between 1801 and 1814. The highest annual rate recorded in England was 10 per cent and that in only two years, and there is no evidence of very rapid rise in other European countries. The rest of the nineteenth century is generally portrayed as a long period of price stability, and while it is true that there were occasional bursts of inflation nowhere do these qualify for inclusion in our list, except for the Confederacy in the American Civil War.

The experience of the twentieth century, of course, is better known and is entirely different. The first major burst of genuine hyperinflation followed or was coterminous with the First World War. The shock of that experience is thought to have helped produce the political climate and policies that led to stable or falling prices until the Second World War. The second major burst of hyperinflation affected three countries at the end of the Second World War. The experience since then around the world has been unremitting inflation, with price increases reaching rates previously unseen in many OECD countries, and of high and accelerating rates in several developing countries. These latter have reached or are at the present time reaching rates in excess of 100 per cent per annum and, at their most rapid, over 1000 per cent per annum.[5]

DATA

In most areas of historical investigation the problem of data availability arises. When data do exist the first question is what exactly they mean - who collected them from where and for what purpose? In other words, how useful are they for present purposes? Generally the striking feature is the fragile nature of most series. But of course discussion of these matters is essentially dull and sounds negative and the temptation often succumbed to under various rationalizations is to say: "Let's not get too

---

[5]In the nature of things this figure will have risen between the writing of the paper and the reading of it.

bogged down with the difficulties; let's press on with the interesting part, the interpretation: - implicitly, "Let's do something positive." When it comes to the kinds of data available, the dangers of pressing on too quickly are immense and must be constantly held in check.

First of all, availability. The applied economist is often puzzled by the difficulties that seem to be manufactured by the historian. For example, we all known there are tolerably good estimates of total output for most industrial countries for the years from 1850 onwards. It so happens, however, that there are few data for GNP, or any reasonable proxy, for the years surrounding the two bursts of hyperinflation in the twentieth century. Equally, when we turn to government revenue and expenditure and national debt, where the data are commonly both extant and accessible, in the years immediately prior to the period of hyperinflation they are less accessible. Even where data do exist and are presented in reputable collections, they must be approached with great caution. Some data that initially appear to have promise have to be completely rejected for a particular purpose.

Take for example basic data on Germany, the country whose hyperinflationary experience of the 1920s has been most intensively researched. One important source is Graham (1930). The major modern data reference volume is Mitchell (1980) <u>European Historical Statistics 1750-1970</u>. A comparison of the information on government finance from these two sources for two of the few years for which they both have data gives the following:

Government Finance (billions of marks, Germany)

	Mitchell			Graham		
	Tot. Rev.	Tot. Exp.	Deficit	Tot. Rev.	Tot. Exp.	Deficit
1917/18	6.8	45.5	38.7	37.1	53.3	16.2
1918/19	9.7	54.9	45.2	34.2	45.5	11.3

Both authors state that these figures are for the fiscal years ending 31st March 1918 and 1919. The differences in the deficit are serious: Mitchell gives a 17 per cent rise in 1919 over 1918, while Graham shows a fall of over 30 per cent - and this for a country and for years when it might be expected that the figures would be reasonably reliable. A check on Mitchell's revenue column reveals that it is in fact tax revenue only, and while it is not clear what else would be included and that tax revenue is probably the best measure for the budget, this still leaves questions and does not explain the differences in expenditure. A more worrying example is that of Hungary. Mitchell gives the 1920/21 deficit as 9.7m Kronen. The major contemporary source was Young (1925) who gave it as 32,000m Kronen, i.e., a figure over three thousand three hundred times as large. To cite one other, for Poland, Mitchell gives a deficit for 1924 as 481m Zlotys while Young's figure is a 74m surplus. There is no obvious way of reconciling these discrepancies and they leave us apprehensive over much of the data underlying the episodes to be discussed. Similar objections apply to many other series. The main point is that while there may be quite good monetary and price data, there is not much else and no scope for econometric testing.

AN ACCOUNT OF MAJOR EPISODES

The following provides an outline of what happened in eleven historical episodes of very rapid inflation - cases where prior to the 1960s there were the most rapid inflations recorded. The episodes are in eighteenth-century America and France, the United States Civil War in the South in the 1860s, five cases from the early 1920s, and three from the 1940s.

AMERICAN WAR OF INDEPENDENCE

At the beginning of the second half of the eighteenth century, grievances amongst colonists against British administrators (in part over restricted expansion in the West) led under further provocation to open rebellion from 1763-1773. The British felt that the Americans should make a proper contribution to their own defense and other expenses of the Empire and attempted to impose duties on sugar imported by the colonies. Protest and riots followed. More taxes were proposed and some withdrawn. Tensions developed and when in April 1775 a detachment of British soldiers went to Lexington to seize arms, the first action of the American Revolution took place. The declaration of Independence was made in 1776, the British suffered important military defeat in 1781, and in 1783 the peace treaty was signed.[6]

The eight-year rebellion (1775-1783) by the colonists was financed in large part by the issue of paper currency - the Continental - which for the time needed bought the necessary arms and troops to resist the British. In fact it was not a costly war but the Continental Congress, which was the only body representative of the Colonies as a whole, had no power to tax. In any case the Colonists hated taxation. The States could tax and the Congress could requisition funds from the States, but only 6 per cent of the revenue needed over the war years was obtained in this way. Some borrowing was done and several European countries, notably France and Spain, made gifts; but in total this came to less than 20 per cent of revenue. The Continental Congress was left to find the balance and resorted to the issue of paper money. It issued $225m by the end of 1779 and by 1783 eleven states had in addition issued paper to the amount of $246m. The inflow of foreign capital helped to hold up the dollar for a while, but after 1777 it began to depreciate quite rapidly. At some points the depreciating currency threatened to undermine the war effort. There was a call for price controls and a few were imposed but as is usually the case, these were relatively easily evaded.

Prices soared across the eastern colonies. In the Philadelphia market, wholesale prices more than doubled in each of the years 1776, 1777, and 1778. But it was in the following two years, 1779 and 1780, that the most rapid inflation took place and prices rose by over 1000 per cent over the two-year period.

FRANCE

In the case of France in the 1790s the fundamental focus of attention was the national debt. Prices had been rising gently between 1730 and the late 1780s. Then in 1788 a bad harvest drove grain prices up sharply. Many French were reduced to penury, and in the summer of 1789 there was widespread rioting and looting of grain convoys. In 1788, a King's edict proclaimed the creation of new interest-bearing money, but there was a storm of disapproval and the edict was revoked.

The revolution brought a change in attitude toward paper money -

---

[6]It is tempting to see the collapse of the Bretton Woods system in a similar fashion, as reflecting the unwillingness of certain countries to pay the inflation tax the U.S. was levying to "defend the West."

Table I

Value of Assignat 1789 - 1796

	1789	1790	1791	1792	1793	1794	1975	1796
January		96	91	72	51	40	18	.46
February		95	91	61	52	41	17	.36
March		94	90	59	51	36	13.28	
April		94	89	68	43	36	10.71	
May		94	85	58	52	34	1.52	
June		95	85	57	36	30	3.38	
July		95	87	61	23	34	3.09	
August	98	92	79	61	22	31	2.72	
September	98	91	82	72	27	28	2.08	
October	97	91	84	71	28	28	1.36	
November	96	90	82	73	33	24	.77	
December	95	92	77	72	48	20	.52	

Source: Henri Sée, Histoire Economique de la France.

indeed it was quite widely asserted that the people's revolution would be impossible without such a change. The pressure in 1790 for issues of irredeemable paper was immense, and there were discussions on issues of notes based on the property of the church. In April 1790, 400m livres of assignats were issued based on appropriated church land bearing 3 per cent. (One priest threatened people handling such money with eternal damnation, but the majority seemed prepared to run that risk.) This first issue appeared to go quite well. None of the dire short-run consequences prophesied by its opponents materialized, but five months later the government had spent the money. The great statesman Mirabeau, who had once called paper money "a loan to an armed robber," now felt that the French had become more enlightened and that assignats should be created to an amount sufficient to cover the national debt. More and more issues of assignats followed over the next five years so that by 1795 a total of 45,000m livres had been issued, though 6,000m livres had been annulled and burned. The early issues were interest-bearing but they later came to be used as money, and later issues carried no interest and were issued for increasingly smaller denominations. Prices rose rapidly - from 100 in 1790 to 3100 in 1795 (September) and then more dramatically to 38,850 in May 1796 (Harris, 1930).

UNITED STATES

An example of very rapid inflation that has captured much interest is that of the United States in its Civil War. This is in fact better explained by the importance of that country and by the divergent experiences of the North and South than it is by the rate of inflation. The worst inflationary experience came in the eastern part of the Confederacy in the course of 1863 and 1864. Taking January 1861 as the base of 100, the price index had risen to 762 in January 1863 and to 2801 by January 1864. It peaked at 9211 in December 1865. This is very rapid inflation but when translated into percentage monthly changes in the price index, there are not many months when the rate is in double figures and only one when it was over 20 per cent March 1864, when it reached 40 per cent.

The experience in the North was wholly different and the contrast doubtless played an important part in the course of the next fifty years in shaping American economists' views on money. In January 1862 the Federal Congress learned that it was unable to pay for necessary supplies and men. If the rebellion in the South was to be stopped, the Union must meet its outstanding commitments with paper money. Nevertheless there seemed to be no alternative and notes were issued to meet the immediate problem. However, the distaste for the action forced other means of finance and greatest reliance was placed upon taxing and borrowing. Neither of these was popular in the North, as the experience of Alexander Hamilton had shown, but rebellions induce different behavior. In fact the total unbacked note issue amounted only to $450m which was of the order of 16 per cent of the total public debt. The resulting increase in prices was relatively modest - about 20 per cent per annum.

Table 2 presents the course of output and debt for the whole country during the war and immediate post-war years. In the course of the war, the Federal Government deficit rose from $25m to $963m and the public debt rose from $90m to $2,677m. Even by present-day standards, these figures would be quite exciting, a budget deficit of about 15 per cent of GNP. But it lasted only a short time and was converted to a fairly substantial surplus immediately after the war. Total public debt grew considerably but leveled off and fell immediately after the war. In short the experience of the United States in the Civil War was fairly orderly.

The experience in the South captured particular attention. The Confederate Government obtained war supplies by turning to the printing press. According to Lerner (1955) notes in the South increased by 82,600 per cent. Banks were justifiably nervous over this and increased their reserve ratios, but the money supply in the South rose by 1,100 per cent between January 1861 and January 1864. Since output in the South declined somewhat, velocity of circulation obviously increased to produce the price rises that we noted at the beginning.

1920s

The early 1920s are well-known for the exceptional rates of inflation experienced in several countries in central and eastern Europe. There were in fact five countries which at some points between 1919 and 1925 suffered severe inflation bursts. They were Austria, Hungary, Poland, Russia, and Germany, and the respective rates of price rises from the beginning to the end of the hyperinflation were: 14,000, 23,000, 2.5m, 4m, and 1,000m. Most of the rest of Europe suffered some inflation but only in these five cases did inflation soar into these astronomical regions.

Some see the fundamental cause of these inflations as the overwhelming pressure to restore (leaving aside Russia for the moment) some resemblance of the standard of living that had prevailed before the war. The important

Table 2

United States

	Col. 1	Col. 2	Col. 3	Col. 4	Col. 5
				Govt.	
			Consumer	Deficit	Public Debt
	GNP $b.	Real GNP $b.	Price Index	000s $	000s $
1861	3.677	6.613	101	- 25,037	90,582
1862	4.012	6.368	113	-422,775	524,178
1863	5.096	6.542	139	-602,044	1,119,174
1864	6.479	5.960	176	-600,696	1,815,831
1865	6.560	6.296	175	-963,840	2,677,929
1866	6.884	7.017	167	+ 37,224	2,755,764
1867	6.869	7.474	157	+133,091	2,650,168

Source and Notes:

Columns 1 and 2 - Thomas Senior Berry, Ph.D. "Estimated Annual Variations in Gross National Product 1789-1909," The Bostwick Press, University of Richmond 23173, 1968, p. 32.

Column 1:   Estimated GNP in current dollars.

Column 2:   Estimated GNP in constant dollars.

Columns 3, 4 and 5 - Source: Historical Statistics of the United States: Colonial Times to 1970, Part 1 and 2, U.S. Department of Commerce, Bureau of the Consumer, Washington, D.C., 1975.

Column 3:   Ethel D. Hoover: Prices in the 19th Century, National Bureau of Economic Research, New York.

Column 4:   Difference between Federal Government Receipts (where figures relate to years ending June 30) and outlays of the Federal Government (again figures relate to year ending June 30).

Column 5:   Public Debt of the Federal Government. (Figures relate to June 3).

126

point stressed in this argument is the extent of the devastation and the sense of exhaustion that hung over most of Europe at the end of the war. The need to rebuild was urgent and the governments who embarked on reconstruction programs faced massive expenditure and little prospect of raising revenue (Aldcroft, 1977). This is not to say that the inflations were inevitable.

Apart from the strong desire for reconstruction, there were several additional burdens and difficulties faced by these countries. Poland was at war with Russia until 1921. All of the countries faced huge reparation payments and the German burden for all practical purposes proved impossible. In Austria and Hungary there was the problem of huge numbers of administrative personnel left over from the Empire.

In the face of these actual and desired expenditures, taxation was inadequate and the tax system in any case was inefficient. The League of Nations said their technical advisers "were powerless to repress the inefficient accountancy, the slowness with which arrears of taxes were collected and even the wholesale corruption..." Even where there was good intent there quickly came a point where real taxes yielded less than the cost of collection.

In addition to the domestic pressures there was an external one in the form of a growing deficit as imports replaced domestic production and exports were negligible. This put additional pressure on the foreign exchanges, and while the depreciating currency might in normal circumstances have restored equilibrium, in these times there was an inelastic demand for imports and inelastic supply of exports. One slightly offsetting factor at least initially was that the depreciated currency attracted a capital inflow as long as there was a prospect of return to the pre-war parity. As soon as the expectation of return to prewar parity became remote the capital inflow was reversed, the exchange rate weakened further and this added to pressure on prices. In these circumstances, it is not surprising that weak or inexperienced governments succumbed to the attractions of inflationary finance, though in defense of some governments it should be borne in mind that with the Russian Revolution as the backdrop there was a widespread desire to take whatever action needed to avert social unrest. It is ironical, though, that Lenin is said to have looked to the destruction of a country's currency as the quickest road to the overthrow of capitalism.[7] Certainly, it was the printing of money that gave governments the real resources they sought, but the effectiveness of the method declined over time as ever larger issues were required. If there is one thing common to all these countries, it is the weakness of government.[8] In and outside Austria there were general doubts about the viability of that new state. In Germany the new and inexperienced socialist government was thwarted in its attempts to pass tax reforms. In addition, in Germany the suggestion has often been made, and not without foundation, that there was an element that looked to inflation to defeat the reparation burden. One reason this argument is not without foundation is that the Reichsbank could have supported the exchange rate in January 1923 and prevented the collapse of the currency, for its gold reserve was five times the total circulation at existing rates. Poland saw its own experienced officials leave the country and the new state was left without proper civil administration; and added to this was the Policy population's greater-than-average distaste for the tax collector. In the Soviet Union's case the new regime had a clear desire for rapid inflation to wipe out the middle classes and speed the revolutionary cause.

In all five countries in the 1920s the episodes occurred either in new states or new regimes where one problem was of coping with the needs/-desires of the mass of the people for some restoration of their living standards. This was of such a nature that civil war was a distinct possibility or reality. Yet there were at least two countries that faced similar problems which escaped hyperinflation. One was Latvia and the other Czechoslovakia. In these countries rigorous fiscal programs enforced from the beginning of the new republic checked incipient hyperinflation by 1921.

1940s

In the 1940s there were three cases of hyperinflation: Hungary, Greece, and China. These three cases are enlightening in certain ways, especially in relation to what has just been said about the 1920s.

---

[7]"Lenin is said to have declared that the best way to destroy the capitalist system was to debauch the currency. By a continuing process of inflation, governments can confiscate, secretly and unobserved, an important part of the wealth of their citizens ... Lenin was certainly right." J.M. Keynes, The Economic Consequences of the Peace (MacMillan 1920) p. 220. But see Frank W. Felter, "Lenin, Keynes and Inflation" Economic Vol. 44.

[8]Obviously a measure of weakness would be difficult to construct, and it is doubtful if anything could be arrived at that would be an improvement on the qualitative judgment.

The case of Hungary is interesting. This was a country that had experienced hyperinflation in the 1920s and yet in the 1940s went through the most rapid inflation on record at any time anywhere. In the thirteen months between July 1945 and August 1946, prices rose by 3×10^{25}. The reason this episode is of particular interest is that there are distinct similarities between the 1940s and 1920s in Hungary in the conditions surrounding the hyperinflation. In particular there were reparation payments and military expenditures that far out-ran the possibilities for raising revenue. But on this second occasion there was a popular government in power and a central bank that clearly understood the dangers of inflation and warned against them. The interest lies in the role that the Allied Commission played in this, and within the Commission the part played by the Soviet Union. When the Central Bank objected to the huge volume of Treasury Bills issued to finance the inflation, the Soviets turned a deaf ear. Again the suggestion is that the Soviets were happy to see inflation proceed and destroy the middle class (Bomberger and Makinen, 1983).

CHINA

Between 1937 and 1949, China was either at war with Japan or all but cut off from the world and experiencing its own revolution. The Japanese invaded North China and Shanghai in 1937 and by 1949 the Communists under Mao Tse Tung had control of mainland China. When the Japanese attacked, the leader of the Nationalist Government pledged total war without regard to cost, and in the next few years no attempt was made to match increased expenditure with increased revenues. The data are very fragile in a case such as this, but the indices in Tables 3 and 4 of wholesale prices for the whole country together with the cost of living index for Shanghai provide a basic picture.

There were clearly a long and accelerating inflation through these years with prices rising first by 27 per cent then 68 per cent, then more than doubling and so on until in 1947 monthly rates in excess of 50 per cent were reached (Huang, 1948, p. 255). Table 5 presents data on government finance. A budget deficit had opened up consequent to the war with Japan, and industrial and agricultural output had fallen drastically as resources were devoted to the war effort. No sooner was VJ Day over than the Communists and Nationalists began fighting for former Japanese-controlled territory. Civil war had broken out and the already substantial budget deficit began to soar. In the budget of 1946 there was a hugh increase in the military outlay and as the deficit moved from CN$266 to

Table 3

Price Movements in China 1937-49

(Average of Monthly Prices 1937 = 100)

	Wholesale Prices	C of L Shanghai
1937	100	100
1938	127	129
1939	214	172
1940	498	360
1941	1258	-
1942	3785	-
1943	12556	-
1944	41927	-
1945	158362	24978
1946	367406	337601
1947	2617781	3078000

Source: Huang Q.J.E.

Table 4

Inflation in China 1945–48
Percentage Change Over Previous Month

	Wholesale prices	Cost of Living in Shanghai
1945		
October		
November	13.7	131.5
December	4.6	-7.5
1946		
January	-14.1	12.4
February	29.2	73.8
March	23.6	49.2
April	6.1	-2.1
May	12.6	52.1
June	7.8	-1.3
July	10.0	11.2
August	3.4	0.9
September	11.0	9.5
October	15.6	5.1
November	8.4	8.9
December	5.6	13.8
1947		
January	20.4	22.8
February	46.1	55.4
March	10.6	7.4
April	14.0	14.5
May	41.6	62.5
June	26.1	17.9
July	25.8	10.7
August	10.1	12.5
September	11.6	22.9
October	54.6	43.3
November	29.6	8.7
December	34.5	26.9
1948		
January	33.4	51.7
February	33.7	44.4
March	63.5	15.3

Source: Huang

131

Table 5

China

Revenue and Expenditure of the Nationalist Government

1930 - 1948

(1936-37 = 100)

Year		Expenditure	Revenue	Deficit
1930-1		41	43	+2
1936-7		100	100	--
1941-2		429	92	337
1942-3		1331	524	807
1943-4		2767	898	1869
1944-5		9704	3086	6618
1945-6		67221	10890	56331
Calendar	1946	295504	146303	149201
	1947	1901581	1064439	837142
Jan-Jul	1948	36580389	17274079	19306310
Aug-Dec		1587821475	501582876	1086238600

Source: CHOU,S-H.

CN$1, 276b. in 1946, there was an expansion in the money supply; it grew by almost 700 per cent between 1946 and 1947. Price and wage controls introduced in 1947 were largely ineffective. By 1948 the war initiative was passing to the Communists and they entered Peking in 1949. On 1st October of that year the People's Republic was founded.

Over the whole period of war, the money supply grew by 15,000 per cent, wholesale prices rose by over 100,000 per cent, and the difference is made up by the change in velocity - the manifestation of a flight to goods. The vastly increased note issue of the Central Bank of China lay behind the huge expansion in the money supply.

GREECE

The Greek economy was just one that was devastated by war. German occupation lasted from 1940 to 1944, and the government installed by the Germans provided the requirements of the occupation forces. The Germans extracted various payments from the government and progressively these were met by turning to the printing press. Circulation rose from a base of 100 in 1940 to 13,769 and 49,854,000,000 in 1944. The respective cost-of-living figures are 100 in 1940, 34,846 in 1943, and 163,910,000,000 in 1944. The fiscal system broke down for there was, in effect, no recognized government for a large section of the community. By October 1944 when the Germans withdrew, 99 per cent of all expenditures were being covered by note issue. When the British liberated Athens from the Germans in 1944 much of the groundwork had been done by two resistance groups. One group, the Monarchists and the other, the Communists, began fighting each other after the German defeat. The events leading up to the Civil War are obviously much more complicated than this suggests, but for our purposes the point that matters is that monetary anarchy continued and the worst hyperinflation came in the period 1944-1946. British troops were still in Greece and they supported the anti-Communists. Stalin kept to commitments made to Churchill and did not intervene. The result was that although there was renewed fighting in 1947-1949, the outcome was not really in doubt and the pro-Western group won in 1949.

Table 6

	Inflation	Inflation Index	Govt. Finance	Govt. Finance GNP	Balance of Payments	Balance of Payments GNP	GNP
Austria (A)			Mil. of paper crowns	(%)	Schillings 000s	(%)	M. Schillings GDP
1915	60	100	....	.....	-1079	.....	.....
1916	112.5	187.5	....	.....	832	.....	.....
1917	97.06	161.8	....	.....	1113	.....	.....
1918	73.13	121.9	.....	.....	792	.....	.....
1919	115.52	192.5	2,704	.....	3689	.....	.....
1920	104	173.3	10,578	.....	-3089	.....	.....
1921	95.5	159.2	41,118	.....	1708		
1922	2553.1	425.5	137,700	.....	203	.....	.....
1923	312.2	520.2		.....	-2115	-12.2	.....
1924					-1130		9257
Germany (B)			Mil. of Marks				Bil. of gold Marks
1919	.....	.....	-45,155	.....	-1859917	.....	.....
1920	.....	.....	-92,209	-297.4	-469317	-7.97	31
1921	20.2	100	-149,196	-39.6	-1516250	-3.99	38
1922	379.72	1879.8	.....	.....	-185867	-0.55	34
1923	6817.5	3375.0	.....	.....	-3497	-0.013	27
1924	.....	.....	-377	.....	-213362	.....	.....
Hungary (C)			Mil. of Kronen		Courannes or gold crowns, 000s		Mil. of Pengo*
1919	183.8	100	.....	.....	.....	.....	.....
1920	92.85	50.5	.....	.....	-20813	.....	.....
1921	-19.91	-10.8	-32089	.....	-22234	.....	4258
1922	316.9	172.4	-21056	.....	-17442	.....	.....
1923	1336.7	727.3	-69732	.....	-7075	.....	.....
1924	626.07	340.6	-3967930	.....	-10649	.....	.....
1925							5058
Poland (D)			Mil. Zlotys		Zlotys		
1919	.....	.....	.....	.....	.....	.....	.....
1920	.....	.....	.....	.....	.....	.....	.....
1921	130.1	100	.....	.....	.....	.....	.....
1922	206.5	158.7	.....	.....	.....	.....	.....
1923	.....	.....	.....	.....	.....	.....	.....
	.....		.....	.....	-15850	.....	.....
(zlotys prices)					6592		
1924	101.3	101.3 (?)	-481	.....	-17697	.....	.....
1925		.....	.....	.....	-21820	.....	.....

134

Russia (E)	Price Index P 1913 = 100		Rubles		Rubles		
1919	682*	100	.....	.....	-6880	.....	.....
1920	7083.3*	1038.6	.....	.....	-3010	.....	.....
1921	63266.7*	9276.6	.....	.....	-16017	.....	.....
1922	5584476.7*	818838.2	.....	.....	-15741	.....	.....
1923	414684916.6*	60804239.97	.....	.....	5090	.....	.....
1924		.....	-184	.....	7072	.....	.....
1925		.....	-98	.....	-14663	.....	.....

Sources:

Column 1: Index number of retail price; cost of living. Source: League of Nations; Monthly Bulletin of Statistics

Column 2: [Except for Austria.] Source: Mitchell, European Historical Statistics, 1750-1970 Pasvolsky, Leo., Economic Nationalism of the Danubian State, George Allen and Unwin, 1928, p/102

Figure for 1919 is for a period of 6 months

Figure for 1920, 21 relate to a period of one year starting at July 1st and ending at June 30th of the following year.

For Hungary, Column 2: Figures for government finance are given in Pasvolsky but these are in millions of paper crowns whereas the figure presented in the table are in million kronen. Similarly figures for Hungary's balance of Trade are given in Pasvolsky p/319.

Column 3: Source: League of Nations, Monthly Bulletin of Statistics, (1925).

* Monthly figures corrected to annual average from Young, J.P. "1925, European Currency and Finance".

Table 6 (continued)

	Internal Debt	Internal Debt / GNP	External Debt	External Debt / GNP	Exchange Rate	Money	Money (Index)	Central Bank Discount Rate
Austria (A)		(%)		(%)	Millions	Millions		(%)
1915								5.14
1916								5
1917								5
1918								5
1919						Kronen		5
1920					4357.4	30646	100	5
1921					12322.4	174115	568.1	5.92
1922					203225.6	4080177	13313.9	7.67
						Schillings	Schillings	
1923					1447286	713		9
1924								
Germany (B)						Mil. of Marks		
1919					.....	14109	100	5
1920					1463.4	12349	87.5	5
1921					2480.3	8523	60.4	5
1922					44218.5	13663	96.8	6.58
1923					16947.7	860	6.1	38.48
1924					103730.6			10
Hungary (C)	Mil. of Kronen		Mil. of Kronen					
1919	17,475	.....	66,869	.....	.....	.....	.....	.....
1920	27,489	.....	96,854	.....	5848.9	14308	100	.....
1921	57,300	0.108	128,047	0.245	9519.2	25172	175.9	6
1922	82,398	.....	424,246	.....	29308	75887	530.4	8
1923	416,392	.....	3,370,659	.....	219841.8	931337	6509.2	13.64
1924	.....	.....	.....	.....	1417784.3	4513990	31548.7	14.06
1925	.....	.....						
Poland (D)	Bils of Polish Marks		Bils of Polish Marks			Marks + Zlotys		
1919	8.9		.....		.....			
1920	69.3		.....		5350.9	49362	100	6
1921	251.2		.....		49458.1	229538	465	6.33
1922	743.4		.....		173901.1	793437	1607.4	7
1923					17268			
1923 [					403.2	125371955	253984.8	16.98
1924			1,840		100.3	3314000	6713.7	11.41
1925			.....		108.7	2770200	5612	
Russia (E)						Notes in circulation Rubles	Bils	
1919					.....	..... *	100	.....
1920					.....	107.65*	488.06	.....
1921					.....	525.40*	3034.70	.....

136

1922		.....	3266.85*	42087.52	.....
			45307.21*		
1923		107.7			9
1924		101.7	640	100	8.25
1925		99.9	1115	174.2	.....

Column 4: Figures relate to national product. Source: A. case Protopapadakis "The Endogeneity of Money during the German Hyperinflation: A Reappraisal" Economic Inquiry, Vol. 21, No. 1, Jan 1983, p/90.

Column 5: Young, J.P. "1925, European Currency and Finance"

Column 6:

Column 7: Percentage at which cost of $ is at its cost at par. Source: League of Nations, Monthly Bulletin of Statistics (19

Column 8: Notes in circulation. Source: League of Nations, Central Banks 1913-25.

Column 9: League of Nations Monthly Bulletin and Statistics 1925.

?   Rudolf Notel, "Money, Banking and Industry in Interwar Austria and Hungary", Journal of European Economic History (1984)

*   One Pengo = 12,500 Korona.

Table 7

	1 Inflation	2 Govt. Finance	3 Govt. Finance GNP %	3 Balance of Payments	3 Balance of Payments GNP %	4 GNP	5 Internal Debt.	6 External Debt.	7 Exchange Rate	8 Money	8 Money (Index)	1 Inflation (Index)	9 Central Bank Discount Rate
Hungary (A)				Forint 000s		m. Pengos			Forint per $	Mil. Pengos			
1940	8.08	...	...	-87	-37.11	6743			28.769	1387	100	100	3
1941	18.7	...	...	59	20.54	8311			28.935	1984	143.0	231.1	3
1942	16.5	...	...	206	...	10348			...	2958	200.3	204.2	3
1943	19.6	...	...	152	...	15431			...	4392	316.7	242.6	3
1944	23.7	...	...	141	...	...			...	12180	878.2	293.3	3
				Pengo									
1945	...	...	...	-3	...	...			8.519	77×10^4	55515.5	...	3
1946	...	...	...	49	...	12285			...	63×10^4	45421.8	...	3.8
1947	...	...	...	...	...	17007			8.519	968	69.8	...	
Greece		Mil. Drachmas		Drachmas 000s		1000 Mil. Drachmas			Drachmas per $	Mil. Drachmas			
1938	1.00	719	1.17	-4610	-7.52	61.3			0.888	8	100	100	6
1939	-1.00	3	0.005	-3081	-4.83	63.8			0.800	10	125	-100	6
1940	11.00	-1396	...	-3165	...	...			0.661	15	187.5	1100	5.58
1941	14.4	...	...	-485	...	...			...	49	612.5	1140	6
1942	...	...	...	-7184	...	...			...	335	4187.5	...	6.42
1943	...	...	...	-17980	...	...			...	3199	39987.5	308090	6
										New Drachmas			
1944	...	...	...	...	...	...			0.667	2	25(100)		7
1945	380.9	...	...	-1575	...	...			...	104	1300(5200)		7

China	a. %	b. %	Mil of CN$	Mil of CN$	Mil of CN$	%	Bil. of CN$		(a)	(b)
1937	-	-			2,523	28.41	3.6	100	-	-
1938	27	29			3,018	24.94	5	138.9	100	100
1939	68.5	33.3			4,190	22.68	7.4	205.6	253.7	114.8
1940	132.7	-	-3,164*		5,371	22.73	13.5	375	491.5	-
1941	152.6	-	-6,805*		7,747		25	694.4	565.2	-
1942	200.9	-	-17,932		8,712		52	1444.4	744.1	-
1943	231.7	-	-38,636*		8,765		104	2888.9	858.1	-
1944	233.9	-	-117,000*		11,797		270	7500	966.3	-
1945	277.7	-	-266,400*	...	9,396		1,472	40888.9	1028.5	-
1946	132.0	1251.6	-1,276,000*	1647.39	9,910	14.20	8,532	237000	488.9	4315.9
1947	612.5	811.7	-2,222,000*	5454.6	23,393	14.18	55,000	152777.8	2268.5	2798.9

Sources:

Column 1:   Except for China; figures relate to cost of living index
             Source: United Nations, Statistical Yearbook, (1948)

For China, Column 1(a):   Year to Year changes in wholesale prices
               (b):   Year to Year changes in cost of living in Shanghai
             Sources (Columns 1(a) and (b): A.C. Huang "The Inflation in China", Quarterly Journal of Economics, (1948), p. 565.

Column 2:   Source: Mitchell, European Historical Statistics 1750-1970
For China, Column 2:   Sources: Huang, p. 566
             *: Actual figures
             +: These are budgetary figures announced by the Ministry of Finance. The actual deficit is much larger.

Column 3:   Sources: United Nations Statistical Yearbook, 1949-50
Columns 4, 5 and 6:   Source: United Nations Statistical Yearbook, (1940)
Column 7:   U.S. cents per unit of national currency
             Source: United Nations Statistical Yearbook, 1948
Column 8:   Except for China, figures relate to currency in circulation
             Source: United Nations Statistical Yearbook, 1948.
For China, Column 8:   figures relate to money supply
             Source: Huang, p. 569
             The 1947 figure relates to December figure
             The June figure is 20, 390 bill of CN dollars.
Column 9:   Source League of Nations Monthly Bulletin of Statistics 1937-1947

COMMON ELEMENTS

The main purpose of this survey of experience is to see if there are common elements in the conditions in which rapid inflation occurred - some generalizations that might be made - generally of the kind suggested by economic theory. What were the conditions in which inflation appeared and rapidly accelerated? (Tables 6 and 7 bring together some of the basic data that are available on the principal variables that are suggested by the foregoing account.) In most of the qualitative accounts of the episodes there emerge certain variables that are clear contenders for inclusion in the list of "proximate conditions". Obviously increasing money supply is the first of these. Also budget deficits are invariably found in parallel with or preceding the rapid inflation. Not surprisingly growth in public debt is generally found accompanying the growing deficit. Trade deficits, too, sometimes appear since as we have seen, the conditions were generally ones in which imports rose and exports fell as the domestic economy was unable to meet the demands being placed upon it. This was true in spite of floating exchange rates; in some instances where there were flexible rates the depreciating currency has been regarded as a further source, or at least accelerator, of inflationary pressure.

The relatively scarce data available for the eleven cases allow limited comment to be made. The variables sought were: the rate of inflation, budget deficit, balance of payments, public debt, the exchange rate, and the money supply. Columns 1 - 9 of Tables 6 and 7 provide the data for the twentieth-century cases, but the number of gaps and the earlier caution on data reliability remind us that any rigorous testing is impossible and that in the end it is difficult to conclude with any certainty about a number of hypotheses. As can be seen from a glance at column 4, there are frequently no aggregate output data against which to set whatever other data are available. In seeking evidence on the conditions in which hyperinflation occurred, the emphasis in these Tables has been placed on the period immediately prior to the worst phase of the inflation.

The first and striking feature common to all the episodes is that of an unbacked paper currency. It can readily be seen from the Tables that the growth in money supply in all cases was enormous. Such a growth was impossible without a paper currency. Kent (1920) claims that copper-coin debasement at the end of the third century was the main cause of the inflation in the Roman Empire: "Copper coins could very easily be manufactured; numismatists testify that the coins of the fourth century often bear signs of hasty and careless minting; they were thrust out into circulation in many cases without having been properly trimmed or made tolerably respectable. This hasty manipulation of the mints was just as effective as our modern printing presses, with their floods of worthless or nearly worthless money" (Kent, p. 47). But as we have seen the rate of price increase was not on a par with what we have in the cases we examine, and it is not believable that sufficient coins could either be minted or carried around to produce the inflation of modern times.[9] The fact that paper currency was rare prior to the twentieth century undoubtedly explains why very rapid inflation was rare. Without a paper currency, the technology available would not allow a sufficient expansion of the money supply or a rise in velocity sufficient to produce the rapid rise in prices. All experiences with unbacked paper money resulted in inflation, though they did not always degenerate into very rapid inflation. For example, in Spain, in the period, 1779-1788 when paper money was issued, prices rose quite steeply. And of course in Britain during the period of inconvertibility, during the Napoleonic Wars, the same was true. But vast increases in unbacked paper characterize all very rapid inflations. The Americans had the Continental and the French the Assignat.

In France the experience of John Law was well remembered so that even in the 1780s the French were still vehemently opposed to the issue of paper money. On a King's edict proclaiming new money in 1788 one parish argued, "Above all, we will not countenance the introduction of paper money or a national bank, either of which can only produce a great evil ...." (Harris, 1930, p. 8). But the Revolution came, and as we have noted the attitude toward paper money change. The people's revolution was impossible without it. The same was true of the Confederacy in the 1860s and of all the episodes of the twentieth century.

A vast expansion in paper currency preceded all these rapid inflations. This brings us to the second feature, for what comes out of most of the qualitative accounts is that the monetary growth derived from fiscal deficits. The view that deficits ultimately require monetizing and inexorably lead to inflation is quite widespread. It is implicit in much of

---

[9]The same was true of the period of the great debasement and of the English Civil War. The coins would not be stamped with a different value for they carried with them the value that they had.

the literature and explicit in some. In previous periods the view was not
a controversial one. The monetary historian with a rough and ready ac-
quaintance with periods of rapid price rises thinks first of all of heavy
and usually war-induced government expenditure that could not be covered by
revenue. For example as far as the post-World War I inflations are concerned, the bulk of informed opinion at the time (represented, for
instance, at the Brussels Financial Conference in 1920) was that governments could prevent inflation development if they balanced their budgets.
The "Brussels doctrine was emphatic in pointing to budget deficits as the
cause of inflation" (League of Nations, 1946). When government was unable
to cover the gap by borrowing it resorted to the printing press. Where
there was little prospect of revenue meeting expenditure, the whole debt
had to be monetized. It is true that for a few years in the mid-twenties
the opposite view took hold - that budget deficits were a consequence
rather than a cause of inflation. The argument was that inflation reduced
the real tax revenue and that the general rise in prices affected the goods
and services that were the object of State expenditure and so raised State
expenditure. This is rather an explanation for continuing inflation rather
than an explanation of its origins.[10] The view that was to dominate was
that deficits were warning lights of inflation to follow.[11]

In the examples of very rapid inflation before the twentieth century,
there is little doubt that when deficits and debt soar monetary growth
follows quickly. The data again do not allow rigorous testing of even an
examination of the precise timing in the relationship, but the accounts of
these cases all suggest that sequence in the variables and that this preceded the price explosion. Fiscal needs led to monetary growth and to
inflation. The American Revolution, the French Revolution, and the
Confederacy in the American Civil War are all example. In the 1920s the
evidence is very similar. Austria, Germany, Hungary, and Poland all had
substantial and growing deficits built up prior to or coincidental with the
inflation. There is little doubt that this was also the case with Russia

---

[10]Obviously both views could have validity. If spending increased and led to the
deficit, then inflation follows the deficit. However, if spending were stable but tax
revenues fell as a result of inflation, then of course inflation caused the deficit. There
are insufficient data to test for the timing of the relationship.

[11]Though recently there has been some work that has failed to find the precise
connection. See for example King and Prosser (1984).

though, as noted earlier, there the intention was to float the revolution on a tide of paper that not only paid for the required resources but in the process destroyed the currency and wiped out the bourgeoisie. There are fewer examples in the 1940s but a striking one is that of China and the case of Greece provides further support, and we also now know in greater detail the experience of Hungary at the end of the Second World War (Bomberger and Makinen, 1983). All these cases confirm the story of deficits leading to very rapid inflation.

Given that very rapid inflation has always appeared in a period of monetary expansion following or contemporaneous with growing budget deficits, the question arises - what circumstances produced the latter? A second question would be: did such deficits and monetary growth lead inexorably to high inflation?

As to what produces the deficit, one suggestion is that it is war:

> "The association of wars...with hyperinflation is easy
> to rationalize. The needs of war demand a major pro-
> portion of the nation's resources to be devoted to
> production that does not satisfy consumption goods.
> Thus shortages develop relative to the normal standard
> of living that exercises a major influence on price
> expectations" (Ball, 1964, p. 262).

But such an answer is clearly unsatisfactory. After all it is obvious that the history of the world is essentially a chronicle of conflict, frequently on a huge and prolonged scale; and in two world wars in the twentieth century, when scores of countries were involved, there are still only a few cases of very rapid inflation. In the seventeenth and eighteenth centuries there were many wars and they often lasted longer than in the nineteenth and twentieth centuries, but the cases of very rapid inflation were fewer.

On some occasions prices actually fell during wars. According to Hamilton (1977) the first war that exerted an upward pressure on prices was the war of the Spanish Succession (1702-1713). But even there and in spite of Madrid being a battlefield for more than a decade, prices rose by only 6 per cent over the whole war. Sometimes inflationary pressures did emerge as in the War of Austrian Succession (1740-1748) and again in the Seven Years War (1756-1815). But in none of these major wars nor in a whole string of others did any danger of very rapid inflation appear. War of itself is certainly not sufficient. It is perhaps worth recalling here that Germany's deficits in the First World War grew rapidly from 1914 onwards and were accompanied by a substantial growth in the money supply, but the very rapid inflation did not develop until 1923, and the First World War cannot really be seen as the prime source of that inflation.[12]

A closer look at the episodes we have gathered together reveals that it was not simply war but civil war or revolution or at minimum serious social unrest that was present in almost all the cases: The American Revolution, the French Revolution, the American Civil War, Russia after 1917, Hungary in 1919, and Poland in the early 1920s. In Germany, too, there were attempted Communist coups. In 1922 and 1923 there were armed uprisings and major breakdowns in public order. In Austria the situation was similar.[13] China and Greece in the years immediately after the Second World War suffered civil war - that is, in ten of the eleven cases. The recent view (Journal of Political Economy) expressed on Hungary in the 1940s is that Soviet influence in the Allied Commission prompted that case.[14]

Governments have always been keen to get hold of resources, and in times of great difficulty the temptation has been in the extreme to confiscate the resources. The easiest way of achieving this is to generate inflation and benefit from the inflation tax. The authorities maximize their revenue when inflation is in excess of a rate of 100 per cent per annum, but at these rates the government must be in serious danger of losing power. In other words while the inflation tax may look to be a tempting short-run policy, it is clearly potentially calamitous in anything except the shortest term. The production of very rapid inflation may be profitable for the authorities but the political consequences are potentially dire. Why then, or in what circumstances, would it be worth taking such a risk? The answer must be -- when the state is seriously threatened from

---

[12]Of course on many occasions price controls were introduced and in many cases were effective in the sense that they held down prices. They undoubtedly distorted the market, but the costs here have been reckoned to have been offset by the benefits of dampening inflation (Rockoff 1984). This does not prove that controls work but rather that they probably have a role to play in time of war. It is war that provides the common purpose and induces a toleration of the loss of economic freedom. Price controls backed with severe penalties were features of most periods of inflation, but outside of war time they have been easily evaded.

[13]Some measures of the lesser known unrest there are given in Teichova (1983).

[14]Again the problem of measurement arises in what constitutes serious social unrest. Whether or not an indicator of social unrest could be constructed is an interesting question and perhaps some researcher will take it up.

within. The reason that an external threat is not critical is, of course, that that usually stimulates patriotism and tax revenue can be raised more easily and borrowing, too, is easier. When the threat is internal there is an immediate loss of tax revenue. If then there were a threat of overthrow from within, the government may calculate that the risk attached to very rapid inflation is worth running and the cost worth bearing. It could be argued that, in many cases, such a view was rational and in the end correct. After all, how many Americans would sooner have lost in the 1780s just to avoid the inflation?

Civil war is obviously a prime reason behind deficits. Expenditure rises sharply as the established authority fights to resist rebellion, but the revenue falls as tax revenue from the rebellious section is one of the first things to disappear. A deficit has opened up and resort to the printing press is immediate. But, or course, there have been many more revolutions and civil wars than there have been very rapid inflations, so why do some wars allow rapid inflation to develop and others do not.

One line of explanation that might be pursued is derived from the explanation offered recently by Sargent (1982) for ending big inflations. The essence of this view is that monetary growth does not of itself lead to inflation. The prevailing and the anticipated fiscal position has to be considered in conjunction with monetary policy. The argument is that in a fiat money regime, an appropriate fiscal policy can implicitly back the money stock. The view has been expressed as follows: the value of government liabilities is determined in the same way as the value of the firm's liabilities. An issue of additional shares in the absence of prospective improvement in the future stream of income leads to a fall in the price of the shares. In the case of government, an increase in its liabilities (notes) without an increase in prospective tax receipts provokes an expectation of a fall in the value of the liabilities - that is, in inflation (Smith, 1984).[15]

It is interesting to look at this argument in relation to certain

---

[15]Smith took this explanation back to an examination of Massachusetts in the first half of the eighteenth century and found support for it. However, it should be said that he was dealing with a highly specific set of circumstances. Deficits did not lead to inflation not simply because there was a strong expectation that the deficit would not be monetized but rather because there was more or less a guarantee that they would not. The circumstances were that when a deficit opened up money was issued to cover it, but as soon as tax receipts came in the money was retired.

examples in this paper and elsewhere. Take for example the case of Britain
in and immediately after the First World War. Britain, too, developed huge
budget deficits and ran down her foreign assets on a huge scale. The
national debt rose from £650m in 1913 to £8000m in 1920, equal in value to
about two and one-half times national income. Yet by the standards of the
time the rate of inflation, while gathering pace in the course of the
period 1914-20, was not high, never higher than 20 per cent per annum. Why
did higher rates of inflation not develop? What prevented Britain from
suffering very rapid inflation? An explanation from the above would be
that it must have been widely believed at some point in the course of the
war - perhaps when victory seemed assured - that fiscal rectitude would
follow and that surpluses would result in some debt being retired, money
supply falling, and prices falling. Certainly deficits were enormous in
1916-1919 - of the order of £1800m or 70 (seventy) per cent of GNP. But
the deficit fell to £326m in 1919-1920 and moved sharply into a surplus of
£230m in 1920-1921. Of course, whether it was the belief that this would
happen because of Britain's traditional adherence to Gladstonian finance or
because of the actual reversal of the deficit requires closer examination.[16]

For this thesis to be supported, detailed studies of the state of
belief in these and other instances would have to be carried out. Sargent
(1982) suggests it was the case for the 1920s, and Makinen (1984) and
Bomberger and Makinen (1983) point to a similar conclusion for Greece and
Hungary in the 1940s. There would seem to be a prima facie case for
investigation in the case of the North in the United States Civil War. The
danger, however, (perhaps particularly in trying to explain the origins of
rapid inflation) would seem to be that of explaining the state of belief by
the outcome. In other words -- is it really testable?

In a civil war or revolution or even in a period of some social
unrest, the course of events is uncertain in varying degrees. The future
stream of income from taxation is likewise uncertain. In the absence of
any commitment to the future, there can be little "backing" for the note
issue in a fiat money regime. But this explanation might prove useful in
directing attention to some critical point which might constitute the

---

[16]There are many other such examples that come to mind. England immediately after the
French experience with the assignat had an unbacked paper currency.

necessary shock to the system that carries it over a critical threshold on the inflationary path.

RECENT

Set against the background described above it can readily be seen that the experience of inflation in the recent past - largely the last two decades and particularly in Latin American - has not been severe and indeed does not qualify as hyperinflation. However, using the very rapid inflation definition of 100 per cent per annum as the qualifying rate we get the countries appearing in Table 8. Again the objective here has been to provide annual data for the period preceding the worst rate of inflation. Given the greater data availability in this period, however, it has also been possible to present monthly data for the eighteen months that surround the worst month. This shows the accelerating rate and the falling away in all the cases where the experience is not currently taking place. The monthly data were limited to money, prices, and exchange rates except in the case of Argentina where there are some data on government finance.

Again the data must be treated with caution. Even with these very recent data it is not always possible to reconcile two different sources. But the annual data allow some comment even if several columns are of limited value.[17]

The experience of rapid inflation in the modern world has not been limited geographically but the dominance of Latin America is obvious. The other possible generalization is that all the countries are primary producers, though there are many different levels or stages of economic development.

There are nine cases involving eight countries - Argentina being the culprit with two experiences. Six were in Latin America, one in Africa, one in the Middle East, and Indonesia in the Far East. Argentina experienced a rapid inflation in the mid-1970s when an annual rate of 443 per cent was recorded. This fell steadily to about 100 per cent in 1980 and has risen since to 364 per cent in 1983. Chile, too, had its worst experience in the mid-seventies with a rate of over 500 per cent in 1974.

---

[17]The fact that International Financial Statistics shows a balanced budget for Brazil over the last few years will alert readers to the kind of caution required.

Uruguay had its worst experience in the late sixties. The other countries who qualify on the basis described (Ghana, Israel, Brazil, and Peru) are all currently in the grip of their worst experience. Bolivia should now be added.

Part of the information is of limited value and can be disposed of quickly. First, the exchange rates. These all move in the direction expected though on occasion not quite on the scale expected. This is interesting only up to a point for the chief deficiency in the data is that they do not represent a market rate. The figures on debt are less reliable, but insofar as the trend goes it is an unsurprising parallel rise. The other column that yields little that is consistent is that on the balance of payments. There were several large deficits but the interesting point here is that these were almost never overwhelming. They were not large as a share of income - not out of line with many other countries at other times who experienced no rapid inflation. If the figures are to be believed in the Argentinian case (1) there was no connection at all. In Ghana there were alternating surpluses and deficits, and in the years of the worst inflation the balance of payments was in surplus. Peru was similar as were Chile and Brazil.

The data about which there is little ambiguity are in money supply and budget deficits. Money supply soared in all the countries on which there is information, and the best guide to budget deficits suggests that they grew too and were strongly negative at the worst point of the inflation. To pursue the explanation found above may not be wise, but the first thing that stands out is that there are several cases of civil war or serious social unrest. Argentina and Chile (and to varying degrees other Latin American countries) and Indonesia at the time of the overthrow of Sukarno are all example. Others such as Israel do not fit the mold so neatly, though some would argue that Israel has certainly had weak government and has tried, in much the way described above, to buy off social unrest so that there is now a large division in its society.[18] However, no pretense is intended here that the complexities of modern politics (especially Latin American) have begun to be disentangled. Simply put, there are hints that some similarities exist.

In summary, before the recent experience all historical episodes of

---

[18]One seminar participant offered to help fit Israel better into the main conclusion by suggesting that it had "externalized" its civil war.

Table 8

Macroeconomic Variables

| | 1 | 2 | 3 | 4 G.N.P. | | 5 Debt | | | 6 | 7 |
	Prices Yearly Change	Govt. Finance Mil. of Pesos	Balance of Payments Mil. of $	a. Domestic Currency Mil. of Pesos	b. U.S. $m. U.S. $ Mil.	a. Domestic Mil. of Pesos	b. Foreign Mil. of Pesos	c. External Mil. of $	Exchange Rate Pesos per $, Market Rate	Money 1980=100
Argentina (A)										
1970	12.2	-0.2	-163	8.7	28,920	...	...		0.0004	0.1
1971	34.9	-0.4	-390	12.4	30,970	...	...	2,150.5[a]	0.0005	0.1
1972	58.9	-0.7	-227	20.6	39,760	...	...	2,374.6[a]	0.0005	0.1
1973	61.2	-1.7	711	35.2	37,380	...	...	2,783.3[a]	0.0005	0.2
1974	23.3	-2.6	118	48.5	39,330	...	...	3,247.3[a]	0.0005	0.4
1975	182.5	-14.9	-1,287	144.0	40,730	23.4	3.3	3,120.6[a]	0.0061	0.8
1976	443.2	-54.3	651	747.2	48,710	97.8	20.1	4,428.5[a]	0.0274	3.3
1977	176.1	-57.7	1,126	2,031.0		205.1	46.9	5,036.1[a]	0.0598	8.1
Argentina (B)										
1978	175.5	-167.9	1,856	5,125.1	53,430	365.0	125.0	9,850.0	0.1003	20.0
1979	159.5	-370.8	-513	13,788.7	60,310	815.7	251.3	13,996.2	0.1618	46.3
1980	100.8	-1,011.5	-4,774	27,893.8	71,750	1,346.3	355.3	16,779.8	0.1992	100.0
1981	104.5	-4,415.4	-4,712	52,404.1	72,120	5,965.0	3,154.8	22,671.7	0.7248	153.9
1982	164.8	...	-2,477						4.88545	455.2
1983	343.8	...							23.261	
1984										

Chile (C)

Year	Billions of Pesos	Mil. of Pesos	Mil. of Pesos	a. Domestic Borrowing (Mil. of Pesos)	b. Foreign Borrowing (Mil. of Pesos)	c. External Debt (Mil. of $)	Billions of Pesos	Pesos per $	Mil. of N.C.
1968	23.5	-138	...	...	...	...	...	0.008	...
1969	28.6	89	...	...	...	...	...	0.010	6,068
1970	33.3	-91	...	-3	...	...	...	0.012	10,049
1971	19.4	-198	7,550	-10	...	2,573.8	...	0.016	21,523
1972	79.1	-471	8,030	-30	-2	2,963.0	...	0.025	54,201
1973	351.9	-279	7,360	-81	-62	177.2	1.20	0.360	224,625
1974	500.0	-292	8,680	-495	-189	4,325.0	9.53	1.870	836,712
1975	374.2	-490	10,130	46	1,016	4,371.9	40.75	8.500	2,994,800

Israel ( )

				Debt					
Year	Mil. of Shekels	Mil. of Shekels	Mil. of Shekels	Mil. of Shekels	a. Domestic Borrowing (Mil. of Shekels)	b. Foreign Borrowing (Mil. of Shekels)	c. External Debt (Mil. of $)	Shekels per $ market rate/par or central rate	Mil. of N.C.
1978	50.6	-3,202	-901	23,035	13,760	26,191	20,271	9,224.1[a]	1.902(1.747)	44.6
1979	78.3	-6,663	-863	42,732	15,980			10,339.1[a]	3.535(2.544)	59.0
1980	131.0	-19,268	-805	100,085	17,560			12,632.7[a]	7.548(5.124)	100.0
1981	116.8	...	-1,383	237,098	20,420			13,867.7[a]	15.604(11.431)	193.9
1982	120.4	...	-2,099	528,261					33.650(24.267)	388.1
1983	145.6	...	...	...					107.770	...
1984	...	...	...	...					...	...

Ghana ( )

				Debt					
Year	Mil. of Cedis	Mil. of Cedis	Mil. of Cedis	Mil. of Cedis	a. Domestic Borrowing (Mil. of Cedis)	b. Foreign Borrowing (Mil. of Cedis)	c. External Debt (Mil. of $)	$ per Cedis Market Rate	Mil. of N.C.
1976	56.1	-734.6[+]	-74.1	6,478	3,860	2,320.6[*]	482.2[+]	665.5[a]	0.8696	21.7
1977	116.4	-923.9[*]	-79.7	11,123	3,940	3,259.4[*]		783.7[a]	0.8696	32.8
1978	73.1	-1056.8[+]	-45.9	...	4,160	5,136.0[+]		802.8[a]	0.3636	57.0
1979	54.4	-1896.7[+]	256.4	...	4,470	6,159.2[+]		906.6[a]	0.3636	74.4
		-1800.0[+]								

(continued — New Pesos)

Year	Mil. of New Pesos	Mil. of New Pesos	Mil. of New Pesos	a. Net Borrowing (financing) Mil. of New Pesos	c. External Debt Mil. of $	New Pesos per $	
1980	50.1	-1808.1+	-93.5	7,621.1+	992.5[a]	0.3636	100.0
1981	116.5		-208.9		978.7[a]	0.3636	135.0
1982	22.3					0.3333	174.8

Uruguay ( )

Year	Mil. of New Pesos	Mil. of New Pesos		Mil. of New Pesos	a. Net Borrowing (financing) Mil. of New Pesos	b.	c. External Debt Mil. of $	New Pesos per $
1963	10.2	...	0.2	22	...	...		0.016
1964	45.2	...	-0.8	32	...	...		0.019
1965	55.6	-1.9	72.0	52	0.1	...		0.060
1966	71.4	-0.3	59.3	98	-0.3	...		0.076
1967	90.0	-4.7	-4.2	167	0.4	...		0.200
1968	125.0	-4.1	23.4	369	5.8	...		0.250
1969	21.1	-11.8	-19.1	499	12.4	...		0.250

Brazil ( )

Year	Bil. of Cruzeiros	Bil. of Cruzeiros	Bil. of Cruzeiros		a. Net Borrowing (Monetary Authority + other) Financing	c. External Debt Mil. of $	Cruzeiros Per $	Bil. of Cruzeiros
1978	38.7	4.9	-7,036	3,646	180,020	-4.8	46,467.6	20.920	454.2
1979	52.7	2.3	-10,478	6,077	206,600	-2.3	51,486.0	42.530	788.5
1980	82.8	2.0	-12,806	12,700	255,070	-2.0	55,759.1	65.500	1,349.1
1981	105.6	10.1	-11,751	25,816	267,730	-10.0	63,790.5	127.800	2,357.8
1982	98.0	6.6				-6.6		252.670	4,036.2
1983	142.0	14.4				-14.4		984.00	

Peru ( )

Year	Bil. of Soles	Bil. of Soles	Bil. of Soles		a. Financing Bil. of Soles	b. Financing Bil. of Soles	c. External Debt Mil. of $	Soles per $	Bil. of Soles
1978	57.8	-80.3	1,613.9	11,440	72.4	7.9	5,402.1[a]	196.18	265.3
1979	66.7	-18.0	2,924.5	14,520	48.7	-30.7	5,933.6[a]	250.12	451.7
1980	59.2	-140.0	4,857.2	17,970	124.7	15.3	6,167.9[a]	341.17	712.6
1981	75.4	-405.9	8,348.0	19,980	282.8	123.1	5,973.7[a]	506.17	1,044.8
1982	64.4	-553.1			885.1	-332.0		989.67	1,408.4
1983	111.2							2,272.2	
1984									

Sources: The sources for all columns are from the International Financial Statistics Yearbook, IMF, various issues, March 1984 No 3, Vol. XXXVII.

Except: Column 2, 5a and 5b; + figures are from Government Finance Statistics Yearbook, IMF, 1982, p. 281.

Column 2, 5a and 5b; ■ figures are from International Financial Statistics Yearbook

Column 4b, GNP at market price (U.S. $ mil.). Source: World Bank Atlas, Issues 1973-1981 and 1983.

Column 5c; external debt excluding short-term debt. Source: World Debt Tables, (IMF), 1982 Edition (Row entitled; Total Debt.)

Column 5c[a]; total debt figure not available, the next best alternative i.e., "public/publicly guaranteed debt" is taken. This is total debt excluding private non-guaranteed debt (the latter of which is not available).

Column 7; M3 figures for Chile from Statistical Abstract of Latin America, Vol. 18, 1977, James W. Wilkie

	(8) $\frac{GF}{GNP} \times 100$	(9) $\frac{BP}{GNP} \times 100$	(10) $\frac{Internal^{(a)}}{GNP} \times 100$	$\frac{External^{(b)}}{GNP} \times 100$	$\frac{External^{(c)}}{GNP} \times 100$	(11) Inflation Index	(12) Money Index	(13) Central Bank Discount Rate
	%	%	%	%	%			
Argentina (A)						1970=100	1970=100	
1970	-2.3	-	-	-	-	100	100	
1971	-3.2	-1.35	-	-	7.43	286.1	100	
1972	-3.9	-0.73	-	-	7.67	482.8	100	
1973	-4.8	1.79	-	-	7.00	501.6	200	
1974	-5.4	0.32	-	-	8.69	190.9	400	
1975	-10.3	-3.27	16	2.3	7.93	1495.9	800	
1976	-7.3	1.60	13	2.7	10.87	3032.8	3300	
1977	-2.8	2.31	10	2.3	10.34	1443.4	8100	
Argentina (B)						1978=100	1978=100	
1978	-3.3	3.47	7.1	2.4	18.44	100	100	
1979	-2.7	-0.85	5.9	1.8	23.20	90.89	231.5	
1980	-3.6	-6.65	4.8	1.3	23.29	57.43	500	
1981	-8.4	-6.53	11.4	6.0	31.44	59.55	769.5	
1982	-	-	-	-	-	93.90	-	
1983	-	-	-	-	-	195.90	-	
1984	-	-	-	-	-	-	-	
Chile (C)						1968=100	1968=100	
1968	-	-	-	-	-	100	100	
1969	-	-	-	-	-	121.7	-	
1970	-	-	-	-	-	141.7	165.60	
1971	-	-2.62	-	-	34.09	82.6	354.70	
1972	-	-5.87	-	-	36.90	336.6	893.23	
1973	-2.55	-3.79	-0.0003	-0.005	2.41	1497.4	3701.80	
1974	-9.71	-3.36	0.0010	-0.002	49.83	2153.2	13788.9	
1975	-0.96	-4.84	-0.0023	-0.002	43.16	1592.3	49353.99	

153

Israel (D)

Year						1978=100	1978=100
1978	-13.9	-6.55	113.7	88.0	67.03	100	100
1979	-15.6	-5.40	–	–	64.70	154.7	132.29
1980	-19.3	-4.58	–	–	71.94	258.9	224.22
1981	–	-6.78	–	–	67.91	230.8	434.75
1982	–	–	–	–	–	237.9	870.18
1983	–	–	–	–	–	287.7	–
1984	–	–	–	–	–	–	–

Ghana (E)

Year						1976=100	1976=100	
1976	-11.3	-1.92	35.8	7.4	17.24	100	100	8
1977	-14.3	-2.02	29.3	–	19.89	207.5	151.15	8
1978	-9.5	-1.10	–	–	19.30	130.3	262.67	13.5
1979	–	5.74	–	–	20.28	97.0	341.01	13.5
1980	–	-2.08	–	–	22.10	89.3	460.83	19.5
1981	–	-4.38	–	–	20.52	207.7	622.12	–
1982	–	–	–	–	–	39.8	805.53	–

Uruguay (A)

Year				1963=100	1963=100
1963	–	0.014	–	100	100
1964	–	-0.046	–	235.4	–
1965	-3.6	8.304	0.192	289.6	100
1966	-0.31	4.600	0.306	371.9	200
1967	-2.8	-0.503	0.240	468.8	300
1968	-1.1	1.585	1.572	651.0	500
1969	-2.36	-0.957	2.485	109.9	900

Brazil (B)

Year					1978=100	1979=100	
1978	0.13	-2.91	-0.13	25.81	100	100	33
1979	0.04	-5.07	-0.04	24.92	136.2	173.6	35
1980	0.02	-5.02	-0.015	21.86	213.95	297.0	38
1981	0.04	-4.39	-0.39	23.83	272.86	519.1	–
1982	–	–	–	–	253.2	886.6	–
1983	–	–	–	–	366.9	–	–
1984	–	–	–	–	–	–	–

Peru (C)

1978	-4.98	-1.68	4.48	0.49	47.22	100	100	28.5
1979	-0.62	5.41	1.67	-0.01	40.87	115.4	170.3	29.5
1980	-2.82	0.35	2.57	0.31	34.32	102.4	268.6	29.5
1981	-4.86	-8.22	3.39	1.47	29.90	130.4	393.8	-
1982	-	-				111.4	530.9	-
1983	-	-				192.4	-	-
1984	-	-				-	-	-

Sources: The sources for all columns are from the International Financial Statistics Yearbook, IMF, various issues, March 1984. No 3. VOl., XXXVII.

Except: Column 13; United Nations Statistical Yearbook, (1982).

155

very rapid inflation took place when there was an unbacked paper currency which was issued at a time of civil disorder, which in turn had produced a budget deficit.   Of course, it is clear that there have been cases of serious disorder and even revolution where there was no rapid inflation. The question to be pursued there is: was that because the outcome was imminent and widely desired and anticipated? Or it may be that the conditions for raising taxes provide part of the explanation. A system based on indirect taxation would be less elastic than a direct system.   The tax base in the former could not be rapidly expanded when required.   Thus a country (and perhaps Britain is an example) with a direct tax system would be less likely to run into budget difficulties.   In the circumstances we have been discussing, a wide variety of alternative policies to choose from is unlikely, and the inflation can hardly be regarded as a consequence of the wrong choice of policy other than abandonment of a backed currency.

Another point to be made in summing up is that this thesis goes some way towards identifying the direction of causation involved in social unrest and rapid inflation.   Many have argued that inflation leads to social upheaval. Keynes wrote:

> "There is no subtler, no surer means of overturning the existing basis of society than to debauch the currency, the process engages all the hidden forces of economic law on the side of destruction and does it in a manner which not one man in a million can diagnose" (Keynes 1920, p. 220).

However, in the examples of very rapid inflation where the events are quite dramatic the sequence is rather: unrest leading to government difficulties and deficits and on to rapid inflation. No doubt the inflation produced further social disorder and the causality can be seen to run both ways, but in seeking the origins of these extreme examples it runs from social disorder to inflation.

156

Table 9

	1	2	3	4
	Prices, Yearly Change	Govt. Finance	Exchange Rate	Money
Argentina (A)	%	Mil. of Pesos	Pesos per $	Mil. of Pesos
March 1975	7.6	-3,442	10.000	11
April	9.9	-3,496	10.000	11
May	3.8	-3,905	10.000	12
June	20.9	-7,728	26.000	13
July	35.3	-8,637	28.080	13
Aug.	22.3	-14,180	34.450	15
Sept.	10.8	-16,420	36.400	18
Oct.	13.9	-17,570	37.70	20
Nov.	8.8	-24,170	52.88	22
Dec.	19.5	-51,400	60.89	28
Jan. 1976	8.9	-27,230	65.59	31
Feb.	18.95	-30,100	74.40	34
March	37.6	-62,730	140.17	39
April	33.9	-44,390	140.17	43
May	12.1	-46,970	140.17	50
June	2.7	-37,230	140.17	59
july	4.2	-39,920	140.17	65
Aug.	5.5	-55,870	140.17	72
Argentina (B)		Bil. of Pesos		
April 1982	4.2	-3,048	11,790.0	6,255
May	3.1	-3,078	14,575.0	6,204
June	7.9	-3,270	15,725.0	6,494
July	16.2	...	38,975.0	9,874
Aug.	14.7	...	38,975.0	9,968
Sept.	17.1	...	38,975.0	10,315
Oct.	12.7	...	38,975.0	10,826

157

		Mil. of Pesos	Bils. of Pesos	
Nov.	11.3	−1,422.4	4.3375	12,200
Dec.	10.6	−2,751.3	4.8545	16,234
Jan. 1983	15.99	...	5.4045	16,711
Feb.	130	...	6.0305	17,396
March	11.3	−3,603.4	6.7345	18,230
April	10.3	...	7.4385	20,252
May	9.1	...	8.1105	23,267
June	15.8	−3,692.4	8.8810	27,647
July	12.5	−5,458.4	9.9610	29,532
Aug.	17.2	−7,940.3	11.2720	32,735
Sept.	21.4	...	13.076	37,429

Chile (C)	%		Escudos per $	Mil. of Pesos
March 1973	6.2		25.00	73
April	10.2		25.00	77
May	19.5		25.00	88
June	15.6		25.00	98
July	15.3		25.00	112
Aug.	17.1		25.00	124
Sept.	16.9		25.00	134
Oct.	87.6		280.00	146
Nov.	5.7		340.00	176
Dec.	4.73		360.00	224
Jan. 1974	4.1		360.00	261
Feb.	24.5		450.00	292
March	12.3		525.00	349
April	16.6		550.00	350
May	8.7		660.00	405
June	20.1		790.00	430
July	12.2		860.00	473
Aug.	10.9		930.00	520

Israel (D)	%		Shekels per $	Mil. of Shekels
April 1982	10.6		20.55	16,744
May	6.22		21.905	17,293

June	6.0		24.080	18,395
July	9.2		25.760	19.196
Aug.	7.9		27.440	20,140
Sept.	7.6		29.060	23,021
Oct.	8.4		30.490	23,375
Nov.	6.5		...	25,722
Dec.	5.5		...	26,543
Jan. 1983	8.6		...	...
Feb.	6.1		...	...
March	5.6		...	...
April	13.2		41.920	35,963
May	5.5		44.650	37,497
June	3.6		47.520	40,566
July	6.2		50.891	43,260
Aug.	7.1		58.839	45,612
Sept.	9.0		63.687	47,012
Oct.	21.1		83.740	53,395
Nov.	15.2		95.620	...
Dec.	11.6		107.770	...
Jan. 1984	14.9		123.720	...

Ghana (E)	%		$ per cedis	Mil. of cedis
Jan. 1980	5.39		0.3636	5,326
Feb.	1.22		0.3636	5,272
March	7.45		0.3636	5,179
April	8.09		0.3636	5,175
May	5.81		0.3636	5,252
June	6.10		0.3636	5,252
July	1.09		0.3636	5,148
Aug.	2.85		0.3636	5,302
Sept.	2.91		0.3636	5,192
Oct.	5.02		0.3636	5,413
Nov.	11.18		0.3636	5,917
Dec.	8.10		0.3636	6,085
Jan. 1981	13.17		0.3636	6,433
Feb.	10.14		0.3636	6,266
March	8.87		0.3636	6,510
April	6.80		0.3636	6,849

May	5.73	0.3636	7.170
June	5.45	0.3636	7.251
July	2.32	0.3636	7.108
		0.3636	7.371

Uruguay	Cost of living	Pesos per $ (Free Rate)	Mil. of new pesos
March 1967	5.1	86.20	16
April	2.72	86.00	16
May	0.53	88.40	18
June	7.4	88.80	17
July	15.7	99.50	18
Aug.	6.78	127.00	19
Sept.	8.73	124.00	20
Oct.	5.11	136.00	22
Nov.	...	198.50	25
Dec.	...	199.00	31
Jan. 1968	16.22	199.75	30
Feb.	6.2	199.75	31
March	5.1	199.75	33
April	3.47	250.00	34
May	7.4	250.00	35
June	13.75	250.00	36
July	0.55	250.00	36
	Consumer Prices		
Aug.	-1.64	250.00	37

Brazil (G)		Cruzeiros per $ (Market Rate)	Bil. of Cruzeiros
Aug. 1982	5.15	193.67	2,840.0
Sept.	4.22	207.23	2,961.6
Oct.	4.28	221.73	3,204.8
Nov.	4.74	237.25	3,503.9
Dec.	7.77	252.67	4,036.2
Jan. 1983	8.96	275.28	4,137.7
Feb.	6.73	381.44	3,961.1

160

March	9.14	417.54	3,931.2
April	8.29	454.93	4,296.3
May	6.86	493.61	4,512.5
June	11.12	542.97	5,056.6
July	12.53	611.92	5,135.0
Aug.	8.21	671.00	5,435.7
Sept.	9.85	738.00	5,862.7
Oct.	9.67	842.00	6,382.4
Nov.	6.66	914.00	...
Dec.	8.81	984.00	...
Jan. 1984	9.91	1,080.00	...
Feb.		1,213.00	...

Peru (H)		Soles per $ (Market Rate)	Bil. of Soles
Aug. 1982	4.44	755.10	1,139.0
Sept.	4.73	794.75	...
Oct.	6.91	851.85	1,177.0
Nov.	4.53	909.03	1,172.0
Dec.	4.45	989.67	1,408.4
Jan. 1983	7.64	1,061.55	1.403.8
Feb.	7.75	1,131.80	1.437.5
March	9.94	1,238.57	1,548.1
April	7.80	1,343.83	1,676.9
May	5.34	1,460.12	1,784.2
June	...	1,585.96	1,998.4
July	...	1,727.31	...
Aug.	8.81	1,964.9	...
Sept.	6.83	2,041.1	...
Oct.	4.86	2,118.8	...
Nov.	4.63	2,194.5	...
Dec.	4.55	2,272.2	...
Jan. 1984	7.30	2,371.1	...
Feb.		2,482.6	...

Sources:

Argentina:

Column 1: Consumer prices, percentage change over previous month, International Financial
          Statistics Yearbook (IFS), various issues.

Column 2: Government finance (deficit or surplus)

Column 3: Pesos per dollar, IFS monthly

Column 4: IFS, Supplement on money, No. 5, IMF 1983, pp. 70 and IFS Vol. 36, Sept.-Dec., 1983,
          pp. 67

Chile:

Column 3: Import rate, IFS, Vol. 27, Sept.-Dec., 1974, pp. 93

Column 4, 5,   Quarterly IFS

    6,2:

Ghana:

Column 3: Market rate

          Figures in two different volumes for the same months do not match: Vol. 36, Sept.-
          Dec., 1983 and VOl. 36, May-Aug., 1983.

REFERENCES

Aldcroft, H.
(1977)   *From Versailles to Wall Street 1919–1929.* London: Allen Lane.

Ball, R.J.
(1964)   *Inflation and the Theory of Money.* London: George Allen & Unwin.

Bezanson, A.
(1948)   Inflation and Controls, Pennsylvania, 1774-1779. *Journal of Economic History.* Vol. VIII Supplement, pp. 1-20.

Bomberger, W.A. and Makinen, G.E.
(1983)   The Hungarian Hyperinflation and Stabilization of 1945-1946. *Journal of Political Economy*, 91: 801-25.

Braudel, F.P.
(1981)   *Civilization and Capitalism, Vol. 1, The Structure of Everyday Life.* London: Collins.

_____
(1979)   Prices in Europe from 1450-1750. Rich and Wilson (eds.), *The Cambridge Economic History of Europe.* Cambridge: Cambridge University Press.

Bresciani-Turroni, C.
(1937)   *The Economics of Inflation: A Study of Currency Depreciation in Post War Germany.* London: George Allen & Unwin.

Cagan, P.
(1972)   *The Channels of Monetary Effects on Interest Rates.* (NBER) New York: Columbia University Press.

_____
(1956)   The Monetary Dynamics of Hyperinflation. M. Friedman (ed.), *Studies in the Quantity Theory of Money.* Chicago: University of Chicago Press.

Campbell, C. and Tullock, G.
  (1954)   Hyperinflation   in   China   1937-1949.   *Journal   of   Political Economy*, 62: 236-245.

Chou, S-H,
  (1963)   *The Chinese Inflation, 1937-1949*.   Columbia: New York.

Delivanes, D. and Cleveland, Wm. C.
            Greek Monetary Developments, 1939-1948.   Indiana.

Friedman, M.
  (1952)   Prices,   Income   and   Monetary   Changes   in   Three   Wartime Periods.   *American Economic Review*, 42: 612-25.

Graham, F.D.
  (1930)   *Exchange, Prices and Production in Hyperinflation, Germany 1920-1923*.   Princeton: Princeton University Press.

Halikias, D.J.
  (1980)   *Money and Credit in a Developing Economy*.   New York: New York University Press.

Hamburger, M.J. and Zwick, B.
  (1981)   Deficits, Money and Inflation.   *Journal of Monetary Economics*, 7: 141-150.

Hamilton, J.
  (1977)   The Role of War in Modern Inflation.   *Journal of Economic History*, 37:, 13-19.

Hammond, B.
  (1961)   The North's Empty Purse, 1861-1862.   *American Historical Review*, 67:, 1-18.

Harris, S.E.
  (1930)   *The Assignats*.   Cambridge, Massachusetts: Harvard University Press.

164

Harlow, R.V.
(1929)   Aspects of Revolutionary Finance 1775-1783. *American Histori-cal Review*, 35: 46-68.

Heilperm, M.A.
(1945)   *Post War European Inflations, World War I.*   (NBER)   Chicago: Chicago University Press.

Holtfrerich, C.L.
(1984)   *The Road to Hyperinflation: Fiscal Problems and Policies in Germany 1914-1923.* Mimeograph, Freie Universität Berlin.

Huang, A.C.
(1948)   The Inflation in China.   *Quarterly Journal of Economics*, 62: 562-75.

Kent, R.
(1920)   The Edict of Diocletian Fixing Maximum Prices.   *The University of Pennsylvania Law Review*, 23: 1-30.

Keynes, J.
(1971)   *A Tract of Monetary Reform.   The Collected Writings of J.M. Keynes.*   E. Johnson and D.E. Moggridge (eds.), Vol. IV. London: MacMillan.

_____
(1920)   *The Economic Consequences of the Peace.*   London: MacMillan.

Kia-Hgau, C.
(1958)   *The Inflationary Spiral.*   Boston: MIT.

King, R.G. and Prosser, C.I.
(1984)   *Money Deficits and Inflation.*   Mimeographed, University of Rochester.

Laursen, K. and Pederson, J.
The German Inflation, 1918-1923.   Amsterdam: North Holland.

Lerner, M.

    (1954)   The Monetary and Fiscal Programs of the Confederate Government 1861-1865. *Journal of Political Economy*, 62: 506-22.

    ——————

    (1955)   Money, Prices and Wages in the Confederacy 1861-1865. *Journal of Political Economy*, 63: 20-40.

League of Nations,

    (1946)   *Monthly Bulletin of Statistics*. Various, 1922-

Makinen, G.E.

    (1984)   The Greek Stabilization of 1944-1946. *American Economic Review*, 74: 1067-1075.

Marcel, M.

    (1927)   *Histoire Financiere de la France, Vol II, 1789-92; Vol III, 1792-1797.* (Paris).

Michell, H.

    (1947)   The Edict of Diocletian: A Study of Price Fixing in the Roman Empire. *The Canadian Journal of Economic and Political Science*, 13: 1-17.

Mitchell, B.R.

    (1980)   *European Historical Statistics 1750-1970.* Cambridge: Cambridge University Press.

Notel, R.

    (1984)   Money, Banking and Industry in Interwar Austria and Hungary. *Journal of European Economic History*, 13: 137-202.

Nurkse, R.

    (1945)   *The Course and Control of Inflation after World War I.* Princeton, New Jersey: League of Nations.

Pasvolsky, L.

    (1928)   *Economic Nationalism of the Danubian States.* London: George Allen & Unwin.

Pearce, D.W.

(1981)   *The Dictionary of Modern Economics.*   London: MacMillan.

Rockoff, H.

(1984)   *Drastic Measures, A History of Wage and Price Controls in the United States.*   Cambridge: Cambridge University Press.

Sargent, T.J.

(1982)   The Ends of Four Big Inflations.   R.H. Hall (ed.), *Inflation: Causes and Effects.*   Chicago: Chicago University Press.

Schmukler, M.E.

(1983)   *Inflation through the Ages.*   New York: Columbia University Press.

See, H.

(1885)   *Histoire Economique de la France.*   Paris: Robert Schnerb.

Smith, B.D.

(1984)   Money and Inflation in Colonial Massachusetts.   *Federal Reserve Bulletin, Minneapolis.*   No. 8.

Sommariva, A. and Tullio, G.

(1985)   *Inflation and Currency Depreciation in Germany 1914-1923: A Disequilibrium Model of Prices and the Exchange Rate.* Mimeographed, Washington.

Spechler, M.C.

(1984)   Ending Big Inflations: Lessons from Comparative European Economic History.   *Economic Quarterly* (Hebrew), 9: 17-35.

Stourn, R.

(1885)   *Les Finances de l'ancien regime et de la Revolution*, 2 Vols.   (Paris).

Teichova, A.

(1983)   A Comparative View of the Inflation of the 1920s in Austria and Czechoslovakia.   M.E. Schmukler, (ed.), *Inflation Through the Ages.*   New York: Columbia University Press.

167

Vilar, P.

    (1969)   *A History of Gold and Money 1450–1920.* London: New Left Books.

White, A.D.

    (1959)   *Fiat Money Inflation in France.* New York: Foundation for Economic Education, Inc.

Wicker, E.

    (1985)   *Colonial Monetary Standards Contrasted: Evidence from the Seven Years War.* Mimeographed, Indiana University.

    ―――――――

    (1984)   *Terminating Hyperinflation in the Dismembered Habsburg Monetary.* Mimeographed, Indiana University.

Witte, W.E.

    (1984)   *Ending Hyperinflations: The Lessons Which Can Be Drawn.* Mimeographed, Indiana University.

World Bank

    Debt Tables (*Various*) 1983 and 1984.

Young, J.P.

    (1925)   *European Currency and Finance.* Washington: United States Senate.

Excerpt from *Studies in the Quantity Theory of Money*, M. Friedman (ed.)

[2]

*The Monetary Dynamics of Hyperinflation**

I. GENERAL MONETARY CHARACTERISTICS
OF HYPERINFLATIONS

Hyperinflations provide a unique opportunity to study monetary phenomena. The astronomical increases in prices and money dwarf the changes in real income and other real factors. Even a substantial fall in real income, which generally has not occurred in hyperinflations, would be small compared with the typical rise in prices. Relations between monetary factors can be studied, therefore, in what almost amounts to isolation from the real sector of the economy.

This study deals with the relation between changes in the quantity of money and the price level during hyperinflations. One characteristic of such periods is that the ratio of an index of prices to an index of the quantity of money (P/M) tends to rise. Row 6 of Table 1 gives one measure of its rise for seven hyperinflations. (These seven are the only ones for which monthly indexes of prices are available.) Another way to illustrate this characteristic is by the decline in the reciprocal of this ratio, which represents an index of the real value of the quantity of money —real cash balances (M/P). Row 15 in Table 1 gives the minimum value reached by this index. Figures 1–7 also illustrate its tendency to decline. In ordinary inflations real cash balances, instead of declining, often tend to rise. The term *"hyperinflation"* must be properly defined. I shall define hyperinflations as beginning in the month the rise in prices exceeds 50 per cent[1] and as ending in the month before the monthly rise in prices drops below that amount and stays below for at least a year. The definition does not rule out a rise in prices at a rate below 50 per cent per month for the intervening months, and many of these months have rates below

---

* I owe a great debt to Milton Friedman for his helpful suggestions at every stage of the work. I also benefited from discussions with Jacob Marschak on certain theoretical points. The following people read the manuscript in semifinal form and offered useful suggestions: Gary Becker, Earl J. Hamilton, H. Gregg Lewis, Marc Nerlove, and my wife.

1. The definition is purely arbitrary but serves the purposes of this study satisfactorily. Few ordinary inflations produce such a high rate even momentarily. In Figs. 1–7 rates of change are given as rates per month, compounded continuously. A rate of 41 per cent per month, compounded continuously, equals a rate of 50 per cent per month, compounded monthly.

TABLE 1

MONETARY CHARACTERISTICS OF SEVEN HYPERINFLATIONS*

	COUNTRY						
	Austria	Germany	Greece	Hungary	Hungary	Poland	Russia
1. Approximate beginning month of hyperinflation	Oct., 1921	Aug., 1922	Nov., 1943	Mar., 1923	Aug., 1945	Jan., 1923	Dec., 1921
2. Approximate final month of hyperinflation	Aug., 1922	Nov., 1923	Nov., 1944	Feb., 1924	July, 1946	Jan., 1924	Jan., 1924
3. Approximate number of months of hyperinflation	11	16	13	10	12	11	26
4. Ratio of prices at end of final month to prices at first of beginning month	69.9	1.02×10^{10}	4.70×10^{8}	44.0	3.81×10^{27}	699.0	1.24×10^{5}
5. Ratio of quantity of hand-to-hand currency at end of final month to quantity at first of beginning month	19.3	7.32×10^{9}	3.62×10^{6}	17.0	1.19×10^{25}†	395.0	3.38×10^{4}
6. Ratio of (4) to (5)	3.62	1.40	130.0	2.59	320.0	1.77	3.67
7. Average rate of rise in prices (percentage per month)‡	47.1	322.0	365.0	46.0	19,800	81.4	57.0
8. Average rate of rise in quantity of hand-to-hand currency (percentage per month)§	30.9	314.0	220.0	32.7	12,200†	72.2	49.3
9. Ratio of (7) to (8)	1.52	1.03	1.66	1.41	1.62	1.13	1.16
10. Month of maximum rise in prices	Aug., 1922	Oct., 1923	Nov., 1944	July, 1923	July, 1946	Oct., 1923	Jan., 1924
11. Maximum monthly rise in prices (percentage per month)	134.0	32.4×10^{9}‖	85.5×10^{9}#	98.0	41.9×10^{15}	275.0	213.0
12. Change in quantity of hand-to-hand currency in month of maximum change in prices (percentage per month)	72.0	1.30×10^{3}***	73.9×10^{9}#	46.0	1.03×10^{15}	106.0	87.0
13. Ratio of (11) to (12)	1.86	24.9	1,160	2.13	40.7	2.59	2.45
14. Month in which real value of hand-to-hand currency was at a minimum	Aug., 1922	Oct., 1923	Nov., 1944	Feb., 1924	July, 1946	Nov., 1923	Jan., 1924
15. Minimum end-of-month ratio of real value of hand-to-hand currency to value at first of beginning month	0.35	0.030††	0.0069‡‡	0.39	0.0031†	0.34	0.27

* All rates and ratios have three significant figures except those in row 15, which have two.

† Includes bank deposits.

‡ The value of x that sets $(1 + [x/100])^{t}$ equal to the rise in the index of prices (row 4), where t is the number of months of hyperinflation (row 3).

§ The value of x that sets $(1 + [x/100])^{t}$ equal to the rise in the quantity of hand-to-hand currency (row 5), where t is the number of months of hyperinflation (row 3).

‖ October 2 to October 30, 1923, at a percentage rate per 30 days.

October 31 to November 10, 1944, at a percentage rate per 30 days.

** September 29 to October 31, 1923, at a percentage rate per 30 days.

†† October 23, 1923.

‡‡ November 10, 1944.

The Monetary Dynamics of Hyperinflation 27

that figure. (The three average rates of increase below 50 per cent per month shown in row 7 of Table 1 reflect low rates in some of the middle months.)

Although real cash balances fall over the whole period of hyperinflation, they do not fall in every month but fluctuate drastically, as Figures 1–7 show. Furthermore, their behavior differs greatly among the seven hyperinflations. The ratios in rows 6 and 15 have an extremely wide range. Only when we bypass short but violent oscillations in the balances by striking an average, as in row 9, do the seven hyperinflations reveal a close similarity. The similarity of the ratios in row 9 suggests that these hyperinflations reflect the same economic process. To confirm this, we need a theory that accounts for the erratic behavior of real cash balances from month to month. This study proposes and tests such a theory.

The theory developed in the following pages involves an extension of the Cambridge cash-balances equation. That equation asserts that real cash balances remain proportional to real income (X) *under given conditions.* ($M/P = kX; k =$ a constant.) Numerous writers have discussed what these given conditions are. Indeed, almost any discussion of monetary theory carries implications about the variables that determine the level of real cash balances. In the most general case the balances are a function, not necessarily linear, of real income and many other variables.

The following section discusses the most important of these variables. Because one of them—the rate of change in prices—fluctuates during hyperinflations with such extreme amplitude relative to the others, I advance the hypothesis that variations in real cash balances mainly depend on variations in the expected rate of change in prices. Section III elaborates this hypothesis and relates it to observable data on money and prices. It is supported by the statistical analysis presented in Section IV. The hypothesis, with an additional assumption, implies a dynamic process in which current price movements reflect past and current changes in the quantity of money. Sections V and VI explore certain implications of the model that describes this process. Section VII analyzes the revenue collected from the tax on cash balances, which is the counterpart of the rise in prices. A final section summarizes the theory of hyperinflation that emerges from this study.

II. The Demand for Real Cash Balances

Because money balances serve as a reserve of ready purchasing power for contingencies, the *nominal* amount of money that individuals want to hold at any moment depends primarily on the value of money, or the absolute price level. Their desired *real* cash balances depend in turn on

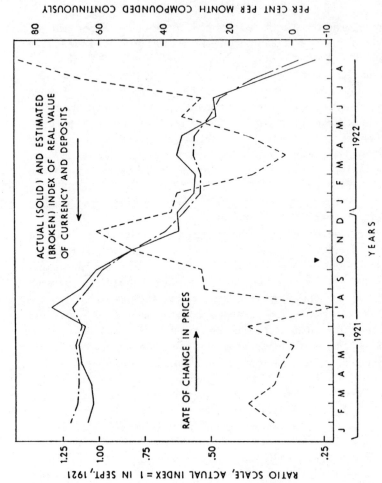

Fig. 1.—Austria—end-of-month rate of change in prices and index of real value of hand-to-hand currency and bank deposits, January, 1921, to August, 1922. (▼ Indicates beginning month of hyperinflation.)

The Monetary Dynamics of Hyperinflation   29

numerous variables. The main variables that affect an individual's desired real cash balances are (1) his wealth in real terms; (2) his current real income; and (3) the expected returns from each form in which wealth can be held, including money.

If an individual's real wealth increases, he will usually desire to hold part of the increase in the form of money, because money is readily accepted in payment for goods and services or debts—it is an asset with a high liquidity.

If his current real income increases, an individual will want to substitute cash balances for part of his illiquid assets, for now he can more readily afford to forego the premium received for holding his assets in an illiquid form, and he may need larger balances to provide conveniently for his expenditures in the periods between income payments.

If the rate of interest on an asset increases, an individual is inclined to substitute this asset for some of his other assets, including his cash balances. His desired real cash balances will decrease. In addition, an increase in the rate of interest reflects a fall in the price of the asset and a decline in the wealth of holders of the asset; this decline in wealth reduces desired real cash balances.

Thus desired real cash balances change in the same direction as real wealth and current real income and in the direction opposite to changes in the return on assets other than money.

A specification of the amount of real cash balances that individuals want to hold for all values of the variables listed above defines a demand function for real cash balances. Other variables usually have only minor effects on desired real cash balances and can be omitted from the demand function. In general, this demand function and the other demand-and-supply functions that characterize the economic system simultaneously determine the equilibrium amount of real cash balances.

A simplified theory of this determination is that the amount of goods and services demanded and supplied and their relative prices are determined independently of the monetary sector of the economy. In one version of this theory—the quantity theory of money—the absolute level of prices is independently determined as the ratio of the quantity of money supplied to a given level of desired real cash balances. Individuals cannot change the nominal amount of money in circulation, but, according to the quantity theory of money, they can influence the real value of their cash balances by attempting to reduce or increase their balances. In this attempt they bid the prices of goods and services up or down, respectively, and thereby alter the real value of cash balances.

During hyperinflation the amount of real cash balances changes

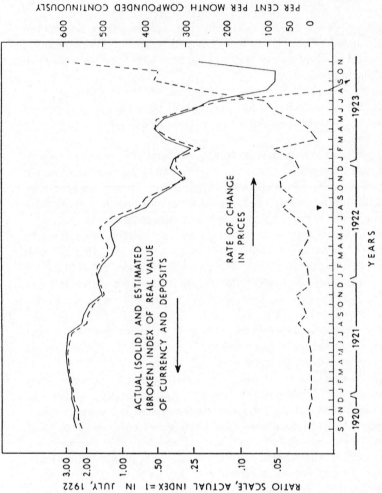

FIG. 2.—Germany—mid-month rate of change in prices and index of real value of hand-to-hand currency and bank deposits, September, 1920, to November, 1923. (▼ Indicates beginning month of hyperinflation.)

The Monetary Dynamics of Hyperinflation 31

drastically (see Table 1). At first sight these changes may appear to reflect changes in individuals' preferences for real cash balances—that is, shifts in the demand function for the balances. But these changes in real cash balances may reflect instead changes in the variables that affect the desired level of the balances. Two of the main variables affecting their desired level, wealth in real terms and real income, seem to be relatively stable during hyperinflation, at least compared with the large fluctuations in an index of real cash balances. Thus to account for these fluctuations as a movement along the demand function for the balances instead of a shift in the function, we must look for large changes in the remaining variables listed above: the expected returns on various forms of holding wealth. Changes in the return on an asset affect real cash balances only if there is a change in the difference between the expected return on the asset and that on money. If this difference rises, individuals will substitute the asset for part of their cash balances. I turn, therefore, to a more detailed consideration of the difference in return on money and on various alternatives to holding money—the cost of holding cash balances.

There is a cost of holding cash balances with respect to each of the alternative forms of holding reserves, and in a wide sense anything that can be exchanged for money is an alternative to holding reserves in the form of cash balances. For practical purposes, these alternatives can be grouped into three main classes: (1) fixed-return assets (bonds); (2) variable-return assets (equities and titles to producers' goods); and (3) non-perishable consumers' goods. The cost of holding cash balances with respect to any of these alternatives is the difference between the money return on a cash balance and the money return on an alternative that is equivalent in value to the cash balance. The money return on a cash balance may be zero, as it typically is for hand-to-hand currency; negative, as it is for demand deposits when there are service charges; or positive, as it is for deposits on which interest is paid. The money return on bonds includes interest and on equities includes dividends, as well as any gains or losses due to a change in the money value of the assets. Variations in the cost of holding cash balances when the alternative is to hold consumers' goods can be determined solely by the change in the real value of a given nominal cash balance—the rate of depreciation in the real value of money. The variation in the real value of goods because of their physical depreciation is fairly constant and can be ignored.

The only cost of holding cash balances that seems to fluctuate widely enough to account for the drastic changes in real cash balances during hyperinflation is the rate of depreciation in the value of money or, equivalently, the rate of change in prices. This observation suggests the hy-

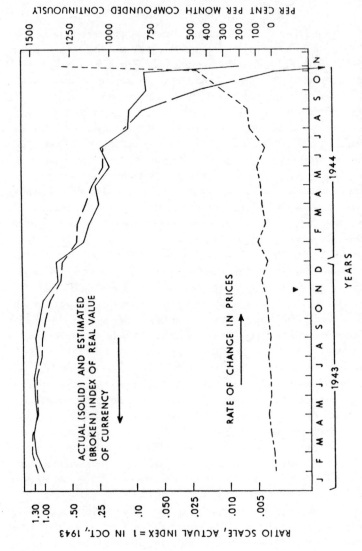

FIG. 3.—Greece—end-of-month rate of change in prices and index of real value of hand-to-hand currency, January, 1943, to October, 1944, and including November 10, 1944. (▼ Indicates beginning month of hyperinflation.)

The Monetary Dynamics of Hyperinflation 33

pothesis that changes in real cash balances in hyperinflation result from variations in the expected rate of change in prices.

To be valid, this hypothesis requires that the effects of the other variables discussed above be negligible during hyperinflation. For the most part the statistical tests in Section IV uphold the hypothesis that variations in the expected rate of change in prices account for changes in desired real cash balances. For the periods in which the data do not conform to the hypothesis, what evidence there is (see Sec. IV) suggests that taking account of changes in real income would not remedy the limitations of the hypothesis. Another explanation of why the hypothesis fails to hold for these periods is offered instead as a plausible possibility.

In order to test the hypothesis statistically, the two variables, desired real cash balances and the expected rate of change in prices, must be related to observable phenomena. The assumption made about the former is that desired real cash balances are equal to actual real cash balances at all times. This means that any discrepancy that may exist between the two is erased almost immediately by movements in the price level.[2] The assumption made about the expected rate of change in prices is that it depends on the actual rate of change in a way to be explained in the next section.

With the above two assumptions, the hypothesis asserts that time series for the price level and the quantity of money are related by some

2. This assumption can be formulated as follows: Let M^d/P and M/P represent desired and actual real cash balances. Then write

$$\frac{d \log \frac{M}{P}}{dt} = \pi\left(\log \frac{M^d}{P} - \log \frac{M}{P}\right), \tag{1}$$

where π is a positive constant. This says that, when desired and actual real cash balances differ, the percentage change in the latter is proportional to the logarithm of their ratio. Prices rise and diminish the actual balances when the latter exceed desired balances. Prices fall and increase the actual balances when the latter fall short of desired balances. If we write the equation as

$$\log \frac{M^d}{P} = \log \frac{M}{P} + \frac{1}{\pi} \frac{d \log \frac{M}{P}}{dt},$$

the assumption in the text is equivalent to asserting that π is so large that

$$\frac{1}{\pi} \frac{d \log \frac{M}{P}}{dt}$$

is always almost zero.

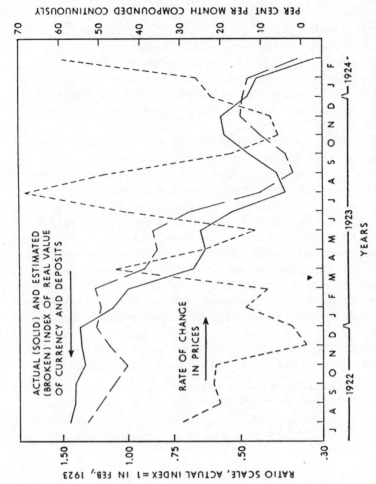

Fig. 4.—Hungary—end-of-month rate of change in prices and index of real value of hand-to-hand currency and bank deposits, July, 1922, to February, 1924. (▼ Indicates beginning month of hyperinflation.)

The Monetary Dynamics of Hyperinflation 35

equation that determines real cash balances. An equation of the following form is able to account for most of the changes in real cash balances in seven hyperinflations:

$$\log_e \frac{M}{P} = -\alpha E - \gamma. \tag{2}$$

Equation (2) shows the demand for real cash balances for different levels of the expected rate of change in prices. M is an end-of-month index of the quantity of money in circulation, and P is an end-of-month index of the price level. α (which is necessarily positive) and γ are constants. E represents the expected rate of change in prices and is assumed to be a function of the actual rate of change, denoted by C. C stands for $(d \log P)/dt$ and is approximated by the difference between the logarithms of successive values of the index of prices. This difference represents the rate of change in prices per month, compounded continuously, if the logarithms have the base e.[3]

E, being the expected level of C, has the same units of measurement as C, namely, a pure number divided by the number of months. M/P is an index and therefore a pure number. Consequently, the unit of α is "months."

An implication of the above relation is that variations in the expected rate of change in prices have the same effect on real cash balances in percentage terms regardless of the absolute amount of the balances. This follows from the fact that equation (2) is a linear relation between the expected rate of change in prices and the logarithm of real cash balances. This implication seems proper for an equation that is supposed to provide an accurate approximation to the true demand function.

If we write equation (2) in the equivalent form,

$$\frac{M}{P} = e^{-\alpha E - \gamma}, \tag{3}$$

the elasticity of demand for real cash balances with respect to the expected change in prices, implied by the above relation, is

$$\frac{d \dfrac{M}{P}}{dE} \cdot \frac{E}{M/P} = -\alpha E, \tag{4}$$

where αE is a pure number. The elasticity is proportional to the expected rate of change in prices. It is positive when E is negative, and negative when E is positive. The elasticity is zero when E is zero.

3. If we view the change in prices from P_{i-t} to P_i in t months as a continuous rate of change at a rate of C per month, $P_i = P_{i-t} e^{ct}$. When t is one month, $P_i = P_{i-1} e^{c}$; hence $C = \log_e P_i - \log_e P_{i-1}$.

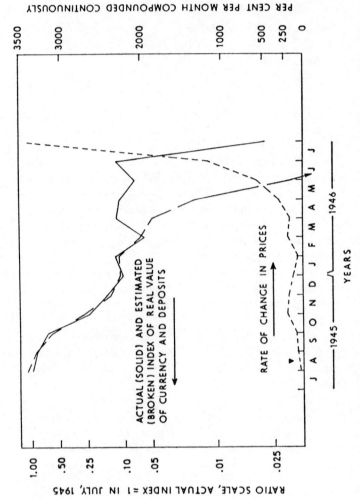

FIG. 5.—Hungary—end-of-month rate of change in prices and index of real value of hand-to-hand currency and bank deposits, July, 1945, to July, 1946. (▼ Indicates beginning month of hyperinflation.)

The Monetary Dynamics of Hyperinflation 37

III. The Expected Rate of Change in Prices

The time series for the seven hyperinflations, displayed in Figures 1–7, indicate that, if desired and actual real cash balances are always equal, the actual rate of change in prices at any moment does not account for the amount of the balances at the same moment. In many months when the rates of change in prices were very low, sometimes even zero or negative, real cash balances were still much lower than they were in previous months when the rates were higher. The expected rate of change in prices seems to depend in some way on what the actual rates of change were in the past. One way is implied by the following assumption, which underlies the statistical analysis described in the next section. *The expected rate of change in prices is revised per period of time in proportion to the difference between the actual rate of change in prices and the rate of change that was expected.*

This assumption is expressed by

$$\left(\frac{dE}{dt}\right)_t = \beta\,(C_t - E_t)\,, \qquad\qquad \beta \geq 0\,, \quad (5)$$

where C_t represents $(d \log P)/dt$ at time t, and E_t is the expected level of C_t. β is a constant,[4] which can be described as a "coefficient of expectation," since its magnitude determines the rapidity with which expected rates of change in prices adjust to actual rates. The smaller is β, the slower is the adjustment.

The solution of (5) indicates what the assumption implies about the expected rate of change in prices. Equation (5) is a linear first-order differential equation in E and t with the solution,[5]

$$E_t = H\,e^{-\beta t} + e^{-\beta t} \int_{-T}^{t} \beta C_x\, e^{\beta x} d\,x\,, \qquad\qquad (6)$$

where H is the constant of integration and $-T$ is an arbitrary lower limit of the integral. If prices had been almost constant before time $-T$, it is reasonable to assume that E was zero at time $-T$; hence

$$E_{-T} = H\,e^{\beta T} = 0\,, \qquad \text{and} \qquad H = 0\,. \qquad (7)$$

4. Since C and E have the units "per month" and dE/dt, the units "per month per month," the units of β are "per month." Equation (5) is mathematically equivalent to

$$E_t = \beta \left(\log P_t - \int_{-\infty}^{t} E_x d\,x \right) + \text{a const.},$$

where the integral term represents the expected level of prices at time t.

5. See any textbook on differential equations.

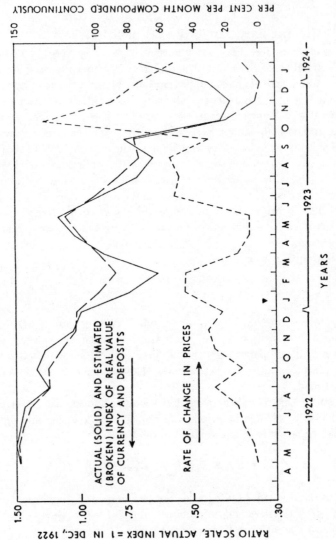

FIG. 6.—Poland—end-of-month rate of change in prices and index of real value of hand-to-hand currency and bank deposits, April, 1922, to January, 1924. (▼ Indicates beginning month of hyperinflation.)

The Monetary Dynamics of Hyperinflation 39

E_t can then be written as

$$E_t = \frac{\int_{-T}^{t} C_x e^{\beta x} dx}{\frac{e^{\beta t}}{\beta}}. \tag{8}$$

In this form the expected rate of change in prices is a weighted average of past rates of change with weights given by the exponential function, $e^{\beta x}$. The denominator of the expression represents the sum of the weights, because

$$\int_{-T}^{t} e^{\beta x} dx = \frac{e^{\beta t}}{\beta} (1 - e^{-\beta[T+t]}),$$

and because $-T$ is chosen so that $e^{-\beta(T+t)}$ is sufficiently small to neglect (see [10], p. 41, below).

Since at best there are only monthly observations of prices during most of the hyperinflations, the expected rate of change in prices is approximated by a weighted average of a series of terms, each representing the rate of change in prices for a whole month. That is, if we approximate C_x for $t - 1 < x \leq t$ by C_t,

$$\int_{t-1}^{t} C_x e^{\beta x} dx = C_t \int_{t-1}^{t} e^{\beta x} dx = \frac{C_t e^{\beta t}}{\beta} (1 - e^{-\beta}).$$

Equation (8) is then replaced by a series of terms, each representing a monthly period, as follows:[6]

$$E_t = \frac{(1 - e^{-\beta}) \sum_{x=-T}^{t} C_x e^{\beta x}}{e^{\beta t}}, \qquad t \geq 0. \tag{9}$$

6. A convenient procedure to follow in computing E for a series of months is to calculate the accumulated products of $C_x e^{\beta x}$ for all the months $x \geq -T$, noting the sum of the products for the months $x \geq 0$. Then E_t is simply the quotient of these accumulated products for $x = t$ divided by $e^{\beta t}/(1 - e^{-\beta})$. However, when β is large, say above .7, it is more convenient to compute each E_t separately by the following form of formula (9),

$$E_t = (1 - e^{-\beta}) \sum_{i=0}^{T} C_{t-i} e^{-\beta i}. \tag{9a}$$

In this procedure the weighting pattern, $(1 - e^{-\beta}) e^{-\beta i}$, is the same for each E_t and need only be calculated once for each value of β.

We can set the sum of the series of weights at a predetermined level by extending the

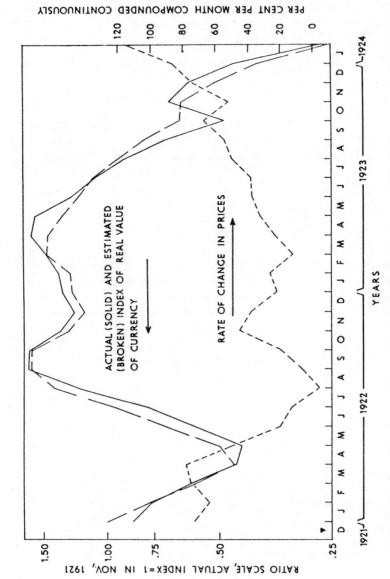

Fig. 7.—Russia—end-of-month rate of change in prices and index of real value of hand-to-hand currency, December, 1921, to January, 1924. (▼ Indicates beginning month of hyperinflation.)

The Monetary Dynamics of Hyperinflation 41

Table 2 illustrates the weighting patterns by the number of months that it takes the weights in equation (9a) to fall by specified percentage amounts for different values of β. The average length of each weighting pattern, shown in the last column, is defined as follows:

$$\frac{-\int_{-\infty}^{0} x\, e^{\beta x} d x}{\frac{e^{\beta t}}{\beta}} = +\frac{1}{\beta}.$$

It serves as a measure of the average length of time by which expectations of price changes lag behind the actual changes.

TABLE 2

CHARACTERISTICS OF EXPONENTIAL WEIGHTS
FOR DIFFERENT VALUES OF β

β (PER MONTH)	VALUE OF WEIGHT WHEN $t=0$ (ROUNDED TO HUNDREDTHS)	APPROXIMATE NUMBER OF MONTHS FOR WEIGHTS TO FALL BY			AVERAGE LENGTH OF WEIGHTING PATTERNS $(1/\beta)$ (MONTHS)
		50 Per Cent	75 Per Cent	90 Per Cent	
.01........	0.01	70	139	230	100.0
.05........	0.05	14	28	46	20.0
.10........	0.10	7	14	23	10.0
.15........	0.14	5	9	15	6.7
.20........	0.18	3	7	12	5.0
.25........	0.22	3	7	9	4.0
.30........	0.26	2	5	8	3.3
.35........	0.30	2	4	7	2.9
.40........	0.33	2	3	6	2.5
.50........	0.39	1	3	5	2.0
.75........	0.53	1	2	3	1.3
1.00........	0.63	1	1	2	1.0
5.00........	0.99	0	0	0	0.5
10.00........	1.00	0	0	0	0.1

IV. STATISTICAL ANALYSIS OF DATA FROM SEVEN HYPERINFLATIONS

Equation (2) and the approximation to the expected rate of change in prices given by equation (9) imply the following equation. The random variable ϵ_t is inserted to account for deviations of the left-hand side from zero.

series. In this study T was set such that

$$(1 - e^{-\beta})\, e^{\beta(-T-t)} < .00005 \qquad (10)$$

for $t = 0$ (the first month used in the regressions); using the same T, the inequality is sure to hold for any $t \geq 0$. We are then sure that the series of weights for $t \geq 0$ adds up to $1 \pm .00005$ for $\beta \geq .01$.

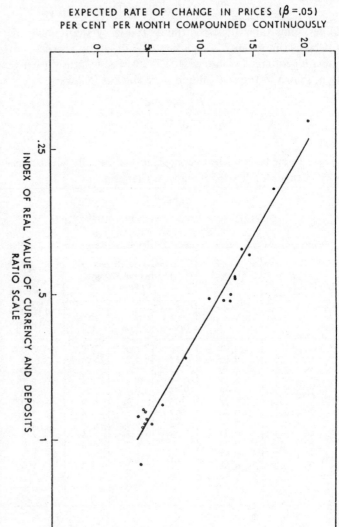

EXPECTED RATE OF CHANGE IN PRICES (β =.05)
PER CENT PER MONTH COMPOUNDED CONTINUOUSLY

INDEX OF REAL VALUE OF CURRENCY AND DEPOSITS
RATIO SCALE

FIG. 8.—Austria—scatter diagram of end-of-month expected rates of change in prices and indexes of real value of hand-to-hand currency and bank deposits, and regression line (α = 8.55), January, 1921, to August, 1922.

The Monetary Dynamics of Hyperinflation 43

$$\log_e \left(\frac{M}{P}\right)_t + a \, \frac{(1 - e^{-\beta})}{e^{\beta t}} \sum_{x=-T}^{t} C_x e^{\beta x} + \gamma = \epsilon_t. \tag{11}$$

Table 3 contains estimates of the parameters a and β and the correlation coefficients derived by fitting equation (11) to the data from seven hyperinflations.[7] The method of fitting was by least squares. Figures 8-14 show the scatter diagrams of the regressions. Time series of real cash balances estimated from the regression functions have been plotted in

TABLE 3

LEAST-SQUARES ESTIMATES OF a AND β AND CORRELATION COEFFICIENTS
FOR SEVEN HYPERINFLATIONS*

COUNTRY	TIME PERIOD (END OF MONTH)	DE-GREES OF FREE-DOM	ESTI-MATED VALUE OF a (MONTHS)	ESTI-MATED VALUE OF β ($\pm$.05) (PER MONTH)	CONFIDENCE INTERVALS†		TOTAL CORR. COEF.
					a (Months)	β (Per Month)	
Austria........	Jan., 1921–Aug., 1922	17	8.55	.05	4.43–31.0	.01 – .15	.989
Germany.....	Sept., 1920–July, 1923	32	5.46	.20	5.05– 6.13	.15 – .25	.992
Greece‡.......	Jan., 1943–Aug., 1944	17	4.09	.15	2.83–32.5§	.01§–.30	.980
Hungary......	July, 1922–Feb., 1924	17	8.70	.10	6.36–42.2§	.01§– 20	.926
Hungary‡.....	July, 1945–Feb., 1946	5	3.63	.15	2.55– 4.73	.10 – 30	.998
Poland.......	Apr., 1922–Nov., 1923	17	2.30	.30	1.74– 3.94	.10 –.60	.972
Russia‡.......	Dec., 1921–Jan., 1924	23	3.06	.35	2.66– 3.76	.25 –.45	.971

* The estimates were computed by maximizing the total correlation coefficient for given values of β rather than by solving the normal equations. The value of β was estimated within an interval of $\pm$ .05. The correct value of the correlation coefficient for each sample is therefore slightly greater than the values given in the table. The method of computing the estimates is discussed in Appendix A, and the data used are given in Appendix B.

† Confidence coefficient for intervals of a and β is .90. The confidence intervals for β are the extreme limits of a .05 interval. That is, the lower limits could be as much as .05 higher, and the upper limits could be as much as .05 lower.

‡ Greece has no adjustment to include deposits because the required data are not available. An adjustment to include deposits is not necessary for Russia. The figures for the quantity of money in Hungary following World War II include deposits for each month. See Appendix B.

§ End of confidence interval lies beyond the figure given. The correct figure was not computed because of the unreliability of the estimates of the expected change in prices for the earlier months when β is very small.

Figures 1–7. For all hyperinflations except the Russian, the regressions include observations before the beginning month shown in Table 1 in order to raise the number of degrees of freedom. But observations were not used from earlier periods in which real cash balances were subject to erratic movements. These movements were mostly increases in the balances in periods of rising prices before the beginning of hyperinflation and are inconsistent with the behavior implied by the demand function formulated above. They are discussed more fully below.

For the periods of hyperinflation covered the results indicate that an exponentially weighted average of past rates of change in prices adequate-

7. The method of deriving the estimates is discussed in Appendix A (pp. 92–96).

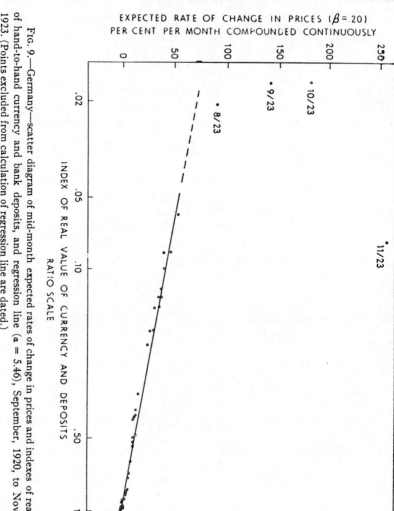

FIG. 9.—Germany—scatter diagram of mid-month expected rates of change in prices and indexes of real value of hand-to-hand currency and bank deposits, and regression line ($a = 5.46$), September, 1920, to November, 1923. (Points excluded from calculation of regression line are dated.)

The Monetary Dynamics of Hyperinflation 45

ly accounts for movements in real cash balances. Furthermore, the confidence intervals for the estimates of β clearly indicate that expected rates of change in prices are not equal to current actual rates. The value of β that produces this equality is 10.0 (see the second column of Table 2). The highest value of β that does not differ from any of the estimates at the .10 level of significance is only .60.[8]

TABLE 4

ESTIMATES OF α AND β FOR SEVEN HYPERINFLATIONS TAKEN TO-
GETHER AND TEST OF SIGNIFICANCE BETWEEN ESTIMATES FOR
THE HYPERINFLATIONS TAKEN TOGETHER AND SEPARATELY*

ESTIMATED VALUE OF		TOTAL CORR. COEF.	LIKELIHOOD-RATIO TEST OF SIGNIFICANCE BETWEEN ESTIMATES OF α AND β FOR THE HYPERINFLATIONS TAKEN TOGETHER AND SEPARATELY	
α (Months)	β ($\pm.05$) (Per Month)		Likelihood Ratio	.005 Level of Significance for Likelihood Ratio
4.68	.20	.894	72.53	28.3

* See Appendix A for statistical methods.

Table 4 gives estimates of α and β derived by fitting equation (11) to the data for all the hyperinflations taken together. These estimates differ significantly from those computed for each hyperinflation separately.[9]

8. The confidence intervals must be accepted with some caution. Besides relying on asymptotic properties of the likelihood ratio, the method of calculating these intervals assumes the independent normal distribution of the residuals from the least-squares fit. The confidence intervals can at best serve to indicate the approximate amount of random variability in the estimates of the two parameters.

9. Table 4 gives the results of fitting equation (11) to all the data under the assumption that the value of α is the same and the value of β is the same in all the hyperinflations. The value of γ varies among the hyperinflations. That the level of the likelihood ratio is significant for this fit means that the correlation coefficient of the fit is significantly lower than the correlation coefficient based on estimates derived for each hyperinflation separately.

Two other fits of equation (11) were made to all the data. In the first fit, all the hyperinflations have the same value of β, and the values of α and γ vary among the hyperinflations. In the second fit, the value of α is the same in all the hyperinflations, while the values of β and γ vary. The correlation coefficient in these two fits is smaller significantly at the .005 level than the coefficient based on the estimates derived for each hyperinflation separately.

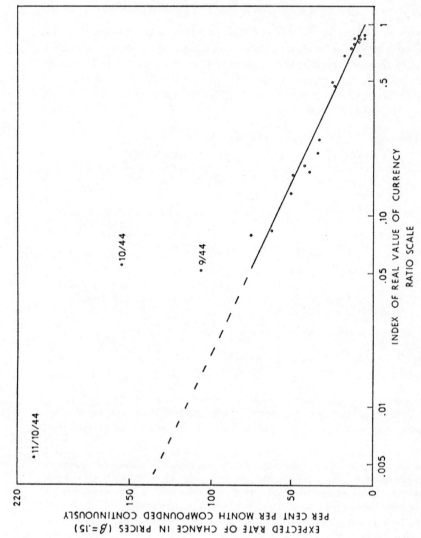

Fig. 10.—Greece—scatter diagram of end-of-month expected rates of change in prices and indexes of real value of hand-to-hand currency, and regression line (α = 4.09), January, 1943, to October, 1944, and including November 10, 1944. (Points excluded from calculation of the regression line are dated.)

The Monetary Dynamics of Hyperinflation 47

Consequently, the differences in the values of the parameters for each hyperinflation cannot be ascribed to random variability in the estimates.

However, we should not overstress these differences. The similarity in the results for the different countries is striking in some important respects. Later sections explore the economic significance of the estimated values of the parameters and point out differences and similarities in the seven hyperinflations. This section deals with the general question of the accuracy of the statistical results. They require certain reservations, not only because of unreliable data but even more because of other difficulties of an economic and statistical nature. These difficulties are taken up below under the following headings: (1) reliability of the data; (2) economic variables ignored in the regression function; (3) observations that do not fit the regressions; and (4) increases in the coefficient of expectation.

1. RELIABILITY OF THE DATA

The data for the statistical analysis are indexes of prices and the quantity of hand-to-hand currency adjusted for all the countries except Greece and Russia to include the quantity of bank deposits. As indicated in Appendix B, which describes the data, they have limited coverage. Hand-to-hand currencies are usually issued by one governmental agency, and official publications report the quantity in circulation with unquestioned accuracy. However, illegal and counterfeit currencies, which are excluded from the money figures because of the unavailability of monthly data, circulated freely in at least one hyperinflation—the German—and were issued to some extent in most of the others. The quantity of bank deposits is based on figures that lack complete coverage. As is shown below, however, an adjustment of the money figures to include deposits has only a small effect on the estimates and cannot be a source of much error. Little can be said about the price indexes except that most of them are averages of prices of economically important commodities. The indexes are far from comprehensive in scope, and their accuracy can be checked only by independent sources. When these exist, they agree on the whole with the index used.

If, as these remarks imply, much of the data could be subject to large errors, why are the correlation coefficients in Table 3 so high? Poor data tend to increase the residual errors of a least-squares fit. The high correlation coefficients suggest that the bulk of the figures are not subject to large random errors. One factor that enhances the reliability of the data is their extreme rates of change. The differences in the rates at which the prices of various commodities rise in hyperinflation are, while no doubt

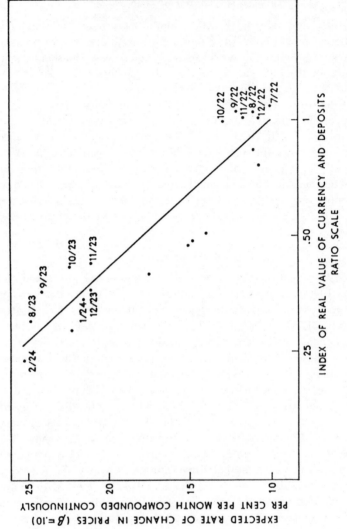

Fig. 11.—Hungary—scatter diagram of end-of-month expected rates of change in prices and indexes of real value of hand-to-hand currency and bank deposits, and regression line (α = 8.70), July, 1922, to February, 1924. (Points before January, 1923, and after July, 1923, are dated.)

The Monetary Dynamics of Hyperinflation 49

large in absolute terms, probably small relative to the rates themselves. Therefore, a price index restricted in scope reflects fairly accurately the rate of rise of an index of all prices. The money figures also, while incomplete, are adequate for approximating large changes.

Although apparently free from large random errors, the data could be consistently biased in one direction. The exclusion of illegal and counterfeit currencies tends to lower the estimates of α.[10] Also limiting a price index to wholesale or retail commodities exclusively, as is necessary for want of comprehensive data, tends to make the index too high or too low, respectively. Note, however, that, if the price index used is a constant multiple of a "correct" index, α and β are estimated without bias. To produce bias in the estimates of β, an index must misrepresent the rates of change in prices. Even then, estimates of β will not be biased if there is a linear relation between the rates used and the "correct" rates. It is not unlikely that such a relation holds approximately. In hyperinflation all prices rise so rapidly that almost any group of them registers more or less accurately the time pattern of the movements in all. Consequently, bias resulting from a consistent error in the price index would appear mainly in estimates of α. But they exhibit no signs of this bias. There is no relation between the size of the estimates of α in Table 3 and the kind of index used. The estimates of α for the Austrian and first Hungarian hyperinflations are the two largest, and they are based on indexes of the cost of living and wholesale prices, respectively. The Polish and Russian estimates, which are the two smallest, depend on indexes of wholesale and retail prices, respectively. The bias is apparently not large enough to determine the rank of the estimates. Therefore, we should be able to rely at least on their general magnitude.

The data for the estimates in Table 3 include indexes of hand-to-hand currency and monthly interpolations of an annual index of the quantity of bank deposits held by individuals and enterprises. As one of the notes to Table 3 points out, the data for Greece and Russia do not include deposits; for Hungary after World War II monthly figures on deposits are available, and no interpolations are necessary. For the other four hyperinflations Table 5 gives estimates of α and β computed from data that exclude deposits. A comparison of Tables 3 and 5 indicates that including an estimate of deposits improves the correlation coefficient twice (Germany and Hungary after World War I) and diminishes it twice (Austria

10. Figures for the quantity of money that understate the correct amount by an increasing percentage over time also make the index of real cash balances progressively too low by an increasing percentage and bias the estimate of α downward.

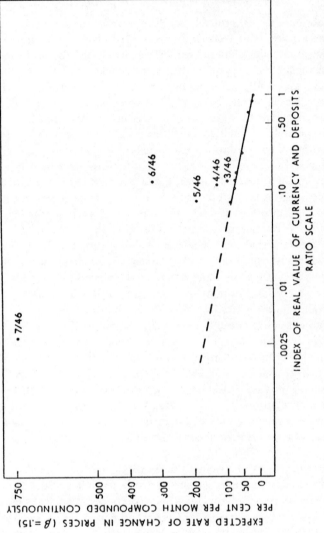

FIG. 12.—Hungary—scatter diagram of end-of-month expected rates of change in prices and indexes of real value of hand-to-hand currency and bank deposits, and regression line (α = 3.63), July, 1945, to July, 1946. (Points excluded from calculation of the regression line are dated.)

The Monetary Dynamics of Hyperinflation 51

and Poland).[11] The net effects on the estimates of including deposits are unimportant. It is likely, therefore, that the use of deposit figures in the other hyperinflations would not make an appreciable difference. Moreover, the ratio of deposits to currency is not likely to change rapidly, so that the use of monthly deposit figures, if they were available, would probably not alter these results.

TABLE 5

ESTIMATED VALUES OF α AND β EXCLUDING
BANK DEPOSITS FROM THE DATA*

Country	Estimated Value of α (Months)	Estimated Value of β ($\pm .05$) (Per Month)	Total Correlation Coefficient
Austria....................	8.78	.05	.996
Germany...................	5.04	.25	.987
Hungary (after World War I)..	6.16	.10	.886
Poland....................	2.84	.25	.978

* The monthly periods and the degrees of freedom are the same as in Table 3. The remarks in n. * of Table 3 apply to these estimates.

2. ECONOMIC VARIABLES IGNORED IN THE REGRESSION FUNCTION

The figures for the quantity of money exclude all money in circulation during the hyperinflations that did not have a fixed rate of exchange with the depreciating currency. One important type of excluded money is foreign bank notes. In addition, in Russia a stable-valued currency first issued by the government at the end of 1922, the chervonets, circulated along with the depreciating rubles. The Hungarian government issued a new currency in 1946, the tax pengö, which was supposed to keep a constant purchasing power. Its issue was partly successful in that it never depreciated in value at the tremendous rates reached by the regular pengö.

These issues are not counted as part of the quantity of money, because this study concerns the cash balances of rapidly depreciating currencies only. However, the sudden introduction of these other issues opened up new alternatives to holding the depreciating currency in cash balances. The fact that a stable-valued money does not pay interest means little

11. Including deposits should improve the results, because the trend of deposits and that of hand-to-hand currency may differ from each other by a great deal. It is to be expected that using monthly interpolations of an annual index of deposits might increase the residual errors about the regression lines. Therefore, the fact that the variance of the residual errors was increased by the adjustment in two cases does not indicate that the estimates of the parameters were not improved.

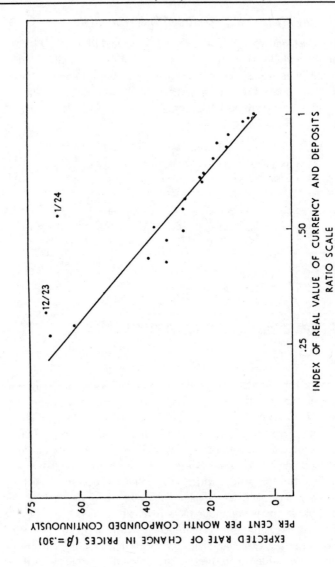

Fig. 13.—Poland—scatter diagram of end-of-month expected rates of change in prices and indexes of real value of hand-to-hand currency and bank deposits, and regression line ($\alpha = 2.30$), April, 1922, to January, 1924. (Points excluded from calculation of regression line are dated.)

The Monetary Dynamics of Hyperinflation 53

in time of hyperinflation. The main concern is to prevent balances of future purchasing power from completely vanishing. Therefore, the effect of issuing a stable-valued currency along with a depreciating one is to hasten the liquidation of balances composed of the latter. It is difficult, however, to find evidence of this effect. As for foreign bank notes, the quantity in circulation during the hyperinflations is not known. It can only be assumed that they could always be held and that their quantity in circulation increased gradually as the rapidly diminishing value of the domestic currency encouraged their use. If so, their gradual increase in circulation does not disrupt the continuity of the data but does make *a* higher than it would be if they could not be obtained. The quantities of chervontsi issued in Russia during 1922–23 are known. The magnitude of their effect on the real value of rubles is difficult to judge. In any event, real cash balances of rubles were not comparatively low in Russia during the last part of the hyperinflation, as the introduction of the chervonets may suggest. There are apparently no figures on the circulation of the tax pengö issued in Hungary in 1946, and so there is no way to determine the magnitude of its effect on the value of the regular pengö.

Other errors in the estimates arising from sources of an economic nature are probably minor. The main variable that was neglected in formulating the demand function for real cash balances is real income. Conceivably, changes in real income could have large effects on the balances. Such changes, however, are probably not a source of much error in the estimates. For some countries there are annual indexes of production and agricultural output to indicate the change in real income. These indexes have small movements compared with the fluctuations in real cash balances, at least until prices rise drastically in the last stages of hyperinflation. A semiannual index of output for Germany declines in the final stage of hyperinflation by as much as one-third in less than half a year.[12] Even so, an adjustment of the data to take account of real-income changes in Germany that assumes income elasticity of demand for the balances to be unity has little effect on the parameter estimates. This effect largely offsets that of the adjustment to include deposits. For the other countries, indexes of output suggest either no great change in real income during the months of hyperinflation or conflicting tendencies from which no conclusions can be drawn.

12. In so far as this drop in real income resulted from measures intentionally adopted to restrict the use of money, there need be no further effect on desired real cash balances.

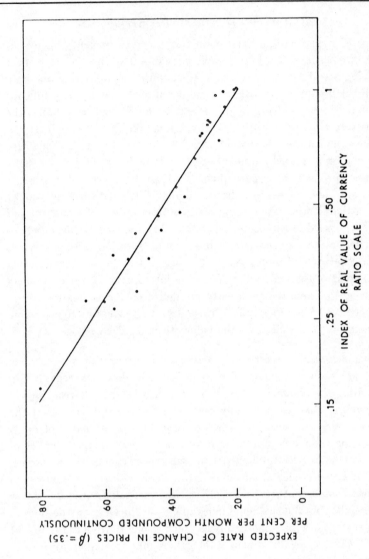

FIG. 14.—Russia—scatter diagram of end-of-month expected rates of change in prices and indexes of real value of hand-to-hand currency, and regression line ($\alpha = 3.06$), December, 1921, to January, 1924.

The Monetary Dynamics of Hyperinflation · 55

3. OBSERVATIONS THAT DO NOT FIT THE REGRESSIONS

The periods covered by the statistical analysis exclude some of the observations near the end of the hyperinflations. The excluded observations are from the German, Greek, and second Hungarian hyperinflations, and they are dated in Figures 8–14. (Some of the points on the scatter diagram for the first Hungarian hyperinflation are also dated, but they were not excluded from the statistical analysis.) All the excluded observations lie considerably to the right of the regression lines, and their inclusion in the statistical analysis would improperly alter the estimates of α and β derived from the earlier observations of the hyperinflations.

One or both of two hypotheses could explain these observations with a much higher level of real cash balances than equation (2) implies. The first one is that in hyperinflation rumors of currency reform encourage the belief that prices will not continue to rise rapidly for more than a certain number of months. This leads individuals to hold higher real cash balances than they would ordinarily desire in view of the rate at which prices are expected to rise in the current month. As long as currency reform remains improbable for the near future, individuals adjust their real cash balances according to the rate at which they expect prices to change for some time. When they believe that the current rate at which they expect prices to rise will not last indefinitely, they are less willing to incur certain costs involved in keeping their balances low. For example, individuals would be unwilling to invest in risky equity stocks or secondhand durable goods whose principal attraction consists in the lack of better alternatives, unless there appeared to be no end to currency depreciation. Firms would not lease warehouses to maintain high inventory stocks as a substitute for cash assets, if the lease were expected to far outrun the rise in prices. Thus, when hyperinflation is expected to end in the near future, real cash balances will gradually rise, even though the expected rate of change in prices for the period preceding the end of hyperinflation remains constant or increases.

The second hypothesis is that the function that determines the demand for real cash balances does not conform to equation (2). This hypothesis suggests that the regression function shown on the scatter diagrams would fit the observations better if it curved upward on the left. To be consistent with the data, this hypothesis requires that all observations that lie to the right of the linear regressions shall fall in order along some curved regression function or, equivalently, that the value of α shall decline as the expected change in prices increases.[13]

13. It is conceivable, of course, that these high levels of real cash balances could be explained by more radical revisions of the model than are considered in the text. For

It would be difficult to test these two hypotheses, and I shall not attempt to do so. But it is not difficult, and is certainly worthwhile, to see to what extent they are consistent with the data plotted on the scatter diagrams. The evidence from these diagrams can be summarized briefly.

The Austrian data (see Fig. 8) do not support either of the two hypotheses. All the observations lie close to a linear regression line. The Russian data (see Fig. 14) only slightly support the two hypotheses. The four observations that lie substantially to the right of the upper half of the linear regression line refer to the last four months of hyperinflation. If these four observations were lowered to take into account the effects of expectations of currency reform, then all the observations might lie near a regression function that curved upward slightly. The Hungarian data after World War I (see Fig. 11) do not seem to support the two hypotheses. However, the four observations that lie to the right of the upper half of the regression line may show a high level of real cash balances because of expectations of currency reform. Figure 4 showed that the observations for August, September, and October, 1923, refer to a period in which the rate of change in prices fell sharply. It is possible that during these three months and the following month, November, there was an expectation that hyperinflation would soon end. A similar expectation may have affected the observations to the right of the lower half of the regression line. August through October, 1922, was a period of falling rates of change in prices. The difficulty of explaining the Hungarian data after World War I in this way is that some of the data from the other hyperinflations are inconsistent with the same explanation. In the Polish hyperinflation, for example (see Fig. 6), the rate of change in prices declined from February to March, 1923, but the data for this period indicate that the estimated level of real cash balances was *not* above the actual level for the entire period.

Observations near the end of the other hyperinflations lie at varying distances to the right of the regression lines, and regression functions that

---

example, new currency could be issued at such a high rate that people could not prevent the real value of their balances from rising even though expenditures rise at an increasing rate. However, a lag in the adjustment of actual real cash balances to their desired level, like that expressed by equation (1) in n. 2, fails to remedy the limitations of the model in the final months of hyperinflation. The lag suggests that the balances should decline when their actual level exceeds the desired level. In fact, they frequently rose still more in the ending months when the model indicates they already exceeded their desired level by large amounts. The failure of this lag to account for the facts reinforces the supposition that the first hypothesis in the text, while it cannot be directly supported, is the main explanation of these limitations.

The Monetary Dynamics of Hyperinflation 57

curved upward would not fit them closely. However, expectations of currency reform may account for these observations. If they were adjusted for the effects of these expectations, it is possible that curvilinear regression functions would then fit the observations better than linear ones. The German hyperinflation provides a good example of this possibility (see Fig. 9). Prices had almost stopped rising in Germany by the middle of November, 1923. (This explains why real cash balances in the middle of that month were relatively so high.) The horizontal distance between the regression line and observations for the three preceding months is progressively greater for the months nearer to the end of hyperinflation. The configuration of these observations is thus consistent with an increasing effect on real cash balances of expectations of currency reform. If taking this effect on the balances into account shifted the points for August, September, and October, 1923, slightly to the left, there is some curvilinear regression function that would fit the data for these three months fairly well.

Similar remarks apply to the later observations for the Greek and Hungarian hyperinflations after World War II and the Polish hyperinflation after World War I (see Figs. 10, 12, and 13). The horizontal distance between the regression line and observations for the later months in these three hyperinflations is progressively greater for the months nearer to the end of the hyperinflations, which, according to the first hypothesis, suggests an increase in the effects of expectations of currency reform. Nevertheless, the observations from these hyperinflations, as well as those from the German one, are not inconsistent with the second hypothesis. Regression functions that curved upward slightly would fit the observations better than linear ones. The scatter diagrams indicate that the functions should begin to curve upward for an expected percentage rate of change in prices per month (compounded continuously) greater than 90–100, except for the Polish hyperinflation where the function should curve upward for a rate greater than 60–70.

The preceding discussion does not provide a direct test of the two hypotheses advanced above, but it does suggest possible revisions to make equation (2) more consistent with the data. Whether these revisions stand up in the light of all the relevant evidence has yet to be confirmed. The first is that expectations of currency reform acted to raise real cash balances near the end of hyperinflation. It is difficult to infer the extent to which this revision is required, because the second revision is also consistent with the data. What the second revision comes to is the possibility that the value of α falls at the higher levels reached by the expected change in prices.

58   *Studies in the Quantity Theory of Money*

4. INCREASES IN THE COEFFICIENT OF EXPECTATION

Figures 1–7 reveal that the residual errors by which estimated real cash balances differ from the actual levels have marked serial correlation. It is statistically significant at less than the .05 level in all hyperinflations except the second Hungarian.[14] And that one is probably not significant only because so few months were included in the regression. The regressions essentially involve fitting difference equations, in which uncorrelated random disturbances typically produce serial correlation, and its appearance in the results is not surprising. However, some, if not nearly all, of it can be attributed to shifts over time in the true value of the coefficient of expectation. Even if these shifts were purely random, the expected price change, being a sum of terms that contain past values of the coefficient (see eq. [6]), would include a component that involved the sum of successive values of a random variable. As is well known, such a sum will show positive serial correlation.

But random movements in the coefficient account for only part, probably a small part, of the serial correlation, because the evidence indicates that the coefficient does not shift in a purely random fashion but tends to increase over time. The index of real cash balances estimated from the regression functions tends to register in the early months a larger response to fluctuations in contemporaneous price changes than the actual index does, and in the later months a smaller response (see Figs. 1–7). This tendency implies that the estimated coefficients are too high for the early months and too low later on.[15] The tendency stands out clearly in five of the hyperinflations when they are divided into two parts: the Austrian, divided at June, 1921; the Greek, divided at November, 1943; the first Hungarian, divided at August, 1923; the Polish, divided at December, 1922; and the Russian, divided at April, 1923. Of the other two, the second Hungarian was too short for this tendency to show up, and the German (discussed in a moment) seems to show, if anything, the opposite tendency.

This tendency in five of the hyperinflations is confirmed by computed estimates of the coefficient, which have a higher value when the regression

14. For a description of the test for serial correlation used see J. von Neumann, "Distribution of the Ratio of the Mean Square Successive Difference to the Variance," *Annals of Mathematical Statistics*, XII (December, 1941), 367–95. For the significance tables see B. I. Hart and J. von Neumann, "Tabulation of the Probabilities for the Ratio of the Mean Square Successive Difference to the Variance," *Annals of Mathematical Statistics*, XIII (June, 1942), 207–14.

15. This cannot be due to a rising value of a, for then we should observe that points on the scatter diagrams, plotted for a given coefficient, curved downward to the left. Actually the points curve upward, if they curve at all.

The Monetary Dynamics of Hyperinflation 59

fit includes only the later months than when the fit includes all the months. Table 6 gives estimates that were derived by fitting the regression to an arbitrary number of the later months. The three hyperinflations represented in the table were the only ones with an estimate for the later months that exceeded the estimate for all months by .05 or more. For these three, the last column in the table shows that the estimate for the later months as a percentage of the estimate for all months was 150 to over 200 per cent, that is, the former *exceeded* the latter by 50 to over 100 per cent. For Austria and Greece, computations not shown suggest that the estimate for the later months also exceeded the estimate for all months by as much as 50 per cent. However, for these two countries the

TABLE 6

ESTIMATES OF α AND β FOR THE LATER MONTHS
OF THREE HYPERINFLATIONS*

COUNTRY	PERIOD	DEGREES OF FREEDOM	ESTIMATE OF		ESTIMATE OF β FOR LATER MONTHS AS PERCENTAGE OF ESTIMATE FOR ALL MONTHS†
			α (Months)	β (Per Month)	
Hungary...	Feb., 1923–Feb., 1924	10	4.72	.15($\pm$.05)	150
Poland.....	Aug., 1922–Dec., 1923	14	1.72	.45($\pm$.05)	150
Russia.....	Apr., 1923–Jan., 1924	7	2.37	.80($\pm$.10)	230

* Method of estimation and sources are the same as for Table 3.

† Preceding column in this table as a percentage of the corresponding estimates of the coefficient for all months shown in Table 3.

percentage difference between the two estimates could not be judged precisely without more exact estimates than have been computed. (The period covered by the regression for Hungary after World War II was too short to detect any change in the coefficient.) These estimates are of average values of the coefficient in the periods covered. If the coefficient was increasing within the periods, the results indicate that its percentage increase from the beginning to the end of these hyperinflations was at least greater than 50 per cent. Based on so few observations, these estimates are certainly subject to considerable error,[16] but they do suggest that increases in the coefficient over time may have been substantial.

16. It is likely that the percentages in the last column of Table 6 are somewhat too high. Errors of measurement in the index of prices, which is used in the index of real cash balances and of current change in prices, will produce a spurious correlation between these two and thus tend to bias estimates of the coefficient upward. This bias will be

For Germany, on the other hand, an estimate for the later months was about the same as the estimate for all months. The failure of the German data to indicate that the coefficient increased is puzzling in view of the other evidence. It is possible that the estimate for all months is too high for the early months even though the regression appears to fit equally well throughout. This result could occur if the extreme fluctuations in real cash balances for the later months dominated the regression, as appears probable only for Germany, and the relatively stable level of the balances from September, 1920, to July, 1921, contributed little. It is not clear, therefore, that the coefficient did not increase, though the amount could not have been very much.

That the coefficient should generally increase over time is certainly reasonable. It would be strange indeed if the public did not become conditioned by recent inflation to conclude that a fresh spurt in prices was not temporary but foretold more intense inflation to come. The assumption about expectations made in Section III pictured them as determined by a trial-and-error process, whereby expected price changes were adjusted to actual changes at a rate proportional to their difference. That assumption seems to provide an adequate approximation to the facts and sufficed for the model. But there is no reason to stop there. It is also reasonable to assume that with experience the public should make these adjustments more rapidly. We have found this assumption to be generally consistent with the data, though the effect of increases in the coefficient on the level of real cash balances is small compared with the major fluctuations that the balances undergo. Nevertheless, this assumption is important, for it ought to account for the level of the coefficients at the beginning of hyperinflation. The coefficient should be higher when past price rises have been more prolonged or larger.

Table 7 compares the level of the coefficient with the price changes preceding hyperinflation. The figures reveal some relation, though it is far from precise, between the level of the coefficient and the extent of past inflation. To what degree errors in the estimates of the coefficient account for the lack of precision in this relation is difficult to say. The very wide confidence intervals for the estimates (see Table 3) suggest that too

---

greater the shorter is the time period covered by the regression, because the variance of errors in the series, which is unrelated to the length of period covered, is then a larger fraction of the total variance, which is larger for longer periods. The amount of bias is difficult to judge. Indirect evidence that it might be fairly sizable is presented in the next section. But, since over-all fluctuations in the series in the periods covered are so large, it is unlikely to account entirely for all the increase in the coefficient over time shown by the estimates.

The Monetary Dynamics of Hyperinflation 61

much reliance should not be placed on them. Yet it is possible to make sense of these figures "after the fact" and to reach some tentative conclusions. The low Austrian coefficient corresponds to relatively mild inflation in the preceding period, and the high Russian one to vigorous war and postwar inflation. For these two the relation seems clear cut. For the others it is less so. If we disregard Germany for the moment, we can attribute the high Polish coefficient to the large rise in prices over the entire

TABLE 7

COMPARISON OF EXPECTATION COEFFICIENT WITH PRICE
CHANGES PRECEDING HYPERINFLATION*

HYPERINFLATION	COEFFI-CIENT OF EXPECTA-TION	PRICE CHANGE PRECEDING BEGINNING MONTH OF REGRESSIONS		
		Since Prewar (1913–14 or 1937–39) (Per Cent)	One Year (Per Cent)	Two Years (Per Cent per Year)
Austrian.........	.05	6,500	94	82
Hungarian I.....	.10	17,300	314	N.a.
Hungarian II.....	.15	10,400	3,460†	520‡
Greek...........	.15	9,750	424	940§
German.........	.20	1,400	206	156
Polish...........	.30	75,000‖	241#	N.a.
Russian.........	.35	28,800,000	1,610	990

N.a. = Not available.
* For sources see Appendix B.
† 13 months at an annual rate.
‡ 25 months at an annual rate.
§ 22 months at an annual rate.
‖ Wholesale price index. A cost-of-living index gives 58,500 per cent.
Cost-of-living index. A wholesale-price index linked to an index of retail food prices gives 137 per cent.

period since 1913–14, and the lower coefficient for Greece and Hungary to a smaller rise over that period, in spite of their larger figures for the year immediately preceding hyperinflation. Apparently the rapid inflation preceding the second Hungarian hyperinflation was also too short to affect the coefficient much. Thus Hungary's experience with hyperinflation the first time does not seem to have influenced behavior appreciably the second time it occurred. This result suggests that memories of currency depreciation fade away in a quarter-century, at least the first time, and that speed of adjustment depends on how prolonged recent experience with inflation has been.

The medium-sized German coefficient at first sight seems out of line

with the others in view of the mild inflation there during and immmediate-
ly after the war. The comparatively high level of this coefficient conceivably results from the advanced development, both financial and industrial, of the German economy at that time. Depreciation in the value of
money may be more apparent, and its effects sooner felt, in an economy
with proportionately less agriculture. Industrial firms and workers rely
on the value of money in selling their products and services; in less urban-
ized economies, money is used much less. While these facts were also
likely to make the coefficient for Austria higher relative to the others, its
value was low primarily because hyperinflation there was milder and
much shorter, ending just about the time the others, after World War I,
were getting started.

By and large, it appears that the coefficient usually increased in response to continual inflation. This increase probably accounts for most
of the serial correlation in the regression residuals. Whether the coefficient increased steadily or suddenly jumped to a higher level during
the hyperinflations cannot be determined, since the data cover too short
a period of time for gradual changes to show up. However, there is some
evidence on this question in the behavior of real cash balances in the
months preceding those included in the regressions. This evidence points
to rather sudden increases in the coefficient from very low or even
negative levels. A negative coefficient in the initial stages of inflation
would indicate that the public expects prices to decline eventually. In
Germany the balances rose throughout World War I, even though prices
were continually going up. Shortly after the war the balances fell sharply
by far more than the model can account for. Moreover, there is no indication that real income fell sharply at the same time. In Austria and Poland
as well, the balances rose in the months preceding hyperinflation, despite
continual inflation. There was also a rapid fall in real cash balances in
these two countries shortly after the war. This fall seems to reflect a belated adjustment to inflation after a long period in which prices were
expected to return to their prewar level.[17] (The figures on money do not
go back far enough in time for Hungary during both world wars and for
Greece during World War II to observē whether the same phenomenon
occurred in these countries.)

17. In Russia, however, real cash balances fell continuously throughout World
War I, even though the rate of change in prices fluctuated fairly closely about the same
average level from the middle of 1917 to the end of 1921. The decline in real income and
political uncertainties during the same period probably account for this steady fall in
the balances.

The Monetary Dynamics of Hyperinflation 63

The erratic changes in the balances preceding hyperinflation imply that the coefficient of expectation makes a sudden upward shift, presumably when the public first loses confidence in the prospect for stable or lower prices.[18] After that, if inflation persists and speeds up, the coefficient (as we have seen) appears to become higher, possibly again by sudden shifts rather than gradual increases. While the exact timing and pattern of these shifts remain unexplained, they bear at least some relation to both the rate and the duration of past inflation. Duration is important, for there is no one rate acting as a threshold that, if pierced, causes the coefficient to jump up. Thus even very mild inflation, if continued long enough, ought eventually to produce a fairly high coefficient. The further question about how high it might go cannot be given a definite answer. After it reaches a certain level this question might seem to lose significance. Russia's coefficient reached close to .8, which gives an average lag in expected behind actual price changes of only one and a quarter months. At that point expectations are extremely responsive to current price movements, and there is not much room for shortening the lag. Yet the exact value of the coefficient at high levels becomes very important in determining whether the price rise is stable or not, that is, whether the rise becomes self-generating. This question forms the subject matter of the next section. The evidence presented there suggests that the coefficients did not, and perhaps never would, reach levels that produce self-generating price rises.

An increasing coefficient of expectation produces an upward bias in estimates of α, because the constant value of the coefficient used in computing the expected rate of change in prices falls short of the true value by increasing amounts for successively later months of hyperinflation. The expected rate of change is then understated by a greater amount for successively later months, since the actual rate of change tends to increase. This understatement biases estimates of α upward.[19] Such bias would partly account for the fact that the estimates of α in Table 6 are lower than those in Table 3. The former would be the more accurate estimates if they were derived with the better estimates of the coefficient. However, the upward bias in estimates of the coefficient (described in n. 16), which bias is larger when the estimates are based on shorter

18. See A. J. Brown, *The Great Inflation, 1939–51* (London: Oxford University Press, 1955), pp. 190–92.

19. It should be pointed out that for this reason an increase in the coefficient is not responsible for pulling observations for the later months of hyperinflation above the regression lines. This could only result from a fall in the coefficient. These high observations can indeed be interpreted as a fall in the coefficient.

periods, also makes the estimates of α in Table 6 somewhat lower than those in Table 3. The true value, therefore, lies somewhere in between the estimates in these two tables, but which estimate is more accurate cannot be determined.

V. The Stability of Equilibrium in Hyperinflation

The coefficient of expectation determines the speed with which individuals revise their expectations of the rate of change in prices. The amount by which they change their real cash balances in accordance with their revised expectations depends on the elasticity of their demand for the balances, which is proportional to the value of α. But the total reaction of a given series of changes in the quantity of money on the price level, and therefore the condition for the stable moving equilibrium of prices, depends on the product of the two parameters.[20] This is proved by deriving the condition for stability from the model.

In a self-generating inflation, a small rise in prices causes such a "flight from money" that prices go up more than in proportion to the initial rise. This cannot occur if, for any change in the price level, its rate of change moves in the opposite direction. Then any increase in prices is dampened by a fall in their rate of rise. This condition for stable moving equilibrium is expressed by

$$\frac{\partial \left(\dfrac{d \log P}{dt} \right)}{\partial P} < 0 .$$

The condition can be derived for hyperinflations from equations (2) and (5). If the indexes of P and M are set at unity in the same month in which E is zero, γ in equation (2) vanishes, and the two equations can be written as follows:

$$\log \frac{M}{P} = - \alpha E , \qquad (2a)$$

$$\frac{dE}{dt} = \beta \left(\frac{d \log P}{dt} - E \right) . \qquad (5a)$$

20. This dependence means that, for given data, the lower is the value of β, the higher is the value of α. As β becomes smaller, the individual weights for the average of past rates of change in prices become more equal, and the weighted average produces a smaller variation in the values of the expected changes. Consequently, a lower β implies a higher α, because the smaller variations in the expected rates of change in prices have to explain the same given variations in real cash balances.

The Monetary Dynamics of Hyperinflation 65

The logarithms have the base e. To reduce the two equations to a single relation between observable variables, equation (2a) is first differentiated with respect to time, which gives

$$-\frac{1}{a}\left(\frac{d \log M}{dt} - \frac{d \log P}{dt}\right) = \frac{dE}{dt}.$$ (2a′)

Substituting (2a) and (2a′) into (5a) produces the following relation between P and M only:

$$\beta (\log P - \log M) = \frac{d \log M}{dt} - (1 - a\beta)\frac{d \log P}{dt}.$$ (12)

From this it follows that

$$\frac{\partial \left(\dfrac{d \log P}{dt}\right)}{\partial P} = \frac{-\beta}{1 - a\beta}\left(\frac{1}{P}\right),$$ (13)

since M is independent of P, and, therefore, partial derivatives of M and of its rate of change with respect to P are zero. Since P is never negative, it is apparent from (13) that prices are in stable equilibrium if $a\beta$ is less than unity and that they are not so if $a\beta$ is greater than unity.[21]

What the stability or instability of equilibrium implies about the course of hyperinflation can be inferred from the function that determines prices through time. The function can be derived by solving equation (12) for $\log P$. This equation is a linear first-order differential equation in $\log P$ and t, where M is assumed to be a function of t, independent of P. The solution of $\log P$ in terms of t, assuming for the moment that $a\beta$ is not unity, can be written as

$$(\log P)_t = (\log M)_t + H e^{-\beta t/(1-a\beta)}$$

$$+ \frac{a\beta}{1 - a\beta} \frac{\left(\int_{-T}^{t} \dfrac{d \log M}{dx} e^{\beta x/(1-a\beta)} dx\right)}{e^{\beta t/(1-a\beta)}},$$ (14)

where $-T$ is an arbitrary number to be specified and H is the constant of integration. H is determined by specifying the values of the variables at a particular time. Without any loss of generality we can assume that, prior to the time when $t = 0$, M and P were unity and that, at $t = 0$, M began to increase at the rate $(d \log M/dt)_0 = r_M$ and that prices began

21. The limiting case, when $a\beta$ is unity and the partial derivative in (13) is zero, turns out to be equivalent to stable equilibrium (see eq. [16]). I am indebted to Professor Jacob Marschak for drawing my attention to this way of formulating the criterion of the stability of equilibrium.

to increase at the rate $(d \log P/dt)_0 = r_P$.[22] With these initial conditions, equation (14) takes on the following form:

$$(\log P)_t = (\log M)_t + \frac{\alpha\beta}{1 - \alpha\beta} \frac{\left(\int_0^t \frac{d \log M}{d x} e^{\beta x/(1-\alpha\beta)} d x\right)}{e^{\beta t/(1-\alpha\beta)}}$$

$$+ \left(\frac{r_M}{\beta} - \frac{1 - \alpha\beta}{\beta} r_P\right) e^{-\beta t/(1-\alpha\beta)} . \tag{15}$$

The course of inflation depends crucially on the value of $\alpha\beta$, the "reaction index."

When the reaction index is less than unity, the terms following the integral in equation (15) approach zero as t increases, so that prices eventually depend on two factors: the quantity of money and the integral, which is an exponentially weighted average of the past rates of change in the quantity of money. The logarithm of real cash balances thus becomes proportional to the negative of this integral.

When the reaction index equals unity, the last term in the original equation (12) drops out, and the level of prices can be derived immediately. We have

$$\log P = \log M + \frac{1}{\beta} \cdot \frac{d \log M}{dt} ,$$

or, since $\alpha\beta = 1$,

$$\log \frac{M}{P} = - \alpha \frac{d \log M}{dt} . \tag{16}$$

Real cash balances in this case are related to the current rate of change in the quantity of money. Adjustments in the balances are not influenced by the past costs of holding money.[23]

22. It is necessary to specify that $r_P > r_M$. In the identity

$$\frac{d \log \frac{M}{P}}{dt} \equiv \frac{d \log M}{dt} - \frac{d \log P}{dt} ,$$

the assumed initial rates can be substituted in the right-hand side, so that

$$\left(\frac{d \log \frac{M}{P}}{dt}\right)_0 \equiv r_M - r_P .$$

Since real cash balances fall when prices and the quantity of money are rising, it is necessary that each side of the preceding identity be negative.

23. The expected change in prices may still lag behind the actual change in prices unless β (or $1/\alpha$) is sufficiently large. In fact,

$$\left(\frac{d \log P}{dt} - E\right) = \frac{1}{\beta} \frac{d^2 \log M}{dt^2} ,$$

The Monetary Dynamics of Hyperinflation 67

When the reaction index is greater than unity, the terms following the integral in (15) are positive. The integral term is negative. The exponential weights in the integral are now turned around, so that the largest weight is given to the past rates of change in money. The integral term eventually stays relatively constant,[24] and the price level depends mainly on the logarithm of money and the two terms following the integral. These two terms following the integral rise at an exponential rate. Therefore, $\log P/M$ eventually rises at roughly an exponential rate.

The solution of equations (15) and (16) with the quantity of money rising at a constant percentage rate will illustrate the three cases of a reaction index less than, equal to, or greater than unity. Before $t = 0$, suppose that $\log P$ and $\log M$ are zero and, when $t \geq 0$, that $\log M = r_M t$. The equations for prices, the change in prices, and real cash balances are then as follows for $t \geq 0$:

$$(\log P)_t = r_M t + a r_M - \frac{1 - \alpha\beta}{\beta} (r_P - r_M)\, e^{-\beta t/(1-\alpha\beta)}, \quad (17a)$$

$$\left(\frac{d \log P}{dt}\right)_t = r_M + (r_P - r_M)\, e^{-\beta t/(1-\alpha\beta)}, \quad (17b)$$

$$\left(\log \frac{M}{P}\right)_t = - a r_M + \frac{1 - \alpha\beta}{\beta} (r_P - r_M)\, e^{-\beta t/(1-\alpha\beta)}. \quad (17c)$$

---

or, since $\alpha\beta = 1$, the difference also equals $a(d^2 \log M/dt^2)$. This means that, when the quantity of money increases at an increasing rate, the expected rate of change in prices lags behind the actual rate. Actual real cash balances are then never as low as they would be if individuals could foresee the actual rates. This result is a consequence of the form of equation (5a) in the model, which shows how expectations are revised per period of time. Higher orders of revision of expectations are not taken into account. In fact, however, when prices actually rise at increasing rates for some time, individuals appear to revise their expectations with increasing rapidity. Equation (5a) nonetheless is adequate to account for most of the data.

24. This statement is true as long as $\log M$ rises at less than an exponential rate. If $\log M$ were to start rising at an exponential rate greater than $-\beta/(1 - \alpha\beta)$, the integral term takes on an increasing negative value. The price level would have to become infinite immediately. (This can be done by setting $r_P = \infty$). Otherwise, sooner or later $\log P$ would begin to fall even though $\log M$ were rising. This is inconsistent with our premises. There is no rising level of prices in this equation that does not immediately rise to infinity and yet is consistent with a $\log M$ that rises at an exponential rate greater than $-\beta/(1 - \alpha\beta)$.

The situation in the intermediate cases, in which $\log M$ rises exponentially at a rate less than or equal to $-\beta/(1 - \alpha\beta)$ can be found by referring to equation (15). The fact that, when $\log M$ rises at a great enough rate, $\log P$ must go to infinity, if it is to increase at all, arises more from the limitations of the model than from the realities of hyperinflation. The model is a first approximation to those realities only.

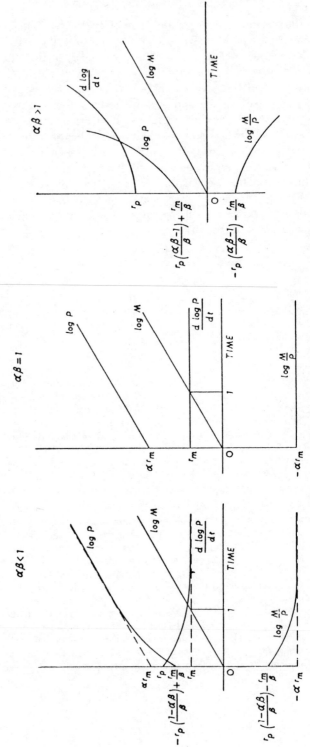

Fig. 15.—Three cases of model for constant rate of increase in quantity of money

The Monetary Dynamics of Hyperinflation 69

These equations are plotted in Figure 15. When the index equals unity, the last term in (17a) and (17c) becomes zero. For this case, direct substitution of the assumed changes in the quantity of money in (16) yields the same result.

Table 8 gives estimates and confidence intervals of the reaction indexes. Only the German and Russian hyperinflations, of those examined, seem to have an index that is greater than unity. Except for the Austrian, Greek, and second Hungarian hyperinflations, however, the confidence intervals are too wide to conclude that the true value of the index is less than unity.

TABLE 8

REACTION INDEXES*

Country	Estimate of $\alpha\beta$	Confidence Intervals for $\alpha\beta$†
Austria............................	.43	.31 – .66
Germany..........................	1.09	.92 –1.26
Greece............................	.61	.32‡– .85
Hungary (after World War I)........	.87	.42‡–1.27
Hungary (after World War II).......	.54	.47 – .76
Poland............................	.69	.39 –1.04
Russia............................	1.07	.94 –1.20

* For method of estimation see Appendix A.
† The confidence level for the intervals is .90. See Appendix A.
‡ End of confidence interval lies beyond the value shown. See n. § to Table 3.

Increases in the coefficient of expectation over time (for which supporting evidence was discussed under subsection 4 in the last section) do not necessarily produce larger reaction indexes for the later months than the indexes for all months listed in Table 8. As was pointed out, when a constant coefficient is used, these increases bias estimates of α upward and so those in Table 8. Taking these increases into account places only the Russian index above unity. Based on the estimates in Table 6 for the later months, the index for Russia becomes 1.90; but for Poland it becomes only .77, and for Hungary I it falls to .71. Computations not shown for the others indicate that the index does not come up to unity; estimates for the last half of the German hyperinflation reduce its value to .96. This evidence implies that only the Russian index clearly exceeds unity. For the later months the German index seems to stand slightly below; and the others, considerably below.

But this estimate of the Russian index may spuriously exceed unity, because there is another bias making estimates of the indexes too high that has to be considered, even though we cannot exactly calculate its

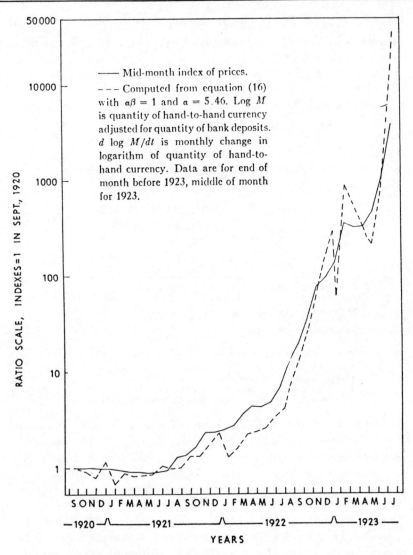

RATIO SCALE, INDEXES = 1 IN SEPT., 1920

—— Mid-month index of prices.

– – – Computed from equation (16) with $\alpha\beta = 1$ and $\alpha = 5.46$. Log M is quantity of hand-to-hand currency adjusted for quantity of bank deposits. $d \log M/dt$ is monthly change in logarithm of quantity of hand-to-hand currency. Data are for end of month before 1923, middle of month for 1923.

S O N D J F M A M J J A S O N D J F M A M J J A S O N D J F M A M J J

— 1920 —⋀— 1921 ———⋀——— 1922 ———⋀—— 1923 —

YEARS

Fig. 16.—Index of prices generated by model and actual index of prices for Germany, September, 1920, to July, 1923.

The Monetary Dynamics of Hyperinflation 71

effect. It is the upward bias in the estimated level of the coefficient of expectation (see n. 16). While this bias makes estimates of a too low, it does not in fact make them proportionately lower; correction for it would mean that the reaction indexes should be lowered somewhat. Its effect on estimates for the whole period of hyperinflation is probably small, but on those for a short period the effect could be substantial. Whether this bias is sufficient to account entirely for the fact that the Russian index exceeds unity is uncertain. There are other minor sources of bias, some operating in the other direction, that might be important when small amounts are crucial.[25] Thus while the true values of the others would all appear to lie below unity, the existence of many sources of possible error places even this conclusion in doubt. The estimate of the German index, being so close to unity, is especially doubtful.

Indirect evidence that the Russian index, as well as the German and others, are actually not greater than unity is provided by the estimated level of prices that can be computed from equation (15). Using the estimated value of the parameters for Germany and Russia from Table 8 in equation (15) to estimate the actual level of prices gives very poor results. Moreover, any other values of the index greater than unity are also unsatisfactory. On the other hand, values equal to, or slightly lower than, unity for Germany and Russia give more reasonable results, as indicated for the German hyperinflation by Figure 16, which compares the actual level of German prices with that generated by equation (16).

25. The two most important sources, which produce downward biases in the parameters, are described below. It is hard to believe that either of them could be very important, even though there is little basis on which to compute the exact amounts involved.

a) The exclusion of illegal currency issues from the series on money undoubtedly makes these data progressively too low by greater percentage amounts, because the incentives to issue without authorization were greatest in the peaks of hyperinflation coming at the end (see the discussion under subsection 1 in Sec. IV). By understating the series for real cash balances, this exclusion makes the estimates of a too low.

b) Least-squares estimates of the coefficient in a first-order difference equation are biased downward. This results from the failure of these estimates to take account of the serial correlation in the regression residuals, which is produced by difference equations even when the original random variable is not autocorrelated (see T. C. Koopmans [ed.], *Statistical Inference in Dynamic Economic Models* [New York: John Wiley & Sons, 1950], pp. 365–83). The regression function (11) is a difference equation of the Tth order. To what extent the estimates in Tables 3 and 8 are subject to the bias found for first-order equations is not known. Such bias, which has nothing to do with any of those mentioned heretofore, implies that estimates of the two parameters are too low. Conceivably it accounts for some of the actual serial correlation in the regression residuals, which was discussed under subsection 4 in Section IV and attributed to increases in the coefficient.

The reason why parameter values estimated from the model in one form are not always appropriate to it in another form is that one introduces biases not present in the other. While the two forms are mathematically identical, the regression functions derived from them involve different time series. For any point in time, the regression used relates the current money supply and prices to past changes in prices. The regression for the other form of the model relates current money and prices to past changes in money. While the former method of estimating the parameters does not sharply distinguish between values of the reaction index above or below unity, the latter does. Thus, even though the true index may lie below unity, the estimated value by the method used will sometimes turn out greater than unity because of random errors and bias.

This interpretation of the results seems inescapable, because a reaction index that exceeds unity is not consistent with the general characteristics of the hyperinflations. When the index exceeds unity, equation (15) implies that changes in the quantity of money, once the quantity initially rises, have very little to do with the course of inflation. The fall in real cash balances is so large that prices continue to rise under the impetus of falling balances *ad infinitum*.[26] This situation did not characterize the whole of the German and Russian hyperinflations, or the others either. Price changes did not always tend to increase at exponential rates. Yet if the reaction index were above unity, the *logarithm* of actual prices would have to rise at no less than an exponential rate before any solution of equation (16) would estimate prices with reasonable accuracy, unless perhaps there were continual changes in expectations. Even in the last part of the Russian hyperinflation, although the rate of change in prices climbed steadily, it was nowhere near exponential. In view of the actual price rises that occurred, therefore, none of the hyperinflations appears to have been self-generating.

Does it also follow that self-generating inflations are somehow im-

26. In such a situation the inflation is self-generating in the sense that diminishing real cash balances create a continual rise in prices, which in turn leads to a continual fall in the balances. It is possible to prescribe values of the parameters so that, according to the model, even certain rates of *decrease* in the quantity of money will not stop the inflation once it gets under way. But we should not expect this solution of the model to apply. In the light of the sharp rise in the balances when a reform in the currency approaches, any diminution in the rate at which notes were issued would likely alter the prevailing expectation of a certain rate of future inflation to one of a less rapid rate, whether the reaction index were greater than unity or not. If so, the balances would rise at once if the policies of the note-issuing authorities justified more confidence in the future value of the currency. These sudden revisions in expectations cannot be accounted for in a model that predicts future prices on the basis of past changes in prices or money alone.

The Monetary Dynamics of Hyperinflation 73

possible? There seems to be no reason why they could not occur; so far they have just not been observed. The world has seen inflations that go on for decades but do not develop self-generating characteristics. This evidence, combined with that from these seven relatively brief hyperinflations, suggests that price increases would become self-generating only after a prolonged period of hyperinflation. Even when the reaction index exceeded unity, if the percentage increase in the money supply were less than exponential, expectations would probably not sustain a percentage increase in prices at an exponential rate for very long. Prices would more likely exhibit a high degree of instability, with the percentage change in real cash balances alternately falling and rising at exponential rates depending on whether the increase in money in the immediate future were expected to accelerate or taper off. Under these circumstances it seems likely that reform of the currency would become a political and economic necessity. This could be the reason why self-generating price increases have never been observed—hyperinflation that otherwise proceeded to the stage where they began would not last long enough after to permit their detection.

VI. A Note on Lags

We have seen that, if the lag in expectations in the model is too short, inflation becomes self-generating. When the coefficient of expectation is quite large, which means that expected price changes follow the actual changes without a perceptible lag, the reaction index exceeds unity. Then, once the money supply increases, the logarithm of prices begins to rise at no less than an exponential rate. Subsequent increases in the money supply only add to the rate of rise in prices;[27] a reduced rate of increase in the supply will not make the rate of price rise less than exponential, except perhaps through indirect effects on expectations. The condition for stable moving equilibrium given in Section V confirms this statement by showing that a reaction index greater than unity creates unstable conditions.

Actually, any function that relates real cash balances to the rate of change in prices without a lag violates the condition for stability. For, given such a function,

$$f\left(\frac{M}{P}\right) = \frac{d \log P}{dt},\qquad(18)$$

the condition for the stable moving equilibrium of prices requires that

$$\frac{\partial \left(\frac{d \log P}{dt}\right)}{\partial P} = \left(\frac{-M}{P^2}\right) f'\qquad(19)$$

27. Subject to the conditions set forth in n. 24.

be less than zero, provided that M is independent of P. Since real cash balances generally fall in response to a rise in the rate of change in prices, f' is usually negative; hence this partial derivative is positive, implying instability. An increase in the rate of change in prices occurs whenever they rise. The inflation will thus continue under its own momentum, as it were.

Certainly no mild inflation exhibits the properties of instability, and the seven hyperinflations do not appear to have them either. Therefore, some lag (or other restraint on changes) affects the dependence of real cash balances on the rate of change in prices to a significant degree. The lag in expectations, which conforms to the data in most months of the seven hyperinflations exceptionally well, appears to be unusually long. Estimates of its average length (see Tables 2 and 3) range from three to twenty months. On the other hand, a lag associated with another variable in the model—the desired level of the balances—is assumed to be extremely short.[28] This section points out that these two lags cannot be empirically distinguished. The extreme length estimated for the first lag may thus result from the additional effects of the second, as well as from those of a third, also discussed below, which concerns the expected duration of any rate of rise in prices. These three seem to be the main lags that require consideration in a monetary analysis of hyperinflation.

To begin with, what can we say about a lag in the balances?[29] Suppose that the actual levels of real cash balances were not always equal to desired levels but were adjusted at a rate proportional to the difference in their logarithms:

$$\frac{d \log \frac{M}{P}}{dt} = \pi \left(\log \frac{M^d}{P} - \log \frac{M}{P} \right), \tag{20}$$

where the superscript d denotes desired levels, and π is a positive constant. This assumption is analogous to the one used to describe how the unobserved expected price changes adjust to the actual changes, except that here the actual level of real cash balances adjusts to the unobserved desired level. Suppose further that expectations involve no lag and that the desired balances depend on the actual change in prices as follows:

$$\log \frac{M^d}{P} = - a \frac{d \log P}{dt}. \tag{21}$$

28. See above, n. 2.

29. The argument that follows has benefited from discussions I have had with Marc Nerlove.

The Monetary Dynamics of Hyperinflation 75

Combining equations (20) and (21), we get

$$\frac{d \log \dfrac{M}{P}}{dt} + \pi \log \frac{M}{P} = - a\pi \frac{d \log P}{dt}. \qquad (12a)$$

This is identical to the reduced equation for the model derived in preceding sections, which used a lag in expectations instead. Compare equation (12a) with (12). The only difference is the substitution of π for β. When we treat (12a) as a differential equation and solve for log (M/P) in terms of $(d \log P)/(dt)$, the result is identical to the combination of equations (2) and (8), which underlies the regression function (11). The two lags thus imply the same relation between prices and money.

This equivalence of the two lags is perfectly reasonable. Individuals may well behave with only one or the other lag, but we cannot observe which one it is. Indeed, the behavior of two individuals who differed completely in this respect has identical effects on the data. One might adjust his expectations to current price changes rapidly but only slowly bring his cash balances in line with the amount desired. Another might tardily adjust his expectations but quickly change his cash balances. For both, we would observe a certain lag of changes in cash balances behind current price changes, and unless we assumed that the two lags affected the data differently,[30] we would not be able to distinguish between them.

The model can be viewed as an approximation, therefore, to a more general model involving both lags. By attaching the superscript d to real cash balances in (12a) and combining that equation with (20), we get the following second-order differential equation:

$$\frac{1}{(\beta + \pi)} \frac{d^2 \log \dfrac{M}{P}}{dt^2} + \frac{d \log \dfrac{M}{P}}{dt} + \left(\frac{\beta\pi}{\beta+\pi}\right) \log \frac{M}{P}$$
$$= - a \left(\frac{\beta\pi}{\beta+\pi}\right) \frac{d \log P}{dt}. \qquad (22)$$

This, too, confounds the two lags. Interchanging β and π does not alter the equation in any way.

The model that was used is equivalent to this equation except for the first term, and what I have previously called the "coefficient of expectation" here approximates $(\beta\pi)/(\beta + \pi)$, an amalgam of two lags.[31] If

30. Suppose eq. (1) in n. 2 had $-d \log P/dt$ for its left-hand side. It would then be similar to (20) but would give a lag in the balances with implications that are not all equivalent to a lag in expectations.

31. Under the original assumption made in Sec. II that π is very large, this expression is only slightly less than β. For, as π increases, $(\beta\pi)/(\beta + \pi)$ approaches the value of β from below.

$\beta + \pi$ is fairly large or the second derivative fairly low, the first term contributes little to the relation. That the contribution of this term was fairly small in the seven hyperinflations is suggested by the good results obtained with the model used. The model describes most months quite well,[32] even though it ignores the first term. Of course, the above equation, incorporating both lags, would probably fit the data better than the model, though whether much better is questionable. Because of the many statistical difficulties as well as extensive computations involved, however, a fit using this equation has not been attempted.

Even though the coefficient of expectation in the model must be interpreted as a mixture of two lags that cannot be distinguished, it hardly seems possible that the lag in the balances could be more than a fraction as long as the lag in expectations. Once a person decides on the desired level of his balances, he can easily adjust his actual balances by spending them or by selling other assets for cash. The time required is negligible, because he adjusts his balances not so much by changing the level of his consumption over a period of time as by altering the form in which he holds his wealth. In forming his expectations, however, he may very well look far back in time in order to assess the current trend of prices. Nevertheless, there is no direct evidence on the relative importance of the two lags, and it should be understood that to some extent the estimates of the coefficient of expectation also reflect a lag in the balances and are to that extent too low as a measure of the lag in expectations alone. For simplicity of exposition, I have referred throughout only to the lag in expectations.

The estimates of α, on the other hand, are not subject to any such ambiguity, and the elasticity of demand defined by equation (4) does represent, as was intended, the percentage change in desired real cash balances with respect to changes in the expected rate of increase in prices.

Another kind of expectation that may be important, although it was not explicitly taken into account, concerns the expected duration of a rate of price change. It affects the desired level of the balances. A rate of price rise of 50 per cent per month may be entirely ignored if the rate is expected to last only one day; but balances will be considerably reduced if the rate is thought likely to continue for six months. Expected duration might follow rumors and conjectures about the future level of prices instantly without regard to the past. Then it would tend to produce erratic and unpredictable changes in desired real cash balances. But, if it depended primarily on the extent and duration of inflation in the recent

32. Moreover, neither lag accounts for the high levels of the balances in the ending months of hyperinflation (see n. 13).

The Monetary Dynamics of Hyperinflation 77

past, it would behave much like the expected price change. Since the model describes most months of hyperinflation fairly well even though the effects of expected duration on the balances were not explicitly taken into account, quite likely the model implicitly incorporates these effects. Thus the exponentially weighted average of the rates of change in prices probably represents not the expected rate for the immediate future, as was assumed, but the average rate that is expected to last long enough to justify the trouble and expense of reducing cash balances. This rate could fall far short of the rate that might be expected to prevail in the coming weeks or months and thus could explain why the estimated values of the coefficient of expectation are so low. An average lag as long as twenty months may reflect not so much a failure to revise expected rates (or to adjust cash balances) rapidly as an unwillingness to incur the costs of low cash balances before the continued tendency for prices to rise is viewed as relatively permanent. Throughout the hyperinflations the expected duration of the price rise seems to have exercised considerable restraint on reductions in desired real cash balances.

Other factors than the past performance of prices undoubtedly influenced the expected duration at certain times. The balances rose near the end of all but two of the seven hyperinflations, while the model predicts they should have fallen (see Sec. IV). Prospects for the probable end of currency depreciation apparently made the public willing to hold larger balances immediately. Before the beginning months, too, the expected duration of inflation apparently underwent a sudden rise (see Sec. IV). The sharp decline in the balances following their long rise in the months preceding hyperinflation seems to reflect a sudden realization by the public that greater price increases lay ahead. The precise timing of such shifts in expectations appears incapable of prediction by economic variables, even though we may be certain such shifts will eventually occur under the circumstances. But, when the shifts are absent, expectations of price changes depend closely on past events.

VII. The Tax on Cash Balances

The analysis so far has linked the large price increases during hyperinflation to large increases in the quantity of money. But there is still the question, "Why did the quantity of money increase and by so large an amount?" The answer is twofold: (1) printing money was a convenient way to provide the government with real resources, though it tended to preclude other methods; and (2) the effectiveness of this method declined over time and so required ever larger issues.

In the unsettled conditions following the two world wars, governments were too weak to enact adequate tax programs and to administer them effectively. Issuing money was a method of raising revenue by a special kind of tax—a tax on cash balances. This tax is often appealing because it does not require detailed legislation and can be administered very simply. All that is required is to spend newly printed notes. The resulting inflation automatically imposes a tax on cash balances by depreciating the value of money.

The base of the tax is the level of real cash balances; the rate of the tax is the rate of depreciation in the real value of money, which is equal to the rate of rise in prices. Revenue (in real terms) from the tax is the product of the base and the rate,

$$\frac{M}{P}\left(\frac{dP}{dt}\frac{1}{P}\right).$$

The note-issuing authorities "collect" all the revenue; however, when prices rise in greater proportion than the quantity of money, that is, when real cash balances decline, part of the revenue goes to reduce the real value of the outstanding money supply.[33] Thus total revenue per period of time is the sum of two parts: first, the real value of new money issued per period of time,

$$\frac{dM}{dt}\frac{1}{P};$$

and, second, the reduction in outstanding monetary liabilities, equal to the decline per period of time in the real value of cash balances,

$$\frac{d\left(\dfrac{M}{P}\right)}{dt}.$$

This is demonstrated by the following identity:

$$\frac{dM}{dt}\frac{1}{P}-\frac{d\left(\dfrac{M}{P}\right)}{dt}\equiv\frac{M}{P}\left(\frac{dP}{dt}\frac{1}{P}\right). \tag{23}$$

The note-issuing authorities do not set the tax rate directly. They set the rate at which they increase the money supply, and this rate determines the tax rate through the process described in preceding sections.

Typically, institutions other than the government also have the authority to issue money. In so far as they exercise this authority, they

33. Inflation also reduces the real value of the principal and interest charges of debt fixed in nominal terms. However, amortization of debt cannot have required a very large fraction of government expenditures once hyperinflation began.

The Monetary Dynamics of Hyperinflation 79

receive some of the revenue from the tax, even though the initiating factor is government creation of money. In the hyperinflations, as government issues swelled the reserves of private commercial banks, an expansion of bank credit could and did take place. Banks largely dissipated the revenue from their share of the tax by making loans at nominal rates of interest that did not take full account of the subsequent rise in prices, so that the real rate of interest received was on the average below the real return that could be obtained on capital. The revenue dissipated by the banks went to their borrowers.[34]

The revenue received by the government thus depends on the tax rate and on the fraction of the revenue that goes to banks and their borrowers. In addition, it depends on the tax base, that is, the level of real cash balances. A higher tax rate will not yield a proportionately higher revenue, because the balances will decline in response to the higher rate. Indeed, the balances may ultimately decline more than in proportion to the rise in the rate, so that a higher rate may yield less revenue. This will not be so immediately, however, because of the lag in expectations.[35] It takes time for expected price changes to adjust to the actual changes. Consequently, a rise in the tax rate, that is, in the rate of change in prices, will at least initially increase the revenue from the tax.

This fact helps to explain why a similar time pattern of revenue emerged in all the seven hyperinflations. The revenue was high at the start, when the expected rate of price increase was still low; tended to decline in the middle, as the expected rate started to rise considerably; and rose near the end, when the rate of new issues skyrocketed.[36] The

34. The government's share of total revenue depends on the proportion of money issued by governmental agencies. If this proportion is not the same for the quantity of money outstanding as for the amount currently issued, the government's share of the two parts of total revenue will differ. To compute the government's share of the total, we must multiply each part in (23) by separate fractions. For the first part, the appropriate fraction is the ratio of money currently issued by the government to total issues in a period of time; for the second, the fraction is the ratio of outstanding government issues to the total money supply.

35. This follows from the relation

$$\frac{d \log \frac{M}{P}}{dt} = - \alpha\beta \, (C - E) \, ,$$

derived from equations (2) and (5), and from the condition that $\alpha\beta < 1$, found to hold for all the hyperinflations (see Sec. V).

36. Part of this rise in revenue resulted from the failure of real cash balances to make further declines in the final months, apparently because the end of hyperinflation appeared imminent (see Sec. IV).

note-issuing authorities in all the hyperinflations evidently responded to the belated decline in the balances in much the same manner. In the beginning months, when the quantity of money rose at rates much higher than those previously attained, the revenue was also much higher than before. Because of the lag in expectations, many months passed before real cash balances declined very much. When the balances finally began to decline by substantial amounts, the revenue decreased from the high level of the beginning months. The revenue could be enlarged, as for a short time it was, only by inflating at successively higher rates. Rates were quickly reached, however, that completely disrupted the economy, and they could not be long continued. The attempt to enlarge the revenue in the closing months thus produced the characteristic pattern of the hyperinflations: price increases did not peter out; they exploded.

The time pattern aside, the productivity of the tax can be analyzed most simply by comparing the revenue that was actually raised in the seven hyperinflations with the revenue that could have been raised if the quantity of money had risen at a constant rate. Under the latter condition, the actual and expected rate of rise in prices would eventually become practically equal to this constant rate,[37] and C can replace E in equation (3), the demand function for real cash balances. This substitution gives

$$\frac{M}{P} = e^{-aC-\gamma}. \tag{24}$$

Since total revenue, R, equals the rate of rise in prices times real cash balances, we have, substituting (24),

$$R = C e^{-aC-\gamma}. \tag{25}$$

Total revenue is a maximum when the derivative of this expression with respect to C is zero and the second derivative is negative, namely:

$$\frac{dR}{dC} = (1 - aC)\, e^{-aC-\gamma} = 0,$$

$$\frac{d^2R}{dC^2} = (a^2C - 2a)\, e^{-aC-\gamma} < 0. \tag{26}$$

These conditions are satisfied when $(1 - aC)$ equals zero. Therefore, the rate of tax on cash balances, that is, the rate of inflation, that yields the maximum revenue in (25) is $1/a$. At this rate of tax, the demand for real

37. We can then refer to these three rates simply as "the rate of inflation." Their equality follows from the constancy of real cash balances, which in turn follows from equation (15), given the constant rate of increase in money.

The Monetary Dynamics of Hyperinflation 81

cash balances has an elasticity of −1. Table 9 shows this rate for the seven hyperinflations. It must be emphasized that the rates in columns 1 and 2 yield the maximum revenue only in the special sense of the revenue that can be maintained indefinitely. When the tax is first imposed, that is, at the beginning of inflation, there is no maximum yield; the higher the rate, the higher the yield, thanks to the delayed adjustment in the balances produced by the lag in expectations.

TABLE 9

RATE OF INFLATION THAT MAXIMIZES THE ULTIMATE
REVENUE FROM A TAX ON CASH BALANCES*

| COUNTRY | RISE IN PRICES AND QUAN-TITY OF MONEY THAT MAXIMIZES ULTIMATE REVENUE | | AVERAGE ACTU-AL RATE OF RISE IN PRICES (PER CENT PER MONTH) |
	Rate per Month Com-pounded Con-tinuously $(1/a)$ (1)	Per Cent per Month $[(e^{1/a}-1)100]$ (2)	(3)
Austria.................	.117	12	47
Germany................	.183	20	322
Greece.................	.244	28	365
Hungary (after World War I)	.115	12	46
Hungary (after World War II)	.236	32	19,800
Poland.................	.435	54	81
Russia.................	.327	39	57

* Rate of change in quantity of money is assumed constant. The values of a used are the estimated values shown in Table 3. Column 3 is reproduced from Table 1, row 7.

The table also lists for comparison the average rates of rise in prices that actually prevailed. The actual rates were well above the constant rates that would have maximized the ultimate revenue. With Table 10 we can compare the yield of the actual rates with the ultimate yield that could have been attained with a constant rate.

Table 10 presents various measures of the average revenue. The closing months of some of the hyperinflations were omitted (see note * to Table 10). To make comparisons among the countries, it is necessary to express the revenue relative to some standard of reference. Two alternative stand-ards were used for Table 10. The first is the level of real cash balances in the beginning month of hyperinflation. Its use allows for differences in the base of the tax. The second is national income in a "normal" year. Its use allows for differences in economic resources.

TABLE 10

REVENUE FROM THE TAX ON CASH BALANCES

COUNTRY AND PERIOD*	RATIO OF GOVERNMENT MONEY TO TOTAL QUANTITY† (1)	AVERAGE MONTHLY REVENUE AS A PERCENTAGE OF‡				
		Real Cash Balances in Beginning Month of Hyperinflation			National Income in a Base Year	
		Ultimate Maximum for a Constant Rate of Increase in Quantity of Money (2)	Total $\left(\dfrac{M}{P}\dfrac{dP}{dt}\dfrac{1}{P}\right)$ (3)	From Issues of New Money $\left(\dfrac{dM}{dt}/P\right)$ (4)	From Issues of New Money $\left(\dfrac{dM}{dt}/P\right)$ (5)	From Issues of Government Money (Cols. [1] × [5]) (6)
Austria Oct., 1921—Aug., 1922.	.30	9	24	18	26	8
Germany Aug., 1922—July, 1923.	.46–.59	30	30	25	12	6–7
Greece Nov., 1943—Aug., 1944	(.50)	22	30	· 22	(11)§	(6)§
Hungary Mar., 1923—Feb., 1924.	.66–.95	19	25	21	20	13–19
Hungary Aug., 1945—Feb., 1946.	.83–.93	18	32	21	7	7‖
Poland Jan.—Nov., 1923......	.65–.75	36	36	31	4	3
Russia Dec., 1921—Jan., 1924.	1.00	41	41	41	0.5	0.5

* The period of the averages in cols. 3–6 is from the beginning month of hyperinflation to the last month included in the calculation of the regression lines (see Tables 1 and 3). For two reasons this period was not carried to the end of all the hyperinflations, shown in Table 1. First, the closing months frequently had extreme fluctuations in real cash balances. Using the end-of-month level of the balances would provide a poor approximation to their average level during the months. Second, in the closing months the level of the balances was sometimes unaccountably high in view of the large expected change in prices (see Sec. IV). These high levels very likely resulted from an expectation that hyperinflation would soon end. They temporarily made the revenue from the tax much higher than in the preceding months.

† "Government money" comprises notes issued by governmental agencies and deposits held by the public in the national bank and postal savings accounts. The total quantity of money comprises all notes and bank deposits held by the public. With one exception the ratios are rough approximations, since they were built up from annual figures for deposits that lack complete coverage. The exception refers to Hungary after World War II, for which fairly complete monthly data were used. Owing to the unavailability of Greek deposit figures during the war, the figure for Greece refers to 1941 and is apt to be a poor estimate for the hyperinflationary period, but it is the only one obtainable. For sources see Appendix B.

‡ Column 2: Product of the rate of change in prices shown in col. 1 of Table 9 and the index of real cash balances (with appropriate change of base) corresponding to this rate on the regression lines in Figs. 8–15.

Column 3: Average product for the period covered of the rate of change in prices ($\log_e P_t - \log_e P_{t-1}$) from the beginning to the end of the month and an end-of-month index of the real value of notes. Since the index tended to fall over most months, the use of its value at the end of the month makes this average an understatement of an average based on daily figures.

Column 4: The total revenue less the average change in real cash balances per month (see eq. [23]). This average change is equivalent to the difference between an index of the real value of notes at the beginning and at the end of the period, divided by the number of months covered.

Column 5:

$$(\text{Col. 4}) \times \left(\frac{\text{Index of real cash balances in beginning month of hyperinflation}}{\text{Index in earlier months}}\right) \times \left(\frac{\text{Quantity of money in the normal year}}{\text{Average monthly national income in the normal year}}\right)$$

Though desirable, using months from the normal year in the third factor for the earlier months in the second factor would involve difficulties and was not attempted. The earlier months used, except for Hungary I and Poland, were prewar months to which the index of real cash balances could be readily extended. The normal years were later years for which reasonably reliable data on national income were available. The above product assumes that the third factor holds for the earlier months used in the second factor. This assumption is likely to be approximately correct, because the earlier months and the normal year had relatively stable prices. The normal year and earlier months used, respectively, were for Austria, 1929 and all of 1914; Germany, 1927 and all of 1913; Greece, 1949–52 and June, 1941; Hungary I, 1936 and July, 1921; Hungary II, 1936 and August–December, 1939; Poland, 1929 and January, 1921; and Russia, 1926–29 and December, 1913. The ratios of money to income in the normal years were calculated by Martin J. Bailey (see his "The Welfare Cost of Inflationary Finance," *Journal of Political Economy*, Vol. LXIV [April, 1956], Table 2

The Monetary Dynamics of Hyperinflation 83

Column 3 gives the actual total revenue. It is the average product of the monthly rate of change in prices and an end-of-month index of real cash balances. Column 4 gives the amount of total revenue collected by banks and the government from spending new money. The total revenue in column 3 exceeds this amount by the average reduction in real cash balances per month. Column 2 shows the maximum ultimate revenue under the restriction that the rate of inflation is held constant, which is equivalent to the condition that the balances eventually remain constant. A comparison of columns 4 and 2 indicates that, in all countries except Austria, a constant rate of inflation could have yielded a revenue as large, on the average, as the amount actually collected.

This outcome seems surprising in view of the high and rising tax rates that were imposed. No purpose was served by such high rates unless the authorities intended to take advantage of the lag in expectations to collect more revenue than could ultimately be obtained with a constant rate. They could succeed in this intention by a policy of inflating at increasing rates and so repeatedly take advantage of this lag. The authorities successfully pursued this policy in the beginning and ending months and in much of the period preceding hyperinflation. The policy was temporarily abandoned in the middle months of all the hyperinflations, when the rate of price increase stopped rising and even fell somewhat. The average revenue exceeds the maximum amount in column 2 if most of the middle months are excluded. It is not clear why the authorities allowed the revenue to decline during these months. Perhaps they hesitated to continue a policy that promised to destroy the monetary system, and they hoped to restore some of the public's confidence in the currency. Apparently the need for revenue soon overrode whatever considerations prompted them to let the revenue decline, for the cumulative process of inflating at increasing rates was resumed in the closing months.

On this interpretation, the actual rate of rise in prices depended pri-

---

col. 5). These ratios do not apply to years as close to the periods of hyperinflation as the data sometimes permit, but they seem adequate for use in the above estimates.

Columns 3, 4, and 5 were derived from changes in figures for notes (except for Hungary II) that were used to approximate changes in notes and deposits combined. This derivation involves the assumption that notes and deposits increased at equal rates. The assumption is obviously not precisely true, since the ratio of notes to deposits varied (see Appendix B). Moreover, relatively small variations in this ratio imply large differences in their rates of increase. Where notes rose faster than deposits (Germany and Hungary I), the percentages in cols. 3 and 4 are somewhat overstated; and, where notes rose less rapidly (Poland), the percentages are understated.

Column 6: This gives the revenue from new issues collected by the government; private banks received the remaining revenue from new issues. These figures use changes in notes to approximate changes in government money, which was composed almost entirely of all the notes in circulation. Consequently, the figures are almost wholly free from the error to which cols. 3-5 are subject, discussed above.

§ The figures for Greece are inclosed in parentheses to emphasize their unknown reliability. Their derivation involves the assumption that the ratio of notes to total money given for 1941 holds for the later hyperinflationary period without alteration.

‖ Monthly data on deposits were used for the later Hungarian hyperinflation, and its revenue was multiplied by the ratio of government money to the total supply for each month before taking the average. Column 1 indicates the range of these monthly ratios for this hyperinflation.

marily on the revenue needs of the governments. We cannot measure these needs directly. But it will facilitate judging the outcome in terms of need to express the actual revenue as a percentage of national income rather than of initial real cash balances.

Rough estimates of this percentage are given in columns 5 and 6 of Table 10. Because data on national income are not available for the periods of hyperinflation, it was necessary to assume that the ratio of the quantity of money to national income in a later "normal" year, for which data on income are available, was the same as in earlier months, to which the index of real cash balances can be readily extended (see note to Table 10 for column 5). This assumption allowed a conversion of column 4 into percentages of national income. These percentages are shown in column 5. In so far as output during the hyperinflations fell below its level in the normal year, revenue as a percentage of contemporaneous national income would be somewhat higher. The government's share of this revenue was found by multiplying column 5 by the ratio of government money to the total supply. Unfortunately, this ratio cannot be estimated very closely, except for Hungary after World War II. Monthly data on deposits are unavailable for the other hyperinflations. Ratios based on annual data only, shown in column 1, were used. Column 6, which is the product of columns 1 and 5, shows the revenue going to the governments as percentages of normal-year national income. These percentages are not subject to one main error affecting those in columns 3–5 (see next to last paragraph of note ‡ to Table 10) and, while rough, are probably reasonably accurate.

In printing money to provide revenue, the governments of these countries collected on the average less than 10 per cent of normal levels of income. Hungary after World War I was the only exception.[38] Even a figure of 10 per cent seems low for ordinary governmental needs, which, as indicated by the little evidence available, probably ranged at the lowest from 10 to 20 per cent of national income. Germany, for example, collected 12 per cent of national income from all taxes in 1925, the second year after the hyperinflation. These results are consistent with the assumption made above that the authorities imposed increasing tax rates in the attempt

38. The range given for its revenue in that period may be too high, because the calculation of this range involved a comparison with the postwar year 1921, when real cash balances were probably somewhat below normal levels.

This qualification applies to the figures for Poland also, but any tendency for them to be too high was counteracted by the unusually low level to which real cash balances had fallen in the beginning month relative to their level in the year 1921 used for comparison. This fall reflects the high rate of inflation there during and after the war (see Table 7).

The Monetary Dynamics of Hyperinflation 85

to collect somewhat more revenue than could be obtained with a constant rate. Other taxes yielded some revenue, of course, though presumably an amount insufficient for desired total expenditures. As the rate of price increase rose, however, the real value of whatever funds were raised by other taxes undoubtedly diminished, and during the later stages of hyperinflation these funds must have become nearly worthless owing to delays in collecting them.[39] Then the only recourse of the government for procuring all the funds needed immediately was to increase the tax on cash balances.

The results of this tax as recorded by the percentages in column 6 are remarkably similar in outcome, except for Russia,[40] despite the greater possible differences due to errors in the data. Certainly the differences are very much smaller than the corresponding differences in the behavior of prices. If, as these results suggest, the different countries sought and, by and large, collected from this tax a percentage of national income roughly of the same order of magnitude, the differences among the hyperinflations in the rate of increase in the quantity of money can be explained by corresponding differences in the factors affecting the amount of revenue. The rate of new issues required for a given revenue is larger when a higher fraction of the revenue goes to banks and when the tax base is smaller; and conversely. Variations in the tax base, namely, real cash balances, are

39. In 1945 Hungary instituted a scheme, which was only temporarily successful, for collecting taxes in a money of constant purchasing power (see Bertrand Nogaro, "Hungary's Recent Monetary Crisis and Its Theoretical Meaning," *American Economic Review*, XXXVIII [September, 1948], 530 ff.).

40. Its low percentage reflects the unusually low level of real cash balances already reached in 1921 before hyperinflation began, and the low ratio of the balances to national income relative to that of the other countries in the later years used for comparison. The low level of the balances in 1921 was undoubtedly due to the social upheaval in that country during 1914–21, which along with war reduced output to about one-half of prewar levels and shook the public's confidence in the currency. In the other countries the balances declined over this period but not to the same extent. The low ratio for Russia in the later years may possibly reflect special circumstances and may be too low as an estimate of prewar levels. The implication is that Russia's revenue was low because the yield of the tax for any feasible rates was exceptionally low. To a great extent this was undoubtedly true. But very likely the revenue the government wished to collect with this tax was also fairly low. The Russian currency reform, unlike those bringing the other hyperinflations to a close, was accomplished gradually. Between the end of 1922 and March 10, 1924, when the depreciating rubles were completely abandoned, the Russian government issued a stable-valued currency, the chervonets, which gradually replaced the old rubles. In so far as the government collected its regular taxes in chervontsi, the revenue did not lose value in the process of collection, and these taxes retained their productivity.

determined in turn by the reaction index and past rates of change in the quantity of money.

The model implies that there is no limit to the revenue that can be collected if the rate of increase in money can be raised to any level. Whether this implication holds for *any* rate, no matter how high, is an interesting but largely irrelevant question, for the rate cannot in fact be raised to any level, except perhaps momentarily. The disruption of the economy caused by extreme rates would arouse political pressures on a scale that would quickly force the government to curtail its issues. The most spectacular of all recorded hyperinflations, that in Hungary after World War II, did not last long. Price increases quickly built up to rates that must have made it impossible for the economy to function effectively. All rates of price increase in the other hyperinflations much above even 150 per cent per month came in the final months preceding a currency reform. In varying degrees all the hyperinflations showed that rising rates imposed in an attempt to collect a larger revenue than can be obtained with a constant rate very soon reach such tremendous heights that the monetary system verges on chaos, and a return to orthodox taxing methods becomes an economic and political necessity.

VIII. Summary of Findings: The Theory of Hyperinflation

This study set out to explain the monetary characteristics of hyperinflation as displayed by seven such episodes following the two world wars. These characteristics are summarized by the pattern of time series for money and prices: (1) the ratio of the quantity of money to the price level—real cash balances—tended to fall during hyperinflation as a whole but fluctuated drastically from month to month and (2) the rates at which money and prices rose tended to increase and in the final months preceding currency reform reached tremendous heights. This second pattern supplies the identifying characteristic of hyperinflation, but the explanation of the first holds the key to an explanation of the second and logically comes first in order of presentation.

1. FLUCTUATIONS IN REAL CASH BALANCES

The evidence given in the preceding sections verifies the hypothesis that these fluctuations result from changes in the variables that determine the demand for real cash balances. With a change in demand, individuals cannot alter the nominal amount of money in circulation, but they can alter the real value of their collective cash balances by spending or hoarding money, and so bid prices up or down, respectively. Only one of the variables that determine this demand has an amplitude of fluctua-

The Monetary Dynamics of Hyperinflation 87

tion during hyperinflation as large as that of the balances and could possibly account for large changes in the demand. That variable is the cost of holding money, which during hyperinflation is for all practical purposes the rate of depreciation in the real value of money or, equivalently, the rate of rise in prices.

To relate the rate of price rise to the demand for the balances, it is necessary to allow for lags. There are two lags that could delay the effect of a change in this rate on the demand. First, there will be a lag between the expected and the actual rate of price rise; it may take some time after a change in the actual rate before individuals expect the new rate to continue long enough to make adjustments in their balances worthwhile. Second, there will be a lag between the desired and the actual level of the balances; it may take some time after individuals decide to change the actual level before they achieve the desired level. The method used to take account of these lags relates actual real cash balances to an average of past rates of price change, weighted by an exponential curve, so that price changes more recent in time are given greater importance. The weights never fall to zero, but past price changes sufficiently distant in time receive too small a weight to have any influence on the weighted average. The steepness of the weighting pattern indicates the length of period over which most of the weight is distributed. This method of allowing for the two lags does not distinguish between them. However, the period of time required for adjusting the balances to desired levels seems negligible compared with the past period of time normally reviewed in forming expectations. For this reason I have assumed that the actual level of real cash balances always equals desired levels and that the weighted average of past rates of price change measures only the "expected rate of price change." But there is no direct evidence on the relative importance of the two lags, and the name given to the weighted average may be lacking somewhat in descriptive accuracy.

The specific form of the hypothesis, restated to allow for lags, asserts that variations in the expected rate of price change account for variations in real cash balances during hyperinflation, where the expected rate is an exponentially weighted average of past rates. The hypothesis was tested by fitting a least-squares regression to time series for the balances and the expected rate. The regression fits the data for most months of the seven hyperinflations with a high degree of accuracy, and thus the statistical results strongly support the hypothesis.

The regression functions derived from these fits provide good approximations to the demand function for the balances and so reveal certain characteristics of this demand during hyperinflation. The elasticity of demand with respect to the expected rate of price change increases in absolute value as this expected rate rises. This contradicts the often stated view that the degree to which individuals can reduce their holdings of a depreciating currency has a limit. The demand elasticity indicates that they reduce their holdings by an increasing proportion of each successive rise in the expected rate. Indeed, the reason why issuing money on a grand scale does not almost immediately lead to extreme flight from the currency is not due to inelasticity in the demand for it but to individuals' lingering confidence in its future value. Their confidence maintains the lag in expectations, whereby the expected rates of price change do not at first keep pace with the rapidly rising actual rates. However, the weighting pattern for the lag appears to become much steeper in the later months, indicating that the lag in the expected behind the actual rates tends to shorten in response to continual inflation.

Thus the large changes in the balances during hyperinflation correspond to large changes in the rate of price change with some delay, not simultaneously. The demand function that expresses this correspondence can be interpreted to represent a dynamic process in which the course of prices through time is determined by the current quantity of money and an exponentially weighted average of past rates of change in this quantity. The process implies that past and current changes in the quantity of money cause the hyperinflation of prices. This link between changes in prices and money is only broken when the absolute value of the slope of the demand function is especially high or the lag in expectations is especially short. In that event price increases become self-generating. What this means is that the rise in prices immediately produces a proportionately greater decline in real cash balances. Then the effect of percentage changes in prices and the balances on each other does not diminish, as a stable moving equilibrium of prices requires, but grows. Such a process sends up the *percentage* change in prices at no less than an exponential rate, even if the quantity of money remains constant. Apparently the demand slope and the lag never reached the critical level in the seven hyperinflations, for none had self-generating price increases. Instead of running away on their own, price increases remained closely linked to past and current changes in the quantity of money and could have been stopped at any time, as they finally were, by tapering off the issue of new money.

2. THE TREMENDOUS INCREASE IN MONEY AND PRICES

If in fact price increases were not self-generating, what accounted for their tremendous size? The above explanation of their behavior in terms of large increases in the quantity of money only raises the further ques-

The Monetary Dynamics of Hyperinflation 89

tion, "Why did this quantity increase so much?" Clearly, issuing money on a large scale serves as a major source of funds for government expenditures. The inflation resulting from new issues places a tax on cash balances by depreciating the value of money. The revenue in real terms raised by this tax is the product of the rate of rise in prices (the tax rate) and real cash balances (the tax base). By setting the rate of increase in the quantity of money, the note-issuing authorities indirectly determine the rate of tax through the process implied by the demand function. The simplicity of administering this tax undoubtedly explains why governments resorted to continual issues of money in the difficult periods after the two world wars. An explanation of why those issues became so large, however, is found in the response of the tax base to the tax rate.

If the tax rate remains constant, the tax base and, therefore, the revenue ultimately become constant. Among all constant rates, there is one that yields a maximum ultimate revenue. With a tax rate that increases rapidly enough, however, the revenue forever exceeds this maximum amount for a constant rate because of delays in adjusting the tax base produced by the lag in expectations. In the beginning and closing months of the seven hyperinflations, the authorities successfully pursued a policy of inflating at increasing tax rates to take advantage of this lag and collected more revenue thereby than they could have obtained with any constant rate. This policy led to actual rates far above the constant rate that would have maximized ultimate revenue and produced the tremendous increases in money and prices characteristic of hyperinflation.

In the middle months the rate of increase in the money supply tapered off, for what reason it is not entirely clear, and the revenue temporarily decreased. As a result, the revenue collected with the actual tax rates was not greater on the average than the amount that could have been obtained with a constant rate. The resumption of increasing rates in the closing months restored the revenue to amounts at least as large as those in the beginning months. In order to compensate for the low level to which the tax base fell after many months of hyperinflation, the tax rates rose to astronomical heights. This explosion of the rates in the final months completely disrupted the economy and forced the government to substitute a traditional tax program for a policy of printing money.

In Section I it was suggested that the seven hyperinflations represent the same economic process because of the similarity in the ratios of the average change in prices to the average change in the quantity of money (row 9 in Table 1). The model of hyperinflation described above depicts the nature of this process. But these ratios of averages cover up an extraordinary dissimilarity. Rows 13 and 15 also present ratios involving prices and the quantity of money but not averages, and they differ wide-ly. The model shows that these differences originate, not in the differing responses of the public to a depreciating currency, but in the varying rates at which money was issued. The average share of national income that these new issues procured for the different governments was 3 to about 15 per cent, except in Russia, which had the unusually low percent-age of 0.5. The differences in these percentages are not large when com-pared with the very much larger differences between the hyperinflations in the rates at which money rose. To some extent the governments may have collected less revenue than was planned. But, in so far as the actual collections met budgetary plans, the rates required to procure the in-tended amount in any month roughly equal the actual rates. The differ-ences between the hyperinflations in the required rates that can be de-rived from the model thus account to a great extent for the corresponding differences in the actual rates at which money rose.

The model used has definite limitations: it only applies accurately to large price increases, and it fails to describe the closing months in four of the hyperinflations. In the closing months real cash balances sometimes rose when the model indicates they should have fallen. This limitation likely results from expectations that current price increases would not last very long. Such expectations are not related in any direct or obvi-ous way to past changes in prices. To take account of this limitation of the model does not seem to require revisions that would contradict the premise of this study that domestic monetary factors alone explain hyper-inflations.

Many prevailing theories of economic disturbances emphasize external monetary factors like the foreign-exchange rate, as well as real factors like the level of employment and real income, the structure of trade union-ism, the rate and extent of capital formation, and so on. These factors are prominent primarily in discussions of depression. Yet they also enter into discussions of inflation. The theory of the cost-price spiral, which borrows its concepts and framework from theories of income and employment common in discussions of depression, has been applied to inflation with the suggestion, sometimes explicit, that it applies to hyperinflation as well. Closely related and often identical to the theory of the cost-price spiral is the explanation of hyperinflation in terms of the depreciation of the foreign-exchange rate.[41]

41. References to discussions of the cost-price spiral are too extensive to give even a partial list here. The most explicit application of this theory to hyperinflation that I

The Monetary Dynamics of Hyperinflation 91

These theories postulate that a rise in prices results from increases in wages or prices of imported goods and precedes increases in the quantity of money. This study points to the opposite sequence and indicates that an extreme rise in prices depends almost entirely on changes in the quantity of money. By implication, the rise in wages and the depreciation of the foreign-exchange rate in hyperinflations are effects of the rise in prices. Extreme changes in a short period of time in exchange rates will primarily reflect variations in the real value of the currency. It is quite true that the public might well expect depreciation of the currency to show up more accurately in depreciation of exchange rates than in any set of readily available commodity prices and so follow these rates in adjusting their balances. Circumstances are easy to imagine in which *for a short time* the exchanges might depreciate faster than prices rise and so appear to move in advance of prices. But this result would not mean that the rise in prices had become the effect rather than the cause of exchange depreciation. Real cash balances would be related to this depreciation only so long as it remained a good indicator of price changes.

The model suggests in addition that the spiral theory places emphasis on the wrong factors. *Hyper*inflation at least can be explained almost entirely in terms of the demand for money. This explanation places crucial importance on the supply of money. While the monetary authorities might capitulate to pressures for sustaining wage increases, as the spiral theory presumes, they will typically attend to many other considerations. The most important of these in hyperinflation is the revenue raised by issuing money, which was analyzed above. More precise analysis than this of the determinants of the money supply goes beyond a mechanistic account of the inflationary process and involves the motives of governments, with whom the authority to open and close the spigot of note issues ultimately lies.

---

have found is by Mrs. Joan Robinson in "Review of Bresciani-Turroni's *The Economics of Inflation,*" *Economic Journal*, XLVIII (September, 1938), 507.

To my knowledge no one has argued that depreciation of the foreign-exchange rate alone is sufficient to explain hyperinflations, but it is often considered to be a causal factor. The attempts to find statistical confirmation of this view are inadequate and unconvincing. Probably the best attempt is that by James Harvey Rogers (see his *The Process of Inflation in France* [New York: Columbia University Press, 1929], chap. vii), on which Frank Graham based his interpretation of the German episode (see his *Exchange, Prices, and Production in Hyper-inflation: Germany, 1920–23* [Princeton, N.J.: Princeton University Press, 1930], esp. p. 172).

APPENDIX A
STATISTICAL METHODS

Equations (2) and (9) were combined to give the regression function (11), which has the form,

$$Y_t + aE_t + \gamma = \epsilon_t , \tag{27}$$

where Y_t stands for $\log_e (M/P)_t$ and ϵ_t is a random variable. The method of computing E_t was given in note 6. The variance of the random variable is estimated by

$$V(\epsilon) = \frac{\Sigma (Y + aE + \gamma)^2}{N} . \tag{28}$$

For simplicity the subscripts have been dropped with the understanding that the summation is over the values of Y and E that refer to the same period of time. N is the number of observations in the summation.

The parameters a and β can be estimated by the method of least squares. The estimates of a and β are those values that make (28) a minimum for all values of γ. The estimates in Table 3 were computed by maximizing the total correlation coefficient after making a substitution for a and γ, a procedure that is equivalent to minimizing (28). The total correlation coefficient, R, is defined as

$$R^2 = 1 - \frac{\Sigma (Y + aE + \gamma)^2}{\Sigma Y^2 - N\bar{Y}^2} , \tag{29}$$

where the bar indicates the average value of the variable.

The values of γ and a that make R^2 a maximum for given values of β are $\hat{\gamma}$ and $\hat{a}$ and are found as follows:

$$\frac{\partial R^2}{\partial \gamma} = \frac{-2\gamma N - 2N\bar{Y} - 2aN\bar{E}}{\Sigma Y^2 - N\bar{Y}^2} = 0 ,$$

$$\hat{\gamma} = -\bar{Y} - a\bar{E} , \tag{30}$$

$$\frac{\partial R^2}{\partial a} = \frac{-2a\Sigma E^2 - 2\Sigma YE - 2\gamma N\bar{E}}{\Sigma Y^2 - N\bar{Y}^2} = 0 ,$$

and, if $\hat{\gamma}$ is substituted for γ,

$$-\hat{a} = \frac{\Sigma YE - N\bar{E}\bar{Y}}{\Sigma E^2 - N\bar{E}^2} . \tag{31}$$

R^2 is derived as a function of β by inserting (30) and (31) in (29).

$$R^2(\beta) = \frac{(\Sigma YE - N\bar{Y}\bar{E})^2}{(\Sigma E^2 - N\bar{E}^2)(\Sigma Y^2 - N\bar{Y}^2)} . \tag{32}$$

The Monetary Dynamics of Hyperinflation 93

The value of β, $\hat{\beta}$, that makes $R^2(\beta)$ a maximum can be found by trying successive values of β that differ by .05 in (32). Given $\hat{\beta}$, $\hat{a}$ is computed from (31). This was the procedure used to calculate the estimates in Tables 3 and 5. It gives the same estimates as would minimizing (28), because the substitutions for a and γ, $\hat{\gamma}$ in (30) and $\hat{a}$ in (31), give, for every β, the maximum of R^2 for all γ and a. The maximum of $R^2(\beta)$ for all β gives the maximum with respect to all the variables, which is equivalent to the minimum of (28).

The reason for choosing a β that gives the maximum value of $R^2(\beta)$, instead of directly solving for the values that set to zero the partial derivatives of (28) with respect to each of the three variables, was one of computational efficiency. The length of the weighted average for computing E is determined by the value of β and can be fixed only by first assuming a value for β, which was the procedure that was followed. But, in the method of solving the partial derivatives simultaneously, the value of β remains to be determined, and therefore the minimum number of items that the accumulated product (9) should include to satisfy (10) (shown in Sec. III) cannot be fixed beforehand. This procedure would in this respect result in more computations than would be strictly necessary. Also, the method of finding the value of β that maximizes $R^2(\beta)$ gives as a byproduct the values of $R^2(\beta)$ for different values of β, which are necessary for calculating confidence intervals for the estimates. One further advantage to the method used is that, by knowing many values of $R^2(\beta)$ over a wide range, we are sure that there is a unique maximum for all positive values of β. As β becomes large, E approaches C, and $R^2(\beta)$ quickly approaches a limit.

A method of finding confidence intervals for the estimates of a and β that utilizes information gained in estimating the two parameters is afforded by the likelihood ratio. If the residuals from the regression function (27) are assumed to be independent and normally distributed with mean zero and variance σ^2, the likelihood function, L, is defined as

$$L = \left(\frac{1}{\sqrt{2\pi}\,\sigma}\right)^N \exp\left\{\frac{-1}{2\sigma^2}\sum_1^N (Y + aE + \gamma)^2\right\}. \qquad (33)$$

The likelihood ratio is then defined by

$$\lambda = \frac{L(\hat{w})}{L(\hat{\Omega})}, \qquad (34)$$

where $L(\hat{w})$ is the maximum of L over the region w of the null hypothesis, and $L(\hat{\Omega})$ is the maximum of L over the region Ω of all alternative hypotheses. As N becomes large, the distribution of $-2 \log_e \lambda$ approaches $\chi^2(r)$, where r is the number of restrictions on the values of the parameters specified in the null hypothesis.[42]

To find confidence intervals for the estimates of β, the values of σ, γ, and a that maximize L are inserted in (33). These values are found by partial differentiation of log L.

$$\frac{\partial \log L}{\partial \sigma} = \frac{-N}{\sigma} + \frac{1}{\sigma^3} \Sigma (Y + aE + \gamma)^2 = 0 .$$

The maximum likelihood estimate of σ is

$$\hat{\sigma}^2 = \frac{\Sigma (Y + aE + \gamma)^2}{N} ,$$

which, by (29), can be written as

$$\hat{\sigma}^2 = (1 - R^2) \Sigma (Y - \bar{Y})^2 . \tag{35}$$

The values of γ and a that maximize L are $\hat{\gamma}$ and $\hat{a}$, as given by (30) and (31). The value of β that maximizes L is the same as the estimated value, $\hat{\beta}$, which was found to an accuracy of $\pm .05$. The components of the likelihood ratio are therefore expressed as follows:

$$\log L (\hat{w}) = \log L (\hat{\sigma}_0^2, \hat{\gamma}, \hat{a}, \beta_0) =$$

$$-\frac{N}{2} \log 2\pi - \frac{N}{2} \log \hat{\sigma}_0^2 - \frac{1}{2\hat{\sigma}_0^2} \Sigma [Y + \hat{a}E (\beta_0) + \hat{\gamma}]^2 , \tag{36}$$

where $\hat{\sigma}_0^2$ is computed using $\hat{\gamma}$, $\hat{a}$, and β_0; and $E(\beta_0)$ is computed using β_0.

$$\log L (\hat{\Omega}) = \log L (\hat{\sigma}^2, \hat{\gamma}, \hat{a}, \hat{\beta}) =$$

$$-\frac{N}{2} \log 2\pi - \frac{N}{2} \log \hat{\sigma}^2 - \frac{1}{2\hat{\sigma}^2} \Sigma [Y + \hat{a}E (\hat{\beta}) + \hat{\gamma}]^2 , \tag{37}$$

where $\hat{\sigma}^2$ is computed using $\hat{\gamma}$, $\hat{a}$, and $\hat{\beta}$; and $E(\hat{\beta})$ is computed using $\hat{\beta}$. Consequently,

$$-2 \log \lambda = N \log \hat{\sigma}_0^2 - N \log \hat{\sigma}^2 , \quad \text{or}$$

$$-2 \log \lambda = N \log [1 - R^2 (\beta_0)] - N \log [1 - R^2 (\hat{\beta})] , \tag{38}$$

which is distributed as $\chi^2(1)$. Only the right-hand tail of the chi-square distribution should be used in this test.

Confidence intervals for β in Table 3 were computed by inserting numbers that differed by .05 for β_0 in (38). The lowest and highest values,

42. S. S. Wilks, *Mathematical Statistics* (Princeton, N.J.: Princeton University Press, 1950), p. 151.

The Monetary Dynamics of Hyperinflation 95

β_L and β_U, that just make (38) significant at the .10 level are the bounds of the confidence interval. This gives a confidence coefficient of .90.

Confidence intervals for estimates of a were found in a similar manner from the likelihood ratio. $L(\hat{w})$ is the maximum of L for given values of a. The lowest and highest values, a_L and a_U, that make the likelihood ratio significant at the .10 level are the bounds of the confidence interval. Since the value of β that maximizes L for given a cannot be found directly, a trial-and-error procedure was followed using values of β that differed by .05.

The confidence intervals for the estimates of $a\beta$ in Table 8, $(a\beta)_L$ and $(a\beta)_U$, are based on the likelihood ratio. $L(\hat{w})$ is the maximum of L under the one restriction that $a\beta = (a\beta)_0$. $(a\beta)_L$ and $(a\beta)_U$ are the extreme values of $a\beta$ that make the likelihood ratio significant at the .10 level. It turns out that $(a\beta)_L = a_U\beta_L$ and $(a\beta)_U = a_L\beta_U$. Computations by trial and error for each hyperinflation verified that they are the extreme values at the .10 level of significance for all β that differ by .05.

The significance tests summarized in Table 4 and described in note 9 are based on the likelihood ratio and its asymptotic properties. The likelihood function of this ratio for the tests is defined as

$$L = \sum_{i=1}^{7} \left(\frac{1}{\sqrt{2\pi}\,\sigma_i}\right)^{n_i} \exp\left\{\frac{-1}{2\sigma_i^2}\sum_{j=1}^{n_i} (Y + a_i E\,(\beta_i) + \gamma_i)_j^2\right\}. \quad (39)$$

The major summation is over the seven hyperinflations. The number of observations from each hyperinflation is given by n_i. The total number of observations from all seven hyperinflations is

$$\sum_{1}^{7} n_i = 149 .$$

The likelihood ratio, (34), for the tests is defined as follows: The denominator, $L(\hat{\Omega})$, is the same in all the tests. It is the unrestricted maximum of the likelihood function. The values of a_i, β_i, and γ_i, which determine σ_i from (35), are those estimated from the observations of each hyperinflation separately. In the test of significance used for Table 4, the numerator of the likelihood ratio, $L(\hat{w})$, is the maximum of the likelihood function under the twelve restrictions that for all seven hyperinflations a_i is the same and β_i is the same. Here the appropriate number of degrees of freedom for chi square is twelve. In the tests of significance for the two fits described in note 9, $L(\hat{w})$ is the maximum of the likelihood function under six restrictions, which makes six the appropriate number of degrees of freedom to use in finding the significance level of the chi-square distribution. For the first fit the restrictions are that β_i is the same for all seven hyperinflations. For the second fit the six restrictions are that a_i is the same for all seven hyperinflations.

Finding the values of α, β, and γ that maximize the likelihood function under these various restrictions is equivalent to finding the values that minimize the following sum of squares under the given restrictions:

$$\sum_{i=1}^{7}\left\{\sum_{j=1}^{n_i}\left(Y + a_iE\left(\beta_i\right) + \gamma_i\right)_j^2\right\}. \tag{40}$$

There is no direct way to minimize the above relation, and the procedure followed was to approximate the minimum for values of β that differ by .05. The minimum is particularly difficult to compute under the six restrictions that all a_i are the same. Consequently, for these six restrictions the minimum of (40) was only shown to lie above a certain number. Greater accuracy was not necessary to prove that the appropriate likelihood ratio based on these restrictions is significant at the .005 level.

APPENDIX B
DATA AND SOURCES

This appendix contains the following three monthly time series for each hyperinflation:

1. *Logarithm of real cash balances.*—In the tables this series is shown as $\log_{10}(P/M)$, where P and M are indexes of prices and the quantity of authorized hand-to-hand currency.[43] This logarithm, when multiplied by $-1/\log_{10}e$, becomes $\log_e(M/P)$, which appears in equation (11). This series, as well as those described below, was computed more easily in its present form, and it could be used for all the statistical work of this study without conversion into natural logarithmic form. The values of the parameters α and β are independent of the base of the logarithms in the equations.

2. *Rate of change in prices per month.*—In the tables this series is shown as $\log_{10}(P_i/P_{i-1})$, where P_{i-1} and P_i are successive values of an index of the price level, the latter on the date opposite the item of the series and the former on the preceding date.[44] Multiplication of this series by $1/\log_{10}e$

---

43. Counterfeiting was widespread in all the countries during hyperinflation (see J. van Walré de Bordes, *The Austrian Crown* [London: P. S. King & Son, Ltd., 1924], Annex III), but it does not seem unreasonable to assume that the amount of counterfeit notes was negligible compared with the tremendous quantities of legal notes issued.

44. When this period between the two dates differs appreciably from thirty days, the logarithm is multiplied, unless otherwise noted, by the appropriate factor to make the figure a rate per thirty days. Where no earlier date is shown after the last item in the column, the period between the values of the price index used for this item is one month.

The Monetary Dynamics of Hyperinflation 97

gives $\log_e(P_i/P_{i-1})$, which is the form of the series used in the equations. This series measures the average rate of change in prices during each month. When the rate is fairly steady, the series is a good approximation to the daily rate throughout the month; but, when the rate rises considerably, this series represents the daily rate at the end of the month more closely than it does the rate at the middle of the month.

3. *Expected rate of change in prices per month, $E(\beta)$*.—The derivation of this series is presented in Section III, and methods for its computation are given in note 6. The value of β used for each hyperinflation is the estimated value shown in Table 3. This series is shown in logarithms to the base 10. To convert to natural logarithms, multiply by $1/\log_{10} e$.

The tables of these series start with the final month of hyperinflation and carry back in time to include all the observations used in the regressions. The series of the rate of change in prices are carried back even further to include all the rates used to compute all the values of E that are included in the regressions.

Notes on sources and comments on the comprehensiveness and reliability of the data accompany each table. Series on deposits and real output are included along with supporting notes.

NOTES ON AUSTRIAN DATA

For 1919 and 1920 P is an index of the cost of living. Rents are excluded, since they were controlled and would bias the index downward compared with an index of the general price level. For 1921 and 1922 P is a different index of the cost of living that excludes rents but includes many prices not included in the earlier index.[45] The earlier index is linked to the later one by a factor that expresses the ratio of the averages of the indexes over the six-month period in which they overlap.

The rate of change in prices for the period preceding January 15, 1919, was found by assuming that the price index was unity on December 30, 1914. If, however, it was unity on June 30, 1914, the last rate in the second series should be changed to .0024, a difference that would have a negligible effect on the series for E. It is not clear whether the base for P in 1914 should be June or December of that year.

M is an index of the quantity of bank notes in circulation.[46] For the base year 1914 the quantity was taken as five hundred million crowns, a figure that Walré de Bordes considers slightly too low.[47] The bank notes were those of the Austro-Hungarian National Bank and were stamped by

45. Walré de Bordes, *op. cit.*, pp. 88 ff.

46. *Ibid.*, pp. 48 ff.

47. *Ibid.*, pp. 38, 64.

98   *Studies in the Quantity Theory of Money*

the Austrian government. Unstamped bank notes also circulated, but they disappeared gradually, probably completely by June, 1920.[48]

Table B2 gives figures on deposits less bank reserves (since reserves are included in M above) and the ratio of an index of bank notes to an

TABLE B1

TIME SERIES FOR AUSTRIA

Date	$\log_{10}(P/M)$ (1914 = 1) (1)	$\log_{10}(P_i/P_{i-1})$ (Per Month) (2)	$E(.05)$ (Per Month) (3)
1922			
Aug. 31.........	1.5988	.3699	.0885
July 31.........	1.4654	.2842	.0740
June 30.........	1.3365	.1247	.0633
May 31.........	1.3522	.1492	.0601
Apr. 30.........	1.2625	.0648	.0555
Mar. 31.........	1.2553	.0117	.0550
Feb. 28.........	1.3118	.0557	.0573
Jan. 31.........	1.3139	.1550	.0573
1921			
Dec. 31.........	1.2742	.1630	.0523
Nov. 30.........	1.2718	.2511	.0467
Oct. 31.........	1.1430	.2154	.0362
Sept. 30.........	1.0414	.1230	.0270
Aug. 31.........	.9956	.1193	.0221
July 31.........	.9085	− .0467	.0171
June 30.........	.9956	.0604	.0204
May 31.........	.9731	.0025	.0183
Apr. 30.........	.9731	.0187	.0191
Mar. 31.........	.9956	.0296	.0191
Feb. 28.........	.9956	.0611	.0186
Jan. 31.........	.9777	.0261	.0166
1920			
Dec. 31.........	....	.0427	....
Oct. 15.........	....	.0127	....
July 15.........	....	.0126	....
Apr. 15.........	....	.0248	....
Jan. 15.........	....	.0334	....
1919			
July 15.........	....	.0065	....
Jan. 15.........	....	.0027	....
1914			
Dec. 30.........	....	....	....

index of bank notes plus deposits in circulation for Austria. The deposit figures include postal savings, deposits in savings banks, sight liabilities of the national bank, and an estimate of deposits in commercial banks. Cash reserves are those in commercial banks.

The figures for the post office include savings but not current accounts

48. *Ibid.*, p. 45.

The Monetary Dynamics of Hyperinflation 99

(i.e., sight deposits),[49] the amounts of which are unavailable. In 1923 the total debits of current accounts in the post office were 25 per cent of the debits of current accounts in the national bank.[50] If the amount of these accounts in the post office were also roughly 25 per cent of their amount in the national bank in the preceding years, the deposits in the post office that are excluded were a negligible proportion of total bank deposits, because all deposits in the national bank were a small proportion of the total.

The deposits of savings banks included above comprise all but about 1 per cent of the total deposits in such banks.[51]

Sight liabilities of the national bank[52] were held by the public and are properly included.[53]

TABLE B2

DEPOSIT DATA FOR AUSTRIA

End of Year	Bank Deposits *less* Cash Reserves (Million Kronen)	Ratio of Index of Bank Notes to Index of Bank Notes *plus* Deposits in Circulation
1913.........	7,423.1	1.00
1920.........	71,371.0	4.75
1921.........	494,914	4.12
1922.........	9,475,665	4.77

Figures for deposits held by the public less cash reserves in commercial banks for the years 1920–22 are based on the deposits and cash-reserve ratios of seven large Vienna banks.[54] To estimate deposits in commercial banks, the deposits in these seven banks were increased by 78.85 per cent, the percentage by which they fell short of the deposits (current, savings, and *Giro* accounts) of twenty-seven Vienna banks in 1920.[55] These twenty-

49. League of Nations, *Memorandum on Currency and Central Banks, 1913–1925* (Geneva: Publications Department of the League of Nations, 1926), II, 61.

50. B. H. Beckhart and H. Parker Willis, *Foreign Banking Systems* (New York: Henry Holt & Co., 1929), chap. ii.

51. League of Nations, *op. cit.*, p. 61.

52. Walré de Bordes, *op. cit.*, p. 53.

53. See Beckhart and Willis, *op. cit.*, pp. 133–34, and League of Nations, *Memorandum on Central Banks, 1913 and 1918–1923* (Geneva: Publications Department of the League of Nations, 1924), pp. 83, 91.

54. League of Nations, *Memorandum on Commercial Banks, 1913–1929* (Geneva: Publications Department of the League of Nations, 1931), pp. 62 ff.

55. Walré de Bordes, *op. cit.*, p. 56.

seven Vienna banks constituted almost the whole body of commercial banking proper within Austrian territory at the time. A great number of new banks established during the hyperinflation remained small.[56]

The above figures of bank deposits exclude deposits in the following institutions:[57]

1. Wiener Giro- und Cassen-Verein and Soldierungs-Verein, which were engaged in clearing transactions. The former's business was large, but most of its activities involved stock-exchange transactions. Before 1924 the latter's deposits can probably be considered negligible, since its debits were only 10 per cent of deposit debits for the national bank in 1923.

2. Provincial mortgage institutions, credit associations, and agricultural credit associations, which held savings deposits and greatly declined in importance during hyperinflation.[58]

Even though the coverage of bank deposits in the above figures is fairly comprehensive, the inadequacy of the data for commercial banks means that the figures in Table B2 must be taken as rough approximations.

Changes in real income in Austria during the hyperinflation were apparently not great.[59] Unemployment figures available show a rise in 1922, but there is no evidence that the relative amount of unemployment became important.[60]

NOTES ON GERMAN DATA

P is an index of wholesale prices compiled by the Statistisches Reichsamt.[61] For the months before 1923 P is the average monthly level of prices and is used to approximate the level of prices at the middle of the month. For the first half of 1923 P is the level of prices on a particular day and is available for ten-day intervals. For the second half of 1923 it refers to a particular day at weekly intervals. Where the period covered by the rate of change in prices in 1923 differs from thirty days, the figures were adjusted to give the rate per thirty days. In computing E, each rate of change in prices was treated as though it pertained to the fifteenth of the month. Adjusting the exponential weights to take account of observations not falling on the fifteenth would have involved an unnecessary complication.

56. League of Nations, *Memorandum on Commercial Banks, 1913–1929*, p. 66.

57. Beckhart and Willis, *op. cit.*, chap. ii.

58. *Ibid.*, p. 169.

59. Walré de Bordes, *op. cit.*, p. 158.

60. Statistisches Reichsamt, *Statistisches Jahrbuch für das Deutsche Reich* (Berlin: Reimar Hobbing, 1925), Vol. XLIV: *1924–25*, International Section, Table 12.

61. Sonderhefte zur Wirtschaft und Statistik, *Zahlen zur Geldentwertung in Deutschland 1914 bis 1923* (Berlin: R. Hobbing, 1925), pp. 33 ff.

The Monetary Dynamics of Hyperinflation 101

M is an index of the quantity of authorized bank notes in circulation.[62] For the months before 1923 the quantity of these bank notes is available for the end of the month, and linear interpolations of these figures were used to estimate M for the middle of the month. For 1923 the gold value of the quantity of bank notes is available weekly. These figures were converted to marks by multiplying by the dollar-exchange rate and by 4.198 (the number of gold marks that equaled one dollar before November, 1923). Weekly figures for the quantity of bank notes were interpolated to estimate M for the same day in each month in 1923 to which P refers. By that time the quantity of bank notes was increasing so rapidly that ordinary arithmetic interpolation would have been subject to large errors. Therefore, interpolations for 1923 were linear between the logarithms of the quantity of bank notes up to June and were linear between second logarithms thereafter. These interpolations are probably in error by negligible amounts for the months preceding September.

Illegal currencies issued in Germany in 1923 were estimated not to have exceeded 192 quintillion marks.[63] These currencies comprised over two-thirds of the outstanding legal bank notes on November 15, 1923, though a rapidly diminishing fraction thereafter. There is some reason to believe that the circulation of the illegal currencies was somewhat localized and that most of them were issued when the so-called needs for currency became acute, which occurred at the peaks of hyperinflation and would imply that they were issued at a rate roughly in proportion to that of the authorized bank notes. In so far as failure to take account of illegal currencies has made the figures for real cash balances for Germany in 1923 too low, the estimate of the parameter a is too high. While similar sources of upward bias in the estimates of a may exist for the other countries, there seems to be no indication that substantial amounts of illegal currencies were issued. Apparently, only in Germany were unauthorized currencies issued by local governments and private organizations.

Table B4 gives figures on deposits less bank reserves (M above includes these reserves) and the ratio of an index of bank notes to an index of bank notes plus deposits in circulation for Germany. The figures include deposits in the post office, savings banks, the Reichsbank, and a rough estimate of deposits in all commercial banks. Cash reserves are those of commercial banks.

The amount of deposits with the post office[64] are available for the years

62. *Ibid.*, pp. 45 ff.

63. German Government, *Germany's Economy, Currency and Finance* (Berlin: Zentral-Verlag G.m.b.H., 1924), p. 67.

64. Statistisches Reichsamt, *op. cit.*, p. 314.

TABLE B3

TIME SERIES FOR GERMANY

Date (Middle of Month unless Otherwise Noted)	$\log_{10}(P/M)$ (1913 = 1) (1)	$\log_{10}(P_i/P_{i-1})$ (Per Month) (2)	$E(.20)$ (Per Month) (3)
1923			
Nov. 13*......	1.9445	2.5560	1.1155
Oct. 16.......	2.6263	1.5881	.7965
Sept. 18.......	2.6415	1.6259	.6212
Aug. 14.......	2.5717	1.1385	.3987
July 17.......	2.1303	.4842	.2349
June 15.......	1.9868	.3789	.1797
May 15.......	1.7782	.1542	.1356
Apr. 14.......	1.7076	.0155	.1315
Mar. 15.......	1.8261	− .0587	.1571
Feb. 15.......	2.0755	.3899	.2049
Jan. 15.......	1.9445	.1546	.1640
1922			
Dec..........	1.9381	.1066	.1661
Nov.........	2.0481	.3094	.1792
Oct..........	1.9247	.2949	.1503
Sept.........	1.7747	.1746	.1183
Aug..	1.7084	.2807	.1058
July.........	1.5024	.1556	.0671
June.........	1.3955	.0369	.0476
May.........	1.3983	.0070	.0501
Apr.........	1.4231	.0681	.0597
Mar.........	1.3886	.1219	.0579
Feb..........	1.2934	.0490	.0438
Jan..........	1.2550	.0218	.0427
1921			
Dec..........	1.2608	.0088	.0473
Nov.........	1.2975	.1426	.0559
Oct..........	1.1855	.0756	.0367
Sept.........	1.1351	.0327	.0281
Aug.........	1.1225	.1279	.0271
July.........	1.0043	.0192	.0048
June.........	.9978	.0189	.0017
May.........	.9886	− .0059	− .0021
Apr.........	.9983	− .0040	− .0013
Mar.........	1.0056	− .0121	− .0007
Feb..........	1.0220	− .0195	.0018
Jan..........	1.0370	− .0003	.0065
1920			
Dec..........	1.0410	− .0203	.0081
Nov.........	1.0730	.0126	.0144
Oct:.........	1.0652	− .0094	.0148
Sept.........	1.0884	.0141	.0202

* Prices still rose sharply but at diminishing rates until November 20, 1923, when the mark exchange rate with the dollar was officially fixed and prices became relatively stable.

TABLE B3—*Continued*

Date (Middle of Month unless Otherwise Noted)	$\log_{10}(P/M)$ (1913=1) (1)	$\log_{10}(P_i/P_{i-1})$ (Per Month) (2)	$E(.20)$ (Per Month) (3)
1920—*Continued*			
Aug...........	....	.0256	....
July..........	....	− .0047	....
June..........	....	− .0379	....
May..........	....	− .0167	....
Apr...........	....	− .0376	....
Mar..........	....	.0061	....
Feb...........	....	.1276	....
Jan...........	....	.1943	....
1919			
Dec...........	....	.0735	....
Nov...........	....	.0815	....
Oct...........	....	.0569	....
Sept..........	....	.0675	....
Aug...........	....	.0951	....
July..........	....	.0416	....
June..........	....	.0158	....
May..........	....	.0164	....
Apr...........	....	.0186	....
Mar..........	....	.0064	....
Feb...........	....	.0131	....
Jan...........	....	.0291	....
1918			
Dec...........	....	.0200	....
Nov...........	....	.0000	....
Oct...........	....	.0075	....
Sept..........	....	− .0094	....
Aug...........	....	.0530	....
July..........	....	.0020	....
June..........	....	.0126	....
May..........	....	− .0021	....
Apr...........	....	.0129	....
Mar..........	....	.0000	....
Feb...........	....	− .0129	....
Jan...........	....	.0021	....
1917			
Dec...........	....	.0000	....
Nov...........	....	.0043	....
Oct...........	....	.0043	....
Sept..........	....	− .0086	....
Aug...........	....	.0720	....
July..........	....	.0180	....
June..........	....	.0053	....

104   *Studies in the Quantity Theory of Money*

1913–22 but not for 1923. The magnitude of these deposits was relatively
small before 1923, and their slow growth up to 1923 suggests that their
magnitude in that year was insignificant.

The figures for savings banks include all deposits of almost all such
banks.[65]

The figures for deposits with the Reichsbank cover private (non-
government) current accounts.[66] They are not separated in the figures
from government current accounts for the years before 1921, however.
For 1913 and 1919 this item is omitted from the estimate of deposits.
This understates the estimate by probably no more than 5 per cent for

TABLE B4

DEPOSIT DATA FOR GERMANY

End of Year	Bank Deposits *less* Cash Reserves (Million Marks)	Ratio of Index of Bank Notes to Index of Bank Notes *plus* Deposits in Circulation
1913.........	29,640	1.00
1919.........	93,340	2.09
1920.........	138,261	2.22
1921.........	197,800	2.29
1922.........	272,220	1.93
1923.........	$1,959 \times 10^{12}$	3.33

1919 and by even less for 1913, since the total of all Reichsbank deposits
was less than 15 per cent of all bank deposits at the end of 1919. Furthermore, cash reserves of commercial banks, included in the figures for these
two years, were mostly balances in the Reichsbank and account for over
one-half of its private accounts.

Private accounts in the Reichsbank for 1920 were estimated by the
figure for January, 1921, since the private accounts seem to have been
stable during this period. Even if this January figure is not applicable to
the preceding month, the greatest amount by which it could differ from
the actual figure for the end of 1920 would not greatly bias the estimate
of bank deposits.

Commercial bank deposits held by the public less cash reserves were

65. League of Nations, *Memorandum on Commercial Banks, 1913–1929*, p. 135.
66. League of Nations, *Memorandum on Central Banks, 1913 and 1918–1923*, p. 199.

The Monetary Dynamics of Hyperinflation 105

extrapolated from figures for almost all commercial banks.[67] Benchmarks for the estimates were provided by complete figures for all commercial banks for the end of 1913 and 1923.[68] The figures for the two years 1921 and 1922 were estimated by a linear interpolation of the second logarithms of the figures for December 30, 1920, and January 1, 1924, including an adjustment for deviations from the same kind of trend in the deposits of the eight major Berlin banks. These estimates could have a substantial error but probably not enough to create the relative fall in the ratio of bank notes to deposits in 1922.

Data on deposits in mortgage, public, and co-operative banks are not available for the relevant years, but their position in 1913 and 1924 indi-

TABLE B5

INDEX OF OUTPUT FOR GERMANY

Year	Index of Output (1913 = 100)	Year	Index of Output (1913 = 100)
1914	82	1920	66
1915	74	1921	73
1916	69	1922	80
1917	67	1923	61
1918	66	1923 (Sept.–Dec.)	42
1919	55		

cates that they declined greatly during the hyperinflation.[69] Their deposits in 1923 were probably less than 10 per cent of those of commercial banks alone.

Table B5 gives an index of output for Germany that is a simple average of indexes of industrial production, agricultural output, and commercial transportation figures. The index portrays in a general way changes in real income.[70]

The index of output for the last part of 1923 is the midpoint of an interval estimate of the aggregate real income of German industrial workers. It is likely to be an understatement of total real income. The

67. League of Nations, *Memorandum on Commercial Banks, 1913–1929*, pp. 129 ff., and P. Barret Whale, *Joint Stock Banking in Germany* (London: Macmillan & Co., Ltd., 1930), p. 191.

68. League of Nations, *Memorandum on Commercial Banks, 1913–1929*, pp. 129 ff.

69. *Ibid.*

70. Graham, *op. cit.*, p. 316.

figures in Table B5 take into account territorial changes resulting from the loss of Upper Silesia to Poland on October 12, 1921. However, the German marks in that area continued to circulate in fixed number along with the Polish marks, which were introduced in March, 1923. By the time the Polish mark was made sole legal tender in November of that year, the value of the German marks had depreciated to nothing.[71]

NOTES ON GREEK DATA

P is an index of the cost of food in Athens.[72] The rate of change in prices for the period before 1941 is based on the fact that prices rose no more than threefold over the entire period 1938–41.[73] In computing E, however, the rate for the period June, 1938, to December, 1940, was taken to be zero. If the rate was actually as high as .0145 for this entire period, the error in E for any of the months would be no greater than .0005.

M is an index of the quantity of bank notes issued by the Bank of Greece.[74] The circulation of these bank notes was largely limited to the area near Athens,[75] which provides some justification for having confidence in a price index of food in Athens only. Nevertheless, little stock can be placed in figures of such limited coverage. Furthermore, data on deposits and changes in real income are apparently nonexistent. Bank deposits should not be dismissed as entirely insignificant, though their effects in the other hyperinflations were minor, because deposits in Greece were as large in value as the quantity of bank notes in circulation during the hyperinflation.[76]

The series are not shown for dates later than November 10, 1944. On this date the country made a second attempt at currency stabilization, which was not entirely successful. Prices continued to rise afterward, though at rates far below those that prevailed before November, 1944.

71. League of Nations, *Memorandum on Currency and Central Banks, 1913–1924* (Geneva: Publications Department of the League of Nations, 1925), II, 128.

72. William C. Cleveland and Dimitrios Delivanis, *Greek Monetary Developments, 1939–1948* ("Indiana University Publications Social Science Series," No. 6 [Bloomington: Indiana University, 1949]), Appendix.

73. Vera Lutz, "The Record of Inflation: European Experience since 1939," chap. iii of preliminary draft for "The American Assembly" (Graduate School of Business, Columbia University, n.d.), p. 86. (Mimeographed.)

74. Cleveland and Delivanis, *op. cit.*

75. *Ibid.*, p. 99.

76. Lutz, *op. cit.*, p. 96.

TABLE B6

TIME SERIES FOR GREECE

Date	$\log_{10}(P/M)$ (June, 1941 = 1) (1)	$\log_{10}(P_i/P_{i-1})$ (Per Month) (2)	$E(.15)$ (Per Month) (3)
1944			
Nov. 10	3.5580	5.9320	.9095
Oct. 31	2.5369	1.9540	.6694
Sept. 30	2.5310	1.3030	.4615
Aug. 31	2.3491	.6524	.3253
July 31	2.3213	.6077	.2724
June 30	2.0752	.2040	.2181
May 31	2.1626	.4120	.2204
Apr. 30	2.0192	.3022	.1894
Mar. 31	2.0554	.2800	.1712
Feb. 29	1.9499	.1832	.1536
Jan. 31	1.8791	.3884	.1488
1943			
Dec. 31	1.5867	.1294	.1101
Nov. 30	1.5999	.2790	.1069
Oct. 31	1.4442	.1687	.0791
Sept. 30	1.4002	.1331	.0646
Aug. 31	1.3553	.0590	.0535
July 31	1.3835	.1278	.0526
June 30	1.3419	.0465	.0405
May 31	1.3538	.0268	.0395
Apr. 30	1.3732	.1224	.0415
Mar. 31	1.3310	.0446	.0284
Feb. 28	1.3505	− .0514	.0258
Jan. 31	1.4402	− .0704	.0383
1942			
Dec. 31		− .1268	
Nov. 30		− .0590	
Oct. 31		.1730	
Sept. 30		.0887	
Aug. 31		.1030	
July 31		.1065	
June 30		.1414	
May 31		.0577	
Apr. 30		.1190	
Mar. 31		.1231	
Feb. 28		.0630	
Jan. 31		.0328	
1941			
Dec. 31		.1696	
Nov. 30		.1472	
Oct. 31		.1569	
Sept. 30		.1200	
Aug. 31		.1012	
July 31		.1776	
June 30		.1396	
May 31		.0969	
Apr. 30		.0000	
Mar. 31		.0215	
1940			
Dec. 31		.0145	
1938			
June 30			

108   *Studies in the Quantity Theory of Money*

NOTES ON HUNGARIAN DATA FOR AFTER WORLD WAR I

For the years before December, 1923, P is an index of retail prices based on the year 1913. Thereafter, P is an index of wholesale prices based on the year 1914. The two indexes were linked together on the assumption that prices changed very little between the two base years.[77]

TABLE B7

TIME SERIES FOR HUNGARY FOLLOWING WORLD WAR I

Date (End of Month)	$\log_{10}(P/M)$ (July, 1921 = 1) (1)	$\log_{10}(P_i/P_{i-1})$ (Per Month) (2)	$E(.10)$ (Per Month) (3)
1924			
Feb.	1.7332	.2536	.1086
Jan.	1.5514	.1124	.0934
1923			
Dec.	1.5051	.0958	.0914
Nov.	1.4472	.0340	.0909
Oct.	1.4728	.0253	.0969
Sept.	1.5490	.0784	.1044
Aug.	1.6385	.2086	.1072
July	1.6776	.2966	.0965
June	1.5453	.1867	.0755
May	1.4713	.0514	.0638
Apr.	1.4969	.1022	.0651
Mar.	1.4800	.1983	.0611
Feb.	1.3201	.0357	.0463
Jan.	1.2923	.0618	.0479
1922			
Dec.	1.2201	.0105	.0464
Nov.	1.2304	−.0040	.0502
Oct.	1.2480	.0923	.0559
Sept.	1.2330	.0945	.0520
Aug.	1.2405	.0898	.0476
July	1.2330	.1300	.0432
June	....	.0691	....
May	....	.0099	....
Apr.	....	.0359	....
Mar.	....	.0662	....
Feb.	....	.0209	....
Jan.	....	−.0078	....
1921			
Dec.	....	−.0026	....
Nov.	....	.0898	....
Oct.	....	.0334	....
Sept.	....	.0634	....
Aug.	....	.1092	....
July	....	.0193	....
1914			
July	....	....	....

77. John Parke Young, *European Currency and Finance* (Commission of Gold and Silver Inquiry, U.S. Senate, Serial 9 [Washington, D.C.: Government Printing Office, 1925]), II, 322.

The Monetary Dynamics of Hyperinflation 109

M is an index of the quantity of notes issued by the State Note Institute.[78] These figures neglect issues of *bons de caisse* in 1923, which apparently circulated as a media of exchange. However, they remained below about 3 per cent of the number of notes in circulation.[79]

Table B8 gives figures on deposits less bank reserves (M above includes reserves) and the ratio of an index of notes to an index of notes plus deposits in circulation for Hungary for the years after World War I. The figures include deposits of all the important commercial banks, current accounts (excluding checking and savings deposits) of the post office, and deposits in savings banks.[80] Cash reserves are those of commercial banks.

TABLE B8

DEPOSIT DATA FOR HUNGARY FOLLOWING
WORLD WAR I

End of Year	Bank Deposits *less* Cash Reserves (Million Kronen)	Ratio of Index of Notes to Index of Notes *plus* Deposits in Circulation
1920........	18,398	1.00
1921........	28,496	1.07
1922........	53,038	1.35
1923........	159,958	1.95
1924........	5,201,805	1.06

Current accounts in the State Note Institute are excluded, because the Institute served mainly as a bankers' bank.[81] Even if these accounts are included in the totals, the pattern of the ratios in Table B8 still retains the peak in 1923. The same kinds of deposits as are included in the figures in the table accounted for 83 per cent of total bank deposits held by the public in 1925.[82] Besides figures on checking and savings deposits in the post office and deposits in small commercial banks, such figures on deposits in municipal savings banks and co-operative credit societies are also excluded, because they are unavailable. These last two institutions probably lost business during the hyperinflation, in which case the coverage of deposits in Table B8 would be nearly complete.

78. *Ibid.*, p. 321.

79. League of Nations, *Memorandum on Currency and Central Banks, 1913–1924*, I, 123.

80. League of Nations, *Memorandum on Currency and Central Banks, 1913–1925*, II, 65, 85.

81. League of Nations, *Memorandum on Currency and Central Banks, 1913–1924*, II, 92.

82. League of Nations, *Memorandum on Commercial Banks, 1913–1929*, p. 170.

An unusual aspect of deposits for this period in Hungary was the phenomenal growth of current accounts in the post office. They increased over a thousand times from 1920 to 1924. Deposits in commercial banks, which seem to account for most of the growth in deposits during other hyperinflations, increased only a little over two hundred times.

Data on output for Hungary after World War I are apparently unavailable.

NOTES ON HUNGARIAN DATA FOR AFTER WORLD WAR II

For the months after July, 1945, P is an index of prices compiled by Professor Varga.[83] For the earlier period P is an index of the cost of living in Budapest.[84] The rates of change in prices based on the cost-of-living index differ in level from those given in the second column of Table B9

TABLE B9

TIME SERIES FOR HUNGARY FOLLOWING WORLD WAR II

Date (End of Month)	$\log_{10}(P/M)$ (Dec., 1939 = 1) (1)	$\log_{10}(P_i/P_{i-1})$ (Per Month) (2)	$E(.15)$ (Per Month) (3)
1946			
July.........	4.5879	14.6226	3.2211
June.........	2.9782	4.9264	1.3758
May.........	3.1740	2.4992	.8011
Apr.........	3.0255	1.2821	.5263
Mar.........	2.9761	.6323	.4040
Feb.........	3.2040	.7804	.3670
Jan.........	2.9718	.2411	.3001
1945			
Dec.........	3.0655	.5041	.3097
Nov.........	2.8954	.7283	.2783
Oct.........	2.6866	.8070	.2055
Sept.........	2.2630	.3456	.1081
Aug.........	2.1359	.2118	.0696
July.........	2.0825	.1352	.0466
June.........	....	.0003	....
May.........	....	.0004	....
Apr.........	....	.0520	....
1944			
June.........	....	.0077	....
1943			
June.........	....	.0056	....
1942			
June.........	....	....	....

83. Stefan Varga, "Zerfall und Stabilisierung der ungarischen Währung," *Neue Zürcher Zeitung*, January 7, 1947, p. 4.

84. Statistical Office of the United Nations, *Monthly Bulletin of Statistics*, June, 1947, No. 6, p. 120.

The Monetary Dynamics of Hyperinflation 111

for the final months of the hyperinflation; however, the former rates do not show a materially different pattern from the rates in the table.

M is an index of the quantity of bank notes issued by the National Bank of Hungary and the quantity of deposits in the thirty major commercial and savings banks.[85] The ratio of deposits to bank notes rose astronomically during the hyperinflation. In view of the fact that this ratio ordinarily declined in the other hyperinflations, a breakdown of deposits into various kinds would be desirable, because deposits in a new unit of currency, which was stable in real value when it was first introduced, appeared in January, 1946.[86] Deposits of this new currency should be excluded from the figures as long as the currency had a stable value. Presumably they are excluded from the published figures,[87] but, since the data on deposits are not broken down, this presumption cannot be verified.

Output in Hungary seems to have been stable during the hyperinflation following World War II, though the evidence is spotty. Production figures on basic raw materials do not decline, and unemployment figures only increase after the date of the reform in the currency.[88] Undoubtedly real income was much below prewar levels.

NOTES ON POLISH DATA

For the months before September, 1921, *P* is an index of the retail prices of foods only. Thereafter it is a geometric average of fifty-seven commodity prices at wholesale.[89] The two indexes were linked together.

M is the quantity of bank notes issued by the Bank of Poland.[90] The Polish mark was introduced into Upper Silesia on March 1, 1923, and was made legal tender in November of that year. It gradually replaced the German mark during this period.[91] One result of transferring this territory to Poland from Germany was that the former's currency was given a larger area within which to circulate, and more Polish marks could be issued without affecting the Polish price level. The ratio of *M* to *P* could

85. *Ibid.*, pp. 54, 106.

86. Nogaro, *op. cit.* (The tables in Nogaro's article contain some errors. Original sources were used.)

87. L'Office Central Hongrois de Statistique, *Revue hongroise de statistique*, October–December, 1946, Nos. 10–12, p. 154.

88. Statistical Office of the United Nations, *op. cit.*, esp. p. 20.

89. League of Nations, *Memorandum on Currency and Central Banks, 1913–1924*, II, 298, and Young, *op. cit.*, p. 349.

90. Young, *op. cit.*, p. 347.

91. League of Nations, *Memorandum on Currency and Central Banks, 1913–1924*, II, 128.

112   *Studies in the Quantity Theory of Money*

thus rise, even if real cash balances within the original borders were constant. This no doubt partly explains the slight rise that occurred in real cash balances in October and November, 1923, above the level at which the expected rate of change in prices suggests they should have been.

TABLE B10

TIME SERIES FOR POLAND

Date (End of Month)	$\log_{10}(P/M)$ (Jan., 1921 = 1) (1)	$\log_{10}(P_i/P_{i-1})$ (Per Month) (2)	$E(.30)$ (Per Month) (3)
1924			
Jan............	2.2279	.2309	.2860
1923			
Dec............	2.3962	.3211	.3053
Nov...........	2.4472	.3947	.2997
Oct............	2.4150	.5740	.2665
Sept..........	2.1553	.1396	.1590
Aug...........	2.2279	.2367	.1657
July..........	2.1761	.2127	.1409
June..........	2.0645	.2232	.1158
May..........	1.9542	.0264	.0782
Apr...........	1.9956	.0299	.0963
Mar..........	2.0719	.0609	.1196
Feb...........	2.2041	.1979	.1401
Jan...........	2.1173	.1966	.1199
1922			
Dec............	1.9823	.0992	.0930
Nov...........	1.9590	.1364	.0908
Oct............	1.8808	.1210	.0749
Sept..........	1.8573	.0501	.0588
Aug...........	1.8865	.1260	.0618
July..........	1.8195	.0639	.0394
June..........	1.8062	.0473	.0308
May..........	1.7924	.0199	.0250
Apr...........	1.7993	.0097	.0268
Mar..........	....	.0636	....
Feb...........	....	.0299	....
Jan...........	....	.0164	....
1921			
Dec............	....	.0115	....
Nov...........	....	−.0488	....
Oct............	....	.0368	....
Sept..........	....	.0526	....
Aug...........	....	.0676	....
July..........	....	.1105	....
June..........	....	.0353	....
May..........	....	.0126	....
Apr...........	....	−.0159	....
Mar..........	....	.0142	....
Feb...........	....	.1024	....
Jan............	....	.0304	....
1914			
June...........	....	....	....

The Monetary Dynamics of Hyperinflation 113

Table B11 gives figures on deposits less bank reserves (M above includes reserves) and the ratio of an index of bank notes to an index of bank notes plus deposits in circulation for Poland. The figures include deposits held by the public in the Bank of Poland,[92] in the post office (savings deposits only),[93] and in almost all commercial banks.[94] Cash reserves are those of commercial banks.

Non-government deposits in the Bank of Poland were held by banks, businesses, and individuals.[95] The part held by banks was largely excluded by deducting that part of commercial banks' cash reserves that includes balances with the national bank. However, the portion of total deposits in the Bank of Poland not held by the government in 1920 and

TABLE B11

DEPOSIT DATA FOR POLAND

End of Year	Bank Deposits *less* Cash Reserves (Million Marks)	Ratio of Index of Bank Notes to Index of Bank Notes *plus* Deposits in Circulation
1920.......	12,094	1.00
1921.......	47,857	1.03
1922.......	224,290	0.97
1923.......	64,229,000	0.94

1923 had to be estimated, because it is not differentiated from government deposits for those two years. The estimates for 1920 and 1923 are based on the proportion of non-government to government deposits in the Bank of Poland at the end of 1921 and in September, 1923, respectively. Since deposits in the Bank of Poland not held by the government were large compared with total bank deposits in Poland at the time, the figure for total bank deposits in the table depends heavily on the accuracy of these estimates. Their accuracy will be only fair at best, because they are based on ratios that were not necessarily constant.

Furthermore, figures on deposits in commercial banks for 1923 are unavailable and had to be estimated from deposits in the sixteen major

92. League of Nations, *Memorandum on Central Banks, 1913 and 1918-1923*, p. 285.

93. League of Nations, *Memorandum on Currency and Central Banks, 1913-1925*, II, 86.

94. League of Nations, *Memorandum on Commercial Banks, 1913-1925* (Geneva: Publications Department of the League of Nations, 1931), p. 230.

95. League of Nations, *Memorandum on Central Banks, 1913 and 1918-1923*, p. 292.

114   *Studies in the Quantity Theory of Money*

commercial banks.[96] The deposits in these sixteen banks at the end of 1923 were increased by 91 per cent to serve as an estimate of total commercial-bank deposits in that year. Ninety-one is the percentage by which deposits in the sixteen banks at the end of January, 1923, fell short of deposits in all commercial banks at the end of 1922. The 91 is a slightly low percentage to use, because it would have been desirable to use a figure for deposits in the sixteen banks for the first of January, 1923, rather than for the end of that month. Deposits at the first of that month were undoubtedly somewhat smaller than deposits at the end, but a figure for the ending date is not available. The cash-reserve ratio of commercial banks at the end of 1923 is taken to be 40 per cent, the approximate ratio that it had been at the end of the previous four years.

The figures in Table B11 exclude deposits in the National Economic Bank and the State Land Bank. At the end of 1925 the kinds of deposits included in the table were 65 per cent of the total deposits in all forms not held by the government in Poland.[97] Even under the assumption that the banks whose deposits are included in the above table gained relatively to the smaller non-commercial banks whose deposits were excluded, the estimates of total deposits cannot be considered very comprehensive. Yet, since the figures cover a large proportion of total deposits, the ratios in the table reflect to some extent the major movements in total deposits relative to bank notes.

The only evidence available related to real income is figures on unemployment. These show a decline for the period from 1922 to August, 1923, except for a short rise in the early part of 1923. Unemployment seems not to have risen until after the first of 1924.[98]

NOTES ON RUSSIAN DATA

P is an index of retail prices for all of Russia published by the Central Bureau of Labor Statistics.[99] Two other available indexes, one of retail prices and the other of wholesale prices, agree substantially with the index used.[100]

M is an index of the quantity of paper rubles in circulation.[101] The total circulation of paper money and coins at the beginning of 1914 is estimated

96. League of Nations, *Memorandum on Currency and Central Banks, 1913–1925*, II, 86.

97. League of Nations, *Memorandum on Commercial Banks, 1913–1929*, pp. 230 ff.

98. Statistisches Reichsamt, *op. cit.*, Table 13.

99. Young, *op. cit.*, Table 81, p. 360.

100. League of Nations, *Memorandum on Currency and Central Banks, 1913–1924*, I, 199, and Young, *op. cit.*, p. 360.

101. Young, *op. cit.*, p. 359.

The Monetary Dynamics of Hyperinflation 115

at 2,512 million rubles.[102] All coins had disappeared from circulation by 1916. The figures for 1923 are given in either chervontsi or chervonets gold rubles. The procedure for converting these units into those that apply to the rubles in circulation before 1923 is as follows: Convert ten chervonets gold rubles into one chervonets. Then convert chervontsi into

TABLE B12

TIME SERIES FOR RUSSIA

Date (First of Month)	$\log_{10}(P/M)$ (1913=1) (1)	$\log_{10}(P_i/P_{i-1})$ (Per Month) (2)	$E(.35)$ (Per Month) (3)
1924			
Feb.............	3.1106	.4958	.3478
Jan.............	2.8854	.3728	.2858
1923			
Dec.	2.7694	.3226	.2493
Nov............	2.7126	.2224	.2186
Oct............	2.8633	.2938	.2170
Sept...........	2.7033	.2360	.1848
Aug............	2.5944	.2192	.1633
July...........	2.5145	.1677	.1399
June...........	2.4548	.1644	.1283
May............	2.3541	.1443	.1131
Apr............	2.3424	.1012	.1000
Mar............	2.3820	.0503	.0996
Feb............	2.4183	.1153	.1202
Jan............	2.4281	.0975	.1223
1922			
Dec............	2.4594	.1667	.1327
Nov............	2.4232	.1972	.1185
Oct............	2.3365	.0880	.0855
Sept...........	2.3345	.0305	.0844
Aug............	2.4713	−.0158	.1070
July...........	2.6571	.0566	.1585
June...........	2.7767	.0872	.2011
May............	2.9079	.2172	.2489
Apr............	2.8949	.3403	.2622
Mar............	2.7767	.3254	.2295
Feb............	2.6656	.2770	.1894
Jan............	2.6160	.3195	.1527

old paper rubles according to the official daily rate of exchange.[103] (One new ruble, issued in 1923, equaled one hundred 1922 rubles and one million pre-1922 rubles.) The official daily exchange rates were based on the free-market rates. The difference between the two quotations was rarely more than $3\frac{1}{2}$ per cent in Moscow, though it sometimes reached as high as

102. League of Nations, *Memorandum on Currency and Central Banks, 1913–1924*, II, 140.

103. S. S. Katzenellenbaum, *Russian Currency and Banking, 1914–1924* (London: P. S. King & Son, Ltd., 1925), p. 111.

116   *Studies in the Quantity Theory of Money*

20 per cent in the provinces.[104] Gold treasury bonds (certificates of the *centrocassa* of the Commissioner of Finance) were not included in M, because they circulated mainly among state enterprises and institutions.[105]

In December, 1922, the government began to issue a separate currency called the chervonets ruble, which was not increased in such quantities as to depreciate much in value. The two currencies circulated together and exchanged according to free-market rates, as noted above. An index of wholesale prices in chervontsi is available.[106] The chervontsi were perfect

TABLE B13

TIME SERIES FOR RUSSIA

Date (First of Month)	$\log_{10}(P_i/P_{i-1})$ (Per Month)	Date (First of Month)	$\log_{10}(P_i/P_{i-1})$ (Per Month)
1921		Sept..........	.0076
Dec..........	.1599	Aug..........	.0470
Nov..........	.0667	July..........	.0930
Oct..........	.0302	June..........	.0557
Sept..........	−.0216	May..........	.0834
Aug..........	−.0022	Apr..........	.0976
July..........	.1145	Mar..........	.0909
June..........	.1620	Feb..........	.1062
May..........	.0777	Jan..........	.1309
Apr..........	.1118	1919	
Mar..........	.1064	Dec..........	.1194
Feb..........	.1092	Nov..........	.1683
Jan..........	.1461	Oct..........	.0546
1920			
Dec..........	.0580		
Nov..........	.0380		
Oct..........	.0180		

substitutes for the depreciating rubles. The amount outstanding of the former is not included in M, which comprises rubles only, because only prices quoted in rubles were undergoing hyperinflation. The fact that such a perfect substitute for rubles existed undoubtedly contributed to the speed at which the rubles declined in value.

All forms of private bank credit soon disappeared after the nationalization of Russian banking in December, 1917. At the beginning of 1914 deposits of all commercial banks totaled 2,545 million rubles; by 1920 deposits of the public were virtually extinct.[107] Credit was extended by the

104. *Ibid.*, pp. 120–21.

105. League of Nations, *Memorandum on Currency and Central Banks, 1913–1924*, II, 143.

106. Statistisches Reichsamt, *op. cit.*, Table 14.

107. Katzenellenbaum, *op. cit.*, pp. 150, 152.

The Monetary Dynamics of Hyperinflation 117

new State Bank established in 1922, but very few of its deposits were held by the public.[108] With the establishment of the State Bank, private banking was also allowed, but it did not develop to any degree until 1923. By 1923 all banking was conducted in relatively stable chervontsi rather than in regular rubles.[109] Consequently, if state enterprises are considered to be a part of the government, deposits held by the public were small enough to neglect.

The currency reform that finally resulted in the complete abandonment of the ruble was begun in February, 1924. It was completed on March 10, 1924, when 1 chervonets officially exchanged for 500,000 1923

TABLE B14

INDEXES OF OUTPUT FOR RUSSIA

YEAR	INDEX OF (1913 = 100)	
	Industrial Production	Agricultural Output
1920.	. . . .	65
1921.	13	55
1922.	24	69
1923.	35	76
1924.	49	69

rubles or 500 billion old (pre-1922) rubles. Russian data during these years are based on the Julian calendar. Add thirteen days to the above dates to convert to the Gregorian calendar.

Table B14 gives an index of industrial production and an index of agricultural output.[110] On the supposition that agricultural output dominated the total product of the economy, the movement in its index suggests that total real income rose until sometime in 1923 or 1924 and then fell. Another index of real income for the fiscal years 1922–23 and 1924–25 is 58 and 77 per cent, respectively, of the 1913 level.[111]

108. *Ibid.*, p. 159.

109. *Ibid.*, pp. 183 ff.

110. Jean Dessirier, "Indices comparés de la production industrielle et de la production agricole en divers pays de 1870 à 1928," *Bulletin de la statistique générale de la France*, XVIII, Sec. 1 (October–December, 1928), 104.

111. Serge N. Prokopovicz, *Histoire économique de l'U.R.S.S.* (Paris: Chez Flammarion, 1952), p. 567.

Excerpt from *Inflation Causes and Effects*, R.H. Hall (ed.)

[3]

2 The Ends of Four Big Inflations

Thomas J. Sargent

2.1 Introduction

Since the middle 1960s, many Western economies have experienced persistent and growing rates of inflation. Some prominent economists and statesmen have become convinced that this inflation has a stubborn, self-sustaining momentum and that either it simply is not susceptible to cure by conventional measures of monetary and fiscal restraint or, in terms of the consequent widespread and sustained unemployment, the cost of eradicating inflation by monetary and fiscal measures would be prohibitively high. It is often claimed that there is an underlying rate of inflation which responds slowly, if at all, to restrictive monetary and fiscal measures.[1] Evidently, this underlying rate of inflation is the rate of inflation that firms and workers have come to expect will prevail in the future. There is momentum in this process because firms and workers supposedly form their expectations by extrapolating past rates of inflation into the future. If this is true, the years from the middle 1960s to the early 1980s have left firms and workers with a legacy of high expected rates of inflation which promise to respond only slowly, if at all, to restrictive monetary and fiscal policy actions. According to this view, restrictive monetary and fiscal actions in the first instance cause substantial reduc-

Thomas J. Sargent is with the Federal Reserve Bank of Minneapolis and the Department of Economics, University of Minnesota.

The views expressed herein are solely those of the author and do not necessarily represent the views of the Federal Reserve Bank of Minneapolis or the Federal Reserve System. Helpful comments on earlier drafts of this paper were made by Preston Miller, John Kennan, Peter Garber, and Gail Makinen. General conversations on the subject with Michael K. Salemi and Neil Wallace were most helpful. Gail Makinen directed the author's attention to the unemployment figures for Poland. Carl Christ of the NBER reading committee made several comments that improved the manuscript.

tions in output and employment but have little, if any, effects in reducing the rate of inflation. For the economy of the United States, a widely cited estimate is that for every one percentage point reduction in the annual inflation rate accomplished by restrictive monetary and fiscal measures, $220 billion of annual GNP would be lost. For the $2,500 billion United States economy, the cost of achieving zero percent inflation would be great, indeed, according to this estimate.

An alternative "rational expectations" view denies that there is any inherent momentum in the present process of inflation.[2] This view maintains that firms and workers have now come to expect high rates of inflation in the future and that they strike inflationary bargains in light of these expectations.[3] However, it is held that people expect high rates of inflation in the future precisely because the government's current and prospective monetary and fiscal policies warrant those expectations. Further, the current rate of inflation and people's expectations about future rates of inflation may well seem to respond slowly to isolated *actions* of restrictive monetary and fiscal policy that are viewed as temporary departures from what is perceived as a long-term government *policy* involving high average rates of government deficits and monetary expansion in the future. Thus inflation only *seems* to have a momentum of its own; it is actually the long-term government policy of persistently running large deficits and creating money at high rates which imparts the momentum to the inflation rate. An implication of this view is that inflation can be stopped much more quickly than advocates of the "momentum" view have indicated and that their estimates of the length of time and the costs of stopping inflation in terms of foregone output ($220 billion of GNP for one percentage point in the inflation rate) are erroneous. This is not to say that it would be easy to eradicate inflation. On the contrary, it would require far more than a few temporary restrictive fiscal and monetary actions. It would require a change in the policy *regime*: there must be an abrupt change in the continuing government *policy*, or *strategy*, for setting deficits now and in the future that is sufficiently binding as to be widely believed. Economists do not now possess reliable, empirically tried and true models that can enable them to predict precisely how rapidly and with what disruption in terms of lost output and employment such a regime change will work its effects. How costly such a move would be in terms of foregone output and how long it would be in taking effect would depend partly on how resolute and evident the government's commitment was.

This paper describes several dramatic historical experiences which I believe to be consistent with the "rational expectations" view but which seem difficult to reconcile with the "momentum" model of inflation. The idea is to stand back from our current predicament and to examine the measures that successfully brought drastic inflations under control in

43   The Ends of Four Big Inflations

several European countries in the 1920s. I shall describe and interpret events in Austria, Hungary, Germany, and Poland, countries which experienced a dramatic "hyperinflation" in which, after the passage of several months, price indexes assumed astronomical proportions. The basic data to be studied are the price indexes in figures 2.1–2.4. These data are recorded in a logarithmic scale, so that they will fit on a page. For all four countries, and especially Germany, the rise in the price level was spectacular. The graphs also reveal that in each case inflation stopped abruptly rather than gradually. I shall also briefly describe events in Czechoslovakia, a country surrounded by neighbors experiencing hyperinflations, but which successfully achieved a stable currency itself. My reason for studying these episodes is that they are laboratories for the study of regime changes. Within each of Austria, Hungary, Poland, and Germany, there occurred a dramatic change in the fiscal policy regime which in each instance was associated with the end of a hyperinflation. Further, though it shared some problems with its four neighbors, Czechoslovakia deliberately adopted a relatively restrictive fiscal policy regime, with the avowed aim of maintaining the value of its currency.

While there are many differences in details among the Austrian, Hungarian, Polish, and German hyperinflations, there are some very important common features. These include the following:

i) The nature of the fiscal policy regime in effect during each of the hyperinflations. Each of the four countries persistently ran enormous budget deficits on current account.

ii) The nature of the deliberate and drastic fiscal and monetary measures taken to end the hyperinflations.

iii) The immediacy with which the price level and foreign exchanges suddenly stabilized.[4]

iv) The rapid rise in the "high-powered" money supply in the months and years after the rapid inflation had ended.

I shall assemble and interpret the facts in the light of a view about the forces which give money value and about the way the international monetary system worked in the 1920s. Before interpreting the historical facts, I now turn to a brief description of this view.

2.2   The Gold Standard

After World War I, the United States was on the gold standard. The United States government stood ready to convert a dollar into a specified amount of gold on demand. To understate things, immediately after the war, Hungary, Austria, Poland, and Germany were not on the gold standard. In practice, their currencies were largely "fiat," or unbacked. The governments of these countries resorted to the printing of new

44   **Thomas J. Sargent**

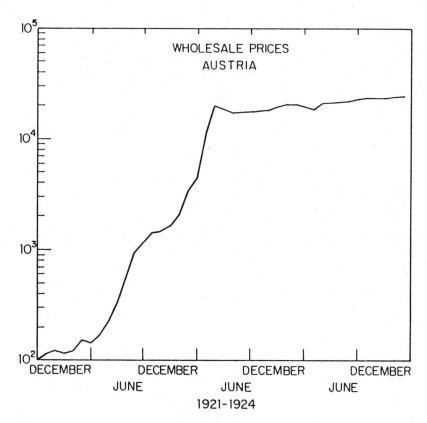

Fig. 2.1   Wholesale prices in Austria.

unbacked money to finance government deficits.[5] This was done on such a scale that it led to a depreciation of the currencies of spectacular proportions. In the end, the German mark stabilized at 1 trillion (10^{12}) paper marks to the prewar gold mark, the Polish mark at 1.8 million paper marks to the gold zloty, the Austrian crown at 14,400 paper crowns to the prewar Austro-Hungarian crown, and the Hungarian krone at 14,500 paper crowns to the prewar Austro-Hungarian crown.[6]

This paper focuses on the deliberate changes in policy that each of Hungary, Austria, Poland, and Germany made to end its hyperinflation, and the deliberate choice of policy that Czechoslovakia made to avoid inflation in the first place. The hyperinflations were each ended by restoring or virtually restoring convertibility to the dollar or equivalently to gold. For this reason it is good to keep in mind the nature of the restrictions that adherence to the gold standard imposed on a government. Under the gold standard, a government issued demand notes and

45   The Ends of Four Big Inflations

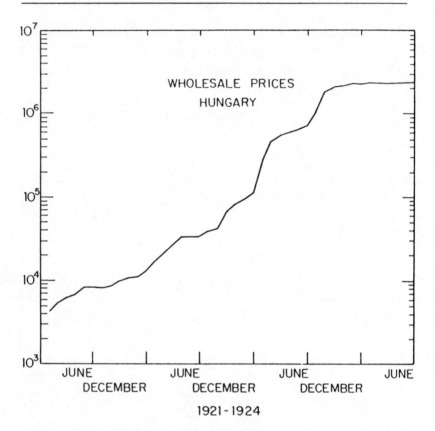

Fig. 2.2   Wholesale prices in Hungary.

longer-term debt which it promised to convert into gold under certain
specified conditions, i.e. on demand, for notes. Presumably, people were
willing to hold these claims at full value if the government's promise to
pay were judged to be good. The government's promise to pay was
"backed" only partially by its holding of gold reserves. More important in
practice, since usually a government did not hold 100% reserves of gold,
a government's notes and debts were backed by the commitment of the
government to levy taxes in sufficient amounts, given its expenditures, to
make good on its debt. In effect, the notes were backed by the government's pursuit of an appropriate budget policy. During the 1920s, John
Maynard Keynes emphasized that the size of a government's gold reserve
was not the determinant of whether it could successfully maintain convertibility with gold: its fiscal policy was.[7] According to this view, what
mattered was not the current government deficit but the present value of
current and prospective future government deficits. The government was

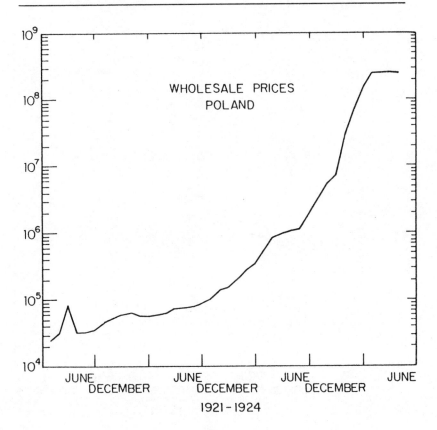

WHOLESALE PRICES
POLAND

1921 - 1924

Fig. 2.3   Wholesale prices in Poland.

like a firm whose prospective receipts were its future tax collections. The
value of the government's debt was, to a first approximation, equal to the
present value of current and future government surpluses. So under a
gold standard, a government must honor its debts and could not engage in
inflationary finance. In order to assign a value to the government's debt,
it was necessary to have a view about the fiscal policy regime in effect,
that is, the rule determining the government deficit as a function of the
state of the economy now and in the future. The public's perception of the
fiscal regime influenced the value of government debt through private
agents' expectations about the present value of the revenue streams
backing that debt.[8] It will be worthwhile to keep this view of the gold
standard in mind as we turn to review the events surrounding the ends of
the four hyperinflations.[9]

However, it will be useful first to expand a little more generally on the
distinction between the effects of isolated *actions* taken within the context

47   The Ends of Four Big Inflations

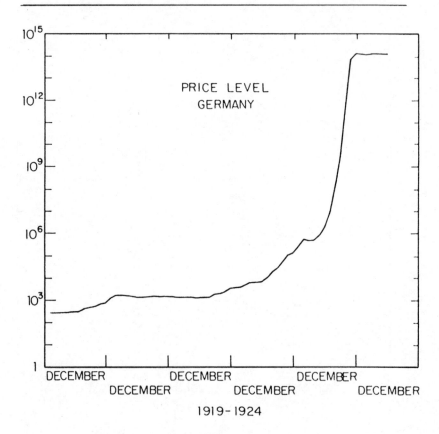

Fig. 2.4   Wholesale prices in Germany.

of a given general strategy, on the one hand, and the effects of choosing among alternative general strategies or rules for repeatedly taking actions, on the other. The latter choice I refer to as a choice of regime. The values of government expenditures and tax rates for one particular quarter are examples of actions, while the rules, implicit or explicit, for repeatedly selecting government expenditures and tax rates as functions of the state of the economy are examples of regimes. Recent work in dynamic macroeconomics has discovered the following general principle: whenever there is a change in the government strategy or regime, private economic agents can be expected to change their strategies or rules for choosing consumption rates, investment rates, portfolios, and so on.[10] The reason is that private agents' behavior is selfish, or at least purposeful, so that when the government switches its strategy, private agents usually find it in their best interests to change theirs. One by-product of this principle is that most of the empirical relations captured in standard econometric models cannot be expected to remain constant across contemplated changes in government policy regimes. For this reason, predictions made under the assumption that such relations will remain constant across regime changes ought not to be believed. The estimate that a 1% reduction in inflation would cost $220 billion GNP annually is one example of such a faulty prediction. When an important change in regime occurs, dynamic macroeconomics would predict that the entire pattern of correlations among variables will change in quantitatively important ways.

While the distinction between isolated actions and strategy regimes is clear in principle, it is an admittedly delicate task to interpret whether particular historical episodes reflect isolated actions within the same old rules of the game or whether they reflect a new set of rules or government strategies.[11] All that we have to go on are the recorded actions actually taken, together with the pronouncements of public officials, laws, legislative votes, and sometimes constitutional provisions. Out of this material we are to fashion a view about the government strategy being used. Common sense suggests and technical econometric considerations confirm the difficulties in making such interpretations in general. Having said this, I believe that the examples discussed below are about as close to being laboratories for studying regime changes as history has provided.

2.3 Austria

At the end of World War I, the Austro-Hungarian empire dissolved into a number of successor states, of which Austria was one. From having been the center of an empire of 625,000 square kilometers and 50 million inhabitants, Austria was reduced to a mere 80,000 square kilometers and 6.5 million inhabitants. Having suffered food scarcities during the war that were produced by an effective Allied blockade, Austria found itself confronted with new national borders and trade barriers that cut it off from the food sources formerly within its empire. Further, the government of Austria reabsorbed a large number of Austrian imperial bureaucrats who were no longer welcome in the other successor states. Austrians also faced a large-scale unemployment problem stemming from the need to reconvert the economy to peaceful activities and to adjust to the new national borders. If this were not enough, as a loser of the war Austria owed the Reparation Commission sums that for a long time were uncertain in amount but were presumed eventually to be substantial. The Reparation Commission, in effect, held a blanket mortgage against the assets and revenues of the Austrian government.

Austria responded to these pressing problems by making large expenditures in the form of food relief and payments to the unemployed. In addition, the state railroads and monopolies ran deficits, as taxes and prices were kept relatively low. The government did not collect enough

49   The Ends of Four Big Inflations

taxes to cover expenditures and so ran very substantial deficits during the years 1919–22 (see table A1). As table A1 shows, in these years the deficit was typically over 50 percent of the total government expenditures. The government financed these deficits by selling treasury bills to the Austrian section of the Austro-Hungarian bank. The result was a very rapid increase in the volume of "high-powered" money, defined as the notes and demand deposit obligations of the central bank (see table A2). As the figures in table A2 indicate, between March 1919 and August 1922 the total note circulation in Austria[12] of the Austro-Hungarian bank increased by a factor of 288. This expansion of central bank notes stemmed mainly from the bank's policy of discounting treasury bills. However, it also resulted partly from the central bank's practice of making loans and discounts to private agents at nominal interest rates of between 6 and 9% per annum, rates which by any standard were far too low in view of the inflation rate, which averaged 10,000% per annum from January 1921 to August 1922 (table A3).[13]

In response to these government actions and what seemed like prospects for their indefinite continuation, the Austrian crown depreciated internationally and domestic prices rose rapidly (see tables A3 and A4). While between January 1921 and August 1922 the note circulation of the central bank increased by a factor of 39, the retail price index increased by a factor of 110 (see tables A3 and A4) so that the real value of the note circulation diminished during the currency depreciation.[14] The "flight from the crown" occurred as people chose to hold less of their wealth in the form of the rapidly depreciating crown, attempting instead to hold foreign currencies or real assets.[15] From the viewpoint of financing its deficit, the government of Austria had an interest in resisting the flight from the crown, because this had the effect of diminishing the resources that the government could command by printing money. Therefore the government established a system of exchange controls administered by an agency called the Devisenzentrale. The essential function of this

Table A1   **Austrian Budgets, 1919–22 (in millions of paper crowns)**

	Receipts	Expenditures	Deficit	Percentage of Expenditures Covered by New Issues of Paper Money
1 January–30 June 1919	1,339	4,043	2,704	67
1 July 1919–30 June 1920	6,295	16,873	10,578	63
1 July 1920–30 June 1921	29,483	70,601	41,118	58
1 January–31 December 1922	209,763	347,533	137,770	40

Source: Pasvolsky [25, p. 102].

50   Thomas J. Sargent

Table A2   Total Note Circulation of Austrian Crowns
                    (in thousands of crowns)

1919	January	—		May	397,829,313
	February	—		June	549,915,678
	March	4,687,056		July	786,225,601
	April	5,577,851		August	1,353,403,632
	May	5,960,003		September	2,277,677,738
	June	7,397,692		October	2,970,916,607
	July	8,391,405		November	3,417,786,498
	August	9,241,135		December	4,080,177,238
	September	9,781,112	1923	January	4,110,551,163
	October	10,819,310		February	4,207,991,722
	November	11,193,670		March	4,459,117,216
	December	12,134,474		April	4,577,382,333
1920	January	13,266,878		May	4,837,042,081
	February	14,292,809		June	5,432,619,312
	March	15,457,749		July	5,684,133,721
	April	15,523,832		August	5,894,786,367
	May	15,793,805		September	6,225,109,352
	June	16,971,344		October	6,607,839,105
	July	18,721,495		November	6,577,616,341
	August	20,050,281		December	7,125,755,190
	September	22,271,686	1924	January	6,735,109,000
	October	25,120,385		February	7,364,441,000
	November	28,072,331		March	7,144,901,000
	December	30,645,658		April	7,135,471,000
1921	January	34,525,634		May	7,552,620,000
	February	38,352,648		June	7,774,958,000
	March	41,067,299		July	7,995,647,000
	April	45,036,723		August	5,894,786,367
	May	45,583,194		September	7,998,509,000
	June	49,685,140		October	8,213,003,000
	July	54,107,281		November	8,072,021,000
	August	58,533,766		December	8,387,767,000
	September	70,170,798	1925	January	7,902,217,000
1922	January	227,015,925		February	7,957,242,000
	February	259,931,138		March	7,897,792,000
	March	304,063,642		April	7,976,420,000
	April	346,697,776			

Source: Young [36, vol. 2, p. 292].

agency was to increase the amount of Austrian crowns held by Austrians, which it accomplished by adopting measures making it difficult or illegal for Austrians to hold foreign currencies and other substitutes for Austrian crowns.[16] Despite these regulations, it is certain that Austrian citizens were holding large amounts of foreign currencies during 1921 and 1922.

Table A4 reveals that the Austrian crown abruptly stabilized in August 1922, while table A3 indicates that prices abruptly stabilized a month

51   The Ends of Four Big Inflations

Table A3   **Austrian Retail Prices, 1921–24**

		Retail Price Index, 52 Commodities
1921	January	100
	February	114
	March	122
	April	116
	May	121
	June	150
	July	143
	August	167
	September	215
	October	333
	November	566
	December	942
1922	January	1,142
	February	1,428
	March	1,457
	April	1,619
	May	2,028
	June	3,431
	July	4,830
	August	11,046
	September	20,090
	October	18,567
	November	17,681
	December	17,409
1923	January	17,526
	February	17,851
	March	18,205
	April	19,428
	May	20,450
	June	20,482
	July	19,368
	August	18,511
	September	20,955
	October	21,166
	November	21,479
	December	21,849
1924	January	22,941
	February	23,336
	March	23,336
	April	23,361
	May	23,797
	June	24,267

Source: Young [36, vol. 2, p. 293].

52   Thomas J. Sargent

Table A4   Exchange Rates, Austrian Crowns
                  per United States Dollar, in New York Market

	1919	1920	1921	1922	1923	1924
January	17.09	271.43	654.00	7,375.00	71,500.00	70,760.00
February	20.72	250.00	722.50	6,350.00	71,150.00	70,760.00
March	25.85	206.66	676.00	7,487.50	71,000.00	70,760.00
April	26.03	200.00	661.00	7,937.50	70,850.00	70,760.00
May	24.75	155.83	604.00	11,100.00	70,800.00	70,760.00
June	29.63	145.00	720.00	18,900.00	70,800.00	70,760.00
July	37.24	165.00	957.00	42,350.00	70,760.00	70,760.00
August	42.50	237.14	1,081.50	77,300.00	70,760.00	70,760.00
September	68.50	255.00	2,520.00	74,210.00	70,760.00	70,760.00
October	99.50	358.33	4,355.00	73,550.00	70,760.00	70,760.00
November	130.00	493.66	8,520.00	71,400.00	70,760.00	70,760.00
December	155.00	659.40	5,275.00	70,925.00	70,760.00	70,760.00

Source: Young [36, vol. 2, p. 294].

later. This occurred despite the fact that the central bank's note circulation continued to increase rapidly, as table A1 indicates. Furthermore, there occurred no change in currency units or "currency reform," at least not for another year and a half.

The depreciation of the Austrian crown was suddenly stopped by the intervention of the Council of the League of Nations and the resulting binding commitment of the government of Austria to reorder Austrian fiscal and monetary strategies dramatically. After Austria's increasingly desperate pleas to the Allied governments for international aid had repeatedly been rejected or only partially fulfilled, in late August 1922 the Council of the League of Nations undertook to enter into serious negotiations to reconstruct the financial system of Austria. These negotiations led to the signing of three protocols on 2 October 1922 which successfully guided the financial reconstruction of Austria. It is remarkable that even before the precise details of the protocols were publicly announced, the fact of the serious deliberations of the Council brought relief to the situation. This can be seen in tables A3 and A4, and was described by Pasvolsky as follows:

The moment the Council of the League decided to take up in earnest the question of Austrian reconstruction, there was immediately a widespread conviction that the solution of the problem was at hand. This conviction communicated itself first of all to that delicately adjusted mechanism, the international exchange market. Nearly two weeks before Chancellor Seipel officially laid the Austrian question before the Council of the League, on August 25, the foreign exchange rate ceased to soar and began to decline, the internal price level following suit three weeks later. The printing presses in Austria were

53   The Ends of Four Big Inflations

still grinding out new currency; the various ministries were still dispersing this new currency through the country by means of continuing budgetary deficits. Yet the rate of exchange was slowly declining. The crisis was checked.[17]

The first protocol was a declaration signed by Great Britain, France, Italy, Czechoslovakia, and Austria that reaffirmed the political independence and sovereignty of Austria.[18] The second protocol provided conditions for an international loan of 650 million gold crowns to Austria. The third protocol was signed by Austria alone and laid out a plan for reconstruction of its fiscal and monetary affairs. The Austrian government promised to establish a new independent central bank, to cease running large deficits, and to bind itself not to finance deficits with advances of notes from the central bank. Further, the government of Austria agreed to accept in Austria a commissioner general, appointed by the Council of the League, who was to be responsible for monitoring the fulfillment of Austria's commitments. The government of Austria also agreed to furnish security to back the reconstruction loan. At the same time, it was understood that the Reparation Commission would give up or modify its claim on the resources of the government of Austria.

The government of Austria and the League both moved swiftly to execute the plan outlined in the protocols. In legislation of 14 November 1922, the Austrian National Bank was formed to replace the old Austrian section of the Austro-Hungarian bank; it was to take over the assets and functions of the Devisenzentrale. The new bank began operations on 1 January 1923 and was specifically forbidden from lending to the government except on the security of an equal amount of gold and foreign assets. The bank was also required to cover its note issues with certain minimal proportions of gold, foreign earning assets, and commercial bills. Further, once the government's debt to the bank had been reduced to 30 million gold crowns, the bank was obligated to resume convertibility into gold.

The government moved to balance its budget by taking concrete steps in several directions. Expenditures were reduced by discharging thousands of government employees. Under the reconstruction scheme, the government promised gradually to discharge a total of 100,000 state employees. Deficits in government enterprises were reduced by raising prices of government-sold goods and services. New taxes and more efficient means of collecting tax and custom revenues were instituted. The results of these measures can be seen by comparing the figures in table A5 with those in table A1. Within two years the government was able to balance the budget.

The stabilization of the Austrian crown was not achieved via a currency reform. At the end of 1924 a new unit of currency was introduced, the schilling, equal to 10,000 paper crowns. The introduction of this new unit

Table A5 The Austrian Budget, 1923–25 (in millions of schillings)

Item	Closed Accounts		
	1923	1924	1925
Total revenue	697.4	900.6	908.5
Current expenditures	779.6	810.0	741.4
Deficit (−) or surplus (+)	− 82.2	+ 90.6	+ 167.1
Capital expenditures	76.0	103.6	90.6
Total balance	− 158.2	− 13.0	+ 76.5

Source: Pasvolsky [25, p. 127].
Note: 1 schilling = 10,000 paper crowns.

of currency occurred long after the exchange rate had been stabilized and was surely an incidental measure.[19]

Table A2 reveals that from August 1922, when the exchange rate suddenly stabilized, to December 1924, the circulating notes of the Austrian central bank increased by a factor of over 6. The phenomenon of the achievement of price stability in the face of a sixfold increase in the stock of "high-powered" money was widely regarded by contemporaries as violating the quantity theory of money, and so it seems to do. However, these observations are not at all paradoxical when interpreted in the light of a view which distinguishes sharply between unbacked, or "outside," money, on the one hand, and backed, or "inside," money, on the other hand. In particular, the balance sheet of the central bank and the nature of its open market operations changed dramatically after the carrying out of the League's protocols, with the consequence that the proper intrepretation of the figures on the total note obligations of the central bank changes substantially. Before the protocols, the liabilities of the central bank were backed mainly by government treasury bills; that is, they were not backed at all, since treasury bills signified no commitment to raise revenues through future tax collections. After the execution of the protocols, the liabilities of the central bank became backed by gold, foreign assets, and commercial paper, and ultimately by the power of the government to collect taxes. At the margin, central bank liabilities were backed 100% by gold, foreign assets, and commercial paper as notes and the deposits were created through open market operations in those assets (see table A6). The value of the crown was backed by the commitment of the government to run a fiscal policy compatible with maintaining the convertibility of its liabilities into dollars. Given such a fiscal regime, to a first approximation, the intermediating activities of the central bank did not affect the value of the crown so long as the assets purchased by the bank were sufficiently valuable. Thus the sixfold increase in the liabilities of the central bank after the protocols ought not to be regarded as inflationary. The willingness of Austrians to convert

Table A6   **Austrian National Bank Balance Sheet**
                    (end of month, in millions of crowns)

	Gold	Foreign Exchange and Currency	Loans and Discounts	Treasury Bills	Notes in Circulation	Deposits
1923:						
January	49,304	1,058,244	731,046	2,556,848	4,110,551	279,092
February	83,438	1,029,134	728,884	2,552,682	4,207,992	178,752
March	86,097	1,336,385	821,397	2,550,159	4,459,117	329,109
April	73,270	1,439,999	741,858	2,550,159	4,577,382	226,273
May	73,391	1,682,209	875,942	2,550,159	4,837,042	343,339
June	73,391	2,532,316	730,848	2,547,212	5,432,619	362,237
July	73,391	2,947,216	658,966	2,539,777	5,684,134	535,121
August	73,391	3,050,085	647,936	2,538,719	5,894,786	413,383
September	73,391	3,126,599	863,317	2,537,661	6,225,109	373,673
October	62,117	3,356,232	1,069,340	2,536,604	6,607,839	414,882
November	62,117	3,504,652	1,094,620	2,535,547	6,577,616	617,321
December	83,177	3,832,132	1,325,380	2,534,490	7,125,755	649,424
1924:						
January	91,274	3,811,148	1,253,110	2,533,434	6,735,109	536,982
February	105,536	3,921,594	1,737,334	2,532,379	7,364,441	558,800
March	106,663	3,953,872	1,733,400	2,295,428	7,144,901	752,814
April	107,059	3,669,333	2,131,984	2,294,471	7,315,471	696,141
May	107,443	3,344,337	2,660,449	2,259,839	7,554,620	641,001
June	107,762	3,178,339	3,092,470	2,237,794	7,774,958	741,400
July	108,342	3,254,477	3,304,876	2,231,173	7,995,647	896,032
August	108,256	3,453,177	3,226,962	2,219,459	8,002,142	997,677
September	108,950	3,724,916	2,852,688	2,210,527	7,998,509	890,537
October	109,327	4,032,485	2,379,700	2,202,106	8,213,003	502,579
November	110,643	4,312,355	1,945,627	2,196,181	8,072,021	484,750
December	110,890	4,770,548	1,881,593	2,178,185	8,387,767	533,450
1925:						
January	111,314	3,337,911	1,545,295	2,172,491	7,902,217	438,390
February	111,474	3,310,032	1,285,158	2,150,151	7,957,242	315,771
March	111,649	3,202,802	1,047,719	2,107,949	7,897,792	295,498
April	112,168	3,474,672	1,059,069	2,088,777	7,976,420	236,957

Source: Young [36, vol. 2, p. 291].

hoards of foreign exchange into crowns which is reflected in table A6 is not surprising since the stabilization of the crown made it a much more desirable asset to hold relative to foreign exchange.[20]

The available figures on unemployment indicate that the stabilization of the crown was attended by a substantial increase in the unemployment rate, though unemployment had begun to climb well before stabilization was achieved (see table A7). The number of recipients of state unemploy-

56   Thomas J. Sargent

Table A7   Number of Austrian Unemployed
                  in Receipt of Relief (in thousands)

Beginning of	1922	1923	1924	1925	1926
January	17	117	98	154	208
April	42	153	107	176	202
July	33	93	64	118	151
October	38	79	78	119	148

Source: League of Nations [14, p. 87].

ment benefits gradually climbed from a low of 8,700 in December 1921 to 83,000 in December 1922. It climbed to 167,000 by March 1923, and then receded to 76,000 in November 1923.[21] How much of this unemployment was due to the achievement of currency stabilization and how much was due to the real dislocations affecting the Austrian economy cannot be determined. However, it is true that currency stabilization was achieved in Austria very suddenly, and with a cost in increased unemployment and foregone output that was minor compared with the $220 billion GNP that some current analysts estimate would be lost in the United States per one percentage point inflation reduction.

2.4 Hungary

Like its old partner in the Hapsburg monarchy, Hungary emerged from World War I as a country much reduced in land, population, and power. It retained only 25% of its territory (down from 325,000 square kilometers to 92,000) and only 37% of its population (down from 21 million to about 8 million). Its financial and economic life was disrupted by the newly drawn national borders separating it from peoples and economic institutions formerly within the domain of the Hapsburg monarchy.

At the end of the war, Hungary experienced political turmoil as the Hapsburg King Charles was replaced by the government of Prince Karolyi. In March 1919, the Karolyi government was overthrown by the Bolsheviks under Bela Kun. The regime of Bela Kun lasted only four months, as Romania invaded Hungary, occupied it for a few weeks, and then withdrew. A new repressive right wing regime under Admiral Horthy then took power. The "white terror" against leftists carried out by supporters of Horthy took even more lives than the "red terror" that had occurred under Bela Kun.

At the end of the war, the currency of Hungary consisted of the notes of the Austro-Hungarian bank. By the provisions of the peace treaties of Trianon and St. Germain, the successor states to the Austro-Hungarian empire were required to stamp the notes of the Austro-Hungarian bank that were held by their residents, in effect, thereby recognizing those

57   The Ends of Four Big Inflations

notes as debts of the respective new states. Before Hungary executed this provision of the Treaty of Trianon, the currency situation grew more complicated, for the Bolshevik regime had access to the plates for printing one- and two-crown Austro-Hungarian bank notes and it used them to print more notes. The Bolshevik government also issued new so-called white notes. Each of these Bolshevik-issued currencies was honored by the subsequent government.

The Austro-Hungarian bank was liquidated at the end of 1919, and it was replaced by an Austrian section and a Hungarian section. The functions of the Hungarian section of the old bank were assumed in August 1921 by a State Note Institute, which was under the control of the minister of finance. In August 1921, the Note Institute issued its own notes, the Hungarian krone, in exchange for Hungarian stamped notes of the Austro-Hungarian bank and several other classes of notes, including those that had been issued by the Bolshevik regime.

As a loser of the war, Hungary owed reparations according to the Treaty of Trianon. The Reparation Commission had a lien on the resources of the government of Hungary. However, neither the total amount owed nor a schedule of payments was fixed for many years after the war. This circumstance alone created serious obstacles in terms of achieving a stable value for Hungary's currency and other debts, since the unclear reparations obligations made uncertain the nature of the resources which backed those debts.

From 1919 until 1924 the government of Hungary ran substantial budget deficits. The government's budget estimates in table H1 are reported by Pasvolsky substantially to understate the size of the deficits.[22] These deficits were financed by borrowing from the State Note Institute, and were a major cause of a rapid increase in the note and deposit liabilities of the institute. An additional cause of the increase in liabilities of the institute was the increasing volume of loans and discounts that it made to private agents (see table H2). These loans were made at a very

Table H1   **Hungarian Budget Estimates, 1920–24**
             (in millions of paper crowns)

	Revenue	Expen-ditures	Deficit	Percentage of Expenditures Covered by Issues of Paper Money
1920–21	10,520	20,210	9,690	47.9
1921–22	20,296	26,764	6,468	24.1
1922–23	152,802	193,455	40,653	21.0
1923–24	2,168,140	3,307,099	1,138,959	34.4

Source: Pasvolsky [25, p. 299].

Table H2   Balance Sheet of Hungarian Central Bank or State Note Institute (millions of kronen)

	Gold Coin and Bullion	Silver Coin	Foreign Currency and Exchange	Bills Discounted	Advances on Securities	Advances to Treasury	Notes in Circulation	Current Accounts and Deposits
1921:								
January	—	—	—	10,924	195	—	15,206	3,851
February	—	—	—	13,202	162	—	15,571	5,531
March	—	—	—	12,862	160	—	15,650	5,246
April	—	—	—	12,178	110	—	13,114	6,802
May	—	—	—	11,847	111	—	13,686	5,760
June	—	—	—	11,693	108	—	18,096	1,162
July	—	1	—	11,787	107	—	15,799	3,532
August	4	1	—	17,799	1,199	—	17,326	2,975
September	5	1	—	20,994	1,194	—	20,845	2,407
October	12	1	—	22,403	1,185	900	23,643	2,154
November	12	1	—	23,650	1,176	1,000	24,742	2,353
December	12	1	—	23,859	1,158	900	25,175	2,240
1922:								
January	13	1	—	24,195	1,147	1,300	25,680	2,488
February	13	1	—	23,952	1,504	1,900	26,758	2,354
March	13	1	—	24,574	1,565	3,000	29,327	2,224
April	13	1	—	25,120	1,565	4,100	30,580	2,901
May	13	1	—	25,326	1,560	5,500	31,930	3,289
June	13	1	—	25,445	1,556	6,900	33,600	3,741
July	13	1	—	28,783	1,546	7,200	38,357	3,929
August	13	1	—	37,617	1,773	7,600	46,242	5,417
September	14	1	—	46,963	1,848	8,900	58,458	5,929

October	14	1	—	51,631	1,728	12,000	70,005	5,189
November	15	1	—	49,246	1,861	12,500	72,016	6,408
December	16	1	—	50,702	2,016	16,500	75,887	4,761
1923:								
January	14	1	—	54,516	2,007	20,000	73,717	5,888
February	23	1	—	58,358	2,013	24,000	75,135	6,600
March	23	1	—	71,284	2,584	29,000	82,205	11,152
April	23	1	—	83,800	2,817	37,000	100,101	9,793
May	23	1	—	93,396	1,763	47,200	119,285	10,609
June	23	1	—	120,608	2,490	59,700	154,996	12,742
July	22	1	—	165,927	1,762	79,700	226,285	21,977
August	22	1	—	273,605	1,789	143,000	399,487	23,629
September	22	1	—	380,454	1,776	243,000	588,810	60,246
October	23	1	—	494,501	1,663	269,000	744,926	60,176
November	23	1	—	531,403	1,047	306,000	853,989	74,970
December	23	1	—	582,117	935	401,000	931,337	84,791
1924:								
January	24	1	—	654,294	9,346	526,000	1,084,677	105,481
February	23	1	—	746,471	34,023	699,000	1,278,437	164,838
March	24	1	—	802,756	4,598	824,000	1,606,875	253,935
April	24	1	—	1,125,898	12,456	944,000	2,098,091	308,121
May	24	1	—	1,420,385	13,437	1,054,000	2,486,257	527,137
June[1]	246.947	9.823	681.268	1,192,517	17,566	1,980,000	2,893,719	1,135,710
July	441.832	13.545	1.110.926	1,257,597	—	1,980,000	3,277,943	1,424,578
August	449.945	13.558	1.382.385	1,438,454	—	1,978,130	3,659,757	1,473,231
September	540.425	13.560	1.385.880	1,756,636	—	1,977,306	4,115,925	1,416,400
October	503.377	13.301	1.658.674	1,872,385	—	1,976,455	4,635,090	1,465,356
November	508.411	13.301	1.816.102	1,984,540	—	1,975,631	4,442,644	1,929,754
December	532.842	13.299	1.933.356	1,976,888	—	1,974,781	4,513,990	2,069,468

Table H2 (continued)

	Gold Coin and Bullion	Silver Coin	Foreign Currency and Exchange	Bills Dis- counted	Advances on Securities	Advances to Treasury	Notes in Circu- lation	Current Accounts and Deposits
1925:								
January	509,848	12,373	1,967,314	1,848,620	—	1,973,930	4,449,650	2,138,629
February	596,334	12,374	1,989,096	1,676,594	—	1,973,163	4,237,985	2,542,262
March	669,107	12,374	1,984,006	1,514,532	—	1,969,809	4,270,096	2,552,762
April	653,534	12,136	2,081,998	1,485,898	—	1,968,987	4,526,216	2,470,507

Source: Young [36, vol. 2, p. 321].

Note: Figures prior to June 1924 are those of the State Note Institute. The Hungarian National Bank opened 24 June 1924 and took over the affairs of the institute.

[1]After this date gold and silver holdings are shown in terms of paper crowns. Other changes were also made in the presentation of accounts after the opening of the new Hungarian National Bank in June.

low interest rate, in view of the rapid rate of price appreciation, and to a large extent amounted to simple gifts from the Note Institute to those lucky enough to receive loans on such generous terms. These private loans account for a much larger increase in high-powered money in the Hungarian than in the other three hyperinflations we shall study.

As table H3 shows, the Hungarian krone depreciated rapidly on foreign exchange markets, and domestic prices rose rapidly. Between January 1922 and April 1924, the price index increased by a factor of 263. In the same period, the total notes and deposit liabilities of the Note Institute increased by a factor of 85, so that the real value of its liabilities decreased substantially. As in the case of Austria, this decrease was symptomatic of a "flight from the krone," as residents of Hungary attempted to economize on their holdings of krones and instead to hold assets denominated in more stable currencies. As in the case of Austria, the government of Hungary resisted this trend by establishing in August 1922 a Hungarian Devisenzentrale within the State Note Institute.

Table H3 indicates that in March 1924, the rise in prices and the depreciation of the krone internationally both abruptly halted. The stabilization occurred in the face of continued expansion in the liabilities of the central bank, which increased by a factor of 3.15 between March 1924 and January 1925 (see table H2). This pattern parallels what occurred in Austria and has a similar explanation.

As in Austria, the financial reconstruction of Hungary was accomplished with the intervention of the League of Nations. Together with the Reparation Commission and the government of Hungary, the League devised a plan which reduced and clarified the reparations commitment of Hungary, arranged for an international loan that would help finance government expenditures, and committed Hungary to establish a balanced budget and a central bank legally bound to refuse any government demand for unbacked credit. On 21 February 1924, the Reparation Commission agreed to give up its lien on Hungary's resources so that these could be used to secure a reconstruction loan. A variety of Western nations also agreed to give up their liens on Hungary so that the new loan could successfully be floated.

The League's reconstruction plan was embodied in two protocols. The first was signed by Great Britain, France, Italy, Czechoslovakia, Rumania, and Hungary, and guaranteed the "political independence, territorial integrity, and sovereignty of Hungary." The second protocol outlined the terms of the reconstruction plan, and committed Hungary to balance its budget and form a central bank truly independent of the Finance Ministry. The government was also obligated to accept in Hungary a commissioner general, responsible to the League, to monitor and supervise the government's fulfillment of its commitment to fiscal and monetary reform.

62   Thomas J. Sargent

Table H3   **Hungarian Price and Exchange Rate**

	Hungarian Index of Prices[1]	Cents per Crown in New York
1921:		
July	4,200	0.3323
August	5,400	.2629
September	6,250	.1944
October	6,750	.1432
November	8,300	.1078
December	8,250	.1512
1922:		
January	8,100	.1525
February	8,500	.1497
March	9,900	.1256
April	10,750	.1258
May	11,000	.1261
June	12,900	.1079
July	17,400	.0760
August	21,400	.0595
September	26,600	.0423
October	32,900	.0402
November	32,600	.0413
December	33,400	.0430
1923:		
January	38,500	.0392
February	41,800	.0395
March	66,000	.0289
April	83,500	.0217
May	94,000	.0191
June	144,500	.0140
July	286,000	.0097
August	462,500	.0056
September	554,000	.0055
October	587,000	.0054
November	635,000	.0054
December	714,000	.0052
1924:		
January	1,026,000	.0039
February	1,839,100	.0033
March	2,076,700	.0015
April	2,134,600	.0014
May	2,269,600	.0012
June	2,207,800	.0011
July	2,294,500	.0012
August	2,242,000	.0013
September	2,236,600	.0013

63   The Ends of Four Big Inflations

Table H3 (continued)

	Hungarian Index of Prices[1]	Cents per Crown in New York
October	2,285,200	.0013
November	2,309,500	.0013
December	2,346,600	.0013
1925:		
January	2,307,500	.0014
February	2,218,700	.0014
March	2,117,800	.0014

Source: Young [36, vol. 2, p. 323].

[1]From July 1921 through November 1923, the index numbers represent retail prices and are based on 60 commodities with July 1914 = 100. From December 1923 through March 1925, the figures are based on wholesale prices computed by the Hungarian Central Statistical Office. They refer to the prices of 52 commodities on the last day of the month with 1913 = 100.

A reconstruction loan of 250 million gold krones was successfully placed abroad in July 1924. The loan was secured by receipts from customs duties and sugar taxes, and revenues from the salt and tobacco monopolies. The purpose of the loan was to give the government a concrete means of converting future promises to tax into current resources while avoiding the need to place its debt domestically.

By a law of 26 April 1924, the Hungarian National Bank was established, and it began operations on 24 June. The bank assumed the assets and liabilities of the State Note Institute and took over the functions of the foreign exchange control office, the Devisenzentrale. The bank was prohibited from making any additional loans or advances to the government, except upon full security of gold or foreign bills. The bank was also required to hold gold reserves of certain specified percentages behind its liabilities.

The government of Hungary also tried to establish a balanced budget. Both by cutting expenditures and raising tax collections, the government was successful in moving quickly to a balanced budget (see table H4). Indeed, the proceeds of the reconstruction loan were used perceptibly more slowly than had been anticipated in the reconstruction plan.

As table H2 confirms, the stabilization of the krone was accompanied by a substantial *increase* in the total liabilities of the central bank. But as with Austria, the drastic shift in the fiscal policy regime that occasioned the stabilization also changed the appropriate interpretation of these figures. As table H2 indicates and as the regulations governing the bank required, after the League's intervention the note and deposit liabilities

64   Thomas J. Sargent

Table H4   Hungarian Budget, 1924–25 (in millions of crowns)

Period	Preliminary Treasury Accounts			Reconstruction Scheme		
	Re-ceipts	Expen-ditures	Surplus (+) or Deficit (−)	Re-ceipts	Expen-ditures	Surplus (+) or Deficit (−)
Jul.–Dec. 1924	208.0	205.9	+ 2.1	143.8	186.3	− 42.5
Jan.–Jun. 1925	245.1	216.9	+ 28.2	150.0	207.6	− 57.6
Fiscal year 1924–25	453.1	422.8	+ 30.3	293.8	393.9	− 100.1

Source: Pasvolsky [25, p. 322].

of the central bank became backed, 100% at the margin, by holdings of gold, foreign exchange, and commercial paper. In effect, the central bank's liabilities represented "fiat money" before the League's plan was in effect; after that plan was in effect, they represented more or less backed claims on British sterling,[23] the foreign currency to which Hungary pegged its exchange as a condition for British participation in the reconstruction loan.

Figures on unemployment in Hungary are reported in table H5, and unfortunately begin only immediately after the price stabilization had already occurred. All that can be inferred from these figures is that immediately after the stabilization, unemployment was not any higher than it was one or two years later. This is consistent either with the hypothesis that the stabilization process had little adverse effect on

Table H5   Number of Unemployed in Hungary (figures relate only to members of Union of Socialist Workers, in thousands of workers)

End of	1924	1925	1926
January	—	37	28
February	—	37	29
March	—	37	29
April	22	36	26
May	23	30	28
June	25	34	26
July	31	32	
August	30	27	
September	20	25	
October	30	23	
November	31	26	
December	33	27	

Source: League of Nations [15, p. 50].

65   The Ends of Four Big Inflations

unemployment or with the hypothesis that the adverse effect was so
long-lasting that no recovery occurred within the time span of the figures
recorded. The former hypothesis seems more plausible to me.

2.5   Poland

The new nation of Poland came into existence at the end of World War
I, and was formed from territories formerly belonging to Germany,
Austro-Hungary, and Russia. At the time of its formation, Poland possessed a varied currency consisting of Russian rubles, crowns of the
Austro-Hungarian bank, German marks, and Polish marks issued by the
Polish State Loan Bank, which had been established by Germany to
control the currency in the part of Poland occupied by Germany during
the war. For Poland, the armistice of 1918 did not bring peace, a costly
war with Soviet Russia being waged until the fall of 1920. Poland was
devastated by the fighting and by Germany's practice of stripping it of its
machinery and materials during World War I.[24]

The new government of Poland ran very large deficits up to 1924 (see
table P1). These deficits were financed by government borrowing from
the Polish State Loan Bank, which the new government had taken over
from the Germans. From January 1922 to December 1923, the outstanding notes of the Polish State Loan Bureau increased by a factor of 523
(table P2). Over the same period, the price index increased by a factor of

Table P1   Polish Receipts and Expenditures (in thousands of zloty)

	1921	1922	1923	1924	1925
Receipts:					
Administration	261,676	467,979	—	—	1,491,743
State Enterprises	11,413	14,556	—	—	133,530
Monopolies	72,222	47,893	—	—	356,611
Total	345,311	530,428	426,000	1,703,000	1,981,884
Expenditures:					
Administration	765,263	734,310	—	—	1,830,231
State Enterprises	115,589	145,003	—	—	106,343
Monopolies	—	—	—	—	45,019
Total	880,852	879,313	1,119,800	1,629,000	1,981,593
Deficit	535,541	348,885	692,000	—	—
Surplus	—	—	—	74,000	251

Source: Young [36, vol. 2, p. 183].
Note: Conversion from marks to zloty was made on the following basis: 1921, 1 zloty =
303.75 marks. First quarter 1922, 1 zloty = 513.52 marks; second quarter, 691.49 marks;
third quarter, 1,024.97 marks; and fourth quarter, 1,933.87 marks.

Table P2   Balance Sheet of Bank of Poland, 1918–25 (end of month figures)

Polish State Loan Bank figures (prior to May 1924) in millions of marks

Month	Gold[1]	Silver[1] (including base coin)	Balances with Foreign Banks	Discounts	Advances		Note Circulation
					Commercial	Government	
1918:							
October	—	—	—	7.0	180.8	—	880.2
November	—	—	—	7.0	184.0	13.9	930.5
December	—	—	—	6.4	183.7	117.8	1,023.8
1919:							
January	—	—	—	5.0	194.7	209.9	1,098.1
February	—	—	—	4.2	196.4	315.0	1,160.0
March	3.7	4.2	3.9	3.5	189.7	400.0	1,223.2
April	3.7	4.4	9.4	2.5	192.8	575.0	1,346.0
May	3.7	8.9	5.8	1.8	193.2	925.0	1,548.3
June	4.9	14.8	14.6	1.3	185.9	1,125.0	1,784.6
July	5.7	20.1	13.3	1.1	193.9	1,925.0	2,087.9
August	6.1	20.5	20.3	.7	107.4	2,525.0	2,466.6
September	6.3	21.6	69.8	.1	218.9	3,225.0	2,964.7
October	6.5	24.3	91.0	.3	242.4	4,375.0	3,723.6
November	6.6	24.6	151.6	3.4	270.2	5,375.0	4,236.2
December	6.6	25.5	344.6	3.9	243.8	6,825.0	5,316.3

1920:

January	6.6	25.5	244.1	3.7	278.5	8,275.0	6,719.9
February	6.8	25.9	565.7	6.4	303.0	10,775.0	8,300.3
March	6.8	25.9	685.4	8.2	319.1	14,775.0	10,690.6
April	6.8	25.9	685.5	14.8	316.7	19,375.0	16,027.9
May	6.8	25.9	565.7	47.2	320.9	22,375.0	17,934.7
June	6.8	25.9	894.7	161.4	488.2	27,625.0	21,730.1
July	6.8	25.9	1,130.9	325.9	847.5	33,375.0	26,311.4
August	9.0	33.8	1,273.4	465.8	1,466.1	39,625.0	31,085.8
September	9.1	34.1	174.9	333.9	1,862.9	40,625.0	33,203.5
October	9.5	34.4	236.7	259.1	2,527.0	46,925.0	38,456.8
November	10.1	35.4	203.8	396.0	3,278.4	49,625.0	43,236.2
December	12.4	37.6	80.7	611.6	3,999.2	59,625.0	43,236.2
December	12.4	37.6	80.7	611.6	3,999.2	59,625.0	49,361.5

1921:

January	12.7	39.2	205.8	1,040.2	4,100.2	65,625.0	55,079.5
February	12.8	39.2	476.0	955.1	4,143.5	77,125.0	62,560.4
March	13.1	39.8	908.5	781.0	4,745.7	93,625.0	74,087.4
April	13.4	40.3	870.7	927.0	4,994.4	106,625.0	86,755.3
May	13.5	40.1	536.5	1,395.2	4,979.0	117,625.0	94,575.8
June	14.3	41.1	49.36	1,557.3	5,306.5	130,625.0	102,697.3
July	19.1	41.5	601.3	2,504.2	6,291.5	140,625.0	115,242.3
August	19.2	42.0	368.7	3,885.4	7,776.9	158,000.0	133,734.2
September	19.4	42.5	1,217.5	6,237.3	9,878.6	178,000.0	152,792.1
October	20.2	42.9	2,341.3	9,529.5	12,022.3	198,500.0	182,777.3
November	22.6	43.5	7,040.1	14,347.2	15,144.3	214,000.0	207,029.0
December	24.9	43.9	12,707.9	15,334.4	19,300.0	221,000.0	229,537.6

Table P2 (continued)

Month	Gold[1]	Silver[1] (including base coin)	Balances with Foreign Banks	Discounts	Advances Commercial	Advances Government	Note Circulation
1922:							
January	26.3	44.2	13,614.2	15,951.6	21,776.9	227,350.0	239,615.3
February	28.3	44.4	14,207.7	19,555.0	22,327.7	230,600.0	247,209.5
March	29.0	44.7	1,156.4	25,451.1	25,473.3	232,100.0	250,665.5
April	29.5	45.2	7,388.0	28,688.8	29,063.7	220,000.0	260,553.8
May	30.1	45.3	23,073.4	34,555.0	26,067.0	217,000.0	276,001.1
June	30.9	45.3	20,521.4	46,629.8	24,499.5	235,000.0	300,101.1
July	31.5	45.4	21,741.0	47,661.2	24,054.4	260,000.0	335,426.6
August	31.6	45.4	51,747.2	56,366.6	21,079.9	285,000.0	385,787.5
September	32.4	45.4	67,384.1	64,093.0	22,239.4	342,000.0	463,706.0
October	33.5	45.4	64,060.9	81,781.9	26,576.5	453,500.0	579,972.7
November	33.8	45.4	78,959.0	107,320.1	41,278.1	519,500.0	661,092.4
December	41.0	45.4	48,580.4	133,400.8	47,904.1	675,600.0	793,437.5
1923:							
January	41.1	44.1	34,721.8	174,950.1	51,899.9	799,500.0	909,160.3
February	41.4	44.1	71,883.7	219,610.7	61,037.1	1,085,000.0	1,177,300.8
March	41.7	44.2	29,868.7	274,657.8	85,323.2	1,752,000.0	1,841,205.6
April	41.9	44.2	50,851.9	304,725.4	156,815.4	2,161,500.0	2,332,396.8
May	41.9	44.3	43,900.7	449,440.7	217,162.3	2,377,000.0	2,733,794.1
June	43.9	39.8	276,506.3	627,339.5	310,862.7	2,996,500.0	3,566,649.1
July	46.9	34.8	384,375.1	758,112.8	390,850.9	4,190,500.0	4,478,709.0
August	48.0	32.9	340,354.4	1,372,150.9	637,268.2	6,473,000.0	6,871,776.5

September	53.2	20.7	857,084.5	2,077,128.6	670,019.6	10,265,500.0	11,197,737.8
October	54.2	19.1	1,510,794.3	3,540,434.4	1,836,712.7	19,080,500.0	23,080,402.2
November	54.3	19.5	6,499,791.5	8,467,033.7	3,951,781.9	42,854,000.0	53,217,494.6
December	54.9	19.6	57,499,741.7	20,588,037.9	28,065,396.8	111,332,000.0	125,371,955.3
1924:							
January	66.2	19.8	91,533,085.2	43,916,802.8	54,181,445.2	238,200,000.0	313,659,830.0
February	66.7	19.8	172,626,128.8	67,216,289.7	83,829,440.5	291,700,000.0	528,913,418.7
March	68.0	20.3	220,658,210.7	138,649,934.8	81,231,988.5	291,700,000.0	596,244,205.6
April	55.7	21.1	277,340,925.7	199,248,956.4	60,589,081.0	291,700,000.0	570,697,550.5

After conversion of State Loan Bank into Bank of Poland, figures in gold zlotys; no ciphers omitted; 1 zloty = 19.3 cents

May	11,684,963[2]		214,191,336	126,522,906	1,801,936	—	244,977,010
June	83,392,914[2]		256,972,386	138,862,243	5,826,971	—	334,405,730
July	93,683,430[2]		272,137,898	166,713,469	8,236,693	—	394,262,550
August	98,288,324[2]		266,390,583	199,710,736	8,224,610	—	430,263,045
September	99,900,015[2]		233,646,562	233,788,177	9,230,850	—	460,383,770
October	100,686.634	16,521,223	241,894,738	245,054,984	12,374,342	—	503,701,830
November	102,809.285	21,951,828	247,034,974	249,560,999	12,371,166	—	497,600,470
December	103,362.870	27,543,698	269,045,551	256,954,853	23,897.766	—	550,873,960
1925:							
January	104,249.258	27,658,749	242,115,258	270,423,615	23,468.829	—	553,174,980
February	107,032.735	27,481,871	206,317,320	286,229.180	28,467.930	18.222.212	549,637,420
March	116,619.825	28,158,597	259,392,902	306,562.690	25,477.638	403.354	563,171.945
April	117,428.697	28,358.000	216,114,621	294,632,508	27,319,944	35.977.630	567,178,830

Source: Young [36, vol. 2, p. 348].
[1] Gold at par; silver coin at face value.
[2] Gold and silver.

2,402 while the dollar exchange rate decreased by a factor of 1,397 (see tables P3 and P4). As in the other inflations we have studied, the real value of the note circulation decreased as people engaged in a "flight from the mark." Extensive government exchange controls were imposed to resist this trend.

Tables P2 and P3 indicate that the rapid inflation and exchange depreciation both suddenly stopped in January 1924. Unlike the cases of Austria and Hungary, in Poland the initial stabilization was achieved without foreign loans or intervention, although later in 1927, after currency depreciation threatened to renew, a substantial foreign loan was arranged.[25] But in terms of the substantial fiscal and monetary regime changes that accompanied the end of the inflation, there is much similarity to the Austrian and Hungarian experiences. The two interrelated

Table P3   **Polish Index Numbers of Wholesale Prices, 1921–25**

Year	Month	Wholesale Price Index[1]	Year	Month	Wholesale Price Index[1]
1921	January	25,139	1923	April	1,058,920
	February	31,827		May	1,125,350
	March	32,882		June	1,881,410
	April	31,710		July	3,069,970
	May	32,639		August	5,294,680
	June	35,392		September	7,302,200
	July	45,654		October	27,380,680
	August	53,100		November	67,943,700
	September	60,203		December	142,300,700
	October	65,539	1924	January	242,167,700
	November	58,583		February	248,429,600
	December	57,046		March	245,277,900
1922	January	59,231		April	242,321,800
	February	63,445		May	
	March	73,465		June	
	April	75,106		July	
	May	78,634		August	
	June	87,694		September	
	July	101,587		October	
	August	135,786		November	
	September	152,365		December	
	October	201,326	1925	January	
	November	275,647		February	
	December	346,353		March	
1923	January	544,690		April	
	February	859,110		May	
	March	988,500			

Source: Young [36, vol. 2, p. 349].
[1]1914 = 100.

71   The Ends of Four Big Inflations

Table P4   **Polish Exchange Rates, 1919–25**

Year	Month	Cents per Polish Mark	Year	Month	Cents per Polish Mark
1919	July	6.88	1922	September	.0127
	August	5.63		October	.0095
	September	3.88		November	.0065
	October	3.08		December	.0057
	November	1.88	1923	January	.0043
	December	1.29		February	.0025
1920	January	.70		March	.0024
	February	.68		April	.0023
	March	.67		May	.0021
	April	.60		June	.0013
	May	.51		July	.0007
	June	.59		August	.0004
	July	.61		September	.00035
	August	.47		October	.00001113
	September	.45		November	.0000502
	October	.37		December	.0000234
	November	.26	1924	January	.0000116
	December	.16		February	.0000109
1921	January	.145		March	.0000113
	February	.130		April	.0000114
	March	.132		May	—

Year	Month	Cents per Polish Mark	Year	Month	Cents per Zloty
	April	.130			
	May	.124			
	June	.082		June	10.29
	July	.0516		July	19.25
	August	.0489		August	19.23
	September	.0256		September	19.22
	October	.0212		October	19.22
	November	.0290		November	19.21
	December	.0313		December	19.20
1922	January	.0327	1925	January	19.18
	February	.0286		February	19.18
	March	.0236		March	19.18
	April	.0262		April	19.18
	May	.0249		May	19.18
	June	.0237		June	19.18
	July	.0185			
	August	0.0135			

Source: Young [36, vol. 2, p. 350].

changes were a dramatic move toward a balanced government budget and the establishment of an independent central bank that was prohibited from making additional unsecured loans to the government. In January 1924, the minister of finance was granted broad powers to effect mone-

72   Thomas J. Sargent

tary and fiscal reform. The minister immediately initiated the establishment of the Bank of Poland, which was to assume the functions of the Polish State Loan Bank. The eventual goal was to restore convertibility with gold. The bank was required to hold a 30% reserve behind its notes, to consist of gold and foreign paper assets denominated in stable currencies. Beyond this reserve, the bank's notes had to be secured by private bills of exchange and silver. A maximum credit to the government of 50 million zlotys was permitted. The government also moved swiftly to balance the budget (see table P1).

In January 1924, a new currency unit became effective, the gold zloty, worth 1.8 million paper marks. The zloty was equal in gold content to 19.29 cents.

Table P2 reveals that, from January 1924 to December 1924, the note circulation of the central bank increased by a factor of 3.2, in the face of relative stability of the price level and the exchange rate (see tables P3 and P4). This phenomenon matches what occurred in Austria and Hun-

Table P5   **Polish Unemployed**

1921:		1923:	
January	74,000	January	81,184
February	90,000	February	106,729
March	80,000	March	114,576
April	88,000	April	112,755
May	130,000	May	93,731
June	115,000	June	76,397
July	95,000	July	64,563
August	65,000	August	56,515
September	70,000	September	—
October	78,000	October	—
November	120,000	November	—
December	173,000	December	67,581
1922:		1924:	
January	221,444	January	100,580
February	206,442	February	110,737
March	170,125	March	112,583
April	148,625	April	109,000
May	128,916	May	84,000
June	98,581	June	97,870
July	85,240	July	149,097
August	69,692	August	159,820
September	68,000	September	155,245
October	61,000	October	147,065
November	62,000	November	150,180
December	75,000	December	159,060

Source: *Statistiches Jahrbuch fur das Deutsche Reich* [33].

gary and has a similar explanation. As table P2 reveals, the increased note circulation during this period was effectively backed 100% by gold, foreign exchange, and private paper.

The available figures on unemployment are summarized in table P5. The stabilization of the price level in January 1924 is accompanied by an abrupt rise in the number of unemployed. Another rise occurs in July of 1924. While the figures indicate substantial unemployment in late 1924, unemployment is not an order of magnitude worse than before the stabilization, and certainly not anywhere nearly as bad as would be predicted by application of the same method of analysis that was used to fabricate the prediction for the contemporary United States that each percentage point reduction in inflation would require a reduction of $220 billion in real GNP.

The Polish zloty depreciated internationally from late 1925 onward but stabilized in autumn of 1926 at around 72% of its level of January 1924. At the same time, the domestic price level stabilized at about 50% above its level of January 1924. The threatened renewal of inflation has been attributed to the government's premature relaxation of exchange controls and the tendency of the central bank to make private loans at insufficient interest rates.[26]

2.6 Germany

After World War I, Germany owed staggering reparations to the Allied countries. This fact dominated Germany's public finance from 1919 until 1923 and was a most important force for hyperinflation.

At the conclusion of the war, Germany experienced a political revolution and established a republican government. The early postwar governments were dominated by moderate Socialists, who for a variety of reasons reached accommodations with centers of military and industrial power of the prewar regime.[27] These accommodations in effect undermined the willingness and capability of the government to meet its admittedly staggering revenue needs through explicit taxation.

Of the four episodes that we have studied, Germany's hyperinflation was the most spectacular, as the figures on wholesale prices and exchange rates in tables G1 and G2 reveal. The inflation became most severe after the military occupation of the Ruhr by the French in January 1923. The German government was determined to fight the French occupation by a policy of passive resistance, making direct payments to striking workers which were financed by discounting treasury bills with the Reichsbank.

Table G3 estimates the budget of Germany for 1920 to 1923.[28] The table reveals that, except for 1923, the budget would not have been badly out of balance except for the massive reparations payments made. The disruption caused to Germany's finances by the reparations situation is

74   Thomas J. Sargent

Table G1   German Wholesale Prices, 1914–24

Year	Month	Price Index	Year	Month	Price Index
1914	January	96	1918	January	204
	February	96		February	198
	March	96		March	198
	April	95		April	204
	May	97		May	203
	June	99		June	209
	July	99		July	208
	August	109		August	235
	September	111		September	230
	October	118		October	234
	November	123		November	234
	December	125		December	245
1915	January	126	1919	January	262
	February	133		February	270
	March	139		March	274
	April	142		April	286
	May	139		May	297
	June	139		June	308
	July	150		July	339
	August	146		August	422
	September	145		September	493
	October	147		October	562
	November	147		November	678
	December	148		December	803
1916	January	150	1920	January	1,260
	February	151		February	1,690
	March	148		March	1,710
	April	149		April	1,570
	May	151		May	1,510
	June	152		June	1,380
	July	161		July	1,370
	August	159		August	1,450
	September	154		September	1,500
	October	153		October	1,470
	November	151		November	1,510
	December	151		December	1,440
1917	January	156	1921	January	1,440
	February	158		February	1,380
	March	159		March	1,340
	April	163		April	1,330
	May	163		May	1,310
	June	165		June	1,370
	July	172		July	1,430
	August	203		August	1,920
	September	199		September	2,070
	October	201		October	2,460
	November	203		November	3,420
	December	203		December	3,490

75   The Ends of Four Big Inflations

Table G1 (continued)

Year	Month	Price Index	Year	Month	Price Index
1922	January	3,670	1923	July	7,478,700
	February	4,100		August	94,404,100
	March	5,430		September	2,394,889,300
	April	6,360		October	709,480,000,000
	May	6,460		November	72,570,000,000,000
	June	7,030		December	126,160,000,000,000
	July	10,160	1924	January	117,320,000,000,000
	August	19,200		February	116,170,000,000,000
	September	28,700		March	120,670,000,000,000
	October	56,600		April	124,050,000,000,000
	November	115,100		May	122,460,000,000,000
	December	147,480		June	115,900,000,000,000
1923	January	278,500		July	115[1]
	February	588,500		August	120[1]
	March	488,800		September	127[1]
	April	521,200		October	131[1]
	May	817,000		November	129[1]
	June	1,938,500		December	131[1]

Source: Young [36, vol. 1, p. 530].
[1]On basis of prices in reichsmarks. (1 reichsmark = 1 trillion [10^{12}] former marks.)

surely understated by the reparations figures given in table G3. For one thing, considerably larger sums were initially expected of Germany than it ever was eventually able to pay. For another thing, the extent of Germany's total obligation and the required schedule of payments was for a long time uncertain and under negotiation. From the viewpoint that the value of a state's currency and other debt depends intimately on the fiscal policy it intends to run, the uncertainty about the reparations owed by the German government necessarily cast a long shadow over its prospects for a stable currency.

As table G4 reveals, the note circulation of the Reichsbank increased dramatically from 1921 to 1923, especially in the several months before November 1923. As pointed out by Young [36], at the end of October 1923, over 99% of outstanding Reichsbank notes had been placed in circulation within the previous 30 days.[29] Table G4 reveals the extent to which the Reichsbank note circulation was backed by discounted treasury bills. During 1923, the Reichsbank also began discounting large volumes of commercial bills. Since these loans were made at nominal rates of interest far below the rate of inflation, they amounted virtually to government transfer payments to the recipients of the loans.

Especially during the great inflation of 1923, a force came into play which was also present in the other hyperinflations we have studied.

76   Thomas J. Sargent

Table G2   **German Exchange Rates, 1914–25**

Year	Month	Cents per Mark	Year	Month	Cents per Mark
1920	January	1.69	1922	August	.10
	February	1.05		September	.07
	March	1.26		October	.03
	April	1.67		November	.01
	May	2.19		December	.01
	June	2.56			
	July	2.53	1923	January	.007
	August	2.10		February	.004
	September	1.72		March	.005
	October	1.48		April	.004
	November	1.32		May	.002
	December	1.37		June	.001
				July	.000,3
1921	January	1.60		August	.000,033,9
	February	1.64		September	.000,001,88
	March	1.60		October	.000,000,068
	April	1.57		November	.000,000,000,043
	May	1.63		December	.000,000,000,022,7
	June	1.44			
	July	1.30	1924	January	22.6
	August	1.19		February	21.8
	September	.96		March	22.0
	October	.68		April	22.0
	November	.39		May	22.3
	December	.53		June	23.4
				July	23.9
1922	January	.52		August	23.8
	February	.48		September	23.8
	March	.36		October	23.8
	April	.35		November	23.8
	May	.34		December	23.8
	June	.32			
	July	.20	1925[1]	January	23.8

Source: Young [36, vol. 1, p. 532].

[1]Cents per rentenmark and (after October 1924) per reichsmark. 1 rentenmark is equivalent to 1 reichsmark or 1 billion former paper marks. The reichsmark is the equivalent of the gold mark worth 23.82 cents.

Table G3   **Real German Revenues and Expenditures, Calculated on the Basis of the Cost-of-Living Index (in millions of gold marks)**

	Revenue				Expenditures					
	Taxes	Sundries	Deficit Covered by Loan Transactions	Total	Repayment of Floating Debt	Interest on Floating Debt	Subsidies to Railroads	Execution of Versailles Treaty	Sundries	Total
1920–21	4,090.8	132.9	7,041.9	11,265.6	821.7	—	—	—	—	11,265.6
1921–22	5,235.7	100.5	6,627.4	11,963.6	1,039.5	811.6	1,114.4	5,110.6	5,738.4	11,963.4
1922–23	3,529.1	51.4	6,384.5	9,965.0	81.0	344.4	1,685.5	3,600.0	4,254.1	9,965.0
1923–24 (first 9 months)	1,496.1	180.6	11,836.5	13,513.2	—	931.0	3,725.0	—	—	13,513.2

Source: Young [36, vol. 2, p. 393].

Table G-4   Balance Sheet of German Reichsbank, 1914-24

	Discounted Bills		Total Discounted Treasury and Commercial Bills	Advances	Securities
	Treasury Bills	Com-mercial Bills			
1921:					
January	50,594,540	2,742,406	53,336,946	8,881	147.126
February	53,690,412	2,760,927	56,451,339	11,522	185.788
March	64,533,894	2,268,745	66,802,639	2,805	217.044
April	58,841,630	2,052,099	60,803,729	9,238	225,777
May	62,953,604	1,809,936	64,763,540	16,624	258,664
June	79,607,790	1,565,406	81,172,196	6,079	282,716
July	79,981,967	1,135,529	81,117,496	10,686	283,381
August	84,043,891	1,002,497	85,046,388	7,704	258.319
September	98,422,137	1,142,218	99,564,355	3,289	277,977
October	98,704,768	881,474	99,586,242	47,775	282,179
November	114,023,417	1,445,667	115,469,084	90,370	247,699
December	132,380,906	1,061,754	133,392,660	8,476	195,912
1922:					
January	126,160,402	1,592,416	127,752,818	20,548	198,725
February	134,251,808	1,856,936	136,108,744	62,305	215,362
March	146,531,247	2,151,677	148,682,924	20,688	205,936
April	155,617,524	2,403,044	158,020,568	134,314	229,242
May	167,793,922	3,376,599	171,170,521	54,361	199,314
June	186,125,747	4,751,748	190,877,495	58,994	307,564
July	207,858,232	8,122,066	215,980,298	141,276	313,488
August	249,765,773	21,704,341	271,470,114	172,966	241,162
September	349,169,650	50,234,414	400,004,064	61,516	416,193

October	477,201,494	101,155,267	578,356,761	624,368	502,348
November	672,222,197	246,948,596	919,170,793	51,425,030[1]	381,068
December	1,184,464,359	422,235,296	1,606,699,655	773,974	469,972
1923:					
January	1,609,081,121	697,216,424	2,306,297,545	95,316,552	483,318
February	2,947,363,994	1,829,341,080	4,776,705,074	27,422,282	1,209,935
March	4,552,011,661	2,372,101,757	6,924,113,418	2,132,906	1,690,011
April	6,224,899,348	2,986,116,724	9,211,016,072	20,466,948	1,207,105
May	8,021,904,840	4,014,693,720	12,036,598,560	61,030,322	697,611
June	18,338[2]	6,914,198,630	25,252,198,630	188,548,574	344,819
July	53,752[2]	18,314[2]	72,066[2]	2,553,177,597	1,422,291
August	987,219[2]	164,644[2]	1,151,863[2]	25,261[2]	15,539,853
September	45,216,224[2]	3,660,094[2]	48,876,318[2]	98,522[2]	1,801,579,570
October	6,578,650,939[2]	1,058,129,855[2]	7,636,780,794[2]	41,787,532[2]	9,536,953[2]
15 November	189,801,468,187[2]	39,529,577,254[2]	229,331,045,441[2]	535,714,637[2]	8,901,495[2]
30 November	96,874,330,250[2]	347,301,037,776[2]	444,175,368,026[2]	7,742,665,263[2]	336,495,629[2]
December	(3)	322,724,948,986[2]	322,724,948,986[2]	268,325,819,530[2]	65,791,385[2]
1924:[4]					
January	—	—	755,866	336,520	12
February	—	—	1,165,649	306,618	25
March	—	—	1,767,443	143,102	533
April	—	—	1,916,969	156,362	91,984
May	—	—	1,954,930	128,597	80,011
June	—	—	1,897,959	108,789	76,378
July	—	—	1,798,097	62,489	76,509
August	—	—	1,860,843	59,983	76,331
September	—	—	2,169,684	54,424	78,305
15 October[5]	—	—	2,153,943	15,947	77,517
31 October	—	—	2,339,616	33,443	77,699
November	—	—	2,290,166	18,628	77,808
December	—	—	2,064,094	16,960	77,999

(*Footnotes appear on p. 82*)

Table G-4 (continued)

	Notes in Circulation	Demand Deposits			
		Public	Other	Total Demand Deposits	Due to the Rentenbank
1921:					
January	66,620,804	4,055,904	11,778,060	15,833,964	
February	67,426,959	7,291,052	10,066,036	17,357,088	
March	69,417,228	15,206,381	12,836,292	28,042,673	
April	70,839,725	11,595,618	9,260,271	20,855,889	
May	71,838,866	3,548,492	10,545,201	14,093,693	
June	75,321,095	5,647,805	14,744,903	20,392,708	
July	77,390,853	4,810,026	11,014,130	15,824,156	
August	80,072,721	4,850,843	8,798,756	13,649,599	
September	86,384,286	4,618,087	15,362,208	19,980,295	
October	91,527,679	5,239,628	13,063,035	18,302,663	
November	100,943,632	5,144,615	20,168,499	25,313,114	
December	113,639,464	7,591,343	25,314,330	32,905,673	
1922:					
January	115,375,766	5,286,950	18,125,502	23,421,452	
February	120,026,387	5,806,922	20,719,150	26,526,072	
March	130,671,352	7,743,735	25,614,597	33,358,332	
April	140,420,057	7,577,862	24,038,306	31,616,168	
May	151,949,179	7,711,279	25,416,711	33,127,990	
June	169,211,792	10,125,837	27,047,908	37,173,745	
July	189,794,722	9,197,727	30,778,489	39,976,216	
August	238,147,160	13,708,213	42,416,241	56,124,454	
September	316,869,799	30,034,309	79,978,068	110,012,377	

October	469,456,818	34,270,926	106,508,333	140,779,259	
November	754,086,109	50,353,945	190,615,514	240,969,459	
December	1,280,094,831	153,190,991	377,335,296	530,526,287	
1923:					
January	1,984,496,369	157,058,537	605,205,692	763,264,229	
February	3,512,787,777	253,915,266	1,329,065,770	1,582,981,036	
March	5,517,919,651	368,550,293	1,903,533,291	2,272,083,584	
April	6,545,984,355	454,403,079	3,399,871,714	3,854,274,793	
May	8,563,749,470	652,575,366	4,410,494,865	5,063,070,231	
June	17,291[2]	1,648,114,327	8,304,602,339	9,952,716,666	
July	43,595[2]	3,779,235,298	24,078[2]	27,857[2]	
August	663,200[2]	206,168[2]	384,912[2]	591,080[2]	
Setember	28,228,815[2]	8,186,467[2]	8,781,150[2]	16,966,617[2]	
October	2,496,822,909[2]	606,660,673[2]	3,261,424,030[2]	3,868,085,703[2]	
15 November	92,844,720,743[2]	72,457,230,513[2]	57,095,366,904[2]	129,552,597,417[2]	
30 November	400,267,640,302[2]	120,478,936,906[2]	253,497,803,653[2]	373,976,740,559[2]	
December	496,507,424,772[2]	303,114,560,004[2]	244,906,637,001[2]	548,024,197,005[2]	
1924:[4]					
January	483,675	492,985	281,320	281,305	200.000
February	587,875	367,551	282,958	650,509	400.000
March	689,864	352,360	352,334	704,694	800.000
April	776,949	474,411	330,561	804,972	800.000
May	926,874	545,252	259,203	804,455	800.000
June	1,097,309	493,043	280,884	773,927	800.000
July	1,211,038	452,597	290,390	742,987	800.000
August	1,391,895	264,064	297,791	561,855	800.000
September	1,520,511	307,515	362,581	670,096	800.000
15 October[5]	1,396,748	—	—	828,511	800.000
31 October	1,780,930	—	—	708,728	800.000
November	1,863,200	—	—	703,938	684.664
December	1,941,440	—	—	820,865	456.508

(*Footnotes appear on p. 82*)

Given the method of assessing taxes in nominal terms, lags between the time when taxes were levied and the time when they were collected led to reduced revenues as the government evidently repeatedly underestimated the prospective rate of inflation and as the rapid inflation gave people a large incentive to delay paying their taxes. This effect probably partially accounts for the reduced tax revenues collected during the first nine months of 1923. The French occupation of the Ruhr also helps explain it.

In response to the inflationary public finance and despite the efforts of the government to impose exchange controls, there occurred a "flight from the German mark" in which the real value of Reichsmark notes decreased dramatically. The figures in table G1 indicate that between January 1922 and July 1923, wholesale prices increased by a factor of 2,038 while Reichsbank notes increased by a factor of 378. Between January 1922 and August 1923, wholesale prices increased by a factor of 25,723 while Reichsbank notes circulating increased by a factor of 5,748. The fact that prices increased proportionately many times more than did the Reichsbank note circulation is symptomatic of the efforts of Germans to economize on their holdings of rapidly depreciating German marks. Toward the end of the hyperinflation, Germans made every effort to avoid holding marks and held large quantities of foreign exchange for purposes of conducting transaction. By October 1923, it has been roughly estimated, the real value of foreign currencies circulating in Germany was at least equal to and perhaps several times the real value of Reichsbank notes circulating.[30]

The figures in tables G1 and G2 show that prices suddenly stopped rising and the mark stopped depreciating in late November 1923. The event of stabilization was attended by a "monetary reform," in which on 15 October 1923 a new currency unit called the Rentenmark was declared equivalent to 1 trillion (10^{12}) paper marks. While great psychological

Footnotes to Table G4

Source: Young [36, vol. 1, pp. 528–29].

Note: End of month figures, in thousands of current marks; from January 1924 in thousands of rentenmarks or reichsmarks. 1 rentenmark is equivalent to 1 reichsmark or 1 trillion (10^{12}) former paper marks. The reichsmark is the equivalent of the gold mark worth 23.82 cents.

[1] The large increase of advances at the close of November 1922 occurred because the Reichsbank had to take over temporarily the financing of food supplies from the loan bureaus (Darlehuskassen), as the latter were unable to extend the needed accommodation, their outstanding notes having reached the maximum amount permitted by law.

[2] In billions.

[3] A decree of 15 November 1923 discontinued the discounting of treasury bills by the Reichsbank.

[4] See note above.

[5] Date of first statement of reorganized Reichsbank.

83   The Ends of Four Big Inflations

significance has sometimes been assigned to this unit change, it is difficult
to attribute any substantial effects to what was in itself only a cosmetic
measure.[31] The substantive aspect of the decree of 15 October was the
establishing of a Rentenbank to take over the note issue functions of the
Reichbank. The decree put binding limits upon both the total volume of
Rentenmarks that could be issued, 3.2 billion marks, and the maximum
amount that could be issued to the government, 1.2 billion marks. This
limitation on the amount of credit that could be extended to the government was announced at a time when the government was financing
virtually 100% of its expenditures by means of note issue.[32] In December
1923, the management of the Rentenbank was tested by the government
and effectively made clear its intent to meet its obligation to limit government borrowing to within the amount decreed.

Simultaneously and abruptly three things happened: additional government borrowing from the central bank stopped, the government
budget swung into balance, and inflation stopped. Table G5 shows the
dramatic progress toward a balanced budget that was made in the months
after the Rentenbank decree.

The government moved to balance the budget by taking a series of
deliberate, permanent actions to raise taxes and eliminate expenditures.

Table G5   **Ordinary Revenues and Expenditures of the German Federal
                 Government (from Wirtschift and Statistik, issued by
                 the Statistisches Reichsamt, in millions of gold marks)**

	Ordinary Revenue		Ordinary Expen-ditures	Excess of Revenue (+) or Ex-penditure (−)
	Total	Of Which Taxes Yielded		
1923:				
November	68.1	63.2	—	—
December	333.9	312.3	668.7	− 334.8
1924:				
January	520.6	503.5	396.5	+ 124.1
February	445.0	418.0	462.8	− 17.8
March	632.4	595.3	498.6	133.8
April	579.5	523.8	523.5	+ 56.0
May	566.7	518.7	459.1	+ 107.6
June	529.7	472.3	504.5	+ 25.2
July	622.2	583.1	535.1	+ 86.9
August	618.2	592.0	597.6	+ 20.6
September	665.6	609.2	581.6	+ 84.0
October	714.3	686.7	693.0	+ 21.3

Source: Young [36. vol. 1, p. 422].

Young reports that "by the personnel decree of October 27, 1923, the number of government employees was cut by 25 percent; all temporary employees were to be discharged; all above the age of 65 years were to be retired. An additional 10 percent of the civil servants were to be discharged by January 1924. The railways, overstaffed as a result of post-war demobilization, discharged 120,000 men during 1923 and 60,000 more during 1924. The postal administration reduced its staff by 65,000 men; the Reichsbank itself which had increased the number of its employees from 13,316 at the close of 1922 to 22,909 at the close of 1923, began the discharge of its superfluous force in December, as soon as the effects of stabilization became manifest."[33]

Substantially aiding the fiscal situation, Germany also obtained relief from her reparation obligations. Reparations payments were temporarily suspended, and the Dawes plan assigned Germany a much more manageable schedule of payments.

Table G4 documents a pattern that we have seen in the three other hyperinflations: the substantial growth of central bank note and demand deposit liabilities in the months *after* the currency was stabilized. As in the other cases that we have studied, the best explanation for this is that at the margin the postinflation increase in notes was no longer backed by government debt. Instead, in the German case, it was largely backed by discounted commercial bills. The nature of the system of promises and claims behind the central bank's liabilities changed when after the Rentenbank decree the central bank no longer offered additional credit to the government. So once again the interpretation of the time series on central bank notes and deposits must undergo a very substantial change.

By all available measures, the stabilization of the German mark was accompanied by increases in output and employment and decreases in unemployment.[34] While 1924 was not a good year for German business, it was much better than 1923. Table G6 is representative of the figures assembled by Graham, and shows that 1924 suffers in comparison with 1922 but that 1925 was a good year. In these figures one cannot find much convincing evidence of a favorable trade-off between inflation and out-

Table G6   **Index of Physical Volume**
                           of Production per Capita in Germany

Year	Index of Production	Year	Index of Production
1920	61	1924	77
1921	77	1925	90
1922	86	1926	86
1923	54	1927	111

Source: Graham [7, p. 287].

85   The Ends of Four Big Inflations

put, since the year of spectacular inflation, 1923 was a very bad year for employment and physical production. Certainly a large part of the poor performance of 1923 was due to the French occupation of the Ruhr and the policy of passive resistance.

Despite the evident absence of a "Phillips curve" trade-off between inflation and real output in the figures in tables G1 and G6, there is ample evidence that the German inflation was far from "neutral" and that there were important "real effects." Graham [7] gives evidence that the inflation and the associated reduction in real rates of return to "high-powered" money and other government debt were accompanied by real overinvestment in many kinds of capital goods." There is little doubt that the "irrational" structure of capital characterizing Germany after stabilization led to subsequent problems of adjustment in labor and other markets.

2.7   Czechoslovakia

After World War I, the new nation of Czechoslovakia was formed out of territories formerly belonging to Austria and Hungary. Under the leadership of a distinguished minister of finance, Dr. Alois Rasin, immediately after the war Czechoslovakia adopted the conservative fiscal and monetary policies its neighbors adopted only after their currencies had depreciated radically. As a result, Czechoslovakia avoided the hyperinflation experienced by its neighbors.

Under Rasin's leadership, Czechoslovakia early on showed that it was serious about attaining a stable currency. Even before the peace treaties required it, Czechoslovakia stamped the Austro-Hungarian notes then circulating within its border with the Czechoslovakian stamp, thereby recognizing them as its own debt. There was considerable drama associated with this event, as the National Assembly passed the plans for stamping in secret sessions on 25 February 1919. From 26 February to 9 March, the frontiers of the country were unexpectedly closed and foreign mail service was closed. Only Austro-Hungarian notes circulating within the country could be presented for stamping. As part of the stamping process, the government retained part of the notes in the form of a forced loan.[36] About 8 billion crowns were stamped.

A banking office in the Ministry of Finance took over the affairs of the old Austro-Hungarian bank. Czechoslovakia moved quickly to limit by statute the total government note circulation and to prevent inflationary government finance. A law of 10 April 1919 strictly limited the fiduciary or unbacked note circulation of the banking office to about 7 billion crowns. This law was obeyed, and forced the government to finance its expenditures by levying taxes or else issuing debt, which, because of the statutory restriction on government note issues, were interpreted as promises to tax in the future.

From 1920 on, Czechoslovakia ran only modest deficits on current account (see table C1). Among other taxes, Czechoslovakia imposed a progressive capital levy on property, which raised a cumulative amount of about 11 billion crowns by 1925. It also imposed an increment tax on the increased wealth individuals had obtained during the war.

Table C2 shows the note and deposit liabilities of the banking office. The government's abstention from inflationary finance shows up in these figures.

Table C1   **Czechoslovakia, Receipts and Expenditures, 1919–25 (exclusive of expenditures for capital improvements covered by loans)**

	1919		1920		1922		1922	
	Esti-mated	Ac-tual	Esti-mated	Ac-tual	Esti-mated	Ac-tual	Esti-mated	Ac-tual
Revenue:								
Ordinary	2,614	—	7,950	—	15,923	—	17,291	—
Extraordinary	1,096	—	2,477	—	1,376	—	1,593	—
Total	3,710	—	10,427	13,455	17,299	21,894	18,884	17,733
Expenditure:								
Ordinary	2,610	—	7,175	—	10,672	—	13,289	—
Extraordinary	6,005	—	8,103	—	7,354	—	6,524	—
Total	8,615	7,450	15,278	13,931	18,026	18,558	19,813	18,663
Deficit	4,905	—	4,851	476	727	—	929	930
Surplus	—	—	—	—	—	3,336	—	—

	1923		1924		1925	
	Esti-mated	Ac-tual	Esti-mated	Ac-tual	Esti-mated	Ac-tual
Revenue:						
Ordinary	17,961	—	15,987	—	—	—
Extraordinary	851	—	404	—	—	—
Total	18,812	15,664	16,391	—	15,702	—
Expenditure:						
Ordinary	13,605	—	12,200	—	—	—
Extraordinary	5,773	—	4,703	—	—	—
Total	19,378	16,540	16,993	—	15,974	—
Deficit	565	876	603	—	272	—
Surplus	—	—	—	—	—	—

Source: Young [36, vol. 2, p. 71].

87   The Ends of Four Big Inflations

Table C3 shows the path of exchange rates and how, after declining until November 1921, the Czechoslovakian crown rapidly gained to about 3 United States cents.

Table C4 shows the price levels. From 1922 to 1923, Czechoslovakia actually experienced a deflation. Indeed, Rasin's initial plan had been to

Table C2   **Note Issue of Banking Office of Czechoslovakia, 1919–24**
                      (in thousands of Czech crowns)

Year	Month	State Notes in Circulation	Year	Month	State Notes in Circulation
1919	April	—		May	9,717,750
	May	—		June	9,838,205
	June	—		July	9,916,077
	July	161,106		August	10,171,383
	August	664,997		September	10,196,880
	September	1,443,570		October	10,139,366
	October	2,512,199		November	9,996,550
	November	3,513,405		December	10,064,049
	December	4,723,303	1923	January	9,222,434
1920	January	5,574,688		February	8,947,988
	February	6,462,825		March	9,157,407
	March	7,216,438		April	9,567,369
	April	7,216,438		May	9,327,676
	May	8,268,695		June	9,375,991
	June	9,729,233		July	9,448,086
	July	9,267,874		August	9,218,475
	August	9,814,920		September	9,311,378
	September	10,310,228		October	9,278,999
	October	10,920,514		November	9,250,688
	November	10,946,653		December	9,598,903
	December	11,288,512	1924	January	8,820,093
1921	January	10,888,319		February	8,506,467
	February	10,914,786		March	8,280,390
	March	10,921,956		April	8,198,653
	April	10,928,560		May	9,078,418
	May	10,851,403		June	8,081,106
	June	11,167,515		July	8,090,034
	July	11,134,327		August	9,139,792
	August	11,455,175		September	8,222,658
	September	11,570,881		October	8,585,847
	October	12,327,159		November	8,500,942
	November	11,871,647		December	8,810,357
	December	12,129,573	1925	January	7,916,540
1922	January	11,230,065		February	7,727,880
	February	10,743,958		March	7,680,867
	March	10,323,069		April	7,525,934
	April	10,075,757			

Source: Young [36, vol. 2, pp. 305–6].

Table C3   **Czechoslovakian Exchange Rates, 1919–24**

Year	Month	Cents per Crown	Year	Month	Cents per Crown
1919	January	—	1922	April	1.960
	February	—		May	1.921
	March	—		June	1.924
	April	6.135		July	2.185
	May	—		August	2.902
	June	—		September	3.231
	July	5.625		October	3.285
	August	4.575		November	3.176
	September	4.575		December	3.097
	October	3.100			
	November	1.950	1923	January	2.856
	December	1.900		February	2.958
				March	2.969
1920	January	1.425		April	2.978
	February	.975		May	2.979
	March	1.275		June	2.993
	April	1.530		July	2.997
	May	2.195		August	2.934
	June	2.335		September	2.995
	July	2.195		October	2.971
	August	1.810		November	2.906
	September	1.535		December	2.925
	October	1.245			
	November	1.165	1924	January	2.898
	December	1.190		February	2.902
				March	2.902
1921	January	1.300		April	2.957
	February	1.290		May	2.939
	March	1.307		June	2.936
	April	1.365		July	2.953
	May	1.460		August	2.979
	June	1.420		September	2.993
	July	1.312		October	2.981
	August	1.225		November	2.989
	September	1.160		December	3.018
	October	1.049			
	November	1.038	1925	January	3.00
	December	1.249		February	2.96
				March	2.97
1922	January	1.732		April	2.96
	February	1.855		May	2.96
	March	1.733		June	2.96

Source: Young [36, vol. 2, p. 307].

89   The Ends of Four Big Inflations

Table C4   Czechoslovakian Wholesale Prices, 1922–24

Year	Month	Wholesale Price Index	Year	Month	Wholesale Price Index
1922	January	1,675		October	973
	February	1,520		November	965
	March	1,552		December	984
	April	1,491	1924	January	974
	May	1,471		February	999
	June	1,471		March	1,021
	July	1,464		April	1,008
	August	1,386		May	1,015
	September	1,155		June	981
	October	1,059		July	953
	November	1,017		August	986
	December	999		September	982
1923	January	1,003		October	999
	February	1,019		November	1,013
	March	1,028		December	1,024
	April	1,031	1925	January	1,045
	May	1,030		February	1,048
	June	1,001		March	1,034
	July	968		April	1,019
	August	958		May	1,006
	September	957			

Source: Young [36, vol. 2, p. 307].
Note: July 1914 = 100.

restore the Czechoslovakia crown to the prewar gold par value of the old Austro-Hungarian crown. Following Rasin's assassination, this plan was abandoned and the crown was stabilized at about 2.96 cents.

2.8 Conclusion

The essential measures that ended hyperinflation in each of Germany, Austria, Hungary, and Poland were, first, the creation of an independent central bank that was legally committed to refuse the government's demand for additional unsecured credit and, second, a simultaneous alteration in the fiscal policy regime.[37] These measures were interrelated and coordinated. They had the effect of binding the government to place its debt with private parties and foreign governments which would value that debt according to whether it was backed by sufficiently large prospective taxes relative to public expenditures. In each case that we have studied, once it became widely understood that the government would not rely on the central bank for its finances, the inflation terminated and the exchanges stabilized. We have further seen that it was not simply the increasing quantity of central bank notes that caused the hyperinflation, since in each case the note circulation continued to grow rapidly after the exchange rate and price level had been stabilized. Rather, it was the growth of fiat currency which was unbacked, or backed only by government bills, which there never was a prospect to retire through taxation.

The changes that ended the hyperinflations were not isolated restrictive actions within a given set of rules of the game or general policy. Earlier attempts to stabilize the exchanges in Hungary under Hegedus,[38] and also in Germany, failed precisely because they did not change the rules of the game under which fiscal policy had to be conducted.[39]

In discussing this subject with various people, I have encountered the view that the events described here are so extreme and bizarre that they do not bear on the subject of inflation in the contemporary United States. On the contrary, it is precisely because the events were so extreme that they are relevant. The four incidents we have studied are akin to laboratory experiments in which the elemental forces that cause and can be used to stop inflation are easiest to spot. I believe that these incidents are full of lessons about our own, less drastic predicament with inflation, if only we interpret them correctly.

Notes

1. "Most economists believe that the underlying inflation rate—roughly defined as wage costs less productivity gains—now stands at 9 to 10 percent, and that only a long period of restraint can reduce that rate significantly" (*Newsweek*, 19 May 1980, p. 59).

2. Paul Samuelson has aptly summarized the rational expectations view: "I should report that there is a new school, the so-called 'rational expectationists.' They are optimistic that inflation can be wiped out with little pain if only the government makes *credible* its determination to do so. But neither history nor reason tempt one to bet their way" (*Newsweek*, 28 April 1980). The second sentence of this quote is probably as shrewd a summary of the rational expectations view as can be made in a single sentence. However, it is difficult to agree with the third sentence: as for "reason," no one denies that logically coherent and well-reasoned models underlie the claims of the "rational expectationists"; as for history, the evidence summarized in this paper is surely relevant.

3. There is actually no such thing as a "rational expectations school" in the sense of a collection of economists with an agreed upon model of the economy and view about optimal monetary and fiscal policy. In fact, among economists who use the assumption of rational expectations there is wide disagreement about these matters. What characterizes adherents of the notion of rational expectations is their intention to build models by assuming that private agents understand the dynamic environment in which they operate approximately as well as do government policymakers. Adherence to this notion leaves ample room for substantial diversity about the many other details of a model. For some examples of rational expectations models with diverse implications, see Lucas [21], Barro [2], Wallace [35], Townsend [34], and Sargent and Wallace [31]. Despite their diversity, it is true that all of these models impel us to think about optimal government policy in substantially different ways than were standard in macroeconomics before the advent of the doctrine of rational expectations in the early 1970s.

91   The Ends of Four Big Inflations

4. Bresciani-Turroni wrote: "Whoever studies the recent economic history of Europe is struck by a most surprising fact: the rapid monetary restoration of some countries where for several years paper money had continually depreciated. In some cases the stabilization of the exchange was not obtained by a continuous effort, prolonged over a period of years, whose effects would show themselves slowly in the progressive economic and financial restoration of the country, as occurred before the War in several well-known cases of monetary reform. Instead, the passing from a period of tempestuous depreciation of the currency to an almost complete stability of the exchange was very sudden" [3, p. 334]. Compare these remarks with the opinion of Samuelson cited in note 2 above.

5. The notes were "backed" mainly by treasury bills which, in those times, could not be expected to be paid off by levying taxes, but only by printing more notes or treasury bills.

6. League of Nations [13, p. 101].

7. Keynes wrote: "It is not lack of gold but the absence of other internal adjustments which prevents the leading European countries from returning to a pre-war gold standard. Most of them have plenty of gold for the purpose as soon as the other conditions favorable to the restoration of a gold standard have returned" (Keynes [11, p. 132]). Writing about Germany in 1923, Keynes said: "The government cannot introduce a sound money, because, in the absence of other revenue, the printing of an unsound money is the only way by which it can live" (Keynes [10, p. 67]).

8. This view can be expressed more precisely by referring to the technical literature of optimum economic growth. I am recommending that a good first model of the gold standard or other commodity money is a real equilibrium growth model in which a government issues debt, makes expenditures, and collects taxes. Examples of these models were studied by Arrow and Kurz [1]. In such models, government debt is valued according to the same economic considerations that give private debt value, namely, the prospective net revenue stream of the institution issuing the debt. A real equilibrium growth model of this kind can also be used to provide a formal rationalization of my claim below that open market operations in private securities, foreign exchange, and gold should have no effect on the price level, i.e. the value of government demand debt.

9. It is relatively straightforward to produce a variety of workable theoretical models of a commodity money or gold standard, along the lines of note 8. It is considerably more difficult to produce a model of a fiat money, which is costless to produce, inconvertible, and of no utility except in exchange. Kareken and Wallace [9], Wallace [35], and Townsend [34] describe some of the ramifications of this observation. The workable models of fiat money that we do have—for example, those of Townsend [34] and Wallace [35]—immediately raise the question of whether voluntarily held fiat money can continue to be valued at all in the face of substantial budget deficits of the order of magnitude studied in this paper. Such models lead one to assign an important role to government restrictions, particularly on foreign exchange transactions, in maintaining a valued, if involuntarily held, fiat money. Keynes [10] and Nichols [24] also emphasized the role of such restrictions.

10. The sweeping implications of this principle for standard ways of formulating and using econometric models were first described by Lucas [19]. The principle itself has emerged in a variety of contexts involving economic dynamics. For some examples, see Lucas [20] and Sargent and Wallace [30].

11. Sargent and Wallace [32] describe a sense in which it might be difficult to imagine that a regime change can occur. As they discovered, thinking about regime changes in the context of rational expectations models soon leads one to issues of free will.

12. The Treaty of St. Germain, signed in September of 1919, required the successor states of the Austro-Hungarian empire to stamp their share of the notes of the Austro-Hungarian bank. The stamp converted those notes to the currency, i.e. debt, of the new states. The Austrian section of the old Austro-Hungarian bank functioned as the central bank of Austria for several years after the war.

13. Needless to say, the central bank encountered a strong demand for loans at this rate and had to ration credit.

14. At the time, some commentators argued that since the real value of currency had decreased and so in a sense currency was scarce, the increased note issue of the central bank was not the prime cause of the inflation. Some even argued that money was "tight" and that the central bank was valiantly struggling to meet the shortage of currency by adding printing presses and employees. This argument is now widely regarded as fallacious by macroeconomists. Disturbingly, however, one hears the very same argument in the contemporary United States.

15. "In Vienna, during the period of collapse, mushroom exchange banks sprang up at every street corner, where you could change your krone into Zurich francs within a few minutes of receiving them, and so avoid the risk of loss during the time it would take you to reach your usual bank. It became a reasonable criticism to allege that a prudent man at a cafe ordering a bock of beer should order a second bock at the same time, even at the expense of drinking it tepid, lest the price should rise meanwhile" (Keynes [10, p. 51]).

16. See Young [36, vol. 2, p. 16]. That a government might want to adopt such measures if it were using inflationary finance was pointed out by Nichols [24].

17. Pasvolsky [25, p. 116].

18. The content of this protocol is highly sensible when it is remembered that the value of a state's currency and other debt, at least under the gold standard, is determined by its ability to back that debt with an appropriate fiscal policy. In this respect, its situation is no different from that of a firm. In 1922, there was widespread concern within and without Austria that its sovereignty was at risk. (See the desperate note delivered by the Austrian minister to the Supreme Council of the Allied governments quoted by Pasvolsky [25, p. 115]). The first protocol aimed to clarify the extent to which Austria remained a political and economic entity capable of backing its debts. A similar protocol was signed at the inception of Hungary's financial reconstruction.

19. It should be noted that for two years the new bank vigorously exercised its authority to control transactions in foreign currency. Only after March 1925 were restrictions on trading foreign exchange removed.

20. This explanation is consistent with the argument advanced by Fama [6]. There is an alternative explanation of these observations that neglects the distinction between inside and outside money, and that interprets the observations in terms of a demand function for the total quantity of "money." For instance, Cagan [4] posited the demand schedule for money to take the form

(1) $$M_t - P_t = \alpha(E_t P_{t+1} - P_t), \qquad \alpha < 0,$$

where P_t is the logarithm of the price level, M_t is the logarithm of the money supply, and $E_t P_{t+1}$ is people's expectation of the log of price next period. There is always a problem in defining an empirical counterpart to M_t, but it is often taken to be the note and deposit liabilities of the central bank or "high-powered" money. The money demand schedule or "portfolio balance" schedule incorporates the idea that people want to hold less wealth in the form of real balances the faster the currency is expected to depreciate. Equation (1) can be solved to give an expression for the equilibrium price level of the form

(2) $$P_t = \frac{1}{1-\alpha} \sum_{i=0}^{\infty} \left(\frac{\alpha}{\alpha-1}\right)^i E_t M_{t+i},$$

where $E_t M_{t+i}$ is what at time t people expect the money supply to be at time $t+i$.

Consider the following two experiments. First, suppose that the government engages in a policy, *which everyone knows in advance*, of making the money supply grow at the constant high rate $\mu > 0$ from time 0 to time $T-1$, and then at the rate zero from time T onward. In this case, the inflation rate would follow the path depicted in figure 2.N.1.

For the second experiment, suppose that initially everyone expected the money supply to increase at the constant rate μ forever but that at time T it becomes known that henceforth the money supply will increase at the rate 0 forever. In this case, the inflation rate takes a

93   The Ends of Four Big Inflations

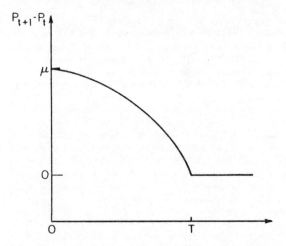

Fig. 2.N.1   Inflation path with an expected decrease in money supply
                        growth from μ to 0 at time *T*.

sudden drop at time *T*, as shown by the path in figure 2.N.2. Now since the inflation and the
expected inflation rate experience a sudden drop at *T* in this case, it follows from equation
(1) that real balances must increase at *T*. This will require a sudden once and for all *drop* in
the price level at *T*.

   This second example of a previously unexpected decrease in the inflation rate provides
the material for an explanation of the growth of the money supplies after currency stabilization. In the face of a previously unexpected, sudden, and permanent drop in the rate of
money creation, the only way to avoid a sudden drop in the price level would be to

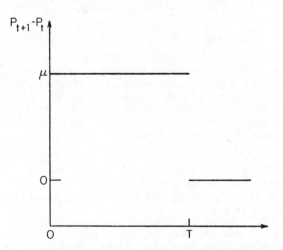

Fig. 2.N.2   Inflation path with a previously unexpected decrease in money
                        supply growth from μ to 0 at time *T*.

accompany the *decrease* in the rate of money creation with a once and for all *increase* in the money supply. In order to *stabilize* the price level in the face of a decreased rate of change of money, the level of the money supply must jump upward once and for all.

What actually occurred in the four countries studied here was not a once and for all jump but a gradual increase in the money supply over many months. This could be reconciled with the observations within the model (1) if people were assumed only gradually to catch on to the fact of stabilization and to decrease the rate of inflation that they expected as the currency stabilization continued to hold. I find this explanation hard to accept, but it is a possibility.

An alternative way to reconcile the preceding explanation with the gradual upward movement of "high-powered" money after the stabilizations is to add adjustment lags to the portfolio balance schedule (1). For example, consider replacing (1) with

$$(1')\qquad (M_t - P_t) = \alpha(E_t P_{t+1} - P_t) + \lambda(M_{t-1} - P_{t-1})$$

$$\alpha < 0,\ 0 < \lambda < 1.$$

In this case, an abrupt stabilization of expected inflation induces only a gradual adjustment of real balances upward at the rate of $1 - \lambda$ per period. My own preference at this point is for an explanation that stresses the distinction between backed and unbacked money.

21. See Pasvolsky [25, p. 161].

22. See Pasvolsky [25, p. 298].

23. Within a year and a half, these became a claim on gold as Britain returned to the gold standard.

24. Unlike Austria, Hungary, and Germany, Poland did not owe war reparations.

25. *League of Nations* [13, p. 111].

26. *Ibid.*, p. 108.

27. See the account in Paxton [26, pp. 146–50].

28. Also see Graham [7, pp. 40–41].

29. Keynes wrote: "A government can live for a long time, even the German government or the Russian government, by printing paper money . . . A government can live by this means when it can live by no other" (Keynes [10, p. 47]).

30. See Young [36, vol. 1, p. 402] and Bresciani-Turroni [3, p. 345].

31. After reading an earlier draft of this paper, John Kennan directed me to the following passage in Constance Reid's biography of the mathematician Hilbert: "In 1923 the inflation ended abruptly through the creation of a new unit of currency called the Rentenmark. Although Hilbert remarked sceptically, 'One cannot solve a problem by changing the name of the independent variable,' the stability of conditions was gradually restored" (Reid [27, pp. 162–63]).

32. Young [36, vol. 1, p. 421].

33. Young [36, vol. 1, p. 422].

34. See Graham [7, chapter 12].

35. Theoretical models of money along the lines proposed by Samuelson [29] predict that too much capital will be accumulated when the government fiscal policy is so profligate that money becomes valueless. See Samuelson [29] and Wallace [35].

36. The frontiers were closed to prevent notes from Austria and Hungary from entering the country. The Treaty of St. Germain, signed 10 September 1919, provided that the successor states should stamp the Austro-Hungarian notes, signifying their assumption of the debt.

37. Of inflationary finance, Keynes wrote: "It is common to speak as though, when a government pays its way by inflation, the people of the country avoid taxation. We have seen this is not so. What is raised by printing notes is just as much taken from the public as is beer-duty or an income-tax. What a government spends the public pay for. There is no such thing as an uncovered deficit. But in some countries it seems possible to please and content the public, for a time at least, by giving them, in return for the taxes they pay, finely

95   The Ends of Four Big Inflations

engraved acknowledgments on water-marked paper. The income tax receipts, which we in England receive from the surveyor, we throw into the wastepaper basket; in Germany they call them bank-notes and put them into their pocketbooks; in France they are termed Rentes and are locked up in the family safe" (Keynes [10, pp. 68–69]).

38. See Pasvolsky [25, pp. 304–7].

39. A deep objection to the interpretation in this paragraph can be constructed along the lines of Sargent and Wallace [30], who argue that for a single economy it is impossible to conceive of a rational expectations model in which there can occur a change in regime. In particular, the substantial changes in ways of formulating monetary and fiscal policy associated with the ends of the four inflations studied here can themselves be considered to have been caused by the economic events preceding them. On this interpretation, what we have interpreted as changes in the regime were really only the realization of events and human responses under a single, more complicated regime. This more complicated regime would have to be described in a considerably more involved and "state contingent" way than the simple regimes we have described. I believe that the data of this paper could be described using this view, but that it would substantially complicate the language and require extensive qualifications without altering the main practical implications.

References

1. Arrow, K. J., and Mordecai, K. 1970. *Public investment, the rate of return, and optimal fiscal policy*. Baltimore and London: John Hopkins University Press.

2. Barro, R. J. 1974. Are government bonds net wealth? *Journal of Political Economy* 82, no. 6 (November/December): 1095–1118.

3. Bresciani-Turroni, C. 1937. *The economics of inflation*. London: George Allen & Unwin.

4. Cagan, P. 1956. The monetary dynamics of hyperinflation. In M. Friedman, ed., *Studies in the quantity of money*. Chicago: University of Chicago Press.

5. de Bordes, J. v. W. 1924. *The Austrian crown*. London: P. S. King & Son.

6. Fama, E. F. 1980. Banking in the theory of finance. *Journal of Monetary Economics* 6, no. 1 (January): 39–58.

7. Graham, F. D. 1930. *Exchange, prices, and production in hyperinflation: Germany, 1920–23*. New York: Russell & Russell.

8. Kareken, J. H., and Wallace, N. 1980. *Models of monetary economics*. Minneapolis: Federal Reserve Bank of Minneapolis.

9. Kareken, J. H., and Wallace, N. 1980. Introduction to *Kareken and Wallace* [8].

10. Keynes, J. M. 1924. *Monetary reform*. New York: Harcourt, Brace & Co.

11. Keynes, J. M. 1925. The United States and gold. In Young [36, vol. 1, pp. 131–33].

12. Layton, W. T., and Rist, C. 1925. *The economic situation of Austria.* Report presented to the Council of the League of Nations, Geneva, 19 August.

13. League of Nations. 1946. *The course and control of inflation.* Geneva.

14. League of Nations. 1926. *The financial reconstruction of Austria.* General Survey and Principal Documents, Geneva.

15. League of Nations. 1926. *The financial reconstruction of Hungary.* General Survey and Principal Documents. Geneva.

16. League of Nations. 1926. *Memorandum on currency and central banks, 1913–1925,* vol. 1. Geneva.

17. League of Nations. 1927. *Memorandum on public finance (1922–1926).* Geneva.

18. League of Nations. 1925. *Memorandum on currency and central banks, 1913–1924,* vol. 1. Geneva.

19. Lucas, R. E., Jr. 1976. Econometric policy evaluation: A critique. In K. Brunner and A. H. Meltzer, eds., *The Phillips curve and labor markets,* pp. 19–46. Carnegie-Rochester Conference Series on Public Policy, Vol. 1. Amsterdam: North-Holland.

20. Lucas, R. E., Jr. 1972. Econometric testing of the natural rate hypothesis. In O. Eckstein, ed., *The Econometrics of Price Determination Conference.* Washington: Board of Governors, Federal Reserve System.

21. Lucas, R. E., Jr. 1980. Equilibrium in a pure currency economy. In Kareken and Wallace [8].

22. Lucas, R. E., Jr., and Sargent, T. J. 1979. After Keynesian economics. Federal Reserve Bank of Minneapolis, *Quarterly Review,* spring.

23. Lucas, R. E., Jr., and Sargent, T. J. 1981. Rational expectations and econometric practice. Introductory essay to R. E. Lucas, Jr., and T. J. Sargent, eds., *Rational expectations and econometric practice.* Minneapolis: University of Minnesota Press.

24. Nichols, D. 1974. Some principles of inflationary finance. *Journal of Political Economy* 82, no. 2, part 1 (March/April): 423–30.

25. Pasvolsky, L. 1928. *Economic nationalism of the Danubian states.* New York: Macmillan.

26. Paxton, R. O. 1975. *Europe in the twentieth century.* New York: Harcourt Brace Jovanovich.

27. Reid, C. 1979. *Hilbert.* New York: Springer-Verlag.

28. Salemi, M. K. 1976. Hyperinflation, exchange depreciation, and the demand for money in post World War I Germany. Ph.D. thesis, University of Minnesota.

29. Samuelson, P. A. 1958. An exact consumption-loan model of interest with or without the social contrivance of money. *Journal of Political Economy* 66 (December): 467–82.

30. Sargent, T. J. 1980. Rational expectations and the reconstruction of macroeconomics. Federal Reserve Bank of Minneapolis. *Quarterly Review*, summer.
31. Sargent, T. J., and Wallace, N. 1975. Rational expectations, the optimal monetary instrument, and the optimal money supply rule. *Journal of Political Economy* 83, no. 2 (April).
32. Sargent, T. J., and Wallace, N. 1976. Rational expectations and the theory of economic policy. *Journal of Monetary Economics* 2, no. 2 (April): 169–83.
33. *Statistiches Jahrbuch fur das Deutsche Reich*. 1924/25.
34. Townsend, R. M. 1980. Models of money with spatially separated agents. In Kareken and Wallace [8].
35. Wallace, N. 1980. The overlapping generations model of fiat money. In Kareken and Wallace [8].
36. Young, J. P. 1925. *European currency and finance*. vols. 1 and 2. (Commission of Gold and Silver Inquiry, United States Senate, serial 9.) Washington: Government Printing Office.

Part II
Inflations before 1900

[4]

Cagan's Hypothesis and the First Nationwide Inflation of Paper Money in World History

Francis T. Lui

University of Minnesota

I. Introduction

More than 25 years ago, Phillip Cagan proposed the hypothesis that the demand for real cash balances depended mainly on the expected rate of inflation, provided that the monetary sector was sufficiently isolated from changes in the real sector (Cagan 1956). To test his hypothesis, Cagan studied seven hyperinflations in modern Europe, during which variations in the real variables were negligible compared with the astronomical increases in prices. It is well known that he got confirmatory results from his studies. However, until recently, it has not been realized that the same hypothesis is also strongly supported by data from a very different socioeconomic context, namely, the first nationwide inflation of paper money in world history.

Paper money was invented in China in the Northern Sung dynasty (A.D. 960–1126) and widely used in the Southern Sung dynasty (A.D. 1127–1278). The first inflation on a national scale occurred from around 1190 to the end of the dynasty when the monetary system collapsed. In this inflation period, available historical records do not suggest significant expansion of the economy or important changes in real income. Modern financial assets such as bonds and equities did

Part of this note is based on an undergraduate term paper that I wrote for a Chinese history course by the late Professor Edward Kracke. Comments and suggestions by John Chipman, Thomas Sargent, Neil Wallace, and the referee are gratefully acknowledged. I am particularly indebted to Edward Prescott, who encouraged me to publish the results in this note. Thanks are also due to Yim Fai Luk, who made some materials used here accessible to me. Remaining errors are of course mine.

[*Journal of Political Economy*, 1983, vol. 91, no. 6]

not yet exist. The real return of holding gold and silver did not seem to fluctuate very much.[1] However, from 1190 to 1240, the supply of paper money and the price level increased more than 6 and 20 times, respectively. In short, although the inflation was not high enough to be called hyperinflation in the modern sense of the word, fluctuations of the real variables then were small relative to changes in the monetary sector. The conditions needed by Cagan's hypothesis were thus still fulfilled. Other than these similar economic conditions, Sung China was drastically different from the modern European environment in culture, social institutions, and technology. If the Cagan hypothesis is supported by evidence from this ancient inflation, then we shall have much greater confidence in its generality. In fact, this will then be another proof that the usefulness of modern economic theory often transcends cultural and historical boundaries.

The novelty of this paper is to present the results of testing the Cagan hypothesis using the Sung inflation data. But before that is done, to make interpretation of the results easier, I shall outline the historical background of paper money. This brief survey is not meant to be original. Other authoritative studies are available (e.g., Yang 1952). The sources and methods of obtaining the data will be discussed in the Appendix.

II. Historical Background

The origin of paper money was often attributed to the *fei-ch'ien* ("flying money") of the T'ang dynasty (A.D. 618–907). The *fei-ch'ien* was in fact only a draft to send money to other places and therefore was not money in the proper sense.

The first true paper money was the *chiao-tzu*, or "exchange medium," which appeared as late as the Northern Sung dynasty. Before this time, iron coins had been the main form of money circulating in the province of Szechwan in central China. During the early years of the dynasty, when Szechwan had just been conquered, copper coins were not allowed to enter the province. Later, the law was abolished, but iron coins remained the main currency in Szechwan. The heavy weight and clumsiness of the coins led people to deposit them in some proto-banks and use the receipts for financial transactions. Many historians believe that these receipts were the origin of paper money. During the reign of Emperor Chen-tsung (998–1023), the governor of Szechwan allowed 16 rich families to form a union to

---

[1] From the second half of the twelfth century to the first half of the thirteenth, the value of gold relative to rice increased only 3 percent, and the value of silver relative to rice decreased 9 percent (see Peng 1965, pp. 506, 512).

CONFIRMATIONS AND CONTRADICTIONS 1069

issue these receipts, which were then called the *chiao-tzu.* Around 1023, these families were no longer rich enough to back up the *chiao-tzu.* The provincial government then decided to take control and set up a *chiao-tzu* bureau. This marked the beginning of government monopoly of paper money.

It should be pointed out that the *chiao-tzu* and, later on, some other forms of paper money were used only in Szechwan and a few other areas during the first century after the invention. Paper money had not yet become a national currency. Metal money coexisted with the latter and continued to be widely used throughout the whole country.

After 1127, most of northern China was conquered by the Nu-chen Tartars, who established the Chin dynasty. The Sung Empire shrank to almost half its former size and had to move its capital to the city of modern Hangchow. In the first 3 or 4 decades after the move south, many kinds of money, including several forms of paper money, circulated in the economy. The monetary system was in disarray.

In 1161, a new kind of paper money, the *hui-tzu,* or "check medium," was issued. The new emperor, Hsiao-tsung (1163–90), soon decided that the government should carefully regulate the supply of *hui-tzu.* The law that those who made counterfeit money should be beheaded was reinstituted and enforced. There were specialists to examine the *hui-tzu* when people exchanged the old ones for the new in government offices. The emperor also tried to make sure that there were enough reserves and that the quantity of *hui-tzu* was not too large. The emperor spent so much effort to regulate the *hui-tzu* that he lamented, "*Hui-tzu* have made me unable to sleep well for ten years" (Hung 1934, p. 8a).

The government's careful regulation and promotion of the *hui-tzu* produced two effects. First, the exchange rate between *hui-tzu* and copper coins was kept constant for more than 20 years. It was only after the 1180s that the exchange rate became variable (see the App.). Second, the *hui-tzu* were soon widely used around the capital. Gradually they spread to neighboring provinces until they were used throughout the entire empire with the exception of Szechwan, which had its own paper currency. Unlike earlier forms of paper money, which were used only in restricted locations, the *hui-tzu* became a truly national currency probably before the end of the twelfth century.

The policy of strict control on the *hui-tzu* supply could not last long. Because of financial difficulties and wars against the Nu-chen Tartars and later on against the Mongols in the thirteenth century, the government resorted to an inflationary policy. Since the *hui-tzu* were then used throughout almost the whole empire, the inflation from the second half of the twelfth century onward was indeed the first nationwide inflation of paper money in world history. Section III will examine the data of the period and show that Cagan's hypothesis is supported.

III. Empirical Results

The model studied by Cagan can be expressed as follows:

$$\ln \frac{M_t}{P_t} = \alpha E_t + \gamma, \tag{1}$$

where M_t is money supply at time t, P_t is price level at time t, E_t is the expected rate of inflation at time t given information available at time t, α and γ are constants, and α must be negative. The model used in this paper, which is a variant of Cagan's, assumes the following expression for E_t:

$$E_t = \beta \ln \frac{P_t}{P_{t-1}} + (1 - \beta)E_{t-1} \quad \text{for } 0 \leq \beta \leq 1. \tag{2}$$

If we further make the strong assumption that $\beta = 1$, that is, expected inflation depends only on current inflation, then equation (1) becomes

$$\ln \frac{M_t}{P_t} = \alpha \ln \frac{P_t}{P_{t-1}} + \gamma. \tag{3}$$

Table 1 presents the data for the estimation of α and γ; M_t is the index of supply of *hui-tzu*. We use the price of rice as a proxy for the aggregate price level, since rice was the most important commodity at the time.

TABLE 1

SUNG DYNASTY INFLATION

Period	Index of Money Supply (M_t)	Index of Price Level (P_t)	$\ln \dfrac{M_t}{P_t}$	$\ln \dfrac{P_t}{P_{t-1}}$
1161–70	100	100		
1171–80	204	86.7	.856	−.14
1181–90	224	107.3	.736	.21
1191–1200	827	183.9	1.503	.54
1201–10	1,429	279.8	1.631	.42
1211–20	2,347	280.2	2.125	0
1221–30	2,755	335.5	2.106	.18
1240	4,949	4,032.2	.205	1.66

SOURCES.—See App. for sources and derivation of data.

NOTE.—The money-supply data are midperiod data. Prices used are averages for each period since midperiod price data are not all available. It is assumed that the average price of a period is equal to the midperiod price. In computing the inflation rate between 1221–30 and 1240, the time span used is 1.5 periods.

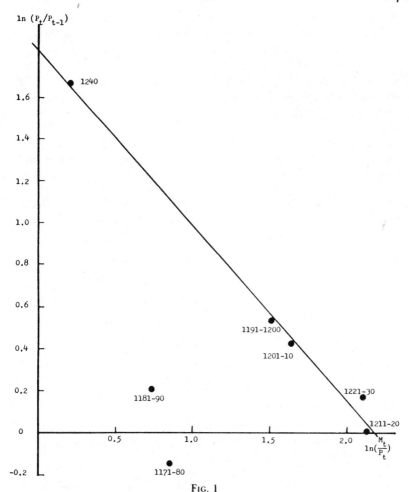

Fɪɢ. 1

After ln (M_t/P_t) is plotted against ln (P_t/P_{t-1}), as in figure 1, it can immediately be seen that the observations for the last 5 periods lie very closely along a straight line, while the first two observations are outliers. Two explanations suggest that these two outliers should be omitted from the least-squares regression.

First, in the earlier periods, *hui-tzu* were used only near the capital. The demand for real balances was therefore lower than in later periods when paper money was used throughout the whole country. Hence, the data of the first 2 periods are not comparable with those of the last 5.

Second, to isolate the monetary sector from the real sector, we need an economy that is not growing too fast. Much historical evidence suggests that the first half of the Southern Sung dynasty was generally characterized by expansion, especially during the relatively prosperous reign of Hsiao-tsung (1163–90). The conquest of north China by the Nu-chen Tartars initiated a series of mass migration to the south. For example, from 1160 to 1166 alone, the number of recorded households increased as much as 8 percent. In fact, China's economic center of gravity was then shifting to the south. However, during the second half of the dynasty, the expansion ceased. Famines and wars were frequent, and the migration came almost to a complete halt. Since the 1170s and 1180s were part of the expansion period, it is unwise to include these two observations in the regression. On the other hand, the last five observations were in the stagnancy period and so fulfill the condition mentioned above. Therefore, these observations only are used in the regression.

The regression results are as follows:

$$\ln \frac{M_t}{P_t} = \underset{(.0715)}{-1.199} \ \ln \frac{P_t}{P_{t-1}} + \underset{(.0577)}{2.186}, \tag{4}$$

$$R^2 = .9894, \text{SE} = .0931.$$

The values in parentheses are standard errors.

It can be seen that the estimated coefficient of α is significantly negative (with a t-value as high as -16.76), a fact consistent with the model. The high R^2 indicates that a single variable, the expected rate of inflation, can explain most of the variations in the demand for real balances.[2] Given the crudeness of historical data and the small number of observations that we have, it is remarkable that Cagan's model fits the 1190–1240 inflation so well.

However, there is an important difference between the results just presented and Cagan's. In computing the results of equation (4), note that the data for the inflation rates represent a decade. In Cagan's paper, data used are monthly inflation rates. As can readily be shown, if we change the data to monthly rates, the corresponding coefficient in equation (4) will be 120 times that of α, that is, around -144. Cagan's study found comparable coefficients ranging from -2.3 to -8.7. It is necessary to find explanations to account for the much larger coefficient in the Sung dynasty inflation.[3]

---

[2] The 1240 observation contributes much to the nice fit of the regression line. It should be pointed out that even without this observation (there is of course no a priori reason to omit it), we still have 98 percent confidence that α is negative. There is also no significant change in the estimate for α. The high inflation rate in 1240 was due largely to wars and famines, which occurred more often after the 1230s until the collapse of the dynasty.

[3] The large coefficient implies a very flat demand curve of paper money. But it does

A natural step is to consider whether there is specification bias in the estimation of α due to omitting some demand-shifting variables. As mentioned above, real income was relatively stable in the period under study. Real returns to holding precious metals did not change much. Paper money by that time was already used more or less throughout the whole country, and therefore there would not be any big expansion of the area of circulation. Hence, these variables could not shift the demand curve sufficiently to produce a large specification bias.

Another way to explain the large coefficient is to note that, unlike the inflations in Cagan's study, metal coins, which were close substitutes of paper money, were also extensively used in the Sung dynasty.[4] It is difficult to know what the "correct" coefficient should be in an environment where there were close substitutes. Nevertheless, it is interesting to compare this coefficient with those from other inflations where close substitutes of paper money also existed. One such example was the inflation in Rhode Island from 1720 to 1750. Paper money was used at that time, but the specie was also in wide circulation. If equation (3) is applied to the data given in Weiss (1970), the estimate for the coefficient with respect to the *monthly* inflation, though not significant, is around − 170, a value even larger than that of the Sung inflation.[5] It does not seem to be necessary to dismiss our estimate of α on the ground that it is too high to be in the correct range.

Appendix

The materials and data in this paper are based on many original documents and several important secondary sources. The *Sung Shih*, especially volumes 180 and 181, and Ma Tuan-lin (1936) provide much of the useful information for Section II. Robert Hartwell (1964) lists many of the primary sources containing information on paper money.

Several secondary works in Chinese have been extensively used. They are Ch'üan (1938), Chang (1957), Peng (1965), and Katō (1944).

The data on money supply are those from Ch'üan (1938, p. 196). The quantity of *hui-tzu* in the base period (1161–70) was 9.8 million strings. The figures for 1191–1200 and 1240 are arithmetic interpolations. If geometric

---

not imply that a particular point on this demand curve of the Sung dynasty is more elastic than points on the demand curves of Cagan's seven hyperinflations. From eq. (1), the elasticity of the demand for real balances with respect to the expected rate of inflation is αE_t. The average of the elasticities in the Sung dynasty is around 0.63, while comparable averages for the seven hyperinflations range from around 1.3 to 20.

[4] If paper money and metal coins were perfectly substitutable, then money supply would be the sum of coins and paper money. However, since the rates of exchange between the two are variable, we can regard them as two different assets. It is therefore meaningful to talk about the demand for paper money.

[5] The *t*-value is only − 1.8. Money supply per capita is used instead of total money supply.

interpolations are used instead, the estimated results are not as good, but the R^2 is still .94.

Most of the price data are reconstructed from Peng (1965, chap. 5.5). In the base period (1161–70), the price of rice was 2.48 strings per *shih*. The data given in Peng are in units of cash per 100 liters. To be consistent with data from other sources, we have to transform the units back to strings per *shih*. It is known that one (Sung) *shih* equals 66.41 liters. The value of *hui-tzu* changed over time with respect to copper cash. The following information can be reconstructed from the sources quoted above and from Yang (1952): in 1161–80, 1 string = 770 cash; in 1181–90, 1 string = 750 cash; in 1191–1200 and 1201–10, 1 string = 620 cash; in 1210, 1 string = 400 cash; in around 1260, the official rate (which was considerably higher than the market rate) was 1 string = 250 cash. Geometric interpolations are used to compute the rates for 2 periods so that in 1215, 1 string = 381 cash, and in 1225, 1 string = 347 cash. The figure for 1215 should be quite accurate, but the 1225 figure is probably too high. Perhaps this is why the 1225 observation deviates from the regression line more than the other points. Geometric interpolations for 1235 and 1240 will not be accurate. Fortunately, we have direct information on the 1240 figure in terms of strings per *shih* from original sources.

References

Cagan, Phillip. "The Monetary Dynamics of Hyperinflation." In *Studies in the Quantity Theory of Money*, edited by Milton Friedman. Chicago: Univ. Chicago Press, 1956.

Chang, Chia-chü. *Liang Sung Ching-chi Chung-hsin Ti Nan-i* [The southward movement of the economic center of gravity in the two Sung dynasties]. Wuhan: Hupei People's Press, 1957.

Ch'üan, Han-shêng. "The Inflation at the End of the Sung Dynasty and Its Effects on Prices." In Academia Sinica, *Li-shih Yü-yen Yen-chiu-so Chi-k'an* [Bulletin of the Institute of History and Philology] 10 (1938): 193–222.

Hartwell, Robert. *A Guide to Sources of Chinese Economic History, A.D. 618–1368*. Chicago: Univ. Chicago, Committee on Far Eastern Civilizations, 1964.

Hung, Mai. *Jung-chai San-pi*. Ssŭ-pu t'sung-k'an hsü-pien, vol. 337, bk. 14. Shanghai: Commercial Press, 1934.

Katō, Shigeru. *T'ang-Sung Shih-tai Chin-yin Chih Yen-chiu* [Study of gold and silver in the T'ang and Sung dynasties]. Chinese translation. Peking: Chung-kuo lien-huo chun-pei yin-hang, 1944.

Ma, Tuan-lin. *Wen-hsien T'ung-k'ao*. Vol. 9. Shanghai: Commercial Press, 1936.

Peng, Hsin-wei. *Chung-kuo Huo-pi Shih* [A monetary history of China]. 3d ed. Shanghai: Shanghai People's Press, 1965.

Sung Shih [Sung dynastic records]. Peking: Chung-hua shu-chü, 1977.

Weiss, Roger. "The Issue of Paper Money in the American Colonies, 1720–1774." *J. Econ. Hist.* 30 (December 1970): 770–84.

Yang, Lien-shêng. *Money and Credit in China: A Short History*. Cambridge, Mass.: Harvard Univ. Press, 1952.

[5]

Some Colonial Evidence on Two Theories of Money: Maryland and the Carolinas

Bruce D. Smith

Federal Reserve Bank of Minneapolis and Carnegie-Mellon University

Recent developments in monetary economics stress the nature of monetary injections, emphasizing that they have implications for the relationship between money and prices. In contrast, traditional approaches posit stable money demand functions that are independent of how money is injected. The former approach implies that certain proportionality relations between money and prices need not obtain. This permits the two approaches to be empirically distinguished, but only if an appropriate "experiment" is conducted. The colonial period is one such experiment. Colonial evidence suggests that the nature of injections is crucial to the effect on prices of changes in the money supply.

One of the most profound recent developments in monetary theory has been a rethinking of how the value of money is determined. In particular, Sargent (1982) and Wallace (1981) have stressed the importance of how money is introduced in determining its value. This contrasts strongly with the view that the value of money is determined by its quantity (or time path) in conjunction with a demand function

The views expressed herein are those of the author and not necessarily those of the Federal Reserve Bank of Minneapolis or the Federal Reserve System. In writing this paper I have had the benefit of extensive conversations with John McCusker, Russ Menard, Tom Sargent, and Neil Wallace. In addition, I would like to thank an anonymous referee for helpful suggestions; Jacob Price for providing me with data on the Maryland sinking fund; the participants of the Monetary and Financial Theory and Policy Conference at the University of Western Ontario (April 1985); and the participants of seminars at Boston College, the Federal Reserve Bank of Richmond, Indiana University, Northwestern University, the University of Wisconsin, and Yale University for their comments. None of these individuals is responsible for any errors or for the views stated herein.

[*Journal of Political Economy*, 1985, vol. 93, no. 6]

for money that is quite stable over time and reasonably invariant with respect to the nature of monetary injections (contractions). The Sargent-Wallace view suggests that one can expect to find in history large monetary expansions (contractions) that were not accompanied by eroding (increasing) currency values if these expansions were produced in an appropriate way. Thus one expects to find historical instances that permit the quantity theory of money to be contrasted with that of Sargent and Wallace.

In fact, several such instances have been examined that provide indirect support for the Sargent-Wallace approach. Sargent (1982) discusses how four hyperinflations were ended by a change in the nature of backing for currency despite continued high rates of growth in the money supply. Riley and McCusker (1983) document sustained per capita growth in the money supply of France (1650–1788) while price levels fell. Also Smith (1985) presents evidence from some of the British colonies in North America (1720–70) that both very rapid growth and contraction of money stocks occurred without resulting in price level changes or exchange rate movements. This is attributed to the nature of backing for money, and cross-sectional evidence from several of the colonies is produced to show (*a*) that better backing of currencies resulted in more stable currency values and (*b*) that when backing was relatively amply provided relative rates of growth in the money stock across colonies were not strongly related to relative rates of inflation or currency depreciation.

This paper is an attempt both to expand the body of evidence against the quantity theory and, for the first time, to present some direct evidence on the Sargent-Wallace approach. In particular, Smith (1985) examined primarily Massachusetts, Rhode Island, New York, Pennsylvania, New Jersey, and Virginia. This paper examines price levels and exchange rates in the Carolinas and shows that they are poorly accounted for by changes in the money supplies of those colonies. It then turns to an examination of the monetary system of Maryland, which is particularly well suited to provide direct evidence for or against the Sargent-Wallace approach to determining the value of money. The experience of the colony turns out to be generally supportive of the Sargent-Wallace view.

The reason for focusing on Maryland derives from the nearly unique method adopted by that colony for backing its currency. Each of the colonies (at least ostensibly) backed its currency in some manner. Typically, currencies were backed either with future tax receipts or with mortgages (usually on land or metal plate). A time path for the value of this backing is generally impossible to obtain from existing data. However, Maryland backed the largest component of its note issues with the proceeds of a sinking fund invested in Bank of

England stock. At preannounced dates (which were met in practice) some portion of the outstanding stock of these notes was to be converted into sterling (or, more precisely, sterling bills of exchange, described below) at a specified rate. Thus a large component of Maryland paper money was a claim to future delivery of sterling. As the Sargent-Wallace view suggests that the value of money can be determined in essentially the same way as the value of privately issued claims, as Maryland notes were a claim against the sinking fund, and as there are fairly complete data on the market value of this sinking fund, a particularly appropriate setting is provided in which to gather some empirical evidence on the Sargent-Wallace view.

The results of the paper are as follows. The quantity of money in circulation does not account well for the time path of prices or exchange rates. In South Carolina, for instance, the per capita stock of paper money more than tripled from 1755 to 1760. The price level increased 7 percent over this same period, while exchange rates between South Carolina currency and sterling remained constant. From 1760 to 1770, on the other hand, the per capita paper money stock declined by 63 percent. The price level rose 1 percent, and exchange rates depreciated 2 percent. Similarly, from 1760 to 1768 the per capita stock of paper money in North Carolina was halved, while the exchange rate between North Carolina currency and sterling appreciated only 5 percent. (There are no existing price indices for North Carolina at this time.) It will be argued that these facts are irreconcilable with the quantity theory.

Evidence shows that the Sargent-Wallace approach finds much more support in the data. Regression results indicate that the quantity of money in circulation in Maryland had no effect on exchange rates. However, both the value of the sinking fund and variables relating to Maryland's track record for redeeming notes on schedule affect the exchange rate strongly and with signs that corroborate the Sargent-Wallace viewpoint. Thus the overall picture arising from the evidence presented here is that the value of money in the colonial period appears to have been determined in much the same way as is the value of privately issued liabilities.

The format of the paper is as follows. Section I provides a brief description of the important features of colonial monetary arrangements. Sections II and III discuss the alternative theories of money that are under consideration here. Section IV discusses the experiences of the Carolinas with regard to currency values and shows that they are inconsistent with the quantity theory. Section V examines the relation between currency values and the value of backing for currency in Maryland. Section VI presents conclusions.

I. Colonial Monetary Arrangements

The term "money" applied to the colonies has been used in different ways by different authors. At its broadest the term "money" includes specie, various kinds of paper money, monetized commodities (i.e., commodities that were legal tender as well as circulating warehouse receipts for commodities), bills of exchange (circulating, privately issued liabilities), and book credit extended by merchants. Of these, contemporary usage included in the term only specie, paper money, and commodity monies. In this section I provide an overview of these various assets as a prelude to examining how the two theories discussed above fit the data.

Local units of account in each colony were pounds colonial currency.[1] There were flexible exchange rates between the currency of each colony and sterling. Colonial currency itself took two forms. One was specie. The specie circulating in North America at this time was coined primarily in Spanish and Portuguese colonies and was denominated in the units of account of those colonies. The amount in circulation was outside of colonial control, being determined by trade flows and the specie holdings of immigrants.

The currency denominated in the local unit of account was paper currency, which was issued in amounts determined by the legislature of each colony (subject to approval of colonial governors, proprietors, and the crown). This paper took two forms: bills of credit issued by colonial institutions known as loan offices or land banks and bills of credit issued directly by colonial treasuries. Notes issued by treasuries were used to cover shortfalls of tax receipts, and these notes were introduced into the economy by direct payment for goods or services provided to the government. One exception to this statement is that Maryland injected some notes via lump-sum transfers.

Notes issued by loan offices were introduced in a more complex way. In the colonies and period under consideration there were no private banks. Rather, most colonies operated land banks, which issued notes that were lent to private individuals and secured by mortgages on land or on plate. The interest rates charged on these loans appear generally to have been below market rates. In addition, a number of rules governed operation of these loan offices, which were meant to provide secure backing for the notes. These included provisions that the amount lent by the loan office was not to exceed half the value of the property mortgaged.[2]

---

[1] Except in Maryland after 1766, where dollars became the unit of account.

[2] This practice of issuing notes backed by land may appear reminiscent of the real-bills doctrine. However, the quantity of notes issued was fixed exogenously by colonial legislatures.

The notes issued in these two ways were (as has been pointed out) the only types of currency actually denominated in the local unit of account. For much of the period under consideration they were legal tender. Colonial governments were obligated to accept these notes at face value in payment of taxes and in repayment of loans issued by colonial land banks. In addition, in the colonies at hand they were issued specifically to provide a medium of exchange in the light of the shortcomings of commodity monies and the problems attendant on the use of specie as a medium of exchange.[3]

It should also be noted that although many authors refer to these notes as fiat money, all colonial note issues were (at least ostensibly) backed in some manner. In the case of notes issued by loan offices, as the principal of a loan was repaid provisions were made for its retirement at specified dates. In the event of default, mortgaged property was to be seized and auctioned off and the proceeds used to retire notes. Notes issued by colonial treasuries were backed by future tax receipts. In particular, at the time such a note issue was authorized, future taxes were earmarked to be used to retire the notes. This system was meant to prevent the accumulation of any long-term government debt, although as we will see, different governments backed their notes with greater or lesser degrees of scrupulousness.

In addition to specie and paper currency, each of the colonies examined in this paper had a commodity money system. In Maryland tobacco was legal tender. Until 1747 people trading in tobacco used the actual commodity in transactions. After 1747 Maryland introduced a system of colonial warehouses and the use of tobacco notes, which were simply negotiable warehouse receipts for tobacco stored. In North Carolina several commodities were legal tender, and the government of the colony established rates at which each was to be accepted in payments due the government. Unlike most other colonies, which discontinued their commodity money systems when sufficient paper money had been issued, this arrangement persisted in North Carolina throughout much of the period in question.

In addition to these types of money, some historians include book credit and bills of exchange as part of the colonial "transactions media." Book credit was simply credit extended by merchants to customers, and bills of exchange were circulating, privately issued

---

[3] There were several such problems. One is that much of the specie circulating in North America was badly worn and underweight. Hence it was necessary to compensate for this in transactions. A second is that much specie circulated in relatively large denominations. For the reason just mentioned, there were not constant returns to scale in the division of specie. Hence the use of specie in standard transactions created problems, as did tax payments in specie. This problem is frequently mentioned in the literature. Two interesting papers on this topic are by Hanson (1979, 1980).

liabilities. In this sense they may appear similar to modern bank liabilities. However, this similarity does not extend very far. Bills of exchange were not convertible into currency on demand, but rather carried a maturity date. Moreover, there were often many copies of a single bill in existence. If the holder of one of these copies presented it for (illegitimate) repayment, the legitimate holder of the bill would need to and often did have to contest payment in court (Gould 1915, p. 38). Finally, bills of exchange appear to have been used only in relatively large denominations. Hence they appear to have been much more like privately issued assets for which secondary markets exist than like bank deposits.

Given this overview of colonial monetary arrangements, we may now turn to a description of the two alternative theories of money that will be used to try to explain the colonial experience.

II.   A Version of the Quantity Theory

According to Lucas (1980, p. 1005), one of the "two central implications of the quantity theory [is] that a given change in the rate of change in the quantity of money induces . . . an equal change in the rate of price inflation." According to Schwartz (1973, p. 264), at least since Alexander the Great, "long-run price changes consistently parallel . . . monetary changes," which is argued to be a verification of quantity-theoretic views.

How are we to check, then, whether these views are consistent with colonial monetary arrangements, in which each colony had its own paper currency exchanging with sterling at market-determined rates? The approach adopted here is one applied to Latin America by Vogel (1974), which is to match price level movements (or in some cases here exchange rate movements) with changes in the quantity of money issued by each of the colonies, that is, with changes in the stock of paper money outstanding in each colony. In fact, because data on specie, quantities of commodity monies, circulating bills of exchange, and so forth are not available, there is really no choice other than to attempt to do this. Moreover, this approach coincides quite well with quantity-theoretic implications when applied to New England before 1750 (Smith 1985). However, because matching paper currency movements with price level (or exchange rate) movements omits many things that a quantity theorist might in principle wish to consider, I argue below that this approach does no great violence to the quantity theory.

What is omitted by focusing on movements in the stock of paper currency? First, as indicated in the previous section, liabilities of private agents such as book credit or bills of exchange are not considered. However, as argued above, bills of exchange appear to have had many of the attributes of modern privately issued liabilities for which secondary markets exist. Such liabilities are not included in modern money supply measures. Similarly, book credit was simply credit extended by merchants to customers. Such credit extensions are also not included in modern attempts to implement the quantity theory empirically. Hence omission of these items would not appear to do any violence to the quantity theory.

With respect to commodity monies, two facts should be noted. One is that in the Carolinas, and in Maryland before 1747, commodity notes were not in use. Thus exchanges with commodity monies were simply trades of commodities. The government of North Carolina, for instance, fixed legal rates at which selected commodities would be accepted in lieu of specie. Since the legal rate established on commodities generally could not have corresponded to market-clearing prices, it seems unlikely that such rates obtained in private transactions. More probably they obtained only in transactions with the government when it was advantageous to make payments with certain commodities. Thus it seems an open question whether these are to be regarded as monetary transactions.

Second, even once the system of commodity notes was introduced,[4] commodity monies did not enjoy the same general acceptability or circulate so widely as paper currency. According to McCusker (1976, p. 97), "the major characteristic distinguishing colonial bills of credit from commodity notes was their widespread acceptability." In fact, it appears that in Virginia (which has been more extensively studied than the other colonies) tobacco notes virtually did not circulate at all, except to transfer title to tobacco. These statements apply even more strongly to commodity money systems without commodity notes. Hence omission of commodity monies does not seem a particularly important problem. Finally, McCusker (1976, p. 95) likens commodity notes to "modern warehouse certificates [which] have a negotiable character." These are not included in modern attempts to implement the quantity theory. Hence their omission does not seem out of line with standard practice.

Last, the approach taken here omits the quantity of specie in circulation from the measured money supply. While it is unfortunate to be forced to omit this, I will still argue that its omission does not bias the results in any important way. First, as has been noted previously, specie circulating in the colonies was primarily of Spanish and Portuguese origin and was not denominated in the unit of account of any

---

[4] Commodity notes were circulating warehouse receipts for the commodity in question, as will be recalled from Sec. I.

colony. Second, money issued by foreign governments circulating within the borders of another country is not included in modern attempts to implement the quantity theory. Hence this omission is not out of line with standard practice. Third, in the colonies under consideration here, specie omission is not particularly detrimental. In North Carolina "it appears certain that there was never any substantial amount of coin in the colony throughout the period" (Brock 1975, pp. 107–8). In Maryland, specie circulated at a market-determined exchange rate with notes within the colony. Hence it would be inappropriate to look at a sum of notes and specie. And finally, even in South Carolina, "a paper bill of credit, with a distinct, explicit value in colonial currency, was naturally to be preferred over any given coin, the value of which in colonial currency was uncertain or, at least, debatable. Not only did a gold or silver coin bear no indication of its value in colonial currency, but its value depended on its weight and condition, factors not easily measured by individual colonists" (McCusker 1976, p. 97). Thus, even in South Carolina, it is not unreasonable to proceed as if there were flexible exchange rates between specie and paper currency.

Lest one be unpersuaded by these arguments, however, I should note the following. In asking whether the quantity theory can confront colonial monetary phenomena, the approach will be to match paper currency movements with movements in prices and exchange rates. It will be seen that for these colonies, as for most of the colonies examined in Smith (1985), these movements match very poorly (even over long periods). It might be suspected that this is due to one of two factors: either (1) paper currency was not a large component of the "money supply" (appropriately defined), or (2) changes in the stock of paper currency were offset by specie flows.

In fact, neither of these views is tenable. With regard to the first point, conservative contemporary estimates placed the components of the money supply (which according to contemporary usage meant specie and paper currency) late in the colonial period at about ¼ specie and ¾ paper currency.[5] As we have seen, this seems conservative for at least some of the colonies at hand. Thus paper currency circulation was not so small that even large increases (or reductions) in it did not have significant impacts on the money supply.

With regard to the second point, this view also does not bear close examination. First, there is no evidence in favor of it. Second, during much of the period at hand there are reasons to think either that the

---

[5] See McCusker (1978, p. 7, n. 9). More strongly, Adam Smith (1776/1937, p. 307) asserts that "almost all the ordinary transactions of its [North America's] interior commerce [are] being thus carried on by paper."

reverse happened or at least that specie flows large enough to offset paper currency movements could not have occurred. In North Carolina, for instance, it has been noted that there was never any significant amount of specie in the colony. In Maryland this view is also not tenable. During the period we examine there were two instances of large increases in the quantity of paper currency: one as this currency was injected into the economy over a period of years and one during the French and Indian War. With respect to the first period, Gould (1915) asserts (without apparent contradiction elsewhere in the literature) that specie stocks rose along with the stock of paper currency. Hence it would appear that movements in the stock of paper currency do not give an overly inaccurate picture of movements in the overall stock of money. During the French and Indian War period (this is true of all of the colonies considered) there is also every reason to think that movements in the stock of specie and of paper currency were generally positively rather than negatively correlated. The reason for this is as follows: During the war each of these colonies made large military expenditures. They were generally financed by the printing of money. Hence note issues rose dramatically (as will be seen) during this period. At the same time British expenditures in the colonies were large, and, in addition, the British government provided sterling grants to each of the colonies. Both of these must have had the effect of increasing specie stocks. Thus paper currency and specie stocks both grew during the war.

After the war paper currency stocks contracted very rapidly. The reason for this is that notes were backed by future tax receipts. At the time of note issue, future taxes were levied. As notes came in in receipt of these taxes they were destroyed. The resultant contraction in paper currency stocks was most likely accompanied by a contraction in specie circulation. The reason is that, as is well known, at the end of the war there was strong sentiment in England that the colonies should help pay for the war. The taxes that were imposed almost certainly led to drains of specie at the same time as paper currency was being retired. Hence in this instance as well it is probable that movements in the stock of paper money were paralleled by similar specie movements. Thus again our approach should provide a reasonably accurate picture of movements in the overall stock of money.[6]

---

[6] One additional comment might be made on the question of paper currency issues displacing specie. Adam Smith (1776/1937) suggested that paper currency issues might have exactly this effect, with new issues of currency displacing equal amounts of specie and having no price level effects. The absence of price level effects is roughly what is observed for parts of the samples. Monetarists should probably not find such an outcome encouraging, if they believe that this is what actually occurred. On this point one might consult Mints (1945, p. 30), e.g., who states that on this issue Smith and others "were completely wrong in their conclusions."

III. The Sargent-Wallace View

In contrast to the quantity theory, the Sargent-Wallace approach is to attempt to determine the goods value of money (inverse price level) in much the same way that the value of privately issued liabilities is determined. In particular, just as the value of privately issued liabilities depends on the issuer's balance sheet, the same is true for government liabilities. Thus issues of money that are accompanied by increases in the (expected) discounted present value of the government's revenues need not be inflationary.

As this approach likens money to privately issued liabilities, it seems appropriate to attempt first to apply it to monetary systems that are not fiat in nature, that is, in which money is backed. However, if paper money is convertible on demand into commodities, then one is perhaps not surprised that its value is not directly linked to its quantity. Thus it seems that the colonial monetary arrangements under consideration, where money was (supposed to be) backed by future income streams but was not convertible on demand into any commodity, are particularly appropriate for study of this view.

What should we expect to observe in the colonial period under the alternate theory, then? We should expect to observe that when money is carefully backed, its value (price levels, exchange rates) should not depend strongly on its quantity. When money is not carefully backed, it should depreciate in value. In fact, when incremental note issues that are essentially unbacked occur, the quantity theory becomes a special case of the Sargent-Wallace approach.

In order to see this, it is useful to consider an analogy. Suppose that a firm doubles the number of its shares outstanding. What happens to its price per share? The answer is that more information is required. In a stock split we expect a halving in the price of the stock. This is analogous to the quantity theory and corresponds to the case where a firm increases its liabilities without a corresponding increase in its future (expected) stream of net revenues. On the other hand, if the quantity of a firm's shares outstanding increases and there is a corresponding increase in its income stream, the change in stock price depends on the relative magnitudes of these increases. Thus whether or not quantity-theoretic propositions apply depends on the nature of backing for government liabilities. If these are poorly backed or unbacked, we expect these propositions to hold. If issues of money are carefully backed by increases in government assets or claims to future income streams, we expect these propositions to fail.

Our approach, then, is to apply Sargent's claim (1982, pp. 45–46) that governments were "like a firm whose prospective receipts were its future tax collections. The value of the government's debt was, to a first approximation, equal to the present value of current and future government surpluses." There are two methods by which this claim will be applied to the data. We will first examine the monetary experiences of North and South Carolina. Both of these colonies had periods in which they issued (nearly) unbacked notes. In these periods the quantity theory applies fairly well to the data. Each colony also had a "currency reform" in which paper currency became much more carefully backed. These reforms served to end currency depreciation. Moreover, inflation and currency depreciation after these reforms were not rekindled by extremely rapid rates of monetary growth. In fact, in these "postreform" periods, large increases and reductions in the money supplies of both colonies occurred. These had virtually no impact on currency values.

There are two conclusions to be drawn from this evidence. One is that the quantity theory does not hold generally. The second is that these episodes provide evidence that the nature of backing is a determinant of currency values.

This evidence on the Sargent-Wallace hypothesis is of an indirect nature, however. In particular, it shows only that the way in which money is backed affects the response of currency values to other economic variables. Therefore, some time will then be spent examining exchange rate determination in Maryland. As indicated previously, Maryland backed a large component of its note circulation with investments in Bank of England stock. At specified dates (1748 and 1764) notes were to be redeemed with this sinking fund. Thus, unlike the notes of other colonies, Maryland notes were backed by a fund whose market value can be followed over time. This presents an opportunity to see how the value of backing for notes affected their purchasing power. As will be seen, the value of backing for notes (and the government's track record for meeting scheduled redemptions) had large and significant effects on Maryland currency values. The quantity of notes circulating did not. Thus the Maryland experience provides direct evidence in favor of the Sargent-Wallace view.

IV. The Evidence: South and North Carolina

A. *South Carolina*

South Carolina was one of the earliest colonies to experiment with paper money and the first to create a loan office. It was also the first colony (along with North Carolina) to experience large depreciations of its paper currency, and, finally, it was the first colony to solve this problem. Initially, South Carolina had issued (in 1703) £4,000 of notes to finance expenditures. Following the general paradigm laid out in Section I, at the same time these notes were issued future tax levies were introduced to retire the notes. The same is true for subsequent note issues (which can be followed in table 1). However, in fact these tax proceeds were generally diverted to other uses, so that very little retirement of notes was actually effected.

In 1712 South Carolina created a loan office, with a resultant large increase in circulating notes. Thus by 1712 South Carolina had created a system of monetary arrangements that were to persist until 1731. Very early on the note issues of the colony were made legal tender, and they were always acceptable in payment of taxes. For a brief period the colony experimented with notes that were redeemable on demand for rice, but this arrangement was short-lived. For our purposes, however, there is only one important feature of South Carolina's note issues: before 1731 they were poorly backed in the sense that as they were issued the government did not succeed in (significantly) raising its flow of future net tax receipts.[7]

Unfortunately, a general price index is not available for South Carolina before 1732. However, table 1 reproduces the sterling exchange rate series reported by McCusker (1978). As can be seen, during the first 20 years of experience with paper currency, depreciation was the rule. By the late 1720s the quantity of sterling purchasable with £1 of South Carolina currency was barely more than one-fifth of its 1710 level. Moreover, quantity-theoretic kinds of predictions perform reasonably well. For instance, as indicated in table 1, from 1710 until 1720 the per capita quantity of paper currency in circulation increased by a factor of slightly more than 4.5. By 1723 the rate of exchange against sterling had increased by a factor of exactly 4.5. In general, in fact, for the first 25 years of this period increases in the stock of paper money tend to precede currency depreciations. Thus the quantity theory appears to apply fairly well to this period, in which paper currency issues were backed only in the most nominal fashion.

After 1727 South Carolina reversed its trend of currency depreciation, maintaining exchange rates at or below their 1727 level until 1736. In fact, during the entire colonial period South Carolina's exchange rate against sterling was never more than 13 percent above its 1727 level. Moreover, South Carolina succeeded in this despite continued growth in its currency stock. For instance, in 1731 the outstanding note issue of the colony nearly doubled. Nevertheless, the exchange rate merely returned to its 1727 level, where it remained for 5 years following this increase. Thus currency depreciation was halted and not rekindled by large changes in the money stock.

The note issue of 1731 and all successive note issues in the colony were not of a legal tender nature. The British government took a

---

[7] On this point see the discussion in Brock (1975, pp. 116–23).

TABLE 1

SOUTH CAROLINA

Date	Paper Currency Outstanding (£) (1)	Pounds per 1,000 Population (2)	Exchange Rate (£ S.C. per £100 Sterling) (3)	Price Level (Average of 1762–74 = 100) (4)
1703	4,000	. . .	150	. . .
1707	12,000	. . .	150	. . .
1708	14,000	. . .	150	. . .
1710	14,000	1,286	150	. . .
1711	20,000	. . .	150	. . .
1712	56,000	. . .	150	. . .
1714	. . .	. . .	200	. . .
1715	. . .	. . .	300	. . .
1716	90,000	. . .	. . .	. . .
1717	. . .	. . .	575	. . .
1718	. . .	. . .	500	. . .
1720	100,000	5,866	400	. . .
1721	. . .	. . .	533	. . .
1722	80,000	. . .	580	. . .
1723	120,000	. . .	675	. . .
1724	. . .	. . .	650	. . .
1725	. . .	. . .	672	. . .
1726	. . .	. . .	700	. . .
1727	106,500	. . .	700	. . .
1728	106,500	. . .	700	. . .
1729	106,500	. . .	700	. . .
1730	106,500	3,550	644	. . .
1731	211,275	. . .	700	. . .
1732	. . .	. . .	700	79
1733	. . .	. . .	700	80
1734	. . .	. . .	700	108
1735	. . .	. . .	700	105
1736	. . .	. . .	743	96
1737	. . .	. . .	753	117
1738	. . .	. . .	775	125
1739	. . .	. . .	792	84
1740	. . .	. . .	796	77
1741	. . .	. . .	691	97
1742	. . .	. . .	699	85
1743	. . .	. . .	700	70
1744	. . .	. . .	700	64
1745	. . .	. . .	700	46
1746	. . .	. . .	. . .	45
1747	. . .	. . .	761	69
1748	. . .	. . .	762	88
1749	133,045	2,142	725	96
1750	. . .	. . .	702	100
1751	. . .	. . .	700	83
1752	. . .	. . .	700	97
1753	152,322	. . .	700	112
1754	156,156	. . .	700	86
1755	221,359	2,801	700	86
1756	311,816	. . .	714	77
1757	542,837	. . .	700	78

TABLE 1 (*Continued*)

Date	Paper Currency Outstanding (£) (1)	Pounds per 1,000 Population (2)	Exchange Rate (£ S.C. per £100 Sterling) (3)	Price Level (Average of 1762–74 = 100) (4)
1758	595,567	...	700	86
1759	521,369	...	700	112
1760	863,827	9,182	700	92
1761	867,744	...	700	80
1762	...	...	700	77
1763	584,916	...	717	92
1764	585,246	...	718	86
1765	472,378	4,327	709	87
1766	446,673	...	707	100
1767	344,147	...	700	94
1768	481,999	...	700	102
1769	497,654	...	...	104
1770	424,154	3,414	717	93
1771	...	...	762	108
1772	...	...	679	137
1773	391,391	...	728	116
1774	258,971	...	700	104

Sources.—Column 1: Brock (1975), pp. 106–26 and table 27; col. 2: Brock (1975) and U.S. Bureau of the Census (1976), p. 1168; col. 3: McCusker (1978), pp. 222–24; col. 4: Taylor (1932).

hand and refused to approve any further legal tender note issues in the colony. To compensate the colony resorted to the use of paper instruments known as public orders and tax certificates. While not legal tender in private transactions, these notes were accepted for taxes and, according to Brock (1975, p. 124), "custom nevertheless caused them to circulate much as the legal tender bills did." As there appears to have been no important difference in practice between public orders and tax certificates, I treat them homogeneously in what follows.

I have already noted that in 1731 outstanding note issue doubled with no apparent effects on the exchange rate. It will now be noted (with reference to table 1) that after 1731 movements in the outstanding stock of notes generally fail to account for price level or exchange rate movements. For instance, from 1730 until 1749 there is a secular decline in the per capita quantity of notes outstanding (a decline of 40 percent). Nevertheless, this reduction in the money supply did not have a salutary effect on exchange rates, and, similarly, it appears that the price level rose rather than declined.

Similarly, after 1749 we see a marked increase in the per capita quantity of notes. From 1749 until 1755 per capita note issue increased 31 percent, and from 1755 until 1760 per capita note issue more than tripled. However, the price level in 1755 was 10 percent *lower* than that in 1749, and the price level in 1760 was only 7 percent higher than in 1755. Thus this extremely large increase in per capita note issue (a factor of 4.3 in 11 years) was not reflected in prices (which fell from 1749 to 1760) or exchange rates (which also appreciated).

After 1760 there was a reduction in the note circulation of South Carolina nearly as dramatic as the increase just considered. From 1760 until 1770 the per capita stock of paper currency was reduced by 63 percent. Despite this large reduction, the price level rose slightly and exchange rates depreciated. Thus after 1731 quantity-theoretic predictions appear to do quite poorly.

Can this poor performance be accounted for in the context of standard theories of money? The answer would appear to be no, for the following reasons. The first way one might attempt to explain the results above in the context of the quantity theory is to argue that specie flows (or changes in the quantity of some other asset) may have "offset" the changes in the stock of paper money noted above. This appears untenable, however, in that it requires implausibly large changes at certain points in time. In particular, the major injections and withdrawals of money after 1750 were associated with (*a*) French and Indian War deficit finance and (*b*) taxes levied for the retirement of these note issues. As noted earlier, movements in the stock of colonial specie almost certainly paralleled these movements as Britain (*a*) sent substantial amounts of specie to the colonies during the war and (*b*) levied substantial taxes on the colonies afterward. In the light of this, the possibility of "offsetting" changes in other components in the money supply seems small.

A second way in which one might attempt to salvage the quantity theory is as follows. It might be supposed that colonial money demand could be characterized, say, by a Cagan money demand function. It might also be noted that (as will be discussed below) after 1731 monetary injections were always followed by promised future monetary contractions. As Sargent and Wallace (1981) have shown, it is possible for the effects of anticipated future monetary changes to dominate current movements in the money supply. Could this account for the observations noted above?

The answer is no. First, the Sargent-Wallace mechanism requires that anticipated future monetary changes exceed current ones in magnitude. As can be seen from table 1, this is not the case for the post-1750 period. Also, the Sargent-Wallace mechanism operates because the anticipated future deflation supposedly associated with future monetary contractions increases money demand sufficiently to offset the effects of current increases in the money supply. However, as table 1 indicates, if colonials expected future deflation as a result of the monetary reductions of the 1760s, they were sorely disappointed. Hence this is not a tenable explanation of our observations.

Last, we might ask whether the observations above can be explained within the framework of conventional money demand functions (or, more broadly, conventional macro models). Some data that one might desire for this purpose are not available, in particular, data on interest rates. However, the period of substantial increase in the money supply is a period of high wartime demand for goods and services, and the period of monetary contraction appears by most accounts to have contained a fairly standard postwar recession (see, e.g., Ernst 1973). In the light of these facts, the nearly insignificant inflations of 1755–60 and of 1760–70 seem difficult to explain absent convenient shifts in money demand functions. In fact, this seems generally true of the post-1731 period. However, this explanation is not consistent with standard presentations of the quantity theory. For instance, Friedman and Schwartz (1963) (see their conclusion) associate the quantity theory with the existence of highly stable money demand functions. Thus this explanation will not salvage the quantity theory.

In the light, then, of the apparent failure of the quantity theory, can the Sargent-Wallace view account for the observations at hand? The answer is yes. As we have seen, when note issues are poorly backed the quantity theory becomes a special case of this view. Thus it is consistent with our pre-1731 observations. After 1731 we observe major fluctuations in the quantity of money. For instance, we have seen that in 1731 the money stock doubled, yet this had no effect on exchange rates. Later monetary changes also had minimal effects on both prices and exchange rates. I will now argue that this is because note issues after 1731 were carefully backed by future tax receipts. Thus the Sargent-Wallace view accounts for the absence of effects on currency values.

It is clear that the post-1750 issues were carefully backed since it was the future tax levies that permitted the post-1760 withdrawal of notes. Note issues between 1731 and 1750 were also carefully backed. Between 1731 and 1745, £259,282 of new issues had occurred. By 1749 only £26,545 of these notes were still in circulation. This indicates that note issues were well backed by future tax levies. Thus the statement of Brock (1975, p. 126) regarding this period appears justified: "the orders of the various issues were all with reasonable promptness drawn in by taxes."

It would seem, then, that the Sargent-Wallace view that the quantity of currency can fluctuate widely without affecting its value (if currency is carefully backed) is borne out by the experience of South Carolina. It will also be noted that its experience is similar to that of the four hyperinflation countries examined by Sargent (1982).

Specifically, South Carolina (as did Sargent's four countries) ended a decline in the value of its (poorly backed) currency by replacing it with a currency that was carefully backed.

Finally, this experience is suggestive of the thought experiment conducted by Barro (1974). Specifically, colonial finance has the feature that current expenditures were financed by government issue of liabilities, accompanied by future tax levies. This is the finance scheme contrasted by Barro with current tax financing of expenditures. The minimal price level impact of money issues seems to bear out Barro's analysis in the sense that it indicates that the timing of tax levies had no significant effect even on price level movements.

B. North Carolina

In most respects, the monetary history of North Carolina parallels that of South Carolina. In 1712, when the Carolinas split, North Carolina had £4,000 of its currency in circulation. As can be seen in table 2, this quantity tripled the next year, and then the stock of paper currency doubled again by 1715. Thus, as was the case in South Carolina, North Carolina's history was one of rapid early expansion of its money stock.

In addition to this paper currency, North Carolina had a number of rated commodities of a legal tender nature (with a legally fixed exchange rate into currency, which could differ from the market price of the commodity). I have already commented above on the general acceptability of this currency. Finally, as noted previously, "it appears certain that there was never any substantial amount of coin in the colony throughout the period" (Brock 1975, pp. 107–8).

As can be seen from table 2, there is no evidence in favor of the quantity theory arising from North Carolina's experience. From 1715 until 1722 (from which point the money stock was held constant until 1729) the money supply of the colony was cut in half. Nevertheless, exchange rates depreciated dramatically. Then in 1729, when North Carolina first instituted its loan office, the money supply of the colony more than quadrupled. While a large depreciation did occur, the exchange rate never much exceeded twice its 1729 level. Moreover, it took 10 years for this doubling to occur. Thus both directions of change before 1748 (I refer here to the 1715–29 period) and relative magnitudes of changes are not supportive of quantity-theoretic predictions for the period.

Before 1748 it is clear from table 2 that currency values declined markedly in North Carolina. In 1748 a currency reform was implemented. A new set of notes was issued to replace those in circulation, with one new note to replace seven and one-half old ones. According

TABLE 2

NORTH CAROLINA

Date	Notes in Circulation (1)	Pounds per 1,000 Population (2)	Exchange Rate (£ N.C. per £100 Sterling) (3)
1712	4,000	...	...
1713	12,000	...	...
1715	24,000	...	150
1722	12,000	...	500
1724	12,000	...	500
1728	12,000	...	...
1729	52,000	...	500
1731	52,000	...	650
1734	54,500	...	...
1735	...	...	720
1736	...	...	700
1737	...	...	867
1739	...	...	1,000
1748*	21,350	...	1,033
1749	21,160	...	...
1750	20,647	283	133
1751	20,119	...	...
1752	19,028	...	...
1753	18,289	...	...
1754	57,951	...	167
1755	56,054	611	160
1756	57,951	...	180
1757	68,255	...	...
1758	70,253	...	...
1759	69,512	...	185
1760	75,806	686	190
1761	95,335	...	200
1762	85,322	...	200
1763	...	...	200
1764	73,378	...	193
1765	...	...	200
1766	67,880	...	...
1767	...	...	173
1768	60,106	334	180

SOURCES.—Column 1: Brock (1975), pp. 108, 112, tables 23, 24; col. 2: U.S. Bureau of the Census (1976), p. 1168, and Brock (1975); col. 3: McCusker (1978), pp. 217–19.
  * Currency reform. New monetary unit employed.

to Brock (1975), this tripled the effective money supply of the colony. Then after 1748, while exchange rates were hardly stable, they never exceeded their 1748 level by more than 50 percent. This constitutes a major success when compared with the nearly 600 percent depreciation of 1715–48. How did North Carolina succeed, then, in slowing so dramatically its rate of currency depreciation? Further examination of table 2 indicates that this was not achieved by reducing rates of money growth. In fact, from 1750 to 1755 the per capita money stock in North Carolina more than doubled. The exchange rate depreciated only 20 percent. From 1750 to 1760 the money stock grew by 142 percent in per capita terms. This occasioned only a 43 percent depreciation in the exchange rate. Hence for the first dozen or so years after the currency reform, money growth far outstripped currency depreciation.

After 1761 the money supply declined, as it did in all colonies, because of the retirement of notes provided for in their emission. By 1768 the per capita money stock was only half of what it had been in 1760. Nevertheless, North Carolina's exchange rate appreciated only 5 percent.

Clearly, then, the quantity theory cannot account for any of the North Carolina experience. How do we account for it according to the Sargent-Wallace approach? First, we should note that prior to 1748 there was no meaningful sense in which North Carolina backed its notes. The reduction in the money supply between 1715 and 1722 represents the *only* time prior to 1748 during which any notes were retired through taxation. Hence monetary expansions were not accompanied by increased future government revenue streams, and we should not be surprised by currency depreciation. Of course, since the quantity theory becomes a special case of the Sargent-Wallace view when money is unbacked, the failure of the quantity theory is also a failure of this viewpoint. Naturally, though, the Sargent-Wallace approach does no worse for this period than the quantity theory.

The Sargent-Wallace approach does permit an explanation for the relative success of the 1748 currency reform, however. We have already noted that, prior to 1748, paper money was essentially unbacked. In fact, the fiscal situation in the colony was generally poor. According to Brock (1975, pp. 112–13),

> With the exception of the years 1715 to 1722, no bills seem ever to have been retired by taxation. The loan office was badly managed. To make matters worse, North Carolina remained a barter colony. Until the law of 1748 provided for payment of taxes in gold, silver, or bills of credit, they had been payable in the rated commodities. The result was, as successive governors complained, that the taxes were paid in the commodity rated highest in proportion to its actual value, and of that commodity each person tendered his most inferior stock. It is small wonder, then, that the sums raised in taxes for the retirement of the outstanding bills were so frequently negligible. But the evil did not stop here. Taxes levied to meet the annual cost of government proved similarly unproductive. The colony fell into debt; and in order to pay the debt, a new issue of bills was emitted.

Thus, it is not surprising that with poor revenue prospects on the part of the government its liabilities were little valued.

After 1748, as pointed out by Brock, taxes were no longer payable in commodities. Moreover, retirement of notes through the provision of taxes for this purpose was much more of a factor. Table 3 reports the cancellation of notes by this method after 1748. As can be seen, this retirement of notes occurred on a regular basis and constituted a generally significant fraction of total notes in circulation. Hence we can, at least partially, account for the success of the currency reform by the superior nature of the backing provided for notes after this date.

Again, one might wonder whether this analysis has failed to pick up important changes in other components of the money supply that account for the poor showing of the quantity theory above. Again, the answer would appear to be no. Some of the reasons for this have been previously elaborated, so we restrict ourselves to two points here. Consider the period of postcurrency reform. This is divided roughly in half in table 2: an initial period of large increase in note circulation followed by a period of large reduction. Could these movements in the stock of paper currency have been offset by changes in other components of the money supply?

It would appear that they could not have been offset to any significant degree by specie movements. In particular, our earlier comment about the scarcity of specie in North Carolina appears to hold for this later period as well (see Brock 1975, p. 443). In addition, changes in the nature of the commodity money system would lead one to believe that the monetary growth of the first half of this period is under- rather than overstated. In particular, in 1754 North Carolina established a system of state warehouses and legal tender commodity notes. This must certainly be viewed as having the effect of a monetary expansion (although probably not to any great extent). In short, then, there is no reason to think that our focus on paper currency alone does any substantial injustice to the quantity theory.

C. Remarks

At this point a few remarks are probably in order. First, when secular movements in the price level fail to mirror secular movements in the money supply, it is typical in studies of this type (see, e.g., Friedman and Schwartz [1963] and their discussion of the greenback period) to explicitly examine movements in real output and velocity. This is not possible for the colonial period, since there is insufficient knowledge of the behavior of real output. However, given the magnitudes of observed variations in real balances, it is clear that these variations cannot be accounted for by changes in the level of real activity. Hence

TABLE 3

NOTE CANCELLATION VIA TAXATION
IN NORTH CAROLINA

Date	Amount Canceled (£)
1748	...
1749	190
1750	514
1751	527
1752	1,091
1753	739
1754	338
1755	1,897
1756	1,809
1757	4,527
1758	9,544
1759	...
1760	5,853
1761	619
1762	10,013
1763	...
1764	11,944
1765	...
1766	5,498
1767	...
1768	7,774

SOURCE.—Sum of cancellations reported by Brock
(1975), tables 23, 24.

velocity must have varied substantially during the colonial period.
And, of course, such variation in velocity is inconsistent with many
presentations of the quantity theory (see, e.g., Friedman and
Schwartz 1963, 1982).

However, some presentations of the quantity theory (Friedman
1956) make velocity a stable function of some limited set of arguments. Most commonly these would involve a measure of the opportunity cost of holding money, such as a nominal interest rate. Then
one might argue that, if the opportunity cost of holding money
moved appropriately over time, the variability of velocity would be
consistent with the quantity theory. Unfortunately, there are no systematic observations on the behavior of interest rates during the colonial period that would allow this argument to be examined explicitly.
However, one observation suggests that the opportunity cost of holding money cannot have varied too substantially during periods of
relative exchange rate stability (such as we observe in South Carolina
after 1727). In particular, it is known that sterling bills of exchange
(discussed above) did not circulate at a discount when they were of

sufficiently short maturity. Hence, these assets, which were sterling denominated, did not bear interest. Moreover, if exchange rates were extremely stable, then the implied nominal return on these assets cannot have varied too greatly over the period of interest. To the extent that bills of exchange might be viewed as substitutes for money, then, this argument suggests that variations in velocity in the colonial period cannot be explained by major variations in the opportunity cost of holding money. Hence simple changes in the specification of the behavior of velocity appear as if they will not salvage the quantity theory.

V. The Evidence: Maryland

We have seen that the Carolinas provide a wealth of evidence against the quantity theory. In addition, experience there suggests that the nature of backing for notes was crucial in determination of their value, as in both Carolinas currency depreciation was halted by the expedient of carefully backing notes. In this section we will delve more deeply into the question of how well the backing of a note issue accounts for its value.

As argued above, Maryland provides a particularly appropriate setting in which to do this. Maryland existed with a monetary system based entirely on specie and a commodity money (tobacco) until 1733. In that year a paper currency was introduced explicitly to provide a medium of transaction for the (by now significant) part of the colony that did not grow tobacco. Most of this currency was injected into the economy via classic lump-sum transfers and was backed in a way unique in colonial experience. The proceeds of designated taxes were to be invested by agents of the colony in Bank of England stock. This investment was to constitute a sinking fund for the notes. Of the £90,000 issued at this time,[8] on the order of £60,000 was backed by this sinking fund. The remainder was issued through land banks. In addition, during the French and Indian War there were additional note issues to finance government deficits. These were not claims against the sinking fund, but rather were backed in conventional (colonial) fashion by future tax receipts.

At specified dates, in 1748 and 1764, notes were to be redeemed for sterling (or, more precisely, sterling bills of exchange). One-third of the outstanding notes were to be redeemed in 1748 and the remaining two-thirds in 1764. These redemptions occurred as scheduled. For our purposes, however, the unique feature of this system is that

---

[8] Actually, the £90,000 was only authorized at this time. It took some years for total circulation to approach this level.

Maryland notes were backed by a fund whose (current) market value is easily ascertainable at any point in time. Thus we may investigate the extent to which changes in the market value of the sinking fund account for exchange rate fluctuations. This seems particularly appropriate as, in addition to serving as a medium of exchange, these notes were simply claims for future delivery of sterling. Since the exchange rate is merely the rate at which sterling could be converted into paper currency, this is the sterling price of a future claim on sterling. We investigate how changes in the market value of this sinking fund affected the value of these claims.

The format of this section is as follows. In order to illustrate the kind of role the market value of backing can play, a highly simplified model of how paper money might be priced as an asset is presented. Then some statistical evidence on the relative importance of the quantity of money, the market value of backing, and the colony's track record for honoring its commitments is presented. It will be seen that currency values in Maryland depended entirely on the latter two factors. The quantity of money is irrelevant in the determination of currency values.

A. An Illustrative Model

It will be recalled that, among their other functions, notes in Maryland were claims to future delivery of sterling (bills of exchange). In this section we attempt to see to what extent empirically an extremely simple asset pricing model can account for movements in Maryland currency values. The model presented is oversimplified, in fact, for brevity of presentation.

What, then, would be the primary factors in any model attempting to explain asset pricing? Obviously the most important factors would be the kinds of promised future payoffs to which assets are a claim and the probabilities that these promises will be honored (or, in a contingent claims setting, that the relevant states will occur). Thus it is necessary to discuss the kinds of promises made by Maryland and how these promises were (in all likelihood) perceived by the residents of the colony.

The promise of Maryland to redeem a third of its notes for sterling in 1748 and the remaining two-thirds in 1764 (at the rate of four Maryland pounds for three pounds sterling) was (at least on its face) uncontingent. However, so were the promises of South Carolina to retire note issues via taxation before 1731. Before Maryland ever had recourse to a paper currency, then, most of the colonies had established by long experience that these promised redemptions or retirements were, in fact, contingent. On what were they contingent, then? First, funds earmarked for retirement of notes were often appropriated in the face of government expenditure needs. The larger the market value of the sinking fund, then, the greater the ability of the government to redeem notes and meet its additional revenue needs (if any) from the proceeds of the sinking fund. Second, when funds provided for the retirement of notes proved insufficient, this retirement was typically postponed. Hence the larger the market value of the sinking fund, the smaller the probability that retirement would not occur as scheduled.

I now introduce some notation. Let MV_t denote the market value of the sinking fund at date t, and let T denote the announced redemption date.[9] In the light of previous remarks, assume redemption will actually occur at T only if MV_T meets or exceeds some critical value, R. Let $F_T[x|MV_t, MV_{t-1}, \ldots]$ be the conditional probability that $MV_T \leq x$ evaluated at t, where in principle there could be a number of variables on which this probability might depend. To simplify matters, I assume that the only relevant conditioning variables are the historical market values of the sinking fund. In addition, I make the plausible assumption that $F_T[x|y_t^*, y_{t-1}^*, \ldots] \leq F_T[x|y_t, y_{t-1}, \ldots]$ for all x and for any sequences $\{y_t\}$, $\{y_t^*\}$ such that $y_t^* \geq y_t$.

Finally, suppose $MV_T < R$. Then a simple assumption is that redemption will occur at the first date for which the value of the sinking fund is at least R. Let $F_{T+i}[x|MV_{T+i-1} < R, MV_{T+i-2} < R, \ldots, MV_t, MV_{t-1}, \ldots]$ be the conditional probability at t that $MV_{T+i} \leq x$, given that $MV_{T+i-s} < R$, $1 \leq s \leq i$, and given the realized sequence of market values.

Given these notational conventions, let us proceed with a simple model in which currency values are determined as if they were conventional asset prices. Let e_t denote the sterling value of a Maryland pound note. Let r be (an exogenously given) discount factor.[10] Then an absence of (expected) arbitrage opportunities implies

$$e_t = \frac{{}_t e_{t+1}}{1 + r}; \quad t < T - 1, \tag{1}$$

where ${}_t e_{t+1}$ is the date t expected value of e_{t+1}. At date $T - 1$ redemption will occur next period if $MV_T \geq R$. Hence for $t \geq T - 1$,

$$e_t = \left(\frac{1}{1 + r}\right)\{[1 - F_T(t)]\tfrac{3}{4} + F_T(t)_t e_{t+1}\}, \tag{2}$$

where $F_T(t) \equiv F_T[R|MV_t, MV_{t-1}, \ldots]$, e_{t+1} is the exchange rate at $t + 1$ if redemption has not yet occurred, and $\tfrac{3}{4}$ is the promised rate at which Maryland pounds were to be converted into sterling.

---

[9] I assume a single redemption date for simplicity.
[10] Data on interest rates are unavailable.

Solving (1) and (2) forward, we obtain

$$e_t = \left(\frac{1}{1 + r}\right)^{T - 1} {}_t e_{T - 1}, \tag{3}$$

$${}_t e_{T - 1} = [1 - F_T(t)]\left(\frac{.75}{1 + r}\right) + F_T(t)[1 - F_{T + 1}(t)]\frac{.75}{(1 + r)^2}$$

$$+ F_T(t)F_{T + 1}(t)\frac{{}_t e_{T + 2}}{(1 + r)^2}, \tag{4}$$

with an obvious notation in (4). When repeated substitutions are applied to (4), the latter term vanishes if, for instance, ${}_t e_{T + k}$ is bounded for all k and if $r > 0$. Then ${}_t e_{T - 1}$ will be, through the relevant conditional probability distributions, a function of the sequence $\{MV_{t - i}\}_{i = 0}^{\infty}$. Let us denote this as ${}_t e_{T - 1} = \psi[MV_t, MV_{t - 1}, \ldots]$. Then (3) and (4) imply

$$e_t = \left(\frac{1}{1 + r}\right)^{T - 1} \psi[MV_t, MV_{t - 1}, \ldots]. \tag{5}$$

Moreover, it is apparent that $\psi(\cdot)$ is monotone nondecreasing in $MV_{t - i}$, $i \geq 0$.

Our method of applying this model is as follows. From equations (3) and (4), our model predicts that the ratio of e_t to the redemption rate (¾) is related positively to market values of the sinking fund. Therefore we estimate below the equation

$$par_t = a_0 + a_1 M_t + a_2 MVI_t + a_3 D_t + \epsilon_t, \tag{6}$$

where $par_t \equiv .75 e_t - 1$, M_t is the quantity of notes in circulation at t, and D_t is a dummy taking the values

$$D_t = 0; \quad t < 1748$$
$$D_t = 1; \quad t \geq 1748. \tag{7}$$

The role of this variable is that Maryland did in fact honor its commitment to redeem notes in 1748. Until this point there was no reason in particular for colonists to believe that this commitment would be honored.[11] According to the view that money is priced in the same way as any other asset, a record of its issuer's honoring promises should enhance the value of this currency. The variable MVI_t is the value of the sinking fund at t divided by its value in 1764. Finally, as should be clear from (3) and (4), par_t—the percentage the exchange rate at t is above the relevant redemption rate—is an appropriate dependent

---

[11] This is certainly the case, as only a minority of other colonies had regularly and strictly honored their commitments with respect to retirement of paper currency.

variable. According to the Sargent-Wallace view, then, we expect $a_2 <$ 0, $a_3 < 0$, and $a_1 = 0$.

Obviously, this is hardly a sophisticated approach to pricing money symmetrically with other assets. In principle far more sophisticated asset pricing models along the lines of Hansen and Singleton (1982) or Mehra and Prescott (1983) could be applied and directly implemented empirically. However, as can be seen from table 4, the number of available observations is small. Hence the best we can hope for is a fairly general indication of whether the Sargent-Wallace hypothesis accounts for the data. In fact, this limited number of observations accounts for the absence of lagged variables in (6).

B. The Evidence

The evidence presented in this section is derived from application of ordinary least squares to (6). This procedure should yield consistent parameter estimates for the following reason. Clearly the only right-hand-side variables whose exogeneity is suspect are the money supply and the market value of the sinking fund. With respect to the money supply, all authorized changes in it either were made in 1733, before any observations on exchange rates were available, or were a result of wartime deficit finance. This latter component might appear partially endogenous, as changes in exchange rates may have altered the nominal value of government expenditures. However, as inspection of table 4 will confirm, exchange rates were fairly stable during the French and Indian War (1756–63), so that this factor should not have been operative.

The market value of the sinking fund at any date was the sum of three factors: tax proceeds from an excise tax on tobacco exports invested in Bank of England stock; dividends paid on the sinking fund, which were reinvested in the fund; and capital gains or losses on the stock held. Certainly we may take Bank of England stock prices and dividends paid on this stock as unaffected by events in Maryland. In principle, tax proceeds on tobacco exports could have been affected by Maryland exchange rate variation to the extent that it influenced tobacco exports. However, this is a question on which some evidence can be produced. In particular, from the results of Sims (1972), it is known that there exists a model in which *MVI* is strictly econometrically exogenous with respect to *par* only if *MVI* is not Granger caused by *par*. In table 5 tests of Granger causality are presented that show that, at a very high marginal significance level, *MVI* is not Granger caused by *par*. Thus we cannot reject that this necessary condition for strict exogeneity is satisfied. In addition, table 5 reports tests of whether *par* Granger causes *EXS* (exports from Mary-

TABLE 4

MARYLAND

Date	Note Circulation (£) (1)	Per Capita Circulation (per 1,000 Population) (2)	Bank of England Stock Price (£ Sterling) (3)	Face Value of Sinking Fund (£ Sterling) (4)	Exchange Rate (£ Md. per £100 Sterling) (5)
1735	56,495	545	140.45	...	140.00
1736	57,864	...	149.10	2,000	230.00
1737	69,856	...	145.88	4,000	250.00
1738	69,856	...	142.11	...	225.00
1739	79,820	...	140.12	6,000	212.34
1740	78,523	676	140.49	7,500	228.08
1741	83,444	...	140.54	9,500	238.17
1742	82,072	...	140.22	...	275.00
1743	82,252	...	146.81	12,500	285.13
1744	83,058	...	145.54	15,000	166.67
1745	83,058	646	142.83	...	200.00
1746	83,058	...	127.34	18,800	210.00
1747	85,309	...	125.48	21,000	225.22
1748	86,040	...	124.15	24,000	200.61

Year					
1749	62,000	...	134.16	12,000	184.58
1750	62,000	439	134.13	...	177.92
1751	62,000	...	139.14	11,000	166.83
1752	62,000	...	145.18	16,000	155.62
1753	62,000	...	139.92	...	151.75
1754	62,000	...	133.63	...	153.75
1755	62,000	409	126.10	19,500	...
1756	96,017	...	117.94	...	170.00
1757	96,017	...	118.84	19,500	145.00
1758	96,017	...	119.59	19,500	150.00
1759	96,017	592	113.81	...	150.00
1760	96,017	...	110.46	27,500	146.25
1761	96,017	...	109.49	...	148.48
1762	96,017	...	101.58	35,500	144.45
1763	62,000	...	120.32	...	140.00
1764	41,295	...	116.50	40,800	136.67
1765	...	...	...	...	133.33

SOURCES.—Column 1: Brock (1975), pp. 104–5, 417–21; col. 2: Brock (1975) and U.S. Bureau of the Census (1976), p. 1168; col. 3: Mirowski (1981), pp. 569–70; col. 4: Scharf Collection, Maryland Historical Society; col 5: McCusker (1978), pp. 202–3.

TABLE 5

EXOGENEITY TESTS

$$A. \quad MVI_t = a + \sum_{i=1}^{q} b_i MVI_{t-i} + \sum_{i=1}^{s} c_i par_{t-i}$$

	q	s	$F(s, 24 - s)$	Marginal Significance Level
(i)	1	1	.57	.57
(ii)	1	2	1.10	.35

$$B. \quad EXS_t = a + \sum_{i=1}^{q} b_i EXS_{t-i} + \sum_{i=1}^{s} c_i par_{t-i}$$

	q	s	$F(s, 20 - s)$	Marginal Significance Level
(iii)	1	1	1.13	.27
(iv)	2	2	.88	.43

SOURCES.—The sources for all data other than exports are reported in the text. Scottish exports are from U.S. Bureau of the Census (1976), pp. 1177–78.

NOTE.—Summary statistics for the regression equations are as follows: (i) R^2 = .15, D-W = 1.51, $Q(13)$ = 8.82 (significance level = .79); (ii) R^2 = .21, D-W = 1.73, $Q(13)$ = 11.40 (significance level = .58); (iii) R^2 = .44, D-W = 1.88, $Q(12)$ = 5.69 (significance level = .93); (iv) R^2 = .44, D-W = 1.94, $Q(11)$ = 4.53 (significance level = .95).

land to Scotland). These would be almost entirely tobacco exports. We use Scottish rather than English exports because the U.S. Bureau of the Census (1976) does not separate Virginia from Maryland in its data on exports to Britain. As can be seen, at a marginal significance level of .43, we cannot reject the hypothesis that exports are not caused by exchange rates. Hence the suspect component of *MVI* does not appear to be correlated with the error term in (6). Therefore, we may proceed with our OLS estimation of (6) with some degree of confidence.

The data used are as follows. Data on exchange rates are taken from McCusker (1978), who reports the number of Maryland pounds required to purchase a sterling bill of exchange. Data on the money supply are taken from Brock (1975). Incidentally, it should be noted that Brock reports that it is not possible to tell exactly how fast authorized wartime monetary increases were actually spent or exactly how fast they were retired. Hence the numbers reported for 1756–62 have some errors, with the earlier and later numbers probably somewhat overstating the true money supply. Thus the usual caveats regarding error-laden variables apply. Finally, data on the sterling value of the sinking fund appear in the Scharf Collection of the Maryland Historical Society, which contains the surviving periodic reports of the London trustees for the sinking fund.[12] Bank of England stock prices are reported by Mirowski (1981). All these data are reproduced in table 4.

In order to get a feel for the magnitudes by which different factors influenced currency values, three different versions of (6) are reported. First, to gauge the extent to which monetary changes affected currency values, (6) was run with the constraints $a_2 = a_3 = 0$ imposed. The resulting equation, with t-statistics in parentheses, was

$$par_t = .310 + (1 \times 10^{-6})M_t,$$
$$(.896) \qquad (.263) \tag{8}$$

$$R^2 = .003, \text{ D-W} = .411, Q(13) = 48.33;$$

D-W is the Durbin-Watson statistic, and $Q(13)$ is the value of the Box-Pierce (1970) serial correlation test statistic with 13 degrees of freedom. The marginal significance level of the Q-statistic is 6×10^{-6}, and for the coefficient a_1 it is .80.

Clearly the quantity of money alone has no impact on currency values. Its coefficient is extremely small, and we cannot reject the hypothesis that it is zero even at extremely high significance levels. Finally, of course, (8) performs extremely poorly.

Next, (6) was run subject to the constraint $a_3 = 0$. The resulting equation is

$$par_t = .84 + (1 \times 10^{-7})M_t - .91MVI_t,$$
$$(2.04) \quad (2 \times 10^{-2}) \quad (2.82) \tag{9}$$

$$R^2 = .364, \text{ D-W} = 1.21, Q(8) = 2.50.$$

This equation is much better behaved than (8). The marginal significance level of the Q-statistic is .96, so this suggests no serial correlation. The coefficient on the money stock continues to be extremely small and highly insignificant. And finally, the coefficient on the (index of the) market value of the sinking fund is large, is significant at the 1 percent level, and has its theoretically predicted sign. In particular, increases in the market value of the backing for notes result in an appreciation in the value of Maryland currency.

Finally, as noted above, Maryland's track record for redeeming notes as promised may significantly affect the value of its currency. The result of running (6) is

$$par_t = .90 - (9 \times 10^{-7})M_t - .37MVI_t - .43D_t,$$
$$(2.92) \qquad (.26) \qquad (1.30) \qquad (3.49) \tag{10}$$

$$R^2 = .671, \text{ D-W} = 2.19, Q(8) = 4.59.$$

---

[12] The relevant data were kindly provided to me by Jacob Price.

Several things should be noted about this equation. First, it is surprisingly successful. For instance, Hodrick (1978) estimates an exchange rate equation between Britain and the United States over the period 1972–75 that contains no lagged terms. His equation has five explanatory variables involving relative money supplies, output levels, and interest rates. In addition, like equation (10), it is estimated on the basis of relatively few (36) observations. Hodrick reports an R^2 of .73. He also estimates a similar regression for the U.S.-German exchange rate with six explanatory variables and 28 observations. An R^2 of .66 is reported for this regression. Equation (10) has similar explanatory power, without the benefit of contemporaneous income or interest rate data. Hence it would appear that the Sargent-Wallace hypothesis applied to Maryland has good explanatory power.

Second, the marginal significance level of the Q-statistic is .80. This, along with the Durbin-Watson statistic, gives no suggestion of serially correlated residuals.

Third, as predicted by the Sargent-Wallace hypothesis, $a_2 < 0$ and $a_3 < 0$. Thus a history of honoring promised redemptions and a large accumulated backing for notes both enhance their value. Moreover, the marginal significance level of a_3 is 4×10^{-3}, so the history of the colony in honoring promised redemption dates is highly significant. The marginal significance level of the market value coefficient is only .22. While this is not particularly high, the value of the sinking fund is far more significant than the quantity of money. In addition, the coefficient on the market value term is fairly large, albeit not very precisely estimated. Hence it is not clear that one should conclude that it is insignificant.

Finally, the coefficient on money has a marginal significance level of .80 and has the wrong sign (according to the quantity theory). Hence it is clearly the case that the nature of promises backing notes, and not the quantity of notes, determines their value.

Again, in defense of the quantity theory, one might ask whether some important component of the money supply is omitted in equations (8)–(10). The answer is no. The exchange rate used in these equations is the rate between Maryland paper currency and sterling. Specie in Maryland as well as tobacco money circulated at market-determined rates with paper currency. Hence it would be inappropriate to aggregate these with paper currency.

VI. Conclusions

The current study encompasses a 70-year period and three colonies with somewhat but not completely similar monetary arrangements. In all of this experience, only that of South Carolina before 1731 is supportive of quantity-theoretic propositions. In this instance, it is also true that the quantity theory is a special case of the Sargent-Wallace approach. However, in contrast to the performance of the quantity theory, the Sargent-Wallace approach generally accounts well for the successes of the Carolina currency reforms and for exchange rate behavior in Maryland.

Moreover, I have argued that the success of the one approach and the failure of the other cannot be accounted for by omissions in monetary figures. Nor can they be accounted for by the effects of anticipated future changes in money stocks that tended to accompany current changes.

How can one attempt to rescue standard approaches to monetary theory, then, in which money is treated asymmetrically from other assets? One suggestion is that standard money demand functions may have characterized colonial currency-holding behavior but that these demand functions shifted at convenient points in time. In addition to having no empirical content, this view is one highly detrimental to the quantity theory. For instance, Friedman and Schwartz (1963) attempt to explain U.S. monetary history in the century following the Civil War on the basis of a stable demand function for money. Then a demonstration that money demand functions were highly unstable for a 70-year period in the colonies would be greatly at variance with their approach.

A second suggestion is that the economy of colonial North America was sufficiently primitive as not to be a "monetized economy." Certainly no one would apply this claim to Europe of the same period. Yet existing indications are that money-income ratios were higher in the (British) North American colonies than in any European country other than Britain itself. Thus such a suggestion would appear to be without basis in fact.

We are left, then, with the conclusion that there is a long period of history and a number of locations to which the quantity theory of money does not apply.[13] Other views of money that do not treat money differently from other assets do appear successful in explaining this period. Thus it would appear that these views deserve greater claim on the attention of monetary economists than they appear to have received.

References

Barro, Robert J. "Are Government Bonds Net Wealth?" *J.P.E.* 82 (November/December 1974): 1095–1117.
Box, G. E. P., and Pierce, David A. "Distribution of Residual Autocorrelations

---

[13] In addition to this work see Smith (1985).

in Autoregressive-Integrated Moving Average Time Series Models." *J. American Statis. Assoc.* 65 (December 1970): 1509–26.

Brock, Leslie V. *The Currency of the American Colonies, 1700–64: A Study in Colonial Finance and Imperial Relations.* New York: Arno, 1975.

Ernst, Joseph A. *Money and Politics in America, 1755–1775: A Study in the Currency Act of 1764 and the Political Economy of Revolution.* Chapel Hill: Univ. North Carolina Press, 1973.

Friedman, Milton. "The Quantity Theory of Money—a Restatement." In *Studies in the Quantity Theory of Money,* edited by Milton Friedman. Chicago: Univ. Chicago Press, 1956.

Friedman, Milton, and Schwartz, Anna J. *A Monetary History of the United States, 1867–1960.* Princeton, N.J.: Princeton Univ. Press (for N.B.E.R.), 1963.

———. *Monetary Trends in the United States and United Kingdom: Their Relation to Income, Prices, and Interest Rates, 1867–1975.* Chicago: Univ. Chicago Press (for N.B.E.R.), 1982.

Gould, Clarence P. "Money and Transportation in Maryland, 1720–1765." *Johns Hopkins Univ. Studies Hist. and Polit. Sci.* 33, no. 1 (1915).

Hansen, Lars P., and Singleton, Kenneth J. "Generalized Instrumental Variables Estimation of Nonlinear Rational Expectations Models." *Econometrica* 50 (September 1982): 1269–86.

Hanson, John R., II. "Money in the Colonial American Economy: An Extension." *Econ. Inquiry* 17 (April 1979): 281–86.

———. "Small Notes in the American Colonies." *Explorations Econ. Hist.* 17 (October 1980): 411–20.

Hodrick, Robert J. "An Empirical Analysis of the Monetary Approach to the Determination of the Exchange Rate." In *The Economics of Exchange Rates: Selected Studies,* edited by Jacob A. Frenkel and Harry G. Johnson. Reading, Mass.: Addison-Wesley, 1978.

Lucas, Robert E., Jr. "Two Illustrations of the Quantity Theory of Money." *A.E.R.* 70 (December 1980): 1005–14.

McCusker, John J. "Colonial Paper Money." In *Studies on Money in Early America,* edited by Eric P. Newman and Richard G. Doty. New York: American Numismatic Soc., 1976.

———. *Money and Exchange in Europe and America, 1600–1775: A Handbook.* Chapel Hill: Univ. North Carolina Press, 1978.

Mehra, Rajnish, and Prescott, Edward C. "The Equity Premium: A Puzzle." Manuscript. Minneapolis: Fed. Reserve Bank Minneapolis, 1983.

Mints, Lloyd W. *A History of Banking Theory in Great Britain and the United States.* Chicago: Univ. Chicago Press, 1945.

Mirowski, Philip. "The Rise (and Retreat) of a Market: English Joint Stock Shares in the Eighteenth Century." *J. Econ. Hist.* 41 (September 1981): 559–77.

Riley, James C., and McCusker, John J. "Money Supply, Economic Growth, and the Quantity Theory of Money: France, 1650–1788." *Explorations Econ. Hist.* 20 (July 1983): 274–93.

Sargent, Thomas J. "The Ends of Four Big Inflations." In *Inflation: Causes and Effects,* edited by Robert E. Hall. Chicago: Univ. Chicago Press (for N.B.E.R.), 1982.

Sargent, Thomas J., and Wallace, Neil. "Some Unpleasant Monetarist Arithmetic." *Fed. Reserve Bank Minneapolis Q. Rev.* 5 (Fall 1981): 1–17.

Schwartz, Anna J. "Secular Price Change in Historical Perspective." *J. Money, Credit and Banking* 5, no. 1, pt. 2 (February 1973): 243–69.

Sims, Christopher A. "Money, Income, and Causality." *A.E.R.* 62 (September 1972): 540–52.

Smith, Adam. *An Inquiry into the Nature and Causes of the Wealth of Nations.* 1776. Reprint ed. New York: Modern Library, 1937.

Smith, Bruce. "American Colonial Monetary Regimes: The Failure of the Quantity Theory and Some Evidence in Favor of an Alternate View." *Canadian J. Econ.*, vol. 18 (August 1985).

Taylor, George R. "Wholesale Commodity Prices at Charleston, South Carolina, 1732–1791." *J. Econ. and Bus. Hist.* 4 (February 1932): 356–77.

U.S. Bureau of the Census. *Historical Statistics of the United States.* Washington: Government Printing Office, 1976.

Vogel, Robert C. "The Dynamics of Inflation in Latin America, 1950–1969." *A.E.R.* 64 (March 1974): 102–14.

Wallace, Neil. "A Modigliani-Miller Theorem for Open-Market Operations." *A.E.R.* 71 (June 1981): 267–74.

[6]

The Role of War in Modern Inflation

S INCE wars occurred far more frequently and lasted much longer
in the first two centuries of modern times than in the last two, it is
indeed fortunate that they generated little, if any, price inflation. The
main reason is that too high a percentage of the people was required
to produce basic necessities for the civilian population for much manpower to be released to fight, produce munitions, and feed and clothe
the armed forces. Consequently, one finds no abrupt price increases
during the wars of Charles V, Philip II, and their Hapsburg successors. Even the construction and outfitting of the so-called Invincible
Armada did not upset the commodity price structure. Spanish prices
sometimes actually fell during wars with maritime powers; because
the wars were not fought in Spain, specie was exported to defray the
cost, and bullion imports from the New World were impeded. Prices
rose after peace came, as specie was no longer sent abroad to finance
the war and bullion imports from Mexico and Peru revived. Charts of
raw data presented by Dr. M. J. Elsas[1] suggest that grain prices
actually fell considerably, and some other agricultural prices to a
lesser extent, in Frankfurt am Main and Leipzig during the Thirty
Years War (1618-1648), but his data are fragmentary and his interpretation questionable.

The first war that clearly exerted upward pressure on prices in
Spain was the War of the Spanish Succession. The coronation of
Philip V, a young grandson of Louis XIV, not only brought internal
conflict in Spain but drew the fleets of the leading powers in Europe
into Spanish waters and their armies onto Spanish soil. Spain became
a battlefield for the massed might of Western Europe. With control of
the world's greatest empire believed to be at stake and bellicose
generals in command on both sides, the war was waged on more than
one front for more than a decade. But by current standards the price
inflation was insignificant. During the entire twelve years of war,
annual prices in New Castile, the heartland of Spain, rose only 6
percent; and in 1710, when Madrid changed hands twice, the price
level was only 9 percent higher than in 1702, when the war began.

Journal of Economic History, Vol. XXXVII, No. 1 (March 1977). Copyright © The Economic
History Association. All rights reserved.
[1] *Unriss einer Geschichte der Preise und Löhne in Deutschland vom ausgehenden Mittelalter
bis zum Beginn des neunzehten Jahrhunderts*, II B (Leiden, 1949), pp. 70ff.

14 *Hamilton*

But inasmuch as nonagricultural prices declined slightly, it seems that poor crops following the winter of 1709, perhaps the coldest that Western Europe has ever experienced, were largely responsible.[2]

Although complaints against scarcity of money in the British colonies of North America had been frequent and widespread, the first government paper money was issued in 1690 by Massachusetts, when it had no other means to pay the soldiers who had participated in a disastrous expedition against Canada during the War of the League of Augsburg. Following this example, South Carolina issued its first paper money in 1703 to liquidate indebtedness incurred in an attack upon Spanish Saint Augustine; and by the end of the War of the Spanish Succession in 1713 New York, Connecticut, New Hampshire, New Jersey, and Rhode Island had resorted to paper money.[3] Most of the colonies outside the mid-Atlantic area inflated with paper currency in war and peace until the outbreak of the Revolution.

Our revolutionary ancestors were willing to fight, and Nathan Hale was not the only one willing to die, if need be, for his country; but hardly anyone was willing to pay taxes for it. Though we denounced lack of representation in legislating taxes, what we really detested was taxation itself. Hence our revolutionary leaders had no greater difficulty than in levying and collecting taxes. "Between November, 1777, and October, 1779, Congress requisitioned the states for $95,000,000 in paper money, but obtained barely half this amount, and the specie value of the sum received was . . . less than $2,000,000." In desperation Congress turned to requisitioning specific supplies such as corn, beef, and pork from the states; but this proved "awkward, difficult, and wasteful, and yielded less than $1,000,000 worth of produce in specie value." Up to 1781 Congress made three requisitions upon the states for $10,000,000 in specie, and received less than $1,600,000.[4]

After the war had been won at Yorktown, Alexander Hamilton utterly failed, as Receiver of Continental Taxes for New York, in collecting the taxes. Only $6,250, less than 2 percent of the amount due, was successfully collected in a whole year by this genius.[5] Yet this was not much below the average for the Thirteen States. They were assessed eight million dollars, and the treasury received from them less than $303,000. North Carolina, Delaware, New Hamp-

---

[2] Earl J. Hamilton, *War and Prices in Spain, 1651-1800* (Cambridge, Mass., 1947), pp. 141ff.

[3] Curtis P. Nettels, *The Money Supply of the American Colonies* (Madison, 1934), pp. 255ff.

[4] Chester W. Wright, *Economic History of the United States* (New York and London, 1941), p. 218.

[5] To whom I am not related.

The Role of War 15

shire, and even Virginia, with a quota of $1,000,000, paid absolutely nothing![6] And the money we could beg or borrow from the enemies of Great Britain who were also our allies would hardly have paid for a single campaign. The amount of genuine savings in America that could have been borrowed was very small. Hence the only way we could have financed the Revolution was by paper money inflation. The result of a protracted Revolution virtually without overt taxation was one of the worst inflationary episodes in modern times.

The War of the Austrian Succession (1740-1748) and the Seven Years War (1756-1763) added to the inflationary pressure resulting from the spread of fractional reserve banking and the greatly increased output of the Latin American (particularly the Mexican) mines. But the wars were not the major factors. The same was true of the war that broke out in 1783.

The wars of the French Revolution financed by the issue of assignats, nominally based on the confiscated landed estates of the Church, the nobility, and the émigrés, gave France its sole experience with hyperinflation and a fascinating venture into price controls. During the Reign of Terror ridiculously low ceilings on grain prices were effectively enforced by ruthless use of the guillotine. Sales above the price ceilings seldom occurred, but the authoritarian regime failed miserably in its efforts to force holders of grain to sell. Threatened starvation, beginning with Paris, forced relaxation of the price controls. From 1790 to 1796 the assignats fell from parity with specie to 1/1000 of par. We must not forget that the assignats were printed to pay for the wars.

Under Napoleon France relied heavily on taxation, particularly in conquered territory, and the British government showed remarkable willingness to tax. Though not perfect, the governors and directors of the Bank of England, constantly maligned by David Ricardo and many others whom I greatly admire, were wise and courageous in restraining monetary expansion after England went off gold. If the amazingly limited commodity price data available (which contrast strangely with the brilliant analyses of the accompanying monetary phenomena by many writers) are correct, British prices rose only about 15-20 percent more than they would have if tied to gold from the beginning of Bank Restriction in 1797 to Waterloo.[7] Price data for

---

[6] Nathan Schachner, *Alexander Hamilton* (New York and London, 1946), pp. 146-52.

[7] Cf. N. J. Silberling, "Financial and Monetary Policy of Great Britain during the Napoleonic Wars," *Quarterly Journal of Economics*, 38 (1924), 214-33, 397-439; Jacob Viner, *Studies in the Theory of International Trade* (New York, 1937), pp. 126-27.

16   *Hamilton*

France are also poor, but it seems safe to guess that prices in France rose less than in England. Owing to unwillingess to tax, which Albert Gallatin not only shared but strongly advised, prices in the United States rose about 120 percent as a result of our participation in the Napoleonic Wars from 1812 to 1815.

Most of the advances in prices during the previous wars of the eighteenth century were relatively mild and largely persisted after the wars were over. But the adjustment required in returning to a peacetime economy after the Napoleonic Wars, the fervid desire to return to prewar conditions after so many years of conflict, and the sharp reduction in silver output resulting from the wars for Latin American independence followed by chaos in the liberated countries—all these brought prices sharply downward with resultant unemployment, bankruptcy, and grave injustice to debtors.

The price decline ended about 1847 in most countries, and gold discoveries in California in 1848 and in Australia three years later pushed the price level upward in Great Britain about 16 percent in 1851-1862.[8] The rise continued until 1873. The U.S. Civil War, mainly financed by inflation, raised prices in the Union about 120 percent (as in the War of 1812) and many times this amount in the Confederacy, which was unable to tax because of its debilitating commitment to states' rights.[9] The sparse data available suggest that commodity price levels in France and Prussia were little, if at all, out of line with the levels in other industrially advanced countries both during the Franco-Prussian War of 1871 and France's payment of the then colossal indemnity. But in spite of neutralization in various ways, the indemnity receipts stimulated a violent boom in real estate and securities, not only in Germany but in Austria, Bohemia, and Hungary as well, which culminated in the worldwide depression that began in 1873.[10] Obviously, if there had been no war there would have been no indemnity. There could have been a depression; but if so, it seems safe to assume that it would have been less severe and would not have lasted six long years.

Discovery of gold in Alaska and South Africa near the end of the nineteenth century and improved processes of extracting bullion from

[8] W. Stanley Jevons, *A Serious Fall in the Value of Gold Ascertained, and Its Social Effects Set Forth* (London, 1863), p. 29.

[9] Cf. Milton Friedman, "Price, Income, and Monetary Changes in Three Wartime Periods," *American Economic Review*, 42 (1952), Papers and Procedings, 612-25. This paper presents extremely valuable data on, and analysis of, our monetary and price experience during the Civil War, First World War, and Second World War.

[10] F. W. Taussig, *International Trade* (New York, 1927), p. 271.

The Role of War 17

ore ended a sharply falling trend of prices that had lasted a quarter century, partly due to demonetization of silver, and raised the price level in most of the Western world something like 40 to 50 percent from 1897 to 1914.

In comparison with what would follow the First World War and its aftermath, this rise was insignificant. Though prices had risen much faster in individual countries on certain occasions, the Western world as a whole had never seen such a sudden and universal price upheaval. Shortages of many commodities, ravaged areas to be restored, mistakes in fiscal policies, and unduly low interest rates engineered by central banks or national governments extended the rise in prices for about two years after the Armistice of November 11, 1918. From 1913 to 1920 prices rose about 120 percent in the United States— nearly the same as in the War of 1812 and the Civil War—145 percent in Canada, 200 percent in Great Britain, and 400 percent in France. Owing to the scarcity and sometimes complete lack of goods formerly imported from belligerents, to the inflow of money to pay for eagerly sought exports, and to mistakes in monetary, fiscal, and central bank policies (criticized so severely by Professor Gustav Cassel[11]), neutral countries did not escape the ravages of inflation. Prices almost trebled in the Netherlands, one of the world's most highly developed countries, and nearly quadrupled in Sweden, a nation famous for its high level of education and its outstanding monetary economists. Switzerland, another extremely enlightened country, also suffered from severe inflation.[12] The hyperinflation which reduced the value of money in Germany to zero from 1919 to 1923 would have been inconceivable without World War I and its aftermath.[13] Neither would we have had the depression throughout the civilized world that began in the autumn of 1929, or at least it would not have been comparable in severity.

World War II again forced commodity prices sharply upward in virtually all countries throughout the civilized world, whether industrial or agricultural, belligerent or neutral. And a large part of our recent inflation, and some part of the inflation in Western Europe, had its origin in our ill-fated venture in Vietnam and the unwillingness of our political leaders in both parties to attempt to pay the cost

[11] In *Money and Foreign Exchange after 1914* (New York, 1930 ed.), pp. 19-25, 101-136.
[12] Cf. *Statistical Yearbook of the League of Nations 1930/31*, II A 16 (Geneva, 1931), pp. 270-72.
[13] Cf. Costantino Bresciani-Turroni, *The Economics of Inflation* (London, 1937), pp. 5-6, 23-182. This is a translation of his *Vicende del marco tedesco* (Milano, 1931). Although the translation is excellent, the original is better.

18 *Hamilton*

of the war through taxation. For this method of payment would have revealed the true cost, and thus ended the war. We should never forget that during the Korean War owners of factories would permit their sons to be drafted for combat but would not tolerate conscription of their industrial plants for war production.

Wars and revolutions without taxation to cover the cost have been the principal causes of hyperinflation in industrial countries in the last two centuries. But in nonindustrial nations, particularly in Latin America, the main cause of both inflation and hyperinflation has not been warfare but welfare, or attempted welfare, without taxation to cover the cost. And in some cases, as in Chile and Uruguay, the hyperinflation has been violent. Attempts to provide more welfare than can be covered by taxation and withholdings seem to be hurting Great Britain badly, and one of my worst fears is that we may tread in the same path.

I shall close by pointing out that from a purely economic standpoint the best possible way to pay for a war is by current taxation. This plan would minimize the cost of the war to the nation adopting it, for normal economic forces would operate in its favor, and the bookkeeping and adminstrative costs would be less than any alternative methods would require. The revenue from taxes could be made to cover exactly the war and non-war expenditures of the government; what was left over could cover civilian expenditures. By its pattern of noninflationary expenditures the government could shift manpower and physical resources from the non-war to the war sectors of the economy, and at the end of the war this could be reversed by an appropriate shift in taxation and public expenditures. What may be still more important is that the heads of government, enterprises, households and the like, as well as private individuals and other makers of economic decisions, could be spared the burden of thinking in both nominal and real terms, for these would be identical. Furthermore, there would be no war debt.

But if this plan is so good, why is it not adopted? Partly because, of all forms of de facto taxation, inflation is the easiest to levy, the quickest to materialize, and the hardest to evade. But the real reason is that educated people would quickly see that the cost of the war was too great and the probable benefits entirely too small for the war to be worthwhile and would clamor for peace. If by some miracle both sides should adopt my utopian plan for paying for wars, conceivably there might be no more wars. But if only one side resolved to pay as it went, it would be one of the surest possible ways to lose the war.

The Role of War 19

All of us should regret the misery inflicted by the inflationary financing of our Revolution, which set the pattern for future wars. But if there had been no inflation, there would be no Bicentennial of our independence in the U.S. today, for we would have remained subjects of George III; and Benedict Arnold, not George Washington, would be the hero of our abortive *rebellion*.

EARL J. HAMILTON, *University of Chicago*

[7]

FIAT MONEY INFLATION IN FRANCE

HOW IT CAME

EARLY IN THE YEAR 1789 the French nation found itself in deep financial embarrassment: there was a heavy debt and a serious deficit.

The vast reforms of that period, though a lasting blessing politically, were a temporary evil financially. There was a general want of confidence in business circles; capital had shown its proverbial timidity by retiring out of sight as far as possible; throughout the land was stagnation.

Statesmanlike measures, careful watching, and wise management would, doubtless, have ere long led to a return of confidence, a reappearance of money, and a resumption of business; but these involved patience and self-denial, and, thus far in human history, these are the rarest products of political wisdom. Few nations have ever been able to exercise these virtues; and France was not then one of these few.[1]

There was a general search for some short road to prosperity: ere long the idea was set afloat that the

---

[1] For this and subsequent footnotes, see pages 117-124.

great want of the country was more of the circulating medium; and this was speedily followed by calls for an issue of paper money. The Minister of Finance at this period was Necker. In financial ability he was acknowledged as among the great bankers of Europe, but his was something more than financial ability: he had a deep feeling of patriotism and a high sense of personal honor. The difficulties in his way were great, but he steadily endeavored to keep France faithful to those principles in monetary affairs which the general experience of modern times had found the only path to national safety. As difficulties arose, the National Assembly drew away from him, and soon came among the members renewed suggestions of paper money: orators in public meetings, at the clubs, and in the Assembly, proclaimed it a panacea—a way of "securing resources without paying interest." Journalists caught it up and displayed its beauties, among these men, Marat, who, in his newspaper, "The Friend of the People," also joined the cries against Necker, picturing him—a man of sterling honesty, who gave up health and fortune for the sake of France—as a wretch seeking only to enrich himself from the public purse.

Against this tendency toward the issue of irredeemable paper Necker contended as best he might. He knew well to what it always had led, even when surrounded by the most skillful guarantees. Among those who struggled to support ideas similar to his was Ber-

[24]

gasse, a deputy from Lyons, whose pamphlets, then and later, against such issues exerted a wider influence, perhaps, than any others. Parts of them seem fairly inspired. Anyone today reading his prophecies of the evils sure to follow such a currency would certainly ascribe to him a miraculous foresight, were it not so clear that his prophetic power was due simply to a knowledge of natural laws revealed by history.

But this current in favor of paper money became so strong that an effort was made to breast it by a compromise; and during the last months of 1789 and the first months of 1790 came discussions in the National Assembly looking to issues of notes based upon the landed property of the Church, which was to be confiscated for that purpose. But care was to be taken; the issue was to be largely in the shape of notes of 1,000, 300, and 200 livres,° too large to be used as ordinary currency, but of convenient size to be used in purchasing the Church lands; besides this, they were to bear interest and this would tempt holders to hoard them. The Assembly thus held back from issuing smaller obligations.

Remembrances of the ruin which had come from the great issues of smaller currency at an earlier day were still vivid. Yet the pressure toward a popular currency

---

° EDITOR'S NOTE: The livre was the common coin of exchange in France at the beginning of the period White describes. The franc became the official monetary unit in 1795, with conversion at the rate of 81 livres to 80 francs.

[25]

for universal use grew stronger and stronger. The finance committee of the Assembly reported that "the people demand a new circulating medium"; that "the circulation of paper money is the best of operations"; that "it is the most free because it reposes on the will of the people"; that "it will bind the interest of the citizens to the public good."

The report appealed to the patriotism of the French people with the following exhortation: "Let us show to Europe that we understand our own resources; let us immediately take the broad road to our liberation instead of dragging ourselves along the tortuous and obscure paths of fragmentary loans." It concluded by recommending an issue of paper money carefully guarded, to the full amount of four hundred million livres, and the argument was pursued until the objection to smaller notes faded from view.

Typical in the debate on the whole subject, in its various phases, were the declarations of M. Matrineau. He was loud and long for paper money, his only fear being that the Committee had not authorized enough of it; he declared that business was stagnant, and that the sole cause was a want of more of the circulating medium; that paper money ought to be made a legal tender; that the Assembly should rise above prejudices which the failures of John Law's paper money had caused, several decades before. Like every supporter of irredeemable paper money then or since, he seemed to

[26]

think that the laws of Nature had changed since previous disastrous issues. He said: "Paper money under a despotism is dangerous; it favors corruption; but in a nation constitutionally governed, which itself takes care in the emission of its notes, which determines their number and use, that danger no longer exists." He insisted that John Law's notes at first restored prosperity, but that the wretchedness and ruin they caused resulted from their overissue, and that such an overissue is possible only under a despotism.[2]

M. de la Rochefoucauld gave his opinion that "the assignats will draw specie out of the coffers where it is now hoarded."[3]

On the other hand, Cazalès and Maury showed that the result could only be disastrous. Never, perhaps, did a political prophecy meet with more exact fulfillment in every line than the terrible picture drawn in one of Cazalès' speeches in this debate. Still the current ran stronger and stronger; Petion made a brilliant oration in favor of the report, and Necker's influence and experience were gradually worn away.

Mingled with the financial argument was a strong political plea. The National Assembly had determined to confiscate the vast real property of the French Church—the pious accumulations of fifteen hundred years. There were princely estates in the country, bishops' palaces, and conventual buildings in the towns; these formed between one-fourth and one-third of the

[27]

entire real property of France, and amounted in value to at least two thousand million livres. By a few sweeping strokes all this became the property of the nation. Never, apparently, did a government secure a more solid basis for a great financial future.[4]

There were two special reasons why French statesmen desired speedily to sell these lands. First, a financial reason—to obtain money to relieve the government. Secondly, a political reason—to get this land distributed among the thrifty middle classes, and so commit them to the Revolution and to the government which gave their title.

It was urged, then, that the issue of four hundred millions of paper, (not in the shape of interest-bearing bonds, as had at first been proposed, but in notes small as well as large), would give the treasury something to pay out immediately, and relieve the national necessities; that, having been put into circulation, this paper money would stimulate business; that it would give to all capitalists, large or small, the means for buying from the nation the ecclesiastical real estate; and that from the proceeds of this real estate the nation would pay its debts and also obtain new funds for new necessities. Never was theory more seductive both to financiers and statesmen.

It would be a great mistake to suppose that the statesmen of France, or the French people, were ignorant

[28]

of the dangers in issuing irredeemable paper money.
No matter how skillfully the bright side of such a currency was exhibited, all thoughtful men in France remembered its dark side. They knew too well, from that
ruinous experience, seventy years before, in John Law's
time, the difficulties and dangers of a currency not well
based and controlled. They had then learned how easy
it is to issue it; how difficult it is to check its overissue;
how seductively it leads to the absorption of the means
of the workingmen and men of small fortunes; how
heavily it falls on all those living on fixed incomes, salaries, or wages; how securely it creates on the ruins of
the prosperity of all men of meager means a class of
debauched speculators, the most injurious class that a
nation can harbor—more injurious, indeed, than professional criminals whom the law recognizes and can
throttle; how it stimulates overproduction at first and
leaves every industry flaccid afterward; how it breaks
down thrift and develops political and social immoral-
ity. All this France had been thoroughly taught by
experience. Many then living had felt the result of such
an experiment—the issues of paper money under John
Law, a man who to this day is acknowledged one of
the most ingenious financiers the world has ever known;
and there were then sitting in the National Assembly
of France many who owed the poverty of their families
to those issues of paper. Hardly a man in the country
who had not heard those who issued it cursed as the

[29]

authors of the most frightful catastrophe France had then experienced.[5]

It was no mere attempt at theatrical display, but a natural impulse, which led a thoughtful statesman, during the debate, to hold up a piece of that old paper money and to declare that it was stained with the blood and tears of their fathers.

And it would also be a mistake to suppose that the National Assembly, which discussed this matter, was composed of mere wild revolutionists; no inference could be more wide of the fact. Whatever may have been the character of the men who legislated for France afterward, no thoughtful student of history can deny, despite all the arguments and sneers of reactionary statesmen and historians, that few more keen-sighted legislative bodies have ever met than this first French Constitutional Assembly. In it were such men as Sieyès, Bailly, Necker, Mirabeau, Talleyrand, Du Pont de Nemours, and a multitude of others who, in various sciences and in the political world, had already shown and were destined afterward to show themselves among the strongest and shrewdest men that Europe has yet seen.

But the current toward paper money had become irresistible. It was constantly urged, and with a great show of force, that if any nation could safely issue it, France was now that nation; that she was fully warned by her severe experience under John Law; that she was now a constitutional government, controlled by an en-

[30]

lightened, patriotic people—not, as in the days of the former issues of paper money, an absolute monarchy controlled by politicians and adventurers; that she was able to secure every livre of her paper money by a virtual mortgage on a landed domain vastly greater in value than the entire issue; that, with men like Bailly, Mirabeau, and Necker at her head, she could not commit the financial mistakes and crimes from which France had suffered under John Law, the Regent Duke of Orleans, and Cardinal Dubois.

Oratory prevailed over science and experience. In April 1790, came the final decree to issue four hundred millions of livres in paper money, based upon confiscated property of the Church for its security. The deliberations on this first decree and on the bill carrying it into effect were most interesting; prominent in the debate being Necker, Du Pont de Nemours, Maury, Cazalès, Petion, Bailly, and many others hardly inferior. The discussions were certainly very able; no person can read them at length in the *Moniteur,* nor even in the summaries of the parliamentary history, without feeling that various modern historians have done wretched injustice to those men who were then endeavoring to stand between France and ruin.

This sum—four hundred millions, so vast in those days—was issued in assignats, which were notes secured by a pledge of productive real estate and bearing interest to the holder at three per cent. No irredeemable cur-

[31]

rency has ever claimed a more scientific and practical guarantee for its goodness and for its proper action on public finances. On the one hand, it had what the world recognized as a most practical security—a mortgage on productive real estate of vastly greater value than the issue. On the other hand, as the notes bore interest, there seemed cogent reason for their being withdrawn from circulation whenever they became redundant.[6]

As speedily as possible the notes were put into circulation. Unlike those issued in John Law's time, they were engraved in the best style of the art. To stimulate loyalty, the portrait of the King was placed in the center; to arouse public spirit, patriotic legends and emblems surrounded it; to stimulate public cupidity, the amount of interest which the note would yield each day to the holder was printed in the margin; and the whole was duly garnished with stamps and signatures to show that it was carefully registered and controlled.[7]

To crown its work the National Assembly, to explain the advantages of this new currency, issued an address to the French people. In this address it spoke of the nation as "delivered by this grand means from all uncertainty and from all ruinous results of the credit system." It foretold that this issue "would bring back into the public treasury, into commerce, and into all branches of industry strength, abundance, and prosperity."[8]

Some of the arguments in this address are worth recalling, and, among them, the following: "Paper money

[32]

is without inherent value unless it represents some special property. Without representing some special property it is inadmissible in trade to compete with a metallic currency, which has a value real and independent of the public action; therefore it is that the paper money which has only the public authority as its basis has always caused ruin where it has been established; that is the reason why the bank notes of 1720, issued by John Law, after having caused terrible evils, have left only frightful memories. Therefore it is that the National Assembly has not wished to expose you to this danger, but has given this new paper money not only a value derived from the national authority but a value real and immutable, a value which permits it to sustain advantageously a competition with the precious metals themselves."[9]

But the final declaration was, perhaps, the most interesting. It was as follows:

"These assignats, bearing interest as they do, will soon be considered better than the coin now hoarded, and will bring it out again into circulation." The King was also induced to issue a proclamation recommending that his people receive this new money without objection.

All this caused great joy. Among the various utterances of this feeling was the letter of M. Sarot, directed to the editor of the *Journal of the National Assembly,* and scattered through France. M. Sarot is hardly able

[33]

to contain himself as he anticipates the prosperity and glory that this issue of paper is to bring to his country. One thing only vexes him, and that is the pamphlet of M. Bergasse against the assignats; therefore it is after a long series of arguments and protestations, in order to give a final proof of his confidence in the paper money and his entire skepticism as to the evils predicted by Bergasse and others, M. Sarot solemnly lays his house, garden, and furniture upon the altar cf his country and offers to sell them for paper money alone.

There were, indeed, some gainsayers. These especially appeared among the clergy, who, naturally, abhorred the confiscation of Church property. Various ecclesiastics made speeches, some of them full of pithy and weighty arguments, against the proposed issue of paper, and there is preserved a sermon from one priest threatening all persons handling the new money with eternal damnation. But the great majority of the French people, who had suffered ecclesiastical oppression so long, regarded these utterances as the wriggling of a fish on the hook, and enjoyed the sport all the better.[10]

The first result of this issue was apparently all that the most sanguine could desire: the treasury was at once greatly relieved; a portion of the public debt was paid; creditors were encouraged; credit revived; ordinary expenses were met, and, a considerable part of this paper money having thus been passed from the government into the hands of the people, trade increased and all difficulties seemed to vanish. The anxieties of Necker, the prophecies of Maury and Cazalès seemed proven utterly futile. And, indeed, it is quite possible that, if the national authorities had stopped with this issue, few of the financial evils which afterwards arose would have been severely felt; the four hundred millions of paper money then issued would have simply discharged the function of a similar amount of specie. But soon there came another result: times grew less easy; by the end of September, within five months after the issue of the four hundred millions in assignats, the government had spent them and was again in distress.[11]

The old remedy immediately and naturally recurred to the minds of men. Throughout the country began a cry for another issue of paper; thoughtful men then began to recall what their fathers had told them about the seductive path of paper-money issues in John Law's time, and to remember the prophecies that they themselves had heard in the debate on the first issue of assignats less than six months before.

At that time the opponents of paper had prophesied that, once on the downward path of inflation, the nation could not be restrained and that more issues would follow. The supporters of the first issue had asserted that this was a calumny, that *the people* were now in control, and that they could and would check these issues whenever they desired.

[35]

The condition of opinion in the Assembly was, therefore, chaotic: a few schemers and dreamers were loud and outspoken for paper money; many of the more shallow and easy-going were inclined to yield; the more thoughtful endeavored to breast the current.

One man there was who could have withstood the pressure: Mirabeau. He was the popular idol—the great orator of the Assembly and much more than a great orator—he had carried the nation through some of its worst dangers by a boldness almost godlike; in the various conflicts he had shown not only oratorical boldness, but amazing foresight. As to his real opinion on an irredeemable currency there can be no doubt. It was the opinion which all true statesmen have held, before his time and since—in his own country, in England, in America, in every modern civilized nation. In his letter to Cerutti, written in January 1789, hardly six months before, he had spoken of paper money as "a nursery of tyranny, corruption, and delusion; a veritable debauch of authority in delirium." In one of his early speeches in the National Assembly he had called such money, when Anson covertly suggested its issue, "a loan to an armed robber," and said of it: "That infamous word, paper money, ought to be banished from our language." In his private letters written at this very time, which were revealed at a later period, he showed that he was fully aware of the dangers of inflation. But he yielded to the pressure: partly because he thought it important

[36]

to sell the government lands rapidly to the people, and
so develop speedily a large class of small landholders
pledged to stand by the government which gave them
their titles; partly, doubtless, from a love of immediate
rather than of remote applause; and, generally, in a
vague hope that the severe, inexorable laws of finance
which had brought heavy punishments upon governments emitting an irredeemable currency in other lands,
at other times, might in some way at this time be ward-
ed off from France.[12]

The question was brought up by Montesquieu's report on August 27, 1790. This report favored, with evident reluctance, an additional issue of paper. It went
on to declare that the original issue of four hundred
millions, though opposed at the beginning, had proved
successful; that assignats were economical, though they
had dangers; and, as a climax, came the declaration:
"We must save the country."[13]

Upon this report Mirabeau then made one of his most
powerful speeches. He confessed that he had at first
feared the issue of assignats, but that he now dared
urge it; that experience had shown the issue of paper
money most serviceable; that the report proved the first
issue of assignats a success; that public affairs had come
out of distress; that ruin had been averted and credit
established. He then argued that there was a difference
between paper money of the recent issue and that from
which the nation had suffered so much in John Law's

[37]

time; he declared that the French nation had now become enlightened and he added, "Deceptive subtleties can no longer mislead patriots and men of sense in this matter." He then went on to say: "We must accomplish that which we have begun," and declared that there must be one more large issue of paper, guaranteed by the national lands and by the good faith of the French nation.

To show how practical the system was he insisted that just as soon as paper money should become too abundant it would be absorbed in rapid purchases of national lands; and he made a very striking comparison between this self-adjusting, self-converting system and the rains descending in showers upon the earth, then in swelling rivers discharged into the sea, then drawn up in vapor and finally scattered over the earth again in rapidly fertilizing showers. He predicted that the members would be surprised at the astonishing success of this paper money and that there would be none too much of it.

His theory grew by what it fed upon—as the paper-money theory has generally done. Toward the close, in a burst of eloquence, he suggested that assignats be created to an amount sufficient to cover the national debt, and that all the national lands be exposed for sale immediately, predicting that thus prosperity would return to the nation and that all classes would find this additional issue of paper money a blessing.[14]

[38]

This speech was frequently interrupted by applause; a unanimous vote ordered it printed, and copies were spread throughout France. The impulse given by it permeated all subsequent discussion; Gouy arose and proposed to liquidate the national debt of twenty-four hundred millions—to use his own words—"by one single operation, grand, simple, magnificent."[15] This "operation" was to be the emission of twenty-four hundred millions in legal tender notes, and a law that specie should not be accepted in purchasing national lands. His demagogy bloomed forth magnificently. He advocated an appeal to the people, who, to use his flattering expression, "ought alone to give the law in a matter so interesting." The newspapers of the period, in reporting his speech, noted it with the very significant remark, "This discourse was loudly applauded."

To him replied Brillat-Savarin. He called attention to the depreciation of assignats already felt. He tried to make the Assembly see that natural laws work as inexorably in France as elsewhere; he predicted that if this new issue were made, there would come a depreciation of thirty per cent. Singular, that the man who so fearlessly stood against this tide of unreason has left to the world simply a reputation as the most brilliant cook that ever existed! He was followed by the Abbe Goutes, who declared—what seems grotesque to those who have read the history of an irredeemable paper currency in any country—that new issues of paper money "will

[39]

supply a circulating medium which will protect public morals from corruption."[16]

Into this debate was brought a report by Necker. He was not, indeed, the great statesman whom France especially needed at this time, of all times. He did not recognize the fact that the nation was entering a great revolution, but he could and did see that, come what might, there were simple principles of finance which must be adhered to. Most earnestly, therefore, he endeavored to dissuade the Assembly from the proposed issue, suggesting that other means could be found for accomplishing the result, and he predicted terrible evils. But the current was running too fast. The only result was that Necker was spurned as a man of the past; he sent in his resignation and left France forever.[17] The paper-money demagogues shouted for joy at his departure; their chorus rang through the journalism of the time. No words could express their contempt for a man who was unable to see the advantages of filling the treasury with the issues of a printing press. Marat, Hébert, Camille Desmoulins, and the whole mass of demagogues so soon to follow them to the guillotine were especially jubilant.[18]

Continuing the debate, Rewbell attacked Necker, saying that the assignats were not at par because there were not yet enough of them; he insisted that payments for public lands be received in assignats alone; and suggested that the church bells of the kingdom be

[40]

melted down into small money. Le Brun attacked the
whole scheme in the Assembly, as he had done in the
Committee, declaring that the proposal, instead of re-
lieving the nation, would wreck it. The papers of the
time very significantly say that at this there arose many
murmurs. Chabroud came to the rescue. He said that
the issue of assignats would relieve the distress of the
people, and he presented very neatly the new theory
of paper money and its basis in the following words:
"The earth is the source of value; you cannot distribute
the earth in a circulating value, but this paper becomes
representative of that value and it is evident that the
creditors of the nation will not be injured by taking it."
On the other hand, appeared in the leading paper, the
Moniteur, a very thoughtful article against paper
money, which sums up all by saying, "It is, then, evident that all paper which cannot, at the will of the
bearer, be converted into specie cannot discharge the
functions of money." This article goes on to cite Mirabeau's former opinion in his letter to Cerutti, published
in 1789—the famous opinion of paper money as "a
nursery of tyranny, corruption, and delusion; a veritable
debauch of authority in delirium." Lablache, in the
Assembly, quoted a saying that "paper money is the
emetic of great states."[19]

Boutidoux, resorting to phrasemaking, called the assignats *"un papier terre,"* or "land converted into paper."
Boislandry answered vigorously and foretold evil re-

[41]

sults. Pamphlets continued to be issued, among them, one so pungent that it was brought into the Assembly and read there—the truth which it presented with great clearness being simply that doubling the quantity of money or substitutes for money in a nation simply increases prices, disturbs values, alarms capital, diminishes legitimate enterprise, and so decreases the demand both for products and for labor; that the only persons to be helped by it are the rich who have large debts to pay. This pamphlet was signed, "A Friend of the People," and was received with great applause by the thoughtful minority in the Assembly. Du Pont de Nemours, who had stood by Necker in the debate on the first issue of assignats, arose, avowed the pamphlet to be his, and said sturdily that he had always voted against the emission of irredeemable paper and always would.[20]

Far more important than any other argument against inflation was the speech of Talleyrand. He had been among the boldest and most radical French Statesmen. He it was—a former bishop—who, more than any other, had carried the extreme measure of taking into the possession of the nation the great landed estates of the Church, and he had supported the first issue of four hundred millions. But he now adopted a judicial tone— attempted to show to the Assembly the very simple truth that the effect of a second issue of assignats may be different from that of the first; that the first was evi-

[42]

dently needed; that the second may be as injurious as the first was useful. He exhibited various weak points in the inflation fallacies and presented forcibly the trite truth that no laws and no decrees can keep large issues of irredeemable paper at par with specie.

In his speech occur these words: "You can, indeed, arrange it so that the people shall be forced to take a thousand livres in paper for a thousand livres in specie; but you can never arrange it so that a man shall be obliged to give a thousand livres in specie for a thousand livres in paper—in that fact is embedded the entire question; and on account of that fact the whole system fails."[21]

The nation at large now began to take part in the debate; thoughtful men saw that here was the turning point between good and evil; that the nation stood at the parting of the ways. Most of the great commercial cities bestirred themselves and sent up remonstrances against the new emission, twenty-five being opposed and seven in favor of it.

But eloquent theorists arose to glorify paper and among these, Royer, who on September 14, 1790, put forth a pamphlet entitled *Reflections of a Patriotic Citizen on the Issue of Assignats,* in which he gave many specious reasons why the assignats could not be depressed, and spoke of the argument against them as "vile clamors of people bribed to affect public opinion."

[43]

He said to the National Assembly, "If it is necessary to create five thousand millions, and more, of the paper, decree such a creation gladly." He, too, predicted, as many others had done, a time when gold was to lose all its value, since all exchanges would be made with this admirable, guaranteed paper, and therefore that coin would come out from the places where it was hoarded. He foretold prosperous times to France in case these great issues of paper were continued and declared these "the only means to insure happiness, glory, and liberty to the French nation." Speeches like this gave courage to a new swarm of theorists. It began to be especially noted that men who had never shown any ability to make or increase fortunes for themselves abounded in brilliant plans for creating and increasing wealth for the country at large.

Greatest force of all, on September 27, 1790, came Mirabeau's final speech. The most sober and conservative of his modern opponents speaks of its eloquence as "prodigious." In this the great orator dwelt first on the political necessity involved, declaring that the most pressing need was to get the government lands into the hands of the people, and so to commit to the nation and against the old privileged classes the class of landholders thus created.

Through the whole course of his arguments there is one leading point enforced with all his eloquence and ingenuity—the excellence of the proposed currency, its

[44]

stability, and its security. He declares that, being based on the pledge of public lands and convertible into them, the notes are better secured than if redeemable in specie; that the precious metals are only employed in the secondary arts, while the French paper money represents the first and most real of all property, the source of all production, *the land;* that while other nations have been obliged to emit paper money, none have ever been so fortunate as the French nation, for the reason that none had ever before been able to give this landed security; that whoever takes French paper money has practically a mortgage to secure it—and on landed property which can easily be sold to satisfy his claims, while other nations have been able only to give a vague claim on the entire nation. "And," he cries, "I would rather have a mortgage on a garden than on a kingdom!"

Other arguments of his are more demagogical. He declares that the only interests affected will be those of bankers and capitalists, but that manufacturers will see prosperity restored to them. Some of his arguments seem almost puerile, as when he says, "If gold has been hoarded through timidity or malignity, the issue of paper will show that gold is not necessary, and it will then come forth." But, as a whole, the speech was brilliant; it was often interrupted by applause; it settled the question. People did not stop to consider that it was the dashing speech of an orator and not the matured judgment of a financial expert; they did not see that

[45]

calling Mirabeau or Talleyrand to advise upon a monetary policy, because they had shown boldness in danger and strength in conflict, was like summoning a prize fighter to mend a watch.

In vain did Maury show that, while the first issues of John Law's paper had brought prosperity, those that followed brought misery; in vain did he quote from a book published in John Law's time, showing that Law was at first considered a patriot and friend of humanity; in vain did he hold up to the Assembly one of Law's bills and appeal to their memories of the wretchedness brought upon France by them; in vain did Du Pont present a simple and really wise plan of substituting notes in the payment of the floating debt which should not form a part of the ordinary circulating medium; nothing could resist the eloquence of Mirabeau. Barnave, following, insisted that "Law's paper was based upon the phantoms of the Mississippi; ours, upon the solid basis of ecclesiastical lands," and he proved that the assignats could not depreciate further. Prudhomme's newspaper poured contempt over gold as security for the currency, extolled real estate as the only true basis, and was fervent in praise of the convertibility and self-adjusting features of the proposed scheme.

In spite of all this plausibility and eloquence, a large minority stood firm to their earlier principles; but on September 29, 1790, by a vote of 508 to 423, the deed was done; a bill was passed authorizing the issue of

[46]

eight hundred millions of new assignats, but solemnly
declaring that in no case should the entire amount put
in circulation exceed twelve hundred millions. To make
assurance doubly sure, it also provided that as fast as
the assignats were paid into the treasury for land they
should be burned, and thus a healthful contraction be
constantly maintained. Unlike the first issue, these new
notes were to bear no interest.[22]

Great were the plaudits of the nation at this relief.
Among the multitudes of pamphlets expressing this joy
which have come down to us the *Friend of the Revolution* is the most interesting. It begins as follows:
"Citizens, the deed is done. The assignats are the key-
stone of the arch. It has just been happily put in position. Now I can announce to you that the Revolution is
finished and there only remain one or two important
questions. All the rest is but a matter of detail which
cannot deprive us any longer of the pleasure of admir-
ing this important work in its entirety. The provinces
and the commercial cities which were at first alarmed
at the proposal to issue so much paper money now send
expressions of their thanks; specie is coming out to be
joined with paper money. Foreigners come to us from
all parts of Europe to seek their happiness under laws
which they admire; and soon France, enriched by her
new property and by the national industry which is pre-
paring for fruitfulness, will demand still another creation of paper money."

[47]

France was now fully committed to a policy of inflation; and, if there had been any question of this before,
all doubts were removed now by various acts very significant as showing the exceeding difficulty of stopping
a nation once in the full tide of a depreciating currency.
The National Assembly had from the first shown an
amazing liberality to all sorts of enterprises, wise or foolish, which were urged "for the good of the people." As
a result of these and other largesses, the old cry of the
"lack of a circulating medium" broke forth again; and
especially loud were the clamors for more small bills.
The cheaper currency had largely driven out the dearer;
paper had caused small silver and copper money mainly
to disappear; all sorts of notes of hand, circulating
under the name of "confidence bills," flooded France—
sixty-three kinds in Paris alone.

This unguaranteed currency caused endless confusion
and fraud. Different districts of France began to issue
their own assignats in small denominations, and this
action stirred the National Assembly to evade the solemn pledge that the circulation should not go above
twelve hundred millions and that all assignats returned to the treasury for lands should immediately be
burned.[23] Within a short time there had been received
into the treasury for lands one hundred sixty million livres in paper. By the terms of the previous acts
this amount of paper ought to have been retired. In-

[48]

stead of this, under the plea of necessity, the greater part of it was reissued in the form of small notes.

There was, indeed, much excuse for new issues of small notes, for, under the theory that an issue of smaller notes would drive silver out of circulation, the smallest authorized assignat was for fifty livres. To supply silver and copper and hold it in circulation everything was tried. Citizens had been spurred on by law to send their silverware and jewels to the mint. Even the King sent his silver and gold plate, and the churches and convents were required by law to send to the government melting pot all silver and gold vessels not absolutely necessary for public worship. For copper money the church bells were melted down. But silver and even copper continued to become more and more scarce. In the midst of all this, various juggleries were tried, and in November 1790, the Assembly decreed a single standard of coinage, the chosen metal being silver, and the ratio between the two precious metals was changed from 15½ to 1, to 14½ to 1—but all in vain. It was found necessary to issue the dreaded small paper, and a beginning was made by issuing one hundred millions in notes of five francs, and ere long, obedient to the universal clamor, there were issued parchment notes for various small amounts down to a single sou.[24]

Yet each of these issues, great or small, was but as a drop of cold water to a parched throat. Although there was already a rise in prices which showed that the

[49]

amount needed for circulation had been exceeded, the cry for "more circulating medium" was continued. The pressure for new issues became stronger and stronger. The Parisian populace and the Jacobin Club were especially loud in their demands for them; and, a few months later, on June 19, 1791, with few speeches, in a silence very ominous, a new issue was made of six hundred millions more—less than nine months after the former great issue, with its solemn pledges to keep down the amount in circulation. With the exception of a few thoughtful men, the whole nation again sang paeans.[25]

In this comparative ease of new issues is seen the action of a law in finance as certain as the working of a similar law in natural philosophy. If a material body falls from a height its velocity is accelerated, by a well-known law, in a constantly increasing ratio: so in issues of irredeemable currency, in obedience to the theories of a legislative body or of the people at large, there is a natural law of rapidly increasing emission and depreciation. The first inflation bills were passed with great difficulty, after very sturdy resistance and by a majority of a few score out of nearly a thousand votes; but we observe now that new inflation measures were passed more and more easily, and we shall have occasion to see the working of this same law in a more striking degree as this history develops itself.

During the various stages of this debate there cropped

[50]

up a doctrine old and ominous. It was the same which appeared toward the end of the nineteenth century in the United States during what became known as the "greenback craze" and the free "silver craze." In France it had been refuted, a generation before the Revolution, by Turgot, just as brilliantly as it was met a hundred years later in the United States by James A. Garfield and his compeers. This was the doctrine that all currency, whether gold, paper, leather, or any other material, derives its efficiency from the official stamp it bears, and that, this being the case, a government may relieve itself of its debts and make itself rich and prosperous simply by means of a printing press—fundamentally the theory which underlay the later American doctrine of "fiat money."

There came mutterings and finally speeches in the Jacobin Club, in the Assembly, and in newspaper articles and pamphlets throughout the country, taking this doctrine for granted. These could hardly affect thinking men who bore in mind the calamities brought upon the whole people, and especially upon the poorer classes, by this same theory as put in practice by John Law, or as refuted by Turgot, but it served to swell the popular chorus in favor of the issue of more assignats and plenty of them.[26]

The great majority of Frenchmen now became desperate optimists, declaring that inflation is prosperity. Throughout France there came temporary good feeling.

[51]

The nation was becoming inebriated with paper money. The good feeling was that of a drunkard just after his draught; and it is to be noted as a simple historical fact, corresponding to a physiological fact, that, as draughts of paper money came faster the successive periods of good feeling grew shorter.

Various bad signs began to appear. Immediately after each new issue came a marked depreciation; curious it is to note the general reluctance to assign the right reason. The decline in the purchasing power of paper money was in obedience to the simplest laws in economics, but France had now gone beyond her thoughtful statesmen and taken refuge in unwavering optimism, giving any explanation of the new difficulties rather than the right one. A leading member of the Assembly insisted, in an elaborate speech, that the cause of depreciation was simply the want of knowledge and of confidence among the rural population and he suggested means of enlightening them. La Rochefoucauld proposed to issue an address to the people showing the goodness of the currency and the absurdity of preferring coin. The address was unanimously voted. As well might they have attempted to show that a beverage made by mixing a quart of wine and two quarts of water would possess all the exhilarating quality of the original, undiluted liquid.

Attention was aroused by another menacing fact:

[52]

specie disappeared more and more. The explanations of this fact also displayed wonderful ingenuity in finding false reasons and in evading the true one. A very common explanation was indicated in Prudhomme's newspaper, *Les Révolutions de Paris*, of January 17, 1791, which declared that coin "will keep rising until the people shall have hanged a broker." Another popular theory was that the Bourbon family were, in some mysterious way, drawing off all solid money to the chief centers of their intrigues in Germany. Comic and, at the same time, pathetic, were evidences of the widespread idea that if only a goodly number of people engaged in trade were hanged, the par value of the assignats would be restored.

Still another favorite idea was that British emissaries were in the midst of the people, instilling notions hostile to paper. Great efforts were made to find these emissaries and more than one innocent person experienced the popular wrath under the supposition that he was engaged in raising gold and depressing paper. Even Talleyrand, shrewd as he was, insisted that the cause was simply that the imports were too great and the exports too little.[27] As well might he explain the fact that, when oil is mingled with water, water sinks to the bottom, by saying that this is because the oil rises to the top. This disappearance of specie was the result of a natural law as simple and as sure in its action as gravitation; the superior currency had been withdrawn be-

[53]

cause an inferior currency could be used.[28] Some efforts were made to remedy this. In the municipality of Quilleboeuf a considerable amount in specie having been found in the possession of a citizen, the money was seized and sent to the Assembly. The people of that town treated this hoarded gold as the result of un-patriotic wickedness or madness, instead of seeing that it was but the sure result of a law working in every land and time when certain causes are present. Marat followed out this theory by asserting that death was the proper penalty for persons who thus hid their money.

Still another troublesome fact began now to appear. Though paper money had increased in amount, prosperity had steadily diminished. In spite of all the paper issues, commercial activity grew more and more spasmodic. Enterprise was chilled and business became more and more stagnant. Mirabeau, in his speech which decided the second great issue of paper, had insisted that, though bankers might suffer, this issue would be of great service to manufacturers and restore prosperity to them and their workmen. The latter were for a time deluded, but were at last rudely awakened from this delusion. The plenty of currency had at first stimulated production and created a great activity in manufactures, but soon the markets were glutted and the demand was diminished.

In spite of the wretched financial policy of years gone by, and especially in spite of the Revocation of

[54]

the Edict of Nantes, by which religious bigotry had driven out of the kingdom thousands of its most skillful Protestant workmen, the manufactures of France had before the Revolution come into full bloom. In the finer woolen goods, in silk and satin fabrics of all sorts, in choice pottery and porcelain, in manufactures of iron, steel, and copper, they had again taken their old leading place upon the Continent. All the previous changes had, at the worst, done no more than to inflict a momentary check on this highly developed system of manufactures. But what the bigotry of Louis XIV and the shiftlessness of Louis XV could not do in nearly a century, was accomplished by this tampering with the currency in a few months. One manufactory after another stopped. At one town, Lodève, five thousand workmen were discharged from the cloth manufactories. Every cause except the right one was assigned for this. Heavy duties were put upon foreign goods; everything that tariffs and customhouses could do was done. Still the great manufactories of Normandy were closed, those of the rest of the kingdom speedily followed, and vast numbers of workmen in all parts of the country were thrown out of employment.[29] Nor was this the case with the home demand alone. The foreign demand which at first had been stimulated, soon fell off.

In no way can this be better stated than by one of the most thoughtful historians of modern times, who says, "It is true that at first the assignats gave the same

[55]

impulse to business in the city as in the country, but the apparent improvement had no firm foundation, even in the towns. Whenever a great quantity of paper money is suddenly issued we invariably see a rapid increase of trade. The great quantity of the circulating medium sets in motion all the energies of commerce and manufactures; capital for investment is more easily found than usual and trade perpetually receives fresh nutriment. If this paper represents real credit, founded upon order and legal security, from which it can derive a firm and lasting value, such a movement may be the starting point of a great and widely-extended prosperity, as, for instance, a splendid improvement in English agriculture was undoubtedly owing to the emancipation of the country bankers. If on the contrary, the new paper is of precarious value, as was clearly seen to be the case with the French assignats as early as February 1791, it can confer no lasting benefits. For the moment, perhaps, business receives an impulse, all the more violent because every one endeavors to invest his doubtful paper in buildings, machines, and goods, which, under all circumstances, retain some intrinsic value. Such a movement was witnessed in France in 1791, and from every quarter there came satisfactory reports of the activity of manufactures.

"But, for the moment, the French manufacturers derived great advantage from this state of things. As their products could be so cheaply paid for, orders poured in

[56]

from foreign countries to such a degree that it was often difficult for the manufacturers to satisfy their customers. It is easy to see that prosperity of this kind must very soon find its limit. . . . When a further fall in the assignats took place, this prosperity would necessarily collapse and be succeeded by a crisis all the more destructive the more deeply men had engaged in speculation under the influence of the first favorable prospects."[30]

Thus came a collapse in manufacturing and commerce, just as it had come previously in France: just as it came at various periods in Austria, Russia, America, and in all countries where men have tried to build up prosperity on irredeemable paper.[31]

All this breaking down of the manufactures and commerce of the nation made fearful inroads on the greater fortunes; but upon the lesser, and upon the little properties of the masses of the nation who relied upon their labor, it pressed with intense severity. The capitalist could put his surplus paper money into the government lands and await results; but the men who needed their money from day to day suffered the worst of the misery.

Still another difficulty appeared. There had come a complete uncertainty as to the future. Long before the close of 1791 no one knew whether a piece of paper money representing a hundred livres would, a month later, have a purchasing power of ninety or eighty or sixty livres. The result was that capitalists feared to

[57]

embark their means in business. Enterprise received a mortal blow. Demand for labor was still further diminished; and here came a new cause for calamity, for this uncertainty withered all far-reaching undertakings. The business of France dwindled into a mere living from hand to mouth.

This state of things, too, while it bore heavily upon the moneyed classes, was still more ruinous to those in moderate and, most of all, to those in straitened circumstances. With the masses of the people, the purchase of every article of supply became a speculation— a speculation in which the professional speculator had an immense advantage over the ordinary buyer. Says the most brilliant of apologists for French revolutionary statesmanship, "Commerce was dead; betting took its place."[32]

Nor was there any compensating advantage to the mercantile classes. The merchant was forced to add to his ordinary profit a sum sufficient to cover probable or possible fluctuations in value; and while prices of products thus went higher, the wages of labor, owing to the number of workmen who were thrown out of employment, went lower.

But these evils, though great, were small compared to those far more deep-seated signs of disease which now showed themselves throughout the country. One of these was the *obliteration of thrift* from the minds of

[58]

the French people. The French are naturally thrifty;
but, with such masses of money and with such uncertainty as to its future value, the ordinary motives for
saving and care diminished, and a loose luxury spread
throughout the country.

A still worse outgrowth was the increase of speculation and gambling. With the plethora of paper currency
in 1791 appeared the first evidences of that cancerous
disease which always follows large issues of irredeemable currency—a disease more permanently injurious to
a nation than war, pestilence, or famine. For at the
great metropolitan centers grew a luxurious, speculative stock-gambling body, which, like a malignant
tumor, absorbed into itself the strength of the nation
and sent out its cancerous fibers to the remotest ham-
lets. At these city centers abundant wealth seemed to
be piled up. In the country at large there grew a dislike
of steady labor and a contempt for moderate gains and
simple living.

In a pamphlet published in May 1791, we see how,
in regard to this also, public opinion was blinded. The
author calls attention to the increase of gambling in
values of all sorts in these words: "What shall I say of
the stockjobbing, as frightful as it is scandalous, which
goes on in Paris under the very eyes of our legislators—
a most terrible evil, yet, under the present circumstances, necessary?" The author also speaks of these
stock gamblers as using the most insidious means to

[59]

influence public opinion in favor of their measures; and then proposes, seriously, a change in various matters of detail, thinking that this would prove a sufficient remedy for an evil which had its roots far down in the whole system of irredeemable currency. As well might a physician prescribe a pimple wash for a diseased liver.[33]

Now began to be seen more plainly some of the many ways in which an inflation policy robs the working class. As these knots of plotting schemers at the city centers were becoming bloated with sudden wealth, the producing classes of the country, though having in their possession more and more currency, grew lean. In the schemes and speculations put forth by stockjobbers and stimulated by the printing of more currency, multitudes of small fortunes were absorbed and lost while a few swollen fortunes were rapidly aggregated in the larger cities. This crippled a large class in the country districts, which had employed a great number of workmen.

In the leading French cities now arose a luxury and license which was a greater evil even than the plundering which ministered to it. In the country the gambling spirit spread more and more. Says the same thoughtful historian whom I have already quoted: "What a prospect for a country when its rural population was changed into a great band of gamblers!"[34]

Nor was this reckless and corrupt spirit confined to

[60]

businessmen; it began to break out in official circles, and public men who, a few years before, had been thought above all possibility of taint, became luxurious, reckless, cynical, and finally corrupt. Mirabeau himself, who, not many months previous, had risked imprisonment and even death to establish constitutional government, was now—at this very time—secretly receiving heavy bribes. When, at the downfall of the monarchy a few years later, the famous iron chest of the Tuileries was opened, there were found evidences that, in this carnival of inflation and corruption, he had been a regularly paid servant of the Royal court.[35]

The artful plundering of the people at large was bad enough, but worse still was this growing corruption in official and legislative circles. Out of the speculating and gambling of the inflation period grew luxury, and, out of this, corruption. It grew as naturally as a fungus on a muck heap. It was first felt in business operations, but soon began to be seen in the legislative body and in journalism. Mirabeau was, by no means, the only example. Such members of the legislative body as Jullien of Toulouse, Delaunay of Angers, Fabre d'Eglantine, and their disciples, were among the most noxious of those conspiring by legislative action to raise and depress securities for stockjobbing purposes. Bribery of legislators followed as a matter of course. Delaunay, Jullien, and Chabot accepted a bribe of five hundred thousand livres for aiding legislation calculated to promote the purposes of certain stockjobbers. It is some comfort to know that nearly all concerned were guillotined for it.[36]

It is true that the number of these corrupt legislators was small, far less than alarmists led the nation to suppose, but there were enough to cause widespread distrust, cynicism, and want of faith in any patriotism or any virtue.

[62]

FIAT MONEY INFLATION IN FRANCE

WHAT IT BROUGHT

EVEN WORSE THAN THIS was the breaking down of the morals of the country at large, resulting from the sudden building up of ostentatious wealth in a few large cities, and from the gambling, speculative spirit spreading from these to the small towns and rural districts. From this was developed an even more disgraceful result—the decay of a true sense of national good faith. The patriotism which the fear of the absolute monarchy, the machinations of the court party, the menaces of the army, and the threats of all monarchical Europe had been unable to shake was gradually disintegrated by this same speculative, stockjobbing habit fostered by the superabundant currency.

At the outset, in the discussions preliminary to the first issue of paper money, Mirabeau and others who had favored it had insisted that patriotism, as well as an enlightened self-interest, would lead the people to keep up the value of paper money. The very opposite of this was now revealed, for there appeared, as another outgrowth of this disease, what has always been seen under similar circumstances. It is a result of previous

[63]

and a cause of future evils. This outgrowth was a vast debtor class in the nation, directly interested in the depreciation of the currency in which they were to pay their debts. The nucleus of this class was formed by those who had purchased the church lands from the government. Only small payments down had been required and the remainder was to be paid in deferred installments. An indebtedness of a multitude of people had thus been created to the amount of hundreds of millions.

This body of debtors soon saw, of course, that their interest was to depreciate the currency in which their debts were to be paid; and these were speedily joined by a far more influential class—by that class whose speculative tendencies had been stimulated by the abundance of paper money, and who had gone largely into debt, looking for a rise in nominal values. Soon demagogues of the viler sort in the political clubs began to pander to it; a little later important persons in this debtor class were to be found intriguing in the Assembly—first in its seats and later in more conspicuous places of public trust. Before long, the debtor class became a powerful body extending through all ranks of society. From the stock gambler who sat in the Assembly to the small land speculator in the rural districts; from the sleek inventor of canards on the Paris Exchange to the lying stockjobber in the market town, all pressed vigorously for new issues of paper; all were

[64]

apparently able to demonstrate to the people that in
new issues of paper lay the only chance for national
prosperity.

This great debtor class, relying on the multitude who
could be approached by superficial arguments, soon
gained control. Strange as it might seem to those who
have not watched the same causes at work at a previous
period in France and at various times in other countries,
while every issue of paper money really made matters
worse, a superstition gained ground among the people
at large that, if only *enough* paper money were issued
and were more cunningly handled, the poor would be
made rich. Henceforth, all opposition was futile. In December 1791, a report was made in the Legislative Assembly in favor of yet another great issue of three hundred millions more of paper money. In regard to this
report Cambon said that more money was needed but
asked, "Will you, in a moment when stockjobbing is
carried on with such fury, give it new power by adding
so much more to the circulation?" But such high considerations were now little regarded. Dorisy declared,
"There is not enough money yet in circulation; if there
were more, the sales of national lands would be more
rapid." And the official report of his speech states that
these words were applauded.

Dorisy then went on to insist that the government
lands were worth at least thirty-five hundred million
livres and said: "Why should members ascend the tri-

[65]

bunal and disquiet France? Fear nothing; your currency reposes upon a sound mortgage." Then followed
a glorification of the patriotism of the French people,
which, he asserted, would carry the nation through all
its difficulties.

Becquet, speaking next, declared that "the circulation
is becoming more rare every day."

On December 17, 1791, a new issue was ordered,
making in all twenty-one hundred millions authorized.
Coupled with this was the declaration that the total
amount in actual circulation should never reach more
than sixteen hundred millions. Before this issue the
value of the 100 livres note had fallen at Paris to about
80 livres;[37] immediately afterward it fell to about 68
livres. What limitations of the currency were worth
may be judged from the fact that not only had the
declaration made hardly a year before, limiting the
amount in circulation to twelve hundred millions, been
violated, but the declaration, made hardly a month
previous, in which the Assembly had as solemnly limited the amount of circulation to fourteen hundred millions, had also been repudiated.

The evils which we have already seen arising from
the earlier issues were now aggravated; but the most
curious thing evolved out of all this chaos was a *new
system of political economy.* In speeches, newspapers,
and pamphlets about this time, we begin to find it declared that, after all, a depreciated currency is a bless-

ing; that gold and silver form an unsatisfactory standard for measuring values; that it is a good thing to have
a currency that will not go out of the kingdom and
which separates France from other nations; that thus
shall manufacturers be encouraged; that commerce
with other nations may be a curse, and hindrance thereto may be a blessing; that the laws of political economy,
however applicable in other times, are not applicable to
this particular period, and, however operative in other
nations, are not now so in France; that the ordinary
rules of political economy are perhaps suited to the
minions of despotism but not to the free and enlightened inhabitants of France at the close of the eighteenth century; that the whole state of present things,
so far from being an evil, is a blessing. All these ideas,
and others quite as striking, were brought to the sur-
face in the debates on the various new issues.[38]

Within four months came another report to the Assembly as ingenious as those preceding. It declared:
"Your committee are thoroughly persuaded that the
amount of the circulating medium before the Revolution was greater than that of the assignats today: but
at that time the money circulated slowly and now it
passes rapidly so that one thousand million assignats do
the work of two thousand millions of specie." The report foretells further increase in prices, but by some
curious jugglery reaches a conclusion favorable to
further inflation. Despite these encouragements the as-

[67]

signats nominally worth 100 livres had fallen, at the beginning of February 1792, to about 60 livres, and during that month fell to 53 livres.[39]

In March, Clavière became Minister of Finance. He was especially proud of his share in the invention and advocacy of the assignats, and now pressed their creation more vigorously than ever; and on April 30, of the same year, came the fifth great issue of paper money, amounting to three hundred millions. At about the same time Cambon sneered ominously at public creditors as "rich people, old financiers, and bankers." Soon payment was suspended on dues to public creditors for all amounts exceeding ten thousand francs.

This was hailed by many as a measure in the interests of the poorer classes of people, but the result was that it injured them most of all. Henceforward, until the end of this history, capital was quietly taken from labor and locked up in all the ways that financial ingenuity could devise. All that saved thousands of laborers in France from starvation was that they were drafted off into the army and sent to be killed on foreign battlefields.

On the last day of July 1792, came another brilliant report from Fouquet, showing that the total amount of currency already issued was about twenty-four hundred millions, but claiming that the national lands were worth a little more than this sum. A decree was now passed issuing three hundred millions more. By this the

[68]

prices of everything were again enhanced save one thing, and that one thing was *labor*. Strange as it may at first appear, while the depreciation of the currency had raised all products enormously in price, the stoppage of so many manufactories and the withdrawal of capital caused wages in the summer of 1792, after all the inflation, to be as small as they had been four years before—viz., fifteen sous per day. No more striking example can be seen of the truth uttered by Daniel Webster, that "of all the contrivances for cheating the laboring classes of mankind, none has been more effective than that which deludes them with paper money."[40]

Issue after issue followed at intervals of a few months, until, on December 14, 1792, we have an official statement to the effect that thirty-four hundred millions had been put forth, of which six hundred millions had been burned, leaving in circulation twenty-eight hundred millions.

When it is remembered that there was little business to do and that the purchasing power of the livre or franc, when judged by the staple products of the country, was equal to about half the present purchasing power of our own dollar, it will be seen into what evils France had drifted. As the mania for paper money ran its course, even the sous, obtained by melting down the church bells, were more and more driven out of circulation and more and more parchment notes from twenty sous to five were issued, and at last pieces of one sou,

[69]

of half a sou, and even of one-quarter of a sou were put in circulation.[41]

But now another source of wealth was opened to the nation. There came a confiscation of the large estates of landed proprietors who had fled the country. An estimate in 1793 made the value of these estates three billions of francs. As a consequence, the issues of paper money were continued in increased amounts, on the old theory that they were guaranteed by the solemn pledge of these lands belonging to the state. Under the Legislative Assembly through the year 1792, new issues were made virtually every month, so that at the end of January 1793, it was more and more realized that the paper money actually in circulation amounted close upon three thousand millions of francs. All this had been issued publicly, in open sessions of the National and Legislative Assemblies; but now under the National Convention, the two Committees of Public Safety and of Finance began to decree new issues privately, in secret session.

As a result, the issues became larger still, and four hundred workmen were added to those previously engaged in furnishing this paper money, and these were so pressed with work from six o'clock in the morning until eight in the evening that they struck for higher wages and were successful.[42]

The consequences of these overissues now began to be more painfully evident to the people at large. Ar-

[70]

ticles of common consumption became enormously dear and prices were constantly rising. Orators in the Legislative Assembly, clubs, local meetings, and elsewhere now endeavored to enlighten people by assigning every reason for this depreciation save the true one. They declaimed against the corruption of the ministry, the want of patriotism among the Moderates, the intrigues of the emigrant nobles, the hard-heartedness of the rich, the monopolizing spirit of the merchants, the perversity of the shopkeepers—each and all of these as causes of the difficulty.[43]

This decline in the government paper was at first somewhat masked by fluctuations. For at various times the value of the currency *rose*. The victory of Jemappes and the general success of the French army against the invaders, with the additional security offered by new confiscations of land, caused, in November 1792, an appreciation in the value of the currency; the franc had stood at 57 and it rose to about 69; but the downward tendency was soon resumed and in September 1793, the assignats had sunk below 30. Then sundry new victories and coruscations of oratory gave momentary confidence so that in December 1793, they rose above 50. But despite these fluctuations the downward tendency soon became more rapid than ever.[44]

The washerwomen of Paris, finding soap so dear that they could hardly purchase it, insisted that all the mer-

[71]

chants who were endeavoring to save something of their little property by refusing to sell their goods for the wretched currency with which France was flooded, should be punished with death; the women of the markets and the hangers-on of the Jacobin Club called loudly for a law "to equalize the value of paper money and silver coin." It was also demanded that a tax be laid especially on the rich, to the amount of four hundred million francs, to buy bread. Marat declared loudly that the people, by hanging shopkeepers and plundering stores, could easily remove the trouble.

The result was that on February 28, 1793, at eight o'clock in the evening, a mob of men and women in disguise began plundering the stores and shops of Paris. At first they demanded only bread; soon they insisted on coffee and rice and sugar; at last they seized everything on which they could lay their hands—cloth, clothing, groceries, and luxuries of every kind. Two hundred such places were plundered. This was endured for six hours, and finally order was restored only by a grant of seven million francs to buy off the mob. The new political economy was beginning to bear its fruits luxuriantly. A gaudy growth of it appeared at the City Hall of Paris when, in response to the complaints of the plundered merchants, Roux declared, in the midst of great applause, that "shopkeepers were only giving back to the people what they had hitherto robbed them of."

[72]

The mob having thus been bought off by concessions and appeased by oratory, the government gained time to think, and now came a series of amazing expedients—and yet all perfectly logical.

Three of these have gained in French history an evil preeminence, and first of the three was the Forced Loan.

In view of the fact that the well-to-do citizens were thought to be lukewarm in their support of the politicians controlling the country, various demagogues in the National Convention, which had now succeeded the National, Constituent, and Legislative Assemblies, found ample matter for denunciations long and loud. The result outside the Convention was increased activity of the guillotine. The results inside were new measures against all who had money, and on June 22, 1793, the Convention determined that there should be a Forced Loan, secured on the confiscated lands of the emigrants and levied upon all married men with incomes of ten thousand francs, and upon all unmarried men with incomes of six thousand francs. It was calculated that these would bring into the treasury a thousand millions of francs.

But a difficulty was found. So many of the rich had fled or had concealed their wealth that only a fifth of the sum required could be raised, and therefore a law was soon passed which levied forced loans upon incomes as low as one thousand francs—or, say, two hundred dollars of American money. This tax was made progressive. On the smaller proprietors it was fixed at one-tenth and on the larger, that is, on all incomes above nine thousand francs, it was made one-half of the entire income. Little, if any, provision was made for the repayment of this loan but the certificates might be used for purchasing the confiscated real estate of the church and of the nobility.[45]

But if this first expedient shows how naturally a "fiat" money system runs into despotism, the next is no less instructive in showing how easily it becomes repudiation and dishonor.

As we have seen, the first issue of the assignats—made by the National Assembly—bore a portrait of the King; but on the various issues after the establishment of a republic this emblem had been discarded. This change led to a difference in value between the earlier and the later paper money. The wild follies of fanatics and demagogues had led to an increasing belief that the existing state of things could not last; that the Bourbons must ere long return; that in such case, while a new monarch would repudiate all the vast mass of the later paper issued by the Republic, he would recognize that first issue bearing the face and therefore the guarantee of the King. So it was that this first issue came to bear a higher value than those of later date.

To meet this condition of things it was now proposed to repudiate all that earlier issue. In vain did sundry

[74]

more thoughtful members of the Convention plead that
this paper money, amounting to five hundred fifty-
eight millions of francs, bore the solemn guarantee of
the nation, as well as of the King; the current was irresistible. All that Cambon, the great leader of finance at
that time, could secure was a clause claiming to protect the poor, to the effect that this demonetization
should not extend to notes below a hundred francs in
value; and it was also agreed that any of the notes,
large or small, might be received in payment of taxes
and for the confiscated property of the clergy and nobility. To all the arguments advanced against this
breach of the national faith Danton, then at the height
of his power, simply declared that only aristocrats could
favor notes bearing the royal portrait, and gave forth
his famous utterance: "Imitate Nature, which watches
over the preservation of the race but has no regard for
individuals." The decree was passed on July 31, 1793,
yet its futility was apparent in less than two months,
when the Convention decreed that there should be issued two thousand millions of francs more in assignats
between the values of ten sous and four hundred francs,
and when, before the end of the year, five hundred
millions more were authorized.[46]

The third outgrowth of the vast issue of fiat money
was the "Maximum." As far back as November 1792,
the Terrorist associate of Robespierre, St. Just, in view

[75]

of the steady rise in prices of the necessaries of life, had proposed a scheme by which these prices should be established by law, at a rate proportionate to the wages of the working classes. This plan lingered in men's minds, taking shape in various resolutions and decrees until the whole culminated on September 29, 1793, in the Law of the Maximum.

While all this legislation was highhanded, it was not careless. Even statesmen of the greatest strength, having once been drawn into this flood, were borne on into excesses which, a little earlier, would have appalled them. Committees of experts were appointed to study the whole subject of prices, and at last there were adopted the great "four rules" which seemed to statesmen of that time a masterly solution of the whole difficulty.[47]

First, the price of each article of necessity was to be fixed at one and one-third its price in 1790. *Secondly*, all transportation was to be added at a fixed rate per league. *Thirdly*, five per cent was to be added for the profit of the wholesaler. *Fourthly*, ten per cent was to be added for the profit of the retailer. Nothing could look more reasonable. Great was the jubilation. The report was presented and supported by Barrère—"the tiger monkey"—then in all the glory of his great orations: now best known from his portrait by Macaulay. Nothing could withstand Barrère's eloquence. He insisted that France had been suffering from a "*Monarch-*

ical commerce which only sought wealth," while what she needed and what she was now to receive was a "*Republican* commerce—a commerce of moderate profits and virtuous." He exulted in the fact that "France alone enjoys such a commerce—that it exists in no other nation." He poured contempt over political economy as "that science which quacks have corrupted, which pedants have obscured, and which academicians have depreciated." France, he said, has something better, and he declared in conclusion, "The needs of the people will no longer be spied upon in order that the commercial classes may arbitrarily take advantage."[48]

The first result of the Maximum was that every means was taken to evade the fixed price imposed, and the farmers brought in as little produce as they possibly could. This increased the scarcity, and the people of the large cities were put on an allowance. Tickets were issued authorizing the bearer to obtain at the official prices a certain amount of bread or sugar or soap or wood or coal to cover immediate necessities.[49]

But it was found that the Maximum, with its divinely revealed four rules, could not be made to work well—even by the shrewdest devices. In the greater part of France it could not be enforced. As to merchandise of foreign origin or mechandise into which any foreign product entered, the war had raised it far above the price allowed under the first rule, namely, the price of 1790 with an addition of one-third. Shopkeepers there-

[77]

fore could not sell such goods without ruin. The result was that very many went out of business, and the remainder forced buyers to pay enormous charges under the very natural excuse that the seller risked his life in trading at all. That this excuse was valid is easily seen by the daily lists of those condemned to the guillotine, in which not infrequently figure the names of men charged with violating/the Maximum laws. Manufactures were very generally crippled and frequently destroyed, and agriculture was fearfully depressed. To detect goods concealed by farmers and shopkeepers, a spy system was established with a reward to the informer of one-third of the value of the goods discovered. To spread terror, the Criminal Tribunal at Strassburg was ordered to destroy the dwelling of anyone found guilty of selling goods above the price set by law. The farmer often found that he could not raise his products at anything like the price required by the new law; and when he tried to hold back his crops or cattle, alleging that he could not afford to sell them at the prices fixed by law, they were frequently taken from him by force and he was fortunate if paid even in the depreciated fiat money—fortunate, indeed, if he finally escaped with his life.[50]

Involved in all these perplexities, the Convention tried to cut the Gordian knot. It decreed that any person selling gold or silver coin, or making any difference in any transaction between paper and specie, should

[78]

be imprisoned in irons for six years; that anyone who refused to accept a payment in assignats, or accepted assignats at a discount, should pay a fine of three thousand francs; and that anyone committing this crime a second time should pay a fine of six thousand francs and suffer imprisonment twenty years in irons. Later, on September 8, 1793, the penalty for such offenses was made death, with confiscation of the criminal's property, and a reward was offered to any person informing the authorities regarding any such criminal transaction. To reach the climax of ferocity, the Convention decreed, in May 1794, that the death penalty should be inflicted on any person convicted of "having asked, before a bargain was concluded, in what money payment was to be made." Nor was this all. The great finance minister, Cambon, soon saw that the worst enemies of his policy were gold and silver. Therefore it was that, under his lead, the Convention closed the Exchange and finally, on November 13, 1793, under terrifying penalties, suppressed all commerce in the precious metals. About a year later came the abolition of the Maximum itself.[51]

It is easily seen that these Maximum laws were perfectly logical. Whenever any nation intrusts to its legislators the issue of a currency not based on the idea of redemption in standard coin recognized in the commerce of civilized nations, it intrusts to them the power to raise or depress the value of every article in the possession of every citizen. Louis XIV had claimed that all property in France was his own, and that what private persons held was as much his as if it were in his coffers. But even this assumption is exceeded by the confiscating power exercised in a country, where, instead of leaving values to be measured by a standard common to the whole world, they are left to be depressed or raised at the whim, caprice, or interest of a body of legislators. When this power is given, the power of fixing prices is inevitably included in it.[52]

It may be said that these measures were made necessary by the war then going on. Nothing could be more baseless than such an objection. In this war the French soon became generally successful. It was quickly pushed mainly upon foreign soil. Numerous contributions were levied upon the subjugated countries to support the French armies. The war was one of those in which the loss, falling apparently on future generations, first stimulates, in a sad way, trade and production. The main cause of these evils was tampering with the circulating medium of an entire nation; keeping all values in fluctuation; discouraging enterprise; paralyzing energy; undermining sobriety; obliterating thrift; promoting extravagance; and exciting riot by the issue of an irredeemable currency. The true business way of meeting the enormous demands on France during the first years of the Revolution had been stated by a true

[80]

statesman and sound financier, Du Pont de Nemours, at the very beginning. He had shown that using the same paper as a circulating medium and as a means for selling the national real estate was like using the same implement for an oyster knife and a razor.[53]

It has been argued that the assignats sank in value because they were not well secured—that securing them on government real estate was as futile as if the United States had, in the financial troubles of its early days, secured notes on its real estate. This objection is utterly fallacious. The government lands of our country were remote from the centers of capital and difficult to examine; the French national real estate was near these centers—even *in* them—and easy to examine. Our national real estate was unimproved and unproductive; theirs was improved and productive, its average productiveness in market in ordinary times being from four to five per cent.[54]

It has also been objected that the attempt to secure the assignats on government real estate failed because of the general want of confidence in the title derived by the purchasers from the new government. Every thorough student of that period must know that this is a misleading statement. Everything shows that the vast majority of the French people had a fanatical confidence in the stability of the new government during the greater part of the Revolution. There were disbelievers in the security of the assignats just as there were

[81]

disbelievers in the paper money of the United States throughout our Civil War; but they were usually a small minority. Even granting that there was a doubt as to investment in French lands, the French people certainly had as much confidence in the secure possession of government lands as any people can ever have in large issues of government bonds. Indeed, it is certain that they had far more confidence in their lands as a security than modern nations can usually have in large issues of bonds obtained by payments of irredeemable paper. One simple fact, as stated by John Stuart Mill, which made assignats difficult to convert into real estate, was that the vast majority of people could not afford to make investments outside their business; and this fact is no less fatal to any attempt to contract large issues of irredeemable paper—save, perhaps, a bold, statesmanlike attempt which seizes the best time and presses every advantage, eschewing all juggling devices and sacrificing everything to maintain a sound currency based on standards common to the entire financial world.

And now was seen, taking possession of the nation, that idea which developed so easily out of the fiat money system—the idea that the ordinary needs of government may be legitimately met wholly by the means of paper currency; that taxes may be dispensed with. As a result, it was found that the assignat printing press

[82]

was the one resource left to the government, and the increase in the volume of paper money became every day more appalling.

It will doubtless surprise many to learn that, in spite of these evident results of too much currency, the old cry of a "scarcity of circulating medium" was not stilled; it appeared not long after each issue, no matter how large.

But every thoughtful student of financial history knows that this cry always comes after such issues—nay, that it *must* come—because in obedience to a natural law, the former scarcity, or rather *insufficiency* of currency, recurs just as soon as prices become adjusted to the new volume, and there comes some little revival of business with the usual increase of credit.[55]

In August 1793, appeared a new report by Cambon. No one can read it without being struck by its mingled ability and folly. His final plan of dealing with the public debt has outlasted all revolutions since, but his disposition of the inflated currency came to a wretched failure. Against Du Pont, who showed conclusively that the wild increase of paper money was leading straight to ruin, Cambon carried the majority in the great assemblies and clubs by sheer audacity—the audacity of desperation. Zeal in supporting the assignats became his religion. The National Convention which succeeded the Legislative Assembly, issued in 1793 over three thousand millions of assignats, and, of these, over twelve hundred millions were poured into the circulation. And yet Cambon steadily insisted that the security for the assignat currency was perfect. The climax of his zeal was reached when he counted as assets in the national treasury the indemnities which, he declared, France was sure to receive after future victories over the allied nations with which she was then waging a desperate war. As patriotism it was sublime; as finance it was deadly.[56]

Everything was tried. Very elaborately he devised a funding scheme which, taken in connection with his system of issues, was in effect what in these days would be called an "interconvertibility scheme." By various degrees of persuasion or force—the guillotine looming up in the background—holders of assignats were urged to convert them into evidence of national debt, bearing interest at five per cent, with the understanding that if more paper were afterward needed more would be issued. All in vain. The official tables of depreciation show that the assignats continued to fall. A forced loan, calling in a billion of these, checked this fall, but only for a moment. The "interconvertibility scheme" between currency and bonds failed as dismally as the "interconvertibility scheme" between currency and land had failed.[57]

A more effective expedient was a law confiscating the property of all Frenchmen who left France after July 14, 1789, and who had not returned. This gave new

[84]

land to be mortgaged for the security of paper money.

All this vast chapter in financial folly is sometimes referred to as if it resulted from the direct action of men utterly unskilled in finance. This is a grave error. That wild schemers and dreamers took a leading part in setting the fiat money system going is true; that speculation and interested financiers made it worse is also true; but the men who had charge of French finance during the Reign of Terror and who made these experiments, which seem to us so monstrous, in order to rescue themselves and their country from the flood which was sweeping everything to financial ruin were universally recognized as among the most skillful and honest financiers in Europe. Cambon, especially, ranked then and ranks now as among the most expert in any period. The disastrous results of all his courage and ability in the attempt to stand against the deluge of paper money show how powerless are the most skillful masters of finance to stem the tide of fiat money calamity when once it is fairly under headway; and how useless are all enactments which they can devise against the underlying laws of nature.

Month after month, year after year, new issues went on. Meanwhile, everything possible was done to keep up the value of paper. The city authorities of Metz took a solemn oath that the assignats should bear the same price whether in paper or specie, and whether in buying or selling, and various other official bodies

[85]

throughout the nation followed this example. In obedience to those who believed with the market women of Paris, as stated in their famous petition, that "laws should be passed making paper money as good as gold," Couthon, in August 1793, had proposed and carried a law punishing any person who should sell assignats at less than their nominal value with imprisonment for twenty years in chains, and later carried a law making investments in foreign countries by Frenchmen punishable with death.[58]

But to the surprise of the great majority of the French people, the value of the assignats was found, after the momentary spasm of fear had passed, not to have been permanently increased by these measures. On the contrary, this "fiat" paper persisted in obeying the natural laws of finance and, as new issues increased, their value decreased. Nor did the most lavish aid of nature avail. The paper money of the nation seemed to possess a magic power to transmute prosperity into adversity and plenty into famine. The year 1794 was exceptionally fruitful, and yet with the autumn came scarcity of provisions and with the winter came distress.

The reason is perfectly simple. The sequences in that whole history are absolutely logical. First, the Assembly had inflated the currency and raised prices enormously. Next, it had been forced to establish an arbitrary maximum price for produce. But this price, large as it seemed, soon fell below the real value of produce; many

of the farmers, therefore, raised less produce or refrained from bringing what they had to market.[59] But,
as is usual in such cases, the trouble was ascribed to
everything rather than the real cause, and the most
severe measures were established in all parts of the
country to force farmers to bring produce to market,
millers to grind, and shopkeepers to sell it.[60]

The issues of paper money continued. Toward the
end of 1794 seven thousand millions in assignats were
in circulation.[61] By the end of May 1795, the circulation was increased to ten thousand millions; at the end
of July, to fourteen thousand millions; and the value of
one hundred francs in paper fell steadily, first to four
francs in gold, then to three, then to two and one-half.[62]
But, curiously enough, while this depreciation was rapidly going on, as at various other periods when depreciation was rapid, there came an apparent revival of
business. The hopes of many were revived by the fact
that in spite of the decline of paper there was an exceedingly brisk trade in all kinds of permanent property. Whatever articles of permanent value certain
needy people were willing to sell, certain cunning
people were willing to buy and to pay good prices for
in assignats.

At this, hope revived for a time in certain quarters.
But ere long it was discovered that this was one of the
most distressing results of a natural law which is sure
to come into play under such circumstances. It was

[87]

simply a feverish activity caused by the intense desire of a large number of the shrewder class to convert their paper money into anything and everything which they could hold and hoard until the collapse which they foresaw should take place. This very activity in business simply indicated the disease. It was simply legal robbery of the more enthusiastic and trusting by the more coldhearted and keen. It was the "unloading" of the assignats upon the mass of the people.[63]

Interesting is it to note in the midst of all this the steady action of another simple law in finance. Prisons, guillotines, enactments inflicting twenty years' imprisonment in chains upon persons twice convicted of buying or selling paper money at less than its nominal value, and death upon investors in foreign securities, were powerless. The National Convention, fighting a world in arms and with an armed revolt on its own soil, showed titanic power, but in its struggle to circumvent one simple law of nature its weakness was pitiable. The *louis d' or* stood in the market as a monitor, noting each day with unerring fidelity, the decline in value of the assignat; a monitor not to be bribed, not to be scared. As well might the National Convention try to bribe or scare away the polarity of the mariner's compass. On August 1, 1795, this gold louis of 25 francs was worth in paper, 920 francs; on September 1, 1,200 francs; on November 1, 2,600 francs; on December 1, 3,050 francs. In February 1796, it was worth 7,200

[88]

francs or one franc in gold was worth 288 francs in
paper. Prices of all commodities went up nearly in proportion.[64]

The writings of this period give curious details. Thibaudeau, in his Memoirs, speaks of sugar as 500 francs
a pound, soap, 230 francs, candles, 140 francs. Mercier,
in his lifelike pictures of the French metropolis at that
period, mentions 600 francs as carriage hire for a single
drive, and 6,000 for an entire day. Examples from other
sources are such as the following: a measure of flour
advanced from two francs in 1790, to 225 francs in
1795; a pair of shoes, from five francs to 200; a hat,
from 14 francs to 500; butter, to 560 francs a pound;
a turkey, to 900 francs.[65] Everything was enormously
inflated in price *except the wages of labor*. As manufacturers had closed, wages had fallen, until all that
kept them up seemed to be the fact that so many
laborers were drafted off into the army.

From this state of things came grievous wrong and
gross fraud. Men who had foreseen these results and
had gone into debt were of course jubilant. He who in
1790 had borrowed 10,000 francs could pay his debts
in 1796 for about 35 francs. Laws were made to meet
these abuses. As far back as 1794 a plan was devised
for publishing official "tables of depreciation" to be
used in making equitable settlements of debts, but all
such machinery proved futile. On May 18, 1796, a
young man complained to the National Convention that

[89]

his elder brother, who had been acting as administrator of his deceased father's estate, had paid the heirs in assignats, and that he had received scarcely one three-hundredth part of the real value of his share.[66]

To meet cases like this, a law was passed establishing a "scale of proportion." Taking as a standard the value of the assignat when there were two billions in circulation, this law declared that, in payment of debts, one-quarter should be added to the amount originally borrowed for every five hundred millions added to the circulation. In obedience to this law a man who borrowed two thousand francs when there were two billions in circulation would have to pay his creditors twenty-five hundred francs when half a billion more were added to the currency, and over thirty-five thousand francs before the emissions of paper reached their final amount. This brought new evils, worse, if possible, than the old.[67]

The question will naturally be asked: *On whom did this vast depreciation mainly fall at last?* When this currency had sunk to about one three-hundredth part of its nominal value and, after that, to nothing, in whose hands was the bulk of it? The answer is simple. I shall give it in the exact words of that thoughtful historian from whom I have already quoted: "Before the end of the year 1795, the paper money was almost exclusively in the hands of the working classes, employees

[90]

and men of small means, whose property was not large enough to invest in stores of goods or national lands.[68] Financiers and men of large means were shrewd enough to put as much of their property as possible into objects of permanent value. The working classes had no such foresight or skill or means. On them finally came the great crushing weight of the loss. After the first collapse came up the cries of the starving. Roads and bridges were neglected; many manufactures were given up in utter helplessness." To continue, in the words of the historian already cited: "None felt any confidence in the future in any respect; few dared to make a business investment for any length of time, and it was accounted a folly to curtail the pleasures of the moment, to accumulate or save for so uncertain a future."[69]

This system in finance was accompanied by a system in politics no less startling, and each system tended to aggravate the other. The wild radicals, having sent to the guillotine first all the Royalists and next all the leading Republicans they could entrap, the various factions began sending each other to the same destination: Hébertists, Dantonists, with various other factions and groups, and, finally, the Robespierrists, followed each other in rapid succession. After these declaimers and phrase-mongers had thus disappeared, there came to power, in October 1795, a new government—mainly a survival of the more scoundrelly—the Directory. It found the country utterly impoverished, and its only

[91]

resource at first was to print more paper and to issue even while wet from the press. These new issues were made at last by the two great committees, with or without warrant of law, and in greater sums than ever. Complaints were made that the army of engravers and printers at the mint could not meet the demand for assignats---that they could produce only from sixty to seventy millions per day and that the government was spending daily from eighty to ninety millions. Four thousand millions of francs were issued during one month, a little later three thousand millions, a little later four thousand millions, until there had been put forth over thirty-five thousand millions.

The purchasing power of this paper having now become almost nothing, it was decreed, on December 22, 1795, that the whole amount issued should be limited to forty thousand millions, including all that had previously been put forth and that when this had been done the copper plates should be broken. Even in spite of this, additional issues were made amounting to about ten thousand millions. But on February 18, 1796, at nine o'clock in the morning, in the presence of a great crowd, the machinery, plates, and paper for printing assignats were brought to the Place Vendome and there, on the spot where the Napoleon Column now stands, these were solemnly broken and burned.

Shortly afterward a report by Camus was made to the Assembly that the entire amount of paper money issued in less than six years by the Revolutionary Government of France had been over forty-five thousand millions of francs; that over six thousand millions had been annulled and burned; and that at the final catastrophe there were in circulation close upon forty thousand millions. It will be readily seen that it was fully time to put an end to the system, for the gold louis of twenty-five francs in specie had, in February 1796, as we have seen, become worth 7,200 francs, and, at the latest quotation of all, no less than 15,000 francs in paper money—that is, one franc in gold was nominally worth 600 francs in paper.

Such were the results of allowing dreamers, schemers, phrase-mongers, declaimers, and strong men subservient to these to control a government.[70]

FIAT MONEY INFLATION IN FRANCE

HOW IT ENDED

THE FIRST NEW EXPEDIENT of the Directory was to secure a forced loan of six hundred million francs from the wealthier classes; but this was found fruitless. Ominous it was when persons compelled to take this loan found for an assignat of one hundred francs only one franc was allowed. Next, a National Bank was proposed; but capitalists were loath to embark in banking while the howls of the mob against all who had anything especially to do with money resounded in every city. At last the Directory bethought themselves of another expedient. This was by no means new. It had been fully tried on our continent twice before that time, and once, since: first, in our colonial period; next, during our Confederation; lastly, by the "Southern Confederacy"—and here, as elsewhere, always in vain. But experience yielded to theory—plain business sense to financial metaphysics. It was determined to issue a new paper which should be "fully secured" and "as good as gold."

Pursuant to this decision it was decreed that a new paper money "fully secured and as good as gold" be

[95]

issued under the name of "mandats." In order that these new notes should be "fully secured," choice public real estate was set apart to an amount fully equal to the nominal value of the issue, and anyone offering any amount of the mandats could at once take possession of government lands, the price of the lands to be determined by two experts, one named by the government and one by the buyer, and without the formalities and delays previously established in regard to the purchase of lands with assignats.

Perhaps the most whimsical thing in the whole situation was the fact that the government, pressed as it was by demands of all sorts, continued to issue the old assignats at the same time that it was discrediting them by issuing the new mandats. And yet in order to make the mandats "as good as gold" it was planned by forced loans and other means to reduce the quantity of assignats in circulation, so that the value of each assignat should be raised to one-thirtieth of the value of gold, then to make mandats legal tender and to substitute them for assignats at the rate of one for thirty. Never were great expectations more cruelly disappointed. Even before the mandats could be issued from the press, they fell to thirty-five per cent of their nominal value; from this they speedily fell to fifteen, and soon after to five per cent, and finally, in August 1796, six months from their first issue, to three per cent. This plan failed—just as it failed in New England in 1737;

[96]

just as it failed under our own Confederation in 1781; just as it failed under the Southern Confederacy during our Civil War.[71]

To sustain this new currency the government resorted to every method that ingenuity could devise. Pamphlets suited to people of every capacity were published explaining its advantages. Never was there more skillful puffing. A pamphlet signed "Marchant" and dedicated to "People of Good Faith" was widely circulated, in which Marchant took pains to show the great advantage of the mandats as compared with assignats—how land could be more easily acquired with them; how their security was better than with assignats; how they could not, by any possibility, sink in values as the assignats had done. But even before the pamphlet was dry from the press the depreciation of the mandats had refuted his entire argument.[72]

The old plan of penal measures was again pressed. Monot led off by proposing penalties against those who shall speak publicly against the mandats; Talot thought the penalties ought to be made especially severe; and finally it was enacted that any persons "who by their discourse or writing shall decry the mandats shall be condemned to a fine of not less than one thousand francs or more than ten thousand; and in case of a repetition of the offense, to four years in irons." It was also decreed that those who refused to receive the

[97]

mandats should be fined—the first time, the exact sum
which they refused; the second time, ten times as much;
and the third time, punished with two years in prison.
But here, too, came in the action of those natural laws
which are alike inexorable in all countries. This attempt
proved futile in France just as it had proved futile less
than twenty years before in America. No enactments
could stop the downward tendency of this new paper
"fully secured," "as good as gold"; the laws that finally
govern finance are not made in conventions or congresses.[73]

From time to time various new financial juggles were
tried, some of them ingenious, most of them drastic. It
was decreed that all assignats above the value of one
hundred francs should cease to circulate after the beginning of June 1796. But this only served to destroy
the last vestige of confidence in government notes of
any kind. Another expedient was seen in the decree
that paper money should be made to accord with a
natural and immutable standard of value and that one
franc in paper should thenceforth be worth ten pounds
of wheat. This also failed. On July 16 another decree
seemed to show that the authorities despaired of regu-
lating the existing currency, and it was decreed that all
paper, whether mandats or assignats, should be taken
at its real value, and that bargains might be made in
whatever currency people chose. The real value of the
mandats speedily sank to about two per cent of their

nominal value, and the only effect of this legislation seemed to be that both assignats and mandats went still lower. Then from February 4 to February 14, 1797, came decrees and orders that the engraving apparatus for the mandats should be destroyed as that for the assignats had been, that neither assignats nor mandats should longer be a legal tender, and that old debts to the state might be paid for a time with government paper at the rate of one per cent of their face value.[74] Then, less than three months later, it was decreed that the twenty-one billions of assignats still in circulation should be annulled. Finally, on September 30, 1797, as the culmination of these and various other experiments and expedients, came an order of the Directory that the national debts should be paid two-thirds in bonds which might be used in purchasing confiscated real estate, and the remaining "Consolidated Third," as it was called, was to be placed on the "Great Book" of the national debt to be paid thenceforth as the government should think best.

As to the bonds which the creditors of the nation were thus forced to take, they sank rapidly, as the assignats and mandats had done, even to three per cent of their value. As to the "Consolidated Third," that was largely paid, until the coming of Bonaparte, in paper money which sank gradually to about six per cent of its face value. Since May 1797, both assignats and mandats had been virtually worth nothing.

[99]

So ended the reign of paper money in France. The twenty-five hundred millions of mandats went into the common heap of refuse with the previous forty-five thousand millions of assignats. The nation in general, rich and poor alike, was plunged into financial ruin from one end to the other.

On the prices charged for articles of ordinary use, light is thrown by extracts from a table published in 1795, reduced to American coinage.

	1790	1795
For a bushel of flour	40 cents	45 dollars
For a bushel of oats	18 cents	10 dollars
For a cartload of wood	4 dollars	500 dollars
For a bushel of coal	7 cents	2 dollars
For a pound of sugar	18 cents	12½ dollars
For a pound of soap	18 cents	8 dollars
For a pound of candles	18 cents	8 dollars
For one cabbage	8 cents	5½ dollars
For a pair of shoes	1 dollar	40 dollars
For twenty-five eggs	24 cents	5 dollars

But these prices about the middle of 1795 were moderate compared with those which were reached before the close of that year and during the year following. Perfectly authentic examples were such as the following:

[100]

A pound of bread	9 dollars
A bushel of potatoes	40 dollars
A pound of candles	40 dollars
A cartload of wood	250 dollars

So much for the poorer people. Typical of those esteemed wealthy may be mentioned a manufacturer of hardware who, having retired from business in 1790 with 321,000 livres, found his property in 1796 worth 14,000 francs.[75]

From this general distress arising from the development and collapse of "fiat" money in France, there was, indeed, one exception. In Paris and a few of the other great cities, men like Tallien, of the heartless, debauched, luxurious, speculator, contractor, and stock-gambler class, had risen above the ruins of the multitudes of smaller fortunes. Tallien, one of the worst demagogue "reformers," and a certain number of men like him, had been skillful enough to become millionaires, while their dupes, who had clamored for issues of paper money, had become paupers.

The luxury and extravagance of the currency gamblers and their families form one of the most significant features in any picture of the social condition of that period.[76]

A few years before this the leading women in French society showed a nobility of character and a simplicity in dress worthy of Roman matrons. Of these were Ma-

[101]

dame Roland and Madame Desmoulins; but now all
was changed. At the head of society stood Madame
Tallien and others like her, wild in extravagance, daily
seeking new refinements in luxury, and demanding of
their husbands and lovers vast sums to array them and
to feed their whims. If such sums could not be obtained
honestly, they must be had dishonestly. The more closely one examines that period, the more clearly he sees
that the pictures given by Thibaudeau and Challamel
and De Goncourt are not at all exaggerated.[77]

The contrast between these gay creatures of the Directory period and the people at large was striking. Indeed, much as the vast majority of the wealthy classes
suffered from impoverishment, the laboring classes, salaried employees of all sorts, and people of fixed income
and of small means, especially in the cities, underwent
yet greater distress. These were found, as a rule, to sub-
sist mainly on daily government rations of bread at the
rate of one pound per person. This was frequently unfit for food and was distributed to long lines of people,
men, women, and children, who were at times obliged
to wait their turn even from dawn to dusk. The very
rich could, by various means, especially by bribery,
obtain better bread, but only at enormous cost. In May
1796, the market price of good bread was, in paper, 80
francs (16 dollars) per pound and a little later provisions could not be bought for paper money at any
price.[78]

And here it may be worth mentioning that there was another financial trouble especially vexatious. While, as we have seen, such enormous sums, rising from twenty to forty thousand millions of francs in paper, were put in circulation by the successive governments of the Revolution, enormous sums had been set afloat in counterfeits by criminals and by the enemies of France. These came not only from various parts of the French Republic but from nearly all the surrounding nations, the main source being London. Thence it was that Count Joseph de Puisaye sent off cargoes of false paper, excellently engraved and printed, through ports in Brittany and other disaffected parts of France. One seizure by General Hoche was declared by him to exceed in nominal value ten thousand millions of francs. With the exception of a few of these issues, detection was exceedingly difficult, even for experts; for the vast majority of the people it was impossible.

Nor was this all. At various times the insurgent royalists in La Vendee and elsewhere put *their* presses also in operation, issuing notes bearing the Bourbon arms—the *fleur-de-lis*, the portrait of the Dauphin (as Louis XVII) with the magic legend *"De Par le Roi,"* and large bodies of the population in the insurgent districts were *forced* to take these. Even as late as 1799 these notes continued to appear.[79]

The financial agony was prolonged somewhat by attempts to secure funds by still another "forced loan,"

[103]

and other discredited measures; but when all was over with paper money, specie began to reappear—first in sufficient sums to do the small amount of business which remained after the collapse. Then as the business demand increased, the amount of specie flowed in from the world at large to meet it, and the nation gradually recovered from that long paper-money debauch.

Thibaudeau, a very thoughtful observer, tells us in his Memoirs that great fears were felt as to a want of circulating medium between the time when paper should go out and coin should come in; but that no such want was severely felt—that coin came in gradually as it was wanted.[80]

Nothing could better exemplify the saying of one of the most shrewd of modern statesmen that "there will always be money."[81]

But though there soon came a degree of prosperity—as compared with the distress during the paper-money orgy—convalescence was slow. The acute suffering from the wreck and ruin brought by assignats, mandats, and other paper currency in process of repudiation lasted nearly ten years, but the period of recovery lasted longer than the generation which followed. It required fully forty years to bring capital, industry, commerce, and credit up to their condition when the Revolution began, and demanded a "man on horseback," who established monarchy on the ruins of the Republic and threw away

[104]

millions of lives for the Empire, to be added to the millions which had been sacrificed by the Revolution.[82]

Such, briefly sketched in its leading features, is the history of the most skillful, vigorous, and persistent attempt ever made to substitute for natural laws in finance the ability of legislative bodies, and, for a standard of value recognized throughout the world, a national standard devised by theorists and manipulated by schemers. Every other attempt of the same kind in human history, under whatever circumstances, has reached similar results in kind if not in degree; all of them show the existence of financial laws as real in their operation as those which hold the planets in their courses.[83]

I have now presented this history in its *chronological* order—the order of events. Let me, in conclusion, sum it up, briefly, in its *logical order*—the order of cause and effect.

And, first, in the *economic* department. From the early reluctant and careful issues of paper we saw, as an immediate result, improvement and activity in business. Then arose the clamor for more paper money. At first, new issues were made with great difficulty; but, the dike once broken, the current of irredeemable currency poured through; and, the breach thus enlarging, this currency was soon swollen beyond control. It was urged on by speculators for a rise in values; by demagogues who persuaded the mob that a nation, by its simple fiat, could stamp real value to any amount upon valueless objects. As a natural consequence, a great debtor class grew rapidly, and this class gave its influence to depreciate more and more the currency in which its debts were to be paid.[14]

The government now began, and continued by spasms to grind out still more paper; commerce was at first stimulated by the difference in exchange; but this cause soon ceased to operate, and commerce, having been stimulated unhealthfully, wasted away.

Manufactures at first received a great impulse; but, ere long, this overproduction and overstimulus proved as fatal to them as to commerce. From time to time there was a revival of hope caused by an apparent revival of business; but this revival of business was at last seen to be caused more and more by the desire of far-seeing and cunning men of affairs to exchange paper money for objects of permanent value. As to the people at large, the classes living on fixed incomes and small salaries felt the pressure first, as soon as the purchasing power of their fixed incomes was reduced. Soon the great class living on wages felt it even more sadly.

Prices of the necessities of life increased. Merchants were obliged to increase them, not only to cover depreciation of their merchandise, but also to cover their risk of loss from fluctuation; and, while the prices of products thus rose, wages, which had at first gone up,

[106]

under the general stimulus, lagged behind. Under the universal doubt and discouragement, commerce and manufactures were checked or destroyed. As a consequence, the demand for labor was diminished; laboring men were thrown out of employment; and, under the operation of the simplest law of supply and demand, the price of labor—the daily wages of the laboring class —went down until, at a time when prices of food, clothing, and various articles of consumption were enormous, wages were nearly as low as at the time preceding the first issue of irredeemable currency.

The mercantile classes at first thought themselves exempt from the general misfortune. They were delighted at the apparent advance in the value of the goods upon their shelves. But they soon found that, as they increased prices to cover the inflation of currency and the risk from fluctuation and uncertainty, purchases became less in amount and payments less sure; a feeling of insecurity spread throughout the country; enterprise was deadened and stagnation followed.

New issues of paper were then clamored for as more drams are demanded by a drunkard. New issues only increased the evil; capitalists were all the more reluctant to embark their money on such a sea of doubt. Workmen of all sorts were more and more thrown out of employment. Issue after issue of currency came; but no relief resulted save a momentary stimulus which aggravated the disease. The most ingenious evasions of

[107]

natural laws in finance which the most subtle theorists could contrive were tried—all in vain; the most brilliant substitutes for those laws were tried; "self-regulating" schemes, "interconverting" schemes—all equally vain.[85] All thoughtful men had lost confidence. All men were *waiting;* stagnation became worse and worse. At last came the collapse and then a return, by a fearful shock, to a state of things which presented something like certainty of remuneration to capital and labor. Then, and not till then, came the beginning of a new era of prosperity.

Just as dependent on the law of cause and effect was the *moral* development. Out of the inflation of prices grew a speculating class; and, in the complete uncertainty as to the future, all business became a game of chance, and all businessmen, gamblers. In city centers came a quick growth of stockjobbers and speculators; and these set a debasing fashion in business which spread to the remotest parts of the country. Instead of satisfaction with legitimate profits, came a passion for inordinate gains. Then, too, as values became more and more uncertain, there was no longer any motive for care or economy, but every motive for immediate expenditure and present enjoyment. So came upon the nation the *obliteration of thrift.* In this mania for yielding to present enjoyment rather than providing for future comfort were the seeds of new growths of wretchedness: luxury, senseless and extravagant, set in. This,

[108]

too, spread as a fashion. To feed it, there came cheatery in the nation at large and corruption among officials and persons holding trusts. While men set such fashions in private and official business, women set fashions of extravagance in dress and living that added to the incentives to corruption. Faith in moral considerations, or even in good impulses, yielded to general distrust. National honor was thought a fiction cherished only by hypocrites. Patriotism was eaten out by cynicism.

Thus was the history of France logically developed in obedience to natural laws; such has, to a greater or less degree, always been the result of irredeemable paper, created according to the whim or interest of legislative assemblies rather than based upon standards of value permanent in their nature and agreed upon throughout the entire world. Such, we may fairly expect, will always be the result of them until the fiat of the Almighty shall evolve laws in the universe radically different from those which at present obtain.[86]

And, finally, as to the general development of the theory and practice which all this history records: my subject has been Fiat Money Inflation in France: how it came; what it brought; and how it ended.

It came by seeking a remedy for a comparatively small evil in an evil infinitely more dangerous. To cure a disease temporary in its character, a corrosive poison was administered, which ate out the vitals of French prosperity.

[109]

It progressed according to a law in social physics which we may call the "law of accelerating issue and depreciation." It was comparatively easy to refrain from the first issue; it was exceedingly difficult to refrain from the second; to refrain from the third and those following was practically impossible.

It brought, as we have seen, commerce and manufactures, the mercantile interest, the agricultural interest, to ruin. It brought on these the same destruction which would come to a Hollander opening the dikes of the sea to irrigate his garden in a dry summer.

It ended in the complete financial, moral, and political prostration of France—a prostration from which only a Napoleon could raise it.

But this history would be incomplete without a brief sequel, showing how that great genius profited by all his experience. When Bonaparte took the consulship, the condition of fiscal affairs was appalling. The government was bankrupt; an immense debt was unpaid. The further collection of taxes seemed impossible; the assessments were in hopeless confusion. War was going on in the East, on the Rhine, and in Italy, and civil war, in La Vendée. All the armies had long been unpaid, and the largest loan that could for the moment be effected was for a sum hardly meeting the expenses of the government for a single day. At the first cabinet council Bonaparte was asked what he intended to do. He replied, "I will pay cash or pay nothing." From this time he conducted all his operations on this basis. He arranged the assessments, funded the debt, and made payments in cash; and from this time—during all the campaigns of Marengo, Austerlitz, Jena, Eylau, Friedland, down to the peace of Tilsit in 1807—there was but one suspension of specie payment, and this only for a few days.

When the first great European coalition was formed against the Empire, Napoleon was hard pressed financially, and it was proposed to resort to paper money; but he wrote to his minister, "While I live, I will never resort to irredeemable paper." He never did, and France, under this determination, commanded all the gold she needed. When Waterloo came, with the invasion of the Allies, with war on her own soil, with a change of dynasty, and with heavy expenses for war and indemnities, France, on a specie basis, experienced no severe financial distress.

If we glance at the financial history of France, during the Franco-Prussian War, and the communist struggle in which a far more serious pressure was brought upon French finances than our own recent Civil War put upon American finance, and yet with no national stagnation or distress but with a steady progress in prosperity, we shall see still more clearly the advantage of meeting a financial crisis in an honest and straightforward way, and by methods sanctioned by the world's most costly experience, rather than by yielding to

[111]

dreamers, theorists, phrase-mongers, declaimers, schemers, speculators, or to that sort of "Reform" which is "the last refuge of a scoundrel."[87]

There is a lesson in all this which it behooves every thinking man to ponder.

CHRONOLOGICAL TABLE

	1789	*Assignats in circulation (millions of livres or francs)*
MAY 5	An attempt to cure the bankrupt state of the public treasury caused Louis XVI to call a meeting of the States-General, which later amalgamated into the single-chamber National Assembly	
JULY 14	Fall of the Bastille, after several days of rioting in Paris	
OCTOBER 5	Declaration of the Rights of Man adopted by Assembly	
NOVEMBER 2	Confiscation of church property	
	1790	
APRIL	First issue of paper assignats, 400 million livres	400
SEPTEMBER 29	Second issue, 800 million	1,200
	1791	
JUNE 19	Third issue, 600 million	1,800
SEPTEMBER	New Constitution; National Assembly dissolved and replaced by Legislative Assembly	
DECEMBER 17	Fourth issue, 300 million	2,100

[113]

		Assignats in circulation (millions of livres or francs)
	1792	
APRIL 30	Fifth issue, 300 million	2,400
	France at war with Russia and Austria	
JUNE-AUGUST	Riots in Paris; King dethroned and royal family imprisoned; Revolutionary Commune takes power; more assignats	2,700
SEPTEMBER	Election of National Convention replacing Legislative Assembly; Monarchy abolished; government by committees; political corruption	
DECEMBER 14	Total assignats issued to date 3,400 million; 600 million destroyed	2,800
	1793	
JANUARY 21	Louis XVI beheaded	
JANUARY 31	More assignats	3,000
FEBRUARY-MARCH	Formation of Committee of Public Safety; rioting in Paris over high prices; Revolutionary Tribunal established; Reign of Terror begins	
MAY 3	Price control on grains	
JUNE 22	Forced Loan decreed—a progressive income tax	
AUGUST 1	Trading in specie prohibited	

[114]

		Assignats in circulation (millions of livres or francs)
SEPTEMBER 29	Law of the Maximum—price control extended to all food	
OCTOBER 16	Marie Antoinette beheaded— Over 3,000 million new assignats issued during the year, of which 1,200 million entered circulation	4,200

1794

JUNE 4	Robespierre elected president of National Convention; thousands executed by decree of Revolutionary Tribunal	
JULY 27	Robespierre beheaded; end of Reign of Terror	
DECEMBER	Law of Maximum repealed Assignats in circulation at end of year	7,000

1795

MAY 31	Assignats in circulation	14,000
	More rioting; business and trade disrupted; shortages persist; uncertain government	
JULY 31	Assignats in circulation	14,000
SEPTEMBER 23	New Constitution adopted and new government formed—the Directory	35,000

[115]

		Assignats in circulation (millions of livres or francs)
	1796	
FEBRUARY 18	Machinery, plates, and paper for printing assignats destroyed	40,000
	First issue of new paper notes—mandats—to displace assignats at 30:1	
AUGUST	Mandats worth only 3 per cent of face value; about 2,500 million mandats issued altogether	
	1797	
FEBRUARY	Legal tender qualities withdrawn from both assignats and mandats, which became worthless after May	
	1798	
	Arbitrary government by the Directory; business disrupted; people discontented; Napoleon gaining military victories abroad	
	1799	
NOVEMBER 10	Napoleon comes into power—"to save the Republic"	

FOOTNOTES

1. For proof that the financial situation of France at that time was by no means hopeless, see Storch, *Economie Politique*, vol. iv., p. 159.

2. See *Moniteur,* sitting of April 10, 1790.

3. *Ibid.,* sitting of April 15, 1790.

4. For details of this struggle, see Buchez and Roux, *Histoire parlementaire de la Révolution française,* vol. iii, pp. 364, 365, 404. For the wild utterances of Marat throughout this whole history, see the full set of his *L'ami du peuple* in the President White Collection of the Cornell University Library. For Bergasse's pamphlet and a mass of similar publications, see the same collection. For the effect produced by them, see Challamel, *Les Français sous la Révolution;* also De Goncourt, *La Société française pendant la Révolution,* etc. For the Report referred to, see Levasseur, *Histoire des classes ouvrierès et de l'industrie en France de 1789 à 1870,* Paris, 1903, vol. i, chap. 6. Levasseur (vol. 1, p. 120), a very strong conservative in such estimates, sets the total value of church property at two thousand millions; other authorities put it as high as twice that sum. See especially Taine, vol. ii, chap. I, who gives the valuation as "about four milliards." Von Sybel, *Geschichte der Revolutionzeit,* gives it as two milliards and Briand, *La séparation,* etc., agrees with him. See also De Nervo, *Finances françaises,* vol. ii, pp. 236-240; also Alison, *History of Europe,* vol. i.

5. For striking pictures of this feeling among the younger generation of Frenchmen, see Challamel, *Sur la Révolution,* p. 305. For general history of John Law's paper money, see Henri Martin, *Histoire de France;* also Blanqui, *Histoire de l'économie politique,* vol. ii, pp. 65-87; also Senior on *Paper Money,* sec. iii, Pt. 1; also Thiers, *Histoire de Law;* also Levasseur, *op. cit.,* vol. i, chap. VI. Several specimens of John Law's paper currency are to be found in the White Collection in the Cornell University Library—some numbered with enormous figures.

6. See Buchez and Roux, *Histoire parlementaire,* vol. v, p. 321, *et seq.* For an argument to prove that the assignats were, after all, not so well secured as John Law's money, see Storch, *Economie Politique,* vol. iv, p. 160.

[117]

7. For specimens of this first issue and of nearly every other issue during the French Revolution, see the extensive collection of originals in the Cornell University Library. For a virtually complete collection of photographic copies, see Dewarmin, *Cent ans de numismatique française*, vol. i, passim.

8. See *Addresse de l'Assemblée nationale sur les emissions d'assignats monnaies*, p. 5.

9. *Ibid.*, p. 10.

10. For Sarot, see *Lettre de M. Sarot*, Paris, April 19, 1790. As to the sermon referred to, see Levasseur, as above, vol. i, p. 136.

11. Von Sybel, *History of the French Revolution*, vol. i, p. 252; also Levasseur, as above, pp. 137 and following.

12. For Mirabeau's real opinion on irredeemable paper, see his letter to Cerutti, in a leading article of the *Moniteur;* also *Mémoires de Mirabeau*, vol. vii, pp. 23, 24, and elsewhere. For his pungent remarks above quoted, see Levasseur, *op. cit.*, vol. i, p. 118.

13. See *Moniteur*, August 27, 1790.

14. *Moniteur*, August 28, 1790; also Levasseur, as above, pp. 139, *et seq.*

15. *Par une seule opération, grande, simple, magnifique.* See *Moniteur*. The whole sounds curiously like the proposals of the Greenbackers, regarding the American debt, some years since.

16. *Moniteur*, August 29, 1790.

17. See Lacretelle, *Histoire de France pendant le XVIII siécle*, vol. viii, pp. 84-87; also Thiers and Mignet.

18. See Hatin, *Histoire de la Presse en France*, vol. v and vi.

19. See *Moniteur*, Sept. 5, 6, and 20, 1790.

20. See Levasseur, vol. i, p. 142.

21. See speech in *Moniteur;* also in Appendix to Thiers' *History of the French Revolution*.

22. See Levasseur, *Classes ouvrières*, etc., vol. i, p. 149.

23. See Levasseur, pp. 151 *et seq*. Various examples of these "confidence bills" are to be seen in the Cornell University Library.

24. See Levasseur, vol. i, pp. 155-156.

25. See Von Sybel, *History of the Revolution*, vol. i, p. 265; also Levasseur, as above, vol. i, pp. 152-160.

26. For Turgot's argument against "fiat money" theory, see A. D. White, *Seven Great Statesmen in the Warfare of Humanity with Unreason*, article on Turgot, pp. 169, *et seq.*

[118]

27. See De Goncourt, *Société française,* for other explanations; *Les Révolutions de Paris,* vol. ii, p. 216; Challamel, *Les Français sous la Révolution;* Senior, *On Some Effects of Paper Money,* p. 82; Buchez and Roux, *Histoire parlementaire,* etc., vol. x, p. 216; Aulard, *Paris pendant la réaction thermidorienne,* passim, and especially *Rapport du bureau de surveillance,* vol. ii, pp. 562, *et seq.* (Dec. 4-24, 1795).

28. For statements and illustration of the general action of this law, see Sumner, *History of American Currency,* pp. 157, 158; also Jevons, on *Money,* p. 80.

29. See De Goncourt, *Société française,* p. 214.

30. See Von Sybel, *History of the French Revolution,* vol. i, pp. 281, 283.

31. For proofs that issues of irredeemable paper at first stimulated manufactures and commerce in Austria and afterward ruined them, see Storch's *Economie Politique,* vol. iv, p. 223, note; and for the same effect produced by the same causes in Russia, see *ibid.,* end of vol. iv. For the same effects in America, see Sumner's *History of American Currency.* For general statement of effect of inconvertible issues on foreign exchanges, see McLeod on *Banking,* p. 186.

32. See Louis Blanc, *Histoire de la Révolution française,* tome xii, p. 113.

33. See *Extrait du registre des délibérations de la section de la bibliothèque,* May 3, 1791, pp. 4, 5.

34. Von Sybel, vol. i, p. 273.

35. For general account, see Thiers' *Révolution,* chap. xiv; also Lacretelle, vol. viii, p. 109; also *Memoirs of Mallet du Pan.* For a good account of the intrigues between the court and Mirabeau and of the prices paid him, see Reeve, *Democracy and Monarchy in France,* vol. i, pp. 213-220. For a very striking caricature published after the iron chest in the Tuileries was opened and the evidences of bribery of Mirabeau fully revealed, see Challamel, *Musée,* etc., vol. i, p. 341. Mirabeau is represented as a skeleton sitting on a pile of letters, holding the French crown in one hand and a purse of gold in the other.

36. Thiers, chap. ix.

37. For this and other evidences of steady decline in the purchasing power of the assignats, see Caron, *Tableaux de Dépréciation du papier-monnaie,* Paris, 1909, p. 386.

38. See especially *Discours de Fabre d'Eglantine,* in *Moniteur* for August 11, 1793; also debate in *Moniteur* of September 15, 1793; also Prudhomme's *Révolutions de Paris.* For arguments of much the same tenor, see vast numbers of pamphlets, newspaper articles, and speeches

[119]

during the "Greenback Craze"—and the craze for unlimited coinage of silver—in the United States.

39. See Caron, *Tableaux de Dépréciation*, as above, p. 386.

40. Von Sybel, vol. i, pp. 509, 510, 515; also Villeneuve Bargemont, *Histoire de l'economie politique*, vol. ii, p. 213.

41. As to the purchasing power of money at that time, see Arthur Young, *Travels in France during the Years 1787, 1788*, and *1789*. For notices of the small currency with examples of satirical verses written regarding it, see Challamel, *Les Français sous la Révolution*, pp. 307, 308. See also Mercier, *Le Nouveau Paris*, edition of 1800, chapter ccv, entitled "Parchemin Monnaie." A series of these petty notes will be found in the White Collection of the Cornell University Library. They are very dirty and much worn, but being printed on parchment, remain perfectly legible. For issue of quarter-sou pieces, see Levasseur, p. 180.

42. See Levasseur, vol. i, p. 176.

43. For Chaumette's brilliant display of fictitious reasons for the decline, see Thiers, Shobel's translation, published by Bentley, vol. iii, p. 248.

44. For these fluctuations, see Caron, as above, p. 387.

45. One of the Forced Loan certificates will be found in the White Collection in the Library of Cornell University.

46. For details of these transactions, see Levasseur, as above, vol. i, chap. 6, pp. 181, *et seq*. Original specimens of these notes, bearing the portrait of Louis XVI will be found in the Cornell University Library (White Collection) and for the whole series perfectly photographed in the same collection, Dewarmin, *Cent ans de numismatique française*, vol. i, pp. 143-165.

47. For statements showing the distress and disorder that forced the Convention to establish the "Maximum," see Levasseur, vol. i, pp. 188-193.

48. See Levasseur, as above, vol. i, pp. 195-225.

49. See specimens of these tickets in the White Collection in the Cornell Library.

50. For these condemnations to the guillotine, see the officially published trials and also the lists of the condemned, in the White Collection, also the lists given daily in the *Moniteur*. For the spy system, see Levasseur, vol. i, p. 194.

51. See Levasseur, as above, vol. i, p. 186. For an argument to show that the Convention was led into this Draconian legislation, not by necessity, but by its despotic tendencies, see Von Sybel's *History of the*

French Revolution, vol. iii, pp. 11, 12. For general statements of theories underlying the Maximum, see Thiers; for a very interesting picture, by an eye-witness, of the absurdities and miseries it caused, see Mercier, *Le Nouveau Paris,* edition of 1800, chapter XLIV.

52. For a summary of the report of the Committee, with list of articles embraced under it, and for various interesting details, see Villeneuve Bargemont, *Histoire de l'economie politique,* vol. ii, pp. 213-239; also Levasseur, as above. For curious examples of severe penalties for very slight infringements on the law on the subject, see Louis Blanc, *Histoire de la Révolution française,* tome x, p. 144. For Louis XIV's claim, see *Memoirs of Louis XIV for the Instruction of the Dauphin.*
For a simple exposition of the way in which the exercise of this power became simply confiscation of all private property in France, see Mallet du Pan's *Memoirs,* London, 1852, vol. ii, p. 14.

53. See Du Pont's arguments, as given by Levasseur.

54. Louis Blanc calls attention to this very fact in showing the superiority of the French assignats to the old American Continental currency. See his *Histoire de la Révolution française,* tome xii, p. 98.

55. See Sumner, as above, p. 220.

56. See Levasseur, as above, vol. i, p. 178.

57. See Cambon's *Report,* Aug. 15, 1793, pp. 49-60; also, *Decree of Aug. 24, 1793,* sec. 31, chapters XCVI—CIII. Also, *Tableaux de la Dépréciation de papier monnaie dans le department de la Seine.*

58. For the example of Metz and other authorities, see Levasseur, as above, vol. i, p. 180.

59. See Von Sybel, vol. iii, p. 173.

60. See Thiers; also, for curious details of measures taken to compel farmers and merchants, see Senior, Lectures on *Results of Paper Money,* pp. 86, 87.

61. See Von Sybel, vol. iv, p. 231.

62. See Von Sybel, vol. iv, p. 330; also tables of depreciation in *Moniteur;* also official reports in the White Collection; also Caron's *Tableaux,* etc.

63. For a lifelike sketch of the way in which these exchanges of assignats for valuable property went on at periods of the rapid depreciation of paper, see Challamel, *Les Français sous la Révolution,* p. 309; also see *Economie Politique.*

64. For a very complete table of the depreciation from day to day, see *Supplement to the Moniteur* of October 2, 1797; also Caron, as above. For the market prices of the *louis d'or* at the first of every

[121]

month, as the collapse approached, see Montgaillard. See also "Official Lists" in the White Collection. For a table showing the steady rise of the franc in gold during a single week, from 251 to 280 francs, see Dewarmin, as above, vol. i, p. 136.

65. See *Mémoires de Tribaudeau*, vol. ii, p. 26, also Mercier, *Le Nouveau Paris*, vol. ii, p. 90; for curious example of the scales of depreciation, see the White Collection. See also extended table of comparative values in 1790 and 1795. See Levasseur, as above, vol. i, pp. 223-224.

66. For a striking similar case in our own country, see Sumner, *History of American Currency*, p. 47.

67. See Villeneuve Bargemont, *Histoire de l'économie politique*, vol. ii, p. 229.

68. See Von Sybel, vol. iv, pp. 337, 338. See also for confirmation Challamel, *Histoire Musée*, vol. ii, p. 179. For a thoughtful statement of the reasons why such paper was not invested in lands by men of moderate means, and workingmen, see Mill, *Political Economy*, vol. ii, pp. 81, 82.

69. See Von Sybel, vol. iv, p. 222.

70. See especially Levasseur, *Histoire des classes ouvrières*, etc., vol. i, pp. 219, 230, and elsewhere; also De Nervo, *Finance française*, p. 280; also Stourm, as already cited. The exact amount of assignats in circulation at the final suppression is given by Derwarmin, (vol. i, p. 189), as 39,999,945,428 livres or francs.

71. For details of the mandat system very thoroughly given, see Thiers' *History of the French Revolution*, Bentley's edition, vol. iv, pp. 410-412. For the issue of assignats and mandats at the same time, see Derwarmin, vol. i, p. 136; also Levasseur, vol. i, pp. 230-257. For an account of "new tenor bills" in America and their failure in 1737, see Sumner, pp. 27-31; for their failure in 1781, see Morse, *Life of Alexander Hamilton*, vol. i, pp. 86, 87. For similar failure in Austria, see Sumner, p. 314.

72. See Marchant, *Lettre aux gens de bonne foi.*

73. See Sumner, p. 44; also De Nervo, *Finances françaises*, p. 282.

74. See De Nervo, *Finance française*, p. 282; also Levasseur, vol. i, p. 236, *et seq*.

75. See Table from *Gazette de France* and extracts from other sources in Levasseur, vol. i, pp. 223-224.

76. Among the many striking accounts of the debasing effects of "inflation" upon France under the Directory, perhaps the best is that of Lacretelle, vol. xiii, pp. 32-36. For similar effect, produced by the

same cause in our own country in 1819, see statement from Niles's *Register*, in Sumner, p. 80. For the jumble of families reduced to beggary with families lifted into sudden wealth and for the mass of folly and misery thus mingled, see Levasseur, vol. i, p. 237.

77. For Madame Tallien and luxury of the stock-gambler classes, see Challamel, *Les Français sous la Révolution*, pp. 30, 33; also De Goncourt, *Les Français sous le Directoire*. Regarding the outburst of vice in Paris and the demoralization of the police, see Levasseur, as above.

78. See Levasseur, vol. i, p. 237, *et seq.*

79. For specimens of counterfeit assignats, see the White Collection in the Cornell University Library, but for the great series of various issues of them in facsimile, also for detective warnings and attempted descriptions of many varieties of them, and for the history of their issue, see especially Dewarmin, vol. i, pp. 152-161. For photographic copies of Royalist assignats, etc., see also Dewarmin, *ibid.*, pp. 192-197, etc. For a photograph of probably the last of the Royalist notes ever issued, bearing the words *Pro Deo, pro Rege, pro Patria* and *Armée Catholique et Royale* with the date 1799, and for the sum of 100 livres, see Dewarmin, vol. i, p. 204.

80. For similar expectation of a "shock," which did not occur, at the resumption of specie payments in Massachusetts, see Sumner, *History of American Currency*, p. 34.

81. See Thiers.

82. See Levasseur, vol. i, p. 246.

83. For examples of similar effects in Russia, Austria, and Denmark, see Storch, *Economie Politique*, vol. iv; for similar effects in the United States, see Gouge, *Paper Money and Banking in the United States;* also Sumner, *History of American Currency*. For working out of the same principles in England, depicted in a masterly way, see Macaulay, *History of England*, chap. xxi; and for curious exhibition of the same causes producing same results in ancient Greece, see a curious quotation by Macaulay in same chapter.

84. For parallel cases in the early history of our own country, see Sumner, p. 21, and elsewhere.

85. For a review of some of these attempts with eloquent statement of their evil results, see *Mémoires de Durand de Maillane*, pp. 166-169.

86. For similar effect of inflated currency in enervating and undermining trade, husbandry, manufactures, and morals in our own country, see Daniel Webster, cited in Sumner, pp. 45-50. For similar effects in other countries, see Senior, Storch, Macaulay, and others already cited.

[123]

87. For facts regarding French finance under Napoleon, I am in-debted to Hon. David A. Wells. For more recent triumphs of financial common sense in France, see Bonnet's articles, translated by the late George Walker, Esq. For general subject, see Levasseur.

[8]

THE ROLE OF WAR IN AMERICAN ECONOMIC DEVELOPMENT

PRICE, INCOME, AND MONETARY CHANGES IN THREE WARTIME PERIODS[1]

By MILTON FRIEDMAN
University of Chicago

The widespread tendency in empirical studies of economic behavior to discard war years as "abnormal," while doubtless often justified, is, on the whole, unfortunate. The major defect of the data on which economists must rely—data generated by experience rather than deliberately contrived experiment—is the small range of variation they encompass. Experience in general proceeds smoothly and continuously. In consequence, it is difficult to disentangle systematic effects from random variation since both are of much the same order of magnitude.

From this point of view, data for wartime periods are peculiarly valuable. At such times, violent changes in major economic magnitudes occur over relatively brief periods, thereby providing precisely the kind of evidence that we would like get by "critical" experiments if we could conduct them. Of course, the source of the changes means that the effects in which we are interested are necessarily intertwined with others that we would eliminate from a contrived experiment. But this difficulty applies to all our data, not to data for wartime periods alone.

To the student of monetary phenomena, the three wartime episodes with which this paper deals—the experience of the United States in the Civil War, first World War, and second World War—offer an especially close approximation to the kind of critical experiment he would like to conduct. As we shall see, in all three cases the rise in prices was of almost precisely the same magnitude, so this critical variable is under control. Yet other crucial features varied, offering the opportunity to test alternative hypotheses designed to explain price changes.

Besides their significance for the general understanding of monetary phenomena, the wartime experiences are unfortunately of interest in their own right. The current period of mobilization raises much the

[1] In this summary of some of the main findings of a larger and still unfinished study, it has not been feasible to describe the sources or method of computation of the figures used. It is expected that these will be presented in full in a later publication. I am greatly indebted to Phillip Cagan and David Fand for able assistance in the research underlying this paper.

same financial problems as previous wartime periods; and the unhappy possibility that the resemblance will become even closer cannot be dismissed.

Price and Income Changes

The appended table summarizes the key magnitudes for the three wartime periods. In all cases, I have taken the outbreak of the war as the starting point, since this seems more nearly comparable for the different wars than the date of our active entry into the war, and the date of the war or first postwar price peak as the terminal point. This gives a period of nearly four years for the Civil War price movement,[2] nearly six years for World War I, and nearly nine years for World War II.

The price peak came approximately at the end of the Civil War, a year and a half after the end of World War I, and three years after World War II. This successively later timing of the peak is one of the most interesting features of the three wartime periods. Measured by the available monthly indexes of wholesale prices, the magnitude of the full price rise was very nearly identical in the three wars (see line 5 of table), prices at the price peak being from 2.1 to 2.3 times their level at the outbreak of the war. This similarity of behavior is not an accident resulting from the use of wholesale prices; it would be shown equally by other broad and equally reliable index numbers. Given the difference in the length of the periods, the rate of rise was of course successively lower in the three wars (line 6).

Unfortunately, no satisfactory data are available on short period movements in national income in the Civil War. General considerations together with some scattered evidence suggest that money income rose in approximately the same or a somewhat higher ratio than prices; i.e., that real output was either unchanged or moderately higher. Money income somewhat more than doubled in the first World War, and more than tripled in the second (line 7).[3] Since prices roughly doubled in both wars, real output changed little in World War I but rose about 50 per cent in World War II (line 9). Somewhat less than half of this rise in output can be attributed to the higher volume of unemployment at the outbreak of the second than at the outbreak of the first World War; the rest, which meant an increase in output of about 2.5 per cent a year, is less readily explained.

[2] All statements for Civil War are for the North ("loyal states") only.

[3] The concept of national income here and elsewhere in this paper is not identical with that currently being used by the U.S. Department of Commerce. To obtain comparability of data for the different wars, it has seemed preferable to use the concept in Simon Kuznets, *National Product in Wartime* (National Bureau of Economic Research, 1945).

The Magnitude of the War Effort

The immediate occasion for the rise in prices and money income was of course the diversion of resources to war use. We can get a rough measure of the magnitude of diversion in each wartime period as a whole by expressing federal expenditures in each year as a fraction of national income, to render the expenditures comparable from year to year and war to war; subtracting the corresponding fraction for an immediate prewar year, to allow for changes from war to war in the "normal" activities of government; and summing the resultant figures for all full fiscal years from the outbreak of the war to the price peak. According to this measure, slightly over one-half of one year's national income was diverted to war use during the Civil War price movement and also during the World War I movement, and about one and two-thirds years' national income during the World War II price movement (line 11). On a per-year basis, the diversion was about 14 per cent for the Civil War, 9 per cent for World War I, and 18 per cent for World War II (line 12).

Numerous qualifications attach to both the statistical and economic significance of these figures. My own judgment is that the aggregate diversion of resources to the war effort was significantly smaller in the first World War than in either of the other two wars in the sense that it raised a less serious economic problem, and probably larger in World War II than in the Civil War.[1] From the point of view of a well-designed experiment, this is a rather happy outcome, since it enables us to distinguish, as it were, the effects of secular change from other effects. If the same factors turn out to explain why the full price rise was roughly the same in the earliest and the latest war as in the first World War despite a more serious economic problem, the results are not rendered questionable by the possibility that would otherwise exist that they merely reflect secular change.

The Problem of Interpretation

How is it that despite substantial differences in the stimulus, the magnitude of the full price rise is much the same in the three wars while the rate of price rise is successively smaller? What features of policy or circumstance account for the less effective handling in the first World War than in either of the other wars of the inflationary threat raised by the wartime need to devote a significant fraction of resources

[1] One set of numbers that brings out dramatically the problem of judging the relative magnitude of diversion is the total number of persons who died in military service in the three wars. The number is roughly 360 thousand for the North in the Civil War, 126 thousand in World War I and 400 thousand in World War II. The corresponding figures for total population at the outbreak of the wars are 22, 99, 131 million. By this index, the Civil War was far and away the costliest.

to the production of goods and services not available for sale on the market?

Three factors are generally cited as explaining part or all of the better performance in the second than in the first World War: first, the larger fraction of government expenditures financed through taxes; second, the greater increase in output documented above; third, the more extensive direct controls over prices, wages, and the distribution of goods. Are these an adequate explanation? And do they also explain the better performance in the Civil than in the first World War?

The Importance of Taxation. Total federal tax receipts averaged about one-fifth of total expenditures during the Civil War price movement, two-fifths during World War I, and three-fifths during World War II, a dramatic and impressive improvement in the tax effort (line 13).

These differences in the level of taxation increase the difficulty of explaining the common behavior of prices in the Civil War and World War I, since not only was the war effort apparently of larger magnitude during the Civil War, but also the fraction of expenditures financed by taxes was smaller. On a per-year basis and as a percentage of the national income, expenditures one and half times as large in the Civil War as in World War I were converted by the smaller tax effort into a deficit nearly twice as large—12 per cent of national income compared with 6.5 per cent (lines 15 or 17).[5] The cumulated deficit over the four years of the Civil War period amounted to about one-half of one year's national income; over the six years of the World War I period, to two-fifths of a year's income (lines 14 and 16).

For the two world wars, on the other hand, the differences in the level of taxation help to explain the common behavior of prices. But they do so only in part, since the higher level of taxation in World War II fell far short of offsetting fully the higher level of expenditures. Despite the larger tax effort, the deficit was substantially higher: 13 per cent of national income per year compared to 6.5 per cent for the total deficit (line 15); and 8.5 per cent of national income per year, compared to 6.5 per cent for the excess deficit (the deficit as a fraction of national income minus the corresponding prewar fraction; see line 17). The cumulated total deficit is nearly three times as large in World War II as in World War I; the cumulated excess deficit nearly twice as large.[6]

[5] The two lines give the same answer because the budget was approximately balanced just prior to both the Civil War and World War I.

[6] I have assumed implicitly that a balanced budget (or the balanced part of the budget) raises no inflationary problem regardless of size. According to the so-called "balanced budget theorem," however, an increase of federal expenditures and taxes by the same amount has a "multiplier" of unity, and hence a larger balanced budget is more infla-

Changes in Real Output. There seems no reason to believe that real output behaved very differently during the Civil War than during the first World War; so this factor is largely neutral as between these two wars.

The substantial rise in real output during World War II, compared to little change during World War I, undoubtedly eased the physical and psychological problems of attaining such an impressively large war output. It is less obvious just how it affected the financial and monetary problem of avoiding inflation. For the increase in real output involved an increase in income payments to the factors of production but, since it was absorbed by government for war purposes, no increase in goods available for purchase on the market.

From the point of view of the quantity theory of money, increased output helps the problem of avoiding inflation by raising the demand for money. In consequence, the government can finance part of its expenditures by creating money without any inflationary pressure on prices. Quantitative estimates along these lines indicate that only a small part of the difference between the deficits in the two world wars can be regarded as noninflationary because of the increase in real output—from one-tenth to one-fifth of the difference, depending on the exact estimate used and on whether the deficit prior to World War II is or is not regarded as "normal."

From the point of view of the income-expenditure theory, the increased output helps the problem of avoiding inflation because at a correspondingly higher income the amount not spent on consumption (or more generally not devoted to "induced expenditures") will be larger, so permitting a larger amount of income-creating or "autonomous" expenditures. Quantitative estimates based on this approach vary more widely than those based on the quantity-theory approach, primarily because there is more uncertainty just how to make them. It turns out that the final result depends critically on two factors: the interpretation placed on the deficit prior to World War II compared with the balanced budget prior to World War I; and the numerical value used for the "multiplier." If the difference in prewar deficits is regarded as "accidental" and hence the total deficits in the two wars regarded as comparable, this approach yields essentially the same result as the quantity-theory approach: between one-twelfth and two-thirds of the difference between the deficits in the two wars can be regarded as non-inflationary because of the increase in real output, the exact estimate

---

tionary than a smaller one. To the extent that this theorem is relevant to the present problem, it strengthens the conclusion reached above; namely, that the difference in the level of taxation cannot account for the difference in performance.

depending on the multiplier that is used. This range includes the whole of the range given earlier. On the other hand, if the pre-World War II deficit is regarded as normal, i.e., as reflecting a secular shift toward "stagnation" so that a deficit of given size was less inflationary, the results are highly ambiguous: between one-half and three times the difference in the excess deficit can then be regarded as noninflationary because of the increase in real output.

In my judgment, the balance of evidence justifies the conclusion that the large increase in output in World War II explains only in part, and probably only in minor part, why the larger per-year and accumulated deficits in that war than in World War I were associated with a price rise that was somewhat smaller in aggregate and decidedly smaller per year.

Direct Controls. Direct controls were completely absent in the Civil War, present to some extent in World War I and extensive in World War II. If they tend to reduce the ultimate inflationary impact of wartime expenditures, they, like the differences in tax effort, increase the difficulty of explaining the common magnitude of the price rise in the Civil War and World War I.

The major channel whereby direct controls can be regarded as reducing inflationary pressure is by inducing income recipients at a given level of prices to accumulate larger cash balances or purchase a larger amount of government securities than otherwise.[7] Figures on holdings of money and of government securities during World War II suggest that the controls may have had such effects when they were in force; but, if so, the effects were not lasting and had completely disappeared by mid-1948 when prices reached their peak. From the outbreak of the war to the subsequent price peak, cash balances as a fraction of national income fell by about the same amount in World War II as in World War I, and cash balances plus government security holdings rose by a smaller amount (lines 18 and 19). So direct controls can be rejected as a factor affecting the ultimate magnitude of the price rise.

Monetary Factors

We have as yet found no answer to the question why the price rise was much the same in the three wars despite substantial differences in the magnitude of the war effort. The three reasons commonly adduced to explain the better performance in World War II than in World War I—larger tax effort, larger increase in real output, and direct controls

[7] I neglect the so-called "wage-price spiral" (more properly, wage-price-money spiral) argument for reasons indicated in my paper, "Some Comments on the Significance of Labor Unions for Economic Policy," in *The Impact of the Union,* edited by David McCord Wright, (Harcourt, Brace and Co., 1951), pp. 217-221.

—seem inadequate even for these two wars and, more significant yet, if anything they increase the difficulty of explaining the better performance in the Civil War than in World War I.

The one set of factors so far left largely out of account are those connected with changes in the quantity of money. Figures on these changes (lines 23 and 24), unlike the figures we have so far been grappling with, tell a simple, coherent, and consistent story and give at least a proximate explanation of price behavior during the three wars. Consider first the two world wars. The stock of money doubled in the first and nearly tripled in the second (line 23). But this difference is more than accounted for by the differential change in total output. The stock of money per unit of output, which is of course the figure that is relevant for price movements, rose somewhat more in World War I than in World War II; and so did prices and in almost exactly the same proportion. During the Civil War, the stock of money rose more than in World War I and less than in World War II.[8] Unfortunately, we cannot reliably translate this figure into the change in the quantity of money per unit of output; we do know enough, however, to demonstrate that if we could, the result might be perfectly in line with those for the other wars and can hardly be drastically out of line with them. The total rise in wholesale prices was the same in the Civil War and in World War I but at a higher rate per year; the higher rate of price rise might be expected to lead to a larger increase in velocity, so the stock of money per unit of output might be expected to have increased somewhat less than in World War I; an increase in output of about 20 per cent would be required for this result;[9] this is not unreasonable in the light of general considerations which suggest that output was relatively stable or rose moderately during the Civil War; even the extreme assumption of no change in output yields results that are not drastically out of line with those for the later wars.

Our conclusions about the three wars do not rest on or require any narrowly restrictive assumption about the constancy of the income velocity of circulation. Income velocity would be expected to rise during a period of rising prices because of the incentive not to hold cash; and it did rise in the two wars for which we have data (line 25). The significant thing is that it rose by roughly the same amount, and that the small difference in the magnitude of the rise is in the expected direction: the rise is somewhat greater in the war in which prices rose at a

[8] It should be noted that the estimates of the stock of money for the Civil War are entirely new estimates constructed by rather roundabout means from a considerable body of fragmentary evidence; so are subject to considerable error.

[9] The 20 per cent is obtained by supposing the rise in income velocity in the Civil War to exceed that in World War I by the same amount as the latter exceeds the rise in World War II (see line 25).

ROLE OF WAR IN AMERICAN ECONOMIC DEVELOPMENT   619

higher rate. Indeed, I would have expected the higher rate of price rise in World War I to have produced an even larger difference in the behavior of velocity.

Reasons for Changes in Stock of Money

The finding that price rises of the same percentage in the three wars can be "explained" by rises in the quantity of money per unit of output of roughly the same percentage is, of course, no final answer to our basic question. What factors account for the common rise in the quantity of money per unit of output despite such wide differences in the magnitude of the war effort, the size of the deficit, the banking structure, and so on? More particularly, why was the rise as large as it was in World War I, given a smaller war effort than in either of the other wars and a larger tax effort than in the Civil War?

Lines 26 through 32 in the appended table are designed to push the analysis one stage farther by giving a particular breakdown of the factors determining changes in the stock of money and the effect of such changes on income. Lines 26 through 29 summarize the factors determining the amount of money created by government; lines 30 through 32, the factors determining its inflationary potency.

World War I involved a substantially smaller issue of money by government than either of the other wars (line 29), and in this sense a smaller inflationary stimulus; smaller than the Civil War despite total expenditures of roughly the same magnitude (line 26) because of both a smaller deficit relative to expenditures (line 27) and the financing of a smaller fraction of the deficit by money creation rather than bond issues (line 28); smaller than World War II, despite a larger deficit relative to expenditures and the financing of the same fraction of the deficit by currency creation, because of a drastically smaller level of total expenditures. Had the inflationary potency of government created money been the same in the two world wars as in the Civil War, wholesale prices would have risen only about 50 per cent in World War I instead of 132 per cent; and only about 60 per cent in World War II instead of 113 per cent. These computations assume that the changes in output would have been as estimated in line 9 of the table and that velocity would have risen by about as much as it did.

But the inflationary potency of government created money was not the same. And it is this factor, summarized in line 32 of the table, that is the key to our basic question. The smaller initial inflationary stimulus in World War I than in either of the other wars was offset by a higher sensitivity to government money creation. Each dollar of money printed by the government meant an increase of $7.00 per year in national income in the Civil War and of nearly $7.50 in the second

World War; it meant an increase of about twice as much, or nearly $15.00, in the first World War.

The increased sensitivity of the economy to government money creation in World War I than in the Civil War is even more remarkable in view of the sharp decline in the income velocity of circulation, which worked in the opposite direction. The villain is the expansion ratio of the banking system, which was more than five times as large.[10] The lower sensitivity in World War II than in World War I is a resultant of a reduction both on the demand side—a decline of more than a quarter in the income velocity of circulation—and on the supply side— a decline of more than a quarter in the expansion ratio of the banking system. Compared to the Civil War, however, World War II shows essentially the same changes as World War I—a drastic decrease in the income velocity of circulation counterbalanced by an even more drastic increase in the expansion ratio of the banking system.

These differences in the expansion ratio in turn reflect changes in our banking structure: the much greater importance of currency relative to deposits in the Civil War than in the two later wars, the abandonment of the gold standard in the Civil War and its retention in the others wars, changes in the reserve ratio of the banking system from war to war, and so on. From this point of view—as, also, if I may add a parenthetical minority view, from almost every other—the establishment of the Federal Reserve System at the outbreak of World War I, far from being the unmitigated boon to war finance that it is generally considered, was a serious handicap. It had the effect of reducing the reserve ratio of the banking system and so increasing the expansion ratio. In addition, it doubtless meant an increase in the amount of money created by the government in both world wars because of the System's rediscount operations (particularly after World War I) and government bond purchases (particularly after World War II). These

---

[10] In calculating the expansion ratios, I have treated as government issued money only net noninterest-bearing obligations issued directly by the government and held outside government agencies. However, the Federal Reserve System has been regarded as part of the government and its accounts consolidated with those of the Treasury. Thus, the total stock of government created money is equal to currency outside Treasury and Federal Reserve plus domestic deposits other than Treasury deposits in the Federal Reserve less gold stock (because regarded as privately created) less state and national bank notes (except for World War II when national bank notes were in the process of retirement) less deposits of U. S. Government and government agencies in commercial and savings banks less Federal Reserve float. The total stock of money used in calculating the numerator of the ratios is currency outside banks and the Treasury plus adjusted demand deposits plus time deposits.

This treatment implicitly makes a distinction between government securities sold to the Federal Reserve banks and other government securities but not between securities sold to commercial banks and securities sold to nonbank purchasers. The sale of securities to the Federal Reserve is not a "real" security sale; it is simply a bookkeeping operation involved in our system in the creation of money by the government. For the rest, little economic importance attaches to the distinction between sales to commercial banks and to others.

involved creation of money, not to meet government expenditures, but to enable private banks to expand.

The secular trend in the income velocity is less readily and satisfactorily explained. Numerous explanations have been offered, but so far as I know, no satisfactory test of their validity has yet been made. In any event, it presumably reflected factors largely outside of government control.

Conclusion

This examination of changes in prices, income, and monetary magnitudes during three wartime periods has led to conclusions which, if accepted, clearly have important implications for both economic theory and economic policy. The explicit statement of a number of these implications will provide a convenient means of summarizing the analysis.

A crucial issue in economic theory in recent years has been the relative value of two competing theories of income determination: the quantity theory of money and the Keynesian income-expenditure theory. These two theories can, of course, be looked on as merely frameworks of analysis—as different languages or assemblies of truisms. In this sense, any statements expressed in the language of one theory can be translated into the language of the other. But I take it that the major issue has been about the theories, not as alternative languages, but as empirical hypotheses. In this sense they are different and competitive: the quantity theory asserts in essence that the velocity of circulation of money is the empirical variable that behaves in a stable or consistent fashion; the income-expenditure theory, that the propensity to consume, or the consumption function, is the empirical variable.

Price and income changes during the three wartime periods seem more readily explicable by the quantity theory than by the income-expenditure theory. The quantity theory instructs us to look for a proximate explanation of the divergent magnitudes of the rise in money income in a similarly divergent rise in the stock of money and for a proximate explanation of the common magnitude of the price rise in a common behavior of the stock of money relative to real output. And it turns out that the percentage rise in the stock of money was larger in the first than in the second war period and larger in the third than in either of the others in roughly the same proportion as the corresponding increases in output; in consequence, the stock of money per unit of output increased by about the same percentage in all three periods. Indeed, even the minor difference between the two world wars in the percentage increase in the stock of money per unit of output is in the same direction and of the same magnitude as the minor difference in the percentage increase in prices. The quantity theory is thus clearly consistent with this empirical test.

The income-expenditure theory instructs us to pay little or no attention to the quantity of money or its behavior but to look for an explanation of the divergent behavior of money income in a correspondingly divergent behavior of "autonomous" or "income-creating" expenditures. But the facts appear inconsistent with this explanation. In all three wars government expenditures are the dominant autonomous expenditures to which the income rise must be attributed by the income-expenditure theory and taxes the chief "leakage" other than savings. The magnitude of government expenditures, measured throughout in units of an appropriate year's national income, was about the same in aggregate during the four years of the Civil War price rise as during the six years of the World War I price rise, hence about one and a half times as large per year; taxes were a smaller fraction of both expenditures and national income; so the per-year deficit was almost twice as large a fraction of the national income during the Civil War price rise. Yet despite not much difference in the behavior of output, prices rose by the same percentage in the two wars. In the second World War, incomes rose more than in either of the other wars though prices did not, thanks to the increase in real output, and total expenditures are larger both in aggregate and on a per-year basis than in either of the other wars. But the per-year deficit, though considerably larger than in the first World War, is no larger than in the Civil War, and the magnitudes of the differences seem to bear no consistent relationship to the magnitude of the changes in income. From an examination of the income or fiscal magnitudes alone, one would expect the rise in income in the second World War to have been much larger relative to the rise in the first than it was, and the rise in prices to have been much smaller relative to the rise in the Civil War than it was. The income-expenditure theory explains part of the difference between the two world wars and, with considerably more difficulty, may perhaps be interpreted as consistent with the whole difference. I have been unable to explain the difference between the Civil War and World War I in its terms. Indeed, the factors it stresses increase the problem of explanation.

This conclusion that the quantity theory is and the income-expenditure theory is not consistent with price and income behavior in the three wars would, I think, be strengthened by examination of the year-to-year changes in prices, incomes, and monetary and fiscal magnitudes, in addition to the changes from the outbreak of the war to the end of the price movement on which I have put major emphasis. The sharp drop in the government deficit and emergence of a surplus shortly after both world wars was not accompanied by a correspondingly sharp drop in income or in prices; at most, they were accompanied by a temporary halt and then a resumption of the rise in prices; and in both cases the stock of money continued rising after surpluses had appeared in the government budget and reached a peak in the general neighborhood of the price peak.

Such an examination would also, I think, provide a plausible explanation for the successively later timing of the price peak. In the Civil War, there was no central bank automatically creating "high-powered" currency at the initiative of commercial banks; so the price rise ended when the government no longer had to print money to meet its expenditures. In the first World War, there was such a central bank and it provided the sinews for continued expansion of the total stock of money after the close of the war through its rediscount operations, but at least there was no bond-support policy to prevent the central bank from calling a halt at long last; so the inflation continued only eighteen months after the end of the war. In the second World War, the bond-support policy had the same effect as the earlier rediscounting operations in providing a base for a larger money supply and in addition served as an excuse for letting the process continue; so the primary postwar inflation lasted thirty-six months after the end of the war.

The implications of our results for policy are, I think, no less clear than for economic theory. The debate between proponents and opponents of monetary policy has in truth been little more than a manifestation of the debate on alternative theories. Our conclusions favor the proponents of monetary policy. If you want to control prices and incomes, they say in about as clear tones as empirical evidence ever speaks, control the stock of money per unit of output. The level of expenditures and of taxation, the extent of increases in real output, are all important for the problem of inflation primarily because of their effects on the stock of money per unit of output, and they are only important insofar as they have such effects. And at least as important as any of these is the expansion ratio of the banking system—the total number of dollars of money created per dollar of direct government money creation. For we found that the major factor that explained the relative income increases in the three wars was not the extent of money creation by the government, for this was less than half as large in the first World War as in either of the others, but the expansion ratio of the banking system. In the Civil War the total supply of money—currency plus deposits—increased about $1.50 for each $1.00 of money created directly by the government; in the first World War, it increased nearly $8.00; in the second World War, $5.50. If direct government money creation had been the same in both world

624   AMERICAN ECONOMIC ASSOCIATION

SELECTED DATA ON PRICE, INCOME, AND MONETARY CHANGES IN
THE CIVIL WAR, WORLD WAR I, AND WORLD WAR II

GENERAL NOTES:
1. With minor exceptions, all figures refer to period from outbreak of war to subsequent price peak.
2. Ratios of a quantity at price peak to its value at outbreak of war are based on averages for a twelve-month period surrounding the price peak and a twelve-month period surrounding the outbreak of war, except for Civil War stock of money ratios.
3. Missing figures for Civil War reflect absence of independent evidence on change in real output.
4. All figures for Civil War are, so far as possible, for the North ("loyal states") only.

Timing Data	CIVIL WAR	WORLD WAR I	WORLD WAR II
1. Date of outbreak of war	April, 1861	July–Aug., 1914	Sept., 1939
2. Date of end of war	April, 1865	Nov., 1918	Aug., 1945
3. Date of price peak	Jan., 1865	May, 1920	Aug., 1948
4. Months from outbreak of war to price peak	45	69	107
Wholesale Prices			
5. Ratio (price peak/outbreak of war)	2.32	2.32	2.13
6. Rate of rise per year	25%	16%	9%
Money National Income			
7. Ratio (price peak/outbreak of war)	—	2.29	3.14
8. Rate of rise per year	—	16%	14%
Real National Income *(Deflated by Wholesale Prices)*			
9. Ratio (price peak/outbreak of war)	—	.99	1.48
10. Rate of rise per year	—	0	4.4%
Magnitude of War Effort			
Federal expenditures as fraction of national income in excess of base year fraction			
11. Sum for all full fiscal years, outbreak of war to price peak	.54	.56	1.65
12. Per year	.14	.093	.18
Fiscal Performance			
13. Taxes as fraction of expenditures	.21	.43	.61
Deficit as fraction of national income:			
14. Sum all full fiscal years, outbreak of war to price peak	.49	.39	1.13
15. Per year	.12	.065	.13
Deficit as fraction of national income in excess of base year fraction:			
16. Sum, outbreak of war to price peak	.46	.39	.76
17. Per year	.12	.065	.085
Money and Government Security Holdings of Nonbanking Public			
Money as fraction of national income			
18. Ratio (price peak/outbreak of war)	—	.86	.88
Money plus securities as fraction of national income			
19. Ratio (price peak/outbreak of war)	—	1.26	1.14
Stock of Money; Velocity			
Ratios (price peak/outbreak of war)			
20. Currency outside banks	2.49*	2.48	4.19
21. Demand deposits adjusted	2.54*	1.98	3.02
22. Time deposits	1.63*	1.83	2.13
23. Total stock of money	2.32*	1.96	2.75
24. Stock of money per unit of output	—	1.98	1.86
25. Income velocity of circulation	—	1.17	1.15

ROLE OF WAR IN AMERICAN ECONOMIC DEVELOPMENT   625

SELECTED DATA ON PRICE, INCOME, AND MONETARY CHANGES IN THE
CIVIL WAR, WORLD WAR I, AND WORLD WAR II—(*continued*)

	CIVIL WAR	WORLD WAR I	WORLD WAR II
Factors Determining Changes in Stock of Money and Their Effect on Income			
26. Ratio of accumulated government expenditures to national income	.62	.69	2.88
27. Deficit as fraction of government expenditures	.79	.57	.39
28. Fraction of accumulated deficit financed by money creation	.23	.11	.11
29. (26)×(27)×(28) = Money created by government as a fraction of a year's national income	.11	.043	.12
30. Expansion ratio of banking system (total money created per dollar of money created by government)	1.49	7.78	5.53
31. Income velocity of circulation	4.70	1.90	1.35
32. (30)×(31) = Dollars of income per year per dollar of money created by government	7.00	14.78	7.47

* Ratios of average for year ending June 30, 1865, to value on June 30, 1861. Data are not available on demand deposits adjusted and time deposits for Civil War. Ratios given are for all deposits other than deposits in mutual savings banks, and deposits in mutual savings banks, respectively.

wars as it was but had been combined with a 100 per cent reserve deposit banking system, a nongold money, and no private creation of money, prices would probably have risen vastly less than they actually did. The Civil War money creation took place in a system that by accident rather than design in effect closely approximated the one just described, which appears to be the main reason why prices rose no more in that war than in the others despite a larger war effort than in the first World War, and a less effective tax effort and a substantially smaller demand for money than in either of the other wars.

[9]

THE MONETARY AND FISCAL PROGRAMS OF THE CONFEDERATE GOVERNMENT, 1861–65[1]

EUGENE M. LERNER

University of Idaho

I

ECONOMISTS have left whole areas of valuable statistical information unexamined because they have considered wartime figures "abnormal." This has been unfortunate. Wars generate sharp changes in prices, wages, and the stock of money during relatively brief periods. These periods, as Friedman has pointed out, "provide precisely the kind of evidence that we would like to get by 'critical' experiments if we could conduct them."[2] The Confederate economy during the American Civil War is particularly important to economists. During these few years prices, wages, and the stock of money rose more than in any comparable period of American history since the Revolutionary War.

I propose to examine these aspects of the Confederate economy in two articles. In this, the first, I discuss the Confederate government's revenue-raising programs and their inflationary consequences. In the second I shall analyze the money, price, and wage series I have prepared for these years. Section II of this paper presents introductory material; Sections III, IV, and V discuss Confederate taxation; Sections VI and VII discuss bond issues; Section VIII discusses note issues; and Section IX discusses the Confederate currency reform.

II

The goods and services raised by the Confederate government to wage its war of secession came, in part, from impressments, donations, and taxes payable in kind. These practices had also been used by earlier wartime governments. Alexander Hamilton, writing during the Revolutionary War, said that "if the farmers do not like the price [offered for their products] they are not obliged to sell . . . and . . . one measure alone can oblige them to contribute to their proper quota to the support of the government: a tax in kind."[3]

Like the taxes in kind during the Revolution, those levied by the South were avoided by the farmers and businessmen who sold their goods (or hid them) before collection time. People in areas hard to reach were exempt by default. Neither the right goods nor the right quantities of goods were collected, and the supplies that were obtained often rotted, became damaged, or were stolen before they could be transported to the areas where they were needed.[4]

---

[1] I should like to thank Professors Earl J. Hamilton and Milton Friedman for their helpful suggestions and comments. I assume full responsibility, of course, for any errors.

[2] Milton Friedman, "Price, Income and Monetary Changes in Three Wartime Periods," *American Economic Review*, XLII (May, 1952), 612.

[3] *Works*, ed. Henry Cabot Lodge (Federal ed.; New York: Putnam, 1885–86), III, 72.

[4] Letter from Allen, chief clerk of the Confederate Treasury Department, to Secretary Memminger, in Raphael P. Thian (ed.), *Appendix* (Washington, D.C., 1878), III, 200. Thian was a chief clerk in the adjutant general's office. He compiled four volumes of incoming correspondence, outgoing correspondence, and reports of the Confederate Treasury Department, under the direction of Brevet

CONFEDERATE FINANCE   507

Donations often came at great personal sacrifice. The farmers of the Shenandoah Valley shared with Lee the corn and wheat they salvaged after Sheridan's men razed their farms. These gifts, of course, were much too small to finance the Civil War; and the Confederacy, like any government, purchased the bulk of its supplies. At times the South impressed goods or paid less than the full market price for them, thereby stimulating "the bitterest feelings against the military authorities."[5] Frequently, impressment agents waited along well-traveled roads and seized the goods of unlucky farmers who happened along, instead of leaving the highways and impressing more equitably the goods of all producers. Farmers who anticipated impressment soon stopped bringing their goods to market and were discouraged from producing more than enough for their own immediate needs.[6]

Large sums of money were required to purchase goods whether the Confederate government impressed them or paid the full market price. The South raised revenue through borrowing, taxing, and printing. Up to October, 1864,[7] almost 60 per cent of all the money received by the Confederacy had come from the printing press. Less than 5 per cent of its revenue came from taxes. Approximately 30 per cent came from bonds

sold to banks, institutions, and private persons and 5 per cent from miscellaneous sources.[8] I shall attempt to account for these proportions and point out some of their implications.

III

On May 10, 1861, Christopher G. Memminger, Secretary of the Confederate Treasury, recommended that for the following fiscal year the Confederate government levy a property tax yielding no more than $15 millions. He further recommended that, if sufficient funds were raised through bond sales and the tariff, "the President should be authorized by proclamation to diminish the quotas called for"[9] under this war property tax. Congress held that the Secretary's $15 million tax request was too high and wanted a program yielding no more than $10 millions.

Secretary Memminger believed that the Confederate government's tax receipts should be at least large enough to meet the interest charges on the rapidly growing national debt, but even such a limited program of taxation met with several difficulties. Entire parts of this new government, such as the Supreme Court, were still unorganized. Machinery for collecting large amounts of taxes was not established.[10] Also, a more am-

Major General E. D. Townsend. These volumes, located in the Treasure Room at Duke University, are titled "*Appendix*, Volumes I, II, III, and IV." The book, to which these are the appendixes, and the publisher are unknown.

[5] John C. Schwab, *The Confederate States of America, 1861–1865* (New York: Charles Scribner's Sons, 1901), p. 207.

[6] Merton Coulter, *The Confederate States of America, 1861–1865* (Baton Rouge: Louisiana State University Press, 1950), p. 207.

[7] My estimates, based on the reports of the Secretary of the Treasury, end on this date.

[8] The North's financial program was vastly more successful than the South's. The North raised almost 21 per cent of its expenditures through taxes. Sixty-two per cent came from interest-bearing bonds, 13 per cent from notes, and 4 per cent from miscellaneous sources (U.S. Department of Commerce, *Historical Statistics of the United States, 1789–1945*, prepared by the U.S. Bureau of the Census with the co-operation of the Social Science Research Council [Washington: Government Printing Office, 1949], pp. 299–306).

[9] "Report of May 10, 1861" (Thian [ed.]., *op. cit.*, III, 10–11).

[10] Memminger, "Report of May 1, 1861" (*ibid.*, p. 5).

508 EUGENE M. LERNER

bitious program would have been strongly opposed by the eleven states that had just seceded from the "despotic" United States government to form the Confederacy. Many southerners believed that large tax payments were not necessary. Cotton was to be king; England would soon recognize the new nation and intervene actively; the Yankees would not fight; and military battles would go well for the South. In July, 1861, at Bull Run these expectations seemed confirmed.

The South was not alone, however, in expecting an easy and early victory. President Lincoln asked men to volunteer for only ninety days, and the United States Congress also failed to enact large revenue-raising bills. It did raise import duties, pass a direct tax of $20 millions, and enact for the first time a 3 per cent tax on incomes over $800. These acts, however, came too late to be of much help to the North during the first fiscal year of the war.

Secretary Memminger saw two immediate and indispensable benefits from levying taxes payable in government notes. First, taxes created a demand for the paper issued by the government and gave it value. Since all taxpayers needed the paper, they were willing to exchange goods for it, and the notes circulated as money. Second, to the extent that taxation raised revenue, it reduced the number of new notes that had to be issued. Memminger's numerous public statements during the war show that he clearly realized that increasing a country's stock of money much faster than its real income leads to runaway prices. They also show that he believed that a strong tax program lessens the possibility of inflation.

Secretary Memminger recommended taxing those forms of property that depended upon southern victory for their future yield and reflected the owner's ability to pay.[11] Slaves, for instance, were appropriate to tax. They "never belong to persons who do not own other property," and the "origin and character of the war makes this species of property particularly bound for its support."[12] He placed business inventories, securities, and money loaned at interest in the same category. On August 19, 1861, the Confederate Congress passed a bill taxing these forms of property as well as certain personal possessions[13] at the flat rate of one-half of 1 per cent.

To administer the tax in the least obtrusive and most efficient manner, Secretary Memminger planned to utilize each state's assessment figures and its collection facilities. He anticipated little difficulty, because "the citizens of each state would in all probability be satisfied with the assessments and modes of collections established by their respective states."[14] To encourage the state governments to co-operate, he recommended that the tax quota of each state assuming responsibility for collecting the tax be reduced by 10 per cent.

Detailed information was requested from the states about their tax systems. When the questionnaires were returned, it was clear that complete integration of

[11] The first law the Confederate Congress passed retained all existing United States legislation not incompatible with the Confederate Constitution. The old tariff, therefore, was the first revenue bill. This was substantially revised on February 18, March 15, and May 21, 1861. On February 18, 1861, an export duty on cotton of one-eighth of a cent per pound was also levied.

[12] Memminger, "Report of July 24, 1861" (Thian [ed.], *op. cit.*, III, 21).

[13] These included cattle, horses, mules, gold watches, gold and silver plate, pianos, and personal carriages.

[14] "Report of May 10, 1861" (Thian [ed.], *op. cit.*, III, 10).

CONFEDERATE FINANCE   509

state and Confederate taxes would be difficult to attain. The revenue systems were so varied that it was "impossible to reduce [them] into one form. Some of the states levy a poll tax on each slave, others value them and impose an *ad valorem* tax."[15] Furthermore, some states prohibited the use of state officials by the Confederate government, and inexperienced assessors and collectors had to be hired.

Forms came to the newly appointed assessors late because paper was scarce, large numbers of printers and binders joined the army,[16] and parts of the law were revised. When the forms finally arrived, property was not uniformly assessed in all areas. "Murmuring and discontent among the people resulted."[17] Capitalizing on this sentiment against the war tax, Governor Pickens of South Carolina arbitrarily exempted all property and all state bonds in parishes "contiguous to the sea and navigable waters that have been subjected to invasion and depredation by the enemy."[18] In Alabama, Governor A. B. Moore, appealing to the doctrine of state rights, reasoned that the states should not co-operate with the government in collecting the tax:

The State should never concede to the General Government the exercise of powers not delegated in the Constitution, and they should never, except in cases of absolute necessity, consent to exercise powers or to perform duties which do not properly belong to them. As a general rule it is dangerous in its tendencies, and precedents of this character are to be avoided. The collection of this tax by the State would be an oner-

[15] Memminger, "Report of July 24, 1861" (*ibid.,* p. 14).

[16] Letter from Allen to Memminger, October 26, 1862 (*ibid.,* I, 71).

[17] Letter from Allen to Memminger, August 1, 1863 (*ibid.,* p. 130).

[18] Letter from Allen to Memminger, January 6, 1863 (*ibid.,* p. 118).

ous and unpleasant duty, as it imposes upon the State the necessity of enforcing the laws of the Confederate Government against her own citizens. . . .[19]

Each state assumed responsibility for collecting its own tax quota to obtain the 10 per cent discount, but only South Carolina actually collected the money in taxes. Texas raised its tax quota by confiscating property owned by people living in the North. Mississippi floated a bond issue and collected the money for the interest payments in taxes. Alabama borrowed the entire amount from the state banks, and the remaining states floated securities to raise the amount needed.[20] To the extent that these securities were bought by banks, the stock of money increased,[21] and the net effect of the tax was to stimulate a rise in prices.[22]

[19] "A. B. Moore to Gentlemen of the Senate and House of Representatives, October 28, 1861," in U.S. War Department, *The War of the Rebellion,* Series IV (Washington, D.C.: Government Printing Office, 1880-1901), I, 698.

[20] Memminger, "Report of December 7, 1863" (Thian [ed.], *op. cit.,* III, 191); Schwab, *op. cit.,* p. 289.

[21] Evidence will be presented later suggesting that, if the states had not sold their bonds to banks, comparable sums of money would not have been loaned to private persons. The risk on a loan to a private person in the South during the war was larger than the risk on a loan to the state government. The private person might be conscripted, his goods confiscated, or his property destroyed. Loans to private persons were, therefore, screened carefully and made with caution. As the war progressed, the reserve ratios of banks increased steadily.

[22] The aversion that the states had to collecting the taxes from the people can be better understood if it is realized that the people themselves were not interested in paying taxes. The following newspaper quotation is probably typical of the attitude:

"The burden of taxation, State and Confederate, should be laid as lightly as possible on our suffering people. We of today are paying the price of our righteous war of defence in blood and wounds and death: in hearts wrung and anguished by the loss of fathers, husbands, sons, and brothers, and in every sort of personal privation and suffering, and it is but just and right that posterity should pay in money the price of that heritage of freedom, property, and

510   EUGENE M. LERNER

No provisions were made for compensating Confederate collectors when the states assumed the tax.[23] Offices remained vacant, and necessary reports were not filed. When compensation was made, the stipend was too small to attract capable men.[24] As a result, later tax laws did not find a staff ready to execute them.

Sixty-one million dollars entered the Treasury in the first year of the war, and $1.2 billions by September 30, 1863. Absolutely nothing came from property taxes in the first year, and only $20.8 millions by September 30, 1863. The property tax accounted for only 1.7 per cent of the total revenue received.

IV

Secretary Memminger believed that increasing the property tax rate to yield "sufficient revenue" operated "with peculiar hardship upon property producing no income."[25] However, he thought that the property tax should not be dropped entirely. More taxation was urgently needed, and the Secretary proposed that the South adopt an income tax for the first time. Stamp duties, excises, and license taxes should be avoided. Taxing these sources required "machinery vexatious in its character and expensive in its operation."[26] Unless an income tax

were passed, "the whole profits of speculation and trade, together with those resulting from skill and labor, would escape contribution."[27] Unfortunately, the income tax was easily evaded and, like any new tax, unpopular.

The Confederate Congress followed only one part of the Secretary's recommendations when it passed its second major tax bill on April 24, 1863. The war property tax bill of August 19, 1861, had been a failure. Unavoidably it had antagonized the strong state rights' governors. Still worse, it increased the stock of money in circulation, because the states sold securities to banks to raise their tax quotas. Ignoring Memminger's cautious recommendations about "vexatious and expensive machinery," Congress seemingly moved in all directions at once to tap new sources of revenue. It enacted the income tax. It also provided for (1) an 8 per cent ad valorem tax on farm and forest products; (2) a 1 per cent tax on the money held on July 1, 1863; (3) professional license fees ranging from $30 to $500, depending on the profession in question; (4) excises ranging from 1 to 10 per cent, depending on the product; and (5) a tax in kind.

Like the old property tax, most of these new taxes were unequally assessed. Once assessed, the invading northern armies often frustrated the attempt to collect them. In Arkansas, for instance, a special treasury agent tried to transmit instructions to A. B. Greenwood, the state's permanent collector. The agent reported that "Mr. Greenwood fled with his property from the state to avoid capture by the enemy and has settled in Texas."[28] This was typical. Ordinary

---

glory which we will bequeath them . . . Let our authorities then fearlessly task and stretch the public credit to the utmost, in order to carry on the war so that taxation may not crush to earth our already overburdened people" (*Wilmington Journal*, April 9, 1863).

[23] Letter from Allen to Memminger, January 6, 1863 (Thian [ed.], *op. cit.*, II, 116).

[24] Memminger, "Report of July 29, 1863" (*ibid.*, pp. 30–31). Under the act of August 19, 1861, the maximum compensation was $800. In the legislation of April, 1863, it was raised to $2,000. When a tax department was created in the Treasury, the maximum compensation for its head was $3,000.

[25] "Report of January 10, 1863" (*ibid.*, p. 108).

[26] *Ibid.*   [27] *Ibid.*

[28] Letter from Allen to Memminger, February 1, 1864 (*ibid.*, II, 250).

CONFEDERATE FINANCE   511

citizens as well as tax-collectors fled from advancing Union troops. There were shortages of forms and men, and the general hostility to paying taxes made the yield of this bill disappointing. These obstacles convinced Secretary Memminger that taxation alone could not "produce such a reduction in the volume of currency afloat as will reduce the price of necessities of life to that standard so essential to the safety of the Government and the happiness of its people."[29] Some new plan of reducing the stock of money must be found.

In his report of December, 1863, Secretary Memminger proposed raising the property tax to 5 per cent and adopting a new corporation profits tax.[30] More important, only one-half of a person's tax should be paid in currency and the other half in bond coupons or specie.[31]

The income and corporation profits tax returns were "so easily evaded that they cannot be estimated beforehand." "Evasions, failure to make returns, expenses, and contingencies" reduced the estimate of property-tax yield by 20 per cent.[32] Under the Secretary's proposed program these difficulties were not serious. The bonds, purchased for their coupons, reduced by several fold the actual amount collected in taxes.

To stimulate the sale of bonds still more, two alternative approaches were suggested. One called for a tax of "at least 25 per cent on all Confederate notes and deposits outstanding."[33] This, the

Secretary said, made it "in the interest of capitalists to invest their surplus monies in Confederate bonds or stocks rather than in speculation or business." The second alternative was to repudiate the currency after a specified date. This left people with the choice of buying bonds immediately or holding paper that would become worthless later.

Congress ignored the Secretary's interesting recommendations to have taxes payable in coupons.[34] Instead, on February 17, 1864, legislation was passed allowing taxes to be paid with bonds.[35] This act gave no new incentive to buy bonds and did not reduce the stock of money by more than the actual tax. The property tax was raised to 5 per cent, but the tax in kind, retained from the act of April 23, 1863, was now counted as part of this payment. To make the tax fall heavily on speculators, the assessment rate on property was determined by the date of purchase. This arbitrary measure assessed property bought before January 1, 1862, at its 1860 price and property bought later at its purchase price. Confederate bonds were taxed for the first time, and the profits of joint-stock companies, after allowing a 25 per cent deduction, were taxed at the rate of 25 per cent.

On May 2, 1864, Secretary Memminger pointed out how far tax collections had deteriorated: "It is probable that no material aid will be derived by the Treasury during the present year

[29] Letter from Allen to Memminger, attached to "Report of December 7, 1863" (*ibid.*, III, 191).

[30] *Ibid.*, p. 182.

[31] In the event that the demand for coupons created a premium on them exceeding 25 per cent, the full tax could be paid in cash. The premium was allowed because "it is necessary to allow some advance in order to furnish inducements to the purchaser of bonds" (*ibid.*, p. 183).

[32] *Ibid.*   [33] *Ibid.*

[34] Several bills were introduced at this time. The most intriguing one, very similar to Keynes's plan in *How To Pay for the War*, wanted a supplementary tax for which the government gave a bond instead of a tax receipt. This bond could be redeemed in thirty years.

[35] The Congress also passed on this date a currency reform repudiating approximately one-third of the outstanding Confederate notes. This act will be discussed later.

512   EUGENE M. LERNER

from any taxes but those in kind."[36] This condition was caused in part by invading Union armies, by southern governors who ordered the Confederate tax-collectors out of their state, and by wholesale public evasion. Some of the blame, Memminger said, also lay with the Congresses that passed "taxation so cumbersome and intricate that delay and disappointment [were] its inevitable results."[37]

Instead of recommending new taxes, Secretary Memminger only requested that "whenever another tax bill is framed, [let] it be a simple tax upon property and income."[38] Congress responded on May 27, 1864, with a resolution declaring Memminger to be unfit for public office, and shortly thereafter he resigned.

(In June and July, 1864, new legislation was enacted that only raised the rates of the existing taxes. On November 7, 1864, Secretary Trenholm, Memminger's successor, repeated the pleas for increasing and simplifying the tax legislation and rendering it more just.[39]

Secretary Trenholm claimed that the taxes on property and income were merely nominal[40] and that, "if Congress does not interpose and by some measures restore the currency, gradually and judiciously, and by some means of voluntary action, it will assuredly rectify itself by some violent and disastrous convulsion."[41] But no new legislation came

until March 11, 1865. Then Congress again only raised the rates under the old laws.)

V

The Treasury was concerned with minimizing outgo as well as maximizing income. Taxes payable in kind, it was asserted, lowered expenditures, reduced prices, afforded abundant subsistence to the army, freed the government from the exactions of speculators, and eliminated the necessity for impressment.[42] Congress enacted taxes in kind on April 24, 1863, and again on February 17, 1864.[43]

The sanguine hopes that taxes in kind would bring abundant and cheap food to the army were never realized. Only seven months after its adoption, the chief clerk of the Treasury recommended that this tax be abandoned because it was "wasteful and expensive to collect."[44] Citizens despised the tax in kind because it was arbitrary, subject to abuse,[45] and not reduced by inflation. The tax was denounced at numerous public meetings in North Carolina in the summer of 1863 as being "unjust," "tyrannical," "unconstitutional," "anti-republican," "oppres-

[36] "Report of May 2, 1864" (Thian [ed.], *op. cit.*, III, 243).

[37] *Ibid.*, p. 265.

[38] The specific sections he recommended repealing were those (1) allowing the value of the tax in kind to be deducted from the 5 per cent tax on property; (2) exempting from the income tax property and capital returns; and (3) discriminating among property owners by varying the dates of assessment.

[39] Trenholm, "Report of November 7, 1864" (Thian [ed.], *op. cit.*, III, 363).

[40] *Ibid.*, p. 364.

[41] On October 28, 1864, Allen reported to Secretary Trenholm that $118.8 millions had been collected in taxes. However, "it is impossible to segregate the amount collected under each law, much less to state in what proportion it is derived from the main sources or subjects of taxation" (letter from Allen to Trenholm [*ibid.*, II, 369]).

[42] Memminger, "Report of April 17, 1863" (*ibid.*, III, 160).

[43] Schwab estimates the return of the tax in kind, in money amounts, at $140 millions. Since this figure is almost 120 per cent of the known amount collected in money, it seems excessively high (*op. cit.*, p. 297).

[44] Letter from Allen to Memminger, November, 1863 (Thian [ed.], *op. cit.*, II, 201).

[45] Hoodlums sometimes posed as tax-collectors, stole the goods, and sold them for personal gain. Legitimate collectors occasionally did the same.

sive," and "taking one-tenth of the people's living."[46] Perhaps the understatement of the war was the comment made to Secretary Memminger that "some dissatisfaction with this law has been exhibited in certain localities where . . . some doubts of its beneficial operation are entertained."[47]

The reasoning that taxes payable in kind reduced prices was also spurious. The prevailing price level is a ratio of money being spent to the goods available for sale. A tax in kind reduces the amount of goods available and, other things remaining constant, raises prices.[48]

In the light of the obstacles faced by the South, the small amount of money collected in taxes becomes understandable. Organizing the government of a

country at any time is difficult; forming the central government during wartime for eleven states, each jealous of its own rights, proved beyond Jefferson Davis' power. The energies of his administration were turned to the more obvious enemy,[49] and each state went its own way, not giving wholehearted support to the newly formed Confederate government. The blockade distorted the income distribution and made any and all taxes unpopular, especially to large landholders. Paper forms as well as experienced tax assessors were extremely scarce. The invading Union armies compounded the evil, and it became impossible for the South to collect large amounts of revenue through taxation.

VI

The Confederacy hoped its tax program would provide sufficient revenue for the government and maintain the value of money. Bonds sold to nonbanking corporations and to private individuals served the same ends. However, to discourage Congress from relying on bond sales alone, Secretary Memminger painted a bleak picture of the amount of money that could be raised from this source. In an agricultural country like the South, "loans are of limited capacity both as to amount and period of payment."[50] Farmers were more likely to buy bonds in autumn when their crops were harvested and sold than in spring when their money was needed for planting. Furthermore, the state governments were placing large bond issues.[51] Taxes,

[46] Schwab, *op. cit.*, p. 295.

[47] Letter from Allen to Memminger, November, 1863 (Thian [ed.], *op. cit.*, II, 200).

[48] Taxation in kind is more inflationary than a tax collected in money, but it is less inflationary than printing money. Consider the following example. Assume an economy at full employment with the technical capacity for 100 units of production in a given period. Assume that the stock of money is $100 and that velocity remains constant throughout. If the government collects $20 in taxes and spends it, the government will receive roughly 20 per cent of the output. Since the number of dollars and the amount of goods remain the same, prices do not rise; only the distribution of real goods changes.

Compare this effect with a tax in kind that takes 20 per cent of the goods but does not reduce the stock of money in people's hands. If people spend their income on goods, prices will rise because the amount of goods available for sale has declined. A tax in kind, therefore, not only changes the distribution of goods but also raises prices.

Printing money is still more inflationary than a tax in kind. With taxes in kind, after an initial rise in prices, there is no reason for prices to continue rising: the stock of money remains the same at $100, and the amount of goods available for purchase remains the same at, roughly, 80. If the government wants to acquire 20 per cent of the goods by printing new money, the stock of money must rise to slightly more than $120 in the first period, $144 in the second, $172 in the third, etc. Since real income remains constant, a continuous rise in prices results.

[49] See William Hesseltine, *Lincoln and the War Governors* (New York: A. A. Knopf, 1948), for a history of Lincoln's successful record in controlling his war governors.

[50] Memminger, "Report of May 1, 1863" (Thian [ed.], *op. cit.*, III, 3).

[51] *Ibid.* Two other impediments to bond sales were mentioned in this report. A $15 million issue had

514 EUGENE M. LERNER

the Secretary urged, are "the only certain reliance under all circumstances"[52] and should be hastily enacted.

Nine days later (May 10, 1863) Secretary Memminger reversed himself. Presumably it was impressed upon him that the efforts of the Confederate Congress were concentrated on organizing itself and studying military affairs; the tax legislation he wanted would be slow in coming. The Secretary's real alternatives for raising revenue were floating bonds or printing money. He, therefore, recommended that Congress authorize an 8 per cent bond issue of $50 million payable "in any resource which can be made available."[53] On May 16, 1861, Congress authorized bonds to be sold for "specie, military stores, or for the proceeds of sales of raw products and manufactured articles."

Immediate confusion arose over the meaning of these words. Not until six months after the legislation was passed did the London *Economist* have "for the first time a distinct account of the nature of the cotton loan." The loan "is not a subscription of cotton at all. It gives the government no right to any specific bales whatever. It is only an engagement on part of the planter to subscribe . . . a certain sum of money out of the proceeds of cotton when sold. The planter retains the produce in his custody, has the exclusive right of declaring when he will sell it and at what price he will sell it. The government gets nothing at present, and it is open [to doubt] . . . whether the government will ever get anything."[54]

To insure that the government received something, an organized campaign raising pledges began at once. Each congressman became an agent to popularize the loan in his home state. The response was so great that Secretary Memminger asked Congress to authorize another bond issue of $50 million to cover all the pledges. He told them that "this large amount of revenue may be counted on with certainty during the winter and spring if sales of the produce can be effected."[55]

At harvest time, however, the market for exported goods was smaller than had been expected. Southern ports were blockaded. Trading with the enemy was discouraged. A grand design forcing Europe to recognize the Confederacy was afoot, and southerners themselves prevented the export of King Cotton. Consequently, the price of cotton was almost 25 per cent lower in September than it had been in June when the pledges were made. Since the general price index for all commodities rose 27 per cent during this period, the real income of the cotton planters fell sharply. Many who planned to buy bonds when they sold their crops became discontented and, instead of buying bonds, demanded immediate government aid. However, Secretary Memminger completely rejected these pleas for state subsidies.[56]

[55] "Report of July 20, 1861" (Thian [ed.], *op. cit.*, III, 14).

[56] The planters proposed two plans for action: the Treasury should either purchase the entire cotton crop outright or advance the planters five cents a pound until it could be marketed. Memminger argued that the Constitution did not permit lending money for relief. But, even if he had had the power, he would not have exercised it. The immediate need was for "measures to relieve the demand for grain and provisions," and "subsidizing cotton eliminated the incentive to change crop outputs." Either plan cost between $100 and $200 millions. For this large investment, "the government receives no benefit whatever. . . . It pays out money which is needful

been floated earlier, on February 28, 1861. (This was largely purchased by banks after they suspended specie payments.) Second, "loans from their nature are contributions" and therefore uncertain.

[52] *Ibid.*

[53] "Report of May 10, 1861" (*ibid.*, p. 10).

[54] *Economist*, November 16, 1861, p. 1261.

CONFEDERATE FINANCE   515

Meanwhile, Secretary Memminger became more convinced than ever that government expenditures had to be reduced to slow down the rise in prices. To avoid increasing the stock of money, he "used every effort in his power to induce the various purchasing officers to buy goods with bonds instead of Treasury notes, and he even ventured upon the compulsory method of holding back his warrants on requisitions unless bonds would be accepted instead of Treasury notes."[57]

Letters immediately began to flood Secretary Memminger's office protesting this policy. Purchasing agents wrote that they were unable to place orders with manufacturers. Planters thought this policy demonstrated a lack of faith in the currency by the government itself, and the Secretary was compelled to find a new plan to reduce money expenditures.

The Confederate bonds issued on February 28, May 16, and August 19, 1861, were long term and yielded 8 per cent interest. Secretary Memminger recommended lowering the interest rate to reduce the annual deficit.[58] He urged the Confederacy to float a short-term bond, redeemable at the will of the holder. On December 24, 1861, Congress passed the legislation requested, and in January, 1862, Memminger announced that new bonds yielding 6 per cent were available.[59]

Probably some southerners bought these certificates with no thought of their return or their capital value. War meant fighting, sacrificing, and buying bonds, whether they yielded 2 per cent or 8 per cent. Others, however, were concerned. The rise in prices made the return on these bonds negative and destroyed their real capital value. The Secretary knew "the inducements to take the bonds are thus destroyed, and the bonds themselves cease to afford relief to the currency."[60] Under the circumstances, pure patriotism was the only reason for buying government bonds.

Secretary Memminger saw clearly the dilemma he faced in trying to maintain the value of money through bond sales. If the bond yields were raised, more would be sold to private individuals, but government expenditures would rise; if the yield stayed the same or was lowered, fewer bonds would be sold, but expenditures would fall.[61] At first the Treasury vacillated between these alternatives: sometimes it urged the payment of interest in coin;[62] at other times it stressed economy in government and lowered interest rates. By October, 1862,

---

[60] "Report of January 16, 1863" (*ibid.*, p. 104).

[61] There is no evidence in the reports to Congress that the Secretary was concerned with the effects of higher interest rates on business costs, war production, the distribution of income, or any of the many problems that plague contemporary war treasury officials. His exclusive concern was with the effect of interest payments on expenditures. The only exception I could find to this statement is a letter to Bocock, speaker of the House, on April 24, 1863. Here Memminger complained that the lowered rate of interest made it impossible to buy goods with bonds. On April 27, 1863, Congress passed a bill providing for government debts incurred before December 1, 1862, to be paid in 8 per cent bonds.

[62] Memminger, "Report of December 10, 1861" (Thian [ed.], *op. cit.*, III, 48). Since gold sold at a premium, this was equivalent to a rise in the rate of interest.

---

to its very existence and receives in exchange planters' notes or produce which it does not need and cannot in any way make use of." Furthermore, "banks were excellently equipped to handle the planters' need for funds until their crops were sold" (Memminger, "Report of October 15, 1861" [*ibid.*, pp. 50–51]).

[57] Letter from Allen to Congress, attached to "Report of May 2, 1864" (*ibid.*, p. 263).

[58] "Report of November 20, 1861" (*ibid.*, p. 37).

[59] Treasury Circular of January, 1862 (*ibid.*, p. 54). The North also followed the policy of lowering the interest rate during the war.

516   EUGENE M. LERNER

the cheap-money policy dominated,[63] and the Treasury's problem was to conceive a plan inducing, or, if need be, coercing, individuals to buy bonds at low rates of interest.

Two plans were proposed by Secretary Menninger in a letter to President Davis on October 6, 1862. The first called for discriminating against specific currency issues by placing a time limit on their eligibility to buy the higher-interest bonds. One week later, on March 23, 1863, Congress enacted this legislation.[64] The Secretary hoped it would "arrest the circulation of these notes and lessen the volume of currency."[65] Though this plan may have encouraged some increase in bond purchasing, it had other, unintended effects as well. Limiting the right to fund certain currency issues penalized the holding of cash. It reduced the amount of cash balances a person wanted to hold and therefore drove prices still higher.

[63] At least two hypotheses can account for this: Secretary Memminger may have imagined a kink in the demand curve for bonds; but, more likely, he wanted to practice economy in all directions regardless of the consequences. Ramsdell noted that a shortsighted policy was also followed in the control of manufacturing.

[64] Congress divided all notes issued by the Treasury into three classes. The first embraced those issued prior to December 1, 1862; the second, those issued between December 1, 1862, and April 6, 1863; the third, those issued subsequent to April 6, 1863.

"The first class are entitled to be funded in 8 per cent bonds. They are subject to a statute of limitation requiring them to claim their right to 8 per cent bonds by April 20, or in default thereof, they can only receive 7 per cent bonds until August 1, 1863, after which date they are wholly debarred from the privilege of funding.

"The second class may be funded in 7 per cent bonds until August 1, 1863, after which they can only be funded in 4 per cent bonds.

"The third class may be funded in 6 per cent bonds for one year from the month of issue, after which they can only be funded in 4 per cents" (Memminger, "Report of April 7, 1863" [Thian (ed.), *op. cit.*, III, 105]).

[65] "Report of January 10, 1863" (*ibid.*, p. 105).

Since the time of Silvio Gessell, taxing cash balances has been a standard plan to attack depressions. Secretary Memminger is the only writer I know of who has claimed it could control inflation as well.[66] He foresaw that, when the final date of limitation approaches, "notes will not pass readily from hand to hand,"[67] and he thought they would simply cease circulating. Instead, as the date of limitation approached, the notes were spent more rapidly. Prices rose, and effective yield of bonds declined further. By December 7, 1863, Memminger was forced to report that "voluntary loans have been offered but have not been taken."[68]

The second plan for selling bonds submitted to President Davis anticipated some of the contemporary war-finance measures of Canada and other countries. Estimating that a loan of one-fifth of current income would end the rise in prices, he wanted legislation compelling "a loan to the government of a portion of all income."[69] Despite repeated requests,[70] Congress did not enact this recommendation.[71]

Another plan often proposed required the states to guarantee the principal and interest of Confederate bonds. Two benefits were to be derived from this backing: "first, the opportunity of converting an 8 per cent debt into a 6 per cent debt, and secondly, the premium . . . realized on

[66] *Ibid.*

[67] *Ibid.*

[68] "Report of December 7, 1863" (*ibid.*, p. 183).

[69] Letter to Davis, October 6, 1862 (*ibid.*, I, 94).

[70] See "Report of January 1, 1863" (*ibid.*, III, 98), and "Report of December 7, 1863" (*ibid.*, p. 191).

[71] A bill was proposed to the House Special Committee on Currency on December 21, 1863, that compelled people to exchange $300 in old notes for $100 in a new issue and $200 in a new issue bond. However, nothing came of this idea either.

CONFEDERATE FINANCE   517

the sale of the bonds."[72] Both Georgia and North Carolina considered the plan an infringement on their "sovereign rights"[73] and refused to co-operate. Since unanimity was required, nothing came of this idea.

A bond issue taking a fresh approach was floated on April 10, 1863. The 6 per cent interest payments on these bonds were paid, at the option of the holder, in either currency or cotton at the rate of 8 pence (British currency) per pound of cotton.[74] "The object of this law was obviously to provide the means of raising money abroad."[75] Secretary Memminger recommended that the price of cotton be lowered to 6 pence per pound, the average price at Liverpool before the war. Congress followed his advice and lowered the price but shifted the option of receiving payment in cotton from the bondholder to the Confederate government. "This converted the bond in the view of a European purchaser to a simple 6 per cent money bond, with the interest payable here."[76]

"It appeared, therefore, that the intention of the law as amended was to provide a means at home for the absorption of Treasury notes."[77] The problem immediately arose of how much cotton was equivalent to 6 pence.[78] No visible answer was found, and the law was repealed on February 6, 1864.

After several informal conferences with European bankers, a second attempt was made to sell securities abroad. A contract was signed on January 28, 1863, with Emil Erlanger and Company for placing a $15 million bond issue. The South lost the battles of Vicksburg and of Gettysburg soon after the bonds were floated, and their price fell sharply. The Confederate government thought this was a temporary decline and attempted to support the market; but the selling continued, and a large part of the foreign exchange just acquired was lost. Contemporaries acknowledged that financially the loan was a failure,[79] and it is a conservative guess that the South raised more money abroad through unintentional gifts—the money that its creditors lost—than she did from this loan.

VII

Until the first quarter of 1864, the price of Confederate bonds at home was primarily determined by the Treasury's interest-rate policy. As new bonds were issued yielding lower rates of interest, the old issues increased in capital value. Fig-

---

[72] Memminger, "Report of January 10, 1863" (Thian [ed.], *op. cit.*, III, 111).

[73] Schwab, *op. cit.*, p. 51.

[74] The reason for paying interest in cotton was that "to negotiate a loan, an assurance must be given that the interest will be paid in a medium of certain value. The departure from this principle has undermined our credit, and our first effort should be to recover our first position. We must make the interest of any loan offered payable in specie or its equivalent" (Memminger, "Report of December 7, 1863" [Thian (ed.), *op. cit.*, III, 181]).

This statement appears to contradict the view that the Treasury was committed to a cheap-money position; but when the conduct of the government is considered, as opposed to its statements, it will be seen that a low-interest-rate policy was followed.

[75] *Ibid.*, p. 193.   [76] *Ibid.*   [77] *Ibid.*

[78] At the legal exchange rate, $4.85 equaled £1. Six pence was, therefore, equivalent to $12\frac{1}{8}$ cents. In the free market, by the end of July, 1863, 6 pence exchanged for $1.50. Cotton then sold for 32 cents a pound in Confederate Treasury notes. If the free-market exchange rate were used, "obviously such bonds would never find a purchaser" (letter from Memminger to Bronwell, December 15, 1863 [*ibid.*, II, 227]). On the other hand, if the "legal" rate of exchange were used, "it would be disadvantageous to the government unless the price paid for the bonds were proportionately advanced" (*ibid.*). Memminger accepted the bids at 50 per cent premium. At the higher price, sales were so small that he recommended the repeal of the legislation.

[79] Optimists thought it indicated an important diplomatic victory. For greater detail see Frank Owsley, *King Cotton Diplomacy* (Chicago: University of Chicago Press, 1931), chap. xii.

518   EUGENE M. LERNER

ure 1 shows the monthly prices of the 8 per cent bonds issued on February 28, 1861.[80] The introduction of the 7 per cent bonds on February 20, the 6 per cent bonds on March 23, and the cotton interest bonds on April 30, 1863, account for the continuing rise in the price of this issue. Strange as it may seem, military victories and defeats, to say nothing of changing political events, passed by without affecting the bond market. Vicksburg, Gettysburg, and the Emancipation Proclamation—all disequilibrating events—did not halt the steady rise in the price of this bond during 1862 and 1863.[81] The bond market first reflected southern military defeat during the opening quarter of 1864. By this time, military supply lines had deteriorated so badly that General Lee's men were living from hand to mouth. It was now impossible for them to take the offensive, and under the circumstances it is a tribute to the loyalty and patriotism of southerners that the price of bonds did not decline further.

Approximately 23 per cent of the total revenue raised by the South came from bonds and 8.5 per cent from call certificates. Unfortunately, these figures cannot be divided into the amounts purchased by banks and by private individuals. The low interest rates and the decline in the gold value of bonds discouraged private purchases. The Confederate tax program also failed in its attempt to reduce the quantity of money. With these two forces inoperative, little stood in the way of further price rises.

[80] Unfortunately, quotations were not available for the price of this bond every month. Where figures were missing, they were interpolated by the straight-line method.

[81] This pattern is consistent with that found in the price of commodities. Here, too, specific military and political events had little effect.

VIII

Unpaid bills began accumulating on Secretary Memminger's desk before revenue could be raised through tax collections or bond sales. Printing notes was the most expedient way of meeting these obligations, and on March 9, 1861, Congress authorized the issue of treasury notes "for such sum or sums as the exigencies of the public service may require, but not to exceed at any one time one million of dollars." During the next four years the Treasury printed over fifteen hundred times this amount.[82]

If the notes issued by the Treasury became part of the circulating medium, prices would rise; but, if the notes were hoarded by the people who received them, inflation could be avoided. Secretary Memminger's problem, therefore, was to devise and issue notes that would be hoarded. On May 10, 1861, he told Congress that two kinds of notes should be issued: "small denominations without interest, say tens and fives, and denominations of twenties and upwards at 8 per cent per annum."[83] Interest-bearing notes would not circulate because banks would invest in them rather than commercial paper, and many persons would

[82] The amount of notes issued by the Confederacy under various acts was obtained from the reports of the Treasury and is shown in the following table:

Date of Act	Total Amount Issued
May 16, 1861	$ 17,347,955.00
August 19, 1861	292,101,830.00
April 17, 1862	128,560,000.00
October 13, 1862	514,768,482.50
March 23, 1863	140,403,200.00
February 17, 1864	456,142,990.50
Total	$1,549,324,458.00

[83] "Report of May 10, 1861" (Thian [ed.], *op. cit.*, III, 10). On July 20, 1861, he changed his recommendation to 7.30 per cent interest or two cents a day on a $100 note (*ibid.*, p. 14). This plan requested legislation similar to that already in effect. On March 9, 1861, the Congress had provided for issuing notes yielding 3.65 per cent interest. The new recommendation simply called for raising the rates.

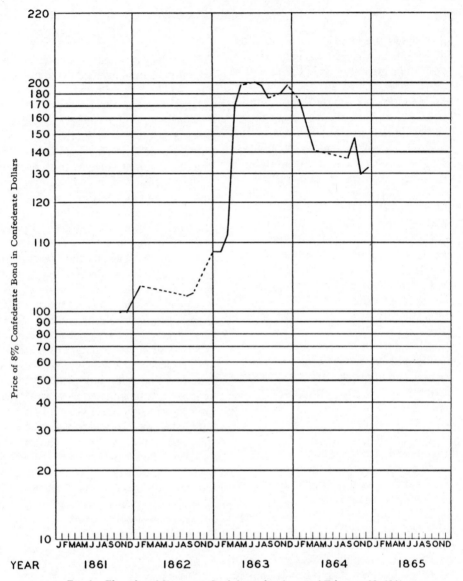

FIG. 1.—The price of 8 per cent Confederate bonds, act of February 28, 1861

[Author's correction: The price of 8 per cent bonds was plotted on a logarithmic scale labeled as though it were arithmetic when it should have been plotted on an arithmetic scale. The highest price at which these bonds sold was $200.]

520 EUGENE M. LERNER

hoard them.[84] Congress ignored this part of his plan and authorized the printing of $20 million in noninterest-bearing notes on May 16, 1861, and $100 million more on August 19, 1861.[85]

These Confederate notes, of course, were not hoarded, and, as southerners spent them, prices rose. The press blamed the inflation on "speculators," "traitors," and "blockade-runners." Secretary Memminger, however, laid the blame for the price rise on his own printing presses[86] and, by implication, on the Congresses that authorized their use, a remarkable honesty illustrating the man's high integrity.

In March, 1862, Secretary Memminger told Congress:

Experience has also established that [printing notes] is the most dangerous of all methods of raising money. . . . Every money value must readjust itself to this increase. . . . The relations of debtor and creditor are disturbed by every successive issue, and the result is a prostration of public credit and private confidence.[87]

In October, 1862, he wrote President Davis: "When it is remembered that the circulation of all the Confederate States before the present war was less than 100 millions, it becomes obvious that the large quantity of money in circulation today must produce depreciation and final disaster."[88] In January, 1863, he repeated his warnings: "The currency continues rapidly to grow in quantity. This increase causes a daily advance in prices . . . which if not arrested must result in consequences disastrous to the best interests of the country."[89] Again Congress did not respond to these warnings. It continued to authorize new issues of notes.

In November, 1861, Secretary Memminger reported that "daily requisitions exceed the supply of money by nearly 50 per cent."[90] He expanded his note-signing bureau from seventy-two employees in July, 1862, to two hundred and sixty-two in July, 1863.[91] Even so, an insufficient amount of currency was issued. As the war continued, paper, suitable engravings, and printers became harder to find.[92] In desperation, Memminger recommended that the South resort to honoring counterfeits. Any person holding a bogus note should be able to exchange it for a 6 per cent call certificate.[93] The

[84] Memminger, "Report of July 29, 1861" (*ibid.*, p. 631).

[85] The Committee on Currency of the Confederate Bankers' Association believed the government could issue this large amount of money without causing a large price rise (Schwab, *op. cit.*, p. 11).

[86] Lack of confidence in the currency was treated as an important contributing cause to inflation in 1864. Velocity increased because of military defeats, price rises, and discriminatiory momentary policy. Earlier, on October 3, 1862, Secretary Memminger denied that military defeats had, as yet, operated to increase velocity: "The large amount of bonds which have been sold in the last month proves the credit of the Government has been improved instead of being impaired" (Memminger, "Report of October 3, 1862" [Thian (ed.), *op. cit.*, III, 91]).

[87] "Report of March 14, 1862" (*ibid.*, pp. 63-64).

[88] Letter from Memminger to Davis, October 6, 1862 (*ibid.*, I, 93).

[89] "Report of July 10, 1863" (*ibid.*, III, 183).

[90] "Report of November 10, 1861" (*ibid.*, p. 30).

[91] Having clerks sign notes was intended to make counterfeiting more difficult. Since so many clerks were employed, it did not accomplish this purpose. Memminger asked Congress to permit him to print his name on the bills and discharge all his signers, but Congress never complied.

[92] Memminger, "Report of January 10, 1863" (Thian [ed.], *op. cit.*, III, 113).

[93] The government felt that no one person should suffer the full loss of accepting them, since some of the "notes were so well counterfeited that they will be freely received in business transactions" (letter from Memminger to Stevens, August 26, 1862 [*ibid.*, IV, 186]). After this legislation was passed, the fear of accepting counterfeits was gone. Banks in Georgia openly included counterfeit notes as part of their assets.

counterfeits could then be stamped "valid" by the Treasury and reissued.[94]

In 1864 Richmond was under siege, and the Treasury Note Bureau moved to Columbia, South Carolina, to escape the danger. Most of the ladies employed in signing the notes resigned, but about a hundred stayed on, and "with cooked ration for three weeks [they] set out by rail for their new abode."[95] Expenditures continued to mount, and on December 15, 1864, Secretary Trenholm reported to the House Ways and Means Committee that "on January 1st, the Treasury will be completely empty and that there will be nothing after that day to satisfy the requisitions."[96]

To conserve money, the Treasury delayed paying Confederate troops, and Secretary of War Seddon wrote to Trenholm:

> You can scarcely realize to what extent the inability or failure to meet the obligations of the Department has been prolific of mischiefs. It has been occasion and excuse for desertion, marauding, sale of clothing and equipments among the soldiers. It has prevented the accumulation of supplies; it has affected the efficiency of transportation; it has produced carelessness or indifference among the contractors; officers are resentful, and soldiers reckless, discontented, and suffering.[97]

Federal troops burned Columbia, South Carolina, in February, 1865. Part of the Treasury Note Bureau's equipment was moved back to Richmond; the rest went to Anderson, South Carolina. Once more operations started, but the war ended shortly thereafter.

[94] Memminger, "Report of January 10, 1863" (*ibid.*, III, 113).

[95] Coulter, *op. cit.*, p. 151.

[96] Letter from Trenholm to Lyon, December 15, 1864 (Thian [ed.]. *op. cit.*, IV, 414).

[97] Letter from Seddon to Trenholm, December 30, 1864 (*ibid.*, II, 417).

IX

When taxes and bond sales failed to halt the steady rise in prices, the Confederacy resorted to more drastic action: on February 17, 1864, Congress passed a bill repudiating part of the currency.

In December, 1863, Secretary Memminger had felt that "the continuance of the notes as a circulating medium to their present extent involves the ruin of public and private credit, and will deprive the government of the means of defending the lives and property of its citizens."[98] To reduce the stock of money, he had proposed floating a new bond issue large enough to absorb the entire stock of money then in existence. All notes must be used to purchase the bonds by a specified date. "The notes not so brought in shall cease to be current or receivable at the Treasury for dues."[99] He went on to state that "if some other mode could be devised; if a tax, or any other means of relief could be found, it would be preferred. But they are all inadequate."[100]

Congress debated numerous bills,[101] and on February 17, 1864, enacted a currency reform. All existing currency, including call certificates, except one-, two-, and five-dollar bills had to be converted into 4 per cent bonds by April 1, 1864.[102] The notes still outstanding on

[98] "Report of December 7, 1863" (*ibid.*, IV, 189).

[99] Memminger, "Report of January 10, 1863" (*ibid.*, III, 183–84).

[100] *Ibid.*, pp. 188–89.

[101] Schwab, *op. cit.*, p. 51.

[102] The small notes had until July 1, 1864. Presumably "poor" people had only these notes (W. H. Bruce, *Suggestions for Financial Relief* [Confederate Congress, House of Representatives (3d Congress, 1st sess.), December 31, 1863]). The five-dollar bills, exempt from the April deadline, were suddenly hoarded and disappeared from circulation. After April they reappeared at a discount. The *Wilmington Journal* of May 5, 1864, claimed "there has been

522   EUGENE M. LERNER

April 1, 1864, had to be exchanged for new issues at the rate of three for two. One-hundred-dollar bills were taxed an additional 10 per cent a month.[103] On January 1, 1865, all old currency still extant was to be taxed 100 per cent. (Later dates were provided for notes west of the Mississippi.) With this one law, one-third of the South's cash was erased.[104]

Anticipating the currency reform, southerners tried to reduce their cash balances. As a result, prices rose faster than they ever had before. The general price index of the South[105] rose 23 per cent in the single month from February to March, 1864. The reform took hold in May, 1864; prices fell sharply and remained stable for the next six months. In medieval times the crown debased the coins in periods of falling prices and restored the specie content in periods of rising prices. Such policies "gave surprising stability to prices in the long run," but Professor Hamilton has indicated that they may have "intensified short-term instability."[106] In the South the attempt to stabilize prices through a well-publicized currency reform had just that result.

----

more trouble and bother with them in the above named weeks than anyone could possibly have imagined. Instead of an accommodation, they have turned out to be a plague and a curse."

[103] Presumably only "speculators" had large denomination notes.

[104] Additional currency was to flow into the Treasury from the tax and bond acts passed the same day. This would further reduce the amount of cash circulating.

[105] A more detailed account of the effect of this reform on prices will be given in a subsequent article.

[106] Earl J. Hamilton, "Prices and Progress," *Journal of Economic History*, XII (Fall, 1952), 329.

The taxes enacted on February 17, 1864, were uncollectible and only succeeded in antagonizing bankers, who felt they were subject to discrimination.[107] Union armies prevented sale of the bonds, and the aid the Treasury had expected to derive from that source was delayed "for at least a month."[108] The Treasury, therefore, began to increase the stock of money to meet the expenditures of the government. By August 1, 1864, $170 million of the new notes had already been issued, but less than $10 million had been collected in taxes.[109] In November, 1864, Secretary Trenholm officially declared the currency reform a failure. "The measures adopted by Congress to reduce the currency did not combine the essential elements of success."[110]

Approximately 58 per cent of the revenue received by the government between February 1, 1861, and October 1, 1864, and 68.6 per cent of the revenue received between July 1, 1861, and October 1, 1863, came from the printing press. No one planned to have the war financed this way; indeed, few in the North or South expected the war to be as long or bitter as it was. The military, the economy, and the government were all pathetically unprepared. Once war began, the large government expenditures, financed as they were, made inflation inevitable.

[107] The law taxed their total assets as of January 1, 1864. But, as a result of the law, their assets were considerably lower than on the assessment date. Secretary Trenholm recommended that the law be changed to remedy their grievance.

[108] Letter from Memminger to Hunter, May 20, 1864 (Thian [ed.], *op. cit.*, IV, 346).

[109] Trenholm, "Report of November 7, 1864" (*ibid.*, III, 358).

[110] *Ibid.*

[10]

MONEY, PRICES, AND WAGES IN THE CONFEDERACY, 1861–65

EUGENE M. LERNER

University of Idaho

I

THE money spent by the Confederate government to purchase war supplies came largely from the printing press; tax collections and bond sales raised relatively small amounts. As the ratio of money to goods available increased, prices rose. Union armies continuously reduced the area in which Confederate notes were accepted as money, and southerners living in captured territory shipped large amounts of these notes to the sections where it still passed as currency. Like government deficits, the Confederate notes received from occupied territory increased the stock of money in areas still controlled by the Confederate government. The rising prices became, in effect, a tax on holding money; to avoid the tax, people spent their money more rapidly, driving prices still higher.

As the war continued, the real output of the Confederacy declined. Many of the most capable white workers left the labor force and joined the army. The northern blockade forced the South to become self-sufficient, isolated the Confederacy from the benefits of foreign trade, and compelled southern labor to be used where it formerly had the least comparative advantage. Worn-out or destroyed machinery was difficult to replace, and northern troops concentrated on razing railroad equipment and entire factories and on cutting the supply lines of raw materials. The increase in the stock of money, the rise in velocity, and the decline in real output in the Confederacy from 1861 to 1865 produced the worst inflation of our history since the Revolutionary War.

In Sections II and III of this paper, I construct money and price indexes for this period; in Sections IV, V, VI, and VII, I describe price movements in various parts of the South and the effect of the northern blockade; in Section VIII, I discuss the real value of money; in Sections IX, X, and XI, wage movements; and in Section XII, the popular response to the inflation.

II

The stock of paper money in the South consisted of Confederate issues, bank notes and deposits, state treasury notes,[1] shinplasters,[2] and legalized counterfeits. I estimated the amount of Confederate notes outstanding from the periodic reports of Secretaries Memminger and Trenholm; and I used United States Treasury figures, southern bank reports, and unpublished bank records to estimate the amount of bank credit issued.[3]

[1] These were issued in Alabama, Florida, Georgia, Louisiana, Mississippi, and North Carolina (John C. Schwab, *The Confederate States of America, 1861–1865* [New York: Charles Scribner's Sons, 1901], pp. 149–51).

[2] This was the name given to notes with a face value of less than one dollar issued by cities, railroads, turnpike companies, factories, insurance companies, savings banks, and other southern businesses.

[3] Scattered bank reports are available for five southern states during the war. Georgia figures can be found in the annual reports of the controller-general. Figures for the Bank of the State of South Carolina are available in South Carolina state documents. Virginia bank figures are available in the *Richmond*

MONEY, PRICES, AND WAGES IN THE CONFEDERACY   21

State treasury notes, shinplasters, and legalized counterfeits were ignored, because their combined total value was insignificant compared with the amount of Confederate notes and bank credit issued.

the light of the large amount of Confederate notes issued, this increase seems remarkably small. The rise in the stock of money was thus limited because banks sharply increased their reserve ratios as the war continued.

TABLE 1

TOTAL STOCK OF MONEY IN THE SOUTH IN MILLIONS OF DOLLARS

Date	Bank Notes and Deposits*	Confederate Government Notes	Total	Index: January, 1861 = 100
1861:				
January	$ 94.6	....	$ 94.6	100
April	121.8	....	121.8	130
June	119.3	$ 1.1	120.4	130
October	146.3	24.5	170.8	180
1862:				
January	165.2	74.6	239.8	250
April	151.1	131.0	282.1	300
June	142.9	166.1	309.0	330
October	181.5	287.3	468.8	500
1863:				
January	239.1	410.5	649.6	690
April	257.1	561.7	818.8	870
June	267.5	637.3	904.8	960
October	274.7	792.4	1,067.1	1130
1864:				
January	268.1	826.8	1,094.9	1160

* These figures are not adjusted for interbank deposits and are therefore biased upward.

My estimates indicate that the stock of money in the South increased approximately eleven fold in the three years from January, 1861, to January, 1864. In

Commercial banks had no central bank to support them during crises. Southern bankers expected mass withdrawals whenever Union troops ap-

Enquirer for January 1, 1861; October 1, 1861; April 1, 1862; January 1, 1863; and January 4, 1864. (Since the same banks are not always included in these reports, link relatives were used to determine percentage increases in notes and deposits.) Figures for Louisiana are available in her state documents, but unfortunately this series ends with the capture of the state. North Carolina figures, available in several documents, are of limited utility, because each bank reported on a different date. In addition to these sources, complete bank records for some banks are available in manuscript form at Duke University, the University of Virginia, and the North Carolina State Archives.

From these sources I calculated the number of times by which bank credit expanded in each of these states during the war. The banks of Florida and Alabama were assumed to have behaved like those

of the neighboring state of Georgia. Tennessee banks were assumed to have behaved like those of Louisiana, because both states were occupied by Union forces at approximately the same time. Banks in Mississippi, Arkansas, and Texas were omitted for lack of data.

The amount of notes and deposits outstanding in southern states on January 1, 1861, was taken from the United States Treasury figures. Unfortunately, no figures are available for Texas, Arkansas, or Mississippi.

By multiplying the number of times bank credit expanded in each state by the number of notes and deposits outstanding in each state on January 1, 1861, I estimated the amount of notes and deposits outstanding during the war. These estimates were added to the amount of Confederate notes issued. They are presented in Table 1.

proached, and they protected themselves the only way they could—by limiting the amount of credit they created.
Georgia banks had 47 per cent reserves
in June, 1862, and 69 per cent in June,
1863; the Bank of Fayetteville had 21
per cent in May, 1861, and 46 per cent in
November, 1863; the Bank of South
Carolina had 5 per cent in January, 1861,
and 30 per cent in October, 1863; the
Bank of the Valley in Virginia had an
average of 41.2 per cent in 1861, 56.5 per
cent in 1862, 57.2 per cent in 1863, and
66.6 per cent in 1864.[4]

In the North during these war years,
$1.49 was created by the banks per dollar
printed by the government.[5] In the
South, as of January, 1864, only $1.20
had been created by the banks per dollar
printed by the government. The stock of
money, and therefore prices, would have
risen still more had southern bankers not
increased their reserve ratios.

III

Abundant price quotations during the
Civil War are available for the cities of
Richmond, Virginia; Wilmington and
Fayetteville, North Carolina; and Augus-
ta, Georgia. Richmond, the capital of the
Confederacy, was overcrowded and un-

der frequent attack throughout the war.
Wilmington was described as a veritable
"fairy city" where boats that ran the
blockade landed and sold their goods.
Augusta became an important supply
base for part of the southern army, and
Fayetteville was a small, inland community. Because each of these cities had
unique characteristics and because they
were several hundred miles apart, any
generalization that is valid for all four
can probably be extended over a somewhat broader area without great error.

Wholesale prices are preferable to retail prices for a study of inflation, because
they "govern" the retail level and are
more uniform and homogenous than retail prices. To depict the price movements of commodities, regularly and systematically reported quotations are necessary. The wholesale-price quotations
used in this study were taken from the
local newspapers that reported regularly
on market conditions.[6] These quotations
are more readily available and much
easier to use than the prices recorded in
the best alternative source, the account-
books of firms.

From newspaper quotations, five unweighted arithmetic price indexes were
constructed:[7] one for each of the four
cities selected, and one averaging the
commodity prices of all four cities.

Continuous price series were con-

---

[4] During the summer of 1864, bank reserves in
some areas declined. In Georgia the reserves were
63.5 per cent in June, 1864. This decline occurred because of the large amount of cash lost by withdrawals for the currency reform of February 17, 1864. The
record books of the Bank of the Valley reflect these
withdrawals as follows:

Date	Total Deposits
Feb. 3, 1864	$416,593.24
Feb. 15, 1864	345,566.62
Feb. 29, 1864	318,616.56
Mar. 14, 1864	264,379.57
Mar. 31, 1864	17,934.34
Apr. 30, 1864	3,747.27

These withdrawals indicate the public's reluctance to deposit money in banks (i.e., to save in this
form) after the currency reform.

[5] Milton Friedman, "Price, Income, and Monetary Changes in Three Wartime Periods," *American
Economic Review*, XLII (May, 1952), 635.

[6] I used the *Richmond Enquirer, Richmond Whig,
Richmond Dispatch, Richmond Sentinel, Wilmington
Journal, Fayetteville Observer, North Carolinian,
North Carolina Presbyterian, Daily Chronicle and
Sentinel* (of Augusta), and *Daily Constitution* (of
Augusta).

[7] A simple average of relatives gives equal weight
to each item; in measuring the rate of rise of prices,
Mitchell felt this was the best kind of index to use
when the price rise was caused by an increase in the
money supply (Wesley C. Mitchell, *The Making and
Using of Index Numbers* [Bureau of Labor Statistics
Bull. 656 (Washington, D.C.: Government Printing
Office, 1938)], p. 8).

structed[8] for 28 commodities in Richmond, 23 in Fayetteville, 34 in Augusta, and 25 in Wilmington.[9] The monthly price relatives of each commodity were calculated, using the commodity's average price during the first four months of 1861 as a base.[10] These price relatives were then averaged to form the price index for each city. The general price index for the entire eastern part of the Confederacy was prepared by averaging

fifty-seven[11] different commodity price series taken from all four cities.[12] This index is presented in Figure 1 and Table 2.

IV

For thirty-one consecutive months, from October, 1861, to March, 1864, the general price index of the Confederacy rose at an almost constant rate of 10 per cent a month. As the real value of money fell, Confederate notes were no longer used as a store of value. Lenders refused to extend credit unless they were repaid in gold, leather, or some other commodity. When debtors tried to use the inflated currency to pay off obligations incurred

[8] To construct these price series, the quotations for each item continuously listed in the newspapers were recorded. (About three times as many quotations were collected from these sources as could be used. Discontinuous series were rejected.) When only one quotation was available for a commodity in a given month, as occasionally happened, this figure was taken as typical of the commodity's price during that month. More often, two or three quotations were available. When I had two quotations for a given month, I took their simple average as typical of the price for the month. When I had three quotations, I gave equal weight to both the beginning and end of the month. (If I had quotations for, say, the first, fifteenth, and thirty-first, I averaged all three quotations. If I had quotations for the first, twenty-fifth, and twenty-eighth, I rejected the twenty-eight and used only the figures for the first and twenty-fifth.) In most cases, however, at least one quotation a week was available, and the four quotations for the month were averaged.

[9] The complete list of commodities for each city is:

Richmond—corn, rye, red wheat, flaxseed, hay, oats, cotton, tobacco, bacon, butter, lard, cornmeal, family flour, extrafine flour, superfine flour, Irish potatoes, rice, salt, sugar, coffee, molasses, tallow candles, adamantine candles, whiskey, sole leather, upper leather, beeswax, lime.

Fayetteville—corn, rye, wheat, flaxseed, cotton, wool, bacon, lard, family flour, peas, molasses, New Orleans sugar, salt, tallow, iron, nails, peach brandy, apple brandy, cotton yarn, sheeting, green hides, beeswax, spirits of turpentine.

Augusta—corn, wheat, hay, cotton, bacon, butter, eggs, chickens, lard, cornmeal, family flour, peas, rice, coffee, molasses, sugar, pork, salt, tea, beef, bagging, 4/4 sheeting, cotton yarn, 7/8 shirting, osnaburgs (defined in n. 43 below), 3/4 shirting, cotton rope, New Orleans whiskey, apple brandy, peach brandy, nails, iron, dry hides, starch.

Wilmington—corn, hay, cotton, bacon, beef, butter, eggs, chickens, live turkeys, dead turkeys, pork, lard, cornmeal, superfine flour, peanuts, sheeting, wool yarn, beeswax.

[10] Since the Confederacy did not reach full strength until May, 1861, when all eleven states had seceded, this base seemed reasonable to me when I constructed these indexes. At the suggestion of Professor Earl J. Hamilton, I investigated the possibility that prices were already inflated by the first quarter of 1861 because southerners had anticipated war and hoarded goods. The best available price study for the South prior to the Civil War, Professor George Taylor's thirteen-commodity index for Charleston, was used. The quarterly figures for 1858 and 1859 were taken as a base. Professor Taylor's index reveals the following rise in prices:

Date	Price Index (1858–59 = 100)
Jan., 1861	109.6
Feb., 1861	111.1
Mar., 1861	110.9
Apr., 1861	110.2

These figures suggest that during the first quarter of 1861 prices were 10 per cent above the 1858 and 1859 average and indicate that the 1858–59 period would have been a more suitable base.

[11] The items in this index are: wool, corn, cotton, flaxseed, hay, oats, rye, tobacco, wheat, bacon, beef, butter, chickens, cornmeal, coffee, eggs, extrafine flour, family flour, superfine flour, lard, molasses, peanuts, peas, pork, Irish potatoes, sweet potatoes, rice, salt, sugar, tea, dead turkeys, live turkeys, adamantine candles, tallow candles, bagging, cotton rope, osnaburgs, 4/4 sheeting, 3/4 shirting, 7/8 shirting, cotton yarn, wool yarn, iron, nails, apple brandy, peach brandy, New Orleans whiskey, hides, soles, upper leather, beeswax, lime, spirits of turpentine, starch.

[12] If the same commodity appeared in two or more cities, its average price relatives were recorded. Where a commodity appeared in only one city, that series alone was recorded. These figures were then averaged to form the general price index.

24   EUGENE M. LERNER

before the war, creditors refused to accept payment. J. D. Davidson, an attorney in Lexington, Virginia, received numerous letters like the following: "Some time about the 1st of the present month, Mr. Jack Jordan again came to me when I refused to take the money [for his debt] owing to the condition of the currency."[13]

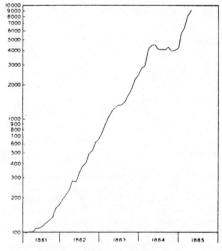

FIG. 1.—The general price index of the Confederacy. (First four months of 1861 = 100.)

Davidson's clients wanted to wait until the war was over and the price level lower before they accepted payment.

As early as 1862 some firms stopped selling their produce for currency alone. Customers had to offer some commodity along with their Confederate notes to complete the purchase, a practice that became widespread during 1863. The Gregg Cotton Mills received numerous letters from other manufacturers requesting the exchange of products. One person wrote: "Money will buy little or nothing here and unless I can find some

[13] University of Wisconsin Historical Society, McCormic Collection, Special Davidson Collection, Charles Aenentrout to James D. Davidson, March 13, 1864, Fol. Jan., 1863–65.

means of getting food for my workmen, I fear I shall lose them."[14]

As the war went on, money continued to fall in value. By April, 1865, the general price index had risen to ninety-two times its prewar base.

Changes in velocity, in the stock of money, and in the supply of goods determined price changes. Contrary to popular opinion, commodity price movements were not directly affected by military events.[15] On February 17, 1864, the Confederate Congress enacted a currency reform. All existing notes except small notes were to be exchanged for new currency at the ratio of three for two by April 1, 1864.[16] In anticipation of the re-

TABLE 2

GENERAL PRICE INDEX OF THE EASTERN
SECTION OF THE CONFEDERACY

(First Four Months of 1861 = 100)

MONTH	YEAR				
	1861	1862	1863	1864	1865
January.....	101	193	762	2,801	5,824
February.....	99	211	900	2,947	6,427
March......	101	236	1,051	4,128	8,336
April.......	101	281	1,178	4,470	9,211
May........	109	278	1,279	4,575	
June........	109	331	1,308	4,198	
July........	111	380	1,326	4,094	
August......	120	419	1,428	4,097	
September...	128	493	1,617	4,279	
October......	136	526	1,879	4,001	
November...	161	624	2,236	4,029	
December....	172	686	2,464	4,285	

form, southerners began to spend their old notes more rapidly. Prices rose im-

[14] Letter from J. Ralph Smith, general supervisor of the State Works of South Carolina, to William Gregg, September 4, 1863 (Raphael P. Thian [ed.], *Appendix* [Washington, D.C., 1878], II, 140).

[15] The single exception that I found was the siege of Richmond during 1864. This will be treated in greater detail later.

[16] For a more complete discussion of this act, see my article in the *Journal of Political Economy*, XLII (December, 1954), 521–22.

mediately; the general price index rose 23 per cent from February to March, 1864. In May, 1864, the currency reform began to take hold. The general price index dropped dramatically and stayed low through December. This decline took place despite the invading Union armies, the reduction in foreign trade, the impending military defeat, and the low morale of the army. The currency reform was more significant than these powerful forces.

V

To compare the price rise of each city with the average price rise in the entire

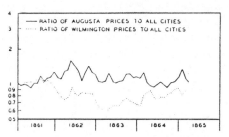

Fig. 2.—Comparison of Augusta and Wilmington prices to prices for all cities. (All cities = 1.0.)

eastern section of the Confederacy, the index for each city was deflated by the general price index. The results are plotted on two graphs, Figures 2 and 3, to facilitate reading. Values greater than 1 indicate that prices rose more from the base period in the city in question than in all four cities; values less than 1 indicate that prices rose less.

Figure 2 compares Wilmington and Augusta, the two cities whose price indexes deviated most from the general price rise during the early years of the war. A large part of the difference between these two price series is explained by their composition. The index for Augusta contains five items not included in the Wilmington index: New Orleans

whiskey, apple brandy, peach brandy, nails, and iron. The prices of these commodities increased considerably faster than an average of all prices. The output of spirits was restricted to save corn for consumption, and the demand for iron increased because of military needs. These commodities give the Augusta index a strong upward bias.

New indexes were constructed that eliminate this bias by including only items common to Augusta and Wilmington. When these new indexes were deflated by the general price index, the two series usually were closer together.[17] This suggests that, had the indexes of all four cities contained a still larger number of common items, the estimated price rises of the four cities would be even more uniform than Figures 2 and 3 indicate.

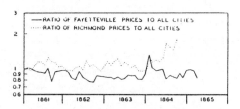

Fig. 3.—Comparison of Fayetteville and Richmond prices to prices for all cities. (All cities = 1.0.)

In Figure 3, Fayetteville and Richmond are compared. The most significant aspect of Figure 3 is the sudden and rapid rise in the Richmond series after January, 1864. This rise, indicating that prices rose faster in Richmond than in the general index, suggests the effectiveness of Union troops in cutting the city's supply lines. They confirm General Sherman's observation that in 1864 goods were scarcer in Richmond than in the Confederacy as a whole.

[17] The new indexes were farther apart in only four months: April, 1861; July, 1861; April, 1864; and October, 1864.

Figures 2 and 3 indicate that prices rose approximately the same amount from the base period in all four cities during the first three years of the war. Only Richmond prices broke away from the general price movement in 1864.[18] These statistics imply that communication and transportation facilities were not so deteriorated that traders could no longer take advantage of large price differentials. Rather, they imply that the businessmen of the South continued to ship goods from one area to another throughout the war, making for uniform price rises.[19]

VI

Since most commodities are substitutes for some others, a student of price movements usually expects all commodity prices to rise or fall at approximately the same rate. Although numerous special circumstances affecting each product cause the rates of price change to vary somewhat, an extremely strong force is necessary to keep the price changes of different commodities radically different over the short run.[20]

During the Civil War the blockade imposed by the North was just such a force. The effect of the blockade was to shift to the right the supply curves for the home market of goods formerly exported, which tended to lower their prices, and to shift to the left those of goods formerly imported, which tended to raise their prices.[21] The more essential foreign markets or foreign producers were to a commodity, the greater was the shift in the product's supply schedule to the home market and the more pronounced its price change.

The effect of the blockade on southern prices can be illustrated by dividing the commodities that make up the general price index into four mutually exclusive categories: imports, partly imported goods, exports, and domestic products.[22] Partly imported goods are those the Confederacy produced only in limited quantities; to satisfy the demand, they were also imported. Domestic products are those neither exported nor imported and therefore not directly affected by the blockade. The price indexes of these four groups are shown in Figure 4.

These figures show in striking fashion the distorted price movements in the Confederacy caused by the northern blockade that closed southern ports. Instead of constantly crisscrossing, as in "normal" times, the prices of these groups fall into four neat rows. Commodities entirely imported had their supply virtually cut off, and their prices rose the most. The blockade did not affect the home production of partly imported goods, and their prices rose less.

[18] These figures suggest a picture different from the one now held by some historians (E. Merton Coulter, *The Confederate States of America, 1861–1865* [Baton Rouge: Louisiana State University Press, 1950], p. 220, and Charles Ramsdell, *Behind the Lines in the Southern Confederacy* [Baton Rouge: Louisiana State University Press, 1944], *passim*).

[19] A hypothesis accounting for these figures is that horses and wagons, not railroads, were the most important form of transportation in the South, and these simple facilities could be repaired or replaced more readily when destroyed than railroad equipment.

[20] Rapid technological advance in the production of one commodity, for instance, could account for different rates of price rise. It is assumed throughout this section that great technological gains were not made in the South during the war.

[21] Legislation passed by both sides to prevent trading with the enemy had the same effect.

[22] These categories include: *imports*—wool, molasses, sugar, coffee, tea, and salt; *exports*—tobacco, cotton, peanuts, peas, rice; *part imported*—bagging, cotton rope, 4/4 sheeting, 3/4 shirting, 7/8 shirting, cotton yarn, wool yarn, iron, cut nails, soles, uppers; *domestic*—corn, flaxseed, hay, rye, wheat, bacon, beef, butter, chickens, cornmeal, eggs, family flour, extrafine flour, superfine flour, lard, Irish potatoes, sweet potatoes, dead turkeys, live turkeys, tallow, osnaburgs.

The prices of domestic goods, which were not directly affected by the blockade, rose still less. The prices of goods formerly exported rose least of all: King Cotton was begging for buyers in southern markets.

These different price rises suggest the reason why blockade-runners carried "Yankee gee-gaws, silks and trinkets" rather than necessities: the price of wheat, corn, and other products produced in limited quantities in the Confederacy simply did not rise fast enough.

Differences in the rates of price rise among commodities caused changes in the income distribution of the Confederacy. The once wealthy planters, who derived the bulk of their income from crops normally exported, lost relative to all other classes. In an attempt to protect themselves from the effects of the blockade, planters demanded immediate government aid.[23] However, their pleas for

[23] In Danville, Virginia, it was reported to the Treasury Department that "there seems to be a strong desire generally to place almost the entire crop under the control of the government. This sentiment is not slight. A general and strong desire prevails that this course is absolutely necessary" (letter from Almanzon Huston to Memminger, June 16, 1861 [Thian (ed.), *op. cit.*, I, 140]).

In a letter to the editor of the *New Orleans Delta*, the alternative to government subsidies to planters was ominously suggested: "If the planters are prohibited from sending their cotton to market until the blockade is raised, and they are to receive no money in the meantime, how are they to get alone? Their negroes must have shoes and winter clothing; their families must have something; their country store debts must be paid, else the country merchants cannot pay their debts to the wholesale city merchants. Therefore, they can get no goods, and the whole business of the country is completely broken up" (October 3, 1861 [*ibid.*, p. 358]).

Other letters to the Secretary of the Treasury pointed out that, because the blockade lowered the price of cotton and tobacco, planters were unable to buy Confederate bonds or to pay their taxes (letter from F. S. Lyon to C. J. McRaie, May 13, 1861 [*ibid.*, p. 98]; letter from C. T. Lowndes to Memminger, June 13, 1861 [*ibid.*, p. 133]; letter from James F. White and J. W. Drake to Jefferson Davis, July 13, 1861 [*ibid.*, p. 211]; and many others).

subsidies were rejected. Mrs. Chestnut's well-known diary portrays in detail the plight of southern planters who tried to maintain their former living standards in the face of their reduced real income.

VII

The blockade was felt in every corner of the southern economy. It not only distorted prices and changed the distribution of income; it also affected the food people ate and the goods they produced.

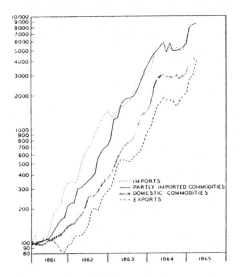

FIG. 4.—Price indexes of commodity groups. (First four months of 1861 = 100.)

The ratio of the price index of imported goods to that of exported goods is shown for each month in Figure 5. This ratio rises very rapidly through November, 1861, indicating that the difference between the price rise of exports and that of imports widened during the early months of the war. Stocks of commodities normally exported accumulated, tending to lower their price;[24] and sup-

[24] Since the southerners tried to coerce European countries into recognizing the Confederacy in 1861, some voluntarily withheld their cotton from the European trade.

plies of goods normally imported declined, tending to raise their price.[25]

The South's small industrial base made it difficult for her to begin producing commodities normally imported. The shift in output was further complicated by the "bottlenecks" caused by shifting production rapidly from peacetime to wartime goods. Like so many countries in Europe during World War I, the Confederacy hoarded manpower in its army and overmobilized. The army drained the economy of necessary laborers, and, as the war continued, troops had to be delegated to work in factories.

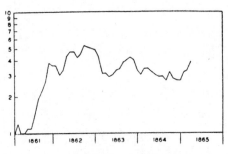

Fig. 5.—Ratio of import prices to export prices. (January, 1861 = 1.0.)

Nevertheless, the effect of the blockade was greatest in the short run. Gradually substitutes, though poor ones, were found for imported goods. Various roots and dried bark replaced coffee; wooden shoes were used instead of leather ones; sorghum took the place of sugar. Other imported goods, such as paper, were used more sparingly; letters were written on crude brown paper, sheets torn out of ledger-books, and the insides of envelopes. A few formerly imported commod-

ities, such as salt, were produced at home; it was not uncommon to see people wash and boil the ground under their smokehouses to salvage the salt drippings from animals slaughtered in earlier years. By these slow, often painful means, the demand for imports was gradually reduced, though until September, 1862, not as rapidly as their supply was falling.

Beginning in October, 1862, the ratio of import prices to export prices followed a downward trend. Planters shifted from growing cotton to growing products whose prices rose faster. "The cotton crop harvested in the fall of 1861 amounted to about 4,500,000 bales; the next year it dropped to about 1,500,000; in 1863 it was somewhat less than 50,000; and the next year it was about 300,000."[26] On the other hand, the demand for cotton rose as wool and other materials became more expensive. The decreased supply and increased demand made the price of cotton, like that of other exports, rise more rapidly.

VIII

The general price index of the Confederacy increased twenty-eight fold from the first quarter of 1861 to January, 1864. During the same period the stock of money increased only eleven fold. The difference between these ratios is attributable to increases in the velocity of money and to decreases in the South's real output. Unfortunately, one cannot determine with strict accuracy from the statistical data now available the extent to which each of these forces changed. However, a measure of their combined strength is given by the real value of the

[25] Ramsdell also attributed much of the rapid rise in the price of cloth in 1861 to the depletion of stocks (Charles Ramsdell, "The Control of Manufacturing by the Confederate Government," *Mississippi Valley Historical Review*, VIII [December, 1921], 234).

[26] Coulter, *op. cit.*, p. 242. These figures appear to me to be extreme. However, they are suggestive of the change in production that went on during this period.

MONEY, PRICES, AND WAGES IN THE CONFEDERACY 29

stock of money.[27] This statistic increases if velocity falls or real income rises and declines if velocity rises or real income falls.

Estimates of changes in the real value of Confederate cash balances are shown in Table 3. Until June, 1862, the index of real value was greater than 100, the level of January, 1861. Instead of reducing their cash holdings immediately, southerners held notes longer, suggesting that they were slow to realize that inflation was under way. In October, 1862, when it was clear that more inflation was in store, the value of cash balances fell below the January, 1861, level. After this date, prices rose more than the stock of money increased.[28]

This pattern, in which the aggregate real value of cash balances first rises, then falls, has been found in every major inflation for which statistical data are available. Keynes, in describing the inflations of post-World War I in Europe, accounted for this repeated occurrence as follows:

At first there may be a change of habit in the wrong direction, which actually facilitates the Government's operation [of collecting taxes by issuing notes]. The public is so much accustomed to thinking of money as the ultimate standard, that, when prices begin to rise, believing that the rise must be temporary they tend to hoard their money and to postpone purchases, with the result that they hold in monetary form a larger aggregate of real value than before. . . . But sooner or later the second phase sets in. The public discovers that it is the holder of notes that suffer taxation and defray the expenses of government and they begin to change their habits and to economize in their holding of notes.[29]

[27] Since $MV = PY$, $M/P = Y/V$, where M is the stock of money; P, the price level; Y, real income; and V, income velocity.

[28] This study ends in January, 1864, the last date for which I was able to obtain figures on the quantity of money in circulation in the South. I believe that the real value of the stock of money continued to decline until the end of the war.

On January 10, 1863, Secretary Memminger stated that velocity had fallen to two-thirds of its prewar rate.[30] If the

TABLE 3

THE REAL VALUE OF MONEY

Date (1)	Increase in Stock of Money (Jan., 1861 = 100) (2)	Index of Commodity Prices (Jan., 1861 = 100) (3)	Real Value of the Stock of Money (Col. 2 ÷ Col. 3) (4)
1861:			
January....	100	100	100
April.......	129	100	129
June........	127	108	117
October.....	180	135	134
1862:			
January....	253	191	133
April.......	298	279	107
June........	337	328	102
October.....	496	522	95
1863:			
January....	687	756	90
April.......	666	1,168	57
June........	959	1,296	74
October.....	1,129	1,858	61
1864:			
January....	1,159	2,776	42

[29] John M. Keynes, *A Tract on Monetary Reform* (New York: Harcourt, Brace & Co., 1924), pp. 50–51.

[30] Secretary Memminger's full statement is as follows: "In a former report it was shown that the circulation of the Confederate States before the war might be estimated at $100 million. [My estimate of the quantity of money outstanding in the South before the war is very close to that of the Secretary of the Treasury. Mine is $94.5 million; his, $100 million.] In the existing state of things, it is probable that a larger amount of currency is required. In time of peace money passes rapidly from hand to hand, and the same money in a single day will discharge many obligations. A large portion, too, of the operations of business is performed by bills of exchange and bank checks. In the present stagnation of commerce and intercourse, larger amounts of ready money are kept on hand by each individual, and the Confederate Treasury Notes and Call Certificates are used as substitutes for bills and drafts to a considerable extent. If this view be just, we may venture to add as much as 50 per cent to the usual amount of currency, and this would raise the sum total at which it might stand to $150 millions. The difference between this sum and the actual circulation will show the redundancy" (Memminger, "Report of January 10, 1863" [Thian (ed.), *op. cit.*, III, 102]).

Secretary's estimate was correct, the real income of the South declined 40 per cent by January, 1863.[31] If he was correct only in that velocity fell, the decline in the real value of money by January, 1863, would still be attributable to the drop in the South's real output.

During the first two years of the war the real income of the South fell because the Confederate army drained large numbers of white men from the labor force. General Clement A. Evans estimated that approximately 40 per cent of the white men of military age were in the army.[32] Colonel Thomas L. Livermore put the number still higher and thought that "substantially the entire military population of the Confederate States not exempted by law were enrolled in the army."[33] The jobs left vacant could not be filled immediately. Old men, women, slaves, or wounded veterans were the replacements for men called to service; these workers were not so productive as the men they replaced.

As war continued, the invading Union armies, the northern blockade, and the reallocation of southern labor tended to reduce output. These disturbing forces, however, were partly offset. Patriotism made workers become more efficient at their jobs, work longer hours, and discover "short cuts" in production. Large numbers of army privates receiving eleven dollars a month deserted to work on their farms back home. Like France during World War I, the Confederacy realized it was overmobilized and sent soldiers home to work in factories; this raised the South's real output. If the conflicting forces just described offset each other, the army's heavy drain on manpower caused a "once and for all" drop in real output,[34] a drop felt most seriously during the first two years of the war.

Though the fall in output was largely responsible for the decline in the real value of cash balances during the early years of the war, the rise in velocity caused its continuing decline. Taxing through printing money was as appealing to the Confederate government as it was to the Continental Congress in earlier years of American history and has been to so many governments since that time. Like all people who live through prolonged and rapid price rises, southerners came to realize that the only way to avoid the tax on holding money was to reduce their cash holdings. Some resorted to limited forms of barter and refused to accept cash alone for their products. Others adopted more stable currencies, such as northern greenbacks, or made their notes payable in commodities. Durable goods, land, precious metals, and jewelry were kept as ultimate reserves instead of notes or bank deposits. As velocity increased, prices rose still higher and the real value of cash balances declined.

[31] The real value of cash balances had declined to 0.9 by January, 1863. If velocity fell to two-thirds, real income must have been only 60 per cent of its January, 1861, amount.

[32] General Evans found 318,000 men enrolled in the army on January 1, 1862; 465,584 on January 1, 1863; 472,781 on January 1, 1864; and 439,675 on January 1, 1865 (Clement A. Evans, *Confederate Military History* [Atlanta: Confederate Publishing Co., 1899], VII, 500).

[33] Livermore is quoted with approval by Rhodes: "The number of men in the Confederate army was 1,082, 119" (James Ford Rhodes, *History of the Civil War* [New York: Macmillan Co., 1904], V, 186). Since "the total number of all white males who came within the final limits of military age was probably under 1,150,000" (Chester Wright, *Economic History of the United States* [2d ed. (New York: McGraw-Hill Book Co., 1949)], p. 434), Livermore's estimates must surely be too high.

[34] According to General Evans' figures, the number of men in the army stayed at roughly their January, 1863, level. This means the effect of mobilization was to reduce suddenly the number of people in the labor force.

MONEY, PRICES, AND WAGES IN THE CONFEDERACY 31

IX

By curtailing foreign trade, the northern blockade compelled the Confederacy to manufacture most of its own war supplies. Undoubtedly, the rapid rise in commodity prices, so bitterly denounced by the people who suffered under it, aided the southern war effort by stimulating the output of war goods, the building of new plants, and the development of industrial processes.

Prices rose much faster than wages in the Confederacy, and southern businessmen made large profits. Describing the period from 1760 to 1800 in London, England, Professor Hamilton writes:

The high level of profits raised large incomes which have supplied practically all the savings in a capitalistic society. As J. M. Keynes has pointed out, savings without investment not only would have proved fruitless, but would have depressed business and thus limited savings. By keeping the normal rate of profits far above the prevailing rate of interest, the lag of wages behind prices stimulated the investment of savings as they took place.[35]

Businessmen in the Confederacy, like those in England a century earlier, responded to their higher profits by trying to build new equipment, expand their labor force, and produce more goods.

Victor S. Clark, after studying manufacturing in the Confederacy, concluded that the lack of competent metalworkers and machinists was never remedied; "It seems to have been the limiting factor in the production of arms and munitions up to the very close of the conflict."[36] The rise in prices had the effect of helping to offset the scarcity of labor. Since prices rose much faster than wages, real wages fell. Southern laborers tried to maintain their prewar living standards by working longer hours and holding down more than one job. In many cases wives and children entered the labor force for the first time to supplement the family income. This increase in the labor force reduced the most important "bottleneck" in southern production.

X

To study wage movements in the Confederacy, I took wage quotations from the account-books of various southern firms.[37] Since the median is not affected by extreme values, it was the statistic

[35] Earl J. Hamilton, "Profit Inflation and the Industrial Revolution, 1751–1800," in *Enterprise and Secular Change*, ed. Frederic C. Lane and Jelle C. Riemersma (Homewood, Ill.: Richard D. Irwin, Inc., 1953), p. 328.

[36] *History of Manufacturers in the United States: 1607–1928* (New York: McGraw-Hill Book Co., 1928), II, 51.

[37] The most fruitful source of quotations was the Tredegar Iron Works. Their account-books have recently been opened to the public and are now available in the Virginia State Library. The pay-roll book for 1863 and 1864 is complete. However, the pay-roll book for 1861–62 was lost or destroyed. Some wage quotations for this earlier period can be gotten from the firm's daily journal. Quotations for foundry and forge workers, pattern-makers, carpenters, blacksmiths, boilermakers, machinists, turners, and fitters are available. The University of North Carolina has the account-book of the Henry Garst Flour and Saw Mill and the John Judge Sock and Yarn Factory. These include quotations for farm hands, butchers, and general labor. In the Moravian Archives at Winston Salem, North Carolina, the account-books of the Fries Cotton and Wool Company are available. Only the total pay roll and the number of people employed are listed. From this source the average take-home pay was recorded. The timebook of the Atlanta, Georgia, arsenal, available at the National Archives in Washington, revealed figures for 1863 and 1864 for guards, machinists, carpenters, cartridge-makers, and superintendents. The accounts of the Central Laboratory of Georgia, also located in the National Archives, give data for 1863, 1864, and 1865 on carpenters, watchmen, overseers, bricklayers, brick-burners, and painters. In the Historical Commission of Columbia, South Carolina, the records for the building of the statehouse are available and reveal the figures for quarrymen, assistant quarrymen, blacksmiths, engineers, watchmen, carpenters, hostlers, architects, and railroad inspectors in 1862–63. The Graham Robinson Iron and Steel Works account-books at the University of Virginia reveal the wages paid to several workers in the mills, not classified by profession, throughout the war.

used as typical of all wages in a trade[38] in any given month.[39] The first quotation listed in 1861 was taken as the base, and successive monthly medians were expressed as a percentage of this value. For some occupations quotations were not available for 1861. To utilize the quotations that were available for later years, I assumed that during 1861 wages increased in these trades as much as the average increase in all other trades.[40] The

TABLE 4

WAGE INDEX FOR THE CONFEDERACY

(January, 1861 = 100)

MONTH	YEAR				
	1861	1862	1863	1864	1865
January.....	100	121	201	397	784
February.....	100	112	207	381	884
March......	99	118	212	462	987
April.......	101	119	237	402	
May........	107	122	233	398	
June........	105	127	241	372	
July.........	100	122	263	385	
August......	100	136	296	394	
September...	106	139	305	450	
October......	101	160	341	527	
November...	116	166	371	528	
December....	114	177	349	521	

first quotation for these occupations in 1862 was therefore given the value of 1.085, a base in 1861 was determined, and the successive monthly quotations were expressed as a percentage of this

[38] In the case of pattern-makers the high wage, rather than the median, was used because for the years 1861–62 it was the only quotation available.

[39] The mode was rejected because some series were bimodal or trimodal, while others had no mode.

[40] There were sixteen cases for which figures were available in both 1861 and 1862. These include forge-workers, pattern-makers, sawmill help, turners, fitters, watchmen, four individuals in the Graham Robinson Mill, foundry help, boilermakers, carpenters, and the help in the Fries Cotton and Wool Company Mill. The average of the first quotation in 1862 to the first quotation in 1861 for these sixteen cases was 1.085.

base.[41] An unweighted average of these relatives was then struck. These values are presented in Table 4 and plotted in Figure 6. They reveal that the average wage increased approximately ten times during the four years of the war, or at a rate of 4.6 per cent a month.

To determine the movement of real wages, the rise in money wages should be deflated by a price index weighted according to workers' expenditures. Unfortunately, no budget studies are currently available for the South during the Civil War.[42] However, the change in real wages may be approximated by deflating the rise in money wages by a wholesale

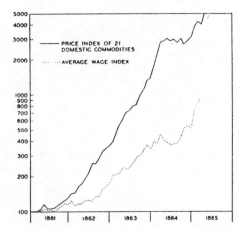

FIG. 6.—Index of prices of twenty-one domestic commodities compared with index of wages. (January, 1861 = 100.)

price index of twenty-one domestic commodities.[43]

[41] If figures were available only for 1863, the trades were not used.

[42] The earliest systematic reports for family living in the United States that have been located are for the years 1816–17 and 1835. The next study available is for the 1870's (see Faith M. Williams and Carle C. Zimmerman, *Studies of Family Living in the United States and Other Countries* [U.S. Department of Agriculture Misc. Publication 223 (Washington, D.C.: Government Printing Office, 1935)], p. 7).

[43] This index includes corn, hay, rye, wheat, bacon, beef, butter, chickens, flaxseed, cornmeal,

MONEY, PRICES, AND WAGES IN THE CONFEDERACY 33

The most serious objection to deflating money wages by a wholesale price index of farm products and textiles is that it overstates the decline in the value of a worker's money wage by between 20 and 40 per cent.[44] The price index used to deflate money wages, plotted in Figure 6, reveals that wholesale domestic prices rose approximately forty times by March, 1865, or at a rate of 9 per cent a month. If this index overstates the rise in the cost-of-living price index by, say, 30 per cent, the cost of living rose approximately thirty times in the Confederacy. Since money wages rose only ten times during the war, real wages declined to approximately one-third their prewar level.

In addition to money wages, workers received part of their wages in kind,[45] and this portion was not reduced by the rise in prices. In February, 1865, the

Henry Garst Sawmill paid its help ninety dollars and a barrel of flour for a month's labor.[46] Undoubtedly, some workers increased their take-home pay, but not their rate of real hourly wages, by working longer hours. Others worked night shifts and received about one and a half times the day rate; still others must have supplemented their family incomes by growing food on their own small plots of land or having other members of their family take jobs also.

These various ameliorations were probably not very large. If they were equivalent to a 10 per cent increase in money wages, real wages in the Confederacy had declined to well under 40 per cent of their prewar level by March, 1865. Southern labor complained bitterly that its wages were "totally inadequate to afford us the merest necessities of life —plain food, shelter, fuel, and clothing. We are literally reduced to destitution."[47]

Physical productivity probably declined during the war. More people were employed in a fixed plant. For example, twenty-one people were employed by the Fries Mills in 1861 and forty-eight in December, 1864. Production was constantly interrupted by Confederate agents who impressed raw materials. The Fries Mill smuggled wool through the Union lines to make Confederate uniforms. When agents seized this wool because the import duty had not been paid, the mill was unable to replace it. The mill did not fulfil its government contract and temporarily halted production.[48] The conscrip-

---

eggs, superfine flour, family flour, extrafine flour, lard, Irish potatoes, sweet potatoes, live turkeys, tallow, and osnaburgs.

As we have seen, the northern blockade curtailed the supply of imported commodities but increased the supply of exported commodities to the home market. It made import prices rise more and export prices rise less than an average of all commodity prices. The prices of farm products and textiles were not directly affected by the blockade. (The supply of wool and cotton, of course, was affected by the blockade. The textile included in my index is osnaburgs, the type of cloth worn by Negroes and manufactured in the South.) The prices of farm products and textiles rose as a result of the increase in the quantity of money and the decrease in real output. By deflating money wages by their average price rise, one approximates the way in which these forces alone affected the value of a worker's income.

[44] I assume that prices in the South behaved like prices in the North during the Civil War and in the United States during the two world wars. In the Civil War an average of textile and farm prices rose 19 per cent more than the cost-of-living index; in World War I, 21 per cent more; in World War II, 40 per cent more.

[45] Some workers received part of their wages in kind before 1861, just as some do today. During the Civil War this practice intensified.

[46] University of North Carolina, Southern Historical Collection, "Henry Garst Payroll Book, 1860–1866," p. 30.

[47] Letter from Taylor to Memminger, October 14, 1863 (Thian [ed.], *op. cit.*, II, 153).

[48] See Moravian Archives (Winston Salem, N.C.), "Fries Letter Books" (MSS), 1863.

tion act also prevented steady and continuous production. The manager of a shoe factory in Montgomery, Alabama, reported:

> It takes fully one half the time of my clerks and about as much of my own to attend to the detailing men. I no sooner have a man trained and somewhat efficient than he is ordered to report to camp, and then, after considerable delay, I have his services replaced by a new

TABLE 5

RATIO OF MEAN SKILLED WAGE TO
MEAN UNSKILLED WAGE

Date	Ratio	Date	Ratio
1861:		February	2.62
January	3.76	March	2.77
February	4.28	April	2.46
March	3.92	May	2.30
April	4.73	June	2.32
May	4.25	July	2.61
June	3.03	August	2.97
July	4.25	September	2.25
August	3.37	October	2.24
September		November	1.69
October	5.30	December	1.86
November		1864:	
December		January	2.96
1862:		February	2.23
January	3.38	March	2.21
February	3.38	April	3.15
March	3.98	May	2.57
April	4.02	June	2.84
May	3.72	July	2.81
June	3.09	August	2.59
July	3.15	September	3.21
August	3.38	October	3.21
September	3.00	November	3.05
October	2.30	December	1.39
November	2.49	1865:	
December	2.38	January	1.16
1863:		February	3.04
January	2.91	March	3.73

one and an invalid, in most cases, who is one half the time in the hospital and the other half not able to do much work.[49]

Machinery worn out through normal use was difficult to replace, and occasionally entire factories were destroyed by fire or northern troops. This hap-

[49] Quoted in Ramsdell, "The Control of Manufacturing by the Confederate Government," *op. cit.*, p. 248.

pened, for example, to some of the furnaces of the Tredegar Mills. These events probably more than offset any increase in productivity caused by patriotically increased endeavor. They reduced the marginal physical product and offset in part the increases in marginal revenue product caused by inflation. They tended to lower wages by causing downward shifts in the demand schedule for labor.

XI

Changes in the dispersion of wages about the average monthly wage reveal that the labor force was undergoing a change during the war. As a measure of dispersion I took a ratio of the mean skilled wage to the mean unskilled wage.[50] These figures are recorded in Table 5. They reveal a downard trend and indicate that the wages of unskilled workers in the South rose faster during the war than the wages of skilled workers. During both world wars and the succeeding inflationary periods there was a similar tendency for the wage spread between occupations to narrow.[51]

Even before Fort Sumter was fired upon, the South had a chronic shortage of skilled workers. The great majority of skilled immigrants coming to America during the 1840's and 1850's settled in the North. Free labor has traditionally feared the competition of slave labor, and the long distances between large southern communities limited the extent of the

[50] I classified the following trades as skilled: engineers, bricklayers, machinists, foremen, boilermakers, pattern-makers, carpenters, blacksmiths, and the highest figure found in a month for foundry and quarry help. As unskilled trades I classified sawmill help, butchers, farm help, watchmen, overseers, yarn-and-sock-factory help, isolated individuals in steel mills, and railroad inspectors.

[51] Philip W. Bell, "Cyclical Variations and Trend in Occupational Wage Differentials in American Industry since 1914," *Review of Economics and Statistics*, XXXIII (November, 1951), 331.

MONEY, PRICES, AND WAGES IN THE CONFEDERACY 35

market that a skilled worker could serve. During the war the persistent demands of the army reduced the small skilled labor force to such an extent that production was seriously impeded.

In May, 1862, the Quartermaster General wrote the Secretary of War:

The supplies of this department are totally inadequate to fill the requisitions made upon it. It has been formally reported to me today that requisitions representing the complete outfit of 40,000 men are necessarily unfilled. . . . The deficiency has been occasioned in a great measure by the interference of the conscription act with the arrangements of manufacturers with whom contracts have been made. Under its operation they have been deprived of the service of their employees to such an extent that they have been rendered incapable of complying with the contracts made with this department for continued supplies of various articles absolutely essential for issue to the Army.[52]

A mill in Selma, Alabama, that would roll "iron enough for all our vessels and cast guns for all the batteries"[53] was scheduled for completion in the fall of 1863. In May, 1864, it was still unfinished for want of skilled mechanics. In May, 1864, it was reported that in Charlotte, North Carolina, "a number of our most important tools are idle a large portion of the time for want of mechanics to work them, and some of these tools, the steam-hammer for instance, are the only tools of their class in the Confederacy."[54] The commander of the Naval Ordnance Works at Atlanta, Georgia, complained that he was "unable to have forged the wrought iron bolts for the Brooke gun for

the want of blacksmiths," and that "nearly all of the lathes are idle for want of hands."[55]

The *Richmond Enquirer* indignantly pointed out:

Nearly the whole operation of this extensive establishment, the shoe bureau like the post office, is stopped now because of the absence of the operatives at the front, where, so far, they have done no work save eating up a certain quantity of bacon, pears, and cornmeal. . . . We understand there is an abundance of leather here, and if the shoemakers were not absent, many thousands of pairs of shoes might now be on hand to supply the present and prospective wants. Men in an army cannot march long without shoes.[56]

One week later the *Enquirer* reported that "considerable trouble" was caused in cotton and woolen mills by the conscripting of a few skilled hands. "Not only were women and children stopped from work, but the Government orders for cotton and cloth had to go unfilled."[57]

The shortage of skilled labor induced firms to raid their competitors' labor force. Banton Duncan, who received a contract from the Treasury Department to print Confederate notes, wrote Secretary Memminger that "Hoyer and Ludwig [another printing firm] has already seduced away two of my journeymen."[58] Two days later the Secretary received a letter from a different printing firm stating that "Mr. Duncan has planned the ruin of Mr. Ball and myself. He has already seduced away our workmen; arson has been tried to destroy our premises. Every other effort failing, he tries to scandalize my past life."[59] Letter fol-

[52] Letter from A. C. Meyers to H. G. Randolph, May 23, 1863 (U.S. War Department, *The War of the Rebellion*, Series IV [Washington, D.C.: Government Printing Office, 1880–1901], I, 1127).

[53] Letter from C. Jones to J. M. Brooke (*ibid.*, III, 523).

[54] Letter from H. Ashton Ramsay, chief engineer, to Commander J. M. Brooke, chief, Bureau of Ordnance and Hydrography, May 5, 1864 (*ibid.*, p. 521).

[55] Letter from D. M. McCorkle to J. M. Brooke (*ibid.*, p. 522).

[56] June 16, 1864.

[57] June 21, 1864.

[58] Letter from Duncan to Memminger, October 21, 1862 (Thian [ed.], *op. cit.*, I, 656).

[59] Letter from E. Ketzinge to Memminger, October 23, 1862 (*ibid.*, p. 657).

lowed letter, until the harassed Secretary ended the raiding of labor among his printers by making it official Treasury policy to cancel the contract of "any contractor, who by offers of higher wages, or in any way incites any person employed by any contractor to leave such service, or who employs anyone in the service of another contractor, even after he may have been discharged, without his written consent."[60]

The skilled workers of the South were essential to production and accounted for only a small fraction of a firm's total pay roll. Under these conditions they could, and did, successfully press for large absolute wage increases.

To maintain output in the face of the large drain of manpower into the army and the shortage of skilled workers, new sources of labor had to be found. Women and children had to be attracted into the labor force and slaves redirected from the farms to factories.

Quartermaster supply depots were located in the larger towns. Many of the women in those areas had never worked in factories before, yet Ramsdell relates that "thousands of women and girls sought employment in the clothing shops."[61] Some women took jobs because it was now patriotic to work for "The Cause." Some wanted to augment the family income and took advantage of the ease of entry into the labor force. A large number, however, must have been attracted by the relatively high wages, for the wages of the unskilled workers in the South during the Civil War rose more than those of skilled workers already in the labor force.

Before the war, slaves were not widely

used in manufacturing.[62] Rather, it was the growing of cotton more than anything else that led to the spread of slavery through the South. Typically, all forced labor has required costly supervision to offset its carelessness, wasteful idling, and wilful destruction. Cotton-growing, however, had several characteristics that made it adaptable to slave labor.[63]

Many slaves, of course, were highly skilled, and some of the more famous southern buildings, such as the old Vicksburg Courthouse, were built by slaves. The wages of Negro and white bricklayers working on the Statehouse of South Carolina reflect this skill: Negro help systematically received 25 cents less per day than white labor. In May, 1863, white labor received $3.25 per day and Negroes $3.00; in February, 1864, whites received $5.00 and Negroes $4.75; in July, 1864, whites received $6.00 and Negroes $5.75.[64] Since the employment of Negro help cost more than that of white help (because of wages for guards and other expenses) and since the wages of slave and free labor, percentage-wise, came closer together as war continued, these quotations suggest that slaves were

---

[60] Correspondence of the Treasury, April 23, 1863 (*ibid.*, III, 444).

[61] "The Control of Manufacturing by the Confederate Government," *op. cit.*, p. 223.

[62] Ulrich B. Phillips, *American Negro Slavery* (New York: D. Appleton–Century Co., 1918), p. 380.

[63] The work involved was simple and routine in character, since only plain tools were used; supervision was relatively easy because more labor was used per acre than for many other crops; at the peak of the labor demand in picking, practically the whole slave family, young and old, could be employed; though the methods employed exhausted the soil and so necessitated either a more careful and varied agriculture, for which slave labor was less adapted, or else resort to new fertile land, this latter alternative was always available, for the rich alluvial soil of the Mississippi Valley was more fertile than that of the older cotton-growing states, and the limit of expansion had not been reached in 1860 (Wright, *op. cit.*, p. 303).

[64] South Carolina State Archives, account-book for the South Carolina Statehouse.

MONEY, PRICES, AND WAGES IN THE CONFEDERACY 37

more skilled than the whites remaining at home.

Before the war, slaveowners generally preferred to keep their slaves on their own plantations. Slaves were not hired out to factories, "because high wages were not adequate compensation for the liability to contagious and other diseases, demoralization, and the checking of the birth rate caused by the separation of husbands and wives."[65] The firms, in turn, preferred free labor because the factories were forced to assume responsibility for a slave's accident.[66] Southern management also recognized that white workers did not work well side by side with slaves. For example, in 1838,[67] white laborers had protested the hiring of Negro carpenters.[68]

The war may not have changed personal attitudes, but it did alter the established pattern of slave usage. Cotton production declined, and the demand for slaves on plantations fell off correspondingly. Plantation owners and their sons, as well as overseers, were in the army, and the women left at home could not organize or direct their field hands. Firms needed labor and advertised widely for Negro help. "The Macon Armory advertised for 100; the Tredegar Iron Works want 1000; the Naval Gun Foundry and Ordnance Works at Selma wanted 200; the salt works in Clarke

[65] Phillips, *op. cit.*, p. 380.

[66] *Ibid.*, p. 379.

[67] J. R. Commons and Ulrich B. Phillips (eds.), *Documentary History of American Industrial Society* (Cleveland: A. H. Clark Co., 1910–11), II, 360.

[68] In 1858 Frederick L. Olmsted stated that, in a mining camp, a group of twenty or thirty white laborers came up to a newly hired white Englishman and told him "they would allow him 15 minutes to get out of sight, and if they ever saw him in those parts again, they would give him hell." The reason given to Olmsted for this action was that the Englishman was "too free-like with the niggers and they thought he'd make 'em think too much of themselves" (*ibid.*, p. 170).

County, Alabama, advertised for 500. Almost every industry was competing for Negro labor."[69] Attracted by relatively high returns, more and more slaves were placed on the labor market and were rented to mills, factories, and railroads.

XII

Most southerners who suffered through this inflation believed it was caused by speculators or government impressment agents. Consequently, they tried to combat inflation largely by denouncing these groups, prohibiting goods from crossing state lines, and instituting price control. Southerners confused the forces that actually instigated inflation—the increase in the stock of money and the decrease in real output—with the process through which these forces operated. They did not concentrate on the basic causes of inflation, and they were unable to formulate a program of reform that might have mitigated some of their hardships.

"The band of harpies preying upon the vitals of the Confederacy,"[70] the speculators and extortioners, was the most widely alleged cause of the inflation. Governor Vance of North Carolina found that, because of extortion and speculation, "it will be impossible to clothe or shoe our troops this winter."[71] One writer in the *Wilmington Journal* claimed that "the speculators have caused the present high prices, and they are determined to make money even if one-half of the people starve."[72] This view was also presented to government officials. Secretary Memminger was told that "the high prices are owing to the wicked spirit that

[69] Coulter, *op. cit.*, p. 258.

[70] *Wilmington Journal*, October 9, 1862.

[71] Letter from Z. B. Vance to Weldon N. Edwards, September 18, 1862 (U.S. War Department, *op. cit.*, I, 85).

[72] July 6, 1862.

infests so many persons to make money upon the downfall of others, overbidding, overreaching, when we are struggling for our most sacred liberty and independence."[73] Two days later another person wrote the Secretary: "The cause of the high prices lies in the bull and bear games carried on by unprincipled speculators who would sacrifice the whole of the South to enrich themselves."[74]

The number of speculators was reputed to be legion.[75] However, a critic of this position pointed out that everyone with products to sell—farmers, merchants, and manufacturers alike—was accused of being a speculator.[76] Another critic suggested that blockade-runners could not justly be called extortioners. "Their operations certainly bring goods into the country and thus tend to relieve prices— they certainly cannot increase scarcity."[77] But these calm voices went unheard; instead, southerners enjoyed the vicarious thrill of concocting suitable punishments for speculators. One could think of no worse punishment for a speculator than placing him "in the ranks of the army and make him live on half rations of raw, stinking, beef, and black bread."[78] The less imaginative felt that the speculators simply "ought to be hung until dead by the side of traitors and tories."[79]

[73] Letter from Joseph Newman to Memminger, March 20, 1863 (Thian [ed.], *op. cit.*, II, 57).

[74] Letter from George F. Gerding to Memminger, March 22, 1863 (*ibid.*, p. 62).

[75] "On Thursday last, our town was full to overflowing with the merchants and speculators, Jews and Gentiles, men from East and West, North and South, who came to attend the advertised auction sale of goods" (*Wilmington Journal*, August 30, 1862).

[76] *Ibid.*, July 10, 1863.

[77] *Ibid.*, September 29, 1864.

[78] *Ibid.*, July 6, 1862.

[79] November 20, 1862.

Poor transportation facilities,[80] droughts,[81] Union armies,[82] and the blockade[83] were also accused of causing the inflation. However, these accusations were neither as bitter nor as frequent as those levied against the agents of the Confederate government who were in daily contact with the public. Except for speculators, these agents were held responsible for high prices more frequently than any other single group or event.

The military authorities, for security reasons, were stringent in granting passports to enter and leave cities. As a result, it was reported that, in Wilmington, "no carts came in with produce. Nothing is brought to market. Nobody comes in to buy or sell."[84] The same events were reported in Richmond.[85]

The specific government agents most despised were the impressment officers.

[If] prices are inconveniently high for poor folks . . . it must be expected so long as the necessities of life are impressed on their way to

[80] January 4, 1862; *Richmond Enquirer*, March 20, 1863; *Richmond Whig*, June 13, 1864.

[81] Letter from Ruffin to Northrop, November 3, 1862 (U.S. War Department, II, 159); *Richmond Whig*, August 15, 1864.

[82] *Richmond Whig*, June 13, 1864; *Wilmington Journal*, June 14, 1862.

[83] *Wilmington Journal*, March 31, 1864; *Richmond Whig*, August 23, 1864.

[84] *Wilmington Journal*, January 24, 1863.

[85] "The owners of a number of country carts that used to bring supplies to this market have of late ceased to come, though the markets are destitute of vegetables common to the season. As many carts as formerly start for the city, but many now stop before reaching their destination, haul up at some convenient place by the roadside, sell their goods and put for home instantly. The market men allege, with show of justice, we presume, that when they come into the city, they are bothered half out of their wits to get out again. When applying for a passport, they have to produce somebody who knows them, as a voucher, a thing not always easy to do. Then, again they say they are stopped on every corner of the street and subjected to cross questioning by the military guard whose importunities are not always to be resisted" (*Richmond Enquirer*, June 15, 1864)

MONEY, PRICES, AND WAGES IN THE CONFEDERACY 39

market by Government agents, who are too lazy to go through the country in search of supplies. Half of the troubles of the army and nearly all of the troubles of the people are due to the existence of the pestiferous commissaries.[86]

Part of this thorough condemnation came because large quantities of impressed goods were never used. They had rotted and decayed.[87] Part also came because commodities were impressed largely from the immediate vicinity of the stationed army.[88] The decreased supply of commodities raised prices to civilians in the area. When it was rumored that impressment officers were near Richmond in 1864, "the people having become alarmed by the interferences of government agents with the sources of supply, cleared the market of flour and produced a heavy advance in the price of that article."[89]

In direct response to the public protests of high prices, "caused" by speculators, extortioners, and impressment agents, the government enacted price control.[90] Secretary of the Treasury

George Trenholm, addressing the Commissioners of Prices, said: "In the function conferred upon you by Congress . . . resides . . . the only power capable of interposing a check on the progress of depreciation [of the currency]."[91]

The price commissioners were constantly harassed by the public to lower their ceiling prices.[92] Secretary Trenholm told Governor Bonham of South Carolina that, when he arrived in Richmond, he found

the commissioners of prices had fixed the schedule rate of wheat and corn at $30 and $24 per bushel, respectively, for the months of August and September. . . . Public meetings were held . . . and resolutions adopted patriotically insisting upon a reduction of the standard rates, and their establishment upon a basis sufficiently low to inspire confidence in the currency. The result was that the commissioners reassembled and reduced the schedule prices to $7.50 for wheat for the month of August and $5 for the month of September. A wiser and more patriotic course was never pursued by any people.[93]

The price ceilings imposed by the Confederate government became more and

---

[86] *Richmond Whig*, October 21, 1864. The *Richmond Whig* of May 2, 1864, reflected public sentiment in its short news item on the impressment of horses: "The horse impressment business seems to have died out. The long legged, white hatted men, with their negroes and bailers, were nowhere to be seen on Saturday. The number of animals secured by impressment in Richmond is said to have been ridiculously small—so many had to be liberated as belonging to Government officers. . . . An attempt was made to seize the President's horse while standing with his carriage in front of his office."

[87] "Last year the country was filled with Government agents impressing the wheat and grinding it before it was dry. The result was thousands of bushels were either bulked up or ground damp and destroyed. The agents were warned of the result, but they were too wise to take advice. Most of them were impudent young men who ought to have been in the ranks. They knew nothing about business and were insulting wherever they went" (*ibid.*, July 19, 1864).

[88] *Richmond Enquirer*, March 13, 1863. (This newspaper is misdated March 13, 1862.)

[89] *Richmond Whig*, September 2, 1864.

[90] Ramsdell has shown that, by controlling the number of conscripts allowed to work in specific factories, the government was able to influence the price of the commodities produced. Early in the war this control extended only to the goods the government purchased for its own use. However, by the end of the war, Ramsdall concluded that the army attempted to regulate the price of commodities going to the consumer as well ("Control of Manufacturing by the Confederate Government," *op. cit.*, p. 239).

[91] Speech delivered in Montgomery, Alabama, September 3, 1864; reported in the *Richmond Whig*, October 12, 1864.

[92] "What do the Confederate Commissioners mean by fixing the prices of wheat and corn at the figures they have? . . . Is it the intention of the Commissioners purposely to increase the price of provisions? . . . It is well known that producers will always demand higher prices from private purchasers than that fixed by schedule, and if the Government attempts to keep up with and outbid the market in this way, by the expiration of the year, prices will have reached a point beyond that which imagination can follow them" (*ibid.*, July 19, 1864).

[93] Letter from Trenholm to Governor Bonham, August 5, 1864 (Thian [ed.], *op. cit.*, IV, 378).

more unrealistic as time passed. In June, 1863, the ceiling prices were, on the average, only 66 per cent of the going market price. By July, 1864, the ceiling prices were only 53.3 per cent, and in October, 1864, only 37.3 per cent of the true market price. The extent to which legal ceilings were flaunted by the public is indicated by the large numbers of newspapers that regularly published a commodity's going market price and its legal ceiling price side by side.

Despite Secretary Trenholm's belief that low price ceilings were essential for the success of the government, the commissioners realistically raised their ceilings when it was urgent that the army procure commodities.[94] When this procedure took too long, the army simply ignored the ceiling rates and paid the full market price.[95]

[94] "Having readopted the schedules for May and June last, in accordance with the clearly manifested wishes of the people, we have thought it advisable and proper to stimulate the sales and delivery of small grain, etc. now so much needed as to be indispensable by advancing the price of wheat, flour, corn, meat, oats, and hay delivered in the month of August" ("Report of the Price Commissioners," in the *Richmond Enquirer*, August 2, 1864).

[95] Letter from the Commissioner of Prices in Virginia to Secretary of War Seddon, August 1, 1864, reprinted in the *Richmond Enquirer*, August 2, 1864.

The controls the South imposed were *ad hoc* measures designed to placate an outraged citizenry. Aggregate spending was not effectively curbed, and every expectation of higher prices was realized in fact. Under these conditions the Confederate controls completely collapsed.

The people of the South did not focus their attention on the basic cause of the rise in prices that plagued their country. Like the people of other countries during every age, they attempted to correct only the abuses of high prices. Had southerners attacked the most basic cause—the increase in the stock of money per unit of real income—with more vigor and understanding, they might have mitigated some of their hardships.

Part III
Inflations in the 1920s

[11]

CHAPTER II

The National Finances, the Inflation and the Depreciation of the Mark*

PART I

I. THE HELFFERICH EXPLANATION OF THE DEPRECIATION OF THE MARK

1. The discussions provoked by the depreciation of the mark in Germany during the decade 1914–1923, present an interesting resemblance to the controversies in England in the years which preceded the publication of the Bullion Report. Throughout the period of the inflation the theory held by the Reichsbank, by successive German Governments, by the great bankers, by great industrialists, by German officials, and by a great part of the Press, was that the depreciation of the mark was caused by the state of the balance of payments. During the war Germany had a "passive" balance because of excess imports over exports; later it was accentuated by the effects of the payment of reparations and of the other burdens imposed by the Treaty of Versailles.

It would be exaggerating to affirm that this was also the point of view of all the German economists. Some of them, as Liefmann, Schlesinger, Pohle, Beckerath, Terhalle, and Lansburgh, clearly recognized the influence of the paper inflation on internal prices and on the exchange rate. But others refused to admit a relation of cause and effect between the increase of the quantity of paper money and the depreciation of the exchange, and they adhered to the "theory of the balance of payments."† This mental attitude, contrary to quantitative monetary conceptions, was the effect of the line of thought which was prevalent before the war, and which preferred that type of monetary approach which Altmann called "Qualitative" as opposed to the quantitative.‡ Writers were attempting to construct a "sociological"

---

* Originally published in *Economia*, 1924.

† According to Diehl (*Über Fragen des Geldwesens und der Valuta*, second edition, 1921, p. 63), "the theory of Liefmann, according to which the exchanges are in close relation to internal prices, has not been sustained lately; indeed, this conception has been decidedly discredited."

‡ In the volume *Die Entwicklung der deutschen Volkswirtschaftslehre im XIX. Jahrhundert*, 1928, vi, p. 4.

NATIONAL FINANCES   43

conception of money. Under the influence of these views, as opposed
to the quantitative theory, such economists stressed the movement of
the value of money as an "historical process," which is not simply a
matter of comparing flows of money and of goods, but which demands
the comprehension of the entire complicated economic structure. To
this was added the influence of the work of Knapp, who diverted
German studies from the analysis of the quantitative relations between
money, prices, and exchange rates.

Dalberg* claims to have been the first to introduce into the post-
1914 literature about monetary problems the theory that the diminution of value suffered by a currency in the internal market is the
determining factor of the movement of the exchanges, i.e. of the
"external value" of that money. In making this claim Dalberg disputes
that of Liefmann, who had claimed that he himself first introduced
this theory into Germany, though he did not claim to be the originator
of the theory—the relation existing between "internal value" and
"external value" being well known outside Germany. "The recognition
of this relation," continues the same author, "has a decisive importançe.
The scientific value of all the publications of the first three years of
the war is doubtful, for those works take no account of this relation;
ignorance of it explains, moreover, many errors or omissions in German
monetary policy."

2. To a great number of writers and German politicians the deficits
in the budgets of the Reich and of the States, and the paper inflation,
were not the cause, but the consequence of the external depreciation
of the mark.†

   * *Die Entwertung des Geldes*, second edition, 1919, p. 93.
   † During the discussions of the "Commission on Socialization" (see *Verhandlungen
der Sozialisierungskommission*, 1921, vol. i, pp. 148 and following) a great diversity of
opinions about the causes of the depreciation of the mark was manifested. The following
are typical opinions:
   BERNHARD (Director of the *Vossiche Zeitung*): "If we had an active balance of
payments it would be a matter of indifference whether the accounts of the State
showed a deficit or no, as it would also be a matter of indifference whether this deficit
were covered by loans or by an increase in the floating debt or by any other means."
   EULENBERG: "A balancing of the Budget is entirely impossible as the exchange
varies in the proportions which we see. First stabilization of the exchange and then
stabilization of the national finances. There is no sense in wishing to take the Budget
and its balancing as a starting-point."
   DIETZEL: "I cannot but contradict the affirmations of my colleague Eulenburg.
It is true that the disequilibrium of the balance of payments has an influence on the
level of internal prices. But at the same time it is true that some price variations are
entirely independent of this and are due to the forced issue of paper into the channels

44 THE ECONOMICS OF INFLATION

The most authoritative representative of this theory is Helfferich, who expounded it in the sixth edition of his work *Das Geld* (Leipzig, 1923).

The increase of the circulation [affirms Helfferich] has not preceded the rise of prices and the depreciation of the exchange, but it followed slowly and at great distance. The circulation increased from May 1921 to the end of January 1923 by 23 times; it is not possible that this increase had caused the rise in the prices of imported goods and of the dollar, which in that period increased by 344 times.

That the collapse of the exchange rate was entirely disproportionate to the increase of the circulation also appears from the following argument: The circulation of the Reichsbank of January 24th, 1923, represented a value in paper marks of 1,654 milliards, but in gold only 330 millions; that is, no more than a twentieth of the value of the circulation in the period preceding the war. . . . It is not to be doubted . . . that the increase of the circulation did not even distantly keep pace with the depreciation of the mark abroad. The theory, according to which the inflation is the cause of the depreciation of the German mark, is based on the *petitio principi* that the external value of money (expressed by the foreign exchange rate) can only be determined by the quantity of paper money.

Now in the present case the causes of the collapse of the money are independent of the conditions of the paper circulation. These causes are obvious; on a country whose balance of payments was passive by about three milliards of gold marks, there was imposed the burden of the reparations bill, amounting annually to about 3·3 milliards of gold marks; to that was added the payments for the redemption of short-term debts; for the costs of occupation, etc., etc.

of circulation. And this issue is in turn due in a great part to the fact that we, up to now, have been unable to satisfy the needs of the Reich by taxation; for example, the need of money for the wages of railwaymen, which are enormously increased. The value of the paper mark depends on the quantity circulating at home: the home value as well as the foreign value. Until the Budget is balanced stabilization of the exchange remains simply impossible."

EULENBERG: "I believe that we need a larger quantity of notes and a bigger floating debt, because we have very high prices."

HILFERDING: "The conception of Bernhard, which holds possible a stabilization of the exchange in spite of the continuation of the unbalanced National Accounts and of the issues, is purely theoretical. It is an economic impossibility. For with the increase of the issues the balance of trade necessarily becomes passive. In effect, the issues increased internal prices, and that stimulated imports and impeded exports."

BERNHARD: "The primary phenomenon is the situation of the bálance of payments. The moment we have an active balance, the internal value of money is entirely independent of the valuation which is given it abroad. The moment the demand in the foreign exchange market for the currency of a country surpasses the supply the question of the internal value of the money of that country comes no longer into consideration."

In Eucken's book, *Kritische Betrachtungen zum deutschen Geldproblem* (1923), the theory, according to which the depreciation of the mark was due to the disequilibrium of the balance of payments, is subjected to a sharp criticism.

NATIONAL FINANCES   45

According to Helfferich, the concatenation of the facts is as follows:

The depreciation of the German mark in terms of foreign currencies was caused by the excessive burdens thrust on to Germany and by the policy of violence adopted by France; the increase of the prices of all imported goods was caused by the depreciation of the exchanges; then followed the general increase of internal prices and of wages, the increased need for means of circulation on the part of the public and of the State, greater demands on the Reichsbank by private business and the State and the increase of the paper mark issues. Contrary to the widely held conception, *not inflation but the depreciation of the mark was the beginning of this chain of cause and effect*; inflation is not the cause of the increase of prices and of the depreciation of the mark; but the depreciation of the mark is the cause of the increase of prices and of the paper mark issues. The decomposition of the German monetary system has been the primary and decisive cause of the financial collapse.*

3. The ideas expressed by Helfferich were also common in the German Press.† The following opinions which were expressed by an authoritative periodical towards the end of 1922 are characteristic:

Since the summer of 1921 the foreign exchange rate has lost all connection with the internal inflation. The increase of the floating debt, which represents the creation by the State of new purchasing-power, follows at some distance the depreciation of the mark. . . . Furthermore, the level of internal prices is not determined by the paper inflation or credit inflation, but exclusively by the depreciation of the mark in terms of foreign currencies. . . . To tell the truth, the astonishing thing is not the great quantity but the small quantity of money which circulates in Germany, a quantity extraordinarily small from a relative point of view; even more surprising is it that the floating debt has not increased much more rapidly.

The theory formulated in German official circles, to explain the causes of the depreciation of the mark, is expounded with clarity also in the following passage from a memorandum of the Central Statistical Office.‡ "The fundamental cause of the dislocation of the German monetary system is the disequilibrium of the balance of payments. The disturbance of the national finances and the inflation are in their turn the consequences of the depreciation of the currency. The depreciation of the currency upset the Budget balance, and determined with an *inevitable necessity* a divergence between income and expenditure, which provoked the upheaval."

The conviction, so widely held, that the depreciation of the mark

* See also the article by Helfferich, "Das deutsche Finanzwesen," in *Börsen-Courier*, February 24th, 1924.

† An exception was the *Frankfurter Zeitung*, which always contested the policy of inflation.   ‡ *Deutschlands Wirtschaftslage*, March 1923, p. 24.

46   THE ECONOMICS OF INFLATION

was only the expression of the disequilibrium of the balance of payments for a long time prevented any serious consideration of monetary reform.

In the congress of German bankers which took place in September 1920, Warburg maintained that the exchange was the expression of the depressed economic, financial, and social conditions of Germany, and that an improvement (or a stabilization) of the exchange could not be achieved until the general situation had been improved from this threefold point of view. Until then every measure of monetary policy would be ineffectual.

In July 1922 the Minister of National Economy elaborated a project for monetary reform which, it was hoped, would have resulted in the stabilization of the exchange. But the project was not carried through, because of the opposition of the Reichsbank. During 1922 the management of the Reichsbank tenaciously refused to allow the gold reserve to be used for monetary reform. At the meeting on August 28th, 1922, of the Central Committee of the Reichsbank, Havenstein, the president, categorically stated that it was not possible to make even an attempt at the stabilization of the exchange while the principal cause of the German crisis remained, that is until Germany succeeded in obtaining a moratorium and a tolerable solution of the reparations question. Havenstein alluded to the failure of the recent intervention of the Reichsbank in the exchange market; 230 millions of foreign exchange had been uselessly sacrificed without the Reichsbank having succeeded in preventing the continued depreciation of the exchange. But Havenstein did not add that the action of the Reichsbank must necessarily be fruitless if at the same time it continued to issue new paper money.

Also in November 1922, after a committee of foreign experts called in by the German Government had declared the stabilization of the German exchange to be possible under certain conditions, the Reichsbank stuck firmly to its theory, according to which it was useless to attempt monetary reform. Fatalistic ideas dominated the governing circles. Once more I quote the opinion of Helfferich: "Inflation and the collapse of the exchange are children of the same parent: the impossibility of paying the tributes imposed on us. The problem of restoring the circulation is not a technical or banking problem; it is, in the last analysis, the problem of the equilibrium between the burden and the capacity of the German economy for supporting this burden."[*]

Opposed to the German theories were those which can be called the "English" (because vigorously upheld by the representatives of

[*] "Die Autonomie der Reichsbank" in *Börsen-Courier* of April 4th, 1922.

NATIONAL FINANCES   47

Great Britain in the Reparations Commission and in the Guarantees Committee) according to which the fundamental cause of the depreciation of the mark was the Budget deficit, which provoked continued issues of paper money. I hold this second theory to be essentially correct, although it is necessary to recognize that in the last stages of the depreciation of the mark the relations between the Budget deficit, the quantity of paper money, prices, and the exchange became more complicated, as we shall see in the course of the present enquiry.

In certain writings of American economists one encounters the influence of the argument advanced by the Germans. For example, according to Professor Williams the causal order of events was the following: "Reparation payments, depreciating exchanges, rising import and export prices, rising domestic prices, consequent budgeting deficits, and at the same time an increased demand for bank credit; and finally increased note-issue."* Commenting on the work of Professor Williams, Professor Angell observed that "The reality of the type of analysis which runs *from* the balance of payments and the exchanges *to* general prices and the increased issue of paper seems to be definitely established."†

II. THE CONDITIONS OF THE NATIONAL FINANCES DURING THE WAR

4. Let us examine, in the light of the facts, the theory according to which the budget deficit was not the fundamental cause but the *effect* of the depreciation of the mark.

In the following table, in millions of marks, the total income and expenditure of the German Reich during the years 1914–1918 are indicated.‡

TABLE VIII

Financial years	Government expenditure	Ordinary and extra-ordinary income
1914	9,651	8,149
1915	26,689	23,207
1916	28,780	22,815
1917	53,261	35,215
1918	45,514	31,590
	163,894	120,976

* "German Foreign Trade and the Reparations Payments" (*Quarterly Journal of Economics*, 1922, p. 503).
† *The Theory of International Prices*, 1926, p. 195.
‡ *Statistisches Jahrbuch für das Deutsche Reich*, 1917–1921.

48   THE ECONOMICS OF INFLATION

The income figures shown in the preceding table include the proceeds from the war loans, subscriptions to which amounted to about 98 milliards of marks. The result was, therefore, that scarcely one-eighth of the expenditure of the years 1914–18 was covered by ordinary income. The difference between the total expenditure and the total income was covered by means of the issue of Treasury bills. The discounting of the Treasury bills at the Reichsbank provided the channel for an inflation which in part is shown directly in the increase of notes in circulation, and in part remained latent for a certain time.

The method adopted by the German Government for financing the war* consisted in funding the floating debt by means of periodical issues of loans. But already by the autumn of 1916 the failure of the method was becoming patent. From then onwards the sums yielded by the loans were always less than the amount of the floating debt. At the end of September 1918, after the issue of the ninth war loan, the floating debt amounted to 48 milliards of marks.

The circulation was not increased in the same proportion, because about half of the Treasury bills had been taken up by the principal banks, public institutions, or some great private firms. From July 23rd, 1914, to October 31st, 1918, the paper circulation (notes of the Reichsbank and those issued by the Loan Office) was increased by 24·2 millions of paper marks.

5. The German Government thought, at first, that the war would be short.† Besides, Helfferich was sure that the conquered enemies would bear the burden of it. Only at the end of 1915 was it resolved to create new sources of ordinary income,‡ but the new taxes were entirely inadequate. The difficulty of increasing the income of the Reich was due also to the particular structure of the German financial system, which was founded on a tripartition of the income between

---

* Germany's war expenses (Helfferich, *Das Geld*, p. 209):

	MILLIARDS OF PAPER MARKS	
Year of the War	Annual total	Monthly Average
1st	20·1	1·7
2nd	24·1	2·0
3rd	34·4	2·9
4th	46·9	3·8
August 1st, 1917–December 31st, 1918	21·8	4·4
	147·3	2·8

† Helfferich, *op. cit.*, p. 212.
‡ For particulars see the admirable book of C. Rist, *Les finances de guerre de l'Allemagne*, Paris, 1921, p. 125.

NATIONAL FINANCES

the Reich, the State, and the Municipalities, which did not provide
the Reich with an income capable of being expanded and easily adapted
to increasing needs. The defects of the fiscal organization, which lacked,
at the centre, a fiscal system of the Reich, to which the fiscal adminis-
trations of the separate States ought to be subordinated, exercised a
damaging influence on the financial policy of the war and the post-war
years.*

If Helfferich affirmed that directly after the outbreak of the war
it was necessary to provide, by issues of paper money, for the expenses
of mobilization which amounted to two milliards of paper marks, and
for the first expenses of the war, one must recognize that in this he was
right. The Government would not have been able to finance the first
phase of the war with taxes, because of the difficulty of obtaining a
sufficient sum by contributions in a few days, nor with loans, because
of the tension of the internal financial market.

But we should recognize that the financial policy followed later
justified the harsh criticisms to which it was subjected in Germany
itself. We may neglect the criticisms of the extreme parties which seem
influenced by political passions. Yet eminent personalities of the Conservative parties have not spared the financial policy of the war some
severe reproaches. Solmssen, director of the Diskonto-Gesellschaft,
affirmed that the whole financial policy, on the base of which Germany
conducted the war, was an error.† The German Government neglected
to draw from taxation the means for continuing the struggle. The
Reichsbank became a pliable instrument in the hands of the Minister
of Finance and renounced the functions of a central organ whose
business it is to regulate the circulation of the country.‡ The facility
of creating the means for covering the expenses made possible a habit
of extravagance not only in public finance but also by private persons,
whose consumption was not limited by heavy taxes.

The fatal theory dominating governing circles and the Reichsbank,

---

* As a justification of the financial policy followed by him during the war, Helfferich has observed, in his book, that the ordinary account was balanced during the
war. But Helfferich has not said that during the war the normal military expenses
were entered in the extraordinary account and perhaps other expenses which ought
to have figured in the ordinary account.

† *Das deutsche Finanzwesen nach Beendigung des Weltkriegs*, 1921, p. 8.

‡ Lotz (*Valutafrage und öffentliche Finanzen in Deutschland*, 1923, p. 7) contrasted
the German policy with the more energetic financial and banking policy followed by
England and France. It is remarkable that the Government did not endeavour to
stimulate private investors to acquire Treasury bills; in that way the inflation would
have been probably less.

the theory which affirmed that inflation did not exist in Germany and that, at any rate, the depreciation of the mark was not the effect of the increase of the circulating medium, made less acceptable the action which would have effectively bridled the increase of the issues. According to the Reichsbank, although the quantity of paper money in circulation increased, one could not speak of "inflation," because this paper money was covered by a one-third reserve. But this reserve included, besides gold, the notes issued by the "Loan Offices" created in August 1914!

Later the Reichsbank, to diminish the issues of notes, favoured the creation of bank deposits, in the belief that by substituting one form of new purchasing power for another inflation would be limited!

Inverting cause and effect, the Reichsbank indicated in its annual report, as a cause of the increasing issues of paper money, the rise of prices, provoked by the scarcity of goods. Helfferich writes in this connection (*Das Geld*, p. 462):

> The president of the Reichsbank, Havenstein—with whom the author was in continual contact during the years of the war (as Secretary of State to the Treasury and later as Secretary of State for Internal Affairs and representative of the Chancellor in the direction of the Bank)—has always upheld the opinion that one could not speak of inflation, when account was taken of the great quantity of money placed to the account of the military administration and of private firms, of the money circulating in occupied territories and of the increased need, which was due to an increase in prices and salaries independent of monetary conditions.*

6. During the war the depreciation of the mark was the consequence of the policy of financing the expenditure of the Reich by having recourse on a very large scale to the central note-issuing authority.†

---

* Also in "Memoranda on Economic Measures," presented by the Government to the Reichstag, it was maintained that the depreciation of the exchange was an effect of the causes which influenced the balance of payments, and had nothing to do with the diminution of the purchasing power of the mark in the home market. (Prion, *Inflation und Geldenwertung*, 1919, p. 48.) To excuse the Reichsbank it is necessary to add that the same erroneous ideas were also held by the issue banks of neutral countries. During the war, Cassel writes: "The central banks in the neutral countries gave earnest assurance that no depreciation in money was taking place, that the rise in the general price level was due to all other possible causes. . . ." (*Money and Foreign Exchange after 1914*, p. 122).

† Hilferding, *Verhandlungen der Sozialisierungskommission*, vol. ii, p. 228: "From 1914 onwards Germany did nothing serious to finance its expenses—not even after the war. In 1918, 1919, and 1920 we had not increased the Reich's income, instead it had diminished enormously in comparison with peace time; it was natural that the mark should fall."

NATIONAL FINANCES

However, the mark depreciated on the whole slowly during the war years. During the whole of that period monetary and financial phenomena developed according to the classical scheme. Budget deficit, increase of issues, increase of internal prices, i.e. diminution of the purchasing power of the paper money: a diminution which necessarily exercised a depressing influence on the exchange.

I have already noted in Chapter I that from 1914 to October 1918 internal prices increased less than the quantity of money existing in Germany. Some circumstances attenuated the influence of the increase of issues on prices (besides the demand for paper marks for circulation in occupied territory),* namely, the increased relative importance of payments in cash, the fact that many hoarded paper money in order to evade taxes or in the hope of an increase in its value after the war, or to have liquid resources in readiness at the coming of peace. It is necessary also to take account of the laws which fixed maximum prices for foodstuffs and for a series of raw or subsidiary materials (the laws of August 4th, 1914, modified by successive orders).

III. INCOME AND EXPENDITURE OF THE REICH FROM 1919 TO 1923

7. In the months which followed the cessation of hostilities the upheaval of the national finances continued to be the principal cause of the increase of note-issues and of the depreciation of the exchange. In November and December 1918 paper circulation increased by about 6·5 milliards of marks, that is by 24 per cent over the level at the end of October 1918. Very heavy expenses burdened the Reich accounts. They were caused by the very heavy burdens imposed by the conditions of the Armistice, by the expenses of demobilization, by the disorder of all life, political, economic, and social, after the revolution of November 1918, by the maintenance of the unemployed, by the purchase of provisions for the people, and by the extravagances of those who were raised to new authority by the revolution. That phenomenon which Wagner had already affirmed to be the consequence of inflation had appeared, i.e. public administration is the less economical the more unlimited are the resources made available by the creation of new money. Wagner quoted† the following words of Hock in support of this: "Once the deficit has become the dominating feature of the situation and has reached a figure of many millions, all saving of small

---

* On this, see the observations of Cassel, who holds that this circumstance could only explain a small part of the increase of the circulation (*Money and Foreign Exchange*, etc., p. 41).   † *Russische Papierwährung*, Riga, 1868, p. 29.

amounts seems useless, it is believed that only great reforms could afford salvation and the financial administration is possessed by a spirit of dissipation and neglect."

To this was added the disorganization of the railway administration, of the post-office, and in general of all activities exercised by the State, all of whose accounts showed enormous deficits. Because of the wretched functioning of the bureaucratic machinery, of the decadence of State authority, and of the tenacious opposition of interested parties, taxes yielded little.

It is true that in the conditions existing after the Armistice it would have been difficult to raise by taxation the means necessary for satisfying the needs of the State. A bold financial reform would have been necessary; but the revolutionary Government either had not the courage to resort to decisive measures or it feared that this would have given a very grave shock to the already weakened political and economic structure of Germany. The increase of note-issues seemed the simplest method. It is curious to observe that it was actually a Socialist Government which resorted to the most traditional and unjust form of taxation.

Meanwhile the German people, impoverished by the blockade, felt the necessity of importing great quantities of foodstuffs and raw materials. For this purpose large credits abroad were needed; but the internal political situation was too uncertain, and foreign creditors did not wish to run the grave risk of lending money to these stricken Germans. The Reichsbank ought itself to have guaranteed such loans. But this was not possible, because in accordance with the financial agreement concluded between Germany and the Allies on December 13th, 1919, the Reichsbank had been forbidden to dispose of its gold reserve.*

In default of foreign credits, it was taking up of paper marks voluntarily by foreigners more confident than the Germans themselves in the future of Germany which made possible large purchases in foreign markets. In a certain sense, therefore, it can be admitted that the increase of the paper-money issues aided Germany in surmounting the post-war crisis; but opposed to this advantage what great dangers were involved!

There weighed also on the balance of payments expenditure on the service of debts to foreigners, contracted during the war. According to an estimate of Schacht,† in the two years between the end of 1918

* Elster, *Von der Mark zur Reichsmark*, 1928, p. 110.
† *Die Stabilisierung der Mark*, 1928, p. 25.

NATIONAL FINANCES   53

and the end of 1920 debts were paid to foreigners amounting to 900 million gold marks.

IV. THE CAUSES OF THE DEPRECIATION OF THE MARK IN 1919

8. In Table I in the Appendix the expenditure and effective income of the Reich and the monthly increase of the floating debt from 1919 to the end of 1923 are shown. Since an examination of the Reich accounts continually adjusted to allow for the variations in the value of the mark cannot lead to any accurate conclusion, I consider that the variations of the floating debt are the best empirical index of the deficit of the Reich.

From the end of October 1918 to the end of March 1919 the floating debt rose by 15·6 milliards of paper marks, equal, according to the monthly average value of the dollar, to 7·741 millions of gold marks.*
In the first three months of the 1919 financial year the deficit of the Reich amounted to 3·063 millions of gold marks. Throughout the period to the end of June 1919 the dollar rate constantly rose. But no one could reasonably assert that in that period the enormous deficit was the consequence of the depreciation of the circulating medium; instead it was certainly due to a fundamental defect in the national financial system in which the income was insufficient to cover the expenditure.

The following period, which began in July 1919, is from more aspects interesting for the study of monetary phenomena. In July 1919 the dollar curve, which in the preceding months had already begun to break away from the other curves, suddenly showed a very rapid increase (see Diagram III). The various curves are spread as a fan; the curve of the internal prices rises less than that of the dollar, and the circulation curve less than that of internal prices. The gold mark, which in October 1918 was worth, on the average, 1·57 paper marks, rose to 3·40 paper marks in July 1919; to 10·8 in December of the

---

* The increase which took place in the separate months may be seen from the following figures:

INCREASE OF FLOATING DEBT

		Paper marks (*Milliards*)	*Gold marks* (*Millions*)
November 1918	..	3·0	1·695
December 1918	..	4·0	2·030
January 1919 ..	..	3·4	1·743
February 1919..	..	3·0	1·382
March 1919 ..	..	2·2	0·891
		15·6	7·741

54   THE ECONOMICS OF INFLATION

same year; and to 23·58 in February of the following year. Such a rapid depreciation had never been known in the past.

9. What is the explanation of this sudden depreciation of the German mark? The financial statistics show that the cause was not a sudden rise in the expenditure of the State. The curve of the floating debt (see Diagram III) shows a rise more or less uniform. Neither is there any indication of large payments having to be made to foreigners about that time. The coincidence of the signing of the Treaty of Versailles with the beginning of the sharp ascent of the exchange curve leads one to suppose that there was some connection between the two phenomena. But since the financial obligations imposed on Germany by the Treaty of Versailles could only have made their influence materially felt later, that connection can only be explained by the existence of psychological influences. Probably the signing of the treaty provoked a psychological crisis in certain German circles, lack of confidence in the future of Germany dominated the German mind and was manifested—for the first time in the history of the mark—in a "flight from the mark," i.e. in a demand for foreign exchange. Fear of revolutionary movements at home and the desire to avoid the heavy taxes with which the Government intended to balance the Budget also contributed to the "flight from the mark."*

In the figures shown in Table I of the Appendix we find evident repercussions of the depreciation of the mark. The gold value of the income was round about 300 million marks in the months April to July 1919. In the following months the gold value rapidly decreased (along with the depreciation of the mark) and touched a minimum in February 1920 (73·8 millions).

But the German authors, who have maintained that the depreciation of the mark was the cause of the disequilibrium between income and expenditure because, given the imperfect adaptation of income to the monetary depreciation, the yield was diminished, have not considered that in the period now under examination the depreciation of the mark influenced both income and *expenditure* in the same direction. Computed in gold marks, the total expenditure also diminished considerably from July 1919 to February 1920 and more rapidly than the income. But

* We must also take account of the following circumstance, recorded by Hawtrey (*Monetary Reconstruction*, London, 1923, p. 71). In January 1920 the fall of the mark and of the Austrian crown was made more rapid by the refusal on the part of the American banks to give credits to those exporters who used to sell in a depressed European money and to hold the proceeds of the sale.

NATIONAL FINANCES

, since the significance of these figures, expressed in gold marks, which were in reality non-existent, could not be intelligible, I prefer to take into consideration the figures which show in paper marks the increase of the floating debt.

They are as follows:

TABLE IX

Increase of Floating Debt

(Milliards of paper marks)

1919			1919		
April ..	..	.. 3·4	November	..	.. 1·9
May ..	..	.. 3·2	December	..	.. 1·4
June ..	..	.. 3·0			
July ..	..	.. 2·7	1920		
August	..	.. 2·1	January	..	.. 1·9
September	..	.. 2·4	February	..	.. 0·7
October	..	.. 2 7	March	..	.. 2·6

We are therefore unable to deduce that the depreciation of the mark, which showed itself in the second half of 1919 and lasted until February 1920, was the cause of an increase in the difference between expenditure and income. On the contrary, never was this difference so small as in February 1920, that is in the month in which the dollar rate reached a maximum, relatively to the rates of 1919 and 1920.

V. THE DEPRECIATION OF THE MARK DURING THE FINANCIAL
       YEAR 1920-21

10. In 1919 and 1920 numerous new laws were promulgated which radically transformed the German fiscal system by the creation of a great system of taxes imposed by the Reich—the States now passing into a completely subordinate position. These charges ought, on the one hand, to have assured to the central power a proper income, sufficient to cover the heavy expenses, and on the other hand to have contributed effectively to that consolidation of Germany which was one of the principal objects of the constitution of Weimar.

This was the famous fiscal reform which is linked with the name of Erzberger. But because of the profound change in the fiscal arrangements the assessment of the new taxes proceeded very slowly. It was a veritable maze of taxes, some of which were difficult to apply. Inspired partly by demagogic conceptions—Erzberger had proclaimed that in the future Germany the rich should be no more—the taxes met with lively opposition from the wealthy classes. The unduly high rates were a stimulus to evasion, and to "the flight of capital" abroad.

Yet the very high rates of the German taxes lose something of their significance if they are considered in relation to the method of valuing real property and industrial plant. The situation of the possessors of securities or of mortgages was very unfavourable as compared with that of the landowners and industrialists. In comparisons which have often been made between the fiscal burden which weighed on the German population and that supported by other countries, the fact that the rates of taxation are only one element in the fiscal burden has not been sufficiently appreciated; the methods of assessing the tax and of the valuation of property, the exemptions and rebates of taxes, the possibility of evasion, and delays in payment have, equally, a great importance.

11. In the financial year 1920-21, thanks to the influence, although slow, of the new fiscal laws, the Reich's income continually increased and reached 400–500 millions of gold marks in the months towards the end of the financial year. But expenditure grew more rapidly. The financial statistics of 1920 are worthy of attention, because study of them leads to the conclusion that even in that year the depreciation of the mark could not have any influence in the sense of provoking the deficit in the Reich accounts. In fact, in that year the value of money remained almost stable, for the gold mark was worth 14·2 paper marks in April 1920 and 14·9 in March 1921. In spite of that, the deficit in Reich accounts amounted to 6,050 millions of gold marks, that is 60 per cent of the total expenses, in the financial year 1920–21. The deficit was covered by the issue of Treasury bills. The circulation of paper money increased by about 20 milliards. Conditions which should conduce to a new fall of the mark were prepared. For the moment a part of the newly issued marks was sold abroad.

It was again possible for the German Government to place a considerable part of the Treasury bills outside the Reichsbank. In March 1921 of the total issue of 166·4 milliards of Treasury bonds, 101·9 milliards were still possessed by private banks, large firms, etc. There was still a check to the increase of note-issues.

As is shown in Diagram IV, in the period from February 1st, 1920, to May 1921 the increase of the floating debt was the factor which dominated and characterized the financial and monetary situation. The increase of the note-issues obviously provoked a continual rise in

NATIONAL FINANCES 57

internal prices, as is particularly shown by the cost of living curve. The psychological crisis which had occurred in the second half of 1919 was gradually calmed, and it seemed that a certain faith in the mark was again established among the German population. In the first months of 1920 a reaction to the sharp depreciation of the preceding months appeared. As the Reichsbank observed in its Report for 1920, there was a tendency on the part of the German public to sell foreign exchange possessed by it; exchange which the Reichsbank willingly bought against marks. It would still have been possible to save the mark if the German Government had taken energetic measures to re-establish a balanced Budget instead of allowing Treasury bills to be discounted continually at the Reichsbank. It should be added that in the financial year 1920-21 the expenditure consequent on the application of the Treaty of Versailles was not relevant in the explanation of the deficit of the Reich.*

VI. DISCUSSIONS CONCERNING THE FINANCIAL REFORM AND THE FINANCIAL COMPROMISE OF MARCH 1922

12. The acceptance of the Ultimatum of London (March 5th, 1921) now imposed on the Government the obligation to prepare a vast fiscal reform which would render existing taxes more productive and procure new receipts sufficient for the payment of reparations. In the following months a violent struggle arose between the different parties, representing definite socio-economic classes, a struggle which resembled the campaign provoked two years previously by the projects of Erzberger.

On one hand the Socialists energetically insisted on the necessity of compelling the wealthy classes to contribute to the expenditure which the State must incur to satisfy its obligations to the Allies. Property (it was said) can and should adapt itself to a sacrifice corresponding to its capacity to contribute. At a time of depreciation of the mark only a direct participation of the exchequer in the profits of industry and agriculture could prevent the continual diminution of the real yield of the taxes. Hirsch, the Secretary of State, published a memorandum proposing that mortgages in terms of gold in favour of the State should be imposed on all property. Interest payments could be made in paper money, on the basis of a coefficient which, for agriculturists, would vary with the price of cereals. It was also proposed

* See Part IV of the present chapter.

58   THE ECONOMICS OF INFLATION

that a certain percentage of the capital of joint-stock companies should be ceded to the State. Only by such a method could a contribution be obtained from the proprietors of "real goods" and of "gold values" (Goldwerte) whom the methods of valuation of property, followed until then, had treated too lightly.

The representatives of the democratic parties also showed themselves favourable to the idea of obliging "capital" to support a much heavier fiscal burden than in the past.* They put it from a realistic point of view: Germany must pay reparations, and if this payment was not well arranged the confusion in economic relations and the depreciation of the exchange which would result would put the foreigner in a position to buy a part of German resources dirt cheap. The wealth of Germany would have been uselessly dissipated. Hence it would be better to regulate the transfer abroad of a part of the "substance" of Germany. Having created a direct participation for itself in agricultural property and industrial firms, the State would have been able to utilize the securities representing this co-proprietorship.

But all the parties on the Right were up in arms against these projects, which were denounced as the beginning of a socialization of the means of production. The Nationalists refused to support the new fiscal proposals, declaring that the attempt to satisfy the obligations imposed under the Ultimatum of London was a "stab in the back" of the German economy, which the parties of the Left apparently would like to disarm and to abandon to the enemy.

It was already clear in August 1921 that the adversaries of the "taxation of material wealth" were so strong as to be able to wreck, in the Reichstag, every project designed with this object. Faced by the violent opposition of the interested classes, the Government, in the fiscal projects published in August, definitely abandoned the idea of a mortgage title in favour of the Reich on rural and urban property and of a participation in industrial and commercial enterprises. The proposal of a new property tax and of a tax on increase in capital were no longer the kernel of the reform, as the Socialists wished, but a mere ornament beside the heavy taxes on consumption goods.

The struggle for fiscal reform continued in the succeeding months. In consequence of the continual modifications recommended by numerous commissions and sub-commissions, the fiscal projects were altered and

---

* An attempt—unsuccessful in practice—at a capital levy, had been made in 1919 with the introduction of "Reichsnotopfer" which should have been one of the cornerstones of Erzberger's reform.

NATIONAL FINANCES   59

mutilated. Representatives of the Labour parties complained that the
new proposals struck especially at consumers, and endeavoured to
reduce the burden of indirect taxes; while the wealthy classes attempted
to undermine the efficiency of the proposals for new direct taxes.
These classes were especially fighting the innovation involved in the
proposals regarding the methods of valuing property, which were no
longer to be based on "rent values" (Ertragswert), which experience
had already shown to be inadequate, but on "selling" value.* Opposition
was especially lively on the part of agriculturists, who denounced the
method of valuing property according to "selling value" as an indirect
way of making the Reich participate in the "gold value." They also
contested any project whatever which was designed to increase the
yield of a tax in proportion to the depreciation of the mark.

On the other hand, towards the end of 1921 the democratic party
saw clearly that the depreciation of the mark threatened to make the
proposed fiscal reform totally ineffective. It presented a proposal
according to which the rates of the taxes should be fixed in gold, and
they should be actually paid in paper marks, according to an index
proportioned to the internal purchasing power of the mark. But
the project was rejected by the Financial Sub-Commission of the
Reichstag.

Finally on March 9th, 1922, a compromise was concluded between
the parties on the base of an authorization given to the Government
to impose a forced loan of a milliard gold marks. It was stipulated that
the money received from this forced loan could not be used in payments
in cash to the Allies but must serve only for internal payments, resulting
from the peace treaty, such as the expenses of occupation, and, above
all, the intended compensation to German industrialists for payments
in kind.†

The wealthy classes, having been obliged to accept against their will
the principle of a forced loan, immediately took their revenge on the
problems of the application of the principle. They secured the concession that the loan should be payable in paper marks at the fixed rate
of 70 paper marks to one gold mark. Consequently the successive
declines in the value of the mark robbed the forced loan of all effect,

* The "rent value" is that which is obtained by capitalizing the return at the
current rate of interest. According to German agriculturists the market value was
notably superior to the capitalized value of current rentals, because of the over-
valuation of land.

† The law which approved the new taxes—forty new taxes or modifications of
existing ones—was promulgated on April 6th, 1922.

60 THE ECONOMICS OF INFLATION

as it did of all the others, even the indirect taxes, regarding which
the error of establishing fixed rates in paper marks had been
committed.

VII. THE CONDITIONS OF THE NATIONAL FINANCES IN 1921 AND 1922

13. After the acceptance of the Ultimatum of London on the part
of Germany, the Reparations Commission created the so-called
"Committee of Guarantees" whose function was to put into execution
the plan of London. The Berlin Delegation of the Committee of
Guarantees made agreements with the German Government and with
the Reichsbank, and collaborated with the latter with the object of
helping the collection of the foreign exchange necessary for the payment
of reparations. The Reichsbank made many efforts in this matter.
Exporters were obliged to hand over to the Reichsbank a part of the
foreign exchange which came into their possession. At the same time
the offices for the control of foreign trade made efforts in order to extend
the custom among exporters of selling abroad for "appreciated" foreign
currencies, rather than for paper marks.

14. In the first months of the financial year 1921 the mark, which,
as we have seen in the preceding year, had shown a notable resistance,
in spite of the continuous increase of the note-issue and internal prices,
once more began to lose value in terms of the dollar. At the same time
both the floating debt and the issues of paper money were increased
continually. From August onwards, the depreciation became more
rapid. A situation was produced analogous to that which we have already
considered while studying the movement of the mark in the second
half of 1919. The sudden collapse of the mark was not preceded by a
sudden expansion of the circulation, such as would give a satisfactory
explanation of the depreciation of the exchange. Diagram v shows that
the dollar rate curve suddenly rose in the last months of 1921, much
above the curves of the circulation and of the floating debt, apparently
pulling up behind it the internal prices and the index number of the
cost of living. The opinion generally held is that the cause of the rapid
depreciation of the mark was the payment of the first milliard for
reparations. We shall discuss this point presently.

15. During 1921, as had already happened in the second half of
1919, the depreciation of the mark considerably depressed the yield

NATIONAL FINANCES

of taxation from about 400 million gold marks, which was the figure at the beginning of the financial year, to 113 million in November, in which month the depression of the exchange rate was greatest (1 gold mark = 63 paper marks). But even the expenditure, computed in gold marks, diminished in a parallel manner, so that not even for the financial year 1921 can it be affirmed that the budget deficit was provoked by the depreciation of the mark. Indeed, the increase of the floating debt did not show, after August 1921, an increase any more rapid than that of the preceding months.

16. In the period of relative stabilization of the exchange which occurred in the first months of 1922 the recovery of the national finances made some progress. The German Government adopted some financial measures to reduce expenditure (e.g. an increase in the "legal" price of bread) and to increase income (as, e.g., the increase of railway rates). A fleeting equilibrium was reached between income and ordinary expenditure; there was even a very small surplus which was set aside for the expenses arising from the Treaty of Versailles. An improvement was also shown in the railway accounts. The extraordinary Budget was not balanced; nevertheless, the increase of the floating debt slackened in the first months of 1922 and the percentage of the total expenditure which was covered by issues of Treasury bills declined.

But confidence in the mark, which the event of September 1921 had profoundly shaken, could not be re-established. On the contrary, after June 1922, a new wave of pessimism swept over Germany. German speculation renewed its attacks against the mark, which once again suffered a sharp fall. The number of people whose interests were favoured by a continuous depreciation of the mark, increased continually in Germany. Not only the great industries and the large merchant firms, but also very numerous classes of investors hoarded foreign bills or currency. The thoughts of all—from the great captain of industry to the modest typist—were concentrated on the dollar rate; and the face of the modest burgher was illuminated by a complacent smile when the daily bulletin, impatiently awaited, revealed to his greedy glance an increase in the dollar rate, while it was clouded if the official quotation showed an improvement in the mark. In a much-frequented cabaret the manager used to address the public in these words: "Many gentlemen are good-humoured this evening, that is to say, the dollar rises!"; or even: "Many people this evening have melancholy faces, that is to say, the mark rises!"

62 THE ECONOMICS OF INFLATION

17. In the summer of 1922 there appeared for the first time a distinct reaction of the depreciation of the mark on the Reich Budget, in the sense that the deficit was aggravated. While in the preceding months the German Government had succeeded in making some progress towards the balancing of expenditure and income, after July 1922 the depreciation of the mark again profoundly disturbed the state of the national finances. The real yield of the receipts lessened rapidly. In September of that year it had fallen, in terms of gold, to less than 100 millions; in November to little more than 60 millions. On the other hand, expenditure was maintained at a high level. The depreciation of the mark, which originally had been the consequence of the dislocation of the national finances, now contributed very much to the aggravation of the disorder and progressive disintegration. It also accentuated the losses of the railway administration, since the rates had not been advanced in proportion to the depreciation of the mark, whilst expenses increased rapidly. The subsidy from the Reich, which had been reduced in the first months of the financial year 1922, had to be continually and considerably increased in the succeeding months.

VIII. THE CONDITIONS OF THE REICH BUDGET AFTER
THE OCCUPATION OF THE RUHR

18. In the first months of 1923 the occupation of the Ruhr gave the *coup de grâce* to the national finances and the German mark. Because of it some important sources of income were lost to the State: the tax on coal, export duties, custom-house dues, and railway receipts. In addition, the German Governments—renewing their wartime errors of financial policy—did not think to cover the heavy expenses caused by Passive Resistance with new taxes. It conceded very large credits to the Ruhr industry to put it in a position to continue production. The continued depreciation of the mark made these loans almost worthless, since only to a very small extent were they subject to the "Valorization Clause," i.e. the obligation on the part of the debtor to restore the real value received by him at the time of the loan.

It was only at the end of August 1923 that the "Ruhrabgabe" was created, that is the tax for the Ruhr, the yield of which was intended to meet the expenses of Passive Resistance.

The nominal value of the notes in circulation, which was 1,280 milliards at the end of 1922, increased to 1,984 milliards on January 31st, 1923; 3,513 on February 28th; 5,518 on March 31st, and 6,546 on April 30th. Whilst at the beginning of 1922 the Treasury bills issued

NATIONAL FINANCES   63

were still placed in almost equal proportions in the portfolio of the Reichsbank and outside the Reichsbank; in 1923 the portion of new ones which was absorbed by the market decreased rapidly. At the end of April 1923 about three-quarters of them were held by the Reichsbank, and at the end of July 93 per cent. To every addition of Treasury bills there now corresponded an equivalent increase in the issues of notes.

The disastrous policy, which consisted in financing the Passive Resistance by means of printing notes, aroused sharp criticism in Germany itself.

Thus, contrary to the opinion of many writers,* the financial policy of the German Government was a fundamental factor also in the last phase of the depreciation of the mark.

19. It is evident that the consequence of that policy could not but be the continual depreciation of the mark, which the Reichsbank opposed in vain by adopting, in February 1923, action to support the mark. Indeed, in the second half of March it was already clear that the Reichsbank could no longer attempt to maintain the mark rate artificially while continuing the issues of paper money. The rise in internal prices, paralysing the export trade, threatened to aggravate the crisis provoked by the violent detachment of the Ruhr. Reserves of notes were collected by the German industrialists, and especially by those of the Ruhr, whom the Government had helped generously by subsidies, and were thrown on to the foreign exchange market. As Havenstein, the President of the Reichsbank, declared before the Committee for research into the causes of the depreciation of the mark: "On the 28th March began the attack on the foreign exchange market. In very numerous classes of the German economy from that day onwards thought was all for personal interests and not for the needs of the country."† The Reichsbank had to sell daily foreign exchange to the amount of about 20 millions of gold marks. But the demand for foreign exchange quickly became more intense and rose to 70 millions. The dam raised by the Reichsbank broke down on April 18th, the Reichsbank not being able any longer to sell foreign exchange at the official rate fixed for the dollar; the mass of paper money accumulated

---

* For example, Professor Angell, who says that "in the later stages of the German experience . . . the degree of the depreciation had absolutely no immediate relationship to Government finance."—*Op. cit.*, p. 446.

† Also Elster, referring to this episode, recognizes that the German industrialists refused to support the measures taken by the Reichsbank to stabilize the mark, and instead thought only of their private interests.—*Op. cit.*, p. 182.

64   THE ECONOMICS OF INFLATION

in four months by the continual issues broke into the market and the
dollar rate rose giddily.

IX. THE INFLUENCES OF THE DEPRECIATION OF THE MARK
       ON THE RECEIPTS OF THE REICH

20. Having reached this point in our treatise, it will be convenient
to pause a moment to examine more thoroughly the varied reactions
which in the advanced stages of the inflation the depreciation of the
mark exercised on the income and expenditure of the State.

(*a*) In the first place the depreciation of the mark rendered difficult—and, in times of the rapid depreciation of the currency,
impossible—the formation of a budget of expenditure. Whatever estimate was made, it was exceeded in a very short
time even before the estimate had been approved by the
Reichstag! Thus arose the necessity for continual corrections
and modifications: they were like a distorting veil which
concealed the true financial situation.

(*b*) The assessment of certain taxes, for example that on income,
met with very great practical difficulties. For example, how
could depreciation be calculated in order to determine the
"real" income and not only the "apparent" income of a firm?

(*c*) Since the nominal value of estates and nominal incomes
normally increased with depreciation of the mark and the
taxes were steeply progressive, there resulted an increase
of the fiscal burden without a corresponding increase in the
contributive capacity of the citizens. In the summer of 1919,
when the preparatory work on the law regarding income
tax was commenced, the mark was still worth 32 gold
pfennigs; in December 1921, when the law was amended,
the dollar was worth 180 paper marks; towards the middle
of May 1922, when a plan for amending the law to the
continuous monetary depreciation was presented to the
Reichstag, the dollar was already worth 295 paper marks,
and towards the end of July—soon after which the proposed
amendments had been approved—it was quoted at 520 paper
marks.

It was continually necessary to change the classes of income
and estates, the regulations about the minimum income and
estates exempt from taxation and the rebates of taxes, etc.

NATIONAL FINANCES 65

Thus was evolved a very great confusion in the financial laws, a continual succession of laws or ordinances which modified the preceding ones,* increasing difficulties of application, an increase of work in the Finance Office and therefore a delay in the assessment of taxes and greater facility for evasion.

(*d*) The basis of the fiscal system was unstable, since the yield of certain important taxes was closely connected with the fluctuations of the exchange and in a particular way with the continually varying phenomenon of the difference between the internal and external value of the paper mark. For example, the yield of the export taxes depended on that difference and should have been continually modified according to whether it rose or fell. But the modifications were always made too late and consequently occasioned disturbance in the economic life of the country. It was proposed to create export taxes towards the end of 1919, when the rapid depreciation of the exchange had increased the divergence between the external and internal value of the German currency. In fact, however, the export taxes were introduced only some months later, when a rise in the foreign exchange value of the mark on the one hand and the rise of internal prices on the other had noticeably diminished that difference. Owing to pressure from interested parties the taxes were perceptibly reduced in the summer of 1920; but they were again increased after a renewed depreciation of the currency. (In September 1923 they were finally abolished.)

Another example is the tax on coal, which had been introduced at a time when there existed a great difference between the German home price of coal and the price in the world market. Later, when the difference between the two prices was lessened, the tax on coal became too heavy for the German economy and threatened to diminish seriously the possibility of German competition in the foreign markets. The tax was first reduced and later, at the beginning of September 1923, when the price of German coal had already reached or surpassed the world price, it was completely abolished.

* For example, the law of July 20th, 1922, was the *sixth* amendment of the law of March 29th, 1920, which instituted the income tax.

c

66 THE ECONOMICS OF INFLATION

21. But the most important influence exercised by the depreciation of the money on the fiscal system was this: Computed in paper money the yield from taxes might even increase; but the real income (the purchasing power of the sum received by the State) declined. This resulted from the following causes:

(a) The depreciation of the currency provoked a true and peculiar destruction of taxable wealth, since the income and property of many social classes were diminished and often completely annihilated. It is true that there was some, though not complete, compensation in the increase of the contributive capacity of the classes for whom the depreciation of the currency was the source of conspicuous profits. But the excess profits derived from the depreciation easily escaped the tax-collector.

Moreover, the continual depreciation of the national currency induced all classes of citizens to invest their savings in foreign currencies, bills, securities, etc., which were easily concealed. The "flight of capital," which in Germany assumed the importance of a "mass phenomenon" and which seemingly vigorous restrictions did not succeed in impeding, continually removed much taxable wealth from the power of the German Exchequer.

(b) Between the moment or period of time in which the transaction occurred which gave rise to any financial obligation, and the moment when the transaction was ascertained by the fiscal organizations and the tax was fixed in figures, and again between this moment and that at which the tax was actually paid, there passed varying intervals of time. If in the meantime the circulating medium depreciated, the tax-payers paid a sum whose real value was the lower the longer were the intervals. Acceleration of the assessment of the tax and shortening of the interval between that assessment and the actual payment reduced the loss suffered by the State; but the interval of time could not be completely eliminated; and in periods of very rapid depreciation even a short interval was enough to cause a grave loss to the Exchequer.

(c) The yield of the duties or taxes, reckoned in paper money, was imperfectly adapted to the currency depreciation. For

NATIONAL FINANCES　　　　　67

this purpose it is possible to arrange the taxes in a scale of sensitiveness.

The case of taxes endowed with a maximum degree of sensitiveness, the yield from which varied exactly with the variations of the exchange rate, is exceptional. An instance of such sensitive taxes is given by customs duties, when they are fixed in gold and payable in paper at a "premium" which is fixed on the basis of the daily rate of exchange. When on the other hand, as was the case for a long time in Germany, the premium is fixed at shorter or longer intervals, the adaptation to the rate of exchange is imperfect, even for customs duties. Another example of a most sensitive fiscal income was the stamp duty *ad valorem* on the buying and selling of foreign exchange.

At the other end of the scale are found those taxes or duties which were completely insensitive to the depreciation of the money; for example, all the fiscal charges for legal documents, passports, etc.; all the indirect taxes fixed by the units of weight, volume, or number of packets of the taxed material (as, e.g., the tobacco, sugar, alcohol, and other taxes).

Between these extremes are a great number of taxes whose yield tended to vary with the variation of the internal value of the paper money, which value remained for some years perceptibly higher than the external value. But even here it is necessary to proceed to a subdivision, rendered necessary by the difference, often considerable, between the internal value of the mark, measured by the index number of the wholesale prices, or the internal value of the mark, measured by the index of the cost of living. The yield of some taxes tended to follow the increase in wholesale prices —for example, the income tax inasmuch as it was levied on the industrial or the commercial classes. The yield of other taxes, on the other hand, was adapted to variations in the cost of living, after a short or a long interval—e.g. income tax, inasmuch as it was levied on wages or stipends, which tended to vary with the variations of the index number of the cost of living.

68 THE ECONOMICS OF INFLATION

X. INFLUENCES OF THE DEPRECIATION OF THE MARK
ON THE EXPENDITURE OF THE REICH

22. From the preceding analysis it may be seen how highly relevant was the divergence between the internal and external value of the mark to the management of the German tax system. Since the nominal incomes of numerous social classes were increased more or less in proportion to the diminution of the *internal* value of the mark; and since internal prices, which formed the basis of many taxes (for example, the "Umsatzsteuer"—turnover tax), were increased less than the dollar rate, it would not have been possible to obtain from existing taxes a constant yield, reckoned in gold. But it may be asked: "Was that necessary for the balancing of the Budget?" To reply to this question it is necessary to examine the relation between the monetary depreciation and the expenditure of the State. For expenses, as for receipts, we can make a scale according to their degree of sensitiveness to the depreciation of the mark.

Some expenses varied exactly with the variations of the exchange rate. Such were the expenses incurred by Germany in the payment of cash reparations for the clearing of pre-war debts and credits, for the purchase of cereals abroad, for the maintenance of representatives abroad, etc.

Other expenses increased in proportion to the rise of internal wholesale prices. The most important example is the expenses incurred by the railway administration in the purchase of coal and materials necessary for the renewal and extension of plant and for the purchase of rolling-stock.

Others tended to increase with the rise of the cost of living in Germany; such were expenditure on stipends and wages, and, in part, pensions.

Finally, certain expenses remained quite insensitive to the depreciation of the currency: the principal example is the interest on the public debt. The relief to the national finances on this account was very considerable. Later the State intervened to help financially the small bondholders ("Kleinrentner"), who were ruined by the depreciation of the currency; but the expenses incurred in these subsidies were not even remotely comparable to the burdens which the State Budget would have had to support if the depreciation of the currency had not occurred.

23. What is the final result of all these influences acting, on one hand on the income and on the other on the expenditure? *A priori* the final

NATIONAL FINANCES   69

result cannot be foreseen since it depends on the effective composition of income and expenses according to the categories elucidated above.

As we have seen, the study of the German finances shows that in the second half of 1919 the depreciation of the mark not only produced a diminution of the real value of the receipts but also greatly reduced the expenses, computed in gold marks. That is explained by the fact that in 1919 by far the greater part of the expenditure of the Reich was internal expenditure. Now, prices and wages had not increased in proportion to the depreciation of the mark; indeed in February 1920 the index number of the prices of goods in the United States was more than three times that of gold prices in Germany. Besides, the payments which were constant in paper marks, i.e. the interest on the public debt and pensions, were still a substantial proportion of ordinary expenditure of the Reich.

But later, in the financial year 1922, the situation changed. As we have already observed, from that year onwards, in the periods of depreciation, the receipts reckoned in gold generally diminished more rapidly than the expenditure. The reaction of prices to the new issues of paper money always came quickly—this was especially true of wholesale prices—and therefore even the internal expenses rapidly reflected the influence of the depreciation of the currency, while the receipts increased later and more slowly. Payments of interest on the public debt had now become a negligible quantity. Therefore a disequilibrium between income and expenditure appeared which aggravated the original sad state of the national finances.

24. The facts just referred to also suggest the following considerations. In these years one often heard repeated the belief that Germany's capacity for paying reparations was measured by the mark rate. To this it was justly objected that a country's capacity for payment is measured not by the foreign exchange value of its money, but by its wealth in real goods, by its production, its exports, etc. However, as the question of reparations is not only a problem of the transfer of goods from one country to another, but also a problem of internal finance—it is certain that the depreciation of the mark, creating a divergence between the internal and external value of the German money, made it more difficult for the German Government to obtain from taxes the necessary sum in paper marks for the purchase of the foreign exchange required for the payment of reparations. There existed, therefore, a relation between the depreciation of the mark and

70   THE ECONOMICS OF INFLATION

the German Government's capacity to satisfy its obligations to the
Allies.

XI. THE ERRORS AND WEAKNESSES OF GERMAN FINANCIAL POLICY

25. But could not the German Government have freed the national
finances from the effects of the depreciation of the currency, by
"valorizing" the taxes from the beginning?

It is true that the incomes of certain social classes were less sensitive
to the depreciation of the exchange, but for other classes the depreciation of the currency was the fount of considerable gains. Exporters
sold to the State foreign bills of exchange at high prices, while their
expenses were not increased in proportion. For many industrialists
the rise in the price of foreign exchange implied a large customs
protection which permitted them to raise their prices. Why did not
the German State think from the beginning of making those classes
who had derived great benefits from the depreciation contribute more
largely to the public expenses? For a long time the democratic parties
and representatives of workers' syndicates in vain demanded a reform
in the method of imposing taxes, which would have saved the Exchequer
from heavy losses. Instead, even towards the end of 1922 the Minister
of Finance declared himself opposed to the introduction of a system
which would permit the adaptation of the yield of taxation to the
depreciation of the mark. In the succeeding months, after the very
great fall in the exchange which followed the occupation of the Ruhr,
the question was examined once more. On March 20th, 1923, a law
was published on "the depreciation of money in relation to the fiscal
laws." But, practically, this law did not give to the State efficacious
means of defence against the effects of the depreciation of money,
because it was limited to imposing a fine of 30 per cent of the amount
of the tax on the taxpayer who delayed for more than three months
the payment of tax owed and a fine of 15 per cent for delays less than
three months.

Later other improvements were timidly undertaken; such as the
change, in certain taxes on consumption goods, from fixed rates to a
percentage of the value of the taxed object; the earlier dating of payments on account of income tax and the turnover tax, the abbreviation
of the time allowed for payment, and the obligation to pay interest
on sums paid late.

There were numerous cases of rates of taxes and tariffs which were
in grotesque contrast to the rise in prices. For a long time some obviously

NATIONAL FINANCES

ridiculous taxes and very low tariffs were maintained. For some time the German railways fixed very much lower fares for passengers, among whom were numerous foreigners, than those charged in any other country. For inexplicable motives the German postal authorities for some time charged less than a gold pfennig for the forwarding of letters abroad (letters sent for the most part by merchants, industrialists, and foreigners); and the natural consequence of that system was a very great fall in receipts.*

* From an official publication (*Zahlen zur Geldenwertung*, 1925) I have deduced the following tables which seem to me important documents of the financial policy followed by the German Government during the inflation.

3rd Class Fare (in gold) for one Person, per Kilometre
(1913 = 100)

1- 1-14—31- 3-18 ..	.. 79·2	1- 6-23—30- 6-23 ..	.. 6·4
1- 4-18—31- 3-19 ..	.. 73·9	1- 7-23—31- 7-23 ..	.. 5·9
1- 4-19—30- 9-19 ..	.. 41·5	1- 8-23—19- 8-23 ..	.. 2·3
1-10-19—29- 2-20 ..	.. 18·3	20- 8-23—31- 8-23 ..	.. 10·7
1- 3-20—31- 5-21 ..	.. 33·4	1- 9-23—10- 9-23 ..	.. 9·3
1- 6-21—30-11-21 ..	.. 21·9	11- 9-23—17- 9-23 ..	.. 7·3
1-12-21—31- 1-22 ..	.. 18·5	18- 9-23—24- 9-23 ..	.. 27·0
1- 2-22—30- 9-22 ..	.. 11·1	25- 9-23— 1-10-23 ..	.. 58·4
1-10-22—31-10-22 ..	.. 3·0	2-10-23— 9-10-23 ..	.. 21·1
1-11-22—30-11-22 ..	.. 2·6	10-10-23—12-10-23 ..	.. 6·9
1-12-22—31-12-22 ..	.. 5·0	13-10-23—17-10-23 ..	.. 12·4
1- 1-23—31- 1-23 ..	.. 4·7	18-10-23—24-10-23 ..	.. 7·1
1-2 -23—28- 2-23 ..	.. 6·0	25-10-23—28-10-23 ..	.. 10·7
1- 3-23—31- 5-23 ..	.. 10·8	29-10-23—31-10-23 ..	.. 41·0

This table shows that in certain periods the railway passenger fares were, in gold, scarcely 2–3 per cent of the pre-war fares! It was objected that it was difficult for the railways to adapt their tariffs to the rapid monetary depreciation. But other companies—e.g. the Berlin Electric Tram Company—adapted their tariffs, if not perfectly, at least in a large measure to the depreciation of the money; and it is impossible to understand why the railways could not do the same.

The following table shows that the postal tariffs for some time were, if reckoned in gold, 1 per cent of the pre-war tariff:

Price (in gold) for Franking a Letter for Home Delivery
(1913 = 100)

1- 1-14—31- 7-16 ..	.. 88·3	1- 7-23—31- 7-23 ..	.. 3·6
1- 8-16—30- 9-19 ..	.. 78·5	1- 8-23—23- 8-23 ..	.. 1·2
1-10-19— 5- 5-20 ..	.. 14·0	24- 8-23—31- 8-23 ..	.. 11·1
6- 5-20—31- 3-21 ..	.. 29·0	1- 9-23—19- 9-23 ..	.. 4·1
1- 4-21—31-12-22 ..	.. 21·3	20- 9-23—30- 9-23 ..	.. 7·4
1- 1-22—30- 6-22 ..	.. 31·8	1-10-23— 9-10-23 ..	.. 14·0
1- 7-22—30- 9-22 ..	.. 12·2	10-10-23—19-10-23 ..	.. 3·7
1-10-22—14-11-22 ..	.. 5·7	20-10-23—31-10-23 ..	.. 0·7
15-11-22—14-12-22 ..	.. 6·5	1-11-23— 4-11-23 ..	.. 1·4
15-12-22—14- 1-23 ..	.. 13·2	5-11-23—11-11-23 ..	.. 7·5
15- 1-23—28- 2-23 ..	.. 7·9	12-11-23—30-11-23 ..	.. 13·3
1- 3-23—30 -6-23 ..	.. 8·1	1-12-23—31-12-23 ..	.. 100·0

72   THE ECONOMICS OF INFLATION

It was only on August 20th, 1923, that the system of increasing the railway fares little by little at varying intervals was abandoned. The multiplication system was adopted. But since a given multiplicator always remained in force for a certain number of days, it was reduced by lagging much behind the rise in the dollar. Railway fares fixed in gold and payable in paper marks at the rate of the previous day were only introduced on November 1st, 1923; tariffs of "constant values" were adopted for the telegraph and telephone services on November 15th, and for postal service on December 1st, 1923.

Even in the summer of 1923—at a time of a very rapid depreciation of the mark—the amount of the tax on wages remained on the average about a fortnight in the hands of the entrepreneurs before being paid into the Exchequer. The entrepreneurs thus used for their advantage a great part of the tax effectively paid by the working classes. The amount of the tax on turnover (Umsatzsteuer) which industrialists and merchants collected from the purchaser at the moment of the sale, was paid a month after the end of each quarter. Even in July 1923 the Railway Administration allowed frequent delays of payment. One must admit this policy of negligence and remissness in the face of the interests of influential groups did much to aggravate the inflation.

26. In the second half of August 1923 the Minister, Cuno, some days before his dismissal, presented some proposals for new taxes. It was a belated attempt to stop, by means of an increase of receipts, the fall of the mark and to repair the errors of the financial policy inaugurated after the occupation of the Ruhr, the policy which had neglected to create the sources of income necessary for financing Passive Resistance. The new "brutal" taxes (as they were called) at first aroused grave prejudice in industrial, commercial, and banking circles. Foreign exchange, securities, and goods were offered on the market by those who had not the liquid resources necessary for the payment of the new taxes. For a brief moment the dollar rate eased and prices of securities fell. But the continued increase of the note-issues and large concessions of credit on the part of the Reichsbank quickly robbed the fiscal reforms of their efficacy. The dollar rate renewed its upward swing and the real value of the sum due to be paid in taxes lessened daily, thanks to the very rapid depreciation of the currency. The last battle fought by the German Government on fiscal ground, to curb the descent of the mark, was definitely lost.

NATIONAL FINANCES   73

27. Only when the disintegration of the monetary system was already complete did the Government decide to "valorize" the payments of those taxes which were collected in arrear, it being prescribed that contributors should pay a sum in paper marks equivalent to the gold value due on the tax claim on the day the tax obligation was incurred. (Order of October 11th, 1923.) The coefficients by which the original sum had to be multiplied were fixed periodically. But even now the valorization was incomplete, since the coefficients were perceptibly below the level corresponding to the depreciation of the mark. For example, for the period from October 17th to 19th, the multiplicator was fixed at 1·08 milliards of paper marks, although the gold mark rate on October 17th was already 1·3 milliards and on the 19th about 2·9 milliards. Then on the insistence of the agriculturists the coefficient was reduced to 936 millions for the days October 20th to 23rd, although the gold mark rate had risen in the meantime to 13·3 milliards! On the 23rd the coefficient was raised to 13·3 milliards, but the gold mark rate was already 15 milliards. At the same time the Finance Officials wasted time and material in exacting very small amounts—amounts much less than the expenses of collecting the money. For example, in October 1923 a passport for the Polish frontier cost only two paper marks!!

In the last phase of the inflation the system of "coefficients" no longer protected the State against the diminution of receipts caused by the depreciation of the circulating medium; indeed, if payment should merely be delayed for a day or two, or if the marks received should remain for a short time in the State Treasury, the latter was bound to suffer heavy losses.

The German fiscal system continued to be based (except in cases cited in the footnote) on the paper mark until the Order of December 19th, 1923, which definitely substituted for it the gold mark, in the fixing of tariffs and in the valuation of taxable goods.*

* In this note are indicated the dates of the most important laws according to which the gold mark was gradually substituted for the paper mark in the German fiscal system.

The law of March 20th, 1923, marked the beginning of a long series of laws or decrees having as their object the adaptation of the fiscal system to the depreciation of the currency. We record the following measures: Decree of March 22nd on the surcharges on customs duties; decree June 5th on automobile tax; laws of July 9th regarding taxes on sugar, matches, beer, salt, and playing cards. Another law of July 9th fixed a system of co-efficients for applying to the interim payments of taxes; but they became insufficient almost at once because of the rapid depreciation of the mark. Also there were: the decree of July 9th regarding the assessment of taxes on export; the law of August 11th about the duties on beer, sugar, salt, matches, coal, mineral waters, etc.; the law of August 11th concerning the tax on industrial and

c*

74 THE ECONOMICS OF INFLATION

28. Do not let us under-estimate the difficulties with which an energetic policy would have had to contend at a time when the exchange rate of the mark was exposed to influence, independent of the financial policy, which provoked continual fluctuations in the exchange rate. But the weakness of the State in the face of the great economic groups, the complications of the German fiscal system, the delay in the collection of taxes and the lack of arrangement for the adaptation of the taxes to the depreciation of the mark, aggravated the financial situation. It is evident from the dates of the decrees referred to in the preceding paragraphs that the measures taken to obviate the dangerous repressions of the depreciation of the money on the income of the State were too late and incomplete.* Consequently, in October 1923 an extraordinary phenomenon in the history of the public finance appeared, *the complete atrophy of the fiscal system.* In the last decade of that month the ordinary receipts covered about 0·8 per cent of the expenses; the State now obtained money exclusively through the discount of Treasury bills.

In the December issue of *Wirtschaft und Statistik*, 1923, some interesting calculations were published of the amount in gold of the yield from taxes and of the other receipts of the State, derived from loans and by the discount of Treasury bills. For the period from 1914 to October 1923 the total results are as follows: taxes, 21·2 milliards; loans, 52·6 milliards; Treasury bills, 59·1 milliards. These statistics clearly display the financial policy followed by the German Government for ten years, which resulted in scarcely 15 per cent of the expenses being covered by means of taxes!

agricultural concerns, a tax payable in gold or in paper according to a co-efficient fixed every Thursday for the week and operating from the following Saturday (this was the first tax fixed on the gold basis); the law of August 11th regarding the increase of the co-efficients fixed for the interim payments of the tax on income and on companies; the decree of September 27th which suppressed, for delayed payments of taxes on income and on companies and for the Ruhrtax, the system of fixed co-efficients, substituting for it the system of a multiplicator fixed each week; the decree of October 11th on the valorization of debts of a fiscal character. The decree of October 17th fixed some specific rates of tax in gold marks on sugar, salt, matches, and playing cards. That of October 3rd decreed that the tax on tobacco should be reckoned and charged on the gold basis. Those of November 9th and 26th and December 7th put on a gold basis the taxes on automobiles, beer, business turnover, and the Ruhr tax. Finally, the decree of December 19th transformed the entire fiscal system, putting it on a gold basis both in assessment and in collection.

* An obscure point in the financial history of post-war Germany is the financial administration of the States. The Budgets of the States were not less disturbed than that of the Reich. The Reich had to intervene continually with subsidies and contribution of various kinds.

PART II

I. THE POLICY OF THE REICHSBANK

1. To the "governmental" inflation, provoked by continual demands made on the Reichsbank by the State, was added a second form of inflation, which Germans called "private," that is, the creation of paper money for business men.

The credit policy adopted by the Reichsbank was based on the idea that a "private" inflation could not occur if the Reichsbank remained faithful to the strict rule of allowing for discount only "commercial" bills, excluding "financial" bills. It would then be certain, if affirmed, that no notes or, in general, credit concessions, would be issued in a measure greater than was necessary and that a normal "reflux" of notes to the bank would be established. Thus old errors were revived.*

The Reichsbank did not recognize that, in a period of continuous "governmental" inflation, and consequently a rise in prices, the rigorous distinction between commercial and financial bills, even if it were practically possible, was not a sufficient guarantee against the danger of a "private" inflation. At a time when prices are rising because of the governmental inflation, the amount of notes issued by the Reichsbank to satisfy the demands of trade must surpass the reflux of notes previously issued. Let us suppose that when the price level is 100 the demand for short-term credit is 1,000. If prices rise later to 120, demand will tend to reach 1,200. At the same time notes for the amount of 1,000 are returned; the reflux will be lower by 200 than the new issues. Moreover, the demand for new credit is stimulated by the prospect of a continual rise in prices.

Consequently, the optimism with which the management of the Reichsbank for a long time considered the concession of credits to private individuals was quite unjustified. It did not realize that the extension of bank credits, like the issue of notes on account of the State, profited some classes and imposed loss on others. It did not realize that there was an abnormal demand for credit, to limit which

---

* Errors exposed by Thornton, *An Enquiry into the Nature and Effects of the Paper Credit of Great Britain*, London, 1802, p. 285.

it was necessary to adapt the discount rate to the rate of the depreciation of the paper mark.

The official discount rate in Germany had remained fixed (at 5 per cent) from 1915 until July 1922. Until the summer of 1922 the Reichsbank exercised, almost exclusively, the function of a State bank, discounting Treasury bills presented to it. The increasing needs of trade were satisfied by private banks, who secured the means by discounting at the Reichsbank the Treasury bills in which they had largely invested the money of depositors during and after the war. At the end of 1920, 25 per cent of the total value of Treasury bills was held by the eight great banks of Berlin, which had invested 60 per cent of their deposits in that way.

But in the summer of 1922 the Reichsbank began to supply directly to commerce and industry the financial means, the need of which, in that period of credit crisis, was urgently felt. To mitigate this crisis the Reichsbank insistently counselled the business classes to have recourse to the creation of commercial bills,* which it declared itself ready to discount at a much lower rate than the rate of the depreciation of the mark, and even than the rates charged by private banks.

Indeed the official discount rate was 6 per cent at the end of July 1922; it was raised to 7 per cent at the end of August; to 8 per cent on September 21st; 10 per cent on November 13th; 12 per cent on January 18th, 1923; and 18 per cent in the last week of April 1923. It is enough to compare these rates with the increase in the dollar rate (a gold mark was worth 160 paper marks at the end of July 1922; 411 paper marks at the end of August, 1,822 at the end of November; and 7,100 at the end of April 1923) to be convinced that the policy of the Reichsbank could not but give a strong stimulus to the demand for credit and to the inflation.† Here are some figures: on June 30th, 1922, the value of the commercial bills in the portfolio of the Reichsbank amounted to 4·8 milliard marks, while its holding of Treasury bills amounted to 186·1 milliard marks. On December 30th of the same year the total of commercial bills had risen to 422·2 milliards, representing about a third of the amount of the Treasury bills (1,184·5

---

* Since the outbreak of the war the commercial bill had fallen into disuse, owing to the spread of cheque payments.

† Prion, *Deutsche Kreditpolitik*, 1919-23—in "Jahrbuch" of Schmöller, 1924, vol. ii, p. 189.

NATIONAL FINANCES   77

milliards). On February 15th, 1923, the amount of commercial bills
(1,345 milliards) had reached almost 60 per cent of the holding of the
Treasury bills (2,301). Hence, besides the governmental inflation,
there had developed a very great banking inflation. On November 15th,
1923, the value of the commercial bills in the portfolio of the Reichsbank amounted to 39·5 trillion marks (a trillion = 1,000,000³). At
the same time deposits on current account at the Reichsbank had also
increased very rapidly.*

2. In Reichsbank circles it was denied that a rise in the discount
rate could exercise a depressing influence on the inflation, and on
prices. On the contrary, such people were more ready to consider a
rise in the discount rate as a cause of the rise in the costs of production
and therefore of prices. Rather than raise the discount rate it was
thought more appropriate to apply a certain rationing of credits, only
the more deserving firms being allowed to benefit therefrom.† But
such a method favoured a privileged class, to whom the Reichsbank
presented enormous sums of money, to the detriment of classes to
whom the depreciation of the mark was disadvantageous. People who
enjoyed the favour of the Reichsbank could make sure of purchasing
goods and foreign exchange. Speculation against the mark was in such
ways financed by bank credits.‡ The credit policy adopted by the
Reichsbank reinforced the effects of the "governmental" inflation and
helped to accelerate the fall of the mark, which, indeed, had never
been so rapid as it became after the summer of 1922.§

* Deposits on Current Account: 32·9 milliards on December 31st, 1921; 33·4
milliards on March 31st, 1922; 37·2 milliards on June 30th, 1922; 530·5 milliards on
December 30th, 1922; 1,165 milliards on February 15th, 1922; 129·6 trillion on
November 15, 1923.

  † In the jubilee volume, *Die Reichsbank, 1901–1925*, Berlin, 1926, the Directors of
the German note-issuing authority attempted to justify themselves against the accusation of having favoured inflation, by asserting that in 1922 and 1923 credit was made
available to clients for economically profitable objects. Credits were not granted which
would have been used to buy gold or foreign bills, with speculative intentions, or for
the purpose of acquiring goods other than the normal necessities of business or to
make up the deficiency of fixed capital. Experience showed that it was not practically
possible to apply a rigorous distinction between legitimate and non-legitimate credits.

  ‡ "The Reichsbank was persuaded to give exceedingly liberal credit concessions
by the laments of the industrialists, who stated that they could not otherwise pay the
salaries and wages of their employees. But if those industrialists had not invested their
available means in goods, securities, and foreign bills, they would not have been
embarrassed."—Pinner in the *Berliner Tageblatt* of February 9th, 1923.

  § In Reichsbank circles it was maintained that the granting of credit to the manu-

78 THE ECONOMICS OF INFLATION

To the credits granted by the Reichsbank it is also necessary to add those of the "Loan Offices" which at certain times were appreciable (they amounted to 252 milliard paper marks at the end of 1922).

3. The policy of the Reichsbank was severely criticized when a committee in the spring of 1923 investigated the causes of the fall of the mark.* The deputy Hertz calculated the presumed profits of those who had taken money on credit on January 1st, 1923, and restored the same after the collapse of the mark, and concluded that it was the Reichsbank itself which had offered to speculators the possibility of counteracting the action for the support of the mark.

It was suggested to the Reichsbank that it should remove the possibility of unjust profits for those to whom it advanced money by compelling the debtor to pay back a sum in paper marks having the same *real value* as the sum taken on loan. The real value could be calculated by means of the rate of exchange or the index number of wholesale prices. But only towards the middle of August 1923 did the President of the Reichsbank announce the adoption of the principle of loans at a "constant value," and commence to apply that principle. The debtor had then to restore the sum received plus four-fifths of the sum corresponding to the amount of the depreciation of the mark, which was calculated on the basis of the sterling exchange rate. If, for example, he had received 1,000 and the sterling exchange rate had risen from 100 to 150, he had to repay 1,400. The "depreciation clause," at first only applied to the advances, was extended, as from the beginning of December 1923, also to the discount of bills of exchange. Until at the

---

facturers was a compensation for the losses of working capital which they had suffered because of the depreciation of the mark. On this point it may be observed that in the summer of 1922, in general, business men had learned to discount in the paper prices the risk of the future depreciation of the paper mark. This is also the opinion of Professor Prion, who thus summarizes the methods adopted by German business men in the second half of 1922: (*a*) the fixing of sale prices on the basis of the cost of "reproduction"; (*b*) the purchaser was obliged to pay in cash on the consigning of the goods; (*c*) recourse, in a large measure, to credit from the Reichsbank. "In reality," concludes Prion, "the object of these methods, the preservation of working capital, was more than achieved, thanks to the courteous invitation of the Reichsbank to discount commercial bills" (Prion, *Deutsche Kreditpolitik*, 1919–23—in "Jahrbuch" of Schmöller, 1924, vol. ii, p. 195).

* An impressive criticism of the policy of the Reichsbank was made by Professor Hirsch in the article "Falsche Kreditpolitik" published in the review *Plutus* of August 1st, 1923.

NATIONAL FINANCES   79

end of January 1924 short-term credits of the Reichsbank were usually issued with this clause.*

Thus the banking policy also, like the financial policy, was characterized by errors in the interpretation of monetary phenomena, by excessive indulgence to the interests of influential groups, and by tardy—and consequently ineffective—innovations. Banking policy was a fundamental cause of the paper inflation and consequently of the depreciation of the mark.

II. THE APPARENT SCARCITY OF THE CIRCULATING MEDIUM

4. The supporters of the theory that the depreciation of the mark was the consequence of events independent of the financial policy of the German Government and of the inflation, stated that the *chronological order* of the phenomena connected with the depreciation of the money confirmed their theories.

The depreciation of the German mark did not proceed in a uniform manner. There were times when depreciation was slow or the exchange was maintained almost stable. Suddenly, often following some political event, the demand for foreign currencies became intense and the exchanges rapidly depreciated. Then, unexpectedly, the money market would settle down and there would be a reaction in the exchange; but generally the latter would remain at a level appreciably higher than before. Then a new period of relative stabilization or of slow depreciation was recommenced, which later was followed by another sudden depreciation of the German currency. These sudden changes from a given level of the price of the dollar to a much higher one occurred, for example, in the autumn of 1921; in July 1922, and in January and

---

* According to the Reichsbank Report for 1923 the interest rates per annum charged in the second half of 1923 were as follows:

Discount on Bills	*Advances*
(*a*) For credits without the "depreciation clause": August 2nd–September 14th, 30 per cent; September 15th–December 31st, 90 per cent.	(*a*) For advances without the "depreciation clause": August 2nd–September 14th, 31 per cent; September 15th–October 7th, 31 per cent (plus a commission of ⅓ per cent per day); October 8th–December 31st, 108 per cent.
(*b*) For "stable value" credits from December 29th, 10 per cent.	(*b*) For "stable value" advances September 15th–December 28th, 10 per cent; from December 28th, 12 per cent.

80   THE ECONOMICS OF INFLATION

July 1923. The sudden falls of the mark which happened at these times were not *immediately* preceded by comparable increases of the issues of paper money.

We must admit that some of the facts which were observed in the last phases of the depreciation of the mark seem to give support to those who deny that the inflation was at the root of the matter.

The characteristic of those last phases was the very close connection between the exchange rate and domestic prices. (See Diagrams VI and VII.) A rise in the exchange spread almost immediately to all prices; not only to those of imported articles but also to purely domestic goods; and to both wholesale and retail prices. The sole preoccupation of industrialists, wholesale, or retail merchants at the time was the dollar rate. An increase in wages, salaries, and fees immediately followed the rise in prices.

5. So long as the disturbance of the exchange exercised only a slow and partial influence on prices, an improvement of the exchange itself was possible and was actually experienced sometimes. But when internal prices, thanks mainly to the influence of psychological causes, commenced to adapt themselves immediately to the sudden increases in the dollar rate, the depreciation of the exchange tended to become permanent because the rise of internal prices quickly established a new level of exchange equilibrium.

The sudden rise of prices caused an intense demand for the circulating medium to arise, because the existing quantity was not sufficient for the volume of transactions. At the same time the State's need of money increased rapidly. Private banks, besieged by their clients, found it practically impossible to meet the demand for money. They had to ration the cashing of cheques presented to them. On some days they declared that they were obliged to suspend payments or open their offices for a few hours only. Panic seized the industrial and commercial classes, who were no longer in a position to fulfil their contracts. Private cheques were refused because it was known that the banks would be unable to cash them. Business was stopped. The panic spread to the working classes when they learned that their employers had not the cash with which to pay their wages.

The economic system reacted to this scarcity of the circulating medium; new forms of credit were invented. In the summer of 1923, when the scarcity of money was most acute, the Berlin banks decided to issue a kind of cheque which was to be acceptable at their branches

NATIONAL FINANCES

and which was also willingly accepted by the public, who were desirous of having any means of payment whatever. Private firms, industrial companies, combines, and public authorities issued every kind of provisional money.

But all these expedients were not sufficient to satisfy the great need of money provoked by the enormous rise in prices, and the eyes of all were turned to the Reichsbank. The pressure exercised on it became more and more insistent and the increase of issues, from the central bank, appeared as a remedy.

These phenomena, which appeared in Germany after a sharp rise in the exchange, made the increase of issues appear as unavoidable as the inevitable consequence of the rise of prices which had been provoked by the depreciation of the exchange. The opinion, on this subject, formed in administrative circles, is clearly expressed in the following words of Helfferich: "To follow the good counsel of stopping the printing of notes would mean—as long as the causes which are upsetting the German exchange continue to operate—refusing to economic life the circulating medium necessary for transactions, payments of salaries and wages, etc., it would mean that in a very short time the entire public, and above all the Reich, could no longer pay merchants, employees, or workers. In a few weeks, besides the printing of notes, factories, mines, railways and post office, national and local government, in short, all national and economic life would be stopped."*

The authorities therefore had not the courage to resist the pressure of those who demanded ever greater quantities of paper money, and to face boldly the crisis which (although painted in unduly dark colours by Helfferich) would be, undeniably, the result of a stoppage of the issue of notes. They preferred to continue the convenient method of continually increasing the issues of notes, thus making the continuation of business possible, but at the same time prolonging the pathological state of the German economy. The Government increased salaries in proportion to the depreciation of the mark, and employers in their turn granted continual increases in wages, to avoid disputes, on the condition that they could raise the prices of their products. A characteristic example of this is given by the discussions of the "Coal Council," where employers and employed easily came to agreement on the basis of higher wages and correspondingly higher coal prices.

Thus was the vicious circle established: the exchange depreciated; internal prices rose; note-issues were increased; the increase of the

* *Das Geld*, p. 650.

quantity of paper money lowered once more the value of the mark in terms of gold; prices rose once more; and so on.

III. THE INCREASE IN THE ISSUES OF PAPER MONEY

6. Certainly the difficulties with which the Government and the Reichsbank had to wrestle in the last phases of the depreciation of the mark were very serious. It is certain that the rise in home prices, which was the immediate consequence of the depreciation of the exchange, had given a definite thrust to the increase of note issues and of the floating debt.

But it is important not to forget that that last stage of the depreciation of the mark was, in a great part, the direct consequence of an erroneous financial policy in the preceding years. Besides, the increase of the note-issues, following the increase of home prices, was not at all a *necessary* action, as some writers seem to believe. An energetic financial and monetary policy and a more circumspect banking policy would have broken the vicious circle; as in fact it was broken by the monetary reform of November 1923.

Instead, for a long time the Reichsbank—having adopted the fatalistic idea that the increase in the note-issues was the inevitable consequence of the depreciation of the mark—considered as its principal task, not the regulation of the circulation, but the preparation for the German economy of the continually increasing quantities of paper money which the rise in prices required. It devoted itself especially to the organization, on a large scale, of the production of paper marks.

Towards the end of October 1923 the special paper used for the notes was made in thirty paper mills. The printing works of the Reich, in spite of its great equipment, was no longer sufficient for the needs of the Reichsbank; about a hundred private presses, in Berlin and the provinces, were continually printing notes for the Reichsbank. There, in the dispatch departments, a thousand women and girls were occupied exclusively in checking the number of notes contained in the packets sent out by the printing press. One of the more extraordinary documents in the history of the German inflation is the memorandum of the Reichsbank, published in the daily papers of October 25th, 1923. In this the issuing institution announced that during the day notes to the total value of 120,000 billions of paper marks had been stamped (a billion $= 1,000,000^2$). But the demand during the day had been for about a trillion ($1,000,000^3$). The Reichsbank announced that it would do its utmost to satisfy the demand and expressed the hope that towards the end of the week the daily production would be raised to half a trillion!

PART III

I. THE DEPRECIATION OF THE MARK AND THE DISEQUILIBRIUM
OF THE BALANCE OF TRADE

1. I have already said that, according to an opinion widely held in Germany, the passive balance of trade was the first and fundamental cause which during the war had already provoked the depreciation of the value of the mark in terms of foreign currencies. After the outbreak of the war the publication of trade statistics ceased; but the Government did not refrain from informing the public that the balance of trade showed a grave disequilibrium.

Later, the excess of imports over exports (including the imports effected on account of the allies) was valued by the Statistical Bureau of the Reich at 15 milliard gold marks, for the period from August 1st, 1914, to the end of 1918.

Obviously, in this argument and in this pretended statistical proof there is much confusion of ideas. If at a given exchange rate between the mark and foreign money the demand for the latter exceeds the supply, the mark is depreciated, and that tends, other things being equal, to re-establish the equilibrium between imports and exports. If, instead, statistics show that for the whole of a long period imports have exceeded exports, it shows that the excess has been compensated for by other items in the balance of payments, such as foreign credits, and sale of stocks and shares; for how, otherwise, could the excessive imports have been paid for?

On the other hand, not even the "Purchasing Power Parity Doctrine" (although certainly more satisfactory than the "adverse balance of payments theory") gives a complete explanation of the foreign exchanges. (See Appendix to this chapter.)

The principal point on which one must insist is this: In a great country like Germany, endowed with vast resources and with a great variety of imports and exports—on which variety was based, even during the war, a considerable elasticity of foreign demand for German products, and of German demand for foreign goods*—a depreciation of the exchanges, when it is provoked only by an increase in the demand for foreign goods, cannot go beyond a certain limit (let us say 15, 20, or 30 per cent of parity) because compensatory forces which the

---

* Rist, *op. cit.*, p. 178.

84   THE ECONOMICS OF INFLATION

depreciation raises prevent it from passing beyond this limit. Although the increase in the demand for foreign goods may be the cause of an initial depreciation of the market exchange, it cannot explain the *continual* depreciation. To explain the *continual* depreciation in this fashion it would be necessary to assume that the real demand curve for foreign goods was moved continually towards the right (see diagrams in the aforesaid Appendix). But that is scarcely probable; besides, the reactions which would arrest the depreciation of the exchange would quickly appear.

2. It is impossible to prove how far the excess of imports over exports during the war was caused by *independent* movements of the international demand for goods; and how far, on the other hand, the movements of Germany's demand curve for foreign goods and of the foreigners' demand curve for German goods were the effect of a rise in the German home prices, provoked by the monetary inflation (see Appendix).

It is doubtful if the theoretical scheme, described in the Appendix, is applicable to the abnormal conditions of the German economy during the war. It may, however, be observed that even at a time when goods traffic and foreign transactions are controlled and limited by restrictions,a disequilibrium between internal and external prices cannot but exercise an influence on the exchange rate. As Diehl (a writer who would not admit the influence of the inflation on the exchange) himself observed, after the outbreak of the war: "*Thanks to the rising prices of many goods in Germany, it was profitable to buy these goods in neutral countries and resell them in Germany.* German buyers went to the neutral countries, carrying with them great quantities of German notes, with the object of doing business of this kind and in this way they depressed the German exchange."*

Those who deny the influence of the rise in home prices on the mark exchange maintain that the causes which determined the prices of goods and the exchange rate respectively were completely different. They argued: the Swiss, Danes, Dutch, etc., who bought marks on the exchanges, did so, not in order to buy German goods but to satisfy their obligations to Germany. Hence these people were not affected by the general level of prices in Germany; the price of bills of exchange payable in marks depended on the demand and supply of those bills.

The weakness of this argument is obvious: the supply and demand

---

* Diehl, *Ueber Fragen des Geldwesens und der Valuta*, Jena, 1921, p. 46.

NATIONAL FINANCES

for foreign bills of exchange, existing at a given moment, were the result of preceding transactions; and exports from Germany were the more discouraged and imports were the more stimulated the higher rose the level of German prices.

Further, it is not true that neutrals bought marks only to pay the debts they owed to Germans. From the outbreak of the war Germany began to pay for her imports partly with marks, which the vendor put aside, hoping for a future rise in the German exchange. Or he opened a credit account in marks at a German bank. As Professor Beckerath rightly observes,* for the foreigner the value of the German mark, now off the gold standard, was measured by the quantity of goods which he could buy with marks, that is, it depended on the German prices of exportable goods. Indeed, many foreign speculators, who had acquired large quantities of marks, proposed to keep them in the hope of the mark exchange rate improving, but to change them quickly for German goods directly the rate had shown signs of depreciating. Thus the internal value of the mark had to be taken into consideration by those speculators. If, for example, German home prices had increased from 100 to 120, the foreign exporter could no longer sell his goods at 100, but had to raise his price in proportion. But that meant a depreciation of the mark relatively to foreign money.

3. According to the Statistical Bureau of the Reich the principal items of the balance of payments during the war were as follows:

TABLE X

Debit Items

(Milliards of gold marks)

Imports of goods into Germany	23
Imports on account of Allied countries	4
	27

Credit Items

(Milliards of gold marks)

Exports of goods	12
Exports of gold .. ..·.	1
Sales of German securities	1
Sales of foreign securities	3
Credits (of which 3 to 4 milliards in terms of foreign currency, the rest in marks)	10
	27

* *Die Markvaluta*, 1920, p. 11.

86 THE ECONOMICS OF INFLATION

II. THE BALANCE OF PAYMENTS AFTER THE END OF THE WAR

4. The German trade journals relate that in the months following the Armistice there was a "goods famine." Great quantities of foodstuffs and raw materials were imported, and therewith stocks, which after the long war were totally exhausted, were replenished. To the imports recorded in the official statistics must be added an unknown but certainly a considerable quantity of goods (especially luxury articles such as cigarettes, chocolates, wines, spirits, etc.) which penetrated into Germany through the "hole" which the occupation of the Rhineland made in the German customs belt. On the other hand the political disorder caused by defeat and revolution, the difficulties of reestablishing commercial relations which the economic blockade had broken, and the impossibility of reorganizing in a day the great industries which for many years had directed all their energy to the production of war goods, impeded in the first months of 1919 a rapid renewal of exports.

Towards the end of 1919 and in the following years, exports increased, but on the whole slowly. According to an estimate of the Statistical Bureau, the disequilibrium between imports and exports amounted, in the four years 1919–1922, to 11 milliard gold marks.

To the disequilibrium between imports and exports was added the influence of the payments which Germany had to make for reparations, for the settlement of private debts and credits, for various inter-allied commissions, and for the repayment of old loans, etc. Moreover, all those credit items (particularly the income from German foreign investments, estimated at about 25 milliard marks) which before the war covered the deficit in the balance of trade, had either diminished or completely disappeared.

In the absence of foreign credits the deficit in the balance of payments was covered, for the most part, by the sale of marks, which for a long time, in spite of bitter past experience, foreign speculators bought in considerable quantities, thinking that the extreme limit of the depreciation was reached. The reports of the banks showed, for the beginning of 1919, great sales of marks and a continuous and very marked rise in deposits by foreigners.* It was the creation of new

---

* The Committee of Experts which, in 1924, made an investigation of the mark credit balances on foreign account in the principal banks of Germany from the end of 1918 to the end of 1923, found that there had been during this five-year period more than a million individual accounts of this kind (*The Experts' Plan for Reparation Payments*, published by the Reparations Commission, p. 125).

NATIONAL FINANCES 87

marks which made it possible to purchase goods abroad beyond the limit set by the value of exports. When foreigners ceased to buy German marks the excess of imports rapidly diminished.*

5. It is not possible to say, on the basis of German trade statistics (which, as we shall see later, are most inaccurate), when the equilibrium of Germany's trade balance was re-established. In 1922 imports, calculated on 1913 prices, amounted to 6·211 million gold marks and exports to 6·199 millions.

From many facts and from opinions of competent authorities it appears that in 1922 (a year in which reparation payments were very small and when exports had increased) the condition of the balance of payments became favourable,† thanks to the expenditure of the numerous travellers who visited Germany in that year, to the activities of the shipping companies, and to the sale of securities, mortgages, houses, land, *objets d'art*, etc. At that time the depreciation of the mark not only continued but did so more rapidly than ever before.

In the months of January to October 1923, according to the calculations of the Statistical Bureau of the Reich, imports amounted to 5,155 million marks and exports to 5,024 millions. But these figures are incomplete, because they include the foreign trade of the occupied territories only in so far as goods destined for them, or provided by them, had to cross non-occupied territory.

III. ABNORMAL CONDITIONS OF THE FOREIGN EXCHANGE MARKET

6. It was alleged in Germany that the favourable conditions of the balance of payments in 1922 could not exercise a beneficial influence on the German exchange because a great amount of foreign exchange was hoarded instead of being offered on the market. To this abnormal shortening of the supply of foreign bills there corresponded a similar abnormal expansion in the demand.

---

* Even in 1922, despite the fact that the great depreciation of the mark had already caused enormous losses to foreign possessors of German money, the sales of marks abroad continued. According to a German official publication (*Deutschlands Wirtschaftslage*, Berlin, 1923), even in October 1922 the quantity of paper marks sold through some few foreign banking houses amounted to 22 milliards.

† See *Plutus* of August 1st, 1923. Also Eucken, *Kritische Betrachtungen zum deutschen Geldproblem*, 1923, p. 15, and Lansburg, "Die Zahlungsbilanz," in *Bank*, July 1923. The latter maintains that in 1922, after exports, the expenditure by foreign travellers represented the most important credit item of the German balance of payments.

The disequilibrium between the demand and supply of foreign bills was the result of the following factors:

(*a*) Having little faith in the political and economic future of Germany and desiring to avoid taxes, German industrialists formed the habit of leaving abroad a part of the profits from exports; that is, the difference between the cost of production and the price which they received by selling abroad.

(*b*) Even a great part of the foreign money which was obtained by the sale of securities, houses, land, etc., was either left abroad (the "flight of capital") or hoarded at home, so that it did not come on to the exchange market.

(*c*) The numerous decrees which surrounded the buying of foreign exchange with difficulties, helped to lessen the supply because the possessor of foreign exchange would not give it up at any price, fearing that he would be unable to re-purchase it later when the need arose. If the authorities wished to relieve the foreign exchange market by prohibiting the purchase of foreign exchange by persons who were not traders, it was necessary to supplement the measures restricting the purchase of foreign exchange by issuing stable value securities which would offer to possessors of paper marks the possibility of investing their savings safely. This was the opinion of financial writers: but the proposal was not accepted because it was feared that, following a further depreciation of the mark, the Reich would have to bear at that too heavy a burden when it had to redeem the securities. But this argument was groundless, because the issue of a stable-value loan should have formed part of a general plan for the stabilization of the mark.

(*d*) There was a brisk demand for foreign exchange on the part of German possessors of paper marks. More and more, as the mark depreciated, the phenomenon was understood by the public and the mark ceased to be wanted as a "store of value." The mark balances of industrial firms and even of private persons were converted into shares and into foreign exchange. A considerable amount of foreign exchange was therefore continually withdrawn from the market for the purpose of more or less permanent investment. At certain times, as in October 1921, July and August 1922, and in January 1923 after the occupation of the Ruhr, the purchase of foreign exchange by the public assumed the proportions of a pathological phenomenon. The feverish acquisition of foreign exchange explained in great part the rapid fall of the mark which occurred at these periods. The situation

NATIONAL FINANCES　　　89

of the foreign exchange market then appeared completely dominated by the purchases of the public, which were the consequence of the panic created by political events.

The very rapid and sharp depreciation of the mark was mainly at those times due to psychological causes, operating especially in Germany. Indeed, it was observed at those times that the impetus for the rise of the dollar originated in the German bourses and not in foreign markets, where the mark was generally quoted at a rate somewhat higher than that in Berlin. No one could blame the German investors, who sought to escape the consequences of the depreciation of the mark, by buying foreign exchange. After the "slaughter of the innocents" occasioned by the depreciation of the currency, it could not be expected that the public should continue to deposit their own money in the savings banks or invest it in Government bonds.

(*e*) As depreciation progressed, the mark was continually rendered more unfit for the function of the circulating medium, and for this purpose foreign exchange took the place of German money. In this way a part of the foreign currencies came to be permanently diverted into the channels of internal circulation.

(*f*) The depreciation of the mark stimulated an ever-growing speculation in foreign exchange. In this way a certain quantity of foreign currency which passed continually from hand to hand in speculating circles, was diverted from the money market.

(*g*) The purchase of foreign exchange was a method frequently used by "real" trade for diminishing the risks arising from the fluctuations of the exchange. Merchants who sold goods for future delivery for payment in paper marks protected themselves against the risk of the future depreciation of the mark by buying, at the time the contract was concluded, a corresponding quantity of foreign exchange. The practice of calculating prices in foreign money, which became widespread in the second half of 1922, as a protection against the risks of the depreciation of the paper mark, also resulted in a marked rise in the demand for foreign exchange, because merchants who assumed the obligation of paying a sum in paper marks, varying according to the rate of exchange on the day of payment, had to protect themselves against eventual losses by buying foreign exchange. This practice of insuring against the risk of the depreciation of the mark, which became more and more common towards the end of 1922, contributed therefore to the deterioration of the situation in the foreign exchange market.

In certain branches of industry, in which it was necessary to take

90 THE ECONOMICS OF INFLATION

account of risks arising from obligations contracted in foreign money, it was felt to be desirable to counteract these risks with guarantee funds in foreign exchange. That happened, for example, in assurance firms.

Hence, under conditions of the depreciation of the circulating medium, the foreign exchange market presented an altogether extraordinary appearance. When the currency is stable the demand for foreign exchange is determined by the necessity of making payments abroad. But in Germany, to this normal demand was added an entirely abnormal demand, which was principally provoked by the desire to invest savings securely in foreign exchange. It is worth mentioning that for a long time there was also a brisk demand for marks by foreigners who speculated for a rise in German money, while in Germany many people speculated for a fall. The large purchases of marks by foreigners for some time checked the rise of the exchanges. But when foreigners ceased to buy marks and a great part of the marks (either notes or bank deposits) possessed by them were offered in Germany for foreign exchange, shares, houses, goods, etc., the depreciation of German money in terms of foreign currencies and goods in the home market was intensified.

7. There is no doubt that the abnormal demand for foreign exchange on the part of the German public who determined to take part in the flight of capital must cause a depreciation of the exchange. This depreciation, however, could not go beyond certain limits if the quantity of marks had not been increased. In fact, the increase in the prices of foreign currencies had immediate effect on the prices of imported goods, and that—had the money income of consumers remained stable—would have meant that prices which passed a certain limit would quickly become prohibitive. It was only due to the rise in money incomes, which was the consequence of .the increase in the circulation, that it was possible that imported goods, which were sold at rising prices because of the depreciation of the exchange, could find buyers.

Besides, if the amount of the circulation and the volume of credit did not increase, there would be limits to the supply of paper marks in the foreign exchange market, and, on the whole, this supply could not be very large. The great mass of the public could not much lessen their normal purchases of consumption goods in order to buy foreign money; and manufacturers needed their money, especially for buying

NATIONAL FINANCES

raw materials, paying workers, etc.* When the public sold securities, houses or land in large quantities with the object of buying foreign money with the receipts from the sales, obviously such sales were only possible while there were people with sufficient means for buying those goods and securities. If the original value (according to the cost of production or of purchase) of the goods or securities offered for sale exceeded the amount of the money saved, then either (*a*) the vendors must sell at a lower cost and suffer losses, which, if they went beyond a certain limit, would check sales, and therefore also the flight of capital; or (*b*) the purchasers must buy the goods and securities with the aid of bank credits. But in this second case it is the bank credits which stimulate the flight of capital abroad; and credit restriction would, therefore, be an efficacious obstacle to this flight.

Sometimes it happens that the demand for foreign money on the part of certain classes in country X is so *inelastic* that the total sum spent, in the money of X, in the purchase of foreign money increases when the currency of X is depreciated. Something like this situation arises in practice when an increase in the price of foreign currencies, instead of reducing purchases of foreign goods, induces importers to anticipate their purchases. If, besides, exports are also rather inelastic, it may be said that the depreciation of the exchange, rather than provoking reactions which re-establish the equilibrium, tend, instead, to increase the disequilibrium of the balance of payments and to accentuate the depreciation of the currency. But even in this case, if the quantity of money in the country with depreciating exchange, and therefore the money incomes of its people, *is not increased*, the rise in the value of foreign currencies will not go beyond a certain limit. In fact, the people of that country cannot spend more than a certain sum on foreign goods and on the purchase of foreign currencies. Besides, depreciating exchange will stimulate foreigners to purchase shares, houses, and land, so that for this reason also the depreciation cannot go beyond a certain limit.

Also, it is most improbable that the *total* curve of the demand for foreign money on the part of a country will remain inelastic for a long time. As soon as the public realizes that the Government has firmly decided not to increase the note issues, confidence in the national currency is re-established and the abnormal demand for foreign currencies ceases. In fact, when the mark was finally stabilized in

* The influence of an increase in the velocity of circulation will be examined in Chapter IV.

92 THE ECONOMICS OF INFLATION

November 1923, the demand for foreign exchange was immediately reduced, and the only demand in the market was that occasioned by the normal needs of trade.

Hence, in order that the abnormal demand for foreign exchange for hoarding should exercise a detrimental influence for a long time on the national paper money (as happened in Germany), it is necessary that this demand should be fed, continually, by new issues of paper money, which also cause distrust to spread continually.

PART IV

I. PAYMENTS UNDER THE TREATY OF VERSAILLES

1. A special item in the German balance of payments was the payment of reparations. Numerous German economists and politicians have stated—an opinion accepted also by several economists outside Germany*—that the principal cause of the depreciation of the mark in the post-war years was the necessity for the German Government to create new money to pay reparations, or, more generally, to satisfy the financial obligations arising from the Treaty of Versailles. In his recent work Elster says that "the stages in the progress of the mark towards depreciation were the same stages which characterized the development of the arrangements between the Allies and the German Government with regard to reparations. . . . The ruin of the German mark was the work of the Allies, while the United States Government looked on in silence."†

Doubtless, the burdens imposed on Germany by the Treaty of Versailles contributed to the deficit shown in the financial years 1920–1923, but as may be seen from German sources, they were not the only causes and never the most important.

In the following table‡ the figures of the deficit are shown (measured

TABLE XI

(*Millions of gold marks*)

Financial year	*Total*	*Expenses under the Treaty of Versailles*
1920	6,053·6	1,850·9
1921	3,675·8	2,810·3
1922	2,442·3	1,136·7
1923 (April–December)	6,538·3	742·4
	18,710·0	6,540·1

* For example, Cassel, *op. cit.*, p. 191.

† *Op. cit.*, pp. 130 and 214. On the other hand, it should be mentioned that some German writers expressed moderate judgment on the influence of reparations on the foreign exchanges—as, e.g., Professor Hirsch (*Deutschlands Währungsfrage*, 1924, p. 12). Also Professor Mises wrote: "The progressive depreciation of the mark could not be the effect of reparations payments; it is simply the result of the Government's financing itself by issuing additional notes" ("Die geldtheoretische Seite des Stabilisierungsproblems," *Schriften des Vereins für Sozialpolitik*, vol. 164, part ii, p. 31).

‡ See art. "Die Reichseinnahmen und Ausgaben in Geldmark" in *Wirtschaft und Statistik*, No. 9 of 1924.

94 THE ECONOMICS OF INFLATION

by the increase in the floating debt) and those of the total expenses borne by the German Treasury under the Treaty of Versailles.

As one may see, even according to German statistics the cost of the application of the Treaty of Versailles could not explain more than a third of the total difference between expenditure and income which existed in the four financial years 1920–1923. Besides, as has already been stated, in the eight months from November 1918 to the end of June 1919, that is *before the signing of the treaty*, the deficit in the Reich Account amounted to a good ten milliard gold marks!

Certainly the expenses imposed on Germany by the treaty and by successive agreements regarding reparations were most considerable, but other countries also came out of the war with a balance of accounts weighted by the formidable burden of interest on debts contracted during the war. In Germany itself, at the end of the war, the public debt, funded and floating, amounted in round figures to 75 milliard gold marks. The service of the debt probably required three or four milliard gold marks a year. Thanks to the depreciation of the mark which occurred in 1919 that burden had been consistently reduced by 1920, when the expenses of the treaty began.

The consolidated public debt of the Reich amounted to 58·5 milliard gold marks at the end of March 1918, to 33·7 milliards towards the end of March 1919, and to 5·4 milliards a year later.*

Let us suppose that the Allies had refrained from imposing any financial burdens whatever on Germany. It is suggested that then the mark would not have depreciated. But the German Government were bound to pay interest on the public debt. There would be two possible courses: either the German Government, finding it impossible to collect the necessary sum by means of taxes, would have to resort to the issue of paper money, and the mark would depreciate even without the influence of the Treaty of Versailles; or it would have to cut down expenses and increase the fiscal burden of the German population: but if it had energetically stated the necessity for this policy in 1920, it would have prevented the further depreciation of the mark in spite of the treaty, so that that cannot have been the fundamental cause of the depreciation of the German mark.

2. Alternatively it is sometimes suggested that the German mark depreciated because the German Government had to buy foreign exchange in order to be able to make reparation payments. Actually

* See the official publication: *Deutschlands Wirtschaft, Währung und Finanzen,* 1924, p. 29.

NATIONAL FINANCES 95

payments in foreign exchange had little relevance until August 31st, 1921. They consisted almost exclusively (in addition to the maintenance of the various commissions instituted by the Treaty of Versailles) of the clearing of pre-war credits and debits resulting from relations between German citizens and those of the allied countries; the balance being adverse to Germany necessitated a payment in foreign money by Germany. On this account Germany had to pay 600 million gold marks before the end of 1922.

According to some writers, among whom was Cassel, it was the attempt made by Germany to fulfil her obligations imposed by the Ultimatum of London of May 1921 which provoked the collapse of the mark. In accordance with the clauses contained in the ultimatum Germany paid, towards the end of August 1921, in foreign money, a milliard gold marks and on November 15th another instalment of 500 million marks.

These were the only disbursements of cash made by Germany under the said ultimatum. On December 14th, 1921, the German Government informed the Reparations Commission that it would not be in a position to pay the instalments due on January 15th and February 15th, 1922. The Commission decided that Germany should continue the payments in kind and every ten days should pay 31 million gold marks in cash. Moreover, the Reparation Recovery Act remained in force. As a result of further negotiations it was agreed that the German Government should pay during 1922 50 million gold marks each month beginning from May 15th and 60 million on the 15th of November and December. But in July 1922 the Government declared that it could not continue to pay even this reduced amount. The last payment was made on July 15th. On August 17th the Government suspended, also on its own initiative, the payments arising from the settlement of private credits and debits.

II. THE INFLUENCE OF REPARATION PAYMENTS ON
THE VALUE OF THE MARK

3. According to official documents the milliard gold marks paid by Germany on August 31st, 1921, was collected in the following manner: Foreign exchange bought on the market or remitted by the Reichsbank, 541 million gold marks; credits conceded by Dutch banks, 270 millions; silver pledged by the Reichsbank, 58 millions; gold bought in the country, 15 millions; credit by the Bank of Italy,

96 THE ECONOMICS OF INFLATION

32 millions; loans conceded by German banks, 16 millions; consigned in gold, 68 millions.

One must admit that the payment of this milliard exercised an appreciable influence on the German exchange, because an excess of exports over imports did not exist. The German exchange remained relatively stable after the summer of 1920. But a slow depreciation appeared once more after the acceptance of the ultimatum. It became more rapid during October 1921, when the German Government had to repay at short notice the credits which it had contracted in Holland on onerous terms.

But those who attributed the rapid rise in the price for foreign exchange which occurred in the autumn of 1921 only to the demand for foreign exchange provoked by the payment of the first milliard, were in error. An even greater influence was exercised by the panic which spread in Germany when the decision of the Council of the League of Nations relating to the division of Upper Silesia was known. German politicians and the more authoritative Press had proclaimed for months that the detachment of Upper Silesia meant the economic ruin of Germany. When the separation was decided, alarm seized the German public, who attributed to it a greater importance than it really had. On October 17th in the Berlin foreign exchange market there was a panic of overwhelming violence.

4. The events which occurred in September 1921 have never been clearly analysed. There is no doubt that in that month there began a violent attack on the mark in the German Bourse. Was this attack the effect of the spontaneous action of speculators who discounted the urgent need for foreign exchange on the part of the Government for reparation payments and who, considering the difficulties arising from the arrangement of Dutch credits, foresaw a further depreciation of of the mark? Was a concerted and systematic attack organized by the adversaries of the "fulfilment policy" to show that every attempt by Germany to pay reparations necessarily conduced to the collapse of the mark?

In those days even the Chancellor of the Reich publicly reproached the want of patriotism in those who, profiting from the fact that the Government had urgent need of collecting a considerable quantity of foreign exchange in a short time, had organized an active speculation on a continual rise in the dollar. According to statements appearing in the more reliable German Press, which severely criticized the actions

NATIONAL FINANCES   97

of the speculators, the fall of the mark did not originate in New York
and was therefore not provoked by foreign speculators; but the origin
of the movement was the Berlin Bourse, where, in fact, the quotations
were generally more unfavourable to the mark than in New York.

The rise in the dollar rate spread panic among German and foreign
holders of paper marks. In the first days of November the lack of
confidence became more serious. The "flight from the mark" became
general. Those who were in Berlin in those days tell of shops besieged
by a crowd ready to buy any object at any price, in order to get rid of
paper marks as quickly as possible. The demand for industrial shares
was very active and the price of them rose rapidly.

That German speculation exaggerated the exchange rates of the
dollar is obvious from the fact that the dollar, which had been pushed
beyond 300 marks at the beginning of November, fell precipitously on
December 1st to 190; industrial share prices following. The result
was an indescribable panic among the mass of small capitalists who
had speculated on the fall of the mark or bought industrial shares at
high prices.

5. A part of the responsibility for the fall of the mark which occurred
in September 1921 also rests on those banks which had supported
numerous purchasers of foreign exchange by means of credits.

That the great German industries were in a position to supply the
Government, owing to the credit they enjoyed abroad, with the foreign
exchange necessary for the payment of reparations is clear from the
offer which the Association of German Industries made to the Government on September 28th, 1921. But this offer was based on conditions
so difficult and humiliating—among other things the great industries
demanded the control of the railways—that the Government had to
reject the proposal.

6. As has been said, in July 1922 reparation payments in foreign
exchange were suspended. In spite of this the depreciation of the
German exchange continued; one of the periods of most rapid depreciation of the mark was the time between July 15th and August 31st,
1922. Even Elster is obliged to acknowledge that the fall of the mark
experienced in those days could not be explained by payments under
the Treaty of Versailles. "Nevertheless," he suggests, "the cause still
rests in the treaty, whose very existence represented for German
economy such a heavy burden that confidence in an improvement of

D

98 THE ECONOMICS OF INFLATION

the governmental finances and of the currency must continually decline."* I willingly admit that the Treaty of Versailles created psychological influences unfavourable to the mark. But, in his study of the consequences of the payments made in 1921, Elster neglected the fundamental question: why were those consequences so serious?

The answer is as follows. The German Government bought foreign exchange with paper money which was not purchasing power collected from German citizens by taxes, but new purchasing power created by the discounting of Treasury bills at the Reichsbank, that is by the increase of note-issues.† If, on the other hand, the quantity of paper money had not been increased, the depreciation of the mark, caused by the payment of reparations, would not have gone beyond a certain limit, which it is reasonable to suppose would have been quickly reached—given the reactions which would have shown themselves in an elastic demand for foreign exchange and in the export of goods and services, and, moreover, in the sale to foreigners of houses, shares, and other parts of the national wealth of Germany. Hence a more energetic financial policy would at least have lessened the effects of reparation payments on the German exchange. But as we have seen in the preceding paragraphs, the wealthy classes were tenaciously opposed to an effective financial reform which would have given the Government the means to begin fulfilling the obligations assumed by the acceptance of the Ultimatum of London.

Certainly, the ultimatum had imposed on Germany the payment of sums which far exceeded her contributive capacity; as was recognized later by the allied countries and was implicit in the celebrated report of the Dawes Committee. It was impossible to squeeze each year from the German people two milliard gold marks, plus a sum equivalent to 26 per cent of the value of exports (five milliard gold marks in 1920); and besides this the expenses arising from occupation, the numerous control commissions, etc. It was not possible for exports to develop so rapidly as to exceed imports by several milliards and to create the source from which the German Government normally had to draw the foreign exchange necessary for reparation payments.

But in Germany the supporters of the so-called "Fulfilment policy"

---

* *Op. cit.*, p. 166.

† One may read on page 14 of the Report of the Deutsche Bank for 1921 that the German Government procured more than a quarter of the sum due to the Allies by means of credits contracted abroad. "To the fact that these credits were covered *by the sale of paper marks abroad*, in default of foreign exchange offered by exporters, was due the rapid depreciation of the mark in the short period from August to November."

NATIONAL FINANCES   99

wanted the German people to make a great effort to pay the *first instalments*, thus showing their good faith; in the meantime world opinion would become more favourable to Germany, the occupation of the Ruhr would be avoided, and the Allies would be persuaded, little by little, of the necessity of alleviating the burdens imposed by the Ultimatum of London. Many people in Germany believed that the first instalments could be paid without excessive difficulty, partly by increasing taxes on income and capital and partly by an internal loan, subscriptions to which should be payable partly in foreign exchange.

But the opposers of the "Fulfilment policy" started from a different premise. In was an illusion to believe—they contended—that the payment of the first instalments would induce the allied Governments to mitigate the hard conditions imposed by London; on the contrary, the idea held abroad that Germany's capacity to pay had not been over-estimated at London would be strengthened. Then to what purpose fling into the bottomless well of reparations some milliards which might be so useful for the economic reconstruction of Germany? Also, if Germany did make an effort to pay some milliards, she could only succeed in covering a part of the interest on the sum fixed in London! Then before continuing reparation payments it was necessary to obtain from the Allies a moratorium of some years and a considerable reduction of the German debt.

It is also worth mentioning that the solution of the reparations question was impeded by those groups of industrialists among the Allies who were opposed to reparations in kind.

As the head of the French Government stated in the House of Deputies in the session of June 19th, 1924, there had been assigned to France for 1922 goods in kind worth 950 million gold marks. Actually, in that year France received only 179 million marks' worth of goods, almost exclusively coal and coke, and that was because certain French industrial groups used their influence to stop the supply of goods which would have competed with their products. At the same session the head of the French Government cited the case of an order for motor cars worth 117 million francs which they were forced to renounce because of the opposition of the French manufacturers.

PART V

I. THE INFLUENCE OF SPECULATION ON THE VALUE OF THE MARK

1. The German Governments were often accused of having wanted the depreciation of the mark in order to show that it was impossible for Germany to pay reparations.

To this accusation Stresemann replied in one of his speeches that a ministry which had "provoked by design the fall of the mark would have been an arch-criminal."

Actually it cannot be admitted that a Government, conscious of the very serious losses which the depreciation of the mark involved to numerous classes of society and of the profound moral disturbance which the experience caused in the whole of the German people, organized the collapse of the mark. Moreover, the manœuvre would have been aimless since it would have been easy for the Allies to tell the German Government that Germany's capacity for payment was not measured by the conditions of the currency but by the other much more important indices, such as her general wealth, the activity of her industries, the amount of her exports, the importance of foreign credits, etc.

For these reasons I cannot consider that accusation seriously. Neither shall I consider another accusation, often raised in Germany itself, according to which the depreciation of the mark was the effect of a conspiracy arranged by the reactionary and nationalist parties, who sought thereby to disorder German finances, to bring discredit on the republican régime and to undermine its (still insecure) foundations, in order to be able to restore the old régime on the ruins of the young republic.*

2. The accusation that the collapse of the German exchange was provoked by bold groups of professional speculators seems better founded. The objection to that is that speculation cannot be the original cause of the depreciation of the currency of a country. On the contrary, speculation appears when for certain reasons, such as the Budget deficit, the continual issues of paper money, the disequilibrium of the balance of trade, and the political situation, the exchanges are unstable. Speculation weakens and eventually disappears when the causes which

* See on this point the article of Professor Valentin in *Börsen-Courier* of August 21st, 1923.

NATIONAL FINANCES

provoked the original depreciation of the currency become less. Speculation in Austrian crowns flourished so long as that currency was unstable; but it disappeared as soon as the stabilization plan was adopted. Directly the monetary reform of November 1923 made the German exchange stable, speculation ceased, after some fruitless attempts to prevent the success of the operation. The well-known movements of international speculators are significant: they first fixed their abode in Vienna; later they passed to Berlin, and after the German monetary reform they transferred their activities to Paris, where the situation of the French franc promised to open for them a field of further activities.

But although the origin of the depreciation of the German mark cannot certainly be traced to the manœuvres of speculation, it appears possible to state that at a certain stage of the depreciation of that currency, speculation played an important part. Recent monetary experiences, in Germany and elsewhere, show that the theories of some economists on the influence of speculation are too optimistic. According to economists, speculators foreseeing the future variations of exchanges and anticipating them with their transactions, lessen the fluctuations themselves. But this theoretical conception often does not correspond to reality. Speculation has continually produced enormous fluctuations in the exchange rates for the German mark. Speculation often anticipated the future variations but exaggerated them, partly because its action was extraordinarily reinforced by the operations of the public, who followed more or less blindly the example of a few professional speculators. The dollar rate was increased rapidly from one day to the next and even from one hour to the next by the expectation of a future rise. But often the rates which had been pushed to a level not corresponding with the fundamental conditions could not be maintained; the first liquidation on the part of wise speculators spread panic among the public, who hastened to sell foreign exchange; hence a fall in the rates as sudden and sharp as the preceding rise had been.

For some time it was foreign speculation (foreigners possessed large sums of marks) which provoked the great fluctuations of the exchanges. In February 1920 the mark had fallen to 4 per cent of its gold parity; in May of the same year it rose again to 12 per cent; and that was mainly due to foreign speculation.* Later the speculation of Germans assumed greater importance.

On November 29th, 1921, the dollar was quoted at 276 marks; on

* Deutsche Bank, Report for 1920, p. 13.

December 1st it fell sharply to 190. By August 1922 the dollar rate had risen beyond 1,900 marks; but a violent reaction set in and the dollar fell to little more than 1,200 marks. On November 1st, 1922, it was quoted at 4,465 marks; November 7th, 8,068; two days later, 6,711; November 21st, 6,791; and on November 28th, 8,480 marks. On December 11th, 1922, it was at 8,337 marks; December 16th, 5,380; and on the 27th, 7,522 marks. Towards the middle of August 1923 the dollar rate rose giddily to 1, 2, 3, and 5 million marks; later falling suddenly to 3 millions. These examples, which could be multiplied, show that speculation did not exercise a stabilizing influence on the exchanges, but had rather the opposite effect.

3. The theorists also maintain that speculation cannot exercise an influence which manifests itself constantly in the same direction. For example, speculation cannot provoke a permanent and continuous rise of the exchanges. In fact, the speculator for a fall in the mark would act in the first place by buying foreign exchange, thus causing a rise in the price thereof; but later would come the moment at which he must sell the foreign exchange and his demand for marks would cause an improvement in the German exchange.

Without doubt this argument is valid for an early phase of the depreciation of the paper mark, when there was no intimate connection between the exchange rate and domestic prices. But in a later phase, when the depreciation of the exchange had immediate effect on prices, the consequences of the operations of speculators were more serious and lasting. In fact, the rise in prices, as we have seen above, was a potent stimulus to the increase of the inflation, as the Government and the Central Bank had not sufficient strength to oppose the demands of business men. Hence the new level of the exchange, provoked by speculators, tended to be justified by internal developments. Subsequent dealings of speculators, who offered on the market the foreign exchange earlier acquired by them, could not depress the exchange rate to its former level, because the foreign exchange was bought with the aid of the new issues of paper money, and a new equilibrium of the exchange was established corresponding to the new level of internal prices.

Experience showed that—whilst every depreciation of the exchange had immediate repercussions on internal prices—an improvement, on the other hand, only exercised a weak and slow influence in lowering the level of prices. As von Siemens, President of the Administrative Council of Siemens and Halske, has observed on this subject: "The

NATIONAL FINANCES 103

internal value of the mark always adapted itself more rapidly to the depreciation of the external value, sometimes it even anticipated it; but when the exchange improved, human nature impeded the adaptation of prices." It is true that the prices of raw materials and foodstuffs decreased; but the vast majority of internal prices remained more or less unaffected. Manufacturers and wholesale merchants preferred not to sell goods rather than adapt themselves to a fall in prices.

Therefore, taking account of these circumstances: (*a*) the great sensitiveness of internal prices to a depreciation of the exchange; (*b*) the great inertia with which they met an improvement in the exchange; (*c*) the scarcity of foreign exchange which was always evident in the German Bourse at times of an increase in the dollar rate; and (*d*) the increase of the inflation which immediately followed the rise in prices—it is obvious that speculators could exercise a great influence in the way of stimulating a continual depreciation of the mark. But it is certain that a financial and banking policy which did not regard the increase of note-issues as an inevitable consequence of the rise in internal prices, would have been able to arrest the effects of speculation on the fall of the mark. In fact the energetic policy, followed after the stabilization of the mark, knocked the bottom out of speculation against the German mark.

II. THE INFLUENCE OF CERTAIN CLASSES OF GERMAN INDUSTRIALISTS ON THE DEPRECIATION OF THE MARK

4. The actions of groups of speculators, unsolicitous for the interests of their own country,* were reinforced by the influence exercised by certain classes of producers.

* The *Berliner Börsen-Courier* of September 12th, 1921, states that "according to all appearances the fall of the mark did not have its origin in the New York exchange, from which it may be concluded that in Germany there was active speculation directed towards the continual rise of the dollar." Also the *Berliner Tageblatt* of September 14th, 1921, laments that "the increase in the number of those who speculate on the fall of the mark and who are acquiring vested interests in a continual depreciation."

The *Frankfurter Zeitung* of September 5th, 1922, condemns the frenzied speculation in foreign currencies. "The enormous speculation on the rise of the American dollar is an open secret. People who, having regard to their age, their inexperience, and their lack of responsibility, do not deserve support, have nevertheless secured the help of financiers, who are thinking exclusively of their own immediate interests."

On the influence of German speculation on the exchanges see Müller (ex Under-Secretary of State) in *8 Uhr Abendblatt* of May 22nd, 1923: "Those who have studied seriously the conditions of the money market state that the movement against the German mark remained on the whole independent of foreign markets for more than six months. *It is the German bears, helped by the inaction of the Reichsbank, who have forced the collapse in the exchange.*"

104 THE ECONOMICS OF INFLATION

The example of all countries with a depreciated currency shows us that the depreciation of money creates a vast net of interests vested in the maintenance and continuation of the depreciation itself; interests which are disturbed by the possibility of a stabilization of the exchange and which, therefore, are assiduously opposed to the return of normal monetary conditions.

Seventy years ago Wagner wrote: "Powerful groups are interested in the maintenance of the premium on gold and even in its increase. If steps are taken for the improvement of the circulation, the powerful party of the protectionists opposes them with all the means at its disposal. Bankers and industrialists are in agreement. This has been proved every time in the numerous attempts made in Austria to re-establish the currency; the same thing happened in Russia in 1862. In the United States the attempt to eliminate the premium was opposed with veritable fanaticism. The adversaries of paper money and of protection are called traitors by the company of industrial egoists."[*]

This is just what happened in Germany. There is no doubt that the paper inflation would not have assumed such vast proportions if it had not been favoured in many ways by the people who drew a large profit from it. It is clear from the discussions held in 1922 and 1923 in the "Economic Council of the Reich," that representatives of those classes used their influence on the Government to impede the reform of the public finances and to sabotage all proposals for the stabilization of the German exchange, which they only accepted when, at last, an economic catastrophe threatened Germany and it was evident that the consequences of the inflation would rebound against their authors. Without making the exaggerated statement that the depreciation of the mark was due to a conspiracy of the industrial classes, it is certain, nevertheless, that they contributed largely to it, aided by the agriculturists who saw the lightening of the burden of their mortgages, which before the war was very heavy, and by all the other people who prospered owing to the continued depreciation of the national money. Such obvious and conspicuous advantages for producers could be derived from this phenomenon, that naturally they became the most convinced supporters of monetary inflation.[†] While sale prices rapidly

[*] Wagner, *op. cit.*, p. 105.

[†] Moulton (*Germany's Capacity to Pay*, London, 1923) refutes the accusation that the industrialists favoured the depreciation of the mark, observing that it was not in their interests to cause misery to vast numbers of German citizens, that is to consumers of the products of industry. Moulton's argument would have been just if based on the hypothesis that man is always wise enough to resist the temptation of an immediate advantage which involves a future danger.

NATIONAL FINANCES   105

approached world prices the industrialists paid wages which for a long time increased only at a great distance behind the rise in sale prices; other elements in the cost of production, such as transport expenses, declined in importance. The fiscal burden was continually lightened, and in addition the payment of certain taxes which industry had to pay into the exchequer, collecting them from others, became for the entrepreneur a source of conspicuous excess-profits. Mortgage debts were rapidly cancelled; bank credits, cleverly used, made possible the acquisition of foreign exchange, freehold property, etc.; and the difference between internal and external prices was a source of considerable gains for exporters.

The Dawes Committee also observed, in its Report, that the wealthy classes in Germany had not, in the last years, borne a fiscal burden adequate to their means. Nothing exasperated and irritated the lower classes so much as the state of affairs in which those who were the strongest economically, and who by the general ruin had been able to reap great advantages, contributed to the payment of taxes less than all the others.

5. Suddenly a theory of the depreciation of the mark was formed which lauded it as a great blessing. By stimulating exports, it revived industrial activity. Industrialists accustomed themselves to consider the depreciation of German money, with the consequent divergence between its internal and external values, as a condition without which industry could not continue to be productive. The possibility of an improvement in the value of the mark was viewed with grave apprehension, because—as Klöckner, a great industrialist observed—"the consequence would be a disaster of incredible magnitude." Another representative of the industrial classes added: "An appreciable and unforeseen improvement in the mark would paralyse the export trades and provoke vast unemployment. But even if it were gradual, any further improvement in our exchange would be a catastrophe."

In June 1922 Stinnes declared himself against a foreign loan "which would raise the exchange rate of the mark to a level which German economy could not endure." Against Stinnes, whom public opinion considered as one of the principal supporters of the depreciation of the mark, Georg Bernhard launched this virulent attack:[*]

He has woven intrigues against every Government which he was afraid would put in order the internal conditions of Germany. Every time any problem

[*] See *Vossische Zeitung*, October 18th, 1923.

D*

whatever was considered—whether it were the question of reparations or that of German finances—he has always raised his voice and declared that the premises necessary for the solution of that problem did not yet exist. He attacked Rathenau after the conclusion of the Wiesbaden Agreement. . . . The classes on which he exercised a great influence opposed in a most violent way all attempts to reconstruct the finances and restore the currency by the issue of a gold loan or in any other way. . . . By means of credits amounting to milliards, whose value was continually reduced by inflation, he bought one firm after another in every possible branch of industry, he appropriated banks, financed shipping firms, acquired participations abroad and controlled numerous commercial enterprises. And all this he co-ordinated with the system of his politics, which aimed at the maintenance of inflation and disorder.

In a memorandum of the German Workers' Association, published in 1925, it is recorded that after the invasion of the Ruhr the great industries continued to buy foreign exchange, thus provoking the anger of Havenstein, the President of the Reichsbank, and succeeded, thanks to the rapid depreciation of the currency, in practically avoiding the payment of taxes. In fact, in March 1923 95 per cent of the total yield from income tax was paid by wage-earners and salaried workers. But the credits conceded by the Government to the industrialists constituted the most scandalous chapter in the history of that unhappy period. The sums received, which were intended to serve to finance Passive Resistance, were partly employed in the purchase of foreign exchange or for the construction of new machinery.

[12]

The Economics of Inflation. By C. BRESCIANI-TURRONI. Translated by MILLICENT E. SAYERS. (London: Allen and Unwin, 1937. Pp. 464. 25s.)

PROFESSOR BRESCIANI-TURRONI'S work, now made available in an excellent translation, will be of great value to English students of inflation, although seven years after its original publication it has a somewhat old-fashioned air.

Theoretical discussion of the great German inflation was for a long time clouded by political prejudices. The German writers regarded reparations payments as the primary source of the trouble, and consequently argued that the collapse of the mark exchange was the cause of the inflation. (*Inflation* is here used in a purely descriptive sense, to mean an inordinately great rise in prices, without any question-begging theoretical significance as to whether the rise in prices is "the fault of money.") While the spokesmen of the Allies blamed the budget deficit, and consequently argued that the inflation was primarily caused by creation of money. Professor Bresciani-Turroni is a strong adherent of the Allied or Quantity Theory school.

At a first glance, as the author freely admits, the facts appear to tell strongly in favour of the German view. There is no dispute as to the fact that the transition from the relatively moderate fluctuating movements in exchange and prices of the immediate post-war years to the violent inflation which set in in the second half of 1921 was inaugurated by a sudden fall in the mark exchange (May 1921, 15 marks = 1 gold mark; November 1921,

63 marks = 1 gold mark). This fall is generally attributed to the commencement of cash payments of reparations. In this period payment of 1 milliard gold marks was carried out, while the total of exports was of the order of 6 milliard gold marks per annum. It is therefore plausible to attribute the fall of the mark to the sudden demand for foreign exchange in respect of reparations. The author, anxious to exonerate reparations, attributes it rather to the shock to confidence caused by the partition of Upper Silesia (p. 96). But this is immaterial to the main theoretical question—whatever the cause of the collapse of the exchange, it seems clear that it was the collapse of the exchange which inaugurated the great inflation. Both the magnitude and the temporal order of price changes in 1921 and 1922 support the argument. If the impulse comes from the side of the exchange, we should expect the fall in exchange to run ahead of the rise in prices, and the prices of traded goods to run ahead of home prices. This is precisely what occurred, the magnitude and speed of change being in this order : exchange, import prices, export prices, home prices, cost-of-living, wages. Moreover, the geographical diffusion of prices supports the argument, the movement spreading from the great ports and commercial centres to the interior of the country (p. 135).

To all this the author opposes a theoretical argument. If home incomes do not rise, exchange depreciation cannot continue indefinitely, but must somewhere come to rest (p. 84). The stimulus to exports and check to imports must wipe out an unfavourable balance of payments and establish a new equilibrium with a constant exchange rate. The author admits that, over a certain range, a fall in exchange rate may reduce the gold value of exports, owing to inelastic foreign demand, and so make the balance of trade still more unfavourable. But, he points out (p. 91), a *sufficient* rise in the home price of imported goods will choke off demand, so that there is always some level of the exchange rate at which the balance of trade will right itself and depreciation come to an end. For this reason he dismisses the view that the depreciation of the mark was the primary cause of the inflation, in spite of the evidence which he admits in its favour, and adheres to an alternative explanation.

His explanation is that the German budget deficit, financed by borrowing from the Reichsbank, led to a continuous increase in the volume of money. From this, in his view, all the rest followed. But this account of the matter must be more closely examined before it can be accepted, or even understood.

1938]   BRESCIANI-TURRONI : THE ECONOMICS OF INFLATION   509

The influence of a budget deficit upon prices can be divided
into two parts. The *direct* effect of a deficit is to increase incomes
and therefore to increase expenditure and business activity,
no matter how the deficit is financed. Even if the Government
is borrowing at long term from the public, an excess of expenditure
over revenue must tend to increase incomes and activity. The
indirect effect of a deficit financed by borrowing from the central
bank is to bring about an increase in the quantity of money, which
continues cumulatively as long as the deficit persists.

Now, so far as the direct effect of the deficit is concerned,
its influence was becoming weaker in the early stages of the
inflation. In 1920 the deficit was 6 milliard gold marks (in this
context a measurement in gold marks, though inaccurate, is
a sufficient guide). In 1921 it was 3·7 milliard gold marks, in
1922 2·4 milliard (p. 438). Only in 1923 was there an increase in
the deficit. From the middle of 1921 to March 1923 the direct
influence of the deficit was declining, and if no other cause had
been at work, activity and prices would have been falling. If
the deficit is to be blamed for the first phase of the inflation, it
can only be because of its indirect effect—the increase in the
quantity of money.

The author assumes, rather than argues, that an increase in
the quantity of money was the root cause of the inflation. But
this view it is impossible to accept. An increase in the quantity of money no doubt has a tendency to raise prices, for it
leads to a reduction in the rate of interest, which stimulates
investment and discourages saving, and so leads to an increase
in activity. But there is no evidence whatever that events in
Germany followed this sequence.

It is true that a very high rate of investment prevailed during
the inflation (p. 291). And it is true that there was a drastic
decline in thriftiness. Saving by the ordinary public ceased
almost completely, investment being financed entirely from
profits. Moreover there was considerable dissaving by individuals
who consumed their past accumulations of wealth. Both the
high rate of investment and the low propensity to save played
a large part in maintaining activity at a high level during the
inflation, but all these effects sprang from the expectation of
rising prices—they reinforced an inflation which was already
under way—not from excessively low interest rates.

Similar objections apply also in regard to his arguments in
relation to the velocity of circulation. If the inflation cannot
be attributed to low interest rates, it cannot be attributed to the

fall in the demand for money which shows itself in increased velocity of circulation.

The author rejects the view that exchange depreciation caused the inflation. But the difficulties of his own explanation are just as great. Neither the budget deficit nor the increase in quantity and velocity of circulation of money can produce the effects attributed to them. Clearly in each explanation some essential item is missing.

The missing item is not far to seek. It is the rise in money wages. Neither exchange depreciation nor a budget deficit can account for inflation by itself. But if the rise in money wages is brought into the story, the part which each plays can be clearly seen. With the collapse of the mark in 1921, import prices rose abruptly, dragging home prices after them. The sudden rise in the cost of living led to urgent demands for higher wages. Unemployment was low (2 per cent. of members of Trade Unions were unemployed August 1921, 0·7 per cent. in 1922), profits were rising with prices, and the German workers were faced with starvation. Wage rises had to be granted. Rising wages, increasing both home costs and home money incomes, counteracted the effect of exchange depreciation in stimulating exports and restricting imports. Each rise in wages, therefore, precipitated a further fall in the exchange rate, and each fall in the exchange rate called forth a further rise in wages. This process became automatic when wages began to be paid on a cost-of-living basis (p. 310). Thus the author's contention that the collapse of the mark cannot have caused the inflation, because the exchange rate will always find an equilibrium level, is deprived of all force as soon as the rise of money wages is allotted its proper rôle.

But though the German theory that depreciation causes inflation can be justified, the Allied theory is not thereby ruled out. A sufficiently great budget deficit, when unemployment is sufficiently low, will raise prices and increase the demand for labour to the point at which the pressure for higher wages becomes irresistible. Each rise in wages raises prices, and so the vicious circle revolves. Meanwhile a collapse of the exchange adds fuel to the fire. It may well have been the budget deficit of 1923 due to passive resistance in the Ruhr, which inaugurated the final downfall of the mark.

It appears, then, that either exchange depreciation or a budget deficit may initiate inflation, and that the German history provides examples of both cases. But the essence of inflation is a rapid and continuous rise of money wages. Without rising money wages, inflation cannot occur, and whatever starts a violent rise in money wages starts inflation.

It is even possible that an increase in the quantity of money might start an inflation. A sufficient fall in the rate of interest might conceivably lead to such an increase in investment that unemployment disappeared, and money wages and prices started their spiral rise. But this is merely a theoretical possibility, not an account of the course of events in Germany.

Actually the quantity of money was important, not because it caused inflation, but because it allowed it to continue. If the quantity of money had not expanded, it may be supposed that the rate of interest would have been driven up, investment impeded and saving encouraged, so that unemployment would have appeared again and the rise in money wages would have been brought to an end. But in fact the budget deficit, the policy of the Reichsbank in " meeting the needs of trade " and the various official and unofficial supplementary currencies which were improvised, combined to meet the demand for money, the short rate of interest did not begin to rise appreciably till July 1922, and no obstacle was put in the way of the inflation.

It is true that in 1923 the short rate of interest rose to such heights that loans were taken at 20 per cent. *per diem* (though the maximum reached by the Reichsbank discount rate was only 90 per cent. *per annum*). But by this time the expectation of a continued rise in prices was so strong that it was impossible for high interest rates to discourage entrepreneurs from investment or to restore the motive for saving to the ordinary public. Thus the fact that high rates did not stop the inflation in 1923 cannot prove that they would have been equally powerless in 1921. The champions of the quantity theory, therefore, may reasonably contend that it was the increase in the quantity of money which permitted the inflation to take place.

In his *Conclusion* the author claims no more than that an increase in the quantity of money is a necessary condition of inflation. A clear grasp of the distinction between a necessary and a sufficient condition seems to be all that is required to settle the controversy. It is true that a train cannot move when the brake is on, but it would be foolish to say that the cause of motion in a train is that the brake is removed. It is no less, but no more, sensible to say that an increase in the quantity of money is the cause of inflation. The analogy can be pressed further. If the engine is powerful and is working at full steam, application of the brake may fail to bring the train to rest.

Similarly, once an expectation of rising prices has been set up, a mere refusal to increase the quantity of money may be insufficient to curb activity.

It is sometimes argued that the stabilisation of the mark in November 1923 indicates that inflation can be stopped at any moment if the quantity of money is strictly controlled. In spite of himself, the author advances evidence for an entirely different interpretation of the facts. Before the stabilisation took place, inflation had reached such a pitch as to bring itself to an end. The stabilisation occurred only when the mark had in effect almost completely ceased to function as money (p. 342). The mark lost the characteristics of money in three stages. By the autumn of 1921 it had ceased to function as a "store of value." When the expectation of a continuous rise in prices became general the demand for money to hold disappeared, as is shown by the fall, which set in at that date, in the real value of the outstanding quantity of money. In the later part of 1922 the mark ceased to function as a "unit of account." It became more and more common to reckon all prices, and to fix wage rates, with reference to the exchange rate, so that, in effect, the dollar was the unit of account. The mark note never ceased altogether to function as a "medium of exchange," but it was to a large extent displaced by foreign currency and the "stable value" instruments of various kinds which were improvised. Finally, in the great slide of 1923 the mark had begun to lose the character of a "standard of deferred payments," for loans began to be contracted in terms of dollars, copper, kilowatt hours and what-not. When this process spread, the expectation of rising prices lost its power to stimulate investment, for there was no expectation that prices in terms of dollars, or of particular commodities, would rise. The force of inflation in stimulating activity was all but spent, and it is significant that unemployment rose sharply in August 1923. The dislocation caused by the invasion of the Ruhr raised unemployment among Trade Unionists to 7 per cent. in April, but the stimulus of inflation reduced it again to 3·5 per cent. in July. In the final slide the stimulus of inflation was exhausted and unemployment rose to 19 per cent. in September (p. 449).

The Rentenmark was in effect no more than an official version of the "stable value" currencies that were already in use (p. 347). The stabilisation was no doubt a firm and courageous act of policy, but it provides no argument to support the view that inflation, at an advanced stage, can be checked by limiting the quantity of money.

JOAN ROBINSON

Cambridge.

Excerpt from chapter 5 entitled 'The Determinants of Monetary Expansion' in *The German Inflation 1914–1923*, Carl-Ludwig Holtfrerich

[13]

War financing: practical proposals, measures and results

In 1914 the authorities in Germany were poorly prepared both for the fiscal problems of a modern war and for its effects on the real economy. More thought had nevertheless been given to the technical aspects of war financing than to any of the other problems. The possibilities of "financial mobilization" for war had been discussed in detail during the closing prewar years by military strategists, academics and bankers. Among early contributions to the debate were those of Moritz Ströll[18] and Josef von Renauld.[19] The latter was

---

[18] Moritz Ströll: "Über das deutsche Geldwesen im Kriegsfall", *Schmollers Jahrbuch*, 23 (1899).
[19] Josef von Renauld: *Die finanzielle Mobilmachung der deutschen Wehrkraft* (Leipzig, 1901).

the only prewar writer to suggest even an approximately accurate forecast of annual war expenditure: assuming an army establishment of ten million men, he suggested twenty two billion marks. Subsequently however he retracted this forecast on the grounds of its financial impossibility.[20] Heinrich Dietzel,[21] Magnus Biermer,[22] Fritz Neubürger[23] and C. Henke[24] tended to advocate long or short-term debt financing. Jakob Riesser,[25] Johann Plenge,[26] Julius Wolf[27] and Wilhelm Gerloff[28] argued on the other side for greater reliance on taxation. In the event, of course, Germany relied less on taxation than England did. Why was this?[29]

Adolph Wagner had recommended a reform of the peacetime tax system which would facilitate the rapid imposition of surcharges on existing taxes if war broke out, thus assuring the state of a rapid increase of revenue.[30] Such a reform was particularly necessary in prewar Germany. According to the 1871 constitution of the Reich, central government had very limited powers to tax. Initially it could levy only certain indirect taxes – customs duties and a number of excises (especially those on tobacco, beer, spirits and salt): beyond this it enjoyed the operating surpluses of the enterprises it owned.[31] Reich expenditure in excess of these revenues was to be covered by so-called "matricular contributions" from the federal states and this effectively turned the Reich into their fiscal dependant. In this arrangement the government of the Reich

---

[20] Josef von Renauld: "Finanzielle Mobilmachung", *Bank-Archiv*, 4 (1904/05). Cp. H. Haller: "Rolle der Staatsfinanzen", p. 116.

[21] Heinrich Dietzel: *Kriegssteuer oder Kriegsanleihe?* (Tübingen, 1912).

[22] Magnus Biermer: *Die finanzielle Mobilmachung* (Giessen, 1913), p. 51: "The treasury certificate is the most appropriate credit instrument while the war lasts."

[23] Fritz Neubürger: *Die Kriegsbereitschaft des deutschen Geld- und Kapitalmarktes* (Berlin, 1913).

[24] C. Henke: "Das deutsche Geldwesen im Kriege", *Vierteljahreshefte für Truppenführung und Heereskunde*, 10 (1913), pp. 260–279.

[25] Jakob Riesser: *Finanzielle Kriegsbereitschaft und Kriegsführung* (Jena, 1909, 2nd edn. 1913).

[26] Johann Plenge: "Zur Diagnose der Reichsfinanzreform", *Zeitschrift für die Gesamte Staatswissenschaft*, 65 (1909), esp. pp. 322–323.

[27] Julius Wolf: *Die Steuerreserven in England und Deutschland* (Stuttgart, 1914).

[28] Wilhelm Gerloff: *Matrikularbeiträge und direkte Reichssteuern* (Berlin, 1908).

[29] Cp. p. 105, note 10 *supra*. For international comparison see the Table in Jens Jessen: "Kriegsfinanzen", article in Ludwig Elster (ed.): *Wörterbuch der Volkswirtschaft* (Jena, 3 vols. 4th edn. 1932–3) vol. 2 (1932), pp. 674–682. See too Karl Theodor Eheberg: "Finanzen im Weltkrieg", article in the *Handwörterbuch der Staatswissenschaften* (Jena, 4th edn. 8 vols. 1921–7), vol. 4 (1927), pp. 75–86. Gerhard Colm: "War Finance", article in the *Encyclopedia of the Social Sciences* (New York, 15 vols. 1930–35), vol. 15 (1935), pp. 347–52.

[30] Cp. H. Haller: "Rolle der Staatsfinanzen", p. 115.

[31] Peter-Christian Witt: *Die Finanzpolitik des Deutschen Reiches von 1903 bis 1913* (Lübeck, 1970), pp. 18–19.

found itself beholden to the Reichstag as well, for the Reichstag had the duty, as part of its general responsibility to approve the budget, of determining aggregate matricular contributions each year, which were then distributed among the states according to a key based on their relative populations. Under the second empire, taxing powers had been allocated according to the principle, "indirect taxes to the Reich, direct to the states."[32] By securing acceptance of this rule in the state whose constitutional relations he influenced so decisively, Bismarck's aim had not been to perpetuate a fiscally weak Reich. On the contrary: in 1875 he had stated, "I declare myself innately in favor of raising revenue entirely out of indirect taxation wherever possible."[33] His intention was not that the Reich should ultimately exploit the sources of direct taxation currently worked by the states, but rather that direct taxation should be pushed back, and indirect taxation extended – thus advantaging the Reich.[34]

From the 1890s the yield of a growing number of stamp duties became increasingly important to the Reich. Eventually, in the years just before the war, it entered the field of wealth taxation.[35] In 1906 a Reich inheritance tax was introduced, but its yield was low. In 1913 a non-recurrent capital levy, the so-called "Defense Contribution", was imposed. Those liable could pay in three annual installments between 1913–15; its eventual yield was pretty near the one billion marks it had been designed to raise. Lastly, a capital gains tax was introduced in the same year, with an intended annual yield of 185 million marks.

The two 1913 taxes were introduced solely in connection with the armament policies of the Reich and must be attributed rather to international tensions and the threat of war than to any reform of fiscal principles designed to improve the Reich's powers of direct taxation.[36] The fact, however, that the demands of the military build-up were met by enlarging the direct tax base and not the indirect, "signifies the victory of a social-democratic/liberal coalition

---

[32] Fritz Terhalle: "Geschichte der deutschen öffentlichen Finanzwirtschaft vom Beginn des 19. Jahrhunderts bis zum Schlusse des Zweiten Weltkrieges", article in the *Handbuch der Finanzwissenschaft* (Tübingen, 2nd edn. 4 vols., 1952–65), vol. 1 (1952), p. 280.

[33] Cited according to Wilhelm Gerloff: "Der Staatshaushalt und das Finanzsystem Deutschlands", article in the *Handbuch der Finanzwissenschaft* (Tübingen, lst edn. 3 vols. 1925–9), vol. 3 (1929), p. 25.

[34] *Ibid.*

[35] F. Terhalle: "Geschichte", p. 286.

[36] *Ibid.* Also Konrad Roesler: *Die Finanzpolitik des Deutschen Reiches im Ersten Weltkrieg* (Berlin, 1967), p. 17.

over the conservatives."[37] Rates of direct taxation can be graduated according to capacity to pay – they can be made progressive; whereas indirect taxation tends to act regressively, bearing more heavily on the lower income groups who consume more and save less. This is an important observation; it means that had taxation played a larger part in financing the war, the additional burden would have been distributed regressively across the population, unless the Reich's fiscal foundations had shifted drastically.

Inelasticity is a further property of a system based on indirect taxation. The yield of the Reich's tax base at the outbreak of war could not be rapidly expanded by the imposition of surcharges. Customs revenue was likely to fall in the event of war, as cross-border trade fell, and in any case certain import duties were suspended – especially on foodstuffs and raw materials – soon after war began, in order to attract urgently required commodities into the country. Excises on non-necessities (especially tobacco, beer, spirits) are also likely to yield falling revenues as the consumption of such goods declines. These things happened in the event: the ordinary revenues of the Reich fell about 25 % between 1914 and 1915 – from 2.47 to 1.83 billion marks (cp. Table 25). The ordinary budget could be balanced only because military expenditure – traditionally by far the largest item on the expenditure side of the Reich budget even in peacetime[38] – was mainly transferred to the extraordinary budget for the duration of the war. Interest payments on the swelling debt by which the "extraordinary war expenditures" were financed were however charged to the ordinary budget, and came to dominate it; debt servicing rose from 26.5 % of ordinary expenditure in 1914 to about 90 % in 1918 (cp. Table 26).

In Great Britain it proved possible to meet a considerable part of war expenditure out of current taxation. The "centrally and efficiently organized English tax system"[39] already possessed powers of direct taxation – income tax in particular.[40]

---

[37] Fritz Neumark: "Die Finanzpolitik in der Zeit vor dem Ersten Weltkrieg", in Deutsche Bundesbank (ed.): *Währung und Wirtschaft in Deutschland 1876–1975*, p. 91.

[38] In 1886/90 military outlays amounted to over 95% of total Reich expenditures, and in 1911/13 still to about 90%. P.-C. Witt, *Finanzpolitik*, p. 380. Cp. also F. Terhalle: "Geschichte", p. 279. A concise survey of the structure of the finances in the last prewar year (1913/14) can also be found in Statistisches Reichsamt: *Die deutsche Finanzwirtschaft vor und nach dem Kriege. Einzelschriften zur Statistik des Deutschen Reichs,* Nr. 14 (Berlin, 1930), pp. 56–57.

[39] H. Jecht: *Kriegsfinanzen*, p. 59.

[40] On U.K. public finances before and during the First World War see, among many works, Paul Haensel: "Der Staatshaushalt und das Finanzsystem Grossbritanniens", article in *Handbuch der Finanzwissenschaft*, 1st edn. vol. 3 (1929), esp. pp. 79–87. Ursula K. Hicks: "Die öffentliche Finanzwirtschaft Grossbritanniens 1799–1949", article in *Handbuch der Finanzwissenschaft*, 2nd

112   Part Two: Explaining the Inflation

Table 25. Ordinary revenues of the Reich 1914–19. Million marks

	1914	1915	1916	1917	1918	1919
Customs	560.8	359.9	348.3	234.4	133.0	1088.8
Excises	775.8	516.2	668.8	1200.2	2032.8	3334.5
of which: Tobacco, cigarettes	68.3	79.7	202.9	419.5	699.4	716.4
Sugar	214.6	168.4	194.7	163.2	184.1	158.7
Brandy	228.0	95.6	73.1	19.6	29.2	120.4
Beer	130.7	78.5	55.2	20.2	33.9	136.8
Wine	–	–	–	–	159.6	414.9
Mineral waters	–	–	–	–	18.1	51.9
Coal	–	–	–	412.9	751.3	1552.2
Stamp duties	183.1	167.1	252.8	468.7	510.8	797.2
of which: on commodity transactions	–	–	24.3	111.7	84.5	–
Turnover tax	–	–	–	–	150.5	823.4
Duty on passenger and freight transport	–	–	–	64.5	291.6	468.3
Duty on postal charges	–	–	89.6	146.8	235.7	173.9
Capital gains tax	2.8	0.7	0.5	1.2	0.7	0.5
Wealth tax	–	–	–	101.5	89.1	76.8
Inheritance tax	43.6	48.8	65.0	69.8	77.8	87.0
Defense contribution	637.4	307.8	19.5	10.4	1.3	–
Extraordinary War levy of 1916	–	–	45.6	4842.7	791.8	93.2
Extraordinary War levy of 1918	–	–	–	–	1617.2	1072.9
Matricular contributions from the states (net)	51.9	51.9	51.9	51.9	51.9	–
Other	215.7	372.8	580.2	818.0	1411.0	2946.7
of which: from the profits of the Reichsbank	43.6	199.7	190.3	206.9	390.5 ⎱	
from the profits of the Loan Bureaux	–	60.0	60.0	275.0	495.0 ⎰	1550.0
Export duties	–	–	25.2	281.4	516.9	849.5
Surpluses from previous years	53.8	71.0	219.7	–	–	–
Total Ordinary Revenues (Excl. Gross revenues of Railways and Post Office)	2471.1	1825.2	2122.2	8010.1	7395.2	10963.2

Source: K. Roesler: *Die Finanzpolitik des Deutschen Reiches im Ersten Weltkrieg* (Berlin, 1967), p. 196.

edn. vol. 1 (1952), esp. pp. 331–334. Ursula K. Hicks: *British Public Finances. Their Structure and Development 1880–1952* (Oxford, 1954). A. W. Kirkaldy: *British Finance during and after the War* (London, 1921). E. V. Morgan: *Studies in British Financial Policy 1914–1925* (London, 1952). Gaston Jèze: *Les finances de guerre de l' Angleterre 1915–1918* (Paris, 1919). Willi Prion: *Steuer- und Anleihepolitik in England während des Krieges* (Berlin, 1918)

Germany's financial preparations for war had been chiefly governed by her experiences during the war with France in 1870/71.[41] The difficulty proved to be that whereas that had been a short war ending in German victory, the war Germany was now entering would be protracted and end in her defeat. The Franco-Prussian war lasted only half a year and cost no more than about one sixth of German national income at the time.[42] These costs were financed initially through loans of the North German Confederation, and of the belligerent German states,[43] and were ultimately more than offset by the French reparations of five billion francs. Over the four years of the First World War however German war expenditure amounted to about one hundred and fifty billion marks[44] – in nominal terms about four times Germany's 1913 national

Table 26. Ordinary expenditures of the Reich 1914–19. Million marks

	1914		1915		1916		1917		1918		1919	
	Marks	%	Marks	%	Marks	%	Marks	%	Marks	%	Marks	%
Deficits of Post Office, Railways, etc.	46.3	2.6	33.0	1.8	40.4	1.3	132.4	1.9	351.5	4.7	–	–
Military Expenditures (Army, Navy)	790.4	44.6	147.0	7.8	73.0	2.4	45.1	0.6	25.4	0.3	469.1	3.5
Costs of servicing the Reich debt	470.4	26.5	1346.0	71.7	2616.8	85.3	6518.8	92.2	6770.5	89.7	8397.1	62.9
Other ordinary expenditures	466.4	26.3	349.9	18.7	336.6	11.0	377.0	5.3	398.2	5.3	4512.8	33.6
Total ordinary expenditures	1773.5	100.0	1875.9	100.0	3066.8	100.0	7073.3	100.0	7545.6	100.0	13379.0	100.0
Surplus (+) or deficit (−) of ordinary revenues over ordinary expenditures	+697.6		−50.7		−944.6		+936.8		−150.4		−2415.8	

Source: K. Roesler: *Finanzpolitik, p. 197.*

[41] Reichsarchiv: *Der Weltkrieg 1914–1918. Kriegsrüstung und Kriegswirtschaft, Bd. 1: Die militärische, wirtschaftliche und finanzielle Rüstung Deutschlands von der Reichsgründung bis zum Ausbruch des Weltkrieges* (Berlin, 1930), p. 417. Cp. also Karl Helfferich; *Der Weltkrieg* (Berlin, 3 Bde. 1919), Bd. 2 pp. 34 ff. On the war of 1870/71, see Rudolf Lenz: *Kosten und Finanzierung des deutsch-französischen Krieges 1870/71* (Boppard am Rhein, 1971).

[42] M. Lanter: *Die Finanzierung des Krieges*, p. 46.

[43] H. Jecht: *Kriegsfinanzen*, pp. 29, 74.

[44] R. Knauss: *Die deutsche, englische und französische Kriegsfinanzierung*, p. 175.

income.[45] Over and above this came Reparations: rather than Germany's enemies defraying her war costs, she was required to help to defray theirs.

It was clear, both from the experience of 1870 and from the tenor of theoretical discussion that the declaration of war would probably be accompanied by a shortage of cash, partly because of hoarding, at the same time as the cash requirements of the Reich would be increasing enormously. Steps had been taken to cope with this eventuality. Certain of the measures for strengthening the credit system recommended by the Bank Inquiry of 1908,[46] and subsequently acted upon, owe their impetus to this consideration – for example the declaration in the Bank Act of 1909 that bank notes were legal tender, the steps taken to centralize gold reserves at the Reichsbank through the issue of smaller denomination notes as substitutes for coin (this began in 1906), and the encouragement of non-cash payment methods. Other measures of this type included the decision, announced in the "Law amending the Fiscal System" of July 3rd, 1913, to add 120 million marks worth of silver to the war bullion reserves, and to increase the circulation of state paper money (*Reichskassenscheine*) by the same amount.[47]

Further steps were taken at the outbreak of war to prevent a domestic run on the gold stock and on the banks, to reinforce the position of the Reichsbank, and to secure direct access for the Reich to the credit and money-creating facilities of the bank of issue. The first step was to suspend the gold convertibility of bank notes; this was done at the end of July 1914. On August 2nd the government turned its war bullion reserves over to the Reichsbank to serve as additional backing for the currency.[48] On August 4th the Reichstag

---

[45] W. G. Hoffmann *et al.*: *Das Wachstum der deutschen Wirtschaft seit der Mitte des 19. Jahrhunderts* (Berlin, 1965), p. 455.

[46] *Bankenquete 1908–1909, Stenographische Berichte nebst Materialien*, H. 1–3 (Berlin, 1909–1910). Summary of findings in L. Cohnstaedt: *Ergebnisse der Bankenquete* (Frankfurt/M., 1908). *Die Reichsbank 1901–1925* (Berlin, n.d.), pp. 26–38. Cp. Alfred Lansburgh: *Die Massnahmen der Reichsbank zur Erhöhung der Liquidität der deutschen Kreditwirtschaft* (Stuttgart, 1914) and the criticisms of the measures by Johann Plenge: *Von der Diskontpolitik zur Herrschaft über den Geldmarkt* (Berlin, 1913).

[47] Goetz Briefs: "Kriegswirtschaftslehre und Kriegswirtschaftspolitik", article in *Handwörterbuch der Staatswissenschaften*, vol. 5 (Jena, 1923), pp. 995–996. All preparatory measures were based on the presumption that the war would be short. "The fact that [the war] became more than we could manage both in its material demands and in its duration showed that we were not adequately prepared for it". Reich Finance Minister E. Schiffer: *Deutschlands Finanzlage nach dem Kriege. Rede gehalten in der Deutschen Nationalversammlung am 15. Februar 1919* (Berlin, 1919), p. 9. On the prevalent prewar expectations about the war's duration, see too Lothar Burchardt: *Friedenswirtschaft und Kriegsvorsorge* (Boppard am Rhein, 1968), pp. 14 ff.

[48] G. Briefs: "Kriegswirtschaftslehre", p. 997.

dispatched a number of laws placing the relationship between Reichsbank and credit system, and Reichsbank and central government, on a new basis. The salient provisions were as follows.[49]

(i) The Reichsbank was released from its duty to redeem its own notes and the *Reichskassenscheine* in gold on demand.

(ii) The tax levied on the Reichsbank when the circulation of its notes exceeded the legal maximum was abolished.[50]

(iii) Treasury bills (*Reichsschatzwechsel*) and interest-bearing treasury certificates (*Reichsschatzanweisungen*) were declared eligible secondary reserves against the note issue, on the same basis as good commercial bills.

(iv) Loan Bureaux were established, and subordinated to the Reichsbank. Their task would be to extend credit to the private sector as well as to public authorities, against the collateral of commodities or stock market securities. Against such collateral they issued non interest-bearing claims upon themselves – *Darlehnskassenscheine* (Loan Bureau Certificates) – which all public offices were obligated to accept at full face-value in discharge of debts. Thus these claims functioned effectively as money. Furthermore, the Reichsbank was empowered to substitute them, along with *Reichskassenscheine*, for bullion in the primary one-third reserve against its note issue. This power gave the Reichsbank autonomy in determining the size of the monetary base, for by varying the credit policy of the Loan Bureaux, it could control the legal limits to its own note issue.[51]

Table 20 reveals the extent to which the government of the Reich took advantage of the opportunities for recourse to the printing presses created by this legislation. During the first half of the war the Reich had considerable success in funding the floating debt that had initially been taken up by the Reichsbank. Successful War Loan flotations (cp. Table 27) were intended by the government to awaken the impression that the economy's excess and inflationary purchasing power was being absorbed, and hence to strengthen

---

[49] Rudolf Stucken: *Deutsche Geld- und Kreditpolitik 1914–1963* (Tübingen, 3rd edn. 1964), pp. 17ff. Hermann Bente: "Die deutsche Währungspolitik von 1914–1924", *Weltwirtschaftliches Archiv*, 23 (1926), I. pp. 117 + ff.

[50] On prewar statutory requirements regarding the note issue, see Jakob Riesser: *The Great German Banks and Their Concentration in Connection with the Economic Development of Germany* (Washington, D.C., 1911), pp. 143ff.

[51] As early as 1915 Friedrich Bendixen made critical notice of this implication, in his *Währungspolitik und Geldtheorie im Lichte des Weltkrieges* (Munich, 1915, 2nd edn. 1919), p. 28. On previous German experience with Loan Bureaux during political crises (1848, 1866, 1870), see Walter Lotz: "Darlehnskassen", article in *Handwörterbuch der Staatswissenschaften*, vol. 3 (Jena, 1926), pp. 209ff.

confidence in the currency. The reality was however that purchasing power placed in War Loans was no less liquid than that placed in treasury bills; the obligation upon the Loan Bureaux to accept them as collateral meant that up to the prescribed limit of 75 percent their cash value could at any time be realized without risk of capital loss. Thus, during the first half of the war more than fifty percent of the Loan Bureau Certificates entering circulation did so against the collateral of War Loan stock.[52] While it is true that only three billion marks worth of such Certificates had been issued by the end of 1916, implying that only a small fraction of aggregate War Loan stock had been employed in this fashion, the important point is the possibility this represented. By it War Loan was constituted as efficient a "potential money" as Reich treasury bills. Indeed the potential of War Loan stock as a source of monetary expansion was theoretically even greater than that of the floating treasury bill stock. The Loan Bureau Certificates which War Loan stock could command were eligible components of the primary reserve cover of the note issue; treasury bills were eligible only as secondary reserves and hence (until 1921) rediscountable only up to the limits dictated by the size of the primary reserves. There was a legal limit on the issue of Loan Bureau Certificates which stood initially at 1.5 billion marks. But a Bundesrat decree was sufficient to raise this limit,[53] and this is what happened whenever the liquidity requirements of the state or the private sector demanded it.

In the spring of 1916 the projections even for the ordinary budget slipped into deficit, despite the fact that military expenditures in their entirety were now debited to the extraordinary budget. The reason was that the cost of servicing the debt now exceeded what the existing sources of taxation could be expected to yield. With the intensified armaments drive called for by the new High Command in the so-called "Hindenburg program" of autumn 1916, this problem could only get worse. Beginning in the spring of 1916, then, the Reichstag agreed to a variety of tax rate increases and new taxes. These new taxes lay within the limits of the Reich's prewar fiscal base however: indirect

---

[52] Monthly data are to be found in a Table on p. 212 of K. Roesler: *Finanzpolitik*. For the 75 percent limit on Loans against the collateral of stock market securities cp. E. Hoppe: *Der Krieg und die deutsche Geldwirtschaft* (Essen, 1919), p. 22. General information on the role of the Loan Bureaux and their relationship with the Reichsbank is to be found in Robert A. v. Ruedorffer: "Reichsbank und Darlehnskassen in der Kriegsfinanzierung 1914–1918" (Dissertation, Cologne, 1968). Cp. also Reinhold Zilch: "Reichsbank und finanzielle Kriegsvorbereitung des deutschen Imperialismus 1907–1914" (Dissertation, Berlin-East, 1976). Rudolf Will: *Die schwebenden Schulden*, pp. 101 ff.

[53] K. Roesler: *Finanzpolitik*, p. 41. Leo Feuchtwanger: *Die Darlehnskassen des deutschen Reiches* (Stuttgart, 1918).

Chapter 5: The Determinants of Monetary Expansion   117

Table 27. Over- or undersubscription of War Loans 1914–18. Million marks

At the flotation of the ... War Loan (W. L.)	Short term treasury paper in current circulation	Amount of War Loan subscriptions	(+) Over- or (−) under- subscription
First W. L. 1914	2.6 M	4.5	+ 1.9
Second W. L. 1915	7.2 M	9.1	+ 1.9
Third W. L. 1915	9.7 M	12.1	+ 2.4
Fourth W. L. 1916	10.4 M	10.7	+ 0.3
Fifth W. L. 1916	12.8 M	10.7	− 2.1
Sixth W. L. 1917	19.9 M	13.1	− 6.8
Seventh W. L. 1917	27.2 M	12.6	−14.6
Eighth W. L. 1918	38.9 M	15.0	−23.9
Ninth W. L. 1918	49.4 M	10.4	−39.0

Source: "Die Finanzen des Deutschen Reiches in den Rechnungsjahren 1914–1918. Denkschrift der Reichsregierung vom 12. März 1919 (Drucksache der Nationalversammlung Nr. 158)", in *Finanzarchiv*, 36 (1919), pp. 797–798.

taxes and stamp duties and, of direct taxes, only an elaboration of the capital gains tax of 1913.[54] No further direct taxes were introduced by the Reich. The highly productive income and wealth taxes remained the preserve of the states and local governments: this did not change till after the war.[55]

The elaboration of the 1913 capital gains tax was the war profits tax of 1916. Under it, private individuals suffered a fifty percent tax rate on the nominal increase in the value of their assets between 31.12.1913 and 31.12.1916. For business companies the tax was assessed on the amount by which their war-time profits exceeded their average profits during the last prewar quinquennium. In 1916 the Reichstag also agreed to a turnover tax, at first confined to the sale of goods but extended in 1918 to the sale of services; the initial rate was one per mille. Consumer excises were increased on tobacco, cigarettes and beer, as were the customs duties on tea and coffee; eventually in 1918 new excises were even imposed on lemonade and mineral waters. A coal tax was

---

[54] Walther Lotz: *Die deutsche Staatsfinanzwirtschaft im Kriege* (Stuttgart, 1927), pp. 59 ff. K. Roesler: *Finanzpolitik*, pp. 105–106 and a summary of tax legislation on pp. 189–194.

[55] Erwin Respondek: *Die Reichsfinanzen auf Grund der Reform von 1919/20* (Berlin, 1921). Klaus Epstein: *Matthias Erzberger and the Dilemma of German Democracy* (Princeton, 1959), pp. 334–348. Johannes Popitz: "Die deutschen Finanzen 1918–1928", in *Zehn Jahre deutsche Geschichte 1918–1928* (Berlin, 1928), pp. 187 ff. Franz Menges: *Reichsreform und Finanzpolitik. Die Aushöhlung der Eigenstaatlichkeit Bayerns auf finanzpolitischem Wege in der Zeit der Weimarer Republik* (Berlin, 1971), pp. 184–228.

introduced in 1917 and proved to be the most productive of the new excises. Various stamp duties were also increased or first imposed after 1916.

These fiscal measures did raise the ordinary revenues of the Reich from 2.1 billion marks in 1916 to 8 billion in 1917 and 7.4 billion in 1918 (see Table 25). This was no more than was required to keep pace with the mounting burden of interest payments on Reich debt. In other words the one hundred and fifty billion marks of German war expenditure over four years were met almost entirely out of War Loan subscriptions (about one hundred billion marks) and, especially during the second half of the war, by increases in the floating debt (fifty billion). The Reich's rising ordinary revenues in the second half of the war did no more than pay the interest on this debt.

The contrast with Great Britain is striking. There tax increases were announced shortly after the commencement of hostilities. In 1914 the rate of income tax was doubled, the excise on beer tripled and that on tea raised by sixty percent.[56] In the following years too the tax screw was turned more tightly than in Germany. The earlier resort to, and the greater success of, taxation policy in Britain than in Germany are alike explained by the differential importance of direct taxes as sources of central government revenues in the two countries; their much greater role in Britain not only before but also during the war can be seen in Table 28. England however also enjoyed the additional advantage that part of her borrowing could be undertaken abroad, particularly in the empire and in the U.S.A., especially after that country had entered the war.

French wartime taxation resembled German: the central government was mainly dependent on indirect taxation for its ordinary revenues, and the taxable base shrank owing to the hostilities on her own territory. As a result tax revenue scarcely increased: it stood at 4.1 billion francs in 1913 and at 4.2

Table 28. Composition of central government ordinary tax revenues in Germany and Great Britain in 1913 and 1918 (%)

| | Great Britain | | Germany | |
	1913	1918	1913	1918
Direct taxes	47.5	77.2	3.5	43.4
Indirect taxes	46.0	21.2	81.3	47.9
Stamp duties	6.5	1.6	15.2	8.7

Source: Robert Knauss: *Die deutsche, englische und französische Kriegsfinanzierung* (Berlin, 1923), p. 148.

---

[56] Karl T. Eheberg: "Finanzen im Weltkrieg", p. 80.

billion francs in 1918,[57] and in fact war costs were met entirely by borrowing. However in her ability to borrow abroad France resembled England and met 21 % of the war-related expenditures in her extraordinary budget from this source.[58] Germany, by contrast, could not borrow abroad at any time during the war; rather, she herself had to make loans to her south-east European allies, and under the terms of the Treaty of Versailles these loans were entirely written off in the end.

Fiscal and monetary policy options in 1919

The German government had financed the war by readier resort to the printing presses than Great Britain, the United States or France. It had turned the tax screw more gently than the British or American governments, and been less able to rely on foreign loans than the British or French. Funding of the floating debt had been less successful in Germany than in any of the three Allied countries, particularly in the second half of the war. Inevitably, then, there *was* a "tax" which had played a larger role in German war finance than in that of her three principal opponents. Price inflation, which suppresses private claims on the domestic product thus releasing productive capacity for war purposes, can itself be viewed as a "tax".[1]

  "Inflation tax" falls indiscriminately on everyone with a net creditor position in domestic currency assets. Those whose access to credit enables them to contract domestic currency debts in excess of their domestic currency assets can easily evade it or indeed convert it into a subsidy, at the cost of very low,

---

[57] R. Knauss: *Die deutsche, englische und französische Kriegsfinanzierung*, p. 148.

[58] Cp. R. Will: *Die schwebenden Schulden*, p. 107.

[1] The conception of inflation as a species of taxation can be traced back to the classical economists. Cp. John Stuart Mill: *Principles of Political Economy. The Collected Works of J. S. Mill, vols. III–IV* (Toronto, 1965), vol. IV, p. 565 (original edition, 1848). Keynes in particular was responsible for reviving the conception during the 1920s in *A Tract on Monetary Reform. The Collected Writings of J. M. Keynes*, ed. E. Johnson and D. E. Moggridge, vol. IV (London, 1971), p. 37: Inflation "is the form of taxation which the public find hardest to evade and even the weakest government can enforce when it can enforce nothing else". The *Tract* was first published in 1923. Philip Cagan also emphasizes the same idea. "In the unsettled conditions following the two world wars governments were too weak to enact adequate tax programs and to administer them effectively. Issuing money was a method of raising revenue by a special kind of tax – a tax on cash balances. This tax is often appealing because it does not require detailed legislation and can be administered very simply." See his "Monetary Dynamics of Hyperinflation", in Milton Friedman (ed.): *Studies*, p. 78. With particular reference to the German inflation, see Friedrich Sommer: "Die Inflationssteuer" (Dissertation, Frankfurt/M., 1924).

even negative, real interest rates. Primarily, then, those whom "inflation tax" affects are those who hold the greatest share of their wealth in assets with fixed domestic-currency value. Real assets, foreign currency assets and "human capital" are not directly "taxed" by inflation, although the income which these yield may be affected as for example when wage, salary or permissible rent increases fail to keep up with the general rise of the price level. Secondly, the incidence of "inflation tax" varies inversely with ease of access to cheap domestic-currency credit. As a result, those who are versed in financial matters are generally speaking in a better position to evade the exactions of "inflation tax" than those who are not. Those who are wealthy to begin with are in a better position than those who are poor, because their wealth improves their ability to borrow. For those whose wealth is in real assets, hard foreign currency assets, or "human capital" and who can use this wealth to command credit in domestic currency, the "inflation tax" shifts into reverse, and becomes a subsidy. Obviously wealth is not *in itself* the passport to evasion of the tax however; many wealthy charities, universities, trade unions and associations, holding their wealth in the form of fixed value domestic-currency assets and not using it to obtain credits, had it wiped out by the inflation, as did wealthy individual rentiers, including many academics.[2]

Thus the incidence of this "tax" is not under the control of the taxing authorities. They can neither determine the class of people to be taxed nor do they determine the distribution of burden between them on the normal equita-

---

[2] Georg Schreiber: *Die Not der deutschen Wissenschaft und der geistigen Arbeiter* (Leipzig, 1923). Alfred Weber: "Die Not der geistigen Arbeiter", in *Schriften des Vereins für Socialpolitik*, Bd. 163 (Munich, 1923), p. 173: "The modern intelligentsia are a rentier-intelligentsia. They depend for their subsistence on their possession of small or moderate independent means – not in the sense (as far as most of them are concerned) that thereby they maintain themselves in professional idleness, but on the contrary that these means enable them to survive the early periods of training in the professions of which I have spoken, until the stage in their careers where they reach their full earning potential. For some, the possession of independent means serves as a permanent supplement to their professional earnings and as such formed the foundation of the intellectual liberty of the prewar intelligentsia…", [p. 174] "… [G]ermany's financial capital has as good as disappeared, and with it, as I have already drawn attention to, the foundation of the intellectual liberty of the intellegentsia". The same matter is dealt with in a larger chronological context by Fritz Ringer: *The Decline of the German Mandarins. The German Academic Community 1890–1933* (Cambridge, Mass.,1969), esp. pp. 62–66, and in a larger social context by Franz Eulenburg:" Die sozialen Wirkungen der Währungsverhältnisse", *Jahrbücher für Nationalökonomie und Statistik*, 122 (1924), pp. 748–794. The importance of the problem in contemporary eyes is shown by the fact that the Provisional Reich Economic Council set up a "Subcommittee for the Economic Advancement of Intellectual Labor" (Unterausschuß zur wirtschaftlichen Förderung der geistigen Arbeit) on October 9, 1920. Cp. Harry Hauschild: *Der vorläufige Reichswirtschaftsrat 1920–1926* (Berlin, 1926), p. 241.

ble principles of equality of sacrifice or ability to pay. The incidence in fact bore no calculable relation to any measurable criterion such as wealth. Rather it depended on the financial adroitness of the individual or of the institutions which he had made responsible for securing his investments and income – banks, business companies or (for the wage earner) trade unions. Under inflation, financial proficiency matters more than status or long established fortune, and the state's power to exact taxation is partially abdicated to its citizens, the most expert of whom turn to profit and subsidy what others experience as severe expropriation.

Periods of high inflation, therefore, resemble those of the classical "laissez-faire" relationship of power between the individual and the state. Such social conditions have been applauded as well as condemned, depending on the individual's political preferences.

In purely economic terms inflation has the following advantage over conventional taxation as a method of converting an economy from a peace to a war footing and back again, that it does not precipitate private sector illiquidity, bankruptcy and unemployment. The adjustments inherent in such large scale changes in the composition of output involve big enough costs without being intensified through illiquidity; resort to the "inflation tax" ensures that the adjustments are undertaken at maximum levels of aggregate output and employment. The economic costs of this method of "taxation" are of course registered in the weakening power of the currency to fulfil its traditional functions, particularly of serving as a store of value. While the war lasts however the time horizon relevant to economic policy-making becomes foreshortened; "the great importance that in normal times is correctly attached to currency stability has to give way to the more urgent objectives dictated by the war."[3] "With the return of peace, however, currency policy objectives which have often been forced into second place by wartime military and political objectives, will regain their former importance. The question then arises, whether official policy should regard as its goal the maintenance of the value which money has acquired during the course of the war, or whether it should seek to bring its value back to what it was before the war."[4] This sums up the currency problem created by the war, already discussed in all the belligerent countries during it, and ultimately requiring to be faced when the war ended and the ground rules for postwar currency policy needed to be fixed.

In the United States the decision to prevent internal currency collapse was taken in December 1919. In that month the Federal Reserve Board, supported

---

[3] Richard Hauser: "Unsere Währung nach dem Kriege", *Bank-Archiv*, 17 (1917/18), p. 3.
[4] *Ibid.*

by the Treasury, acted to break the inflationary pressures set up by the wartime and postwar boom. A high interest rate policy precipitated a fall in economic activity, culminating in the world slump of 1920–21.[5] The recession was sharper than that of 1929–32,[6] as also, however, was the subsequent recovery.

The *external* stability of the dollar and its convertibility into gold was never in question. The war had strengthened the financial solidity of the U.S.A. and substantially enlarged its gold reserves, and postwar developments only reinforced this tendency. The war had the opposite effect on the British financial position and bullion reserves. In Britain the currency debate revolved round the question of whether or not to restore sterling's prewar international parity; a decision on this question also necessarily determining the extent to which the pound's domestic purchasing power could be allowed to depreciate. In 1918 the British government established the so-called Cunliffe Committee to examine the question and make recommendations. It decided that policy should aim to restore the prewar parity under conditions of convertibility (during the war exchange controls and practically unlimited U.S. credits had enabled the near-maintenance of parity), and that exchange controls should be abolished forthwith.[7] Since the floating pound was well below parity after the war, these recommendations dictated a deflationary course for domestic prices and economic activity. The inadequacy of Britain's own bullion reserves compelled her to subordinate her currency policy strictly to that of other major gold standard countries, chief among which was the U.S.A. It forced the United Kingdom to accommodate her own policy fully to the contractionary policy introduced by the U.S.A. at the end of 1919; no other course of action

---

[5] Elmus R. Wicker: *Federal Reserve Monetary Policy 1917–1933* (New York, 1966), pp. 42–43. Milton Friedman and Anna J. Schwartz: *A Monetary History of the United States 1867–1960* (Princeton, 1963), p. 227.

[6] Derek H. Aldcroft: *From Versailles to Wall Street 1919–1929* (London, 1977), pp. 68–9. Cp. also p. 209 *infra*. On the development of economic conditions outside Germany after the war see also Statistisches Reichsamt: *Die Wirtschaft des Auslandes 1900–1927. Einzelschriften zur Statistik des Deutschen Reichs*, Nr. 5 (Berlin, 1928). More particularly on fiscal developments see Statistisches Reichsamt: *Die Staatsausgaben von Grossbritannien, Frankreich, Belgien und Italien in der Vor- und Nachkriegszeit. Einzelschriften zur Statistik des Deutschen Reichs*, Nr. 2 (Berlin, 1927).

[7] Committee on Currency and Foreign Exchanges after the War: *First Interim Report* (London. 1919). This "interim report" contains the essential recommendations. The documents collected by the Committee – submissions from experts, discussions within the Committee, statements by interest groups – are to be found in the Public Record Office, London, T185/1–3. A recent discussion and assessment of the Committee's deliberations and recommendations is offered by Donald E. Moggridge: *British Monetary Policy 1924–31. The Norman Conquest of $ 4.86* (Cambridge, England, 1972), pp. 17–21. Cp. also Albert Feavearyear: *The Pound Sterling. A History of English Money* (Oxford, 2nd edn. 1963), pp. 348–50.

was possible if the depreciation of sterling against the dollar that had followed
the lifting of currency controls in 1919 was to be halted (cp. Diagram 2).

The basis of the British decision was the calculation that the fiscal
economies necessary for the domestic stabilization of the pound were both
achievable and politically desirable and that the deflationary costs of the action
would be compensated both by the restoration of London's role as an international financial center and by the improvement this in turn would cause in
Britain's capacity to trade on world markets. But reality proved different from
the calculation. Britain's international position continued to weaken, partly
because America's policy ran counter to the "rules" of the gold standard.
Gold flows into the U.S.A. were "sterilized" to prevent their causing domestic price rises, and tariff barriers were increased, thus limiting other countries'
capacities to earn the gold and dollars they needed to buy imports and repay
debts. These measures to insulate the American money and goods markets
from outside influences stood in the way of any permanent improvement of
the British external trading position and hence of the position of sterling. At
the same time U.S. policy set its face steadily against European, especially
French, demands for the cancellation of inter-allied debts.[8] In Gottfried
Haberler's view, the increasing protectionism of the U.S.A., the world's
greatest creditor nation, during this period could only be described as "sa-
distic."[9] The American economist B.M. Anderson described the U.S.
government's schizoid economic policy – demanding repayment of debts but
preventing the corresponding real transfers – with the following metaphor:
"The debts of the outside world to us are ropes about the necks of our debtors,
by means of which we pull them toward us. Our trade restrictions are pitch-
forks pressed against their bodies, by means of which we hold them off. This
situation can obviously involve a very painful strain for the foreign debtor."[10]
These were the external strains to which the British economy was exposed in
the twenties and which constrained her economic development.

The decision to "return to gold" not only exposed the British economy to
these deflationary impulses from abroad; it also created a domestic environment inimical to enterprise. The falling price level conferred a bonus on net
holders of fixed value domestic-currency assets – the rentiers who held conser-

---

[8] Statistisches Reichsamt: *Die interalliierten Schulden. Ihre Entstehung und ihre Bedeutung im Youngplan*
(Berlin, 1930), esp. the documents on pp. 115 ff. Cp. H.G. Moulton and L. Pasvolsky: *War
Debts and World Prosperity* (Washington, D.C., 1932), chapters III. – V.

[9] Gottfried Haberler: *The Theory of International Trade with its Applications to Commercial Policy*
(London, 1936), p. 80 (German original, 1933).

[10] In Chase National Bank (ed.): *The Chase Economic Bulletin* (New York), March 14, 1930. Cited
from G. Haberler: *International Trade*, p. 80.

vatively selected asset portfolios including a high proportion of War Loans and other government stocks and who had not used their wealth to contract large debts. Such people, earning nominally fixed-interest incomes, were the beneficiaries of falling prices, whereas the same price falls discouraged the enterprising elements in society from extending their business activities by borrowing to invest in real or "human" capital. Since the state was the largest debtor of all, the chosen deflationary policy entailed an "austerity" policy; debt service charges increased with higher interest rates while tax revenues tended to fall; this compelled so much the greater savings on other classes of expenditure. The "Geddes" axe fell on personnel and infrastructural investment projects. Employment of labor and utilization of capital suffered as a result; business willingness to invest was weakened and the rate of economic growth diminished. An environment was created in which the required adjustments of economic structure necessarily brought heavy structural unemployment in their train.

These comparisons furnish a background against which to consider the corresponding discussion in Germany. The alternatives, "return to the prewar parity" or "stabilization at a depreciated exchange rate", were already being debated during the war itself.[11] Initially, the fiscal implications of the choice played a subordinate part in the discussion; however as early as 1916 the Swedish economist Gustav Cassel[12] had made them the basis of his argument that after the war the mark ought to be stabilized at a lower parity. Drawing attention to the great rise in the national debt during the war he pointed out, "The real burden of an annual interest charge of one billion marks must obviously double, if the purchasing power of the currency unit doubles in which the debt is denominated."[13] German discussion recognized that restoration of the prewar parity would penalize the public household with reduced tax revenues out of which unaltered debt servicing obligations would have to be met.[14] Nevertheless it was steadfastly maintained that domestic prices must be reduced to their prewar level in order to protect the real wealth of prewar creditors. The "goal of speedy restoration of the external parity"[15] of the mark was equally undisputed: restoration of convertibility at a lower parity or, worse still, the retention of an inconvertible paper currency would

[11] R. Hauser: "Unsere Währung nach dem Kriege", pp. 2–6.
[12] Gustav Cassel: *Deutschlands wirtschaftliche Widerstandskraft* (Berlin, 1916), pp. 155–156. Subsequently, Gustav Cassel, *Money and Foreign Exchange after 1914* (London, 1922), pp. 254 ff.
[13] G. Cassel: *Deutschlands wirtschaftliche Widerstandskraft*, p. 151.
[14] R. Hauser: "Unsere Währung nach dem Kriege", p. 4.
[15] *Ibid.*

"seriously jeopardize the reputation of our currency as an international means of settlement, as well as the international position of our banking system... For more than a generation our banks and great merchant houses have been endeavoring to secure recognition for the mark as an international currency alongside the pound and the franc. Success crowned their efforts, so that not only the greater part of German foreign trade but even a portion of the foreign trade of neighboring countries to the south and east was settled in mark currency – a situation bringing German banks pecuniary and other advantages that had previously been enjoyed by London."[16] These sentiments are reminiscent of those which in Great Britain led the Cunliffe Committee to make its – eventually realized – currency recommendations.

However during the war currency theorists in Germany – as in England – did debate whether the return should take the form of a full "gold currency" system or merely a "gold reserve" system in which the nation's gold stocks would be centralized at the Reichsbank and the currency would be convertible only for the purposes of foreign transactions.[17] On the question of the parity itself and of the domestic price level to be aimed at, virtual unanimity reigned – as in the Cunliffe Committee: return to prewar conditions. "Our postwar currency policy must aim at as rapid as possible a restoration of the parity – this is the overwhelming consensus among those practically and theoretically concerned with the question." So wrote Friedrich Bendixen as late as October 18th, 1918.[18]

But in 1919 a fundamental change of opinion came across the discussion. From now on the debate about how to restore currency stability revolved, in principle, round three distinct possibilities. Common to all of them was the long-term goal of pegging the mark to some gold or foreign exchange parity, thereby also securing domestic price stability. They differed however as to the external parity and domestic price level to be aimed at. Disregarding minor differences of detail, the proposals discussed can be reduced to one or other of the following three schools of thought.

(i) Return to the prewar parity, i.e. (relative to the actual situation at the war's end) reduction of the price level and appreciation of the exchange rate. This type of proposal entailed a rigorous fiscal deflation yielding the budget surpluses out of which the state could retire both the floating debt and the long-term debt as it matured.

---

[16] *Ibid.*, pp. 5–6.

[17] The gold reserve currency was explicitly recommended by e.g. Robert Liefmann, Johann Plenge, Otto Heyn and Friedrich Bendixen.

[18] Friedrich Bendixen: "Die Parität und ihre Wiederherstellung", *Bank-Archiv*, 18(1918/19), p. 9.

(ii) Stabilization at the existing price level, thus avoiding the need for domestic price deflation and external exchange rate appreciation. Contemporaries applied the word, "devaluation" (*Devalvation*) to this course of action; in currency history it was sometimes associated with proposals designed to reconstitute original currency relationships in nominal terms: by overprinting banknotes or exchanging existing notes for new in a fixed ratio, and by converting nominal debt values.[19] This type of proposal merely involved the government's renouncing the right to pursue further inflationary financial policies.

(iii) Continued price inflation and exchange rate depreciation. This policy entailed yet further increases in governmental indebtedness at the Reichsbank, hence in the monetary base, using either premature retirement of War Loan stock or continued budget deficits to bring the cash thus created into general circulation. Its advocates recommended this strategy as an alternative to a regular "state bankruptcy,"[20] under which the state suspends retirements of, and interest payments upon, its debt, thus permitting nominal public debt values to collapse. Inflation by contrast reduces the real value not only of public but also of private debts.

This last argument is sufficient to show that the fiscal dilemma of the Reich was becoming an increasingly central element in the currency debate as the war ended. At the heart of the discussion was the question whether and how the Reich was to service and redeem the long term debt of around one hundred billion marks which it had contracted during the war. Including the floating debt, the aggregate had increased to 175 billion marks by the middle of 1919, representing annual interest charges of about 9 billion marks. Helfferich estimated national wealth on the eve of the war at about three hundred billion marks.[21] This gives a perspective on the size of the problem: were prices reduced to the prewar *status quo ante*, the state would have to appropriate more than half the nation's assets to redeem its debts. The nine billion marks interest charges (175 bn. marks at five percent) were four times the Reich's

---

[19] Friedrich Bendixen: "Devalvation, Eine Richtigstellung", *Bank-Archiv*, 19 (1919/20), pp. 163–169. Carl Weill: "Betrachtungen zum Devalvationsproblem", *Bank-Archiv*, 19 (1919/20), p. 183. Cp. too Karl Diehl: "David Ricardo und der finanzielle Wiederaufbau Englands nach den napoleonischen Kriegen", *Bank-Archiv*, 19 (1919/20), p. 122.

[20] Alfred Manes: *Staatsbankrotte. Wirtschaftliche und rechtliche Betrachtungen* (Berlin, 1918). Waldemar Haefner-Hainen: *Der Staatsbankrott in Deutschland unvermeidlich. Ein ernster Mahnruf an die Nationalversammlung in Weimar* (Leipzig, 1919). Paul Bang: *Staatsbankrott oder -erneuerung?* (Munich, 1920).

[21] Karl Helfferich: *Deutschlands Volkswohlstand 1888–1913* (Berlin, 6th edn. 1915), p. 122.

total 1913 revenues of 2.2 billion marks.[22] This was the essence of the fiscal dilemma that had built up by the end of the war. The strategy selected to resolve it simultaneously determined postwar currency policy, as we shall see by further examination of each of the three schools of thought on the subject.

(i) Those who proposed the first type of policy – restoration of prewar parity plus domestic price deflation – generally supported it with a two-stage policy for dealing with the debt problem. They proposed that the floating debt be dealt with as soon as possible, by funding loans. Steps should then be taken to reduce the principal of the funded debt, preferably by means of a non-recurrent capital levy.[23]

The only attempt at a funding loan by the Reich after the war ended however in failure. This was the so-called *Sparprämienanleihe* of 1919[24] and its under-subscription registered the decline of the state's credit worthiness in the eyes of the public. War Loan stock traded at very depressed prices on the stock market;[25] this was a symptom of the same ailment, as Karl Elster confirmed in an article published on July 15th, 1919: "A single observation tells all. On the stock market the price of five percent War Loan stands almost twenty five percent below that of the four percent mortgage bonds of commercial mortgage banks (*Hypothekenpfandbriefe*). There exists only one explanation for this unhappy, indeed shameful state of affairs: War Loan is no longer regarded as a secure investment."[26] The "observation" Elster refers to reflects public anxiety about possible state bankruptcy of the classic type, affecting governmental debts only or at least not affecting private debts in the same measure.

But even had it proved possible to place long-term Reich debt, it must be questioned whether such a "funding" operation would have had a significant counterinflationary impact. This is because of the high liquidity of Reich Loan stock as already described, in virtue of its eligibility as collateral at the Loan Bureaux and of the admissibility of the Loan Bureau Certificates it could thus command as components of the primary currency reserve.[27] The expansionary implications of funded debt for the monetary base were not much less than

---

[22] Peter-Christian Witt: *Die Finanzpolitik des Deutschen Reiches von 1903 bis 1913* (Lübeck, 1970), p. 379.

[23] Fritz Terhalle: "Zum Inflationsproblem der Übergangswirtschaft", *Bank-Archiv*, 18 (1918/19), p. 93 (February 15, 1919).

[24] F. Hesse: *Die deutsche Wirtschaftslage von 1914 bis 1923. Krieg, Geldblähe und Wechsellagen* (Jena, 1938), p. 137.

[25] The stock market prices of War Loans are reproduced in the *Statistische Jahrbücher für das Deutsche Reich*, 1920–1923.

[26] Karl Elster: "Kriegsanleihen und Finanznot", *Bank-Archiv*, 18 (1918/19), p. 212.

[27] See p. 115 *supra*.

those of the floating debt; subscription to the former reduced lenders' liquidity only somewhat more than purchase of the latter. It seems astonishing, then, that to my knowledge not one of the postwar anti-inflationary proposals for consolidating the floating debt even discussed its necessary corollary: the closing of the Loan Bureaux.

Against this it must be conceded that wartime funding issues may have achieved a counterinflationary result by a different route: by building confidence in the solidity of the Reich's financial policy and hence, more generally, in the currency. As long as the Loan Bureaux existed, Reich funding policy could hardly damp inflationary pressures from the supply side (by reducing lender liquidity and the potential growth of the monetary base); it could however act to support the demand for money, by its psychological effect on confidence, and this would help to contain inflation. After the war however general confidence in the Reich's credit worthiness had so much deteriorated that even this effect could not operate.

The second part of this proposal for creating the fiscal prerequisites of a return to prewar currency relationships involved a tax measure: the non-recurrent capital levy.[28] Even before the war ended this possibility had been faced and thoroughly ventilated.[29] Its aim would be to "lighten the burden" of the war debt and it was to be undertaken in the context of wider fiscal reform designed to mobilize new sources of taxation. By making it *non-recurrent*, the *continuing* burden of postwar taxation required to service the remaining part of the debt could be rendered bearable. "Had we the choice between gradual amortization on the basis of a moderate burden of annual taxation, and a non-recurrent capital levy, the gradual amortization would unquestionably be preferable. But in fact we face a different choice: between gradual amortization coupled with an intolerable tax burden, and the non-recurrent levy. The levy is a severe measure indeed, but justifiable as it reduces the permanent burden of taxation considerably."[30]

The proposed levy was partially realized in the "Reich Emergency Contribution" (*Reichsnotopfer*) exacted from the wealthier classes as part of the great Erzberger tax reforms. It was, however, payable in installments, contrary to the original conception, and became a recurrent charge on wealth additional

---

[28] Otto Heyn: "Die Geldentwertung; ihre Ursache und die Mittel zu ihrer Beseitigung", *Bank-Archiv*, 18 (1918/19), p. 72 (January 15, 1919).

[29] Cp. the various contributions on the question of the "non-recurrent capital levy" from Karl Diehl und Felix Somary (both in favor) and from Heinrich Dietzel and Paul Homburger (both against), plus the annexed discussions, in Heinrich Herkner (ed.): *Die Neuordnung der deutschen Finanzwirtschaft. Schriften des Vereins für Socialpolitik Bd. 156 I–III* (Munich, 1918).

[30] Karl Diehl in *ibid.*, Bd. 156 I, p. 11.

to wealth holders' existing liabilities under the "Defense Contribution" of 1919[31] and the extraordinary 'War levy' of 1917. The assessments under the Emergency Contribution were made in nominal terms and the first installment was not due until 1920 by which time the swelling of the floating debt and consequent diminution in the value of the currency had assumed considerably larger proportions than in November 1918 (cp. Tables 1 and 20).

This is the astounding thing. All the time that people were discussing the *reduction* of the floating and funded debt resulting from the war, the Reich in 1919 was finding it impossible to operate without continuing to contract new floating debt at a rapid rate. Reich expenditures in 1919 did show a decline against the last year of the war: 55 as against 76 billion marks.[32] Expenditures by state and communes on the other hand were considerably higher: in Prussia they were 17.3 billion marks in 1919 as against 9.7 billion marks in 1918.[33] Meanwhile the ordinary revenues of the Reich showed only a modest increase: from 7.4 billion marks in 1918 to 11.0 in 1919 (cp. Table 25) and did little to reduce the overwhelming reliance on deficit financing, now almost exclusively through short-term borrowing. The fighting and maintenance costs of a military establishment formed a much smaller proportion of Reich expenditures in 1919 than in the previous year; in their place however came the costs of demobilizing the armed forces and reintegrating them into employment, also the costs imposed by the Armistice terms and the Peace Treaty.

It may be concluded then that the strategy of "lightening the burden" of Reich debt and restoring prewar currency conditions was no longer a realistic alternative even as early as 1918/19, once Germany had lost the war and the burden of Reparations had been superimposed on the crushing load of the Reich's internal debt. Any attempt not only to service but also to redeem this debt out of taxation – recurrent or non-recurrent – would have involved a deflation and depression of unimaginable severity – if it had not first burst the bounds of all tax morality and administrative capacity. No government could have survived such a policy; the newly constituted republic would have been no exception to this judgment. Richard Hauser, who in October 1917 had still been advocating resumption of the prewar parity, came to recognize that circumstances alter cases. In July 1919 he wrote that, "the preconditions on which the judgment [i.e. restoration of the parity] rested have now altered fundamentally."[34] Restoration was now no longer desirable since the greater

---

[31] Boleslav Fux: "Die Vermögenssteuer", article in *Handbuch der Finanzwissenschaft* (Tübingen, 1st edn. 3 Bde. 1925–9), Bd. 2 (1927), p. 153.

[32] F. Hesse: *Deutsche Wirtschaftslage*, p. 422.

[33] A. Jessen: *Finanzen, Defizit und Notenpresse 1914–1922* (Berlin, 1923), Tafel (i.e. Table) 1.

[34] Richard Hauser: "Zur Währungsfrage", *Bank-Archiv*, 18 (1918/19), p. 197 (July 1, 1919).

part of the state's wartime debt had been contracted after the currency had already begun to depreciate; return to 1914 prices would bring the creditors unjustifiable windfall gains. But in any case, Hauser argued, the restoration of the original parity was "simply not possible", in view of the condition of the Reich's finances. Using the argument already expounded that at 1913 prices the Reich's current internal debt would amount to half the aggregate prewar German national wealth, and adding that interest charges on the same debt at a rate of five percent would represent one quarter of the prewar national income at the prewar price level,[35] he concluded, "Annual interest charges to the tune of ten billion gold marks would, in view of the additional obligations toward the Entente, prove a greater burden than the German national income could bear and would inevitably lead to collapse. Consideration of the internal debt problem rules out categorically the restoration of the former parity of our currency."

Richard Hauser emphasized other problems of returning to the prewar parity, notably the implied pressure on wages and prices. "The attempt to reduce workers' wages would create insuperable difficulties... Conflict between wage earners and employers would be interminable... Under present political circumstances such a measure could not be achieved without great damage being done."[36] In October 1918, just before the war ended, Friedrich Bendixen had already warned against restoring the gold parity of the mark, and his reservations had less to do with the associated fiscal problems than with its probable effects on production, social relations and politics. Bendixen's arguments sound in places like a criticism of the English Cunliffe Committee proposals: it would be perverse, he wrote, "to regard the gold value of the currency in itself as a good, directly enhancing the welfare and honor of the people, and worth paying any economic price to achieve."[37] As if passing premonitory judgment on Brüning's policy of deflation, he opined, "No statesman would want to incur responsibility for the odious policy of depressing wages. To drive prices down is, however, likewise the reverse of good policy."[38] Bendixen recommended that those who formulated postwar financial and currency measures pay attention to the consequences of alternative policies for national production. He warned of the effects of traumatic tax increases designed to reduce the quantity of money and the price level. "Un-

---

[35] Cp. Karl Helfferich: *Deutschlands Volkswohlstand*, p. 122, who estimated German prewar national income at forty billion marks.

[36] R. Hauser: "Zur Währungsfrage", p. 198.

[37] F. Bendixen: "Die Parität und ihre Wiederherstellung", p. 13 (October 15, 1918).

[38] *Ibid.*

employment, devaluation of real production and credit crisis would be the hallmarks of this fateful policy. On the contrary, nothing will in fact be so bitterly necessary in Germany after the war as the harnessing of our entire economic capabilities to the task of production."[39]

Thus the first school of thought about postwar currency policy no longer enjoyed serious support after the end of the war, mainly on account of its fiscal implications. Advocates of the second and third types of proposal – stabilization at present price levels or continued inflation – were not lacking: what distinguished them was the importance they attached to production policy.

(ii) Willi Prion may be regarded as the most prominent representative of the second school of thought. In 1918 he had, it is true, prepared a memorandum for the Reich Finance Ministry that bore the title, "Financial Measures for Reducing Prices", but in it he had reached the conclusion that, "price stability would be more advantageous than the objective of achieving a lower price level at some future date, both for the economic life of the country and for the public finances. The same conclusion applies to exchange rate policy."[40] Like Hauser and Bendixen he justified his recommendation with economic, social and political arguments on the one hand, and with reference to fiscal considerations on the other. "The process of reconstituting the former (prewar) price level would set in motion a whole train of new economic disturbances. In particular, owners of real goods... would suffer losses, the production of new goods would come to a standstill, commodity markets would be dislocated, and wage disputes would threaten economic and social life with incalculable damage. It would have the most far-reaching consequences for public finance. The enormous debts contracted by public authorities in depreciated currency would have to be paid back with good money. Creditors would do good business, for they would get back their principal at the same face value, but with greater purchasing power. Quite apart from the harshness and injustice of such a distribution of burdens and benefits, the raising of the required taxation would weigh intolerably on those who shared only the burden."[41] Price reductions should therefore occur only when they could be generated from the side of real supply – that is, from increasing production.[42]

Prion recommended forced loans, income taxes and excises on consumer

---

[39] *Ibid.*

[40] Willi Prion: *Inflation und Geldentwertung. Finanzielle Massnahmen zum Abbau der Preise. Gutachten erstattet dem Reichsfinanzministerium* (Berlin, 1919), p. 108.

[41] *Ibid.*, p. 113.

[42] *Ibid.*, p. 108.

goods as the method of meeting the state's fiscal requirements and hence of attacking the root cause of inflation; the tax increases were to be introduced once increases in production were depressing prices and thus creating an environment where they could be passed on in a non-inflationary manner. Finally he recommended a non-recurrent capital levy, to be paid in a lump sum and not by installments, thus preventing its being passed on in higher prices. He believed that the upward pressure on prices of a capital levy payable in installments would be greater than the corresponding upward pressure exerted by income and consumption taxes. The latter taxes bore on the mass of the population, reducing its purchasing power and this effect would counter-act attempts to pass them on in higher prices. A capital levy affects the rich only who would react by cutting back on saving and hence investment, thus protecting their level of consumption; lump-sum payment would prevent its being passed on. Nonetheless the Reich Emergency Contribution was in the event levied in installment form; it was payable over a maximum of fortyseven years.

(iii) The third school of thought regarding currency policy – that advocat-ing further inflation – remains to be discussed. Prion, Hauser and Bendixen had all at first argued that the price level should be stabilized at its current, depreciated level, but towards the middle of 1919[43] Bendixen[44] made public a proposal which had been the subject of private discussion since March.[45] His immediate concern was simply to propose a method of eliminating the en-larged discount at which the Reich's long-dated issues were standing in the aftermath of the announcement of the Allied peace treaty conditions; in doing so however he explicitly advocated accelerated inflation as a mode of taxation: the Reich should redeem its long-term debt prematurely and at par value, obtaining the requisite cash by recourse to the central bank; alternatively it should convert its long-dated stocks into treasury bills, thus giving the hold-ers immediate access to central bank credit and to additional newly created money. This course of action would remove the threat of state bankruptcy; at the same time the productive economy could enjoy the benefits of plentiful and depreciating currency. For it was preferable, "to exploit to the full the opportunities afforded by money creation, than to cripple the forces of pro-duction and the spirit of enterprise by a confiscatory tax policy."[46]

---

[43] This is clear from an article discussing the proposal: Karl Elster: "Kriegsanleihen und Finanz-not" (July 15, 1919). Elster is ultimately unsympathetic to the proposal.

[44] Friedrich Bendixen: *Kriegsanleihen und Finanznot. Zwei finanzpolitische Vorschläge* (Jena, 1919).

[45] *Ibid.*, p. 18.

[46] *Ibid.*, p. 9.

Keynes drew a similar contrast between the two alternatives a few years later: "Thus inflation is unjust and deflation is inexpedient. Of the two perhaps deflation is...the worse, because it is worse in an impoverished world to provoke unemployment than to disappoint the rentier."[47] Whereas Keynes however saw evils in both alternatives, and believed they could be avoided by a policy of price stabilization,[48] Bendixen regarded stabilization in the existing circumstances as a good deal worse than inflation. "I have never denied that what I propose is an evil, but it is the only means of preventing a still worse evil... We may deprecate the fraudulent excesses of speculation and of entrepreneurial activity that inflation would bring – and not without reason: but are we on this account to prefer the corpse-strewn battlefield into which the repudiation of the War Loans would turn our economy?"[49] Bendixen believed it would be impossible, or at least extremely injurious to the economy, to repay the War Loans out of taxation. He also regarded inflation as preferable to the type of tax system that – under existing political conditions – was threatening wealth holders and high income groups in the manner proposed and partly effectuated under the Erzberger tax reforms. Bendixen's prejudice against the *soziale Republik* and its tax schemes is unmistakable:[50] whether his inflationary proposals flow more from his anxieties regarding government tax proposals, or from his concern about growth and employment, is difficult to decide. It is significant however that even the government itself and the higher levels of the bureaucracy undoubtedly formulated and discussed currency proposals on the lines of Bendixen's, as Prion remarks in his memorandum of 1919.[51]

Bendixen's proposals to convert War Loan stock into cash were never put designedly into effect. The Reich did occasionally make open market purchases of its bonds and sometimes accepted them in discharge of tax liabilities – practices which reduced the one hundred billion marks' worth outstanding at the end of the war to around seventy billion in early 1924[52] – but these were not the principal inflation-accelerating and production-stimulating forces in the early postwar economy. Rather Bendixen's results were achieved by a

---

[47] J. M. Keynes: *A Tract on Monetary Reform. The Collected Writings of J. M. Keynes, ed. E. Johnson and D. E. Moggridge, vol. IV* (London, 1971), p. 36 (original edition, 1923).

[48] Thus too Willi Prion: *Inflation und Geldentwertung*, p. 114.

[49] Friedrich Bendixen: " Die Inflation als Rettungsmittel", *Bank-Archiv*, 19 (1919/20), p. 54 (December 1, 1919).

[50] *Ibid.* where the polemical tone is manifest.

[51] W. Prion: *Inflation und Geldentwertung*, p. 113.

[52] Cp. p. 327 *infra*.

different route – as continuing budget deficits necessitated a continuous expansion of the floating debt. Constantly increasing prices eroded the real receipts from taxes assessed on a nominal basis and payable, as is customary in the case of wealth taxes and taxes on higher incomes, only after a certain lapse of time from the assessment. Even the servicing of War Loans, regarded by Bendixen as a primary cause of the Reich's fiscal difficulties, became an ever more minor element of Reich expenditure as the inflation progressed. Indeed the goal he pursued was far more effectively achieved by the route actually followed than by the means he proposed. Repayment of War Loan would not have greatly increased liquidity in the economy. As long as it could be lodged as collateral at any time at the Loan Bureaux, official repurchase was not necessary to create this effect – War Loan was almost "as good as money" anyway. It was the pressures exerted by a deficitary public household that had the greatest impact on inflation and production, and this mechanism played no part in Bendixen's scheme; he may have envisaged a balanced budget.

Whatever the positive advantages claimed for the postwar inflation as a means of easing the transition to peacetime production, of promoting full employment and of stimulating private investment, its power to rescue the private economy from the clutches of an unacceptable tax system, based on socially equitable criteria and aiming at income and wealth redistribution, is vividly illustrated by the history of the Reich Emergency Contribution. Announced in December 1919 as the successor to two provisional measures of that year – the 'War Levy on Capital Gains' and the 'Extraordinary War Levy for Fiscal Year 1919' – its tax rates were strongly progressive: rising from 10% of the value of assets at five thousand marks to 65% at above seven million marks.[53] According to original estimates the tax would cream off up to one

---

[53] Fritz Terhalle: "Geschichte der deutschen öffentlichen Finanzwirtschaft vom Beginn des 19. Jahrhunderts bis zum Schlusse des Zweiten Weltkrieges", article in *Handbuch der Finanzwissenschaft* (Tübingen, 2nd edn. 4 Bde. 1952–65), Bd. 1 (1952), p. 298. Cp. also Johannes Popitz: "Die deutschen Finanzen 1918–1928", *Zehn Jahre Deutsche Geschichte 1918–1928* (Berlin, 1928), pp. 189–190. More detailed: Robert Eichhorn: *Die einmaligen Vermögensabgaben im Deutschen Reiche* (Jena, 1925), esp. pp. 16 ff. Cp. also *Akten der Reichskanzlei. Weimarer Republik. Das Kabinett Fehrenbach*, pp. 265–266, note 1. Detailed statistical material on the effects of the Reich's financial policies during the war is to be found in the state memoranda: "Die Finanzen des Deutschen Reiches in den Rechnungsjahren 1914 bis 1918", in *Verhandlungen der Verfassunggebenden Deutschen Nationalversammlung, Bd. 335* (Berlin, 1920), Drucksache Nr. 158. "Der künftige finanzielle Bedarf des Reichs und seine Deckung", in *Verhandlungen der Verfassunggebenden Deutschen Nationalversammlung, Bd. 338* (Berlin, 1920), Drucksache Nr. 760. "Die finanzielle Lage des Reichs", in *Verhandlungen des Reichstages, Bd. 363* (Berlin, 1924), Drucksache Nr. 254.

third of German national wealth,[54] which could then be applied to redeeming the state's war debts; it would have been a fiscal exaction without parallel in the history of German public finance. Since the Levy was for the most part payable in cash,[55] the Reich had no choice but to permit payment by installment, and in fact according to its provisions payment could normally be spread over up to twenty-eight and a half years, or in the case of landed property up to forty-seven years. Since aggregate liability was determined according to assessed nominal value of assets on a date fixed at the direction of the tax authorities, the real value of the installments which the exchequer was receiving dwindled rapidly into insignificance. The gold value of what had been paid up to 1922 was only a little more than one billion marks. In this way the currency depreciation made the capital levy into "a sham...indeed a comedy."[56] In 1922 the collection of the now pointless tax ceased; it was replaced by surcharges on the recurrent wealth tax.

A further, more modest, attempt at conscripting the resources of the rich for the financing of the Reich on a non-recurrent basis was the "compulsory loan," announced in the Reichstag in April and agreed to in July 1922. The one billion gold marks it was supposed to raise were earmarked to meet certain Reparations commitments accepted at the Cannes Conference of January 1922. The Loan was actually subscribed in paper marks however at the fixed ratio of seventy paper marks to one gold mark (this corresponded to the dollar rate in April); subscriptions were paid between July 1922 and March 1923, and because of the simultaneous slide into hyperinflation after June 1922 the real value of the sums raised was pitiful. Only fifty million gold marks were ultimately received by the exchequer – a fiasco hardly less total than that of the Reich Emergency Contribution.

This discussion of the options facing fiscal policy in 1919 cannot be concluded without discussion of the question whether those who found the inflation a welcome alternative to confiscatory taxation can be considered responsible for the fiscal policy that stimulated it. This question was heard only indirectly in the contemporary debate itself – namely in discussion of the limits of taxable capacity.

Before answering the question it needs to be spelt out more clearly. Debt servicing out of tax revenue does not enlarge public sector demand at the

---

[54] Heinrich Dietzel: "Abbürdung der Kriegsschuld", in H. Herkner (ed.): *Die Neuordnung der deutschen Finanzwirtschaft*, p. 107.

[55] Criticism of this stipulation can be found in Robert Nöll von der Nahmer: *Lehrbuch der Finanzwissenschaft* (Cologne, 2 Bde. 1964), Bd. 2: *Spezielle Steuerlehre*, p. 38.

[56] Gaston Jèze, cited in F. Terhalle: "Geschichte", p. 298.

expense of private sector demand in the way that the expenditures do which give rise to the debts in the first place. Rather it represents a transfer of purchasing power from the tax payer to the debt holder.[57] As the sums transferred grow larger so does the share of national income subject to state discretion (assuming constant real value of other public expenditures); specifically, the scope widens for employing taxation policy as an instrument of social goals.

Evidence that taxation was beginning to be governed by such considerations, already apparent during the war, became unmistakable after the November 1918 revolution, and many, particularly in business circles, perceived it as a threat. The foregoing discussion of the tax implications of a deflationary policy shows how immeasurably more threatened they would have felt, had a tax-financed policy of funding and redeeming the debt and of restoring the prewar parity been carried through by a state they perceived as hostile to their interests. Inflation however was a form of taxation[58] against which the individual could more or less shield himself, and in any case its incidence could not be controlled according to social criteria. Over the long run inflation could only tend to weaken the state, initially in the measure that rising prices eroded the real value of its conventional tax revenues, and ultimately as the accelerating pace of price increase reduced the resources which the "inflation tax" itself could command.

For those who feared the expansion of state activity – especially of the kind involving fiscal expropriation of private property – inflation acted as a loophole through which they could defend their assets and ward off state interference. Can they on this account be held responsible for it? Were they the authors of the fiscal policy that engendered it? Clearly the propertied classes were not *en masse* its beneficiaries. Those whose wealth was sunk in fixed value monetary assets and who did not learn to protect it by shifting into real assets or by contracting equivalent debts, suffered capital losses through the inflation far greater than the most rigorous tax policy would have caused them. Obviously this group cannot be accused of having fostered inflation to protect their wealth. Nor on the other hand can owners of real assets or paper-mark debtors, however much they gained by inflation, be held responsible that a government, conducted largely by the Social Democrats who at one time had strongly advocated a capital levy,[59] added large demobilization and social expendi-

---

[57] Heinz Haller: *Finanzpolitik. Grundlagen und Hauptprobleme* (Tübingen, 5th edn. 1972), p. 198–199.

[58] Cp. p. 119 note 1 *supra*.

[59] Heinrich Dietzel in H. Herkner (ed.): *Die Neuordnung*, p. 107.

tures to the Reparations outlays it could not escape. These expenditures bore much of the responsibility for the failure to gain control of the budget deficit after the war, and by fuelling inflation reduced the chances of effective progressive taxation of income and wealth. Whether the new republican government had any real alternative, in view of the economic and political exigencies under which it took office and the small confidence placed in it by precisely those wealthier classes from whom the bulk of tax revenues would have to flow, must be doubted. Haller recently calculated that a level of taxation equal to thirty-five percent of national income would have been required to defray postwar expenditures on Reparations, social welfare and the general running costs of government in a noninflationary manner, as against 11–12% before the war. The decisive precondition for such taxation "would have been a strong government that had the entire population behind it and was thus in a position to demand great sacrifices.... The legislative apparatus and machinery of government would have to have been intact and in possession of the sheerly technical competence to devise and organize the collection of new high-yielding taxes in a short space of time. Scarcely any country that had just lost a war would have been in a position to satisfy this precondition... And so, in the circumstances, the Reich had no other means of defraying the flood of expenditure than by further short-term borrowing."[60] "The inflation", according to Haller, had "the great positive effect" that it secured the parliamentary form of government for the duration of the Weimar republic.[61] While Terhalle[62] merely opined that the national exchequer was both author and chief beneficiary of the inflation, Haller stressed the political dilemma which narrowly constrained the spectrum of feasible options for financial policy. "If the state did cause the inflation, it did so in self-defense."[63]

---

[60] Heinz Haller: "Die Rolle der Staatsfinanzen für den Inflationsprozess", in Deutsche Bundesbank (ed.), *Währung und Wirtschaft in Deutschland 1876–1975* (Frankfurt/M., 1976), pp. 140–141.

[61] *Ibid.*, pp. 151–152.

[62] F. Terhalle: *"Geschichte"*, p. 304.

[63] H. Haller: *"Rolle"*, p. 152.

[14]

STEVEN B. WEBB

Government Debt and Inflationary Expectations as Determinants of the Money Supply in Germany

1919–23

1. INTRODUCTION

THE GROWTH OF THE MONEY SUPPLY HAS FIGURED prominently in every account of Germany's inflation. In the 1920s the very word *inflation* referred more to money growth than to the rise of prices. In their models of inflation, especially hyperinflation, recent economists treat the growth of money as an immediate and often as an exogenous cause of inflation of prices. Inflationary expectations play an important intermediary role, and what expectations process was rational depends chiefly on what process determined the money supply (Sargent and Wallace 1973; Webb 1983, pp. 443–46). Unfortunately economists have rarely looked beyond the numbers — at what the Reichsbank did and what it left undone.

To investigate the money supply this paper begins with a model that reflects the central bank's own understanding of its monetary policy. During the inflation period the Reichsbank followed a passive policy that let the size of the money stock be determined by the government and corporate demand for credit and by the private sector's choice of the mix of debt and money in its portfolios. We must see how well such a model explains money growth and whether its coefficients changed signifi-

On earlier versions of this paper the author received helpful comments from David Aschauer, Carl-Ludwig Holtfrerich, Thomas Huertas, Jan Kmenta, Robert Zevin, the Economic History Seminar at the University of Michigan, the Economics Faculty at the University of Saarbrücken, the editor, and two anonymous referees. The author bears full responsibility, of course, for any remaining errors. The Volkswagen Foundation and the National Science Foundation (SES 8200602) have provided financial assistance for this paper; Michael Foley provided valuable research assistance.

STEVEN B. WEBB *is assistant professor of economics, University of Michigan.*

Journal of Money, Credit, and Banking, Vol. 17, No. 4 (November 1985, Part 1)

cantly in different phases of the inflation. We should then compare the performance of the model with that of some other models of the money supply.

2. REICHSBANK CREDIT AND MONEY POLICY

Although the Reichsbank directors realized the significance of the money supply in the inflation process, from 1914 to 1923 their monetary policy primarily derived from their credit policy (Reichs Chancellery Papers, Cabinet of Chancellor Bauer [Reichskanzlei, Kabinett Bauer, henceforth abbreviated RK Bauer etc.], pp. 40–47; RK Stresemann, pp. 37–42). The Reichsbank did not aim for target growth rates of the money supply, but rather aimed to guarantee that neither the corporate sector nor the government would need to restrain its activities because credit was too costly or unavailable. They justified easy credit at first as necessary to win the war and after 1918 as necessary to prevent further political upheaval and socialization (Holtfrerich 1980, pp. 104–5, 109–12; RK Stresemann, pp. 102–7). The Reichsbank and its subsidiaries kept the bank rate at 5 percent from the end of 1914 until mid-1922. After that they raised the rate eight times, but never to levels that approached the average rate of inflation. Political instability in early Weimar Germany made the expedients of easy money and deficit spending appear necessary.

The Reichsbank created most of the money supply by discounting bills — Treasury bills and commercial bills of exchange. The latter were unimportant until the last year and a half of the inflation, when the share of commercial bills in the Reichsbank portfolio regained its prewar level of 30 to 40 percent. The government issued T-bills by selling them at a discount to the Reichsbank, which then traded them with the private sector, especially banks. There was no real open market for T-bills, only an announced discount rate and an open window at the Reichsbank. The Darlehnskassen or loan bureaus were subsidiaries of the Reichsbank, which also created money by making loans against collateral — corporate bonds, stocks, real goods, and government securities. The loan bureau notes could circulate as currency, but the Reichsbank held most of them and issued its own notes in exchange. The Reichsbank could count the loan bureau notes in its portfolio as the equivalent of gold. This possibility was especially important when, prior to May 1921, the Reichsbank had to keep "gold" cover for one-third of its note issue. In short, the central bank would monetize, at an interest rate fixed in the short run, almost any liability of a major corporation or the government. The size of the money supply thus depended on the stock of monetizable assets and the desire of the private sector to monetize rather than to hold them.

The Reichsbank described the German economy as having excess liquidity up to late 1922 and as facing credit scarcity after mid-1922 (Reichsbank Annual Reports for 1919 to 1923; Renell 1926, pp. 20–25). These phrases refer in essence to whether the commercial banks were net lenders to the government or net borrowers at the Reichsbank. Prior to mid-1922, the banks held substantial amounts of government debt and took little of their loan portfolio to be monetized at the Reichsbank. Most of the collateral at the loan bureaus then was government securities (RK Bauer,

p. 42; RK Fehrenbach, pp. 447–48; Holtfrerich 1980, pp. 124–25; Lotz 1926, pp. 212–15). Until mid-1922 the private discount rate was one or two points *below* the 5 percent rate at the Reichsbank, apparently because investors thought that corporate debt had less default risk than government debt (*Statistisches Jahrbuch* 1923, p. 269; Reichsbank Annual Report for 1921, p. 4; Holtfrerich 1980, p. 124). An important source of the banks' liquidity was the deposits of foreigners — some speculating outright on a recovery of the mark and some arbitraging with the cover of the premium on the mark in the forward exchange market. When the foreigners finally became pessimistic about the mark and withdrew their deposits in mid-1922, the banks, on behalf of their corporate borrowers, joined the government at the discount window of the Reichsbank (Holtfrerich 1980, p. 63; Reichsbank Annual Report for 1922, pp. 1, 4). Monetization of corporate debt mainly took place through discounting commercial bills at the Reichsbank. Accounting conventions valued assets at their current market or historical value, whichever was *lower*. So by the time the hyperinflation made the advantages of cheap central bank credit obvious, most assets against which firms could borrow at the loan bureaus were monetizable for only a small fraction of their current value.

The size of the money supply — the nominal value of the forced loan from money holders — depended of course not only on the net position of the private participants in the credit market, but also on the size of the government debt. Another paper of mine examines the spending and tax policies that caused the government debt to grow (Webb 1985; see also Holtfrerich 1980, pp. 126–35; Feldman 1982, pp. 191–93; Witt 1982, pp. 151–79; 1983, pp. 450–72). The long-term changes in the real value of spending and taxes resulted primarily from tax reforms, reparation payments, and the occupation and passive resistance in the Ruhr. Until the stabilization neither tax nor spending policy depended directly on the size of the deficit; neither was adjusted in quick response to changes in the deficit. The government raised taxes as much as the propertied interests would permit and spent as much as necessary to appease the workers and the Allies. Both spending and revenue followed inflation with lags, because of delays in wage payments and indexation and in tax collection. Thus, although it might increase the share of expenditures covered with borrowing, an acceleration of inflation typically reduced the real value of the deficit. In the early postwar years even large fluctuations in current prices, revenue, and spending could have only a small percentage effect on the great flywheel of the accumulated debt. As the subsequent progress of inflation reduced the real burden of the government debt, it also reduced the real inertia in that flywheel. The growth rate of debt rose sharply in fall 1922 (see Table 1) not because the real deficit had risen — actually it fell — but because the hyperinflation greatly reduced the real value of the old debt. Devaluing the debt in this way may have temporarily improved the government's finances, but it also made the inflationary process more unstable.

For modeling the money supply as a function of government debt, the lag between prices and the deficits has the important implication that the government debt was a predetermined variable. If the stock of debt were determined simultaneously with the money supply, it would have been through the effect of current prices on the deficit. To test this hypothesis econometrically, the government deficit was re-

TABLE 1

THE GROWTH OF MONEY AND DEBT AND INFLATIONARY EXPECTATIONS (MONTHLY RATE)

Month	*HPM* Growth Rate	Government Debt Growth Rate	Ratio *HPM* to Debt	Forward Exchange Discount	Adaptive Expectations
1919 Jan			0.30		0.029
Feb	0.01	0.03	0.29		0.028
Mar	0.08	0.02	0.31		0.029
Apr	0.03	0.02	0.31		0.031
May	−0.03	0.03	0.29		0.032
Jun	0.11	0.01	0.32		0.038
Jul	−0.06	0.02	0.30		0.060
Aug	−0.01	0.01	0.29		0.083
Sep	0.06	0.01	0.30		0.094
Oct	0.01	0.02	0.30		0.106
Nov	0.03	0.01	0.30		0.119
Dec	0.15	−0.00	0.35		0.153
1920 Jan	−0.02	0.02	0.34		0.193
Feb	0.03	0.01	0.35		0.186
Mar	0.14	0.00	0.40		0.145
Apr	0.02	0.02	0.40	−0.006	0.108
May	0.03	0.03	0.40	−0.008	0.077
Jun	0.10	0.04	0.43	−0.005	0.054
Jul	−0.03	0.05	0.39	−0.008	0.049
Aug	0.02	0.03	0.39	−0.004	0.048
Sep	0.07	0.03	0.41	−0.006	0.041
Oct	0.00	0.01	0.40	−0.007	0.034
Nov	−0.00	0.03	0.39	−0.006	0.026
Dec	0.08	0.01	0.42	−0.009	0.017
1921 Jan	−0.06	0.02	0.38	−0.012	0.010
Feb	−0.01	0.01	0.38	−0.011	0.002
Mar	0.03	−0.02	0.40	−0.009	−0.002
Apr	−0.03	0.04	0.37	−0.007	−0.004
May	0.02	0.04	0.37	−0.008	−0.000
Jun	0.08	0.02	0.39	−0.006	0.008
Jul	−0.02	0.02	0.37	−0.005	0.037
Aug	−0.00	0.04	0.36	−0.006	0.064
Sep	0.12	0.02	0.39	−0.004	0.075
Oct	0.02	0.02	0.40	−0.004	0.107
Nov	0.14	0.03	0.44	−0.003	0.119
Dec	0.14	0.06	0.48	−0.004	0.104
1922 Jan	−0.04	0.03	0.45	−0.003	0.100
Feb	0.05	0.02	0.46	−0.002	0.117
Mar	0.10	0.02	0.50	−0.000	0.136
Apr	0.05	0.03	0.52	−0.000	0.127
May	0.07	0.02	0.54	−0.000	0.123
Jun	0.10	0.01	0.59	0.001	0.133
Jul	0.12	0.04	0.65	0.003	0.200
Aug	0.23	0.05	0.78	0.023	0.258
Sep	0.33	0.24	0.85	0.041	0.310
Oct	0.36	0.27	0.94	0.120	0.340
Nov	0.48	0.30	1.13	0.107	0.397
Dec	0.56	0.50	1.19	0.066	0.356

TABLE 1 *(Continued)*

Month	HPM Growth Rate	Government Debt Growth Rate	Ratio HPM to Debt	Forward Exchange Discount	Adaptive Expectations
1923 Jan	0.44	0.35	1.31	0.148	0.495
Feb	0.63	0.54	1.43	0.209	0.429
Mar	0.43	0.62	1.18	0.046	0.338
Apr	0.30	0.25	1.24	0.102	0.316
May	0.27	0.18	1.35	0.122	0.364
Jun	0.68	0.75	1.26	0.181	0.485
Jul	0.97	0.97	1.26	0.462	0.725
Aug	2.74	2.84	1.14	0.356	1.040
Sep	3.56	3.52	1.18		1.473
Oct	5.05	5.10	1.13		2.278

SOURCES: *HPM* –High-powered money is the end-of-the-month value of currency plus nongovernment deposits at the Reichsbank (*Zahlen zur Geldentwertung [ZzGew]*, pp. 45–51). For 1919–20 nongovernment deposits were estimated as 0.67 of total deposits, which was their share in 1921. Government debt is bonds plus adjusted T-bills at the end of the month (*Deutschlands Wirtschaft, Währung und Finanzen [DWWF]*, pp. 29, 62). The adjustment excludes T-bills held by the Reichsbank as backing for the government deposits there and deflates T-bills in August–October 1923 by the amount of discounting. The forward exchange discount is the monthly rate for one month forward, interpolated to the end of the month (Einzig 1937, pp. 450–55; Keynes 1923, pp. 119–20). Adaptive expectations were computed with the coefficient of adjustment equal to 0.20 and the WPI log-linearly interpolated to the end of the month (*ZzGew*, pp. 16–18).

gressed on the lagged value of itself; on the WPI lagged 1, 3, 6, 12, and 24 months; and on the current WPI (the log of all variables at the end of the month). This test was tried for four periods: March 1919 to June 1922, to June 1923, to August 1923, and to October 1923. In each case the coefficient on current prices was statistically insignificant (*t* ratios = -0.62, 1.11, 1.46, and 1.65). Perhaps this is just because of collinearity between current and lagged prices. Still, we can at least say that innovations in prices, resulting from innovations in money and from other causes, do not contribute significantly to explaining innovations in the government debt.

To model the supply of money, think of the private sector facing a stock of government debt and deciding what fraction to hold as debt and what fraction to monetize. Table 1 shows the ratio of high-powered money to the government debt. The opportunity to monetize corporate liabilities permitted the ratio of high-powered money to government debt to rise above one. What caused the private sector to vary the ratio as it did? The discount rate at the Reichsbank, to the extent it varied, should have had a negative effect on the ratio. A higher bank rate decreased the attractiveness of money relative to debt within the nominally valued portion of people's portfolios. Inflationary expectations should have had a positive effect on the ratio. With a higher expected opportunity cost of all nominally valued assets, people should have wished to reduce them closer to the minimum needed for transactions. The Reichsbank was aware and concerned that a panic would cause private lenders to have their holdings of debt monetized (RK Bauer, p. 42; RK Fehrenbach, pp. 315–16). Algebraically we can express the relationship as follows:

$$\log M_t = m_t = a + bE_t + cBR_t + d \log D_t + \varepsilon_t ,$$

where M is the money supply; E is inflationary expectations; BR is the bank rate; and D is the government debt, bonds as well as T-bills. The hypothesized money supply process implies that b is positive, c is negative, and d equals one.

3. EMPIRICAL TESTING

The main tests of the money supply model, described above, were done with monthly data, which are all available from April 1920 until August 1923. High-powered money — the sum of (official) currency and nongovernment deposits at the Reichsbank — is the most appropriate measure of the money supply (*Zahlen zur Geldentwertung* [*ZzGew*], pp. 45–51). People could monetize debt into either currency or deposits at the Reichsbank. To reduce the cost of printing currency, the Reichsbank encouraged firms to keep deposits there and to use its direct transfer service (Reichsbank Annual Reports for 1919 to 1922). Since most previous studies have used currency alone as the money supply, it was also tried. Government debt equals (Reichs) bonds and T-bills, adjusted and interpolated as described in Table 1.[1]

Most studies of the demand for real balances in hyperinflations have used one of two indicators of inflationary expectations. Cagan's adaptive expectations are the more venerable:

$$E_t(\Delta p_{t+1}) = E_{t-1}(\Delta p_t) + \beta[\Delta p_t - E_{t-1}(\Delta p_t)].$$

This, of course, implies that currently expected inflation is a distributed lag on all past inflation rates, at least back to a time of price stability. Sargent and Wallace (1973) showed that adaptive expectations would be rational if a constant real deficit were monetized each month. Adaptive expectations here uses β equal to 0.20, which was Cagan's estimate (1956, p. 43). The other expectations indicator is the forward discount on the mark in the foreign exchange market (cf. Frenkel 1977). Although the forward market was much smaller than the goods markets and Germans could not participate freely because of restrictions on holding foreign exchange, the forward discount could react instantly to news and did reflect directly expectations about the future value of the mark (see Table 1). In theory the equations for real balance demand, for revenue, for spending, and for the money supply imply some rational expectations of inflation, but the complexities of such fully endogenous expectations are beyond the scope of this paper.

The regressions reported in Table 2 support most of the hypotheses implied by our model of the money supply. The reported results are mostly with high-powered money as the money supply, because those with currency — two of which are shown at the bottom of the table — have significant serial correlation of the error term even after a first-order Cochrane-Orcutt transformation. (With a second-order transformation, the second-order ρ is not significantly different from zero, and yet its value implies an unstable error structure.) Equations (4), (5), and (6) were also run for the longer period over which the adaptive expectations are available.

The coefficient on inflationary expectations is positive with either indicator, as predicted, and is usually statistically significant at the 10 or 5 percent level. With either expectations measure, the coefficient on expectations is around 0.4 — a one-

---

[1]The adjustments to the statistics on money stock and government debt make them more accurate, I believe, but the changes are too small to affect the qualitative results of the statistical analysis.

TABLE 2

REGRESSIONS OF THE MONEY SUPPLY ON INFLATIONARY EXPECTATIONS, THE DISCOUNT RATE, AND GOVERNMENT DEBT: $\log M = m = a + bE + cBR + d \log(Govdebt) + \varepsilon$

Equation	M	E	Period	Coefficient (standard error)			SSE	D-W
				b	c	d		
(1)	HPM	FXD	4/1920–8/1923	0.482 (0.200)*	0.018 (0.009)	0.902 (0.040)**	0.188	1.55 (?)
(2)	HPM	FXD	same	0.361 (0.198)		0.955 (0.025)**	0.201	1.66 ($=d_u$)
(3)	HPM	FXD	same	0.409 (0.204)*		1	0.221	1.50 (?)
(4)	HPM	AdEx	same	0.442 (0.241)	0.012 (0.009)	0.873 (0.047)**	0.200	1.68 (ok)
(5)	HPM	AdEx	same	0.459 (0.242)		0.912 (0.037)**	0.209	1.71 (ok)
(6)	HPM	AdEx	same	0.023 (0.172)		1	0.244	1.68 (ok)
(4)	HPM	AdEx	1/1919–10/1923–	0.416 (0.212)	0.002 (0.001)	0.918 (0.034)**	0.283	1.90 (ok)
(5)	HPM	AdEx	same	0.340 (0.209)		0.940 (0.031)**	0.294	1.97 (ok)
(6)	HPM	AdEx	same	−0.035 (0.075)		1	0.316	0.195 (ok)
(7)	CURR	FXD	4/1920–8/1923	0.270 (0.170)	0.007 (0.008)	0.927 (0.034)**	0.136	1.24 (s − c)
(8)	CURR	AdEx	same	0.494 (0.187)**	0.003 (0.007)	0.885 (0.037)**	0.122	1.30 (s − c)

NOTES: *HPM* is high-powered money, *CURR* currency, *FXD* the forward exchange discount, and *AdEx* adaptive expectations. SSE is the sum of squared errors. All equations were estimated with a Cochrane-Orcutt transformation to correct for first-order serially correlated residuals. The iteratively estimated ρs were all between 0.98 and 1.00. The reported Durbin-Watson (D-W) statistics are for the residuals of the transformed equations. ("ok" indicates that the D-W was above d_u, "s − c" below d_1, and "?" in the uncertain region, all for the 5 percent level of significance.)
*Significant at the 5 percent level.
**Significant at the 1 percent level.

percentage-point increase in the expected monthly inflation rate would increase high powered money by about 0.4 percent. The coefficient on the bank rate term, however, is always positive — the opposite of the predicted sign — and statistically insignificant. The Reichsbank's changes of the bank rate were too small to have much effect on the portfolio choices of the private sector, and they came so late that they appear more like a reaction to than a determinant of changes in the fraction of debt monetized. Both at the time and in retrospect, the Reichsbank authorities believed that the discount rate was an ineffective weapon with which to combat speculative pressure — the effects of pessimistic expectations (RK Cuno, pp. 77–78; RK Stresemann, pp. 106–7; Schacht 1927, p. 159).

The debt-expectations model, as we shall call it, also suggests that the coefficient on government debt would be 1, which is equivalent to regressing log money/debt on expectations. With the forward exchange discount as expectations we cannot reject this hypothesis, although with adaptive expectations the coefficient on debt is around 0.9 and significantly different from 1. Further analysis uses equations (3) and (5) from Table 2.

Most historical accounts describe Reichsbank policy as more complex and variable than the simple model hypothesized here (Renell 1926, pp. 26–62; Graham 1930, pp. 56–75; Holtfrerich 1980, pp. 115–77; Feldman 1982, pp. 180–206;

Habedank 1982, pp. 37–99). Were the present model in fact too simple, we would expect the fit of the regression to improve significantly if the coefficient values could change at the times of the alleged shifts of policy. To test the impact of changes in Reichsbank procedures, dummy variables were entered into the constant term and the coefficient on expectations.

The Reichsbank frequently bought and sold gold or foreign exchange in order to stabilize the exchange rate. The first important intervention episode came in early 1920, when the Reichsbank stepped in to halt the appreciation of the mark, out of fear of a worsening trade balance (Feldman 1982, pp. 182–91). At the end of January the Reichsbank held about 50 million gold marks worth of foreign exchange (mostly in bills of exchange, checks, and deposits). By the end of May the Reichsbank's holding had climbed to over 1,300 million gold marks and backed one-fifth of its liabilities. After May it declined, although not as fast or as far as it had risen (ZSA, Reichsbank 6435, Bl. 15–17). Because data on the forward exchange discount do not begin until April 1920, the test could only be done with adaptive expectations. A dummy for February to May 1920 showed no trace of explanatory power.

In May 1921 Reichsbank procedures changed with the repeal of the one-third coverage law, mentioned earlier, but again there was no significant change of coefficients at that time. The reason is clear in confidential Reichsbank memoranda (RK Bauer, pp. 41–42; RK Fehrenbach, pp. 447–48). At a discount rate of 5 percent, the private demand for T-bills was so low in 1919–21 that the Reichsbank would have had to buy them until its note issue exceeded three times its gold reserve. Thus the one-third coverage law did bind the Reichsbank in a formal sense. But in practice the Reichsbank sidestepped the legal constraint on their note issue by having the Prussian State Bank (*Seehandlung*) buy T-bills and borrow against them at the loan bureaus, creating loan bureaus' notes, which the Reichsbank could count as gold. The loan bureaus' notes in the Reichsbank portfolio were, in other words, mostly T-bills in disguise. The one-third coverage law, with the amendment elevating loan bureau notes to the status of gold, thus put no effective constraint on the amount of government debt the Reichsbank could monetize.

Another change in Reichsbank practice was its resumption of discounting commercial bills in July 1922. The key issue is whether the Reichsbank changed what it would do, or whether the private credit market merely changed what it asked the Reichsbank to do.[2] If the latter were true and if the change resulted only from a change in inflationary expectations, then the coefficients in equations (3) and (5) (in Table 2) would remain constant. A dummy variable for July 1922 and thereafter does not significantly improve the fits, rejecting the hypothesis of a shift in coeffi-

---

[2]It would have been useful, especially in regard to this issue, to have data on monetizable corporate securities, so that we could look at the ratio of money to total monetizable assets. The only monthly data on corporate securities are the volume of new bills of exchange, computed from the tax on them. Even if the flow of new commercial bills (all very short-term) is a good approximation for the stock, it does not faithfully represent total corporate credit demand. Commercial bills became the main form of corporate borrowing only after mid-1922, mainly because of their discountability at the Reichsbank. Earlier, when banks had enough deposits to meet the needs of their commercial customers, revolving credit accounts and the like were far more important than commerical bills.

cients. The inflation accelerated into hyperinflation in mid-1922 because the Reichsbank would *not change* its basic policy of letting the credit market determine the ratio of money to government debt.

The Reichsbank's second major intervention in the foreign exchange market came in early 1923, when for twelve weeks the Reichsbank stopped the previous (and subsequent) precipitous fall of the mark. The Reichsbank tried to discourage, with sermons and flexible quotas, any speculative or unnecessary credit to firms. The intervention began on February 1, after the French invasion of the Ruhr in early January had caused the mark to plummet, and lasted until April 18 (RK Cuno, pp. 399–402; BAK, R 43/I 632, Bl. 25–26). Because of its short duration and its end in the middle of a month, monthly data could scarcely identify much less tell anything about the statistical significance of a dummy variable for this intervention. For 1923 the relevant variables were reported frequently enough to permit regressions with thrice-monthly observations.[3] With neither expectations measure does a dummy variable for February 10 to April 20, 1923, improve the fit significantly. This result does not imply that the Reichsbank's intervention had no effect, for Table 1 shows the obvious effect. The intervention lowered prices and inflationary expectations, which slowed the growth of the money supply, even though the Reichsbank's credit and monetary policy remained unchanged.[4]

To an already chaotic economy August 1923 brought many changes. The Reichsbank's correspondence tells of its increasing insistence on only rediscounting commercial bills with one month or less duration and with an obligation to repay in terms of gold. The Reichsbank also announced to the government that after the end of the year, it would monetize no more government debt, although this announcement was apparently not known outside the upper levels of the government and banking community (RK Stresemann, pp. 37–42, 101–25; Habedank 1982, pp. 89–92). After November 1923, when the hyperinflation had convinced both Germans and Allies of the need to end deficit spending, the Reichsbank actually enforced the requirement of a balanced budget. There were also major changes in fiscal policy. The question is whether these changes altered the money supply process, as modeled here, or only affected the money supply through the government debt and inflationary expectations. The regressions with thrice-monthly data fail in two out of three formulations to reject the hypothesis of no shift in August 1923. The results here need an extra grain of salt because of several problems with the data for the last three months of the hyperinflation. For instance, Notgeld, scrip that circulated as currency, became important then, and much of it was neither counted in the official statistics nor backed by Reichsbank deposits.

Since there is not a significant shift of coefficients at *any* of the times suggested in the secondary literature, we may conclude that, if the money supply was a

---

[3]BAK, R 43 I/2356–58; *Wirtschaft und Statistik* 1923–24, passim; *ZzGew*, pp. 16–18; Einzig 1937, pp. 450–55. Details of the regressions with thrice-monthly data are available from the author.

[4]The effectiveness of the intervention was not a function of the amount of gold reserves that the Reichsbank sold off. The Reichsbank sold half of its gold reserves in 1923, but mostly over the summer in a series of sales, each of which only halted the mark's depreciation for a few days (cf. RK Cuno, pp. 689, 750).

log-linear function of government debt and expectations, the function remained constant from the end of the war to the final stabilization. The Reichsbank kept its money and credit policy constant and separate from its foreign exchange interventions, which had an impact on the money supply only via their effects on government deficits and expectations.

4. COMPARISON WITH ALTERNATE MODELS

Although the results in Table 2 clearly reject the null hypothesis that the money supply was unrelated to government debt and inflationary expectations, the debt-expectations model faces competition from other models, which can also explain most of the variation in the German money supply. A cousin to the debt-expectations model is the inflationary finance story (*INFL-FIN* in Table 3) that the government printed money to cover some portion of each month's deficit (e.g., see Sargent and Wallace 1973; Frenkel 1977). Deflating with the previous month's wholesale price index to reduce heteroskedasticity of the errors gives the equation

$$\frac{M_t - M_{t-1}}{P_{t-1}} = c_0 + c_1 \frac{D_t - D_{t-1}}{P_{t-1}} + \varepsilon_t \,.$$

This model implies that the money supply depended on past and current deficits, but not on agents' portfolio decisions or expectations. Protopapadakis (1983) finds some

TABLE 3

J-TESTS COMPARING THE DEBT-EXPECTATIONS MODEL WITH TIME-SERIES MODELS—
H_0: $m = f(X, \beta) + \varepsilon$; H_1: $m = g(Z, \gamma) + \varepsilon$; $m = (1 - \alpha)f(X, \beta) + \alpha g(Z, \hat{\gamma}) + \varepsilon$
(May 1920–August 1923)

H_0	H_1	α	*t*-statistic of α	ρ^a	D-W[b]
DEBT-FXD	INFL-FIN	−0.01	−0.55	1.00	1.39[c]
DEBT-FXD	AR(1, 0)	0.07	1.70	0.99	1.65
DEBT-FXD	AR(1, 1)	0.04	1.18	1.00	1.56
DEBT-FXD	LLN-AR(1, 1)	0.04	0.96	0.99	1.62
INFL-FIN	DEBT-FXD	1.29	5.18	0.04	1.95
AR(1, 0)	DEBT-FXD	0.96	22.46	0.20	2.01
AR(1, 1)	DEBT-FXD	0.38	6.86	0.97	1.87
LLN-AR(1, 1)	DEBT-FXD	0.95	20.85	0.16	2.01
DEBT-AdEx	INFL-FIN	1.13	25.07	−0.22	2.11
DEBT-AdEx	AR(1, 0)	0.50	19.18	−0.05	1.98
DEBT-AdEx	AR(1, 1)	0.71	21.48	−0.58	2.04
DEBT-AdEx	LLN-AR(1, 1)	0.58	22.68	−0.39	2.17
INFL-FIN	DEBT-AdEx	1.41	4.58	0.06	1.97
AR(1, 0)	DEBT-AdEx	0.96	22.99	0.10	2.01
AR(1, 1)	DEBT-AdEx	0.38	6.83	0.97	1.90
LLN-AR(1, 1)	DEBT-AdEx	−0.00	−0.60	0.11	1.54

[a]Computed with an iterative Cochrane-Orcutt procedure for the linear equations and with GLS for the nonlinear.
[b]D-W statistics for residuals in the transformed regressions, which are all above d_u, except as noted in c.
[c]D-W equals d_l.

problems with models of this type, which he interprets as support for the exogeneity of the money supply process.

The money supply becomes completely exogenous in time-series models, such as those used by Flood and Garber (1980a, 1980b). One of their models is a first-order autoregressive process on the first difference of the log of the money supply [$AR(1, 1)$], which is equivalent to the current value being a weighted average of the previous two:

$$m_t = a_0 + (1 + a_1)m_{t-1} - a_1 m_{t-2} + \varepsilon_t.$$

Burmeister and Wall (1982) also use this model. The other model of Flood and Garber has the same basic time-series structure, but deletes the constant term and uses the log of the log of the money supply [$LLN\text{-}AR(1, 1)$]:

$$m_t = m_{t-1} e^{(\beta_t)}, \qquad \beta_t = \Theta \beta_{t-1} + \varepsilon_t$$

or

$$\log m_t = (1 + \Theta) \log m_{t-1} - \Theta \log m_{t-2} + \varepsilon_t.$$

Burmeister and Wall also tried an undifferenced autoregressive model [$AR(1,0)$], though they do not put much stock in it.

None of the four alternate models can nest within the debt-expectations model, nor vice versa. Consequently they were compared by means of the *J*-test, a technique for testing nonnested hypotheses (see Davidson and MacKinnon 1982). If H_0 is $y = f(X, \beta) + \varepsilon$ and H_1 is $y = g(Z, \gamma) + \varepsilon$, then the statistical significance of the coefficient α in the equation

$$y = (1 - \alpha)f(X, \beta) + \alpha g(Z, \gamma) + \varepsilon$$

implies a rejection of H_0. To identify α, however, the equation is run with γ constrained to the values estimated by running H_1 alone. (If H_0 is linear, we also drop the $1 - \alpha$ term.) Table 3 gives the results of the *J*-tests, both with the debt-expectations model as H_0 and with the alternate models as H_0. In seven out of eight comparisons, the test overwhelmingly rejects H_0 when the debt-expectations model is H_1. On the other hand, the debt-expectations model with the forward exchange discount as the expectations measure [*DEBT-FXD*] is never rejected as the true model, although with adaptive expectations [*DEBT-AdEx*] it is always rejected. The stalemate between the time-series models and the debt-expectations model with adaptive expectations occurs perhaps because the adaptive expectations are built out of a time series of past prices. When the adaptive expectations are adjusting with a delay to match true expectations, the money supply and deficits in recent periods offer some useful information.

490 : MONEY, CREDIT, AND BANKING

5. CONCLUSIONS

The Reichsbank directors correctly understood the money supply process during the inflation as one where they played a passive role, letting the accumulation of government debt and the public's portfolio decisions determine the size of the money stock. The public's decision about how much of the debt to monetize appears to have depended mainly on its expectations of future inflation. To the extent that expectations were endogenous, therefore, we may say that the primal cause of the money growth and the whole inflation was the growth of government debt. While this may seem obvious, as it was to the Reichsbank, econometric models as well as historical accounts often ignore or deemphasize it. Furthermore, at the several times where traditional accounts suggest a change in Reichsbank policy, econometric tests reveal no significant shift in the coefficients of the debt-expectations model of the money supply. The constancy of the Reichsbank's monetary policy implies that historians, wishing to allocate responsibility for the inflation, may blame the Reichsbank for its passivity but not for causing changes in the course of the inflation.

The debt-expectations model of the money supply with the forward exchange discount as the measure of inflationary expectations is clearly superior to the alternate time-series models. Any conclusions about inflationary expectations in Germany's inflation drawn from models with time-series equations for the money supply are suspect.

Models of the demand for real balances and the determination of the price level[5] build upon assumptions about the money supply process. The endogeneity of the money supply means that it was determined contemporaneously, although not simultaneously in a mathematical sense, with the price level. Although it still appears econometrically legitimate to estimate a real balance demand equation with the endogenous variables both on the left-hand side, $\log(M/P) = a_0 + a_1 E + \varepsilon$, one must understand its meaning differently. Rather than nominal M being exogenous and only P depending on expectations, as Cagan and others assumed, both M and P depend on expectations. The price level could be modeled as a function of debt and expectations, leaving out the intervening variable — money. In any case, we should keep in mind that the public was deciding both the fraction of the German government's total liability to hold in the form of money and the nominal value of that liability.

Data for this paper are available from the JMCB *editorial office.*

LITERATURE CITED

BAK. Bundesarchiv, Koblenz. R43 I: Reichskanzlei, 1919–24.

Burmeister, Edwin, and Kent D. Wall. "Kalman Filtering Estimation of Unobserved Rational Expectations with an Application to the German Hyperinflation." *Journal of Econometrics* 20 (November 1982), 255–84.

[5] As typically modeled, these two approaches are equivalent.

Cagan, Phillip. "The Monetary Dynamics of Hyperinflation." In *Studies in the Quantity Theory of Money,* edited by Milton Friedman, pp. 25–117. Chicago: University of Chicago Press, 1956.

Davidson, Russell, and James G. MacKinnon. "Some Non-Nested Hypothesis Tests and the Relations among Them." *Review of Economic Studies* 49 (October 1982), 551–65.

Deutschlands Wirtschaft, Währung und Finanzen. Allied Powers, Reparations Commission. Berlin: Zentral-Verlag GmbH, 1924.

Einzig, Paul. *The Theory of Forward Exchange.* London: MacMillan, 1937.

Feldman, Gerald D. "The Political Economy of Germany's Relative Stabilization During the 1920/21 World Depression." In *The German Inflation: A Preliminary Balance,* edited by Gerald D. Feldman, Carl-Ludwig Holtfrerich, Gerhard A. Ritter and Peter-Christian Witt, pp. 180–206. Berlin: Walter de Gruyter, 1982.

Flood, Robert P., and Peter M. Garber. "An Economic Theory of Monetary Reform." *Journal of Political Economy* 88 (February 1980), 24–58 (a).

———. "Market Fundamentals versus Price-Level Bubbles: The First Tests." *Journal of Political Economy* 88 (August 1980), 745–70 (b).

Frenkel, Jacob A. "The Forward Exchange Rate, Expectations, and the Demand for Money: The German Hyperinflation." *American Economic Review* 67 (September 1977), 653–70.

Graham, Frank D. *Exchange, Prices, and Production in Hyperinflation: Germany, 1920–1923.* Princeton N.J.: Princeton University Press, 1930.

Habedank, Heinz. *Die Reichsbank in der Weimarer Republik: Zur Rolle der Zentralbank in der Politik des deutschen Imperialismus 1919–1933.* Berlin: Akademie-Verlag, 1981.

Holtfrerich, Carl-Ludwig. *Die deutsche Inflation, 1914–1923: Ursachen und Folgen in internationaler Perspektive.* Berlin: Walter de Gruyter, 1980.

Keynes, John Maynard. *A Tract on Monetary Reform.* London: MacMillan, 1923.

Lotz, Walter. "Darlehnskassen." *Handwörterbuch der Staatswissenschaft,* Vol. 3. Jena, 1926.

Protopapadakis, Aris. "The Endogeneity of Money during the German Hyperinflation: A Reappraisal." *Economic Inquiry* 21 (January 1983), 72–92.

Reichsbank. *Reichsbank Jahresberichte* [Annual Reports]. In BAK 43 I/638, 1919–24.

Reichskanzlei. *Akten der Reichskanklei, Weimarer Republik,* edited by Karl. D. Erdmann et al. Boppard am Rhein: Harald Boldt, 1971–78.

Renell, Erich. "Der Warenwechsel in Deutschland in der Geldentwertungszeit 1919–1923." Ph.D. dissertation, University of Berlin, 1926.

Sargent, Thomas J., and Neil Wallace. "Rational Expectations and the Dynamics of Hyperinflations." *International Economic Review* 14 (June 1973), 328–50.

Schacht, Hjalmar. *The Stabilization of the Mark.* London: George Allen and Unwin, 1927.

Statistisches Jahrbuch für das Deutsche Reich. Statistisches Reichsamt, Berlin, 1921–24.

Webb, Steven B. "Money Demand and Expectations in the German Hyperinflation: A Survey of the Models." In *Inflation Through the Ages,* edited by Nathan Schmukler and Edward Marcus, pp. 435–49. New York: Columbia University Press, 1983.

———. "Government Spending and Revenues in Germany, 1919–1923." In *Inflation and Reconstruction in Germany and Europe after World War I,* edited by Gerald D. Feldman, et al. Berlin: Walter de Gruyter, 1985.

Wirtschaft und Statistik. Statistisches Reichsamt, Berlin, 1921–44.

Witt, Peter-Christian. "Staatliche Wirtschaftspolitik in Deutschland 1918–1923." In *The German Inflation* edited by Gerald D. Feldman, Carl-Ludwig Holtfrerich, Gerhard A. Ritter, and Peter-Christian Witt, Berlin: Walter de Gruyter 1982.

_____. "Tax Policies, Tax Assessment, and Inflation: Toward a Sociology of Public Finances in the German Inflation 1914–1923." In *Inflation Through the Ages,* edited by Nathan Schmukler and Edward Marcus, pp. 450–72. New York: Columbia University Press, 1983.

Zahlen zur Geldentwertung in Deutschland 1914 bis 1923. Statistisches Reichsamt, Sonderhefte 1 zu *Wirtschaft und Statistik,* Berlin, 1925.

ZSA: Zentrales Staatsarchiv, Potsdam.

Excerpt from *The Political Economy of Inflation*, F. Hirsch and J.H. Goldthorpe (eds.)

[15]

CHAPTER 2

The Politics of Inflation in the Twentieth Century

Charles S. Maier

The Limitations of the Economic Models

Of the more than sixty years since the outbreak of World War I over half have comprised periods of sharply rising prices: 1914 to 1921 or to 1926 (the terminal date depending upon the particular economy), 1938 to 1953 (with 'creeping inflation' still prevailing from 1953 to the late 1960s), and 1967 or so to the present. Nonetheless, political scientists have only recently begun serious analysis of inflation, while historians of politics and society have been even more laggard. Even economic historians strictly speaking have contributed few studies, although this is not surprising. Until recently most economic historians concentrated on questions of development and growth, and above all on industrialization. Inflation, however, presents an urgent problem of welfare and allocation. Sometimes it involves distributing the dividends of economic growth, but often it serves as the mechanism for sharing out the costs of stagnation and decline. All the more central a theme it should be, therefore, for the historian of twentieth-century politics and society. His investigations cannot avoid the political bitterness that has arisen in epochs when growth faltered or fell. In that distributive conflict, inflation has played important roles, either easing or exacerbating the struggle over shares.

The historian can draw only limited assistance from the economic models proposed to understand inflation. (For the most recent see Gordon, 1975.) On one level they provide the raw material for a history of ideas; they indicate how strongly

37

38   *Charles S. Maier*

theoretical systems are influenced by refractory problems and
policy dilemmas of the day. Quantity theory served economists
writing on the inflationary experiences of the 1920s. They might
differ as to whether balance-of-payments difficulties or internal
budget deficits prodded currency emissions, but they attributed
inflation to growing monetary circulation and in France at least
tended to define inflation as the increasing volume of currency,
not the rise in prices. (Rogers, 1929, pp. 91–128; Aftalion,
1927; Graham, 1930; Ellis, 1934; Bresciani-Turroni, 1937, pp.
79 ff.)

The Keynesian analysis turned from the quantity of money
to levels of income and expenditure. But, as interpreted by
those whom Coddington (1976) has termed 'hydraulic' Keynesians, the problem presented by potential excess demand was
viewed as a mirror image of insufficient demand. An implicit
theoretical parity suggested that if the $C+I+G$ streams of
demand (consumption, investment and government spending)
produced an inflationary gap, macroeconomic adjustments could
reduce them easily to a full-employment non-inflationary equilibrium. This extrapolation from a world of depression to one
of inflation was too simple, and for the historian of economic
ideas, the development of Phillips-curve analysis after World
War II can be interpreted as a defensive retreat on the part
of the Keynesians. They abandoned the presumed mirror-image
symmetry between deflation and inflation and fell back on the
more intractable trade-off. Yet even the Phillips-curve redoubt
has come under heavy bombardment from Friedmanite critics,
and earlier defenders are themselves uncertain of its soundness.

Although the historian can trace these themes as they have
developed since the 1930s, they do not offer an effective starting
point for his or her own sociopolitical analysis. Monetarism
focuses on the keepers of the printing press and summons
them to abstinence, but rarely explains what pressures sustain
or overcome their resolution (Friedman, 1956; Patinkin, 1969;
Teigen, 1972). Keynesian analysis tends to look at consumption
decisions on the part of the generality or sometimes postulates
the coherence of a class of wage earners. Conservatives, regardless
of theoretical camp, postulate gloomy secular changes in a society
undermined by 'growthmania,' dark-skinned immigrants or Cau-
casian egoism. (Mishan, 1974). The point is that the actors

The Politics of Inflation in the Twentieth Century 39

posited by the economists are not the agents a historian or social observer will find critical. Each economic model usually implies a particular sociological model, but not all are useful. Refinement of the implicit sociology can make possible decisive advances in economic theory: one of the basic claims of *The General Theory* (1936) was that the group behaviour alleged by classical orthodoxy did not correspond to actual decision-making in the collectivity. A finer breakdown of savers and investors (at least as roles if not as separate individuals) explained why the presumption of full employment was ill-founded. Keynes did not propose an equivalent sociology of inflation, probably because he felt its origins were more centrally determined by war finance (cf. Keynes, 1940; Weintraub, 1960; Trevithick, 1975). Nor do I think that economic models since Keynes have allowed a sufficiently plausible sociology of inflationary propensity, in part because the different class roles vary in different societies, and in part because class alignments themselves evolve in the course of inflation. Social and political structure helps to shape inflation; conversely inflation alters collective social roles. No economic theories, so far as I know, incorporate these reciprocal influences.

Some economic models, however, have begun from assumptions of institutional or class behaviour and not from the postulates of pure competition or marginal-choice rationality. Analyses of cost-plus or other administered pricing go back to Gardner Means, Joan Robinson and Edward Chamberlain in the 1930s, were incorporated by Fred Holzman in his 1950 analysis of inflationary wage price spirals, and recently have been accredited by William Nordhaus (1975) after being elaborated by French and German economists as well (Koblitz, 1971; Biacabe, 1962, pp. 247–250). Marxist concepts, which link political alignments and economic outcomes even more closely, offer two major theoretical lines of development. James O'Connor (1973) and Ian Gough (1975) stress the contradictory burdens placed upon the public sector in capitalist society—the state's need to bear all the 'externalities' of the profit system, even while it must provide sufficient welfare payments to prevent social upheaval. (Their analysis here converges with many points made by free-market critics of the mixed economy.) This Marxian concentration on the budgetary process derives from Goldscheid's fiscal socio-

40 *Charles S. Maier*

logy of the early twentieth century. Goldscheid (1926) did not break down the different class and sectoral claims impinging on the state but emphasized growing public indebtedness *vis-à-vis* private accumulation, and he called upon the state to 'reappropriate' the assets it had allowed capitalists to assemble.

Other Marxian models look less at the state than at the clash of class claims directly in a society where state and economy have largely interpenetrated. Hilferding's concepts of 'organized capitalism' (1915) and the 'political wage' (1927) pointed to the connection betweeen political strength and market power in the raw pluralism of the Weimar Republic. Labour's success in wage negotiations depended upon the German Social Democratic Party preserving the ground-rules for collective bargaining and arbitration; in turn the SPD could remain powerful only so long as its affiliated trade unions retained leverage in the labour market. Similar ideas, of course, have been offered by liberal theorists who stress interest-group rivalry, from Bentley to McConnell (1966) and Lowi (1969). In what Beer terms the collectivist age (1967) and what I have elsewhere (Maier, 1975, pp. 9–15, 580–6) termed corporate pluralism or just corporatism, several developments may facilitate inflation. The state has become 'spongier', more extensive in function and reach but less distinct in administration *vis-à-vis* private interests. The modern economy seems to increase the disruptive possibilities for organized groups—not necessarily because schoolteachers, dustmen and even truck-drivers are more crucial today than railroad workers half a century ago, but because we seem to feel more uncomfortable when they withhold their services, perhaps because the legitimacy of a pluralist system depends precisely upon the appeasement of grievances short of a group's actual walkout. (How else can we explain the potency of student strikes?) In any case, the brokerage of group demands may seem less painful than showdown; as Tobin argues, 'Inflation lets this struggle proceed and blindly, impartially, and nonpolitically scales down all its outcomes. There are worse methods of resolving group rivalries and social conflict' (Tobin, 1972, p. 13).

While this sort of analysis can remain empty or trivial, it does suggest that the state is no longer just an umpire (even a biased one) but a player deeply enmeshed in the game of social and economic bargaining. This player possesses one trump: control of the money supply. But in its control of money and credit (sometimes shared with central bank authorities who achieve genuine independence), the state does not act qualitatively differently from other groups. Each competing interest under inflationary conditions seeks in effect to monetize the assets it controls, whether by means of commodity currency keyed to agricultural products thereby stabilizing the income of farmers, control of interest rates on the part of banks, or index wages that would make labour time the unit of value. Rapid inflation involves the search for constant income shares and thus the attempted coinage of each group's respective scarce goods. Coinage, however, has been a traditional prerogative of sovereignty. Inflation thereby tends to erode sovereignty. Likewise it usually accompanies the devolution of state regulatory capacities upon private interests and, even more generally, dissolves the very sense that an effective public authority exists to enforce the same rules on haves and have-nots together. The loss of commonwealth is, I would argue, one of the severest tolls of inflation, but a cost that the usual welfare functions of economists cannot accommodate.

The analysis of group bargaining thus begins with a tautology, namely that the granting of price and wage claims beyond the given money value of the national product produces inflation. But this recognition, derived from either Marxian or liberal theories of group rivalry, at least assists in demystifying inflation and understanding it as one of the major forms of distributive conflicts in contemporary society. This at least provides the starting point for linking political and social analysis to economic outcomes. For the specification of particular group conflicts and outcomes, case-by-case analysis is required.

Levels of Inflation and the Configuration of Interests

Efforts to infer a sociology or politics of inflation have often foundered on their over-generalization and their formalism. However, inflation is not a uniform phenomenon; it may rather be a syndrome of very different group conflicts. At the risk of over-simplification we can establish a typology of three infla-

tionary plateaus and a deflationary process as well. They are
labelled here: 'hyperinflation', 'Latin inflation', 'creeping inflation' and 'the stabilization crisis'. The first three cases are analysed
in this section, the stabilization crisis in the following section.
Each case, I submit, is characterized by one or two different
configurations of interests and group alignments.

Table 1 summarizes the respective inflationary types and their
associated socio-political alignments. It is important to note
that the differing levels of inflation may be more or less stable.
There is no inevitable slide from creeping inflation to Latin
inflation or thence to hyperinflation; significant alterations in
group attitudes and/or group behaviour are necessary for these
step-changes. (On the other hand, hyperinflation involves such
a great destruction of the real value of money in circulation
that it usually provokes an economic crisis deep enough to
regroup political forces and impel currency reform. Hyperinflations are the super novas of the monetary firmament, exploding
furiously outward only to collapse into the dark neutron stars
of economic contraction. Likewise a stabilization crisis cannot
continue indefinitely although deflationary pressures can remain
prolonged, as from 1930 to 1933.

It is natural to ask whether the coalitions associated with
different levels of inflation actually help cause the inflation
or merely result from it. Of course, incipient inflation can encourage the crystallization of groups whose very demands will there-
upon aggravate the inflationary pressure. But even beyond this
recursive scenario, the alignments themselves appear to me causa-
tive in important ways. At the least they help determine the
extent and duration of an inflationary experience, even if the
initial shock to the system is provided by an exogenous event
such as the need to finance a war, the changes in prices of
key imports or the sudden cashing in of domestic currency
balances held abroad. Thereafter internal coalitions—not always
prepared in advance but quickly, if sometimes unwittingly, woven
across existing party lines according to patterns of wealth, income
and industrial affiliations—themselves generate inflationary impulses of varying intensity. Likewise, the stabilization crisis is
often triggered by signals from abroad that the time for 'responsibility' has come. The signals include outflows of reserves (under
fixed exchange rates), currency depreciation (under flexible rates)

The Politics of Inflation in the Twentieth Century 43

TABLE 1 *The Coalitions of Inflation*

	Economic characteristics	Coalitions
Hyperinflation (over 1000% year)	Initial economic expansion; crisis of credit and production in final stage.	*De facto* industrialist–trade-union collaboration on basis of wage–price spiral, export premium, hostility to foreign power. Relative expropriation of rentiers, unorganized salaried employees, eventually small businessmen. The inflation of the producers.
Latin inflation (10–1000%/year)	Either real growth and development, or unproductive subsidies of export sector and services. Side-by-side persistence of modern and pre-modern sectors.	Strong interest-group disaggregation and working-class–bourgeois conflict. Redistribution of resources toward working classes, and/or key resistance of middle-class and upper-class elements *qua* consumers and savers. Effort to avoid direct taxes by broad evasion, export of capital. Bourgeois leverage precludes early fiscal redress.
Creeping inflation (up to 10%/year – typically, creeping inflation up to 7%)	Real growth.	General consensus of all classes on high employment and welfare. Remains under control only so long as real increases do not require cutting back any sector in absolute terms.
Stabilization and/or deflation	Initial crisis and recession; then expansion or weak recovery with periodic crises.	Initial collaboration of middle-class *qua* consumers and savers with entrepreneurial spokesmen on basis of capital formation. Can lead to middle-class alienation because of inadequate revaluation of assets, stringent credit, or higher taxes.

or admonitions from the IMF. Nevertheless, while such pressure from guardians abroad is often needed to persuade domestic policy makers to undertake stabilization or to provide politically weak but deflation-minded civil servants with useful symbols of national emergency, the ensuing course of stabilization is still associated with a characteristic domestic structure of interests and classes. Foreign bankers reinforce domestic interests.

Clearly, the classifications proposed here are over-simplified. The initial approach to sorting inflations according to their magnitude represents an effort to rank the 'intensity' of these economic experiences. However, the level of inflation may be less politically relevant than the acceleration of inflation. A rapid slide from an inflation rate of 5 per cent to one of 12 per cent or more, as in the major market economies during 1974, may be more destabilizing than a long period of continuing 50 to 75 per cent inflation as in Brazil. For the hyperinflationary experience, the distinction tends to collapse since only very great accelerations of inflation can produce the astronomic magnitudes that are recorded. Conversely in 'creeping' inflation the rate of change of inflation must be very low or the level of inflation itself would quickly become worrisome. But in the middle range it is possible that what is politically important is the second and not the first derivative of prices with respect to time. Yet the continuing, if stable, high rates of inflation in a country like Brazil do suggest underlying class cleavages of a strong and characteristic type. A society with prolonged but steady Latin inflation has different inner conflicts from a society with prolonged creeping inflation.

Hyperinflation. Hyperinflation is, of course, the most sadly picturesque deterioration of purchasing power. Cagan, who has presented a systematic monetarist treatment (1956), dates the appearance of hyperinflation from the month in which price rises reached 50 per cent. Extended steadily over a year's time this rate would yield 130-fold price increases. Societies in recent times that have lived through hyperinflation by this measure include Austria, Hungary, Germany, Poland and Russia in the wake of World War I; Hungary again, Rumania, Greece and China during and after World War II. The highest rate of inflation was achieved not by Weimar Germany (which stabilized

TABLE 2   *Selected Annual Rates of Inflation*

a.   *Creeping Inflation: the experience of the 1960s*
     Mean annual percentage increases in consumer prices, 1961–71

United States	France	Germany	Britain	All OECD countries
3.1	4.3	3.0	4.6	3.7

b.   *Latin Inflation: some major episodes*
     Percentage increases in consumer prices

	1914–18	1919	1920	1921	1922	1923	1924	1925	1926	1927
France	138.0	21.0	37.7	−21.6	−1.0	17.8	9.6	13.0	27.2	−6.3

	1938–44	1945	1946	1947	1948	1949	1950	1951	1952
France (retail food prices only)	182.0	36.7	71.1	62.2	58.7	9.4	14.3	17.4	8.5
Italy	1120.0	95.9	18.0	62.4	5.7	1.7	–	–	–
Argentina	–	20.7	17.1	12.2	13.0	32.7	24.6	37.2	38.1
Brazil	–	–	27.3	5.8	3.5	6.0	11.4	10.8	20.4

	1958	1959	1960	1961	1962	1963	1964	1965	1966	1967
Argentina	31.4	113.9	27.3	13.5	28.1	24.0	22.1	28.6	31.9	29.2
Brazil	17.3	51.9	23.8	42.9	55.8	80.2	86.6	45.5	41.2	24.1

	1968	1969	1970	1971	1972	1973	1974	1975	1976
France	4.6	6.1	5.9	5.6	5.9	7.4	13.6	11.8	9.6
Italy	1.3	2.7	4.9	5.1	5.4	10.8	19.1	17.2	15.7
Britain	4.7	5.4	6.4	9.5	7.1	9.2	15.9	24.2	16.8
Argentina	16.2	7.6	13.6	34.7	58.5	62.5	23.4	171.2	486.0
Brazil	24.5	24.3	20.9	18.1	14.0	12.6	27.5	29.0	41.7
Chile	27.9	28.9	35.3	20.1	77.9	319.5	586.0	380.0	229.5

c.   *Hyperinflation: two Central European cases*
     Percentage increases in internal prices

	1914–18	1919	1920	1921	1922	1923 (to November)
Germany	140	223	68	144	5,470	75×10^{9}

Percentage increases in government cost-of-living index

	1914–18	1919	1920	1921	1922 (to October)
Austria	1,226	197	87	797	1,603

Sources: Creeping inflation: OECD, *Economic Outlook*, December 1974.
Latin inflation: IMF, *International Financial Statistics*, January, 1948;
January, 1954; October, 1973; and August, 1977. Also Sauvy
(1965), Wachter (1976) and Skidmore (1976).
Hyperinflation: Walré de Bordes (1924); Bresciani-Turroni (1937).

45

CHART 1: *Selected Inflationary Experiences. 1914–76*

Note: The positions show the average annual rate of inflation for the timespan indicated. For simplification. only the maximum annual rates have been used for the hyperinflations. The plottings are approximate only, and are designed to show the relative position of each country within the particular episode.

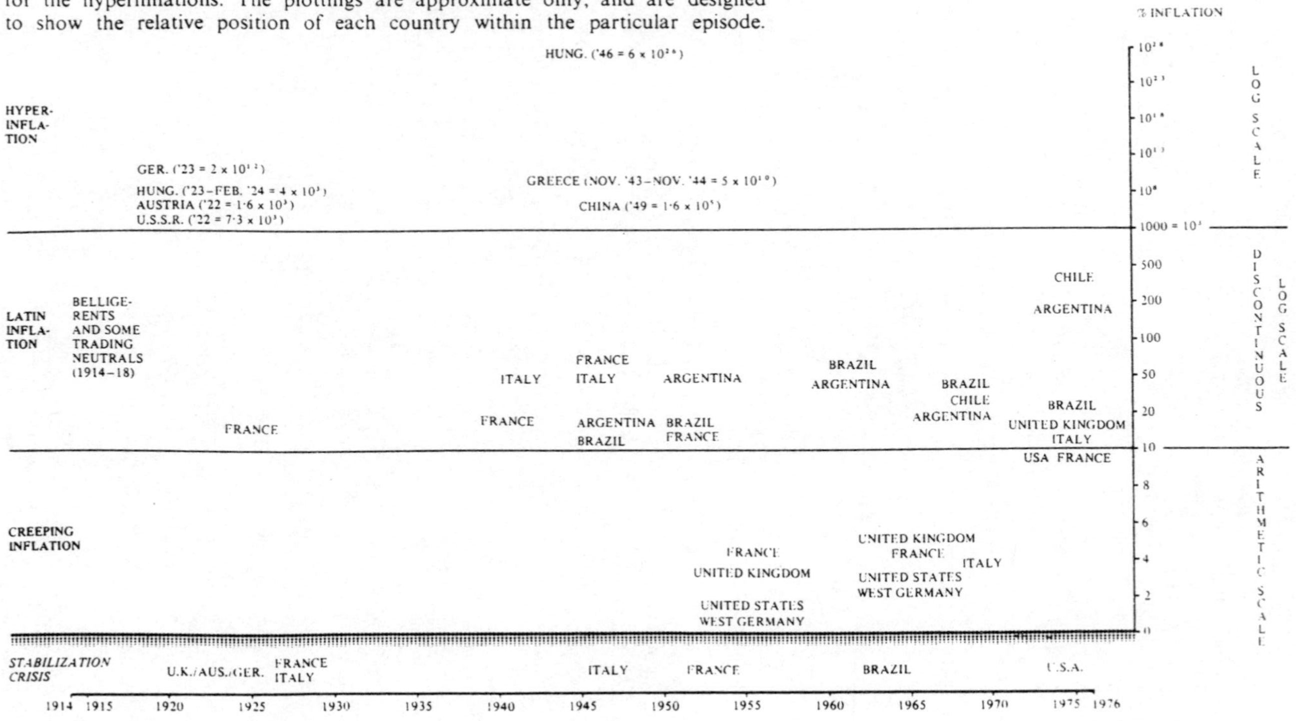

% INFLATION

LOG SCALE

10^{24}
10^{23}
10^{22}
10^{13}
10^{5}
$1000 = 10^{3}$

LOG SCALE DISCONTINUOUS

500
200
100
50
20
10

ARITHMETIC SCALE

8
6
4
2
0

HUNG. ('46 = 6×10^{24})

GREECE (NOV. '43–NOV. '44 = 5×10^{10})

CHINA ('49 = 1.6×10^{5})

GER. ('23 = 2×10^{13})
HUNG. ('23–FEB. '24 = 4×10^{3})
AUSTRIA ('22 = 1.6×10^{3})
U.S.S.R. ('22 = 7.3×10^{3})

HYPER-INFLA-TION

CHILE
ARGENTINA

BRAZIL
CHILE
ARGENTINA

BRAZIL
UNITED KINGDOM
ITALY

USA FRANCE

BRAZIL
ARGENTINA

ITALY   FRANCE
         ITALY   ARGENTINA

FRANCE   ARGENTINA BRAZIL
          BRAZIL   FRANCE

LATIN INFLA-TION

BELLIGE-RENTS AND SOME TRADING NEUTRALS (1914–18)

FRANCE

UNITED KINGDOM
FRANCE   ITALY
UNITED STATES
WEST GERMANY

FRANCE
UNITED KINGDOM

UNITED STATES
WEST GERMANY

CREEPING INFLATION

U.S.A.

BRAZIL

ITALY   FRANCE

FRANCE
ITALY

U.K./AUS./GER.

STABILIZATION CRISIS

1914 1915   1920   1925   1930   1935   1940   1945   1950   1955   1960   1965   1970   1975 1976

GER. = GERMANY   AUS. = AUSTRIA   HUNG. = HUNGARY

46

The Politics of Inflation in the Twentieth Century   47

its new currency at 10^{-12} prewar marks), but by Hungary between August 1945 and July 1946. After a year of frantic issues of Milpengö (10^6 pengö), bilpengö (10^{12}), then tax pengö based on astronomic index numbers, Budapest finally stabilized a new forint at the rate of 4×10^{29} pengö, or about 400 times a billion cubed. (Falush, 1976; Nogaro, 1948).

Effectively, such a degree of inflation destroys money in circulation and substitutes foreign currencies or book-keeping units. Keynes estimated that a government could double the supply of money every three months without entirely destroying its use in retail transactions; the Germans first exceeded this multiple between September and November 1922 and then vastly accelerated by mid-1923 (Keynes, 1923, p. 55 note). Introduction of a new currency or index-money can in fact accentuate depreciation. The Soviets issued a chervonets in November 1922 and allowed the original rouble and successive heavy roubles to sink until a final conversion ratio was established in early 1924. The German authorities consciously drove down the mark in the last two weeks before stabilization in November 1923 in order to prepare the ground for the forthcoming Rentenmark.

What is the political context of such currency disasters? As in other inflations, weakness of the state is an underlying general condition. But that alone specifies little. In certain circumstances hyperinflation accompanies outright civil war, as in Russia from 1917 to 1921 or China between 1945 and 1949. Austria and Germany after World War I, Hungary after World War II were sharply divided polities. Secondly—and as also is the case in other inflations—an important incentive may exist for major socio-political interests to avoid early stabilization. The Bolsheviks felt they might exploit inflation against their class enemies; the Hungarian Communists´ in the coalition of 1945–7 could likewise perceive political and economic advantages; German exporters learned about the advantages of dumping, and the German right in general could see that the inflation effectively paralysed the reparations system they hated. Thirdly—and this seems a distinguishing aspect in societies with a cohesively organized working class—common economic advantages of an inflationary policy bind industrialists and labour together, even if politically they remain at daggers drawn.

None of this is to deny that hyperinflation is proximately

generated by massive fiscal dislocations. Hyperinflation is
amplified by wage price spirals, but at any one time the increase
in money supply represents in effect a frenzied effort at tax
collection. Preobrazhensky pointed this out to the Soviets in
1921 (Erlich, 1967, p. 43 note), and two years later Keynes
wittily explained that the diversion of purchasing power to the
state amounted to a mode of taxation: 'The income-tax receipts
which we in England receive from the Surveyor, we throw
into the wastepaper basket; in Germany they call them bank-notes
and put them into their pocket-books; in France they are termed
Rentes and are locked up in the family safe' (Keynes, 1923,
p. 42).

This taxation operates differently, however, according to the
rate of inflation. While double-digit inflation under a progressive
tax system will increase government revenues by pushing income
earners into higher brackets, hyperinflationary conditions destroy
the normal tax framework. The delay between levying a tax
bill and collection wipes out much of the value of the receipt
with the important exception of weekly withholding. By March
1923, 95 per cent of German income taxes derived from those
wage-earners and employees subject to withholding—a situation
the General Trade Union Federation (ADGB) vigorously protested (Harbeck, ed., 1968, pp. 228–31)[1]. In addition the state
cannot usually raise the price of public services quickly enough
to avoid a massive subsidy. German freight rates were a noted
example. Replacing conventional taxes by currency emissions
provides a heady though ultimately self-defeating alternative.
In the hyperinflations that Cagan reviews, the tax yield of
new currency issues ranged from 3 to 15 per cent of national
income, except for the Soviet state which had a return below
one per cent. But as the real value of cash balances declines,
the yield must fall unless the government can issue paper ever
more rapidly; and it is never rapid enough to keep the money
supply and tax base from shrinking to a tiny fraction, inadequate
for commercial needs or for public revenue (Cagan, 1956, p.
89).

Critical to the unleashing of runaway inflation, therefore, is
the failure of the normal fiscal system. Unexpected demands
of war finance usually trigger such note issues in some degree,
but political factors determine how far the community will there-

The Politics of Inflation in the Twentieth Century 49

after choose direct sacrifice or continued levies through inflation. Soviet finance revealed a situation where an inflationary levy seemed actually purposeful and not just an expedient. After the fact, the Soviets justified their drastic depreciation of the rouble as a way of expropriating the bourgeoisie. During the era of War Communism, Soviet theorists could likewise celebrate a reversion to a moneyless economy characterized by direct requisitioning and provision of goods and services to workers. Even as over 10,000 employees printed roubles (the total value of which by 1921 was no more than a thousandth of the money stock in November 1917), the state pared rents, sought moneyless payments between its agencies and envisaged the elimination of taxes. Still, the monetary collapse remained, it seems, a result of desperation, not calculation in advance.

The advent of the New Economic Policy in the spring of 1921 ended the anti-monetary revery. 'State capitalism' required money and book-keeping criteria of efficiency. Budgeting, which had been largely ignored, was revived, and the expected deficit was reduced from about 85 per cent of government expenditure in 1920 and 1921 to 40 per cent for the first three quarters of 1922. In the same period conventional taxes rose from 1.8 to 14 per cent of government revenue, while the levy derived from the note issue fell from 90 to 56 per cent (with payments in kind making up the remainder). While the old rouble and periodic successors continued to collapse, the chervontsi of November 1922 provided a stable accounting unit until the final currency reform in 1924. In retrospect the Soviet inflation possessed a certain unwitting, costly and ruthless logic for an era of civil war. Ideologists may have made a virtue of necessity when they praised demonetization as an indicator of socialism — a fervour soon after discarded as 'infantile'. But at the price above all of urban–rural exchange, inflation did permit a harsh and coercive control over the allocation of goods and services (Carr, 1952, vol. II, pp. 256–68, 345–59; Katzenellenbaum, 1925; Yurovsky, 1925; Fetter, 1977).

More relevant for other Western countries are the German and the Austrian hyperinflations. Both societies had a cohesive, organized urban working class enjoying critical political influence after the revolutions of 1918–19. At the same time conservative élites were not uprooted and ably resisted incursions into their

50   *Charles S. Maier*

real property and prerogatives. To carry on the Weimar Republic
required the appeasement, if not originally of diehard Junkers,
then of the industrialists whose leadership seemed essential for
recovery and to meet reparation demands. Successive governments
in Berlin reflected either a stalemate among different interests—the
Joseph Wirth–Walther Rathenau cabinets of 1921–2 sought to
keep Social Democratic support and business cooperation simultaneously—or else they reflected the conventional wisdom of
the industrial and financial community as under Wilhelm Cuno
(1922–3). The price of industry's toleration was fiscal paralysis.
If in Russia monetary debasement was a weapon of civil war,
in Central Europe it became its surrogate. Moreover, recourse
to the printing press seemed more attractive because of a widely-
shared unwillingness to meet reparation charges from national
income. Until the last months, hyperinflation was virtually welcomed by many business leaders and bureaucrats as providing
a demonstration that without a change of policy in Paris, the
German monetary disaster could only injure British and American
commerce (Maier, 1975, chs. 4 and 6; Witt, 1974; Feldman,
1977).

From May 1921 through to the summer of 1923, the Wirth
and Cuno ministries by and large accepted the view of the
industrial leadership that further increases in the floating debt
represented the only possible fiscal option. When stabilization
came under consideration in the fall of 1922, leading industrialists
such as Hugo Stinnes raised the spectre of serious recession.
Stabilization would indeed impose transitional costs, which might
involve unemployment for the working class and real taxes
for industry and personal income. The question facing the political
system was which group would pay more. Inflation had disguised
the levies and at first had imposed them on middle-class households, although its results later hit labour too. Finally the government and representatives of industry accepted a stabilization
programme once the alternative appeared grave Communist-led
unrest and once depression threatened as credit dried up in
the summer and fall of 1923. In addition, the export premium
that inflation had provided ended in the summer of 1923 as
domestic price increases outran the mark's depreciation in terms
of foreign currency. (In effect all prices became set in terms
of the daily dollar or pound rate plus a hefty mark-up for

The Politics of Inflation in the Twentieth Century 51

the expected depreciation to follow—a self-defeating form of indexation.) Industry still understood how to alleviate its own costs and the liquidity crisis accompanying stabilization by imposing longer working hours and a disadvantageous calculation of stable-money wages upon the unions. The inflation and Ruhr conflict had almost totally undermined their financial and organizational capacity for resistance (Hartwich, 1967, pp. 67, 102; Maier, 1975, pp. 363–64, 445–50)[2].

Still, the trade unions had accepted the inflation with surprisingly little labour unrest, even before the French occupation of the Ruhr imposed a patriotic front. But then, demand remained strong and employment high, and Germany was spared the brief but severe depression of 1920–1. In part, too, business and the government allowed union wages to keep relative pace with rising prices, although there were painful lags in 1921 and 1922 and growing misery as real income for the society dropped sharply in 1923.

The German Social Democrats and the bourgeois left did indeed suggest alternative fiscal policies between 1919 and 1923. The Catholic Centre leader, Matthias Erzberger, then Social Democratic ministers and advisers, proposed mild capital levies. But even when taxes were theoretically stiffened, as with Erzberger's reforms of 1919–20 and the 'tax compromise' of 1922, they came to nought because payment was stipulated in rapidly depreciating paper marks. Instead of winning needed fiscal reform, working-class representatives won relative wage protection, though not without recurring losses of real income. And by the end of 1923 and early 1924, the stabilization crisis that brought winter unemployment to at least two million allowed industry to renegotiate with labour the terms of the social partnership that had been accepted five years earlier only under menace of revolution. The end of inflation meant the end of tacit union–industry partnership.

The Austrian inflation involved another collaboration of trade unions and entrepreneurs through a formalized index-wage scheme. In November 1919 the Social Democratic prime minister, Karl Renner, summoned employers and employees to an economic summit that accepted an indexation scheme to be worked into collective contracts and which provided bimonthly and later monthly wage. adjustments. Such a compact was facilitated because Austrian industry was enjoying a surge of export demand. As elsewhere, unskilled workers kept their earnings closest to the 'peace parity'; skilled workers emerged relatively protected; while the Viennese middle classes suffered most drastically. By the end of 1921, in fact, the pace of depreciation taxed workers anew. As in Germany, prosperity was dissipated as the volume of money contracted and a credit crisis loomed. By October 1921, the Social Democrats declared themselves ready to cooperate with stabilization measures even at the price of ending their favoured food subsidies. Ending the subsidies, however, only briefly halted the inflation. By a round-robin of diplomatic negotiations that played on the Western powers' fear of Austria's disappearance as an independent state, Chancellor Ignaz Seipel finally extracted a stabilization loan from the League of Nations. The Geneva Protocols of October 1922 also pledged Austria to remove the government's financial measures from parliamentary scrutiny for two years. Seipel's stabilization thus cost the Austrian Social Democrats their latent coalition role, just as in Germany a year later stabilization was to be carried out at the cost of Social Democratic representation in the cabinet and the eight-hour day (Gulick, 1948, vol. I, pp. 149–71; Walré de Bordes, 1924).

Hyperinflation thus involved an implicit coalition of labour and industry at the expense of rentiers, professionals, the civil service and modest entrepreneurs. Industrialists with access to credit stood to profit greatly and industry in general could benefit by heavy demand. Labour avoided postwar lay-offs and preserved relative wage protection until the final months of the monetary collapse. The cost was intermittent lags in real income, harsh unemployment in the transition to stable currency and a sacrifice of collective political influence.[3] Inflation represented a second-best or perhaps maximin strategy of curtailing predictable losses in a situation where the preferred policy of stabilization at full employment appeared unavailable. For any social group the restraint needed to end the spiral of prices and wages seemed doomed to become just a unilateral and costly renunciation. Confidence that restraint would be fairly distributed disappeared; and thus in a sense the true cost of inflation came to involve the very premises of civil society.

This lesson should be sobering today for those who contend

The Politics of Inflation in the Twentieth Century 53

that setting rigid monetary targets can make unions police their own wage demands by making unemployment the logical price of excessive claims. Most workers, of course, will evade the penalty for claiming too much but will surely pay one if they claim too little.

Latin Inflation. The second class of monetary depreciation comprises severe cases of what is usually called double-digit inflation but can range easily up to 100 per cent and sometimes even to several hundred per cent per annum. I have chosen the more playful designation of 'Latin inflation', for salient experiences have included France in the mid-1920s, France again and Italy in the years after World War II and over more protracted periods, Brazil, Argentina, Chile and other Latin American countries. Inflation rates in Latin America in the last few years have ranged up to 700 per cent. Contemporary Britain and Israel also merit inclusion in terms of percentage range, even if not of ethnic designation.

It would be wrong to impose a false unity on these inflationary experiences. Nonetheless, a certain logic of social disaggregation does seem to mark them all. South American inflations are often described as the 'structural' outcome of societies afflicted with concentrated, quasi-feudal distributions of resources while undergoing rapid development. But as Hirschmann has pointed out, since inflation can be conceived of as a failure of production to respond to expectations, almost any social or economic impediment can be invoked as a cause of structural inflation (Hirschman, 1963, pp. 213–16; Lambert, 1959, pp. 43 ff.). Just this perspective, though, suggests a relationship to the heavy inflationary pressures in the developed European economies. The emergence of powerful group interests with divergent policy priorities characterizes all the Latin cases. Of course, this disaggregation of interests marks hyperinflation as well. What, then, distinguishes the politics of Latin inflation from hyperinflation?

First, in Latin inflation the *de facto* coalition of producers is less important. The latent collaboration of labour and industry does not coalesce, and the socio-economic cleavage tends to run horizontally between classes and not sectorally, uniting unions and management.

Second, the relationship to the international economy is also

54   *Charles S. Maier*

a different one in the case of Latin inflation, embodying elements
of dependence more than defiance. Hyperinflation can gather
momentum from the widespread conviction among all classes
that a stable fiscal system will primarily benefit foreign exploiters,
such as Germany's victors seeking reparations after World War
I, or perhaps Hungary's Soviet occupiers in 1945–6. Latin inflations are the expression less of monetary unilateralism than
of relative weakness. In Germany and Austria currency depreciation against the dollar was accepted almost fatalistically as a
condition for maintaining high export demand and relative social
peace. In Latin America devaluation has generally accompanied
conservative efforts at stabilization designed to curb wage
advances and to redress the balance of payments in order to
secure foreign capital. (The Brazilian resort to continual incremental devaluation is more a unilateral recourse but rests simultaneously upon thorough price indexation—and in any case
was a relatively late response to inflationary difficulties.)
Devaluation, however, has in turn triggered new bouts of inflation
led by higher import prices. Thus the susceptible economies
have oscillated between phases of high employment, leading
to international deficits and shortages of foreign capital, and
efforts at stabilization, including currency devaluations that just
renew inflation. Argentina's stop–go cycles in the 1950s were
an exaggerated version of Britain's similar difficulties (Diaz-Ale-
jandro, 1970, pp. 351–390; cf. Vogel, 1974; Pazos, 1972; Skidmore, 1976).

The Latin cases suggest that middle-class or entrepreneurial
elements wager more on foreign capital than upon a continuing
high-growth, high-wage industrial economy. Their strategy often
reflects economic weaknesses and domestic political strength
simultaneously, whereas the German entrepreneurial strategy in
the hyperinflation corresponded to underlying economic strength
but post-revolutionary political weakness. Fearing a decisive rup-
ture with labour, German industry could rely upon the demand
for their advantageously-priced manufactures or industrial semi-
finished products. In contrast, the export capability of most
countries vulnerable to Latin inflation has consisted primarily
of price-inelastic minerals or commodities subject to great price
oscillations and loss of revenue; or it has involved services
ranging from tourism to Britain's banking. The lesser-developed

The Politics of Inflation in the Twentieth Century 55

of the Latin cases reveal the familiar economic dualism that tends to integrate an export-oriented élite into the investing circles of the more economically powerful nations while leaving large backwaters of poverty. The relative factor constraint for the Latin cases is capital, not labour. In fact, once capital became the major constraint in the later stages of the German hyperinflation, the tactic of monetary defiance had to be abandoned.

In a further distinction from the cases of hyperinflation, while the countries afflicted with Latin inflation embark upon stabilization efforts at lower threshholds of depreciation, their attempts seem less likely to stick (Skidmore, 1976). Either a political leadership friendly to labour has secured working-class acquiescence in stabilization—Peron in 1952–3; Britain 1976—or conservatives have resorted to confrontation (army take-overs in Latin America, the Industrial Relations Act in Britain), but the upshot is often just to unleash a new cycle of inflation. Class divisiveness may spare these societies hyperinflation but it seems to condemn them to longer or recurrent periods of double-digit price increases.

The class antagonisms in the Latin cases are often part and parcel of the structural handicaps to real growth: persistent unemployment due to traditional sectors (Italy, Argentina, Brazil, even Britain), or premature expansion of the service class and large bureaucracies (Chile, Uruguay, perhaps Italy). Sometimes the inflationary process itself can help to mobilize savings and to tax incomes on behalf of real development. Brazilian growth seems to have been invigorated by heady price rises in the 1960s, and the French inflation of the mid-1920s may have accelerated reconstruction and stimulated new investment. But the inflation often lingers after growth flags and becomes counterproductive.

Springing as it does from a deeply divided society, Latin inflation can be generated by either of the opposed dichotomous class groupings. In Peronist Argentina, inflation accompanied a redistributive effort on behalf of the urban working-class migrants. But just as significantly a broad defensive reaction on the part of bourgeois holders of money and bonds often plays an important role. Thus middle-class elements end up acting less in their capacity as producers than as savers. In the face of class stalemates, the *de facto* coalition of labour and industry that acquiesces in hyperinflation does not become influential. Therefore, if hyperinflation rests upon a precarious social compact among producers, Latin inflation in Europe has often incorporated the decentralized and sometimes self-defeating choices of savers and rentiers. In seeking to protect their portfolios, middle-class interests, however, often aggravate the very levies they are seeking to avoid.

The French inflation of 1924 to 1926 revealed the capacity of a broad middle-class community to prevent stabilization under the rules of the monetary game. These precluded exchange controls and gave a politicized central bank week-to-week control over advances to the government. From 1919 to 1924 a conservative–centrist parliamentary coalition sanctioned massive credits for reconstruction, which the bourgeois public largely underwrote by subscribing to government bonds. Debt charges accumulating since 1914, however, threw the budget into prolonged deficit. The National Assembly disguised rather than defrayed the deficit by establishing a 'recoverable' budget that would supposedly be covered by German reparations. The governments of the centre and right, which bequeathed an unacknowledged inflationary fiscal policy, were succeeded by those of left and centre, who moved in with inconsistent financial remedies and internal political divisions. The Socialists and left wing of the Radical Socialists around Edouard Herriot advocated a tax on capital of 10 to 12 per cent to be collected over several years. This proposal alienated the votes of the moderates in their own electoral cartel and thus fell short of a majority. The Cartel moderates were willing instead to seek the votes of the conservative opposition to impose further indirect taxes and restore 'confidence' in capital, which amounted to relaxing the controls designed to curtail tax evasion (Goldey, 1961; Schuker, 1976).

The controversies over fiscal policy proved all the more debilitating to the left because of the trumps that monetary policy gave to conservatives. Left as well as right accepted the principle that there should be legal ceilings on the bank notes in circulation and on the advances of the Bank of France to the state. At the same time, however, the bourgeois public held directly large quantities of short-term bonds. When, alarmed by plans for a capital levy, they failed to renew these bills, the Treasury had to draw upon occult Bank of France advances to redeem

The Politics of Inflation in the Twentieth Century 57

the volatile public debt, disguising the overdrafts by covering them weekly with overnight private bank loans. The left thus became hostage both to distrustful private banks as well as to the hostile central bank, even while it was unwilling to cease frightening bondholders with talk of 'radical taxes'.

With the final exposure of the concealed overdrafts the Cartel collapsed, to be succeeded by a parade of ministries which introduced alternately left and right financial expedients. Only after dramatic political crises and flights from the franc did Raymond Poincaré form a ministry of national unity in July 1926, which achieved stabilization with no further technical innovations. By finally demonstrating the political exhaustion of the left wing of the Radical Socialists and persuading Herriot to join his cabinet, Poincaré generated the confidence that proved so crucial in the presence of the diffuse pattern of middle-class thrift, the mass of short-term bonds, and the leverage of the Bank of France (Maier, 1975, pp. 494–507; Moreau, 1954).

Inflation probably imposed a burden just as high as the mild capital levy suggested by Blum and Herriot would have done. Fixed-income patrimonies and deposits stood at about half their 1913 value by 1929 (allowing both for appreciation through interest and the toll taken by inflation). An alternative calculation is that a composite portfolio of money savings, bonds and shares would have been producing perhaps 30 per cent less real revenue by the time the franc was stabilized than two years earlier when the centre–left government came to power. (Of course, equity returns would then have grown again.) The Blum–Herriot capital levy would actually have been collected as a twelve-year surtax on income from assets of perhaps 20 per cent per year (assuming a 5 per cent yield on capital).

Post World War II experiences in France and Italy revealed a similar middle-class tendency to accept the indirect taxation of inflation rather than confront the direct levies needed to avoid it. In 1945 de Gaulle rejected the currency reform proposed by Mendés-France and backed away from any radical amputation of private balances (Parodi, 1971, pp. 66ff.; Brown, 1955, pp. 227–48; Grotius, 1949; Gurley, 1953; Dupriez, 1947). The French price index rose from 285 in 1944 (1938 = 100) to 1817 in 1949, stimulated by state deficits and a four-fold expansion of bank reserves through 1946–7. In Italy, the 1945 price index

58   *Charles S. Maier*

stood already at 16 times that of 1938 and before stabilization
at the end of 1947 had climbed to 49 (retail) and 55 (wholesale)
times 1938 levels. Government borrowing rose from 11 billion
lire in 1938 to 152 billion for the year 1943 and 572 billion
for 1944-5. At the same time the central bank made liberal
credits available to the banking system as a whole, and reserves
at the Bank of Italy rose from less than half a billion lire
in 1938 to 1,920 billion in 1945. These monetary pressures
occurred, moreover, in societies whose 1945 real national income
was reduced to about 50 per cent of the prewar level (Hildebrand,
1965, chapters 2, 8).

Removal of the Communists from the governing coalition
in 1947, the division of the labour movement, and Washington's
declaration of intent to provide 'Marshall Plan' funds that would
ease the constant external pressure against the lira allowed a
stabilization programme to be launched by the successive governors of the Bank of Italy, Luigi Einaudi and Donato Menichella.
This effort involved principally the severe restriction of central
bank credits. Rome, like Paris, rejected the blocking of accounts
and direct levies that other continental countries such as Belgium
adopted. Nor would either emulate the tax severity imposed
in Britain. Italy resorted to a contractionary monetary policy
rather than a severe fiscal policy. The result included a recession
that bottled up labour in the South and effectively passed much
of the burden of stabilization to the popular classes (De Cecco,
1968; Foa, 1949; European Cooperation Administration, 1950;
Barucci, 1973; Ruffolo, 1974).

Stabilization involved a break with the Communists over wage
policy. The post-Liberation governments had not been prepared
to clamp down on wages. Instead the Communist labour leadership initially pledged an effort at full production and won general
wage indexation—an issue that has recently become crucial once
again. As cost-of-living adjustments dwarfed the base-pay differentials, an inflationary levelling of wages took place. This was
a development Communist unions favoured and over which
they separated from the non-Communists during the 1950s.

When stabilization came in France it was, similarly, under
the conservative leadership of Antoine Pinay. The end of the
Resistance-born coalitions with the Communists was probably
a prerequisite for anti-inflationary efforts. Nevertheless, even

The Politics of Inflation in the Twentieth Century 59

as both French and Italian governments shifted to the centre or right, they could make no drastic attempt to cut back into enlarged wage shares (especially when the Korean war and rearmament created new scarcities and inflationary pressure). The governments of the 1950s in Europe ruled out cooperation with the Communists but launched no bourgeois or business counter-revolution. Thus the political logic of the third major type of inflation we encounter: the persistent incremental price rises of the 1950s and 1960s.

Creeping Inflation. The prerequisite for creeping inflation was the remarkable record of economic growth that avoided a harsh distributional conflict between classes. By the early 1950s, bottled-up demand had spent itself; capital building had brought national incomes back to and beyond 1938 levels; international terms of trade began a long-term shift in favour of commodity importers. Marshall Plan assistance eased foreign-exchange constraints; at the same time, United States enthusiasm for currency convertibility helped maintain fiscal and monetary discipline.

The related factor behind the creeping inflation was the balance of social forces. The 1944–49/51 inflation had been a unique legacy of wartime destruction. But the way in which the governments of postwar Europe had sought to allocate the losses reflected their broad political composition and the coalitions that emerged from the Liberation: wage increases for the working class, tax avoidance for the middle classes, relatively easy credit for business. Even after the Catholic–Communist Socialist coalitions fractured, the possibilities of real growth and the felt need to prevent a renewed polarization of the working class precluded any drastic renegotiation of the postwar social bargain. Growth, pursued in an effort to reconcile all important social groups, became the objective of postwar governments.

Some differences persisted between coalitions of the centre right and those of the centre-left. The former stressed capital formation and currency stability whereas the latter emphasized using the new wealth to pay for social insurance schemes. But these were differences of degree. Labour made no serious effort to claim a radically larger allotment of national income, and, in an implicit social contract, Conservative or Christian Democratic ministers made no effort to contest full-employment targets,

60   *Charles S. Maier*

even if keeping demand buoyant involved a persistent upward price trend. (Only when balance-of-payment concerns intervened did this commitment flag.)

In retrospect this era of creeping inflation may appear unique and based upon transitory advantages. The significant increase in agricultural productivity and the continuing exodus from the farms allowed a funnelling of resources to industry and services. The terms of trade favoured food ·and commodity importers, i.e. Europeans, at the expense of their suppliers. Old and new middle classes—employees, small entrepreneurs, bureaucrats—now pressed their own claims effectively through interest-group bargaining. They did not resort to right-radical protest to the same degree as in interwar Europe. The absence of a fascist revival on any significant scale meant in turn that no major ideological attack was levelled against the class collaboration that was occurring.

The international constellation also made its contribution. Thanks in part to the Cold War, the United States proved willing to finance Europe's deficit on current account well into the 1950s if not longer. The Cold War also led to decisions to encourage the reconstruction of Germany and Japan as productive centres for the non-Communist world in general. For many complex reasons, workers in both countries exhibited exemplary wage restraint. Success confirmed its own rewards, as persistent growth focused political dispute less upon the division of the national income than the proper uses of the expected increments. And in turn this level of bargaining did not open larger issues about what groups enjoyed basic power or real legitimacy.

The question for the contemporary observer is whether these conditions were exceptional or potentially durable. The relapse into double-digit inflation after 1973 had its proximate origins in contingent developments: the Vietnamese war with its increase in American deficit financing and its stimulus to international liquidity, and also new price rises in petroleum and food. But the pressures may be more long term. The era of rapid agricultural dividends may be closing; and as growth becomes problematic, disputes over the allocation of national income raise ugly confrontations or require increased dosages of inflation. The very structures of policy making may also heighten vulnerability. The growing role of quasi-independent planning agencies and authorities helped depoliticize distributional conflicts after 1945, but they reinforced a trend in which interests win representation not merely in the legislature, but in the executive agencies of the state. The *de facto* corporatism that eases economic bargaining also facilitates inflation.

Redistribution and Coalition

We have sought hitherto to specify deductively the coalitions that help to generate inflation. This essay presupposes that there exist or are called into being relatively coherent interests which foresee (sometimes incorrectly) different outcomes for different fiscal and monetary policies. No group is likely to be an advocate of inflation absolutely; rather it is the costs of stabilization that will seem more or less acceptable.

Even this assumption, however, is problematic. The stakes of inflation are far more ambiguous than they are often presented as being. Consider some of the obvious difficulties. First, individual interests may not mesh with class interests; the worker may find his own real resources declining even while his class increases its share of national income due to higher employment of previously idle labour. Alternatively his individual wages may decline in real terms but his family income may jump as his wife seeks and finds employment. Second, inflation acts consistently only upon types of income and wealth (or economic roles), not upon real individuals. It is clearly better to be a debtor than a creditor when the value of money is eroding, but most members of the middle classes are both. If the state effectively repudiates a quota of the public debt, it likewise spares taxpayers the burden of servicing it. Third, changes in subjective welfare are hard to sort out. Each individual will certainly feel whether he is better or worse off than he was formerly. But will he also take account of the new comparative rankings of salaries across occupational lines? The formerly well-paid civil servant may feel terribly humbled in terms of his old salary but even more bitter about how close he now ranks with the skilled manual labourer. Conversely the poor charwoman may be closer to her boss but thrown from 'decent' poverty into real impoverishment. And even if the community might choose to trade a degree of wealth for an increment of equality, it may never be fully aware of the equality it purchases; for a few well-publicized cases of inflation profiteering will dominate the public consciousness. Finally, the society as a whole may be sufficiently risk-averse that even equal chances of gains or losses would not compensate for the unpleasant wager entailed.

Do these considerations mean that we must abandon efforts at a political sociology of inflation? No, but they impose great caution about imputing simple correspondence between interests and political behaviour, especially since interests are often far from clear. A further complication emerges from the fact that rational behaviour early in an inflationary surge, may prove less rational later, especially if one passes to a much higher rate of inflation. (Conversely, as is to be explained below, some groups will be vulnerable both during inflation and stabilization.)

Inflation-sheltered assets are by definition more secure than monetary holdings, but such assets become rarer, more expensive and more exposed. What seems a Noah's Ark at the outset of inflation can become a millstone by the end. Rampant inflation, such as the German one, illustrates that few assets are inflation-proof. Ownership of real property, especially if it was mortgaged, seemed a windfall, unless the property was an apartment building subject to the widespread imposition of rent control. In the wake of World War I, landlords in France as well as Germany were locked into property ownership that was more costly than rewarding. On the other hand, this often helped elderly or other middle-class lodgers. Similarly many public services including transportation and higher education became subsidized. The small businessman seemed well-off at the beginning of the inflation and many middle-class investors sunk savings into enterprises. But by the later stages of hyperinflation such proprietors found themselves squeezed by the shortage of credit and working capital, especially as replenishing inventories became ever more costly. Consequently, without knowing when in the inflationary cycle an enterprise was capitalized, it was difficult to determine its value as a shelter. (Eulenburg, 1924; Bresciani-Turroni, 1937, chaps. V, VIII.)

The effect on wages and salaries is also less simple to determine

The Politics of Inflation in the Twentieth Century 63

than initially appears. In Germany real wages periodically fell behind and then spurted forward when the government published new cost-of-living indices and adjustments followed. Organized workers in major industries may have seen their real wages erode as badly in late 1922, when index revisions lagged, as they did at the height of the inflation in the summer and fall of 1923 (Bresciani-Turroni, 1937, pp. 308–13). In Vienna, however, real wages oscillated less but fell behind at the height of the hyperinflation.

Although trade unions may secure relative protection for their memberships (and thereby intensify inflation), there may be greater gains for unorganized workers if inflation accompanies a boom thereby creating new jobs and bidding up low wages (Peretz, 1976, ch. III). In Austria and Germany the fate of civil-service salaries depended upon rank; the real income of the higher grades fell perhaps 70 per cent, but minor clerks were cut much less (Elster, 1928, pp. 444–9). On the other hand, the conditions of employment seemed so secure that the bureaucracy remained a favoured occupational choice (Eulen-burg, 1924, p. 775). Levelling of earnings within each occupational group, the shrinking of differentials between the less and more qualified, seems to be universal in periods of increasing inflation. Data from different countries and periods suggest the greater proportional vulnerability of higher salaries even when conscious redistribution is unintended (Ogburn and Jaffé, 1927, p. 164; Routh, 1965, pp. 108ff.; Hildebrand, 1955, pp. 194ff.). On the other hand, the tendency towards equalization—at least when the tempo of inflation is not too drastic—can be offset by differential relative price increases. Researchers have cited British and American experiences where the outlays for poorer families, with their greater share devoted to necessities, have risen more steeply than the consumption costs of wealthier households (Seers, 1949; Brittain, 1960; Muellbauer, 1974; Williamson, 1976a, 1976b; Piachaud, this volume). In wartime emergencies, when rent and food prices are controlled, however, the poor may benefit relatively on the price as well as the earnings side. Even if we assume that income-equalizing tendencies have prevailed in twentieth-century inflation (cf. Nordhaus, 1973, for possible theoretical results), this still might not determine political (or socio-economic) outcomes in its own right. An increase

in equality that accompanies a growing national product yields
different results from equalization in a stumbling economy. In
the former case, a vigorous demand for labour bids up the
wages of the unskilled without undue penalties for the more
established; while in the latter more painful case, the exposed
higher-income positions are reduced more dramatically.

There are other suggestions that inflation promotes a levelling
of incomes, but the political consequences are far from clear.
Studies of the United States since World War II have suggested
that the inflationary trends have transferred income shares to
wages and salaries at the expense of unincorporated businesses,
farms, rents and net corporate profits (Bach and Stephenson,
1974). These redistributions thus reinforce the longer-term transformations that Kuznets has pulled together for the period
from the late nineteenth century, reflecting the concentration
of economic units and the move out of agriculture (Kuznets,
1959, pp. 45, 86 ff.). The former major regressive toll of inflation —
the erosion of pensions—is now being transformed as social
security pensions are increasingly inflation-proofed, while private-
sector pensions lag behind. At the same time, tax schedules
for nominal income strongly reinforce progressivity under double-
digit inflation. Consequently, income effects in the last few years,
whether in the United States or more drastically in Britain,
have probably been equalitarian. The political implications, however, are far from clear-cut. Levelling has few advocates when
GNP falters in its upward course or falls. And a few spectacular
speculative windfalls may convey to the public a sense that
inequality is rifer and more pernicious, even if aggregate income
differences are actually diminishing.

Changes in wealth and assets may be even harder to sort
out during the course of inflation. The debates over accounting
procedures illustrate the complexity of the issue. To compare
the outcomes upon families in the 1920s I have sought to
measure the inheritances of the late 1920s in Germany and
France against those of 1913. French patrimonies were approximately halved in real terms, and the larger the estate the greater
the percentage sacrifice. German wills were apparently cut down
to less than two fifths real value. The Germans virtually wrote
off their entire public debt and revalued old corporate bonds,
mortgages, bank accounts and life insurance policies up to only

The Politics of Inflation in the Twentieth Century 65

a 25 per cent maximum. The brunt of the loss may have been borne, however, by the more humble legatees, not the largest. All the more reason for a middle-class reaction.[4]

The role of the corporation adds to the difficulty of calculating redistribution. It has been estimated for the United States that perhaps $500,000 million had been transferred from creditors to debtors in the twenty-five years after World War II, largely at the expense of households and to the benefit of business and government. (Bach and Stephenson, 1974, p. 12; cf. Carré, Dubois and Malinvaud, 1972, pp. 362–70) These long-term transfers reflected the lowering of corporate and national indebtedness in real terms. The incidence in terms of individuals and families, however, is hard to ascertain. Individuals might lose on corporate bonds, but their stock portfolios should have risen as corporate indebtedness was reduced, and their tax bills should have been relatively lighter as government debt service became cheaper.

It is just as hard to ascertain the direct effect of inflation on share prices. While investors may initially bid up equity prices, they learned both in Britain and the United States in 1973–5 that shares could not easily keep up with double-digit inflation. Developments in the German hyperinflation might have provided a forewarning. Share prices in Germany tended to follow the dollar exchange until late 1921 largely as a hedge against inflation. Corporate profits seem to have dropped to about 30 per cent of 1913, although this was disguised by inadequate valuation of depreciation. Nonetheless, firms could cut back dividends and add to their reserves as well as seek their own inflation-proof assets through mergers, acquisition and the general process of vertical integration. By 1922, however, share prices could no longer keep up with depreciation, and in October they represented less than 3 per cent of the 1913 values. The assets of the Daimler works, according to the bourse, were worth only 327 of their own automobiles. By late 1922 the growing liquidity shortage precluded investment in the market. Foreigners were dissuaded from takeover bids by the fact that new shares carried no voting rights. However, with the collapse of the 'support action' of February to April 1923 and Berlin's ever more massive recourse to the printing press, investors returned to the bourse. The parity of shares against gold marks

66   *Charles S. Maier*

(1913 = 100) rose from 5.24 in January to 16 in July, and as gold–mark accounting was instituted more broadly from July share prices rose even faster to reach 40 (even 120 when the mark was held artificially high for a few weeks) and to end the year, after stabilization, at 27 (Bresciani-Turroni, 1937, pp. 253–85).

Although Wall Street tended to ignore the lesson during the palmy 1960s, it learned again with a vengeance that share prices cannot easily provide shelter against persistent inflation: The capital base of companies becomes eroded through inventory profits and inadequate depreciation. Of course, share prices become a reflection in part of the cost of holding alternative assets: relative shelter should matter more than intrinsic value. Corporation prosperity, on the other hand, may become divorced from share value and depend upon credit availability. In Germany, in Italy and France after World War II, in the United States until late 1975, access to credit was not seriously limited. The extent to which even high nominal interest rates will inhibit corporate borrowing will depend on how far the market anticipates inflation and on how the monetary authorities respond to it. Fearing a liquidity crisis, guardians of the central bank will often see the continued supply of business needs as vital; for each Einaudi there is a Havenstein—the director of the Reichsbank during the German inflation—who can argue that since advances to the state are so large, further credit to business hardly adds to inflationary pressures.

The cost, if 1975 America was an indication, may well have been at the expense of private housing and of credit availability for mortgages and smaller businesses that did not enjoy privileged relations with their banks. In this sense, inflation taxes households for the sake of corporate expansion. This transfer may help prevent a quick lapse into recession, for the deficiency of private consumption is compensated by vigorous business spending and investment. Office buildings may go up after housing starts to slow down. Ultimately, diminished household resources will dampen industrial expansion.

So long as the economy remains vigorous, however, a trade-off can be expected. If households subsidize corporations, those wage and salary earners tied in to the corporations are generally protected. The corporation may no longer reward its shareholders

The Politics of Inflation in the Twentieth Century 67

concomitantly, but it protects the strong unions and management. Hence there emerges an analogue to the effects of a wage–price spiral at the expense of the rentier or small entrepreneur: credit availability and the delayed tightening of money differentially benefit those organized sectors—labour and management—affiliated with large-scale economic units (Cf. Sylos-Labini, 1974, *passim.*).

These results, however, do not necessarily produce clear-cut political alignments. As noted, inflation taxes economic roles in a society and not necessarily real people. If any major division emerges, it should, of course, separate those who enjoy relative inflation leverage and those who do not. Corporations, their executives, and strong unions (if not necessarily shareholders) should square off against the congeries of vulnerable middle-class proprietors, pensioners and savers. (Since pensioners are increasingly granted indexed benefits their vulnerability has recently been reduced.) One can envisage a coalition of filling-station owners, stenographers and insurance salesmen against the executives of Exxon and the United Auto Workers.

But if this latent coalition emerges under inflation, it rarely corresponds to available political alternatives. To use the jargon of the economists, there is a high search cost for alternative political organizations. Traditional occupational and class identification continues to play a major role in political outcomes.

The consequence of this political lag is often parliamentary incoherence. Any possible coalition, whether of the left or right, includes social groups with disparate interests. The left—whether in the 1924 Cartel des Gauches or the Democratic Party in the United States—includes strong unions and weaker white-collar workers as well as small businessmen. A conservative or Christian Democratic coalition includes entrepreneurs who enjoy relative inflation leverage and vulnerable petty bourgeois of the same social strata as those whom sentiment or anticlericalism or regional tradition places in the opposing camp.

The internal inconsistencies emerge most clearly during the politics of monetary stabilization, the fourth (negative) inflationary case to be considered here. Stabilization is not always welcomed, even by those groups hurt by inflation. The civil servant may find himself furloughed, as occurred in the German *Beamtenabbau* of the mid-1920s. The small proprietor may find himself deprived of credit and operating capital during the period of stringency; likewise the peasant may find that prices for his output have dropped drastically. If his mortgage has been lightened, new short-term operating credit has become costly. What is more, during hyperinflation or even Latin inflation, the aggrieved consumer/saver usually expects stabilization to bring about a recovery of the assets that inflation has eroded. Unless his society is willing to risk a grave depression and heavy tax burden, this expectation must be frustrated (as it was in both France and Germany during the mid-1920s). During the course of inflation it is the levies on real income that appear most preoccupying; the tax on savings is often concealed or believed less definitive. But after stabilization the levy on capital can be totted up. Moreover, any progressive income redistribution that might have taken place now ceases. Thus a direct government reduction or blocking of monetary assets, as carried out in Germany, Austria and Belgium after World War II, produces less resentment than the levy of inflation. Even if it is not a progressive tax, it is a more universal one.

Despite the difficulties, therefore, of accurately foreseeing gains and losses, there does seem to be a natural evolution to the political constellations that superintend inflation and stabilization: (i) workers concerned with high employment, (ii) that segment of entrepreneurs lured by export opportunities or speculative gains or able to exploit increased leverage, and (iii) middle-class constituents originally anxious to avoid heavier taxes, form a natural inflation-prone coalition. If the inflation originates in war finance, this coalition does not preclude conservative sponsorship. Since 1945, however, it has been more often characterized by the participation of the moderate left.

The third group above is especially volatile. When the levy of inflation itself becomes onerous and preoccupying, middle-class constituents revert to a more conservative coalition alongside less 'go-go' businessmen. Moderate and conservative leaders stress the protection of savings and the need for capital formation to compensate for the running down of assets that has characterized inflation. In 1974, as in the societies of the 1920s, business leaders could predict a necessary recession or crisis, what Caillaux termed the 'great penance' that must follow monetary debauch. The penance, however, has often been that of the working classes, which must suffer unemployment even if the real wages of those with jobs may actually increase.

While middle-class constituents may only slowly come to give priority to their stakes as savers and consumers (rather than producers), industry leaders previously acquiescent in inflation can join a stabilization coalition late but with more alacrity. They finally foresee a liquidity crisis being as likely to emerge on the inflationary path as on that of monetary contraction. Although it is difficult in an era of sticky wages, their costs can often be passed along to other sectors of the economy, sometimes by direct government credits. If real growth soon resumes, such a new coalition of (i) reunited business leaders and (ii) inflation-weary middle-class elements can successfully assemble around a programme of capital formation and the restraint of collective consumption.

But if prolonged recession results, or small proprietors get caught by a combination of credit stringency and tax increases, bewildered middle-class elements may turn again: now either to the left anew, or toward the radical right. Not inflation alone, but a harsh ending of inflation has provided the socio-economic ground for radical right-wing movements from the 1920s on. The first electoral success of the Nazis, and of other right-wingers, in 1924 drew in part upon the resentments of those who felt that their paper assets had been insufficiently revalued after the inflation. And the subsequent mass vote for the party depended a great deal upon farmers who had gained relatively in the inflation (by the wiping out of mortgages) but who were hurt by credit and price squeezes after stabilization (Maier, 1975, pp. 483–515). More recently the Poujade movement rose to prominence in the wake of the first major post World War II stabilization program carried out in France (Parodi, 1971, p. 77).

Inflation, Growth and Distribution. The emphasis on capital formation and the reduction of collective consumption has characterized conservative advocacy for a half-century or more. How many times have we heard the Delphic phrase that a country 'is living beyond its means'! What this lament amounts to is that a society is changing the ratio of capital formation to current consumption. The most noticeable way of proceeding is by

70 *Charles S. Maier*

refusing to curtail imports until compelled to by exchange-rate readjustment. Internally, this often signifies to conservatives that the wages and transfer bill of a modern society is growing faster than a normally glacial rate of change would warrant. Again, this is a question of perspective. From one point of view, labour in Western Europe and North America has shown remarkable restraint in view of the enormous differentials of income that persist despite taxes and transfers.

Recent conservative suggestions for indexation may have arisen in part, I believe, from a sense that older arguments on behalf of capital formation and stable money have lost their force (Friedman, 1974b; *The Economist*, June 15, 1974). Why should conservatives become more receptive to indexing? In Austria of the 1920s and Italy of the 1940s cost-of-living escalators reinforced the inflationary process. Supposed success in Brazil has been far from clear (Fishlow, 1974; Lemgruber, 1977; and for more general evaluations see Goldstein, 1975; Braun, 1976). Obviously, to index government bond returns or income tax calculations must be appealing. But wage indexation has also been proposed, perhaps because it seems to offer a way to restore the labour restraint that many feel has disappeared. Indexation appeals when 'guidelines' or social compacts fail. Indexation can work, however, only when labour (or corporations) accept their given share of the national income as satisfactory. It will sufficiently persuade workers to moderate claims only if they accept the productivity-linked concept of wages. The assumption is that labour may accept this concept if reassured that it need not constantly anticipate the next round of price increases. The matter is more complicated when national income is reduced by external forces, such as a deterioration in the terms of trade. The basis of indexation then becomes crucial, as discussed by Flemming (1976, pp. 124–5). This complication aside, indexation offers a chance once again to win a consensus on growth as a surrogate for redistribution.

The concept of growth as a surrogate for redistribution appears, in retrospect, as the great conservative idea of the last generation. By conservative I do not mean militantly right-wing, for indeed wide circles of social democracy and the left have implicitly embraced the covenant it implies. Nonetheless, in the confrontation with Marxism and socialism, conservatives had only three

The Politics of Inflation in the Twentieth Century 71

choices: an outworn insistence on the value of traditional élites and privileges, which had little prospect for success under conditions of universal suffrage; or a fascism requiring that all class rivalry must be submerged in the search to aggrandize national authority and territory (which emerged discredited by the war); or the non-zero-sum pursuit of economic growth in the hope that this might make the older doctrines of class conflict irrelevant. Inflation has played an important role in preserving a broad consensus around the third concept; for when growth could not keep up with expectations, inflation helped disguise the lag. But beyond a certain rate, inflation cannot play this role as social lubricant and instead aggravates the very distributional conflicts it helped assuage.

Thus inflation is integrally linked with the stability conditions of twentieth-century capitalism. Ultimately the society may have to resort to indexation; but at that point the left may well insist that income shares be not frozen, but made an issue of political determination. This will require explicit decisions on equality instead of *ad hoc* and covert ones. Will the result be a gain? Perhaps from the viewpoint of a rational social allocation of income and wealth. But whether it will assure political harmony or even civil peace is far from certain.

NOTES

1. Bresciani-Turroni (1937) also points out (p. 72) that employers might hold the withholding taxes from their workers up to two weeks, thus effectively appropriating much of the real value for their own uses.
2. The best sources for understanding the shifting balance of forces in Germany at the end of the inflation are the stenographic records of two joint employer-employee bodies—the Zentralarbeitsgemeinschaft and the Provisional Reich Economic Council—now held at the State Archives in Potsdam (GDR). They are utilized in Maier (1975), which is drawn upon here.
3. Another cost hits the humbler elements of society that of constant shopping and queueing. Sensitive observers of the Austrian inflation pointed out the sacrifice of family time together because of frenetic shopping expeditions (Arlt, 1925)—a task that servants could be assigned in upper-class households. Twenty years later Kalecki would emphasize this aspect of inequality as an argument for rationing in wartime Britain. (Kalecki, 1947, p. 148)

72   *Charles S. Maier*

4. Data from *Bulletin de la Statistique Générale et du Service d'Observation des Prix*, XIX, f. 2 (Jan Mar. 1930), pp. 206–7, and XX, f. 3 (April June, 1931), 390–1 show the following:

Mean value of inheritance in France (pre-tax; per estate)

	1913	1929	1929/1913
Current value	15,342	40,900	2.67
Retail-price indexed francs	15,342	7,027	0.46

Mean value of inheritances over Fr.50,000

Current value	Fr. 243,634	Fr. 258,706	1.06
Retail-price indexed francs	243,634	44,451	0.18

(Dollar and price indices from Alfred Sauvy, *Histoire économique de la France entre les deux guerres*, vol. I, (Paris: Fayard, 1963), annèxes. Note the greater compression of the wealthier estates.)

For Germany we have comparisons only of the legacies cousins or more distant relatives inherited in 1928 v. those of 1908–13. The number of registered inheritances in 1928 was 16.4 per cent of 1908–13; the amount of bequeathed property involved was 22.9 per cent of the earlier period. The number of inheritances below RM 10,000 was only 15.5 per cent of the equivalent in the earlier period although the individual legacies were of almost 50 per cent higher value. The number of inheritances above RM 10,000 remained between 21 and 26 per cent of the earlier period (save for the inheritances to distant relatives of over RM 1,000,000—down to 17 per cent). Humbler legacies, however, may have escaped registration because they were concentrated in immediate family members, so the results are indeterminate. See *Statistik des deutschen Reichs*, Bd. 276 (Berlin, 1930): *Die deutsche Erbschaftsbesteuerung vor und nach dem Krieg*.

Remember, what these figures measure is the cost of war and reconstruction. Inflation represented a way of allocating that cost, not the cost *per se*.

[16]

RODNEY L. JACOBS*

Hyperinflation and the Supply of Money

1. INTRODUCTION

When a man swaps horse for horse. that's one thing. . . . But
When cash money starts changing hands. that's something else.
William Faulkner, The Hamlet

    Hyperinflation is a somewhat arbitrary term that is used to
describe the monetary experience of six European countries after World War I and
Hungary and China after World War II. All eight countries experienced enormous
growth of the nominal money stock, mainly because governments resorted to the
printing press to finance expenditures.

 The primary focus of economic studies of hyperinflation has been to test quantity theory propositions concerning the stability of the demand for money during
hyperinflation. Cagan's [5] study presented the first formal model whose empirical
results appeared to confirm quantity theorists' beliefs concerning hyperinflation:
i.e.. that hyperinflation was due to growth of the nominal money stock acting
against a stable demand for real money balances. More recently, models of hyperinflation have been derived by Allais [1] and Barro [2]. Both of these models are
developed within the same theoretical framework employed by Cagan. Only the
functional forms of the behavioral equations differ from Cagan's model. The Barro
and Allais models appear to provide even stronger support for a stable demand for

 *This paper is a portion of the author's Ph.D. dissertation at Stanford University. Mordecai
Kurz and Duncan Foley provided many helpful comments and suggestions during the formative
stages of this research. Comments by Phillip Cagan and an unknown referee helped improve the
exposition. Financial support was provided by the American Bankers Association and the Social
Science Research Council.

 *Rodney L. Jacobs is assistant professor of economics, University of California,
Los Angeles.*

money during hyperinflation than did Cagan's model. Not only do the models provide a better fit of the data, but their coefficients satisfy certain theoretical restrictions imposed on the models.

The evidence of Cagan, Barro, and Allais for a stable demand for real money balances during hyperinflation has been questioned by Jacobs [8]. In that paper, the author shows that Cagan, Barro, and Allais solve and estimate the parameters of their models in such a manner as to obtain good empirical results whether or not their structural equations actually represent the dynamics of hyperinflation. When their models are correctly solved and estimated, each model provides a good fit to the data from several of the countries. However, none of the models can match this performance for the entire data set, since the estimated coefficients violate certain theoretical restrictions or appear economically unreasonable.

This paper develops a model that accurately describes the dynamics of hyperinflation. Because of the above-mentioned difficulties with the models of Cagan, Barro, and Allais, the first portion of the paper is devoted to developing a model of the demand for money and the formation of inflationary expectations. In the remainder of the paper the assumption that the money supply is exogenous is dropped, and a model of government behavior is developed that accurately describes the growth of the nominal money stock. In the model, the government attempts to extract some level of real revenue from the economy through the inflation tax. The actual revenue extracted depends on the rate of money issue and on the level of real money balances. If the actual and desired revenue differ, the rate of money issue is varied in an attempt to equate actual inflation revenue with that desired. The hyperinflations become unstable, in the sense of ever increasing rates of money issue, if the desired revenue exceeds the maximum revenue that can be obtained in equilibrium for any constant rate of money issue.

2. A MODEL OF HYPERINFLATION

The model of hyperinflation presented in this section is developed within the same theoretical framework that Cagan employed. That is, we assume a complete dichotomy between the monetary and real sectors of the economy and analyze hyperinflation as a purely monetary phenomenon. We make the standard assumption of lack of money illusion so that the demand for money is a demand for real money balances. Furthermore we assume that the demand for money is a function of only one variable, the expected rate of inflation. The model was developed in a trial and error process using data for the first Hungarian hyperinflation. The impressive empirical results obtained for the remaining countries provide the ultimate justification for the specific functional forms used in the model.

We assume that the demand for real money balances is a nonlinear function of the expected rate of inflation and is given by

$$m_D = \gamma - \alpha \sqrt{E}, \tag{1}$$

where m is $\ln(M/P)$, M is the nominal money stock, P is the price level, γ and α are constants, and E is the expected rate of inflation. Inflationary expectations are formed according to an adaptive expectations model in which the speed of adjustment of expectations increases as the inflation becomes more pronounced. The functional form of the adaptive expectations model is

$$\frac{dE}{dt} = \beta \sqrt{E} \left(\frac{1}{P} \frac{dP}{dt} - E \right), \tag{2}$$

where β is a constant. The model is closed by assuming that equality between the supply and demand for real money balances is continuously maintained by price adjustments. More specifically, we note that by definition

$$\frac{dm}{dt} = \theta - \frac{1}{P} \frac{dP}{dt}, \tag{3}$$

where θ equals $(1/M)(dM/dt)$. The price dynamics of the model are then derived by substituting equation (3) into the derivative of equation (1) to obtain

$$\frac{1}{P} \frac{dP}{dt} = \theta + \frac{\alpha}{2 \sqrt{E}} \frac{dE}{dt}. \tag{4}$$

Thus, the assumption that the supply and demand for real money balances are always equal implies that the rate of inflation instantly adapts to changes in the rate of money issue.

The model given by equations (1) and (2) can be solved by substituting equation (4) into equation (2) and rearranging terms to obtain

$$\frac{dE}{dt} = \frac{\beta \sqrt{E} (\theta - E)}{1 - \beta\alpha/2}. \tag{5}$$

If $\alpha\beta < 2$ the model is stable and inflation can only be sustained through continuous increases in the money stock. If $\alpha\beta > 2$ the model is unstable and self-generating inflations can occur because a small rise in prices produces such a decline in real money balances demanded that the subsequent rise in prices exceeds the initial price increase.

For a given time history of the money stock $\dot{M}$ and values of the constants E_0, α, and β, equation (5) can be numerically integrated to obtain the theoretical value of E as a function of time.[1] The numerical integration for E_t is represented symbolically as

---

[1] The numerical integration was performed using the Runge-Kutta method described in the appendix. The data are available in monthly intervals. For each monthly interval, $x - 1$ to x, θ is set equal to $\ln(\dot{M})_x - \ln(\dot{M})_{x-1}$. To perform the integration we assume arbitrary values of the constants. We then obtain a unique time history of E for the given time history of $\dot{M}$. This provides a unique time history of real money balances from equation (1). The initial constants are then iteratively corrected to obtain a set that minimizes the sum square of residuals.

290 : MONEY, CREDIT, AND BANKING

$$E_t = E_0 + G(\hat{M}, t, E_0, \alpha, \beta), \qquad (6)$$

where E_0 is the initial value of E_t and time is measured from the start of the hyperinflation. Theoretical real money balances can then be computed from equation (1). The hyperinflation data are monthly values of the nominal money stock and the price level, which are denoted as $\ln(\hat{M})$ and $\ln(\hat{P})$, respectively. The data on real money balances are computed from $\hat{m} = \ln(\hat{M}) - \ln(\hat{P})$. Residuals between the actual and theoretical data can then be computed and the parameters of the model $(\gamma, E_0, \alpha, \text{ and } \beta)$ adjusted so as to minimize the sum square of residuals.

Before proceeding with the estimation of the parameters of the model, a short discussion of the problems encountered with the Cagan model is needed to aid understanding of later results. The Cagan technique is to solve equation (2) directly with the rate of inflation computed from the data $\ln(\hat{P})$. We represent this solution technique as

$$E_t = E_0 + F(\hat{P}, t, E_0, \beta). \qquad (7)$$

Simulation studies discussed in [8] show that if the theoretical rate of inflation given by equation (4) accurately reproduces the actual rate of inflation, then the solution techniques represented by equations (6) and (7) will give approximately the same estimation results. This constitutes an indirect test of the structural specification, which the Cagan, Barro, and Allais models fail to pass. If the actual rate of inflation differs systematically from what would be predicted by equation (4), then serious difficulties arise if equation (7) is used to generate the expected rate of inflation. The difficulties arise because $\ln(\hat{P})$ produces compensating differences in the actual and theoretical values of real money balances that insure a good fit of the data.[2] The apparently excellent estimation results obtained by Cagan, Barro, and Allais using equation (7) prove nothing about the ability of their structural models

---

[2] To illustrate this fact consider Cagan's model

$$m = \gamma - \alpha E$$

$$\frac{dE}{dt} = \beta \left(\frac{1}{P} \frac{dP}{dt} - E \right).$$

This model reduces to a linear first-order differential equation that can be solved explicitly. Cagan's solution method, which is equivalent to equation (7), gives

$$m_t = Ce^{-\beta t} - \gamma - \alpha(1 - e^{-\beta}) \sum_{\tau=1}^{t} (\ln(P)_\tau - \ln(P)_{\tau-1})e^{-\beta(t-\tau)},$$

where C is an arbitrary initial condition. Recall that by definition $m_t = \ln(M)_t - \ln(P)_t$ and note that with Cagan's solution method $\ln(P)_t$ will cancel from both sides of the equation if $\alpha(1 - e^{-\beta})$ is equal to unity. My earlier paper illustrates that if the structural model is incorrect, then Cagan's estimation procedure will select values of α and β such that $\alpha(1 - e^{-\beta})$ is biased towards unity. The Cagan solution is then no longer an equation for real money balances but an equation for the money stock as a distributed lag on past prices. Since both M and P grow rapidly at nearly the same rate during hyperinflation, we obtain a good fit whether or not the structural model is correctly specified. As an illustration consider the German data for which

to accurately represent the dynamics of hyperinflation. In retrospect, the fact that three different models accurately fit the same data should have aroused suspicions that the estimation procedure ensured a good fit of the data no matter what the structural specification of the model.

The parameters γ, E_0, α, and β of equations (1) and (6) were estimated from the data for eight hyperinflations using nonlinear techniques described in the appendix. Results of the estimation are presented in Table 1.[3] Except for the Russian data, the model provides a good fit to the data as evidenced by the high values of R^2. In addition, the behavioral parameters α and β are similar for all of the countries.[4] To test the equality of the coefficients α and β across countries, several simultaneous fits of the data were performed with these parameters constrained to be equal for all countries. In performing these simultaneous estimates, we assumed the error term to be independent and heteroscedastic from country to country. To correct for heteroscedasticity the data for the ith country were weighted by $1/\sigma_i$, where σ_i was approximated by the estimate of the standard error given in Table 1. For each constrained estimate we obtain a constrained sum square of residuals $S\dot{S}R_i$ for the ith country. We then construct the statistic

$$\nu = T \cdot \ln \frac{\Sigma \, T_i S\dot{S}R_i / SSR_i}{T},\tag{8}$$

where SSR_i is the unconstrained sum square of residuals taken from Table 1, T_i is the number of data points for the ith country, and $T = \Sigma T_i$. The statistic ν is then

---

the Cagan solution gives $\alpha = 5.14$ and $\beta = 0.21$ so that $\alpha(1 - e^{-\beta}) = 0.99$. The numerical coefficients for Cagan's solution become

$$\ln(M)_t = Ce^{-\beta t} - \gamma + \ln(P)_t - 0.99\ln(P)_t + 0.19\ln(P)_{t-1}$$
$$+ 0.15\ln(P)_{t-2} + 0.12\ln(P)_{t-3} + \cdots.$$

This illustrates the approximate cancellation of $\ln(P)_t$ from the equation and the fact that the equation now describes $\ln(M)$ as a function of past prices.

[3] As an alternative check of the model, the parameters were estimated using equation (7) to generate the expected rate of inflation. This estimation gave approximately the same coefficients listed in Table 1.

[4] Residuals for the estimates of Table 1 show some evidence of first-order serial correlation. A two-stage procedure, which is equivalent to the Cochrane-Orcutt procedure for linear models, was employed. We first iterate the nonlinear model to convergence and compute the serial correlation coefficient

$$\rho = \left(\sum_{i=2}^{T} \Delta q_i \Delta q_{i-1} \Big/ \sum_{i=2}^{T} \Delta \dot{q}_i^2 \right),$$

where Δq are the data residuals. The theoretical data and observations were then transformed according to the equation $m_i^* = m_i - \rho m_{i-1}$ and the model was again iterated to convergence using this transformed data. These results were not significantly different from the results reported in Table 1. For instance, with $\rho = 0.53$, the Austrian data give $\alpha = 2.43$ and $\beta = 0.49$ with standard errors of 0.58 and 0.12 respectively and a D-W statistic of 1.89. A more comprehensive discussion of the effects of serial correlation on models of hyperinflation is contained in [9].

292 : MONEY, CREDIT, AND BANKING

TABLE 1
Empirical Results for Equations (1) and (6)

Country	Interval	T	γ	E_0	α	β	R^2	SSR	SEE	D-W
Austria	1/21–12/22	24	3.029 (0.154)	0.046 (0.028)	2.787 (0.324)	0.466 (0.062)	0.829	0.736	0.192	0.93
China	2/46–7/48	30	−4.762 (0.140)	0.079 (0.020)	3.594 (0.391)	0.338 (0.088)	0.834	0.681	0.162	1.48
Germany	1/21–8/23	32	2.826 (0.058)	0.021 (0.011)	3.029 (0.113)	0.485 (0.034)	0.973	0.579	0.144	1.40
Greece	1/43–8/44	20	−2.847 (0.508)	$3.0.10^{-4}$ (0.004)	3.876 (0.904)	0.176 (0.060)	0.898	1.379	0.294	1.00
Hungary I	10/21–2/24	29	1.182 (0.219)	$3.0.10^{-6}$ (0.003)	2.370 (0.504)	0.337 (0.075)	0.800	1.156	0.215	0.55
Hungary II	6/45–3/46	10	1.078 (0.645)	$1.5.10^{-4}$ (0.006)	2.392 (0.640)	0.355 (0.100)	0.938	0.601	0.317	2.02
Poland	1/22–1/24	25	1.626 (0.239)	$3.9.10^{-4}$ (0.003)	2.617 (0.409)	0.235 (0.059)	0.932	0.559	0.164	1.14
Russia	12/21–1/24	25	−4.170 (0.353)	0.404 (0.146)	2.941 (0.578)	0.478 (0.141)	0.465	2.625	0.354	0.99

Notes: All data are monthly and the unit of time is a month. T is the number of observations, R^2 is the coefficient of determination, SSR is the sum of squared residuals, and SEE is the standard error of the estimate. The approximate standard error of the estimated parameters is in parentheses (see the appendix on the method used to obtain the standard error).

distributed as $\chi^2(\rho)$ where ρ is the number of constraints for the estimate being considered.

In the first simultaneous estimate, the coefficient α was constrained to be equal for all countries. The results of this estimation are summarized in the second column of Table 2. The simultaneous estimation gives a common value of α equal to 3.002 and the individual values of β and $S\hat{S}R$ listed for each country. The statistic v, computed from equation (8), has a value of 11.63, which is distributed as $\chi^2(7)$, since there are seven constraints imposed by restricting α to be the same for all eight countries. The 95 percent cumulative distribution occurs at a value of v equal to 14.07, so we accept the hypothesis that the α_i are equal for all countries. The

TABLE 2
Empirical Results for Simultaneous Estimation

Country	Eight Countries					Four Countries	
	$\alpha = 3.002$		$\beta = 0.430$		$\alpha = 2.890$ $\beta = 0.421$	$\alpha = 3.039$ $\beta = 0.463$	$\alpha = 2.912$ $\beta = 0.272$
	β	$S\hat{S}R_i$	α	$S\hat{S}R_i$	$S\hat{S}R_i$	$S\hat{S}R_i$	$S\hat{S}R_i$
Austria	0.439	0.750	2.928	0.747	0.755	0.769	–
China	0.437	0.719	3.183	0.706	0.750	0.730	–
Germany	0.490	0.579	3.161	0.651	0.803	0.593	–
Greece	0.270	1.603	3.235	2.386	2.446	–	1.612
Hungary I	0.260	1.322	2.157	1.289	1.672	–	1.300
Hungary II	0.268	0.725	2.242	0.691	1.014	–	0.721
Poland	0.196	0.567	2.499	0.612	0.709	–	0.578
Russia	0.469	2.626	3.173	2.639	2.711	2.626	–
Summary Statistic	$v \sim \chi^2(7)$ 11.63		$v \sim \chi^2(7)$ 25.59		$v \sim \chi^2(14)$ 51.44	$v \sim \chi^2(6)$ 3.93	$v \sim \chi^2(6)$ 9.30

simultaneous estimation with β constrained to be equal for all countries gives a common value of β equal to 0.430. The individual values of α and $S\hat{S}R$ are given in column three of Table 2. According to the statistic ν we reject the hypothesis that β is equal for all countries. It is the high value of $S\hat{S}R$ for Greece that causes the hypothesis to be rejected.

For the next simultaneous estimate, both α and β were constrained to be equal for all countries. The estimation gives a value of α equal to 2.890 and a value of β equal to 0.421. The individual values of $S\hat{S}R$ are listed in column four of Table 2. The critical value of ν is 23.68 so we reject the hypothesis that α and β are simultaneously equal for all countries. The values of β_i obtained in column two for the common fit of α indicate that the countries can be split into two groups. The countries Austria, China, Germany, and Russia have a larger expectations adjustment coefficient than do Greece, Hungary I, Hungary II, and Poland. Columns five and six of Table 2 summarize results of a simultaneous fit with α and β constrained to be equal for the two groups of countries. Both fits satisfy the statistical test of equality of coefficients across countries, since the critical value of ν for $\chi^2(6)$ is 12.59.

The estimation results indicate that a money demand function with a common value of α approximately equal to 3.0 accurately fits the data for all eight cases of hyperinflation. One group of four countries with a common value of β equal to 0.46 appeared to adjust expectations more rapidly than the remaining group of four countries with a common value of β equal to 0.27. It is interesting to note that the two Hungarian hyperinflations give almost exactly the same estimates for α and β. The first Hungarian hyperinflation appears to have had no influence on economic agents' reaction to the second hyperinflation.

The model given by equations (1) and (6) was derived under the assumption that the per capita demand for real money balances was homogeneous of degree zero with respect to the price level. This assumption can be tested by assuming a demand function of the form

$$m = \gamma - \alpha \sqrt{E} + \psi \ln(P), \qquad (9)$$

where ψ is the degree of homogeneity with respect to prices. Equation (9) can be rewritten as

$$\ln(P) = \eta(\ln(M) - \gamma + \alpha \sqrt{E}), \qquad (10)$$

so that

$$\frac{1}{P}\frac{dP}{dt} = \eta\left(\theta + \frac{\alpha}{2\sqrt{E}}\frac{dE}{dt}\right), \qquad (11)$$

where $\eta = 1/(1 + \psi)$. Substituting this expression into equation (2) and solving for dE/dt gives

294 : MONEY, CREDIT, AND BANKING

$$\frac{dE}{dt} = \frac{\beta \sqrt{E}\,(\eta\theta - E)}{1 - \beta\alpha\eta/2}. \tag{12}$$

Equation (12) can be numerically integrated to obtain E as a function of time. Given the numerical integration for E_t, represented symbolically as

$$E_t = E_0 + G(\dot{M}, t, E_0, \alpha, \beta, \eta), \tag{13}$$

the logarithm of the price level can be computed from equation (10). The parameters of equations (10) and (13) were estimated from the price data with η constrained to equal unity (actually this is the same as the estimation reported in Table 1) and with η as a parameter to be estimated. These estimation results are summarized in Table 3. The last column of Table 3 contains the statistic $\nu = T \cdot \ln(SSR_{\eta=1}/SSR)$, which is distributed as χ^2 with one degree of freedom. The results given in Table 3 indicate that there is no evidence of money illusion for the eight hyperinflations, since the critical value of $\chi^2(1)$ equals 3.84.

3. THE SUPPLY OF MONEY

For most countries, hyperinflation was not a sudden phenomenon, but was, in fact, the culmination of a historical process that had its origins in the methods used for war finance. The financial policies of China and Germany (discussed comprehensively in [4, 6]) provide a perfect illustration of this point. For almost ten years prior to the Japanese invasion in 1937, the Chinese government had run a deficit amounting to approximately 25 percent of total expenditures. The deficit was financed by the sale of domestic and foreign bonds. After the Japanese invasion, the Chinese government was faced with huge increases in military expenditures, and at the same time did not have a tax system capable of financing these expenditures. The domestic and foreign bond markets would not absorb new government bond issues, and so the Chinese placed increasing reliance on currency issue as a method of financing the war.

The German experience prior to the hyperinflation of 1921–23 closely parallels that of China. The German government believed that the war would be short and

TABLE 3
Money Illusion Results

Country	η	SSR	SSR ($\eta = 1$)	$\chi^2(1)$
Austria	0.913	0.712	0.736	0.796
China	0.987	0.680	0.681	0.044
Germany	0.969	0.570	0.579	0.501
Greece	1.004	1.368	1.379	0.160
Hungary I	0.925	1.140	1.156	0.404
Hungary II	0.937	0.541	0.601	1.051
Poland	1.014	0.558	0.559	0.045
Russia	1.008	2.620	2.625	0.048

made no attempt to increase taxation. For the war years, total government expenditures amounted to 163,894 millions of marks, and government income amounted to only 22,976 millions of marks—scarcely one-eighth of total expenditures. The deficit was initially financed by the sale of foreign and domestic bonds. Toward the end of the war it became increasingly difficult for the government to market its bonds and it had to rely heavily on currency issue to finance the deficit. The postwar government found it politically impossible to expand tax revenue or even to maintain existing tax revenue. As a result it followed the established policy of printing money to finance its expenditures. By October 1923 over 99 percent of government expenditures were financed by currency issue.

Hyperinflation was a natural outcome of continued reliance on the policy of currency issue to finance such a large proportion of government expenditures. To maintain any volume of real revenue from money issue, governments would have had to respond to changes in the price level by changing the rate of money issue. For instance, if the rate of inflation increased, say in response to previous increases in the money supply, the rate of money issue would have had to be increased by a corresponding amount to maintain the level of real revenue. In this process the money supply can no longer be considered exogenous, as in the previous section, but needs to be explained in any complete model of hyperinflation. In this section we will develop a government behavioral equation that describes the growth of the nominal money stock. Hyperinflation is seen as an attempt by governments to extract an excessive level of real income from the economy through the inflation tax. As prices increase in response to increases in the money stock, higher and higher levels of money issue are resorted to in order to maintain the desired level of real revenue.

To develop our model, we assume that the government desires to extract some rate of real revenue R_t^* from the economy through the inflation tax. If the actual rate of revenue deviates from that desired, the government will experience either a deficit or surplus in the volume of revenue extracted in a given time period compared with that desired. The actual rate of real government revenue from inflation is given by

$$R_t = \theta\,(M/P),\tag{14}$$

where θ can be thought of as the inflation tax rate and M/P as the inflation tax base. The deficit between desired and actual revenue becomes

$$V_t = V_0 + \int_0^t (R^* - R)d\tau,\tag{15}$$

where V_0 is the initial value of V_t. (If desired revenue exceeds actual revenue, then the deficit V_t is positive.) The government is assumed to respond to the deficit in the volume of revenue by attempting to increase the rate at which revenue is ex-

296 : MONEY, CREDIT, AND BANKING

tracted from the economy.[5] That is, we assume that the government wishes to change the rate at which real revenue is extracted from the economy according to the relationship

$$dR/dt = \delta V_t, \tag{16}$$

where δ is a positive constant. However, the government cannot control dR/dt directly, but can only increase or decrease the inflation tax rate θ. To derive a relationship between dR/dt and the assumed government control variable, $d\theta/dt$, we differentiate equation (14) to obtain

$$\frac{dR}{dt} = \frac{M}{P}\frac{d\theta}{dt} + \frac{M}{P}\theta\left(\theta - \frac{1}{P}\frac{dP}{dt}\right). \tag{17}$$

Equation (17) illustrates that the rate at which real revenue is extracted from the economy will change if the tax rate changes or if there is any difference between the current rate of money issue and the current rate of inflation, since this changes the tax base. Equations (16) and (17) can be solved for $d\theta/dt$ to obtain an equation that describes government behavior with respect to the issue of nominal money. The government behavior equation can be combined with the model of the previous section to give a complete model of hyperinflation that is represented by the four differential equations

$$\frac{d\theta}{dt} = \frac{\delta V_t}{(M/P)} - \theta\left(\theta - \frac{1}{P}\frac{dP}{dt}\right), \tag{18}$$

$$\frac{dE}{dt} = \frac{\beta\sqrt{E}(\theta - E)}{1 - \beta\alpha/2}, \tag{19}$$

$$d\ln(M)/dt = \theta, \tag{20}$$

$$dV/dt = R^* - R. \tag{21}$$

For a given time history of desired revenue R_t^*, values of the structural parameters γ, α, β, and δ, and values of the initial conditions θ_0, E_0, $\ln(M)_0$, and V_0, equations (18) through (21) can be numerically integrated to yield the theoretical time

---

[5]The model is similar in spirit, but different in its actual form, to an endogenous money supply model used in [7] to explain inflation in Argentina. The control law given by equation (16) implies that the government would continue to increase the rate of money issue if a deficit existed, even if the current revenue rate R_t exceeded that desired. At first glance one might suspect that an adaptive control law of the form $dR/dt = \delta(R^* - R)$, in which the government is only concerned with the current revenue rate, might be more appropriate. However, this type of control rule gives very poor empirical results for a number of the countries. The reason is that this control law allows R_t to exponentially approach R^*, whereas R_t actually oscillates about R^*. The control law given by equation (16) is able to reproduce these oscillations of R_t.

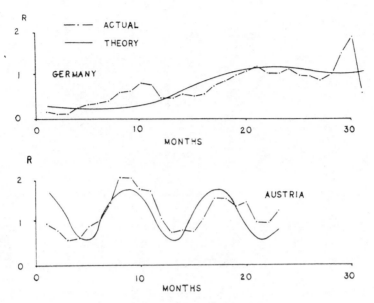

Fig. 1. Government Revenue from Inflation

history of the state variables $\ln(M)$ and E. Theoretical data values can be obtained from $\ln(M)$ and from $\ln(P) = \ln(M) - \gamma + \alpha\sqrt{E}$. The variables M/P, $(1/P)(dP/dt)$, and R, which appear in the differential equations, can be replaced by the functions of θ, E, and dE/dt given by equations (1), (4), and (14) respectively.[6]

All that remains to close the model is to specify R_t^*. To this end we consider the real rate of revenue actually obtained during the hyperinflations. Figure 1 contains a graph of R_t computed from the money and price data for the Austrian and German hyperinflations. The revenue graph for Austria is similar to those of the remaining countries. The real revenue rate does not show any systematic trends, but merely oscillates about some constant value. This suggests that the governments may have been attempting to extract a constant level of real revenue from the economy through the inflation tax. Deviations of the actual revenue from the constant desired rate could be due to lags in the adjustment of the rate of money issue to any shortfalls in desired revenue. For all countries except Germany we will assume that R_t^* is a constant given by the mean of the actual revenue. The German data suggests an increasing desire for revenue as time progressed. For Germany we assume that $R_t^* = a_0 + a_1 t$, where the constants a_0 and a_1 were obtained from a

---

[6] The Runge-Kutta method of integration was also used for these simultaneous differential equations. It is important to note that if the exogenous desired revenue R^* is given, then a complete time history of the theoretical money stock and price level can be generated. This computation depends only on R^* and the eight constants and is independent of the data values $\ln(M)$ and $\ln(P)$. The estimation process will then select the constants for which the theoretical data provides the best fit to the actual data.

TABLE 4

Empirical Results for Complete Model of Hyperinflation

Country	γ	E_0	α	β	θ_0	δ	$\ln(M)_0$	V_0	SSR	$R^2 \ln(P)$	$R^2 \ln(M)$	R^2_m
Austria	2.920 (0.178)	0.004 (0.010)	2.868 (0.282)	0.406 (0.033)	0.118 (0.021)	0.545 (0.036)	8.264 (0.095)	0.191 (0.277)	1.156	0.989	0.997	0.794
China	-4.627 (0.221)	0.039 (0.020)	4.438 (0.802)	0.195 (0.081)	0.115 (0.016)	0.231 (0.031)	0.424 (0.080)	-0.084 (0.331)	1.123	0.992	0.997	0.757
Germany	2.786 (0.075)	0.028 (0.029)	2.961 (0.017)	0.481 (0.053)	0.029 (0.011)	0.088 (0.018)	8.423 (0.113)	0.111 (0.357)	5.433	0.982	0.993	0.901
Greece	-2.840 (0.183)	0.0001 (0.001)	3.953 (0.577)	0.179 (0.029)	0.109 (0.029)	0.200 (0.077)	2.793 (0.084)	-0.482 (0.123)	0.642	0.998	0.997	0.932
Hungary I	1.335 (0.126)	0.00002 (0.0009)	2.627 (0.273)	0.446 (0.093)	0.052 (0.012)	0.052 (0.012)	7.280 (0.077)	-1.573 (0.303)	1.752	0.989	0.984	0.882
Hungary II	1.068 (0.353)	0.00004 (0.002)	2.424 (0.327)	0.309 (0.059)	0.345 (0.038)	0.079 (0.024)	6.900 (0.318)	-0.158 (0.211)	2.464	0.985	0.991	0.920
Poland	2.451 (0.059)	0.060 (0.027)	3.726 (0.747)	0.236 (0.098)	0.081 (0.007)	0.019 (0.005)	7.451 (0.073)	0.960 (0.616)	1.176	0.994	0.997	0.917
Russia	-4.170 (0.107)	0.387 (0.056)	2.921 (0.123)	0.501 (0.138)	0.425 (0.063)	0.079 (0.021)	0.172 (0.133)	-0.183 (0.319)	1.391	0.994	0.997	0.690

RODNEY L. JACOBS : 299

least-squares fit of the actual revenue. The mean of R_t^* is normalized to unity to allow cross-comparisons of δ.

For a given R^* the model works in the following way. Assume that the government is printing money at a certain rate. The rate of money issue (tax rate) and the level of real money balances (tax base) determine the actual rate of real revenue R. If R differs from R^*, then a surplus/deficit between the actual revenue and that desired will build up over time according to equation (21). Say there is a deficit, so that actual revenue has fallen short of that desired. The government will then increase the rate of money issue according to equation (18) and as a result increase R. The increased rate of money issue will eventually increase the expected rate of inflation through equation (19). The higher expected rate of inflation will lower real money balances and also the actual revenue rate. The changing revenue rate will call forth additional changes in the rate of money issue.

Estimates of the parameters of equations (18) through (24) that minimize the sum square of residuals

$$SSR = \sum_{i=1}^{T} \{(\ln(\dot{M})_i - \ln(M)_i)^2 + (\ln(\dot{P})_i - \ln(P)_i)^2\}$$

are presented in Table 4. We see from the values of R^2 for $\ln(\dot{P})$ and $\ln(\dot{M})$ that the model quite accurately describes the time history of these variables. The value of R^2 for real money balances was also computed and is listed in the last column of Table 4.[7] Considerable improvement is noted for the Russian data while the remaining values of R^2 compare favorably with those of Table 1. The coefficients α and β are not significantly different from the values reported in Table 1. Thus, the results obtained with the money supply assumed to be exogenous are not contradicted by the empirical results for the complete model, which treats the money supply as an endogenous variable.[8] The values obtained for δ indicate that the same government response coefficient could not be used for all countries; however, the government response coefficient for Hungary is not significantly different for the two hyperinflations. Figure 1 compares the theoretical revenue rate derived from the model with the actual revenue rate for Austria and Germany. We see that the

---

[7] In the estimation process the money and price data were weighted equally. Estimates using alternative weighting schemes were not significantly different. The values of R^2 for the money and price data measure how closely the theoretical values $\ln(M)$ and $\ln(P)$ explain the variation about the mean of the data $\ln(\dot{M})$ and $\ln(\dot{P})$, respectively. The value of R^2 for real money balances measures how closely $\ln(M) - \ln(P)$ explains the variation about the mean of $\ln(\dot{M}) - \ln(\dot{P})$.

[8] At first glance this result may seem surprising. However, the system of differential equations is similar in some respects to a fully recursive linear system. If θ is given as a function of time, then equation (19) can be integrated to obtain E as a function of time. This computation for E is similar to the integration of the model that treats the money supply as exogenous. Thus, if the money supply model accurately predicts the growth of the nominal money stock, one would expect to obtain similar values of α and β for the two models.

TABLE 5

Maximum Revenue

Country	θ_M	R_M	R^*	θ_T
Austria	0.520	1.196	1.0	0.178
China	0.296	0.944	1.0	0.646
Germany	0.459	1.265	0.18–1.82	1.502
Greece	0.250	0.298	1.0	1.438
Hungary I	0.641	1.377	1.0	0.201
Hungary II	0.657	0.417	1.0	1.870
Poland	0.301	0.492	1.0	0.886
Russia	0.455	0.970	1.0	0.591

theoretical revenue rate accurately reproduces most of the variations in the actual revenue rate.[9]

If we assume that real income is constant and that the rate of inflation equals the rate of monetary expansion, the equilibrium rate of real government revenue from inflation is given by

$$R = \theta e^{\gamma - \alpha\sqrt{\theta}}. \tag{22}$$

The revenue rate is maximized for a value of θ, denoted by θ_M, which is given by

$$\theta_m = (2/\alpha)^2. \tag{23}$$

The maximum rate of real revenue then becomes

$$R_M = \theta_M e^{\gamma - \alpha\sqrt{\theta}_M}. \tag{24}$$

The first two columns of Table 5 contain the values of θ_M and R_M computed from the parameters of Table 4. The value of R_M has been normalized by the same factor used to normalize desired revenue R^* to unity. For China, Greece, Hungary II, Poland, and Russia the level of revenue actually extracted from the economy exceeds the maximum equilibrium level of real revenue. This is also true for the latter stages of the German hyperinflation. During the initial stages of the hyperinflations this high level of desired revenue could be achieved with relatively modest rates of monetary growth. Since the expected rate of inflation lags increases in the current rate of money issue, a higher than equilibrium rate of revenue is initially achieved for any new increase in the rate of monetary growth. As the expected rate of inflation increases, the tax base (real money balances) falls and the real revenue can only

[9]Although the assumption that R^* equals a constant accurately reproduces the actual inflation revenue, an alternative view on government behavior may seem more plausible. We could assume that the government desires a constant level of total revenue that includes both inflation revenue and other taxation. As the inflation progressed it would affect tax collections and the expenditure needs of the government so that R^* would vary as a function of time. This was tested by assuming that the desired revenue varied in proportion to the rate of inflation with the constant of proportionality as a parameter to be estimated. Estimation results from this more general model were not significantly better than the results of Table 4.

be maintained by again increasing the rate at which money is issued. As long as R^* exceeds R_M, the desired revenue can only be maintained by continuous increases in the rate of money issue that rely on the disequilibrium lag in expectations to produce the desired revenue. These cases of inflationary finance were unstable from the very beginning because the desired level of inflation revenue could not be obtained for any equilibrium rate of money issue. The end result of such a policy is rates of monetary expansion that would approach infinity if the process were allowed to continue. The last column of Table 5 shows the rate of money issue for the last month of each hyperinflation. As expected, the value of θ_T exceeds θ_M for these unstable cases of inflationary finance. For Austria and Hungary the revenue rate actually extracted was below the maximum possible rate and the rates of money issue in the final month are less than half of θ_M.

4. CONCLUSION

A model of hyperinflation was developed that accurately fits the data for eight hyperinflations. We first considered a model within Cagan's theoretical framework. That is, hyperinflation was analyzed in terms of an exogenous money supply acting against a stable demand for real money balances. Structural equations different from Cagan's provided an accurate fit to the data on real money balances for the eight hyperinflations. In addition, statistical tests showed that the behavioral coefficient in the demand for money could be constrained to be equal for all countries. The assumption that the money supply was exogenous was then dropped and a government behavioral equation was developed that describes the growth of the nominal money stock. In the model, the government attempts to extract a constant level of real revenue from the economy through the inflation tax. If the actual amount of revenue differs from that desired, the rate of money issue is varied in an attempt to equate the actual inflation revenue with that desired. When the desired level of government revenue exceeded the maximum equilibrium level, the hyperinflations were unstable, and the policy of inflationary finance led to ever-increasing rates of money issue.

APPENDIX

Mathematical and Statistical Methods

The data for Greece and Russia were taken from Cagan [5, Appendix B]. The data given by Cagan are $\log_{10}(P/M)$ and $\log_{10}(P_t/P_{t-1})$. These were converted to $\ln(M/P)$ and $\ln(P_t/P_{t-1})$ by dividing by $-\log_{10}(e)$ and $\log_{10}(e)$, respectively. Data on $\ln(M/P)$ and $\ln(P_t/P_{t-1})$ for Austria, Germany, Hungary I, and Poland were taken from [2, Appendix 1]. The data for Hungary II were taken from [3, Appendix 1]. $\ln(P)_0$ was arbitrarily set equal to 6.0 and a price series was constructed as $\ln(P)_t = \ln(P)_{t-1} + \ln(P_t/P_{t-1})$. The money stock series was computed as $\ln(M)_t =$

302 : MONEY, CREDIT, AND BANKING

$\ln(M/P)_t + \ln(P)_t$. Data on the money stock and price level for China are taken from [6, App. 6, Tables 2.1, 2.3].

The differential equations used in this paper were numerically integrated using the Runge-Kutta method of integration with a step size h of one-half month. For a single differential equation $dy/dt = f(t, y)$ and a value y_t we compute y_{t+h} by the following method. First compute

$$z_1 = f(t, y_t),$$

$$z_2 = f(t + h/2, y + z_1/2),$$

$$z_3 = f(t + h/2, y + z_2/2),$$

$$z_4 = f(t + h, y + z_3).$$

The value of y_{t+h} is then given by

$$y_{t+h} = y_t + h(z_1 + z_2 + z_3 + z_4)/6.$$

For simultaneous differential equations the algorithm is similar and is described in [11].

The parameters of the model were estimated using a nonlinear least-squares algorithm developed in [10]. This method represents an optimum interpolation between the Taylor series and gradient methods, the interpolation being based on the maximum neighborhood in which the linear Taylor series gives an adequate representation of the nonlinear model. To outline the algorithm we define the column vector λ of parameters to be estimated $\lambda_1, \ldots, \lambda_n$, the $n \times T$ matrix of partial derivatives Q containing T row vectors $\partial q/\partial \lambda_1, \ldots, \partial q/\partial \lambda_n$, where q is one of T observations, and the column vector Δq containing T residuals. Next we define the matrix $A = Q'Q$ with elements a_{ij} and the vector $g = Q'\Delta q$ with elements g_j. The first step is to compute the scaled matrix A^* with elements $a_{ij}^* = a_{ij}/(\sqrt{a_{ii}} \sqrt{a_{jj}})$ and the scaled vector g^* with elements $g_j^* = g_j/\sqrt{a_{jj}}$. Scaled parameter corrections are then computed from

$$\Delta\lambda^* = (A^* + \eta I)^{-1} g^*,$$

where η is a constant and I is the identity matrix. The parameter corrections are obtained from $\Delta\lambda_j = \Delta\lambda_j^*/\sqrt{a_{jj}}$. For small η we essentially have the linearized least-squares method, and for large η we essentially have the gradient method. The actual value of η is varied from iteration to iteration in the manner described below. On iteration i the parameter corrections $\Delta\lambda_i$ are computed and SSR_{i+1} is evaluated for the parameters $\lambda_{i+1} = \lambda_i + \Delta\lambda_i$. If $SSR_{i+1} < SSR_i$ the parameter corrections are accepted and on iteration $i + 1$ the value of η_{i+1} is set equal to η_i/ζ, where ζ is a constant. If $SSR_{i+1} > SSR_i$, then η_i is increased to $\zeta\eta_{i-1}$ and a new set of parameters is computed. This process is repeated until, on iteration i, we obtain $SSR_{i+1} < SSR_i$. The choice of η_1 and ζ is arbitrary; Marquardt's suggestion of $\eta_1 = 0.01$ and

ζ = 10.0 worked satisfactorily. The iterative least-squares procedure is stopped when no significant improvement in the fit is obtained from an additional iteration. The specific test used is that if $(SSR_i - SSR_{i+1})/SSR_i$ is less than some input constant, usually 10^{-2} or 10^{-3}, the fit is assumed to have converged. Partial derivatives for the matrix Q were computed from numerical differences. That is, for any parameter λ_i, $\partial q / \partial \lambda_i = (q(\lambda_i + \Delta \lambda_i) - q(\lambda_i))/\Delta \lambda_i$.

The standard errors reported for the parameters were computed from the diagonal elements of the matrix $(A^* + \eta I)^{-1}$. A value of η between 10^{-2} and 10^{-4} was selected to approximate the region over which the linear approximation was valid. Of course it would have been more accurate to evaluate the actual confidence interval for each parameter, but this procedure would have been too expensive computationally.

LITERATURE CITED

1. Allais, Maurice M. "A Restatement of the Quantity Theory of Money." *American Economic Review*, 56 (December 1966), 1123–57.

2. Barro, Robert J. "Inflation, the Payments Period, and the Demand for Money." *Journal of Political Economy*, 78 (December 1970), 1128–63.

3. _____. "Inflationary Finance and the Welfare Cost of Inflation." *Journal of Political Economy*, 80 (October 1972), 978–1001.

4. Bresciani-Turroni, Costantino. *The Economics of Inflation*. London: George Allen and Unwin Ltd., 1937.

5. Cagan, Phillip D. "The Monetary Dynamics of Hyperinflation." In *Studies in the Quantity Theory of Money*, edited by Milton F. Friedman. Chicago: University of Chicago Press, 1956.

6. Chou, Shun-Hsin. *The Chinese Inflation 1937–1949*. New York: Columbia University Press, 1963.

7. Dutton, Dean S. "A Model of Self-Generating Inflation." *Journal of Money, Credit, and Banking*, 3 (May 1971), 244–62.

8. Jacobs, Rodney L. "A Difficulty with Monetarist Models of Hyperinflation." *Economic Inquiry* (Journal of the Western Economic Association), 13 (September 1975), 337–60.

9. _____. "A Comment on Khan's Estimates of Hyperinflation." *Journal of Monetary Economics*, in press.

10. Marquardt, Donald W. "An Algorithm for Least-Squares Estimation of Nonlinear Parameters." *SIAM*, 2 (June 1963), 431–41.

11. Scarborough, James B. *Numerical Mathematical Analysis*, 6th ed. Baltimore: The Johns Hopkins University Press, 1966.

Part IV
Inflations in the 1940s

[17]

HUNGARY'S RECENT MONETARY CRISIS AND ITS THEORETICAL MEANING

By Bertrand Nogaro*

Not many monetary catastrophes similar to those which succeeded the First World War immediately followed the Second World War. Aside from those in Greece, Hungary, Poland, and Rumania, only quite limited currency depreciations have been observed so far. Hungary, however, presents a case of extreme depreciation which leaves the fall of the mark in 1923 far behind. When the fall of the mark was finally arrested, the paper mark was converted into a new mark which equaled the old at the ratio of one trillion[1] depreciated marks to one goldmark. When on August 1, 1946, however, the pengö was replaced by the new forint after less than one year of monetary crisis, the ratio was 400 octillions[2] to one forint and since the 1938 pengö was equal to 2.07 forints, the ratio was actually 828 octillions[3] of depreciated pengö to one prewar pengö.

Hungary's latest monetary crisis is, however, notable not only for the speed and extent of the depreciation, but also for the nature of the measures taken in an effort to check it and for the circumstances in which the currency was stabilized. Finally, this crisis is significant as a novel attempt to neutralize the depreciation through the use of an index-currency.

So far, not all facts relating to the extraordinary features of the Hungarian currency problem are known in every detail. Although the history of this monetary crisis goes back less than two years, the data available are not as complete as one might wish. It is, nevertheless, possible to draw some very instructive conclusions and it is interesting to raise questions even if for the present some of them have to remain unanswered.

I. *The History of Hungary's Monetary Crisis*

A. *The Stages of Depreciation*

When after the First World War the Hungarian government had

---

* The author is professor of economics in the Faculty of Law, University of Paris. This article has been translated from the French version by Dr. Helen Osterrieth Nicol, a member of the staff of the department of economics, George Washington University.

[1] One trillion according to American and French usage, one billion according to English and Central European usage. Figures quoted henceforth will be given in American and French usage.

[2] One octillion $= 1,000,000,000^3$.

[3] As much as 920 octillions according to the pengö-dollar rate.

succeeded in putting an end to the currency depreciation, it adopted
a new monetary unit, the pengö, which was equal to 263.16 milligrams
of fine gold. This new money was put into circulation on January 1,
1927 and remained stable until 1931 when it broke away from gold.
Before the beginning of the Second World War the pengö was sacrificed
on the exchange market because of the existence of a gold premium
of 50 per cent in terms of its original parity. Thus, on the eve of the
last war, the pengö-dollar rate was 5.14 pengö to one dollar.

During the war, Hungary's monetary situation was affected by
government financial policy and by economic circumstances. In 1937
a five-year plan for rearmament had been adopted which entailed, at
the outset, an expenditure of one billion pengö. This was followed by
war expenditures and occupation costs so that from 1939 to the end
of 1944, the national debt increased from 1,659 millions to 15 billion
pengö, while the note issue increased from 831 millions to 10.7 billions.
During the same period, large deliveries made to Germany and Italy,
especially of cattle, very much reduced the country's food supplies.

Accordingly, there existed two conditions for a price rise, that is,
for an internal depreciation of currency—an increase in the monetary
medium (*signes monétaires*) and a decrease in the supply of commodities. Nevertheless, during this first stage, that is from 1938 until the
end of 1944, Hungary's monetary situation was in no way exceptional.[4]

The first months of 1945 marked the beginning of the second phase
of Hungary's currency depreciation. Following the arrival of the Russian armies, there was first a period of about four months during which
note issues ceased almost completely because the Hungarian nazis
had carried off the bank-note reserves of the National Bank. Furthermore, the Russian Army put into circulation only the small amount of
money sufficient for its own needs. On the other hand, all war restrictions such as taxation, rationing, etc., had been suspended, while the
supply of commodities remained very low. During this period the cost
of living rose fifteen times from its former level.

On April 29, 1945 the Hungarian government again put notes
into circulation, but an improvement in the food situation compensated
for the effect of the new issues.[5]

In September, 1945, the depreciation of the pengö accelerated. It
should be noted that a large number of pengö had entered that part of
Transylvania which was annexed by Rumania, where these pengö

---

[4] *Cf. Revue de la Situation Economique à l'Étranger*, published by the French Ministry
of National Economics (le ministère français de l'économie nationale), No. 1 (January,
1946), p. 77.

[5] *Cf.* N. Kaldor's article on "Inflation in Hungary," *Manchester Guardian*, weekly,
(December 7 and 13, 1946).

circulated side by side with the leu. The Roumanian government converted only a part of them and the rest returned to Hungary. The
same thing happened with pengö which had filtered into Austria.
These old pengö were withdrawn from circulation on August 1, 1945,
but the budget expenditures were covered by normal revenues up to
not more than approximately 15 per cent.[6] New issues of pengö increased rapidly. Towards the end of the fall of 1945, the third stage
began when Hungary found itself engulfed in a currency depreciation
which is without historical precedent.

The following table[7] gives the main statistics of this great monetary
crisis.

TABLE I

Dates		Price Index Base: August 26, 1939 = 100	Dollar Exchange on the Black Market
1945	July	105	1,320
	August	171	1,510
	September	379	5,400
	October	2,431	23,500
	November	12,979	108,000
	December	41,478	290,000
1946	January	72,330	795,000
	February	435,887	2,850,000
	March	1,872,913	17,750,000
	April	35,790,361	232,000,000
	May	11,267 millions	59,000 millions
1946	First two weeks in June	862,317 millions	7,600,000 millions
	Second two weeks in June	954 trillions	42,000 trillions
	First two weeks in July	3,066,254 trillions	22,000,000 trillions
	Second week in July	11,426 quintillions	481,500 quintillions
	Third week in July	36,018,959 quintillions	5,800,000 quintillions
	Fourth week in July	399,623 septillions	4,600,000 septillions

Table II shows the increase in the total number of notes issued by
the National Bank of Hungary.

B. *The Devaluation of December, 1945*

The first attempt to check the depreciation of the pengö was made
towards the end of December, 1945. A decree was broadcast December 18 and published by the press on the 19th. By this decree the

[6] This information was given by Professor Eszláry in a lecture delivered at the University
of Pecz (Hungary), during the academic year 1946-47. He was kind enough to transmit
this information to the author.

[7] *Cf.* the first of three articles published by Professor Varga in the *Neue Zürcher Zeitung*,
(January 7, 8, and 9, 1947).

government proclaimed the following regulations: Henceforth, all notes of 1 thousand or more pengö were prohibited from further circulation, unless stamps were affixed to them. The stamps were sold by the government at a cost of three times the face value of the notes. Thus, an owner of four one thousand pengö notes could only keep one of them by sacrificing three others for it. Private currency holdings and the number of notes in circulation were thus reduced by three-quarters. Meanwhile, the face value of bank deposits and other credits and

TABLE II

Date	Notes Issued
December 31, 1945	765,400
January 31, 1946	1,646,000
February 28, 1946	5,238,000
March 31, 1946	34,002,000
April 30, 1946	434,304,000
May 31, 1946	65,589,000,000
June 30, 1946	6,277,000,000,000,000
July 31, 1946	17,300,000,000,000,000,000[a]

[a] 17.3 quintillions.

liabilities was unchanged; and, in particular, wages and salaries were untouched.

When these regulations were announced, many business men thought they had to raise their prices. Subsequently, from these new levels, a very considerable fall in prices took place—amounting to 40 per cent, 60 per cent, and even 80 per cent—for a great many commodities. But it lasted only a few days. At the end of the month, this price fall was completely checked and the movement of prices tended upwards again. Soon the depreciation of the currency advanced so rapidly that it not only was felt from day to day, but even from hour to hour. Employees had hardly received their pay when they rushed outside to buy what they could.

C. *The Creation of the Tax Pengö*

On January 1, 1946, other measures were put into effect. These were designed not to check the pengö depreciation but to neutralize its effects. A new money of a special nature made its appearance. This money was called the tax pengö (*pengoe fiscal*).

The creation of the tax pengö was, at its outset, a simple fiscal expedient. In all countries where an accelerated depreciation of the currency occurs, the tax yields lose a great deal of their purchasing power between the time that the tax is imposed and the time when it is collected and the tax sums expended. It was therefore decided that tax-payers would henceforth pay the treasury the amount of the tax as stipulated on the tax notice, multiplied by a factor corresponding to the daily published price index. In order to achieve this result easily, a new money of account, the tax pengö, was created. Its rate was published every day in accordance with a price index expressed in terms of regular pengö. The taxpayers' liabilities were thus designated in this money of account.

Soon, however, this money was used in business transactions. Beginning with January 10, 1946, commercial banks and savings banks opened valorization accounts which they were obliged to establish in tax pengö. After the depositor had paid in a certain amount of regular pengö, he received, upon withdrawal of his deposit, the same amount of pengö, multiplied by a factor equal to the ratio of the tax pengö's rate of the day of withdrawal to the rate of the day of deposit.

These valorization accounts were encouraged in order to reduce the demand for dollars, the purpose of which was to acquire a stable money. The general use of the valorization accounts meant that the banks receiving deposits in this form were able to grant credits under the same conditions.

Beginning with June 1, 1946, notes of tax pengö were issued. They could be bought in exchange for regular pengö at post offices or savings banks. Owners of tax pengö could keep them or later exchange them for an amount of regular pengö corresponding to the rate of the tax pengö of the day—as if they had a valorization account, with the advantage that they were not required to give advance notice. It was therefore assumed that the tax pengö would be hoarded. But soon many payments were stipulated and settled in tax pengö. The tax pengö thus ceased to be solely a money of account but played the role of a store of value until it became currency which fulfilled all the functions of money.

Soon, however, the tax pengö which on January 1, 1946 was equal to one regular pengö developed a slight premium in relation to the latter, and finally an "astronomical" one. On February 1, it was worth 1.7 regular pengö; at the end of June, it was worth 7.5 billions; on July 5, 1.2 quintillions[8] and on July 27, 2 octillions.

The depreciation of the regular pengö in terms of commodities and in terms of the dollar took place at the same time as its depreciation in terms of tax pengö. This is shown in the first column of Table III.

The tax pengö depreciated as shown in Table III.

Until April 18, that is for almost four months, there was no price

---

[8] One quintillion $= 1,000,000,000^2$; one octillion $= 1,000,000,000^3$.

rise whatsoever in terms of the tax pengö, which meant that it did not depreciate internally until then. Also, not until some time in April did the tax pengö depreciate in terms of the dollar. Beginning with June 20 the depreciation accelerated. It became suddenly more severe between July 16 and 23, precipitous between the 24th and the 27th, and more moderate during the last three days of the month. It should be noted that the extreme depreciation of the tax pengö occurred only

TABLE III

Year (1946)	Average Daily Rise of Prices as Percentage of the Tax Pengö	Prices in Tax Pengö (Jan. 1, 1946 = 1)	Index of the Dollar Rate of Exchange on the Black Market in Tax Pengö
Jan. 2	—	1.0	1.0
April 18	—	1.0	1.5
April 19–May 31	2.8	2.4	1.9
June 1–19	6.9	4.8	5.9
June 20–July 8	19.9	22.8	21.9
July 9–15	43.5	101.0	116.0
July 16–23	95.8	875.0	981.5
July 24–27	258.5	15,454.9	37,037.1
July 28–31	5.4	10,551.0	8,518.5

after the news had leaked out that it was to be withdrawn, without information as to its rate of conversion.

D. *The New Forint*

On August 1 a new monetary unit was put into circulation, called "forint," equal to 75.7 milligrams of gold.[9] The regular pengö were withdrawn from circulation and redeemed at the exchange rate of 400 octillions to 1 forint and the tax pengö, which continued to circulate as auxiliary currency, were converted at the rate of 200 millions to 1 forint. The new forint dollar rate was 1 to 11.74. Since it had been 1 to 5.14 before the war, the exchange multiplier adopted by the National Bank between the 1938 pengö and the 1946 forint was set at 11.74 to 5.14, that is, in round figures, 2.3.

E. *The New Price Structure*

The conversion of prices expressed in prewar pengö to prices expressed in new forints was not made by an equally simple method. The authorities in charge of monetary reform thought that the current price structure needed to be substantially revised. It was deemed neces-

[9] Decrees of July 26 and 28, 1946.

sary to make certain that disposable purchasing power was proportional to actual output so as to avoid another currency depreciation.

National income, that is the value of the total output, was thus estimated at only 60 per cent of that of 1938, but since reparations and reconstruction payments had to be taken into account the rate was lowered to 50 per cent. Consequently, it was decided that wages estimated in 1938 pengö should not rise to more than 55 per cent of their prewar level, at a time when output per industrial worker was at a level of 75 per cent of the prewar rate. As to salaries, a rate of 40 to 42 per cent was adopted, and for rents the rate was fixed at 60 per cent for low rents and 40 per cent for high rents. The price of grain was fixed by means of a factor of 2.2 applied to the price of prewar pengö; the average was 2.7 for farm prices and 4.4 for industrial prices. It was actually planned to adjust the purchasing power of the farmers to the share of the industrial output which was to go to them. An ultimate fall in industrial prices was, however, anticipated.[10]

This price structure was decided on before it was known what the exchange rate of the pengö with the new monetary unit would be. The announcement was made, according to Kaldor, only the night before the stabilization. The prices of forints were on the average three times those of 1938 pengö while income payments, such as wages, etc., which had already been fixed in terms of old pengö, were converted into forints at the rate of 3 to 1.

Official documents[11] emphasize that as soon as the monetary reform was completed, effort was made to establish and maintain a budgetary equilibrium and to avoid any new inflatioñ. These documents do not make allusion to any measure intended to guarantee the regular conversion of the new forint in dollars to maintain a stable exchange rate.

Some commentators, therefore, believed that Hungary's monetary crisis had run its course and had been solved according to classical theories, that it was solely due to inflation and that, in contrast to the monetary experiences which followed the first World War, the monetary reform of Hungary had been effected by internal measures alone and without outside help. A more detailed analysis of the facts, leading to somewhat more complex conclusions, will be developed in the second part of this article while the third and last part will be devoted to the problem of an index-currency.

---

[10] During the year which followed the monetary reform, prices rose an average of 25 per cent which affected agricultural products mostly. *Cf. Gazdazágstatisztikai Tájékoztató* (Journal of Economic Statistics, Sept., 1947).

[11] *Cf.* the decree regarding the establishment of the forint of July 20, 1946, and the announcement published by the National Bank of Hungary on the same day.

II. *Theoretical Considerations*

A. *Deflation and Decline in Demand*

The extraordinary depreciation of the Hungarian currency is undoubtedly linked to an inflation of the classical type, that is an abnormal issue of money by the state in order to offset a budgetary deficit. The interpretation of such a phenomenon appears so simple that one need not make the effort to formulate it more explicitly. While creating money for its own account, the state provides itself with purchasing power which has no counterpart in output. This is added to the purchasing power of individuals rather than being levied on them in form of taxing or borrowing and thus destroys the equilibrium between supply and demand. It should, however, be noted that the enormous increase of issues of money to which the state resorts provides no exact measure of this disequilibrium for when depreciation becomes extreme the excess of purchasing power created by the last issues is generally very small.[12] The acceleration of the depreciation appears then primarily as the result of a psychological phenomenon; it is the "flight from money." This money circulates therefore with extreme rapidity.

On the other hand, the great inflations of history have usually occurred either during wartime or after a war, that is during a period when the output available to consumers is very much reduced. This raises prices and the price rise, which is customarily attributed to inflation (in other words, to the increase in the quantity of money and therefore to the increase in demand), is partially due to the decrease in supply. Hungary's latest monetary crisis underlines the importance of this observation for it illustrates, as we have seen, a period during which prices rise rapidly, even though there was no increase in the quantity of money in circulation.

B. *An Interpretation of the Attempt at Devaluation*

Equally instructive is the attempt made by the Hungarian government at the end of December, 1945 to check the depreciation of the pengö by reducing by three-quarters the quantity of notes in circulation. The announcement of this measure could at other times have had a psychological reaction which would have brought about a price fall; it generated, however, first a price rise due to a contrary psychological reaction, the motives for which were stated above. This price rise was followed by a price fall once the measure had been put into

---

[12] At the time when the tax pengö were withdrawn from circulation, their total value did not exceed fourteen million forints.

effect, but it lasted only a few days. When the mechanism of this operation is analyzed, this is easily explained. The volume of paper currency, that is the quantity of notes existing at a given moment, was reduced by three-quarters and so were the currency holdings of business firms and individuals. Their current liquid funds were thus curtailed which brought about a fall in the price of gold and the dollar, but the volume of bank deposits and other credits, and, related thereto, incomes and especially wages, had not been changed. The measures adopted by the government were therefore not of a nature to reduce incomes on which during the same period the demand for goods and services depended. Entrepreneurs were free to draw on their bank deposits or to borrow in order to avoid a temporary reduction of their cash balances.

This experience confirms that it is wrong to reason in the abstract when contemplating such an operation and thus to assume that a reduction of the monetary stock will necessarily generate a price fall. In order to counteract a price rise, it is necessary to decrease incomes and therefore the quantity of money which enters the market during a given period.[13]

C. *A New Conception of Inflation*

It seems as if the Hungarian monetary authorities learned a lesson from this experience. When they undertook the monetary reform, their fundamental idea, according to Kaldor, was that a monetary system could not be stable unless the total of incomes did not exceed the money value of goods and services available.

This conception should at first sight surprise economists who are used to the idea that total incomes are necessarily equal to the value of output—which is understood, broadly speaking, when taking all economic activities into account. This is because the total value of the output includes the incomes of all those who have helped to produce it. But this equality must be understood to be that of the value of products sold and of the total of incomes already paid out for their production. Thus, if wages are suddenly raised, total incomes will rise higher than the value of the goods actually put on sale, calculated on the basis of wages previously paid for their production. It is therefore possible to state that there is an excess of total incomes over the total value of the output, which is equivalent to saying that there

---

[13] Thus understood, the reduction of the quantity of money does not necessarily bring about a price fall, for if supply is insufficient, a quantity of money which has been reduced may equally well serve to pay at a higher price for a reduced quantity of commodities as to pay at a lower price for a constant quantity of commodities. *Cf.* Bertrand Nogaro, *La Valeur Logique des Théories Economiques,* Chap. I. (Paris, 1947).

is a rise in money incomes without corresponding increase in output.

As a matter of fact, it could be objected that in order to have an increase in money incomes there should have been an increase in the quantity of money in circulation. In the modern economy, however, if incomes are increased, the quantity of money in circulation increases automatically. If entrepreneurs have to face an increase of wages they start by drawing down their deposits thus increasing the quantity of money in circulation. Then, if necessary, they will borrow from their banks and the banks will create paper money or credit instruments (*de la monnaie fiduciaire ou scripturale*[14]).

This is a new conception of inflation, much closer to present reality— and especially as concerns actual conditions in France—than the traditional conception which stated that inflation is solely the result of issues of money made by the state in order to prevent a budget deficit.

D. *Hungary's Depreciation and the Exchange Rate of the Dollar*

It is now better understood how the application of a sliding scale of wages could contribute to accerelating the depreciation of the pengö, by raising the purchasing power in the same proportion as prices rose. It also makes clear why the generalization of the principles of a sliding scale through the creation of a currency with automatic revalorization, in spite of being necessitated by the circumstances, had the same effect. Though the preceding discussion shows how the Hungarian currency depreciated, it does not explain why the rate of depreciation should have become accelerated to the point of surpassing all previously known depreciations.

The data presented here undoubtedly do not solve this problem completely. Nevertheless, it must be said that the depreciation of the Hungarian currency cannot be explained from internal factors alone. This depreciation was not only characterized by a price rise, but also by an equivalent rise of gold and foreign exchange, and espccially, of the dollar rate of exchange.

While it may happen that an internal depreciation of the currency caused by inflation is accompanied by inconvertibility, and therefore by an exchange loss—considered as an additional phenomenon—it also may happen that an exchange loss which follows from a disequilibrium in the balance of payments may bring about a rise of internal prices which requires an equivalent creation of money. It is in this order that the correlative phenomena developed at the end of Germany's great monetary crisis. It would be interesting to discover what role the for-

[14] As to an analysis of the conditions which cause the creation of bank money and a discussion of the dictum "loans make deposits," the author refers to his book, *La Monnaie et les Systèmes Monétaires* (2nd ed., Paris, 1948), p. 18 and following.

eign exchanges and the increase in the exchange rate played in Hungary's monetary crisis.

In any case, it is certain that a dollar-pengö exchange rate continued to be quoted on the official exchange market and on the free market and that during some periods the exchange rate preceded the internal depreciation of the pengö in terms of the price index.

Furthermore, it should be noted that during the great monetary crisis of 1945-46 dollars entered Hungary in the form of bank notes[15] and these dollar notes were purchased, like gold, by those who held reserves of pengö which they were not able to spend immediately and who wanted to exchange them for a stable currency. In all, the premium on the dollar seems to have had largely the nature of an internal exchange rate (*agio intérieur*), and it is quite likely that the comparison constantly made between a currency which keeps its purchasing power and one which melts away, contributed much to accelerate the depreciation of the latter. On the other hand, we know that industrialists adopted the custom of computing their manufacturing costs in dollars which, according to some observers, contributed more than the sliding scale of wages to the accelerated price rise of industrial products.[16] And there is evidence that merchants acted in the same way. The extreme depreciation of the pengö may be explained by the general custom of adopting as a money of account a money, namely the dollar, which fluctuated dizzily upward in a highly speculative market, with consequent impacts on all prices.

The history of monetary crises suggests that great depreciations arise especially if their exists a gap between two currencies, be it external (crisis of foreign exchange) or internal. It may well be that Hungary's monetary experience, if studied more closely, confirms this thought.

E. *The Stabilization of the Hungarian Currency and Its Convertibility*

In any case, it would be a grave error of interpretation to say that Hungary's monetary reform was of a strictly internal character. Whatever the timing and effectiveness of the measures taken to prevent the internal depreciation of a currency, the task remains to guarantee its stability in terms of gold or foreign currencies which have stable parities. If the external stability of the national currency can be facilitated by a combination of adequate economic measures—especially

[15] At the time of the monetary reform, the National Bank of Hungary accumulated about 12 million dollars in foreign exchange especially in United States notes, while the pengö withdrawn from circulation amounted to only 14 million forints.

[16] *Cf.* the *Revue de la Situation Économique à l'Étranger*, published by the French Ministry of National Economics, No. 1 (January 31, 1946), p. 64.

those which tend to stabilize the purchasing power parities[17]—it is also true that, in the last analysis, this follows only from a regulatory mechanism which tends to guarantee stability of the rate of exchange.

From the point of view of the value of the forint in internal exchange, the recovery of gold by the National Bank corresponds to the old-fashioned conception that gold is a "security" or the necessary guaranty of a bank note. The value of the forint in terms of the dollar and in terms of other currencies which have a stable exchange rate with the forint, is, however, an entirely different matter. After all, the stability of the exchange value of a national monetary unit in terms of other national monetary units can only be guaranteed if they are reciprocally convertible at a fixed rate. This conversion can be assured according to traditional methods by converting unit for unit the internal paper money (note) or credit instrument (bank account) into national gold pieces and then converting weight for weight these pieces into foreign currencies. This conversion could, however, be equally well performed by the intermediary of an exchange bureau or agency which buys and sells at a fixed rate in national currency bills of exchange on foreign countries and which supplies, in case of need, official bills of exchange if the number of private bills of exchange offered on the market is insufficient. This supply of bills of exchange may be due to either reserves or foreign credits abroad. Failing rigid conversion at a constant rate, a conversion which is based on parities which are slightly variable could be guaranteed by a banking agency or by an exchange equalization account. The stability of the exchange rate can be assured, discreetly and without official action, by the intervention of the central bank or a large bank which assumes the responsibility of absorbing the excess of bills offered, or on the other hand,

---

[17] This does not refer to Cassel's theory of purchasing power parities. According to Cassel, the rate of exchange of an inconvertible currency would not fluctuate beyond the limits determined by the purchasing power parities, because he thinks that importers will not be willing to pay for a foreign currency such a sum in their own currency, that a commodity bought abroad would be more expensive than a commodity bought at home. After all, one buys abroad only goods which one does not find at home or not in sufficient quantity. When, therefore, the foreign exchange rate rises this tends to restrict purchases abroad, but to the extent that a purchase is necessary, the importer will pay the foreign exchange at the market rate and consequently raise his sales price. The rise of the prices of imported products will then affect the level of prices at home. The purchasing power parity changes, therefore, as a result of the exchange parity.

What the author means is that when a new exchange parity is established the purchasing power parity existing at that time must be taken into account. It is necessary, so as not to encourage importation excessively and in order to be able to export, that goods bought abroad in foreign currency be not much cheaper than similar goods bought at home and that home goods do not become too dear to foreign buyers. An equilibrium in the balance of payments should be maintained so that exchange reserves will not be exhausted and so that it will be possible to maintain a fixed parity in the long run.

of supplying the necessary amount. But the stability of exchange, even of a currency, the purchasing power of which is reasonably stable at home, cannot be maintained without some regulatory mechanism. The fluctuations of the exchange rates, linked as they are to those of the supply and demand of foreign bills of exchange and therefore to the balance of payments, cannot be held within narrow and predetermined limits unless all supply or all demand are in some manner or other immediately balanced at an approximately stable rate of exchange.[18]

When the Czechoslovakian crown stopped fluctuating in 1922, this was not the result of its growing scarcity alone, because it had not stopped fluctuating and falling in spite of a draconic devaluation policy. It remained completely stable afterwards and in spite of a large increase in the issue of notes because the Czechoslovakian government had succeeded in acquiring gold reserves and foreign credits in order to supply the exchange market with a regulatory reserve and because the Prague Banking Commission (*office bancaire*) adopted the policy —which had been traditional with the National Bank of Vienna—of intervening, if necessary, by buying a surplus of bills of exchange or by selling the additional bills of exchange needed at a price equivalent to the chosen parity.

Likewise, the real "miracle of the Rentenmark" at the end of 1923 was not so much that of substituting a "secured currency" (*une monnaie "gagée"*) for the depreciated paper currency, but of collecting and employing the German funds which had fled to the United States in order to create an equalization fund. This served the purpose of supplying dollars at a fixed exchange rate in terms of marks as well as supplying marks in terms of dollars.

In the case of Hungary, in spite of the fact that the official documents do not mention foreign credits nor an equalization fund, one can be just as certain that the new Hungarian forint remained stable in terms of the dollar, not only as a result of the internal measures taken—as shown above—but also because, as a matter of fact, the exchange market was so equipped as to assure the conversion of the forint into the dollar on the basis of an official parity. From this point of view, the accumulation of a gold reserve by the National Bank and its collection of the dollars which circulated in Hungary, represent

---

[18] In a review of a book by the author of this article, *La Monnaie et les Systèmes Monétaires*, published in *Economica* (August, 1937), the reviewer claimed that the author was "unable to conceive of a permanently stable inconvertible currency." If, however, the currency in question is inconvertible into metal, long discussions in this book are, quite to the contrary, devoted to showing that such a currency can be completely stable. But the discussion also brings out that it can only be kept stable because of another mechanism of conversion which, furthermore, may follow from actual fact. This discussion can only be briefly summarized here.

much more than measures taken to satisfy a popular prejudice. The accumulation of gold, foreign currencies, and foreign securities actually furnished 12 million dollars which, added to the 32 million of repatriated gold dollars, supplied the central bank with a reserve of 44 million dollars, that is, more than 517 million forints, when at that time the ceiling for the authorized note issue was 1 billion forints. Although the meaning of the operation was not essentially the amount of "backing" (more than 51 per cent), it was not the less necessary from the exchange point of view and it is probable that this action was rounded out by other appropriate measures.

The Hungarian experience, therefore, need not contradict earlier experiences as concerns the realized stabilization of the national currency in terms of foreign currencies.

III. *The Problem of an Index-Currency*

A. *The Tax Pengö as Money of Account, then as a Complete Currency*

The Hungarian monetary experience did, on the other hand, reveal a discovery. This is the appearance of the index-currency. As shown, this original creation was quite empirical and by accident; it did not follow from any preconceived ideas. Its purpose was to guarantee tax revenues, but it deserves to become the subject of a theoretical analysis.

As mentioned above, the creation of an index-currency, called the tax pengö, developed through two stages. First, it was a simple money of account which was automatically revalorized according to the daily price index. A certain sum in regular pengö was deposited on a given day; this sum was equal to a certain number of tax pengö at the exchange rate of the day, which on the day of withdrawal gave right to another sum of regular pengö, fixed according to the exchange rate of that later day. Since this exchange rate was theoretically determined by the price index in regular pengö, it can be said that the sum deposited had automatically become revalorized by a factor equal to the ratio of the price index on the day of withdrawal to the price index on the day of deposit.[19]

The tax pengö thus assumed the role of a store of value. But the other functions of money—medium of exchange and standard of value —were always fulfilled by the regular pengö, in which prices were established and payments were made.

---

[19] In practice the number of regular pengö was first divided by the exchange rate of tax pengö of the day of their deposit. This figure was then multiplied by the rate of exchange of the tax pengö on the day of withdrawal. Suppose, for instance, that a sum of 10 million regular pengö were deposited on day A. The rate of tax pengö was 50—that means 200,000 tax pengö. On day B the rate of tax pengö rose to 100, which makes 20 million regular pengö, the purchasing power of which is equal to that of the 10 million pengö on day A.

During a second stage, the tax pengö—which was issued in the form of notes—became a complete currency, fulfilling all the functions of money. Prices and wages were little by little established in tax pengö and payments were made in them.

This raises the first question. Is the introduction of an index-currency, such as the tax pengö, of such a nature as to check the depreciation of the circulating medium? Or does it have other purposes than to prevent the consequence of its depreciation?

It has been said that the creation of the tax pengö even in its first form, rather than slowing down the depreciation of the regular pengö, to the contrary accelerated it. Actually, the depreciation of the regular pengö increased following the creation of the tax pengö on January 1, 1946. Was it a matter of cause and effect? It is almost impossible to prove. All that can be said is that the creation of an index-currency by setting up a sort of sliding scale favoring that part of income which is not immediately spent, makes this income extensible; it tends, consequently, to increase monetary reserves and to lower the resistance to the price rise. On the other hand, one can observe that to the extent that an index-currency compensates the effects of high prices, it serves to discourage demands for a wage increase based on high prices.

Moreover, the essential purpose of the creation of an index-currency is to neutralize the effects of high prices. We must therefore ask whether this result can be obtained.

It should first be noted that this neutralization can only occur to the extent that the sums received in regular money and which are not immediately spent, can be laid aside and then used again, after multiplying them by a factor corresponding to the price index. Bank customers in Hungary had adopted the habit of depositing their liquid funds in the evening so as to withdraw them, revalorized, the next morning.

B. *The Theoretical Problem of an Index-Currency*

After allowance is made for the peculiar circumstances which applied to the system, the Hungarian experience gives an idea of its effectiveness. For four months the index of the tax pengö remained stable while the difference between the value of the tax pengö and that of the regular pengö corresponded to the price index. This is easily understood, since any sum deposited in regular pengö and converted into tax pengö was at the time of withdrawal automatically revalorized in terms of the price index. If, beginning with April 19, the price index as expressed in tax pengö reveals an internal depreciation, then this is, according to trustworthy evidence, because from that day on the authorities decided no longer to take full account of the whole of the price rise for the purposes of fixing the price of pengö. Furthermore, for technical reasons, the value of the tax pengö was fixed every day according to the price index of the preceding day—this means with an approximation which during a period of extremely rapid depreciation was far from being negligible.

The experience of the tax pengö confirms therefore the logical deduction that the establishment of a money of account which is destined to fulfill the sole function of a store of value, protects its owners from the fluctuations of internal purchasing power of the current money to the extent that these fluctuations are recorded in a price index.

The circulation of notes drawn up as tax pengö, however, raised an entirely different problem. Henceforth there existed a monetary instrument which was able to fulfill all the functions of money. Prices were established in it and it also served to make payments. Even though the owners of this money were assured of the stability of its purchasing power, this does not exclude the hypothesis that for any reason whatsoever they might have insisted on raising the prices of their products or services. In that case the index-currency itself would have depreciated.

This currency was furthermore exposed to depreciation in terms of foreign currencies provided that its conversion at a fixed exchange rate was not guaranteed for foreign settlements.

This is not all. By what can the stability of the purchasing power of the index-currency itself be expressed?

So far it was said that it was expressed, once the deposit was made in regular money, by automatic revalorization which permitted the withdrawal, still in regular money, of a sum which had increased in the same proportion that prices had increased in this regular money, as recorded by the price index. This assumed that prices were established in this regular money and that this regular money continued to circulate.

It happened, however, after the issue of tax pengö that contrary to Gresham's law, good money drove out bad money, that the regular pengö were abandoned, that the tax pengö became current money, that prices were more and more stipulated in that money and that they rose in relation to it first slowly and then at an accelerated rate. When, therefore, the index-currency became full money and prices rose, the price index henceforth registered this depreciation in terms of itself. From the moment that there was no other money against which the growing sums could be exchanged in terms of a price index, it became imperative that the money instrument in form of the index-currency became valorized of itself. It would, for instance, become necessary if the index rose from 100 to 110, for a note or check of 100 units of index-currency to acquire automatically a value of 110 units.

Theoretically this is conceivable, but in practice it is hardly applicable except when price rises are moderate so that from time to time an adjustment of the value of money instruments can be made in round figures which are easily calculated. It is not surprising that this was impossible in the case of the tax pengö. The theoretical problem of the index-currency, although not completely solved, has nonetheless been formulated. It is a matter for serious thought.

[18]

THE INFLATION IN CHINA[1]

SUMMARY

I. The Wartime Inflation (1937–45), 562. — II. The Postwar Economic Situation: budgetary deficits, 568; industrial and agricultural production, 570; the food situation, 571; other difficulties, 571. — III. Developments in 1947, 571. — IV. Summary and Conclusions, 574.

It is the purpose of this paper to survey China's wartime and postwar inflation in those principal aspects for which relatively complete and reasonably reliable information is available, and to endeavor to single out the paramount factors that influenced prices. No attempt has been made to suggest methods whereby the problems exposed should be solved.

The period examined comprises the years from 1937, when the Sino-Japanese war started following the Liu-Kiu-Chiao Incident on July 7, to the end of 1947, when the country was engaged in the third year of the civil war after V-J Day.

A conclusive study of the development of inflation in China is impossible without more complete data pertaining to the aggregate effect of the wars on China's economy, and it can be made only after the nation has returned to normal. Although the data presented in this paper and the statistics derived therefrom are not all that one could wish for, they are nevertheless more complete than anything hitherto available, and on a number of critical points, are fairly adequate. The use of these provisional data may likewise find justification in the fact that more definitive figures will probably not be obtainable for many years to come.

I. THE WARTIME INFLATION (1937–45)

Perhaps no nation has experienced a more serious inflation than China during the war and postwar years since 1937.[2] In

---

1. The statistical material was obtained from various publications, both official and private. Where sources are not given, the data represent computations of the writer. The abbreviation — CN$ — used in this paper is the standard symbol for Chinese National dollars.

2. Before the war China consisted of Manchuria, Mongolia, Sinkiang, Tibet and Sikang, in addition to the 22 provinces of China proper. As one province after another fell into Japanese hands after the war started in 1937, only about 15 provinces constituted Free China when the war ended in 1945. Today the Republic includes Formosa in addition to its territories prior to the war.

INFLATION IN CHINA 563

order to survey the current situation, it seems appropriate to review first the manner in which inflationary pressures were set up during the war. In this section the survey will be devoted to the developments up to V-J Day in August 1945. Postwar events will be dealt with in the suceeding sections. The movements of prices, as emphasized by the official indices (Tables 1a and 1b) furnish an appropriate starting point.

The movement of prices was comparatively moderate, the increase averaging about 12 per cent per month during most of the war, then showing a slight dip immediately following V-J Day in anticipation of increasing supply, and again around the beginning of 1946 when external supplies actually began to arrive in large quantities. Since then prices have been rising steadily and rapidly with a greater speed than during most of the wartime. Prices in September 1947 were more than eight times the same period of the preceding year.

Trends in the exchange rate for the United States dollar in the free market have been similar. From about CN$12.96 per US$1.00 in December 1939, the Chungking rate rose to CN$545 in December 1944, then to a maximum of CN$3,250 in July 1945 and decreased to a minimum of CN$640 in September 1945 following V-J Day, since which time it has been steadily rising. In December 1945, the Chungking rate again rose to CN$1,350 per US$1, as compared with CN$6,450 in December 1946. In March 1946, the official rate, which had been kept at a nominal figure of CN$20 per US$1 since 1942, was raised to CN$2,020, approximately in agreement with the prevailing free market rate at that time. In August 1946 the official rate was again raised to CN$3,350 per US$1.

While these price indices show the general tendency of the inflationary pressures in China, they do this imperfectly. As a result of extensive war devastation, the inadequate transport system, the enemy's economic blockade, and the collapse of inefficient market organizations, the regional price differentials in China were great. In addition, black market prices, both in the cities and villages, were often higher than the government ceiling prices.

The principal cause of inflation was the tremendous increase in government outlay for military purposes. As the war progressed, half of the country was lost, including almost all of its chief

commercial, financial and industrial centers such as Shanghai,
Tientsin, Canton and Hankow. Receipts of customs revenue,
which was the government's main source of revenue, fell to about
15 per cent of normal. A major portion of the internal tax revenue

TABLE Ia

WHOLESALE PRICES AND COST OF LIVING IN CHINA 1937–1947
(Average of Monthly Prices: 1937 = 100)

	Wholesale Prices	Cost of Living (Shanghai)
1937.............	100	100
1938.............	127	129
1939.............	214	172
1940.............	498	360[a]
1941.............	1,258	—
1942.............	3,785	—
1943.............	12,556	—
1944.............	41,927	—
1945.............	158,362	21,978
1946.............	367,406	337,601
1947.............	2,617,781	3,078,000

[a] January–November.
Source: U. N. Monthly Bulletin of Statistics.

was also lost. With military expenditures mounting rapidly, the
gap between revenue and expenditures became wider and wider
(Table II), and since few people in China have surplus funds to
buy war bonds, only about 20–30 per cent of the deficit was recovered by revenue. The rest was financed by borrowings from four
government banks[3] which resulted in continuous increase of notes
in circulation. Incomes increased as a consequence of government
expenditures. In so far as military requirements were met by
diversion of production, they resulted in a reduction of civilian
goods. Besides, imports were cut off on account of the enemy
naval blockade, and domestic production of consumption goods
in Free China was far below the requirements. The process naturally led to an abrupt rise in prices. The rise in prices increased
the incomes of manufacturers, landlords, farmers and merchants.
Wages of industrial workers rose but less rapidly than prices.

3. The Central Bank of China, the Bank of China, the Bank of Communications, and the Farmers' Bank of China.

INFLATION IN CHINA   565

The main burden of the inflation fell on civil servants, school teachers and others dependent on fixed salaries. The weight of demands resulting from increased money income precipitated a

TABLE Ib

MONTHLY CHANGES IN CHINESE WHOLESALE PRICES AND COST OF LIVING
(1937 = 100)

	Wholesale Prices	Cost of Living (Shanghai)
1945 — October	173,670	37,361
November	197,500	86,492
December	206,495	79,989
1946 — January	177,295	89,924
February	229,033	156,219
March	283,020	233,112
April	300,165	228,041
May	337,953	346,660
June	364,238	341,994
July	400,765	380,381
August	414,307	383,982
September	460,027	420,432
October	531,740	441,689
November	576,245	481,138
December	608,764	547,637
1947 — January	732,796	672,498
February	1,070,450	1,045,000
March	1,183,576	1,122,000
April	1,349,316	1,285,000
May	1,910,668	2,088,000
June	2,409,977	2,462,000
July	3,030,573	2,725,000
August	3,338,056	3,066,000
September	3,723,964	3,767,000
October	5,756,866	5,397,000
November	7,460,448	5,866,000
December	10,035,911	7,444,000
1948 — January	13,384,935	11,293,000
February	17,898,096	16,308,000
March	29,268,172	18,806,000

Source: U. N. Monthly Bulletin of Statistics.

further cumulative rise in prices, causing further drastic reductions in real incomes.

By 1944, although as a result of the government's evacuation policy there were about 5,000 industrial establishments with

TABLE II

GOVERNMENT EXPENDITURES, REVENUE AND DEFICIT[a]

(In millions of CN dollars)

	Government Expenditures	Government Revenue	Deficit
1940[b]	3,798	634	3,164
1941[b]	8,078	1,273	6,805
1942[b]	25,069	7,137	17,932
1943[b]	52,127	13,491	38,636
1944[b]	150,000	33,000	117,000
1945[c]	339,700	73,300	266,400
1946[c]	2,525,000	1,249,000	1,276,000
1947[c]	9,370,000	7,148,000	2,222,000
1948[d]	96,000,000	58,000,000	38,000,000

[a] The Chinese fiscal year begins January 1.
[b] Actual figures.
[c] These are budgetary figures announced by the Ministry of Finance. The actual deficit, expenditures and revenue at the end of each year were much larger.
[d] Budgetary estimates for the first half year.
Source: Directorate of Statistics and Ministry of Finance.

300,000 workers in Free China which had not been there before the war, and some increase in the output in certain branches that were considerable as compared with prewar level, the increase in production of basic commodities was on the whole insufficient.

TABLE III

PRINCIPAL AGRICULTURAL, MINING AND INDUSTRIAL PRODUCTION IN CHINA 1938–1945[a]

	1938	1939	1940	1941	1942	1943	1944	1945
Rice (million piculs)[b]	748	753	619	644	635	609	674	588
Wheat (million piculs)	203	198	201	165	210	199	248	219
Coal (thousand tons)	4,700	5,500	5,700	6,000	6,314	6,617	5,502	5,238
Iron ore (thousand tons)	41	42	55	63	78	70	40	49
Cement (thousand bbls)	120	287	297	150	236	206	239	250
Cotton yarn (thousand packs)[c]	25	27	30	112	114	117	115	69

[a] Production of Free China.
[b] One picul equals 133⅓ pounds.
[c] One pack equals 400 pounds.
Source: Ministry of Economic Affairs.

INFLATION IN CHINA 567

The production trend in some of the most important categories is shown in Table III.

As regards food, actual supply was greatly reduced because of the Japanese occupation of over half of China proper, and the lack of all transport. Farms were deserted after the mass retreat to the Western Hinterland. Implements were carried off or destroyed, animals killed and a large area flooded. Total cereals output in 1945 fell about 15 per cent below 1931–35 level, thus aggravating the inflationary pressure.

Another factor working in the same direction was the shortage of cotton textile products and other manufactured goods which, combined with an imperfect rationing and price control system, resulted in speculative hoarding and generated further price rises. After 1942, still another factor was the complete stoppage of external supplies, in particular of all cotton goods and cereals, owing to the fall of Burma. Since 1900 China had been partially dependent on the import of cereals and cotton manufactures which amounted to CN$136 million and CN$70 million respectively in 1935 out of a total import trade of CN$919 million. As these imports are of great importance to the national economy of China, their unavailability greatly hastened the inflation.

These unfavorable developments, associated with the dislocation of an inefficient transportation system, both by military use and by enemy destruction, resulted in a critical situation in Free China which is on the whole more under-developed industrially than was occupied China.

We have already emphasized the fact that during most of the war period, the price movement in China was more moderate than after V-J Day (although the price indices reflect chiefly government wartime ceiling prices, and therefore tend to understate both the degree of inflation and the wide regional differences in price). There are reasons to explain this existence of a relatively well controlled economy.

In the first place, the budget deficit did not reach its peak until after V-J Day. The second reason was the relatively satisfactory supply situation of food in Free China as a result of good harvests in Hunan and SzeChwan provinces. Industrial production was also at a high level, owing to the concentration of all major plants in Western China and a more effective utilization of productive resources.

The third counterbalancing factor was the more strictly enforced rationing and price ceiling system, which kept prices under better control as compared with what they would have been otherwise, although it was impossible to stabilize them completely. Price ceilings and the partial rationing system of basic commodities such as food, meat and clothing were adopted early in 1942 in the principal cities of Free China. Supplies of rationed goods to the major cities were partly controlled and distributed to the consumers by government agencies at reduced prices which favorably affected the real incomes, particularly of public employees, teachers and organized workers.

However, in small towns and rural areas a free market existed where prices of all kinds of goods were determined solely by the interplay of supply and demand. There were great regional variations in prices on account of transport difficulties, and as a consequence, the people in these rural areas suffered most. In addition, black market dealing and speculative hoarding of rationed and free goods was prevalent in all parts of Free China. Thus, the fact that during this period price behavior was not at any time out of control should not lead us to the conclusion that the situation was in any sense satisfactory. As a matter of fact, the standard of living of the lower and fixed income groups was on the whole drastically reduced by the increase of prices.

II. The Postwar Economic Situation

The predominant influence during the period immediately following V-J Day was the continuously rapid increase in military expenditures as a result of the outbreak of civil war, added to the budgetary deficit to which the war with Japan had given rise. This had its counterpart naturally in the retained conscription of civilians into the armed forces, the maintenance of production of the war industries, and devastation perhaps even more extensive to an economy which had already sustained eight years of modern warfare. We have noted that, on the whole, the effect of the war against Japan was to divert China's economic resources into the conduct of war, rather than to bring about new industrial or agricultural developments. As a matter of fact, the economy was disrupted to such an extent that its transition to peace would have been slow and difficult even if the civil war had not broken out following V-J Day.

INFLATION IN CHINA 569

The principal problems which confronted China in its second year of illusory peace were as follows:

(1) Throughout the war the budgetary deficit, as mentioned above, was large and the actual figures even many times larger. In the budget of 1946 there was a tremendous increase in the military outlay, which accounted for 70 to 80 per cent of the total as compared with previous years, and as a result, there was a rise in the budgetary deficit from CN$266 billion in 1945 to CN$1,276 billion in 1946. This found its expression in a very rapid increase in the quantity of money and a further aggravation of the inflationary pressures. Circulation of notes in 1946 was about three and one-half times higher than the year before and about 2,200 times as high as in 1937. The total supply of money, including total demand deposits of the four government banks, increased in even larger proportions. (See Table IV.)

TABLE IV

THE SUPPLY OF MONEY IN CHINA

(In billion CN dollars)

	Notes in Circulation[a]	Demand Deposits[b]	Total Money Supply
1937	1.6	2	3.6
1938	2.3	2.7	5
1939	3.1	4.3	7.4
1940	8	5.5	13.5
1941	15	10	25
1942	35	17	52
1943	80	24	104
1944	190	80	270
1945	1,000	472	1,472
1946	3,500	5,032	8,532
1947 — June	8,500	11,890	20,390
December	35,000	20,000[c]	55,000

[a] Total note circulation of the four government banks before July 1942, and of the Central Bank of China thereafter.
[b] Total demand deposits of the four government banks.
[c] Estimated.
Source: Ministry of Finance, China's Economic Critic Weekly, Far Eastern Trader, China Weekly Review and China's Statistical Monthly.

The internal national loan increased from CN$3 billion at the end of 1937 to CN$17 billion at the end of 1946.[4]

4. Report of the Loan Department, Ministry of Finance.

(2) Industrial and agricultural production were at a very low level. As a result of the general disintegration caused by the war, China's industrial production in the last quarter of 1945 and during 1946 was far below the prewar level. The chief causes for this low level of production were the shattered state of the transport system which was inadequate even before the war, the shortage of fuel and power, the lack of raw materials, the mismanagement and slow rehabilitation of ex-enemy plants in the liberated areas, the desertion of the wartime industries in the interior, and, above all, the civil war.

The inadequacy of internal transportation prevented an efficient distribution of imports to the interior and of raw materials to the plants. By mid-1946 only about 120,000 tons per month of external supplies could be moved from Shanghai to the interior by waterway which accounted for more than one-half the total tonnage from all of China's ports to the inland cities. About one-half of the locomotives, one-third of the freight cars, and 40 per cent of the passenger cars were destroyed during the war. Postwar railway rehabilitation was very slow owing to the shortage of essential equipment and accessories, and to the Communist interruption. Although China had about 20,000 trucks by the end of 1946 from UNRRA and Lend-Lease, compared with 15,000 in 1938, they could make only a limited contribution to the serious transportation problem, since the availability of these facilities to civilian and commercial uses was very much restricted on account of extensive military activity.

Coal production from Kailan mines, which represented three-fourths of China's domestic coal supply, was at only 75 per cent of its prewar level, while operation of other mines was constantly interrupted by warfare. The internal transport cost was so high that it was cheaper to ship coal from San Francisco to Shanghai than from the Kailan mines. The output of antimony and tungsten, which constituted the bulk of China's mineral exports before the war, was reduced to about 50 per cent owing to the high cost of production.

Rehabilitation of the cotton textile industry, of which the capacity was reduced by 50 per cent during the war, was also very slow owing to the power shortage and to labor disputes. The woolen and silk textile industries were in the same situation on account of war damage to capacity and of the lack of raw materials.

(3) In spite of the relatively large output of rice, which represented about one-half of the total cereal output, at 95 per cent of the prewar standard, China's food situation in 1946 was far from satisfactory, for a considerable amount of foodstuffs had been imported before the war to meet this deficiency. Import of rice alone amounted to about 400,000 tons in 1938 as against 20,000 tons in 1946. Moreover, with the dislocated and inadequate transport system, movement of food supplies from surplus areas to deficient areas within the country was more difficult than before the war.

The livestock population in 1945 was some 20 per cent below prewar level in all kinds except hogs and poultry, which were 30 to 40 per cent below prewar. In 1946 the numbers were estimated at 10 to 20 per cent below prewar standard for all classes of animals.

(4) The effect of a continuously severe inflation and unstable currency tended to encourage speculative hoarding of other daily necessities from the market, to make exports more difficult, to generate successive labor unrest, and to deter any permanent industrial recovery. Most of all, the transition from a war to peace economy was constantly threatened by open civil war on an ever growing scale. Under such conditions the economic rehabilitation could hardly be expected to proceed rapidly without interruption.

III. Developments in 1947

The situation with regard to inflation further deteriorated in 1947 despite some increase in production. The outstanding feature of the Chinese economy in the year was a sharp intensification of inflationary pressures due principally to the vast increase in government expenditures,[5] which, for the fiscal year ending December 31, were almost five times higher than anticipated, or CN$42 trillion, while actual revenue did not exceed CN$16 trillion. It was estimated that over 80 per cent of the year's expenditures were for military outlays. As before,

5. Reviewing the economic position of China during 1947, the Minister of Finance attributed the unbalanced budget to the disruption of communications by the Communists and the consequent slowing down of production.

the deficit was met by printing new paper money, with its natural consequence of an inflationary spiral; the unbalanced budget hoisted the price and the latter, in turn, increased the budgetary deficit. At the same time, money wages moved up.

The United Nations Index of wholesale prices jumped from 733,000 in January to 10,000,000 in December, and the cost of living in Shanghai in December 1947 was approximately eleven times higher than in the first month of the year.

Under this condition, profit incentives associated with industry grew weaker and weaker, while hoarding and speculation increased very substantially, since money could be made more easily by holding raw materials and other goods. These factors, together with those mentioned in the preceding sections, contributed to the rapid increase in prices.

It may be opportune to say something at this point in specific explanation of the substantial disparity between the price rise as shown in Table I and the increase of money supply shown in Table IV, and its significance in analyzing China's inflation. During most of the period under review, both the cost of living and the level of wholesale prices rose more steeply than total money supply. Between 1937 and 1947 the money supply increased about 15,000 per cent, whereas, during the same period, wholesale prices advanced about 100,000 per cent. This disproportion is chiefly accounted for by changes in the velocity of money, and was a manifestation of the widespread practice of a flight to commodities, which became more extensive during the last two years as people were more inflation-conscious.

The velocity of cash changed more significantly than that of demand deposits over the country as a whole. In certain areas of the economy, trade and speculation were particularly brisk, and expectations of a continued decline in the value of money were exceedingly acute, especially among certain groups of the population; here the rate of money turnover, and in particular, of cash, was high. No exhaustive studies have been undertaken of the velocity of various kinds of money, but certain generalizations can be made a priori, and others from such data as are available. It has been estimated that prior to the war the ratio between cash and demand deposits was approximately 1–3.[6] The amount of bank deposits has greatly decreased in relation

6. China Economic Critic Weekly, Shanghai, January 10, 1948.

to cash since 1937, their ratio being about 7–4 at the end of 1947. The most obvious explanation for the diminution of bank deposits is that the quantity of money in existence was much too small for the quantity of goods available at the continuously inflated prices; and individuals with larger money incomes and no faith in their money chose to spend rather than to save. This is the fundamental reason for the high velocity of money and the decline of savings in banks. The propensity among the public to spend, arising from a complete lack of confidence in the value of their currency, constituted one of the most effective stimulants upon China's hyper-inflation.

The food situation in 1947 was slightly improved. It was estimated that rice output was a little over 987 million piculs, showing an increase of 4 per cent over the previous year. However, food distribution to the deficient areas was still greatly handicapped by lack of transport, and the actual supply of grain was reduced by the widening of fighting zones.

Progress was also made in certain branches of industry in 1947.[7] Cotton textile production was estimated at 80 per cent of prewar output, or 176,000 packs, as against 65 per cent in 1946. This improvement was largely the result of an increased supply of raw cotton and of electricity. Production of cement reached about 500,000 tons as compared with 350,000 tons in 1936.

Coal production in China proper in 1947 amounted to about 18 million tons, or 65 per cent of the 1936 level, an increase of 15 per cent as compared with 1946 output. The coal supply in Manchuria was reduced to about 2 million tons in 1947, as against 4 million tons in 1946 and 13 million tons in 1936, while its transport to Shanghai was impeded by sweeping armed conflicts between the Government and Communist troops. The production of coal in Formosa totaled one million tons at about 65 per cent of the 1936 level. As a result of limited supplies of coal and power, industrial rehabilitation was progressing far behind schedule.

The exchange position was still difficult. The gap in the balance of payments for 1947 amounted to US$230 million following a deficit of US$570 million in the preceding year. In January 1947, the free market rate for United States currency was CN$7,233 to the dollar, while the official rate was still pegged at CN$3,350. On February 17, 1947, in an attempt to wipe out the black market

7. Ibid., January 3, 1948.

in exchange, the official rate was advanced to CN$12,000 per US$1.00, which was then considerably above the rate quoted in the black market. After a brief setback, the black market in exchange re-appeared during April, in consequence of the rapid increase in the wholesale prices, with a quotation of CN$22,000 per US$1.00 or about 55 per cent higher than the official rate. The free market rate quoted on December 27,1947 was CN$145,000 per US$1.00 or about 23 times 1946 and 11,150 times the 1939 level. The official rate was still maintained at CN$12,000 to the dollar but its application has since been confined to the financing of imports of absolute necessities. In addition, an open market rate has been adopted, with the first rate set at CN$39,000 per US$1.00 starting August 17, 1947. It is to be adjusted from time to time in correspondence with the free market movement. This is the rate at which exporters and exchange holders are required to sell their foreign currencies to the Central Bank of China, and at which licensed importers of commodities other than absolute necessities are permitted to buy exchange from the Central Bank of China. Since its introduction, and up to the end of 1947 almost twenty adjustments in rates have been made in response to the change of black market quotations. While its efficacy as an instrument for the supression of the black market has been viewed with growing skepticism and disapproval on account of its passivity, it has had its effects in checking the unfavorable balance of trade. In addition, the Central Bank of China reported, in the first month following the institution of the new rate, that it had bought a considerable amount of dollar exchange which would have otherwise gone to the black market.

IV. SUMMARY AND CONCLUSIONS

(1) Between 1937 and 1947, wholesale prices in China increased at least 100,000 per cent. In the same period, the money supply increased about 15,000 per cent. Demand deposits increased 10,000 per cent and currency about 22,000 per cent. The velocity of circulation of currency was extremely variable throughout the eleven year period, and the widespread propensity to spend among the people became increasingly pronounced owing to lack of faith in the currency and to the prolongation of the civil war.

(2) The primary cause of the inflation in China is the phenomenal increase in the quantity of all money, the low level

INFLATION IN CHINA 575

of production being of the second order of magnitude. The increase in the quantity of money is chiefly the consequence of the increased note issues of the Central Bank of China by the National Government, and the inflation of demand deposits resulting from government borrowing from the banks. The dislocation of transport and of the general economy contributed to the inflationary process by their effect on the distribution and utilization of resources, and on the level of production.

The inflation in China began with the Japanese invasion of North China and Shanghai and had been in rapid progress up to V-J Day. After the end of the Sino-Japanese war, inflation gained force, and prices skyrocketed much faster than before. The inflationary pressures in China have become more and more disastrous and unmanageable since the advent of 1948, in spite of the enforcement of various measures, including partial rationing and price-ceilings in major cities, and stringent credit control. Since the existing financial instability is principally a cause as well as a result of the general disorganization of the country, it is difficult to see how economic rehabilitation can be attained without internal political unification.

ANDREW CHUNG HUANG.

INTERNATIONAL BANK FOR RECONSTRUCTION AND DEVELOPMENT

[19]

HYPERINFLATION IN CHINA, 1937–49[1]

COLIN D. CAMPBELL AND GORDON C. TULLOCK

Washington, D.C., and Hong Kong, China

I

THE unusual monetary develop-ments that took place in China from 1937 to 1949 may prove in-structive to Western economists. The period extends from the beginning of the Japanese invasion to the first year of Communist control of the mainland. This monetary experience generally sup-ports our theories. However, events in China suggest a modification of the widely accepted principle that hyper-inflation tends to drive currency out of use. Although rapid inflation lasted a long time, the various Chinese curren-cies served as media of exchange during the entire period.

II

Between 1937 and 1949 three govern-ments—the Nationalists, the Japanese, and the Communists—occupied China, and each of them issued its own money. The National government issued Chi-nese Nationalist Currency until its mone-tary reforms in 1948–49, when the CNC was replaced first by the gold yuan and then by the silver yuan. The Japanese at first used both bank notes from Korea and Japan and a script called "Military Yen." Later, notes were issued by their central banks in North China, Central China, and Inner Mongolia.[2] In North China the Japanese Federal Reserve Bank dollars remained in circulation al-most two years after the surrender of the Japanese. However, since the National-ists actively opposed the use of FRB notes, they eventually passed out of the picture. Between 1930 and 1948 the Com-munists issued approximately thirty local currencies, and ten different paper cur-rencies circulated in the border regions and "liberated" areas in 1948.[3] Soon after the People's Bank of China was estab-lished the Communists replaced almost all of their local issues with a unified pa-per money called "People's Currency." When the Communists took over North China, they converted the Nationalists' gold yuan into People's Currency at a realistic rate. On the other hand, in South China they did not honor the silver yuan which the Nationalists is-sued shortly before they lost the area.

To add to the confusion, the three governments in China engaged in mone-tary warfare. As early as March, 1938, the Japanese declared it illegal for any-one to carry or use Nationalist Cur-rency. Similar policies were adopted by the Communists in the North and the National government in the South. These were accompanied by control of trade across borders in order to prevent the exchange of goods for the enemy's currency. The Nationalists claimed that after the Japanese puppet government

[1] The personal observations of Mr. Tullock have provided the principal data for this study. He was in Tientsin as a Foreign Service Officer from 1948 to 1950.

[2] U.S. Foreign Economic Administration, *The Japanese Occupation Technique in the Field of Money and Banking* (Washington, D.C., 1944), pp. 1–3.

[3] See Chao Kuo-chun, *Source Materials from Com-munist China*, Vol. III: *Fiscal, Monetary, and Inter-national Economic Policies of the Chinese Communist Government* (Center for International Studies, M.I.T., and Russian Research Center, Harvard University, 1952), pp. 45, 75.

recalled Chinese Nationalist Currency in the area they occupied, the Japanese leaders used it to purchase goods and foreign exchange from Free China—thus adding to inflation in Free China and draining away some of their supplies. The Communists accused the Nationalists of counterfeiting their poorly printed notes; however, this was seldom possible because of the efficiency of the Communist police. Propaganda stating that the currency of their enemies was falling rapidly in value was issued on all sides.

In Free China rapid and continuous inflation resulted from extreme budgetary difficulties and the inability to sell bonds on terms acceptable to the government. Expenditures naturally increased to provide for expanded military outlays, and important prewar sources of revenue in the eastern cities were lost to the Japanese. Taxes also were usually in arrears because with inflation this was one way of getting them reduced. The Nationalists financed their deficits primarily by monetary expansion. They had abandoned the silver standard and established a managed currency in 1935. As Mr. Kung, minister of finance, wrote: "When Japan invaded China in 1937, China's monetary system was prepared for the emergency. . . . The new system enabled the government to rely on the increase of bank credit as a means of emergency war finance."[4] Only a small percentage of the deficits were financed by selling bonds to individuals. The Nationalists were unable to sell many short-term securities because they did not offer a positive real rate of return. In 1940, for example, when prices more than doubled, they offered rates of from 5 to 12 per cent a year.[5] Because of the long

[4] H. H. Kung, "China's Financial Problems," *Foreign Affairs*, XXIII (January, 1945), 222–23.

[5] F. M. Tamagna, *Banking and Finance in China* (New York: Institute of Pacific Relations, 1942), pp. 266–67.

civil war and the precarious future of the Nationalist government, the salability of its long-term bonds would have been very low.

In 1938–39 the velocity of money in Free China shifted to a distinctly higher level. Table 1 shows that at this time

TABLE 1*

THE SUPPLY OF MONEY AND WHOLESALE PRICES IN NATIONALIST CHINA
1937–47

YEAR	TOTAL MONEY SUPPLY†		WHOLESALE PRICES‡	
	In Billions of CNC Dollars	Percentage Increase§	1937 = 100	Percentage Increase§
1937....	3.6	......	100	......
1938....	5.0	39	127	27
1939....	7.4	48	214	68
1940....	13.5	82	498	133
1941....	25.0	85	1,258	153
1942....	52.0	108	3,785	201
1943....	104.0	100	12,556	232
1944....	270.0	159	41,927	234
1945....	1,472.0	445	158,362	277
1946....	8,532.0	479	367,406	132
1947....	55,000.0‖	544	2,617,781	612

* Source: A. C. Huang, "Inflation in China," *Quarterly Journal of Economics*, LXII (August, 1948), 564, 569.

† Total note circulation of the four government banks before July, 1942, and of the Central Bank of China thereafter, plus total demand deposits of the four government banks.

‡ Average of monthly prices.

§ Percentage increase from previous year.

‖ December estimated.

prices rose faster than the quantity of money, whereas from 1937 to 1938 they had risen less rapidly than the money supply. In 1938–39 people evidently began to realize that prices would rise continuously. As soon as they tried to hold smaller cash balances because they expected inflation, velocity increased sharply.[6] The shift to a higher velocity must have been abrupt and undoubtedly caused considerable disturbance in the

[6] Although the public was trying to hold smaller cash balances, they actually were holding much larger cash balances because of the new issues by the government.

economy, but it was hidden by other catastrophes of the time.

Even after this initial shift to a higher rate of circulation, velocity continued to rise, but for a different reason. Table 1 shows that in 1938–44 and in 1946–47 wholesale prices rose more rapidly than the money supply.[7] The rate of circulation continuously increased because holding money became more and more costly. During inflation the cost of holding money depends largely on the rapidity of the rise in prices. For example, if prices rise at a constant rate, the cost of holding money will tend to be constant. However, from 1937 to 1947 the quantity of money and prices in Free China generally increased at an increasing rate. Since the cost of holding money rose continuously, people tried to hold less currency, and velocity became more rapid.

Both a deteriorating military situation and an anticipated monetary reform caused runaway inflation in 1948. The Communists claim that in Nationalist China prices in August, 1948, were over sixty-three times the monthly average in 1947. In the fall of 1948 the Nationalists exchanged the CNC for the gold yuan at 3,000,000 to 1. The reform failed to stabilize prices mainly because the Nationalists did not stop printing money. Both the enactment of price controls and the announced limit on currency that could be issued legally had little effect. The limit was so much above the amount in circulation that it was irrelevant. A simultaneous program to buy United States currency, silver, and gold accelerated the issuance of notes. After approximately three weeks of comparative stability, the new currency depreciated faster than the old.

Many small fluctuations in the rate of inflation occurred, but they lasted such a short time that they are not shown in Table 1. To some extent, these correlated with the volume of new notes put in circulation. The rate of printing was so high that persons frequently received neat packets of one hundred brand new notes from banks or in change from merchants. The appearance of many new bills or of new and larger denominations almost always coincided with a sharp fall in the value of money. On the other hand, when new notes became rare, prices were comparatively stable. These periods lasted only a week or ten days. Many Chinese believed that high officials manipulated the rate of inflation by varying the release of new currency.

The Nationalists and later the Communists made several bizarre attempts to stop inflation by refusing to supply currency to banks. When this happened, although one could not cash checks, banks were not considered bankrupt. Since everyone understood that the banks could not pay, a sort of moratorium on obligations occurred until the government issued more notes. The only effect was a disruption of business. If the government had cut off the supply and at the same time required prompt payment of all debts, presumably the value of currency would have shot upward.

The reported use of wheelbarrows for carrying money is a case of seizing upon a conspicuous, but unimportant, detail. This was usually unnecessary because, as inflation progressed, the government issued notes in larger denominations. Ordinarily, the largest bill widely used was worth between three and fifteen cents in American money. This was small, but, by using bundles of ten and one hundred notes, they were adequate for normal usage. Occasionally, the Nationalists at-

[7] In 1945–46 velocity dropped sharply probably because people believed that inflation would cease or, at least, slow up when World War II ended.

HYPERINFLATION IN CHINA 239

tempted to control inflation by collecting old small-denomination bills and insisting that payments be made with them for about a week. At such times, carrying money was a problem; and carts were of considerable assistance. This policy created several other problems. It hurt wage-earners, since merchants usually accepted this paper only at a discount, and firms had great difficulty meeting pay rolls with small-denomination bills.

During inflation in China interest rates rose to allow for depreciation. The computation of future transactions at interest rates that took depreciation into account was difficult and was a social waste compared to computations with a stable currency, but it was a minor one.[8] Because interest rates discounted the depreciation in the value of currency, markets for short-term loans operated as usual, even though political instability precluded long-term lending. The continuous operation of the short-term money markets was extremely significant. It meant that numerous transactions depending on deferred payment were unimpeded. Of course, interest rates were phenomenally high, but, because they primarily discounted anticipated inflation, they did not constitute the almost insuperable barrier to investment claimed by some observers.

Depreciation of Japanese puppet currencies was nearly as severe as that of CNC, for the Japanese also financed the bulk of their expenditures by continuously expanding bank credit. Just before the end of hostilities, prices in Occupied China rose faster than in Free China because of the anticipated defeat of the Japanese. However, after the war, one dollar FRB was worth more than one dollar CNC probably because the Japanese puppet government had received large amounts of aid from Japan.

The numerous Communist currencies undoubtedly depreciated at least as rapidly as the CNC. This is indicated by the following announcement of their new monetary policy in 1950-51:

> Instead of issuing huge quantities of paper money, as we were forced to do previously, we are now collecting taxes in a planned way and the finances of our country thus have a comparatively stable foundation. Since March of this year, we have almost achieved a balanced budget and stability of prices.[9]

Although estimates of the rise in prices in Communist China before 1949 are not available, Communist statisticians admit that in 1949 prices rose more than 7,000 per cent.[10] Twice during this year the People's Currency dropped to one-third its value in a period of one week. This was faster than the decline in the value of the CNC at any time from 1937 to 1949. The Communists claim that the rise in prices was reduced to 93.2 per cent in 1950 and to 13.8 per cent in 1951.

The extreme depreciation in the value of the People's Currency in 1949 was related paradoxically to attempts by the Communist government to stabilize its currency by discontinuing increases in the money supply. They had learned from experience (and partly by reading their own propaganda about the Nationalists) that price stability required limiting the quantity of money. They were unaware of the difficulty of administering a smooth transition from an economy adjusted to continuous inflation to one

---

[8] The close relationship between interest rates and inflation is illustrated by their sharp decline when the Communists eventually stabilized the price level. The official commercial rates charged by the People's Bank of Shanghai dropped from 100 per cent per month in November, 1949, to 2.3 per cent in March, 1952. The decline in black-market rates was probably more rapid than this (Chao, *op. cit.*, p. 62).

[9] *Ibid.*, p. 16.

[10] *Ibid.*, p. 71.

240   COLIN D. CAMPBELL AND GORDON C. TULLOCK

based on price stability. The Communists at first stopped increasing the
money supply. This caused the velocity
of circulation to fall, because the populace no longer anticipated rapid inflation.
Very soon the government gave in to
pressure from its various departments
for more money and also relaxed its restrictions on private credit. The combination of a fall in velocity and an increase in the quantity of money kept
prices stable. However, this could last
only as long as velocity was adjusting to
its new, lower level. Since the Communists kept on issuing large amounts
of currency, an explosive inflation occurred as soon as the populace realized
that prices were not going to be stabilized. Once the fall in the value of their
money began, the Communists undertook severe, and occasionally cruel, methods of reducing the money supply. These
methods probably prevented the value
of currency from falling further than it
did and led to new stabilization efforts.

These unsuccessful attempts to stabilize prices and the explosive inflations
that followed were more upsetting to the
business community than the steady depreciation to which the Chinese had become accustomed. The future level of
prices became completely unpredictable,
and many firms were forced out of business. Imagine the plight of business firms
that had borrowed at rates of 1 or 2 per
cent per day when the government decided to stop printing more money. A
scramble for currency followed, borrowers were unable to pay their debts, bank-
ruptcies flourished, and lenders probably
found their promissory notes worthless.
When the government failed to control
the money supply, the shift back to
continuously rising prices also resulted
in serious market disturbances and ruined
lenders who had invested money at in-

terest rates based on expected price stability. The two unsuccessful attempts by
the Communists to stabilize prices resulted in such extreme uncertainty that
they were a major factor in breaking the
power of the business groups.

There is little basis for the belief that
in monetary affairs the record of the
Nationalists was worse than that of the
Communists. Historians have probably
exaggerated the role of inflation in the
rise of Chinese communism. The following quotation is an example:

> The themes of latter-day Nationalist cor-
> ruption, strategic stupidity, administrative
> ineptitude, and general incompetence have been
> sufficiently elaborated in our press and official
> records; what needs to be more fully under-
> stood is the Nanking government's gradual
> bankruptcy of morale, which in turn sapped the
> morale of its erstwhile supporters and pro-
> duced a general rout and debacle. Loss of morale
> cannot justly be attributed to Chiang Kai-shek
> as an individual, but perhaps it may be traced
> to the power structure which he headed, and
> which had become conservative and anti-
> revolutionary. This sessile spirit affected the
> lower and higher echelons of the KMT party
> organization, the minor officials in the sprawl-
> ing government agencies, and even the clerks,
> shopkeepers, and students in the cities. As the
> war-time and post-war inflation endlessly
> progressed, all these people were consumed by
> it in substance and finally in spirit. Spiralling
> prices made life increasingly precarious and
> hard, month after month and year after year.
> Malnutrition, disease, and depression followed.
> The government in power offered no way out,
> and Free China lost its feeling of support for,
> or tacit acquiescence in, the Generalissimo's
> regime.[11]

Of course, both the Sino-Japanese War
and the Chinese civil war imposed extreme hardships on the Chinese people.
However, the usual conclusion that the
middle class—students, teachers, shopkeepers, office workers, and government

[11] C. Brandt, B. Schwartz, and J. K. Fairbank,
A Documentary History of Chinese Communism (London: Allen & Unwin, 1952), pp. 19–20.

employees—were impoverished assumes incorrectly that these groups received fixed nominal incomes. When inflation is anticipated, as it was in China, persons with fixed nominal incomes become extremely rare. The wages of office workers and other employees almost always rose as fast as prices and even discounted anticipated inflation. Government employees in Nationalist China actually lost a little, since their wages were computed by multiplying their 1937 wage rates by a cost-of-living index that was usually a few days behind the market. This was approximately equivalent to a reduction of 10–20 per cent in their wages, which was not uncommon during this period. The fortunes of shopkeepers were extremely uncertain. Some merchants became wealthy, and others failed. However, as a group they probably did not bear an especially heavy burden. City landlords suffered, since effective price controls existed only on urban real estate. In the country, rents and taxes were usually paid in kind; so landlords and farmers neither gained nor lost.

III

Continuous inflation in China caused the official currencies to be discarded both as units of account and as stores of value. During these years money could not serve as a store of value, because it did not keep its real value. Nonetheless, business firms and individuals needed some relatively liquid funds and quickly replaced Chinese currency as a store of value with other assets. Wealthy persons usually retained United States currency. This type of asset was not available to ordinary persons, since the activities of counterfeiters had made small bills suspect, and the smallest note that was salable without a discount was the five-dollar bill. The Chinese silver dollar was occasionally used, but for the poorer classes even this was too large. In the South, Hong Kong currency was available in small denominations, and in the last days of the Nationalists it was probably more widely used as a store of value than any other foreign currency. However, the poorer Chinese usually saved by buying consumer's goods in larger quantities than they expected to use. Business firms customarily held reserves in United States dollars, Chinese silver dollars, gold, short-term notes, or readily disposable commodities such as rice and flour.

The social costs of using commodities as stores of value undoubtedly were higher than those of using a stable currency. Capital goods were held in reserves instead of being used for production. But this was not the only undesirable effect. Since the basic technique of adjusting to inflation was to retain currency as briefly as possible, businessmen planned to put funds back into their firms immediately. When they sold anything, they rushed out to lay in more stock. This made careful buying difficult and increased the markup. It also resulted in various businesses having all sorts of commodities on hand, depending on what happened to be available. When a loan was repaid unexpectedly, even a bank would purchase commodities to avoid holding an excessive amount of currency.

An institutional change that helped to provide liquid reserves was the expansion of the stock markets in Chinese cities. Securities markets obviously were used to avoid the effects of inflation. On the Shanghai Stock Exchange the monthly turnover increased from about 1.5 million shares in 1937 to 10 million in 1940.[12]

[12] Tamagna, *op. cit.*, p. 233.

Even though corporation stocks were safer stores of value than currency, after World War II the prices of stocks did not keep up with the fall in the value of currency. The Chinese probably understood the political situation well enough to withdraw their money from permanent, capitalistic investments. When the Communists took over in Tientsin, the market value of all stocks outstanding was less than 5 per cent of the book value of the corporations' property. Even so, it was a wonder that stocks at this time had any value at all.

Banks provided another organized method of retaining the value of one's liquid assets. They offered extraordinarily high interest rates on deposits. In Tientsin, 2 per cent a day compounded daily was not unusual following World War II. The bank rate did not fluctuate exactly with the rate of inflation, but at least it was similar. Nonetheless, deposits were not used as much as one would expect. Since a Communist victory was possible, few persons desired to have their money recorded on the books of a bank.

The unusually large holdings of commodities by persons and business firms were very obvious during these years in China. Both Western observers and Chinese writers thought that the purpose of the "hoarding" was to make profits, and they condemned it as a waste of resources. Few of them realized that commodities were replacing currency as a store of value and that the purpose of holding commodities in place of cash was to maintain the real value of one's assets. Instead of diverting businessmen from productive activity, the holding of commodities provided firms with the liquid assets that they needed at all times.

Writers have exaggerated the profitability of hoarding goods in China at this time. Actually, when inflation is anticipated, although the value of goods increases, normally one cannot make real profits by hoarding. This is because buyers who expect inflation immediately bid prices of goods up so high that the opportunity to make real gains by holding commodities disappears. Since hoarders profit only when the rise in prices is greater than generally anticipated, success or failure becomes a matter of chance or exceptional judgment.

The prevalent belief that businessmen were better off under conditions of inflation is questionable. Uncertainties were increased significantly, and many fortunes must have been lost almost overnight. Because the securities and commodities held as reserves were not perfectly liquid, they were not reliable stores of value. In addition, the small size of the markets for many reserve items frequently made it difficult for large firms to secure or sell the quantity of liquid assets desired.

Another effect of inflation was that the Chinese Nationalist dollar and the other currencies were no longer used as units of account. Modern money usually serves both as a medium of exchange and as an accounting unit. This has not always been true. In the days of metallic currency, for example, the unit of account was often a theoretical coin, while the medium of exchange was a real coin. A division in the functions of money also occurred at this time in China.

The Chinese theoretically might have kept their accounts in the deteriorating monetary unit by the use of advanced mathematics and the compound-interest formula. In practice, this would be extremely complex. As a result, and despite the law, small shops in Free China usually kept their accounts in United States dollars. The shopkeepers bought and sold with Chinese currency, but they computed prices by applying the daily exchange rate to a price on their books in United States dollars. Larger businesses ordinarily used elaborate commodity indexes and computed prices by multiplying the price of the product in a base year by their current index number. Long-term loans were occasionally drawn up in terms of commodities or United States dollars; however, because of political uncertainties, few Chinese were willing to enter into long-term contracts. The National government used 1937 prices in its accounts and then multiplied this value by its cost-of-living index to get actual payments. The Communists required all businesses to keep their accounts in terms of corn flour or some other commodity. The *Tientsin Daily News* published the current price of corn flour; and all wages, debts, taxes, and other costs were then paid in currency at this standard rate. If the price of corn flour doubled between the time one borrowed money and the time he repaid it, he would repay twice as much. While the use of the corn flour index was an improvement over the numerous different accounting units prevalent under the Nationalists, it was subject to seasonal fluctuations and other disadvantages of a one-commodity base. Later, for bank deposits, the Communists introduced the "parity unit" based on several commodities. In Shanghai the parity unit was the sum of the price of 1.72 pounds of medium-grade rice, one foot of twelve pound "Dragon Head" cloth, one ounce of peanut oil, and 1.33 pounds of coal briquettes. These "deposits in kind" were kept in terms of the parity unit of account, and, since their monetary value varied with the prices of the four commodities, depositors were protected, at least partially, against loss due to infla-tion. However, since bank accounts often were blocked, the parity unit never was given an adequate trial.

The most significant characteristic of inflation in China from 1937 to 1949 is that Chinese Nationalist Currency and the various Japanese and Communist issues stayed in circulation as media of exchange. There was neither a significant shift to barter nor the use of unofficial means of payment. Westerners in China realized that this was unusual. A reporter wrote: "Ordinarily inflation of the sort that China is undergoing would have brought about collapse several years ago. In fact, orthodox economists predicted it." Some persons have assumed that because both United States and Hong Kong currencies were used as stores of value during this period, they were also substituted for Chinese currencies as media of exchange. Actually, transactions in foreign money were the exception rather than the rule. The agricultural property tax payable in kind which was adopted by the Nationalists was a type of barter, but the enactment of such a tax does not indicate a public preference for barter or the unacceptability of the circulating medium.

There is some evidence that in rural areas the use of barter became more prevalent just before the monetary reforms in Free China and in Communist China in 1949. In February, 1951, the Communists announced that their currency was being used by increasing numbers of peasants and was "replacing steadily the silver coin and the barter system."[13]

[13] A survey in one of the provinces concluded that before August, 1950, 55 per cent of the trade was conducted in silver dollars, 20 per cent by barter, and 25 per cent in People's Currency. In the spring of 1951, 81 per cent of the trade was conducted in People's Currency, 17 per cent in silver dollars, and 2 per cent in barter trade (Chao, *op. cit.*, p. 74).

However, monetary collapse was not the cause either of the monetary reforms in Free China or of the stabilization attempts in Communist China. The purpose of these programs was to stabilize the value of their currencies and especially to reduce the rate of velocity. No evidence exists that commodities took the place of money as a medium of exchange in the cities of China, and even in the rural areas it was never claimed that currency exchange was entirely displaced by barter.

There are several reasons for this extraordinary acceptability of Chinese currencies as media of exchange. Regulations requiring the use of official currencies were strictly enforced, and the Chinese are by nature law-abiding. Even though these laws were related to the monetary wars and primarily sought to prevent circulation of the enemy's money, they also contributed to the acceptability of their own issues. The governments also controlled the terms of many transactions. Taxes in Free China, except for the agricultural property tax, were paid in legal tender, and goods and services distributed by the government were sold for the official medium. Since foreign trade was negotiated through government exchange banking facilities, the official medium also was required for such transactions.

The almost complete lack of effective price controls in China contributed to the use of currency as a means of payment. This is probably the principal reason for the different experiences in postwar Germany and China. In Germany after World War II extensive price controls made barter attractive, even though normally barter exchange is extremely disadvantageous. Since controlled prices were still at their prewar level, individuals insisted on being paid in kind, and business firms also acquired most of the commodities they wanted through barter, even though barter was illegal. The government forced some commodities through legitimate trade channels, and people used money to buy their meager rations, but generally money did not serve as a means of payment. In China, under the Nationalists and later under the Communists, no effective price ceilings existed except on rents and a few goods that were rationed and distributed by government agencies in large cities. The rental ceilings were frequently circumvented by the institution of key money. Since prices could rise freely, monetary transactions were not penalized, and the Nationalists' cost-of-living index even helped merchants compute higher prices.

Finally, by anticipating inflation, the Chinese were able to eliminate many of the disadvantages of a depreciating currency. Because the Chinese expected depreciation, they discarded the official currencies both as stores of value and as units of account and developed their own occasionally ingenious substitutes for these functions of money. In addition, since interest rates rose to allow for depreciation, borrowing and lending of money for short periods were relatively unimpeded. This ability to adjust to inflation required a steady rise in prices, which depended on careful control of new issues and on the absence of monetary reforms and stabilization programs.

IV

The Chinese experience from 1937 to 1949 shows that under conditions of hyperinflation people may retain currency as a medium of exchange but discard it as a store of value and as a unit of account. Many economists have thought that under such conditions the use of currency would have been given up completely. Cannan has stated:

A continuance of rapid change in either direction will cause a currency to go out of use. This is perfectly reasonable, stability of value being one of the most important requisites of useful currency, and Gresham's law that bad money drives out good being fortunately quite untrue of the long run.

The explanation seems to lie in the fact that human intelligence anticipates what is coming. When it is seen that the value of currency is steadily falling, people see that it is more profitable to hold goods than currency, the demand for currency fails to extend in proportion to the enlargement of the supply, and its value consequently falls more rapidly. The issuer very likely redoubles his efforts to keep up with the fall by issuing new currency at a still more rapidly increasing rate, but all to no purpose—he is bound to lose the race.[14]

[14] Edwin Cannan, "The Application of the Theoretical Apparatus of Supply and Demand to

In China, anticipation of inflation had just the opposite effect from that expected by Cannan. Instead of contributing to collapse, it resulted in adjustments that cushioned the impact of inflation. Depreciation significantly increased the cost of using money, but the Chinese apparently were willing to pay a high price to avoid the disadvantages of barter, and price controls which might have made barter more profitable than monetary exchange were not established.

Units of Currency," *Economic Journal*, XXXI (December, 1921), 460-61; reprinted in American Economic Association, *Readings in Monetary Theory* (New York: Blakiston, 1951), p. 12.

[20]

The Greek Hyperinflation and Stabilization of 1943–1946

GAIL E. MAKINEN

The Greek hyperinflation started during the Axis occupation and was the result of an excessive reliance by the puppet government on the inflation tax. The inflation reached a peak in November 1944 after liberation. The Greek government undertook three stabilization efforts spread over eighteen months before price level stability was achieved. The final effort involved fiscal reform and the creation of an independent supracentral bank. Controversy surrounds the origin and nature of the transition costs involved in stabilizing an economy. The Greek stabilization cannot resolve all the issues raised.

Seven episodes of inflation severe enough to be called hyperinflation have occurred during the twentieth century.[1] Among them is the Greek experience of 1943–1944. In terms of average and maximum monthly rises in prices, it would rank below Hungary II but above Germany, though in terms of duration and total rise in prices it would rank behind both. When its initial stabilization occurred the Greek government converted its unit of account, the old drachma, for the new drachma at a rate of 50 billion to one, compared with conversions of one trillion to one for Germany and 400 octillion to one for Hungary II.

Unlike the initial efforts made by Germany, Austria, and Hungary I and II to end their hyperinflations, Greece's first attempt did not result in price level stability. Inflation continued for an additional 15 months, albeit at a much reduced rate. Price level stability was finally achieved when, in a third reform, certain legal and institutional changes deemed essential to the successful stabilizations were put into place. The Greek effort is similar in many respects to that of the Poles, whose success at stabilization required two reforms spread over three years.

Whether stabilizations are costly to enact is controversial. Some contend that the experience in Germany, Austria, Poland, and Hungary

Journal of Economic History, Vol. XLVI, No. 3 (Sept. 1986). © The Economic History Association.

The author is Specialist in Economic Policy, Congressional Research Service, Library of Congress, Washington, D.C. 20540.

The views expressed in this paper are my own and do not represent the views of the Congressional Research Service and the Library of Congress. I am indebted to Phillip Cagan, Gardner Patterson, Thomas Woodward, Robert Anderson, William Bomberger, and two anonymous referees for their numerous comments.

[1] The definition of a hyperinflation belongs to Phillip Cagan. See his "The Monetary Dynamics of Hyperinflation" in *Studies in the Quantity Theory of Money*, edited by Milton Friedman (Chicago, 1956). According to his definition, Austria, Germany, Poland, Russia, Greece, China, and Hungary (after both World Wars) had hyperinflation. China's experience is analyzed in Jarvis Babcock and Gail Makinen, "The Chinese Hyperinflation Revisited," *Journal of Political Economy*, 83 (Dec. 1975), pp. 1259–68.

I and II demonstrates that a convincing change in monetary and fiscal regime can minimize the transition costs in unemployment and lost output. Others dispute this contention, citing the absence of staggered long-term nominal contracts during hyperinflations as the reason the transitions appear to be easy. Still others contend that costs related to the adjustment of expectations are too narrow a concept of transition costs. They cite the longer-term costs of rationalization—as distorted relative prices are adjusted to the new steady state following stabilization.

I. THE HYPERINFLATION

The Greek hyperinflation was set in motion by World War II. At its outbreak Greece was neutral, but not immune to war. Most notably its foreign trade and tariff receipts, a major revenue source, declined. The scarcity of imported raw materials led to a further decline in industrial production (averaging 30 percent lower in 1940 than in 1939). War, especially the Italian conquest of Albania, necessitated unplanned military expenditures. While the budget showed a surplus for fiscal 1939 (September 1, 1938–August 31, 1939) of 271 million drachma, the decline in revenues and the extraordinary expenditures produced a deficit of 790 million drachma for fiscal 1940. Notes advanced by the Bank of Greece covered the deficit. The Greek tax system depended on specific rather than ad valorem taxes, a shortcoming characteristic of other countries with experience of hyperinflation. The system made it difficult for tax revenue to keep pace with inflation.[2]

The Italians invaded Greece on October 28, 1940; the Axis conquest began and was completed by May 1941. During the period of resistance the Greek budget deteriorated further. Tax revenue declined and expenditures for military purposes rose 10-fold. Advances from the Bank of Greece continued to fund the deficit. Prices rose during the period 4.6-fold while the money supply increased from 1.8- to 2.2-fold.[3]

With the installation of a puppet government in Greece, one might have expected the deficit to decline. This did not happen. Two new costs replaced military outlays: an indemnity, and support of the occupation army of about 400,000 men. These varied from one-third to three-fifths of all expenditures during the occupation, and notes advanced from the Bank of Greece again paid the bills.

Indemnities have played a prominent role in hyperinflations—in

---

[2] For the role played by limitations on the ability to tax and specific taxes in the German hyperinflation see Peter-Christian Witt, "Tax Policies, Tax Assessment and Inflation: Toward a Sociology of Public Finance in the German Inflation, 1914–1923," in Nathan Schmukler and Edward Marcus, eds., *Inflation Through the Ages: Economic, Social, Psychological and Historical Aspects* (New York, 1983).

[3] No continuous price series exists for the whole of the inflation period except for quotations of the gold sovereign.

Germany, Austria, Hungary I and II. Sargent, Galbraith, and Teichova believe they played an important role in the German and Austrian episodes because they caused uncertainty about fiscal and monetary policy.[4] Schuker, indeed, suggests that Germany purposefully engineered its hyperinflation to reduce its indemnity.[5] No evidence exists that the Greek puppet government purposefully resorted to inflationary finance to persuade the Axis to reduce its indemnity. And an indemnity is not always present. Poland, China, and Russia had a hyperinflation without an indemnity; and Bulgaria (after World War I), Vichy France, and Finland (after World War II) paid an indemnity without a hyperinflation.

The Greek puppet government, by choice or necessity, did not tax to cover its expenditures. Revenue declined, covering less than 6 percent of expenditures in the final year of occupation. The decline was the result of a disastrous fall in national income. In 1938 the national income was approximately 67.4 billion drachma, declining in real terms to 23 billion in 1941 and 20 billion in 1942. There it remained for the next two years.[6] Unlike inflation in Germany, Austria, and Hungary I, then, the initial stage of the Greek inflation did not produce an economic boom, because of the Axis policy of economic exploitation and the absence of credit. As in Hungary II credit was not an important source of the rise in note circulation.[7]

Prices measured in terms of the gold sovereign rose 155-fold during 1941–1943 (and the money supply rose 72-fold), but their behavior during late 1942 and early 1943 is unusual. The price of the sovereign reached a peak in October 1942, then *declined* dramatically. By December it had fallen to 43 percent of its October value. It fell again slightly in both January and February 1943, when it stood at approximately 38 percent of its October value. Observers linked the fall in prices to the expectation that liberation was at hand, following the successful Allied

---

[4] See Thomas Sargent, "The Ends of Four Big Inflations," in Robert Hall, ed., *Inflation: Causes and Effects* (Chicago, 1982); John Kenneth Galbraith, *Money: Whence It Came, Where It Went* (Boston, 1974); and Alice Teichova, "A Comparative View of the Inflation of the 1920s in Austria and Czechoslovakia" in *Inflation Through the Ages*.

[5] See Stephen A. Schuker, "Finance and Foreign Policy in the Era of the German Inflation: British, French, and German Strategies for Economic Reconstruction after the First World War," in Otto Busch and Gerald D. Feldman, eds., *Historische Prozesse Der Deutschen Inflation, 1914–1924* (Berlin, 1978).

[6] The German economic exploitation of Greece was systematic and many Greeks starved. Large quantities of wheat, other foodstuffs, and drugs to ease the deprivation began to arrive in September 1942. They were furnished by the United States and Canada and distributed by the Red Cross.

[7] Sargent's data show that in Germany, Austria, Poland, and Hungary I a substantial portion of the notes were issued on discount or private commercial paper at negative real interest rates. For the Hungary II experience see William Bomberger and Gail Makinen, "The Hungarian Hyperinflation and Stabilization of 1945–46," *Journal of Political Economy*, 91 (Oct. 1983), pp. 801–24.

798   *Makinen*

TABLE 1
PERCENTAGE RATE OF INFLATION
AND NOTE ISSUE AND INDEX OF REAL NOTE BALANCES[a]

	1940			1941			1942			
	Infla-tion[b]	Note Issue	Real Note Index	Infla-tion	Note Issue	Real Note Index	Infla-tion	Note Issue	Real Note Index	Infla-tion
Jan.	—	—	1.00	—	5.2	1.86	1.7	8.5	.30	−4.8
Feb.	—	—	1.00	—	4.9	1.95	—	10.4	.33	−6.7
March	—	1.1	1.01	—	14.1	2.22	73.5	16.1	.22	19.8
April	—	10.8	1.11	—	c	—	35.4	16.5	.19	5.7
May	1.1	10.3	1.25	364.0	c	—	16.8	16.5	.19	40.5
June	−1.1	4.5	1.32	50.2	24.3[d]	.40	−.3	19.1	.23	28.2
July	—	−.8	1.22	8.2	—	.37	122.0	20.5	.12	4.9
Aug.	—	4.7	1.27	40.3	20.7	.32	50.4	17.2	.10	10.3
Sept.	—	1.8	1.30	8.1	16.1	.34	10.9	19.7	.10	18.0
Oct.	—	11.5	1.45	71.4	15.7	.23	62.3	28.3	.08	81.9
Nov.	—	12.7	1.63	37.7	11.2	.19	−22.6	21.5	.13	64.4
Dec.	—	8.5	1.76	−26.2	12.2	.28	−44.4	15.7	.27	24.8

[a] Percentages computed as the first differences of natural logs.
[b] Rate of inflation measured by the rise in the price of the gold sovereign.
[c] No data exist on the note issue for April and May.
[d] Percentage change from March.
[e] Percentage change calculated to November 10.
[f] Percentage change for December cannot be computed as no observation is available for the end of November.
Source: Dimitrios Delivanis and William Cleveland, *Greek Monetary Developments, 1939–1948* (Bloomington, 1949), Statistical Appendix.

military operations in North Africa. Others linked the fall to the arrival and distribution of aid goods by the Red Cross. Table 1 records the progressive acceleration in prices and money supply and the level of real money balances.

By Cagan's definition, hyperinflation began in October 1943 while Greece was still occupied by the Axis. There was a rapid rise in the velocity of money, motivated by expectations of future inflation. In the initial stage the occupation authority pursued a policy that aggravated the tendency of velocity to rise. Finding some Greeks hesitant to accept notes, the authority began to pay with gold sovereigns and gold 20-franc coins. Over 1,300,000 sovereigns entered Greece in this way. While the practice undoubtedly decreased the rate of issue of paper money, it raised the velocity of money, for two reasons. It reduced public confidence in the future worth of the drachma, encouraging the public to hold its wealth in other forms. And by creating a closer substitute for money than, say, commodities, the practice increased the elasticity of, and reduced the demand for, domestic money (that is, it raised velocity). As a consequence, the tax base against which the inflation tax could be levied was reduced, and the rate of note issue and inflation

Greek Hyperinflation   799

TABLE 1—continued
PERCENTAGE RATE OF INFLATION
AND NOTE ISSUE AND INDEX OF REAL NOTE BALANCES[a]

1943		1944			1945			1946		
Note Issue	Real Note Index	Infla-tion	Note Issue	Real Note Index	Infla-tion	Note Issue	Real Note Index	Infla-tion	Note Issue	Real Note Index
9.8	.31	99.2	24.7	.16	35.5	270.0	.15	−17.6	33.6	.11
9.2	.36	77.4	29.6	.12	7.1	78.0	.24	−4.5	61.6	.19
15.9	.35	166.7	49.5	.06	20.0	42.0	.29	−4.1	27.5	.25
20.2	.40	142.5	118.0	.06	122.2	65.0	.21	—	30.4	.33
11.2	.32	188.4	85.5	.04	58.3	22.0	.16	−.9	7.1	.35
14.5	.28	22.6	95.8	.06	−36.8	17.4	.30	1.7	5.8	.37
22.0	.33	188.5	114.6	.04	33.3	9.2	.25	1.7	7.8	.40
22.1	.36	556.0	321.6	.03	12.5	22.4	.27	—	11.6	.44
22.6	.38	675.1	12.2×10^2	.05	66.7	15.9	.19	.5	3.2	.46
33.3	.28	13.8×10^3	9.4×10^3	.03	46.6	31.3	.17	—	−1.2	.45
32.8	.22	$1.6 \times 10^{2^c}$	$8.0 \times 10^{2^c}$	.02	59.1	25.1	.13	.4	−7.4	.42
38.9	.25	f	f	.05	160.0	31.3	.07	—	14.8	.48

required to yield a constant stream of real resources for the government was raised.[8]

On October 18, 1944, the Greek government-in-exile returned to Athens to confront hyperinflation and wartime destruction. Inflation continued, though indemnity and occupation costs were no longer present; they were replaced by expenditures for unemployment benefits and the care of large numbers of refugees.[9] Moreover, because the government exercised a delicate authority only in the Athens area (the Communists controlled the remainder of the country), it had a limited ability to raise and collect taxes. The daily expenditures and receipts of the government for the month preceding the first attempt at stabilization show that revenues covered about .4 percent of expenditures, with the remainder covered by advances from the Bank of Greece.

The rise in velocity and fall in real money balances forced the government to enact a stabilization program. The government was living off the inflation tax. As the tax base declined toward zero, the government's ability to use it ended. The rise in velocity was dramatically illustrated by the fall in real money balances. On the eve of stabilization the real balances were only about .4 percent of their 1938 average. The Greeks typically held a drachma note for 40 days in 1938 before spending it; by November 10, they typically held the note for about four hours.

[8] See Donald Nichols, "Some Principles of Inflationary Finance," *Journal of Political Economy*, 82 (March 1974), pp. 423–30.

[9] An explanation of the role of unemployment and other social costs in the German and Austrian hyperinflations is given in Carl L. Holtfrerich, "Political Factors of the German Inflation, 1914–23," in *Inflation Through the Ages*; and in Alice Teichova, "A Comparative View."

800   *Makinen*

II. THE STABILIZATION

There is seldom an opportune time to effect a stabilization. The Greeks and their British advisers prepared the initial program in haste. A number of conditions militated against its success. The Greek economy collapsed just 23 days after the government returned to Athens. Because the stabilization occurred during the war, it was impossible to restore Greece's export trade The country's principal prewar trading partners were members of the Axis, and it was difficult to obtain critical raw materials to revive domestic industry and commerce.

The November 11 stabilization program had two essential features. The government was limited to an overdraft of two billion drachma and the old drachma were converted for new at a rate of 50 billion to one. The new drachma converted into British Military Authority pounds at a rate of 600 to one, but only in lots larger than 12,000 drachma. Beside the old and new drachma, the military pound remained legal tender in Greece until May 31, 1945. It was not legal tender in Great Britain nor convertible into ordinary pounds. Moreover, convertibility placed no constraints on the fiscal and monetary policies of the government. The British furnished as many pounds as the Greeks desired (up to a limit of £3.0 million, at which time convertibility would cease—the ceiling was never reached).[10] The government neither changed the tax system nor announced expenditure cuts, assuming that the sale of aid goods would provide some 75 percent of its expected revenue.[11] The civil war of December/January 1945/46 spoiled the scheme and turned the printing press on again.

Prices rose in the first seven months after stabilization, but at a much reduced rate. The cost of living index rose 140 percent (measured as May over November). Because the index contains commodities and services (principally rent) whose prices were officially fixed or controlled, it understates the price rise. When the price of the sovereign is used the rise is shown to be over 800 percent. The government budget deficit declined as revenues rose from 6.5 percent of expenditures in February to more than half in May. Almost half of the revenue came from the sale of aid goods. The net revenue from these sales was small because distribution costs were high. Distribution costs exceeded sales revenue in 1945 largely because the government decided to use the aid

[10] This limit was part of a secret treaty concluded between Britain and Greece on November 10, 1944. See Gardner Patterson, "The Financial Experiences of Greece from Liberation to Truman Doctrine (October 1944–March 1947)" (Ph.D. diss., Harvard, 1948).

[11] The British furnished substantial military and economic aid from the time of liberation. On April 1, 1945, the United Nations took over civilian relief aid. The purpose of the aid was also to raise significantly the daily caloric intake of the population.

program to redistribute income. All materials of war including food and clothing were provided without cost by the British.

The behavior of real money balances indicates the public's acceptance of the reform. The government was successful in remonetizing the economy. Through May 1945, real balances rose 3-fold (using the sovereign price as a deflator), which is comparable to the Hungary II experience (for the other episodes, the increase was: Austria and Hungary I, 2.1-fold; Poland, 1.8-fold; and Germany, 1.3-fold).

During April and May 1945, Greek officials became increasingly concerned, for the economy failed to revive, exports remained a minute fraction of imports, and inflation started to accelerate again. The price of the gold sovereign rose from 6,000 drachma on April 2 to 11,000 on May 1 and to 19,500 on May 31. On June 3, Kyriakos Varvaressos, a prominent economist, was named economic czar. Varvaressos thought Greece's failure to recover was caused by inadequate assistance from abroad and a lack of effective state control. He set in motion an ambitious but somewhat inconsistent recovery program to increase foreign assistance, revive domestic production, and impose controls on wages and prices. The net result seems to have been to redistribute income in favor of the working and poorer classes.

Increased assistance from abroad took the form of an acceleration in foreign aid deliveries ($300 million for 1945) and a $25 million credit from the United States Export-Import Bank. To revive domestic production, the government sought to reduce the amount of savings going into gold hoards by monopolizing the sale and purchase of sovereigns, and to spur work incentives by raising the wages of lower-paid workers (including the civil service) and reducing prices on a large number of items. Controls were then placed on prices at the retail level and on all wages and salaries. A special market police force was created for enforcement. These provisions merely worsened the budget deficit, by reducing revenue and increasing expenditures. Varvaressos responded with a special tax on rents. Because rents had been frozen in Greece since 1940, they were insignificant. To capture this huge subsidy for the state the government classified all commercial, industrial, and professional establishments into three broad categories and imposed monthly assessments equal to 15, 10, and 6 times monthly rents on the occupants. So that the occupants would bear the assessments the market police were to rigidly enforce price controls. The government expected the tax to yield 2.5 to 3.0 billion drachma per month, a sum sufficient to balance the budget.

The Greek civil service, unsurprisingly, was unable to enforce the program. Moreover, the special rent tax antagonized merchants, shopkeepers, factory owners, and doctors, who began closing businesses in massive protests. By mid-August Greek citizens were openly evading the ceiling prices and the market police proved ineffectual. Varvaressos resigned on September 1.

Prices fell in June 1945, rose sharply in July, and again in August. State receipts for the three months covered 47, 75, and 58 percent of expenditures, respectively. The controls imposed by Varvaressos were dismantled and exemptions and exclusions granted from the rent tax. To compensate, the government imposed additional taxes, but the deficit worsened. For the final four months of 1945 receipts covered 52, 51, 56, and 39 percent of expenditures. Despite assistance from the United Nations and Britain the Greeks were unable to deal with their mounting budget deficit. Public confidence declined, as measured by the fall in real money balances which reached a peak in June 1945, six times their December 1944 level. They then fell rapidly and were only 40 percent larger by the end of 1945.

The British offered a plan to restore the financial and economic health of Greece, the Anglo-Hellenic Convention. Concluded on January 24, 1946, it gave top priority to arresting inflation through budget reforms that adjusted the specific tax rates, improved tax collection methods, and increased revenue from the sale of aid goods. To make it difficult for the government to obtain advances from the Bank of Greece, the Convention specified the establishment "of a Currency Committee which will have statutory management of the note issue" and that "new issues of currency will only be made with the unanimous approval of the Committee." The Committee consisted of three Greek cabinet ministers, one Briton, and one American. It met in April 1946 and remained a feature of the Greek economy into the early 1950s. Through its control of the note issue this supracentral bank exercised a pervasive influence on government expenditures, foreign exchange, and credit.

To enforce fiscal and monetary discipline, Greece consented to stabilize the drachma in terms of the pound and dollar through open-market operations in gold sovereigns (the drachma was devalued and parity set at rates prevailing in the black market). This restored internal gold convertibility. The position of the gold reserve became an indicator of the degree of inflationary pressure and the need for action by the Currency Committee.

The Bank of Greece began open-market sales of gold sovereigns. Prices began to fall. Fiscal deterioration continued into early 1946 (in January and February receipts covered only 45 and 36.5 percent of expenditures, but rose to over 50 percent in March), but then the situation improved. For February and March the government borrowed 204 billion drachma from the Bank of Greece but only 196 billion for the final 9 months of 1946. The rise in national income aided stabilization; it increased 62 percent in 1946 and 34 percent in 1947 (in 1946 it was still only about one-half its 1938 level). Public confidence was restored as demonstrated by the 4-fold rise in real balances, comparable to their rise in Germany and Hungary II one year after their successful stabilizations (in Austria and Hungary I the rise was 2.6-fold and in Poland 2.5-fold). By January 31, 1947, the public was, however, holding real money balances only about 40 percent as large as it held, on average, during the final five months of 1939. Hyperinflation may have had a long-lasting influence on asset choices and transaction arrangements.

III. THE TRANSITION COSTS

Historical studies and simulations of Phillips curves for modern industrial countries show that the transition from high inflation to price level stability can be protracted and costly.[12] Critics discount the results, arguing that the behavior of economic agents will not remain invariant when monetary and fiscal regimes change. Rather, they will modify their expectations and compensation demands, permitting brief transition periods and small production and employment losses.[13] Because the stabilization of hyperinflationary economies involves drastic changes in regimes, stabilizations have become a testing ground for the critics. Sargent claims that his evidence supports the rational expectations view because unemployment either fell (Germany), got no worse (Hungary I and Poland), or while it rose (Austria), the rise started before stabilization. Bomberger and I have claimed that in Hungary II the rise in unemployment was less than expected and might have been due to other factors.[14] There are reasons for questioning the relevance of the findings for other episodes. In each country stabilization occurred during major real dislocations, making it difficult to identify its specific cost. For example, Austria and Hungary I were greatly reduced in size and Austria forced to absorb great numbers of civil servants from the old empire. Germany lost substantial territory and Hungary II was a major battlefield. And hyperinflation economies are unlikely to have staggered long-term nominal contracts and economic agents with adaptive expectations. Rapid reductions in inflation can occur without severe costs. Such a finding cannot discriminate between the rationalist and conventional views.

The Greek experience provides no further insight. While real national income and industrial production rose substantially in 1946 and 1947 and

[12] See Robert J. Gordon, "Why Stopping Inflation May Be Costly: Evidence from Fourteen Historical Episodes" in *Inflation: Causes and Effects*; and Arthur Okun, "Efficient Disinflationary Policies," *American Economic Review*, 68 (May 1978), pp. 348–52.

[13] See Thomas Sargent and Robert Lucas, "After Keynesian Macroeconomics" in *After the Phillips Curve: Persistence of High Inflation and High Unemployment*, Federal Reserve Bank of Boston, Conference Series No. 19 (June 1978), pp. 49–73.

[14] Sargent's conclusion for Germany comes from p. 287 of Frank Graham, *Exchange, Prices, and Production in Hyperinflation Germany, 1920–23* (New York, 1930). Graham also shows (p. 317) that the wholly unemployed among trade union members rose from 3.5 percent in August 1923 to 28.2 percent in December while the partially unemployed rose from 26 percent to 42 percent. For the Hungarian experience, see Bomberger and Makinen, "The Hungarian Hyperinflation."

804 *Makinen*

unemployment declined from 197,000 in the summer of 1946 to 122,000 on December 31, 1947, few staggered nominal contracts were likely to have been in force when stabilization occurred.[15]

Garber claims that Sargent's concept of the transition costs is too narrow.[16] He argues that even if economic agents correctly predict and respond to new policy regimes, large unemployment and output costs might still emerge because in severe inflations relative prices are likely to change: wages relative to profits, skilled wages relative to unskilled, consumer goods relative to producer goods, and so forth. The changes create incentives to alter the capital intensity of production, the technical nature of capital, the quantity of capital, and the allocation of resources. The alterations are often made possible by loans at subsidized interest rates and by government using the proceeds of the inflation tax to expand the size of state-owned enterprises such as railroads and public utilities. In addition, the desire to economize on the use of money encourages vertical integration. Once stabilization occurs and relative prices adjust to the new steady state, new incentives changing the industrial structure can cause lost output and unemployment. Garber provides evidence that the costs were considerable for Germany and not incurred until 1925–1926.

Data are not available to quantify the rationalization costs for the other hyperinflations.[17] They may be small in the Greek case as Greece did not experience an industrial boom, its national income was chronically depressed, credit was insignificant, and the proceeds of the inflation tax were not used to expand state-owned enterprises.

IV. CONCLUSIONS

The origin of the Greek hyperinflation is similar to that of other episodes during which governments relied too heavily on the inflation tax. Those governments were forced to enact a stabilization program when the tax base disappeared. The Greek program was also similar to those enacted by the other countries. Unlike the other experiences, price level stability did not follow immediately after the initial effort. It occurred 18 months later when, in a third reform embodied in the Anglo-Hellenic Convention, the fiscal system was strengthened and an

[15] The index of industrial production (1939 = 100) rose from 38.3 in January 1946 to 59.7 in March 1947. Unemployment data were not gathered systematically. The observations for 1946 and 1947 were taken, respectively, from a survey made by the Allied Mission for Observing the Greek Election and the *Annual Report of the Bank of Greece for 1948* (Athens, 1948), p. 72.

[16] Peter M. Garber, "Transition from Inflation to Price Stability," *Carnegie-Rochester Conference Series on Public Policy* (Monetary Regimes and Protectionism), 16 (Spring 1982), pp. 11–42.

[17] For a qualitative discussion of the change in production technique and resource reallocations during the Austrian hyperinflation, see J. van Walras de Bordes, *The Austrian Crown* (London, 1924).

Greek Hyperinflation   805

independent monetary authority (the Currency Control Committee)
which was committed to maintaining stable prices was created.

The total cost of the stabilization cannot be accurately measured, but
the evidence suggests that it may have been small. Because of severe
wartime dislocations and the absence of numerous staggered long-term
nominal contracts, the cost incurred in Greece may not be indicative of
the cost other high-inflation countries contemplating stabilization can
expect to incur.

[21]

The Hungarian Hyperinflation and Stabilization of 1945–1946

William A. Bomberger

University of Florida

Gail E. Makinen

Georgetown University

Inflation in Hungary after World War II was the most intense on record. The reforms of August 1946 were immediately and entirely successful in stabilizing prices. This paper describes and analyzes the unique policies and institutions that produced these phenomena. Despite its severity, the Hungarian experience was consistent with the less extreme inflation and stabilization experiences examined by Sargent. Price stabilization was accomplished by fiscal rather than purely monetary measures and was, paradoxically, accompanied by rapid and prolonged money growth.

Any attempt to study this era is fraught with difficulties. Hungarian state archives are in reality closed. Because this period is now 36 years in the past, few individuals associated with it are still alive, outside Hungary. Fortunately, we located several strategically placed officials in the U.S. and Hungarian governments who provided us with information that made it possible to conclude our study. We were able to locate these individuals through the assistance of Professor Joseph Zrinyi, S.J., of Georgetown University; Aladar Szegedy-Maszak, Hungarian Minister to the United States, 1945–46; and Professor William Fellner. With their assistance, we traced Dr. Arthur Karasz, president of the Hungarian National Bank (the central bank of Hungary) from August to December 1945, and a member of its board of directors until June 1946. Dr. Karasz provided us with a great deal of information on the inflationary process, the unique Hungarian experience with indexed money, and institutional details surrounding the successful stabilization. Dr. L. László Ecker-Racz, economic counselor to the Allied Control Commission (the allied occupational authority in Hungary) and later economic counselor at the American Legation in Budapest, made available two extensive statistical and economic analyses of the Hungarian economy and state finances during and after the hyperinflation. The data used in these studies were provided to the U.S. Legation by the government of Hungary. Many of these data have been hitherto unavailable to researchers. We were unable to inspect the Hungarian archives, but Dr.

[*Journal of Political Economy*, 1983, vol. 91, no. 5]
© 1983 by the University of Chicago.

From July 1945 until August 1946, Hungary experienced the worst hyperinflation on record. In this brief period of 13 months, the price level rose by a factor of 3×10^{25}. When stabilization was achieved on August 1, exchange of old for new currency was at a rate of 400 octillion to one. This contrasts with the conversion in Germany's famous hyperinflation of a trillion to one.

Every hyperinflation offers insight into the inflation process and anti-inflationary policy. Aside from its severity, Hungary's 1945–46 experience is unique in a number of respects. First, of all the countries after World War I experiencing an episode of hyperinflation, only Hungary had the misfortune to suffer a second hyperinflation after World War II. Second, in Cagan's (1956) seminal study of the demand for money in hyperinflations, Hungary stands out as posing the most formidable data problems. Third, Hungary is unique in its extensive experiment with indexed money.

It is remarkable, in the light of the magnitude of this hyperinflation, that it has yet to receive a systematic treatment.[1] We propose to fill this gap. We are able to do so because of newly uncovered data on the Hungarian money stock and public finances and the use of resources unavailable or unexploited by other researchers.

Our paper has three goals. First, we will discuss the origin and magnitude of this hyperinflation in terms of the state of Hungary's public finances, the depressed level of national income, and the use of indexed money. Second, using new money data, we are able to explain the anomalous movement in the deposit to note ratio described by Cagan (1956). Third, we will describe what we believe to be the crucial elements in the Hungarian stabilization program and draw appropriate lessons for contemporary stabilization strategies along lines consistent with rational expectations.[2]

Janos Fekete, currently first deputy president of the Hungarian National Bank, was responsive to our written requests seeking clarification of some of the data on the money stock during this period. We are especially grateful to Professors Zrinyi and Fellner, Doctors Karasz, Ecker-Racz, and Fekete, and Mr. Szegedy-Maszak for the time they shared and the useful data they furnished. We wish to offer special thanks to Professor Phillip Cagan for his encouragement and useful comments on an earlier draft. Finally, we gratefully acknowledge the assistance of James Harris, Vincent Marie, Thomas Woodward, and Eileen Mauskopf as well as the useful comments of an anonymous referee.

[1] The best partial accounts available in English are to be found in Kaldor (1946), Nogaro (1948), Cagan (1956), Falush (1976), and Bomberger and Makinen (1980). See also Kemény (1952), Ecker-Racz (1954), Eckstein (1955), Helmreich (1973), and Berend and Ranki (1974).

[2] In this endeavor, our work is complementary to a recent study by Sargent (1980).

I. The Hyperinflation of 1945–46

*The Depressed Level of National Income and
the State of Public Finances*

It is frequently asserted that the cause of hyperinflation rests in a government whose political survival is so precarious that it cannot levy sufficient explicit taxes. It is, therefore, forced to rely on the issue of new money as the principal source of tax revenue. This is an apt characterization of the situation in Germany, Austria, Hungary, Poland, and Russia following World War I. It has an element of truth when applied to Hungary after World War II, but it is not the whole truth. In Hungary in 1945, unlike post–World War I Hungary, the prevailing political party (the Smallholders) commanded an absolute majority in the National Assembly, having received 60 percent of the vote in the November 1945 election. Hungary was, however, governed by a coalition that included the Communist party. This government appeared to enjoy wide popular support. The coalition was agreed on before the election as a means of achieving political unity during the difficult postwar reconstruction period.

Because Hungary had been one of the lesser Axis powers, its government did not enjoy complete sovereignty. In most matters, especially foreign affairs, the decisions of the government were subject to the approval of the Allied Control Commission, a group dominated by the Soviet Union (in accord with the Yalta agreement). We describe below the role of the Control Commission in the hyperinflation.

In addition, unlike the countries experiencing hyperinflation after World War I, Hungary was a major battleground in World War II. For 6 months beginning in October 1944 the front line moved across Hungary, accompanied by heavy fighting. Budapest was liberated only after a long siege and heavy street fighting. As the German army retreated, it pursued a policy of removing much of the portable capital stock to Germany and destroying much that remained (e.g., the railroad system).[3] A great deal of the remaining physical capital was systematically removed by the Soviet army.[4] It is estimated that World War II destroyed some 40 percent of the nonhuman wealth of Hungary (Commercial Bank of Pest 1947). The mass deportation and

---

[3] For a detailed account of war damage, see Berend and Ranki (1974, pp. 180–82).

[4] Under the Potsdam Agreement, the Soviet Union was entitled to the possession of all German property in Hungary. They interpreted this right broadly and removed much equipment that, while not German owned, had been produced in Germany. There is no doubt that this equipment removal was extensive, for German economic penetration of Hungary was substantial (see Kemény 1952, pp. 169–76). The U.S. government strongly protested this policy (see *New York Times*, July 27, 1946, pp. 1, 11).

extermination of Hungary's Jews and the prisoner-of-war status of many of the young men who formed the basis of the Hungarian army deprived the country of badly needed human capital. While precise calculation of the national income for 1945 is questionable, it is estimated at 40–50 percent of the prewar level.[5]

When Hungary signed the armistice on January 20, 1945, ending its state of belligerence against the Allies, it consented to pay reparations of $300 million.[6] For the first reparations year (ending on January 20, 1946), Hungary was obligated to furnish to the Soviet Union $33 million in goods, exclusive of any costs for preparation and shipment. Should she fail to meet the scheduled payments, an interest penalty of 5 percent per month was to be imposed. In addition, she agreed to pay the full cost of the Soviet army transiting through Hungary to and from Germany. The size of the Soviet garrison was estimated to vary from 500,000 to 700,000 men (see Ecker-Racz 1946b, p. 149). This combination of reparations and occupation costs accounted for 25–50 percent of monthly expenditures by the Hungarian government during the hyperinflation (see table 1).

The revenue and expenditures of the Hungarian government are reported in table 1 on a monthly basis for all except the final 2 months of the hyperinflation. These data show that, for all but 3 months, less than 10 percent of expenditures were covered by revenue.[7] It is es-

---

[5] The Hungarians did not compile their national income accounts according to methods used in the United States. For a detailed discussion of their procedures, see Eckstein (1955) and Spulber (1973). Ecker-Racz (1946b, p. 145), reporting data furnished by the Hungarian Institute for Economic Research, gives national income for 1945–46 as 2,541 million pengö compared with 5,192 for 1938–39 (both in 1938–39 prices). While no figure is available for 1944–45, it might reasonably be set at 55–65 percent of the 1938–39 figure, or from 2,860 to 3,375 million pengö. The United Nations Relief and Rehabilitation Agency (UNRRA) estimated that the real wage declined from a monthly high of 54 percent of the 1938 average in August 1945 to a low of 12.8 percent in July 1946. The monthly average during the hyperinflation was 28.3 percent (UNRRA 1947, p. 77).

[6] Of this sum $200 million was to go to the Soviet Union, $70 million to Yugoslavia, and $30 million to Czechoslovakia. In millions of dollars, the Hungarian reparations payable to the Soviet Union in goods were industrial machinery 36.1; ships 12.9; railway equipment 46.4; metals 70.3; grains and seeds 9.0; animals 17.3; and all other 8.0. The real burden of these payments is discussed below. As the indemnity was to be paid in kind, no transfer problem of the kind discussed by Keynes and Ohlin was to emerge.

[7] Revenue collection in Hungary suffered from many problems. First, the tax administration system was badly disrupted. Many experienced tax administrators fled Hungary with the Nazi government in early 1945. Of those remaining, many were removed by postliberation political committees and replaced by large numbers of inexperienced tax collectors. Second, the war caused a massive destruction of public records. Third, the tax base was seriously eroded, in part because of the land reform policy. In early 1945 the government broke up the large estates, which reduced both output and tax revenues. The tax base eroded also because of the cessation of foreign trade, the sharp reduction in the level of economic activity, and the widespread growth, especially as

TABLE 1

Expenditures and Receipts of the Hungarian Government July 1945–May 1946
(Regular Pengő)

	1945 (Millions)						1946 (Trillions)				
	July	August	September	October	November	December	January	February	March	April	May
Expenditures:											
Ordinary	1,726	4,231	8,903	29,143	132,427	304,437	.689	2.480	17.00	189.5	31,900
Deficits of state enterprises	896	1,713	3,703	13,756	54,757	108,198	.194	.720	3.50	36.4	7,500
Reparations	569	2,293	2,256	8,149	49,318	224,627	.318*	1.500	13.00	222.0	24,500
Soviet occupation costs	148	590	1,348	3,915	29,355	46,656	...	...	...	...	...
Allied Control Commission	64	179	349	1,635	5,999	24,997	...	...	...	...	...
Total	3,403	9,006	16,559	56,589	271,857	744,916	1.191	4.700	33.50	448.0	63,900
Revenues	231	746	1,210	3,222	17,973	53,047	.169	.680	4.35	43.8	4,700
Occupation costs and reparations as percentage of expenditures	23	34	23	24	31	40	26	32	39	50	38
Revenues as percentage of expenditures	6.8	5.3	7.3	5.7	6.6	7.1	14.2	14.4	13.0	9.8	7.3

Source.—Ecker-Racz (1946b, pp. 58, 60).

* In 1946 reparations, occupation and control commission costs are combined and reported in the reparations row.

TABLE 2

TREASURY BILLS ISSUED BY THE HUNGARIAN GOVERNMENT
(Billions of Pengö)

	1945		1946
July 3	5.0	January 8	500.0
July 20	5.0	January 30	800.0
August 11	5.0	February 12	2,000.0
September 3	15.0	February 25	4,000.0
September 15	15.0	March 6	10,000.0
October 5	20.0	March 18	25,000.0
October 24	25.0	April 1	100,000.0
October 30	50.0	April 15	500,000.0
November 10	80.0	May 2	2,000,000.0
November 19	200.0	May 11	10,000,000.0
December 4	350.0	May 24	100,000,000.0
December 20	400.0	June 3	300,000,000.0
		June 8	2,500,000,000.0
Total	1,170.0	Total	2,912,000,000.0

SOURCE.—Ecker-Racz (1946*b*, pp. 74, 76).

timated that for the final 2 months of the hyperinflation less than 5 percent of expenditures were covered by tax revenue (*New York Times*, June 28, 1946, p. 6). In table 2 we show the issue of treasury bills necessary to finance the budget deficits.[8]

Since Hungary has the distinction of having had two hyperinflations, we were curious to learn what role the earlier post–World War I experience played in the actions of the central bank and government. We were told by Arthur Karasz (interview, Washington, February 15, 1981) that the central bank did not believe that it was operating under any kind of real-bills doctrine or that the inflation was due to speculative movements in the foreign exchange rates. Rather, the central bankers were monetarists in the sense that they knew that the policy of discounting treasury bills to finance a large deficit would lead inevitably to a repetition of the earlier episode. The officials of

---

inflation accelerated, of what we now call the underground economy. In 1945, approximately 75 percent of tax revenues came from the turnover tax and from the state monopolies on alcohol and tobacco (see Ecker-Racz 1946*b*, p. 71). To our knowledge, this is the first time these data on state finances and treasury bill issues have been published.

[8] An important distinction between the second Hungarian hyperinflation and the first was the limited role played in the former by credit granted to the private sector by the central bank. The overwhelming proportion of the bills discounted by the central bank (over 90 percent) were those of the Hungarian treasury. This resulted from the presence of a credit allocation system operated by a body called the Economic High Council. Thus, even though the central bank's discount rate remained at only 3 percent throughout the second hyperinflation, the private sector could not obtain unlimited funds at negative real interest rates.

the central bank continually warned the Allied Control Commission of the consequences of this policy. The Soviets, who dominated the Commission, turned a deaf ear to these warnings, which led some to conclude that the hyperinflation was designed to achieve a political objective—the destruction of the middle class.[9]

In summary, even though Hungary was stable in the political sense that one party commanded a majority in the parliament, the very depressed level of national income in 1944, 1945, and 1946 and the fact that the actions of the Soviets indicated that they wanted inflation made it very difficult for any government to raise sufficient taxes to cover expenditures. Resort was made, therefore, to the inflation tax which governments impose when they can impose no other.[10] This was done, one suspects, although it was quite well known what the ultimate result would be.

The Hungarian Tax Pengö

In an earlier paper (Bomberger and Makinen 1980) we discussed the link between indexed deposits supplied by Hungarian banks (at the insistence of the government) and the severity of the hyperinflation. The existence of these deposits decreased the tax base against which the inflation tax could be levied.[11] To obtain the same real resources, the government was forced to accelerate money growth and the rate of inflation rose dramatically.[12]

[9] The Hungarian central bank was nominally independent of the central government. Article 50 of its statutes forbade granting direct credit to the state. This statute was suspended before World War II and remained suspended during the hyperinflation. On May 7, 1946, the government extended its direct control over the central bank through a decree giving it the power to appoint a commissioner who was to ensure that the work of the bank accorded with the laws of the land, the general economic interests of the country, and the government's credit and foreign exchange policy. The powers of the commissioner were so broad that he became, in effect, the central banker.

[10] Initially, money issue was hampered by a lack of paper and the removal of plates to Germany by the Hungarian Nazi government. Dr. Karasz told us that when he returned to the bombed-out central bank, Hungary did not possess sufficient foreign exchange to pay for the imported ink which had been used for note printing; this money had to be borrowed (interview, Washington, D.C., February 15, 1981).

[11] Our early impression that all bank deposits were indexed by the decree of January 10, 1946, was incorrect. Deposits at the Postal Savings Bank, mainly in provincial areas, were not indexed until July 9, 1946, some 3 weeks before stabilization. Quantitatively, these deposits were sigificant, varying from 16 to 54 percent of total bank deposits. On January 31, 1946, they made up 48 percent of total deposits declining to a low of 16 percent at the end of May. After they were indexed, they rose to a high of 54 percent of total deposits on July 31.

[12] Although indexed deposits were instituted to protect state revenues from depreciation, they were extended to the private sector to reduce the velocity of money by providing an attractive alternative to commodities and foreign currencies. In this regard the tax pengö had an interesting but ill-fated antecedent. On February 25, 1924, the Hungarian government attempted to curb the earlier hyperinflation by introducing the saving crown (or *sparkorona*). Regular paper crowns (the unit of account) could be

As inflation intensified, the popularity of the tax pengö accounts grew. This is shown in table 3 by the very sharp rise in the deposit to note ratio January–April 1946 (the subsequent decline is explained below). By June 1946, it was virtually impossible to find regular pengö currency in circulation in Budapest and other cities, especially after 2 P.M., the hour the banks closed. Businesses and individuals would deposit practically all their currency in banks and withdraw a scaled-up sum the following morning with which to conduct business.[13] It should be noted that the tax pengö itself did not remain immune from depreciation. It did, however, depreciate at a more modest rate than the regular pengö.[14]

In addition to the tax pengö deposits supplied by banks, tax pengö notes were also printed. On May 21, 1946, 2 months before stabilization, the minister of finance was authorized to issue tax pengö notes. They made their appearance the following week. Originally they could be used only for the payment of taxes, and in this regard they correspond to tax anticipation notes issued by the U.S. government. Thus, individuals who had future tax liabilities could purchase these notes and use them to discharge their tax liabilities when they came due. The notes had a term of 2 months and were to lose their value on

---

deposited in saving crown accounts, which were indexed. The index was computed daily on the basis of the crown rate in Zurich and Vienna, the dollar exchange rate of the Foreign Exchange Office in Budapest, and the price of six arbitrage securities traded between Budapest and Vienna. This experiment came to an end on May 31, 1924, at which time the regular crown had depreciated by 25 percent relative to the saving crown. It ended because the adjustment formula tended to rise faster than domestic prices. For a discussion of this earlier effort at indexed money, see Humphrey (1924), Donaldson-Rawlins (1925), Mitzakis (1926), and Ecker-Racz (1933). For its possible effect on the currency/deposit ratio, see Makinen (1981). Mr Karasz (interview, February 15, 1981) related that the tax pengö system was proposed by individuals who remembered the experiment with the saving crown. Others in the government opposed the extension of the tax pengö to the banking system. They feared that indexed accounts would have an adverse psychological effect by convincing the public that the government was not serious about curbing inflation.

[13] Mr. Ecker-Racz (interview, Arlington, Va., February 23, 1981) drew our attention to this phenomenon, which was confirmed by a report in the *New York Times* (July 8, 1946, p. 4). The desire to get rid of currency by 2 P.M. caused serious problems in exchange and distribution. To deal with these, the government on July 8 was forced to decree that food stores and the like remain open until 5 P.M. However, after 2 P.M. they were not required to accept regular pengö notes. The decree also specified that any wage earner could refuse his wages if they were tendered later than 2 P.M. and could insist on being paid the following day at that day's quotation for the tax pengö.

[14] At its inception on January 1, 1946, the value of the price index used for scaling up was that prevailing two days earlier. On March 1, it was advanced to the index number for the preceding day (the government announced the value for the coming day by radio at 6 P.M.). Beginning April 19, 1946, the government scaled up the tax pengö by arbitrary values that fell short of the actual increase in the index. The reason for this change in policy is unclear. Ecker-Racz (1946a, p. 4) states that it was to comply with the somewhat obscure price policy of the Economic High Council (the price-setting authority).

TABLE 3

DEPOSIT TO NOTE RATIO
(End of Month)

1945		1946	
June	.32	January	.18
July	.33	February	.30
August	.27	March	.49
September	.22	April	1.03
October	.13	May	.29
November	.10	June	.31
December	.13	July	9×10^{-8}

the date of expiration, without obligation on the treasury for reimbursement.

On June 13, the minister of finance extended the use of tax pengö notes to cover payment for such things as public utility bills, rail fares, and other services supplied by the state or state enterprises. In addition, the government could make payments with these notes for produce delivered to it under the system then in place, which obligated farmers to furnish a portion of their output to the state.

In May, when the tax pengö notes were introduced, the government was experiencing great difficulty in finding individuals or businesses who would accept regular pengö notes. In the face of this massive repudiation of the regular currency, the government decided to extend the use of tax pengö notes further. On June 23, 5 weeks before the hyperinflation ended, it began to disburse all of its expenditures in these notes. In this regard, the notes functioned much like emergency issues of scrip made by U.S. cities during the 1930s or like the greenbacks issued during the Civil War. In table 4, we show the magnitude of this issue in the final weeks of the hyperinflation.

Because it issued its own money, the government had little need to discount treasury bills with the central bank. Discounting ceased on July 9 and on July 12 the central bank issued its last pengö notes—these bearing a denomination of 100,000,000 trillion regular pengö

TABLE 4

TAX PENGÖ NOTES OUTSTANDING, 1946

	Millions of Tax Pengö
May 29	4,447,810
July 15	11,427,723
July 23	276,698,900
July 31	2,798,667,900

SOURCE.—Ausch (1958, p. 116).

(10^{20}). The data on notes outstanding published for the week ending July 15 reveal that the issue of ordinary pengö notes reached their peak of 76×10^{24}. By July 31, the note issue had fallen to 47×10^{24}. At the official rate of exchange, the total note issue could have been purchased for \$23,245 (or approximately \$2,300 on the black market).

On July 9, the tax pengö notes became legal tender and their printing and distribution were taken over by the central bank. During the few remaining days of hyperinflation, these notes became the sole medium of exchange in Hungary. In the August 1 reform, provision was made for the conversion of the tax pengö notes. They were, however, allowed to circulate after stabilization as an auxiliary and fractional currency. They were gradually withdrawn from circulation during 1946 and early 1947.

Once tax pengö notes were introduced, the government was theoretically returning most of its inflation tax revenue to the public. The portion it kept was determined by the fraction of the rise in the price index that it did not allow to be reflected in the scale-up of the tax pengö.

The effect of the notes was the same as if the tax base had been reduced in the absence of their issue. To obtain the same real revenue it would have been necessary to increase further the rate of regular note issue, aggravating the rate of inflation. Thus, the issuance of tax pengö notes served only to accelerate the rate of inflation by reducing the inflation tax base. These notes also drove the remaining regular pengö notes into the banking system, where they served to increase the rate of deposit creation.

It is hard to avoid the conclusion that tax pengö deposits and notes were anything other than a major contributing factor to the severity of the hyperinflation. Clearly, the lesson is that when governments attempt to raise their revenue from inflation taxes, instituting indexed money may be counterproductive.

II. The Tax Pengö and the Deposit to Note Ratio

Movements in the deposit to note ratio have played the major role in cyclical movements in the money multiplier. Cagan (1956, p. 111) drew attention to this ratio in his examination of the hyperinflation episodes. He observed that, except for the 1945–46 Hungarian episode in which it rose astronomically, this ratio declined as inflation increased.

It was the movement in this ratio that (in our earlier work) caused us to question Cagan's interpretation of the available data. He was aware that both indexed deposits and notes had been issued in Hungary, but he assumed that the data on both notes and deposits reported only the unindexed components. Unfortunately, the data sources available to him (see Hungary, Central Statistical Office 1946; UN Statistical Office 1947) were silent on the important issue of the degree to which indexed and unindexed monies were commingled. We can now state with certainty that the data on deposits do commingle indexed and unindexed components. By July 31, 1946, all deposits were indexed.[15] The currency data used by Cagan (1956) report only the note issue of the central bank. They exclude the indexed currency issued by the Hungarian treasury shown in table 4. The deposit to note ratio was, therefore, computed using indexed deposits and unindexed notes.

The issuing of tax pengö notes and their emergence as the dominant medium of exchange raise the question of their effect, if any, on the deposit to note ratio. We show in table 3 the movement of this ratio incorporating indexed currency. In making these computations, we have used a more complete data set than was available to Cagan. In particular, we have uncovered monthly data on the deposits of the Postal Savings Bank, which were of considerable importance, and, of course, data on the stock of tax pengö notes.[16]

As shown in table 3, the ratio rose after indexed deposits were introduced, reaching a maximum in April. The introduction of the tax pengö notes in May caused the ratio to decline once again, indicating that the Hungarian experience corresponds to the others studied by Cagan.[17]

[15] Several sources confirm this conclusion. Our primary reference is a work by Ausch (1958), available only in Hungarian; we have had portions translated into English. Ausch provides information on the proportion of bank deposits which were indexed (p. 116) and the extent to which indexed currency was issued (p. 119). To learn more about his data sources, we wrote to Ausch (using the good offices of Janos Kornai, Hungarian Academy of Science); but, unfortunately, he had died in 1974. However, Janos Fekete of the Hungarian central bank was able to answer many of our data questions through correspondence. Additional confirmation was provided by Karasz (interview, 1981) and Ecker-Racz (1946b, p. 86).

[16] The only money data still missing are monthly observations on the deposits in provincial banks. Data for these banks are available on a monthly basis for the poststabilization period (August 1946 until the series ends in 1948). These data reveal that the deposits in provincial banks varied between 4 and 10 percent of the total deposits in the Budapest banks and the Postal Savings Bank.

[17] Strictly speaking, the note component of this ratio should measure only currency in circulation outside the banking system. The available data do not allow such a computation. For the July observation, however, the stock of tax pengö notes is so large relative to regular pengö notes that it would make no difference if all regular pengö notes were held by banks. Tax pengö notes were converted to regular pengö using the established conversion ratios in the National Bank of Hungary *Monthly Bulletin* (September 1946, p. 81). The ratio for June is only an approximation as no data are available on the outstanding tax pengö notes for June 30. As a point of interest, the ratio in the poststabilization period (August 1946–April 1948) rose gradually from 0.23 to 0.71.

III. The Stabilization Program

Contemporary views on the success of stabilization efforts generally follow one of two lines. For one group, inflation is generally held to depend on the trend growth of per unit labor costs. This trend growth is frequently called the core or underlying rate of inflation. According to this view, any attempt to bring down the core rate will not be successful in the short run. Rather, a prolonged period of high unemployment is necessary to accomplish a significant reduction in the core rate. The cost of such a policy in lost output is often judged to be too high when fiscal and monetary policy are used alone.

This view is discounted by advocates of rational expectations. They claim that major regime changes lead to major behavioral changes on the part of market participants. That is, once the public believes the government is sincere in reducing inflation, as evidenced perhaps by substantial reductions in budget deficits and moderation in the rate of growth of money, it will modify its behavior accordingly and stabilization will occur without the necessity of a prolonged period of high unemployment. To provide evidence that discriminates between these alternative views, the stabilization phase of hyperinflation episodes has recently attracted attention (Sargent 1980).

We conclude this paper with two sections that examine the Hungarian experience. Although our approach is basically descriptive, we construct our account with the controversy above in mind. In discussing the design of the stabilization program, we emphasize the attempts to provide not only the substance but also the appearance of a regime change. In describing the results of this policy we focus on events that may be used to discriminate between alternative views. The Hungarian experience not only adds another observation to the sample collected by Sargent but also provides an opportunity to examine the effect of the severity of the hyperinflation on the success of the subsequent stabilization.

Preliminaries

A basic goal of a stabilization program is the restoration of the public's faith in the value of money so that monetary exchange will take place once again. The essential ingredients usually include a complete overhaul of the fiscal system designed to achieve a balanced budget both in the near term and over the longer run. Frequently, stabilization programs also involve the additional step of restoring the convertibility of domestic money into gold or stable-value foreign currencies. This step imposes an additional constraint on fiscal policy and serves to reinforce the belief of the public that a serious attempt is being made to balance the budget.

Monetary and fiscal reform may be aided by the availability of foreign loans. On the other hand, it may be made more difficult if the nation in question must pay an indemnity whose amount or amortization schedule is uncertain. Uncertainty here makes individuals uncertain about the resources the government has available for fiscal stability and for currency convertibility.

We have already mentioned several aspects of the Hungarian situation relevant to stabilization: the very depressed state of the economy, the great imbalance in the state budget, the indemnity of $300 million,[18] and the cost to provision the Soviet army of occupation.

Of additional uncertainty was the geographic area of Hungary and the population that was to bear the reparations burden. Under the Treaty of Trianon signed on June 4, 1920, Hungary lost 71 percent of her territory and 60 percent of her population. Hungary's support of the Axis powers during the 1930s led to a restoration of a portion of these so-called lands of the crown of St. Stephen. These territories almost doubled the geographic area of Hungary and increased her population from 9 to 14.6 million. When Hungary signed the armistice on January 20, 1945, she agreed to evacuate all her troops and officials to within the limits of her frontiers as they existed on December 31, 1937 (the Trianon frontiers). The armistice did not, however, settle the question of the size of Hungary. It remained an issue pending a formal treaty.

The August 1 Reform

On August 1, 1946, the Hungarian government introduced an ambitious stabilization program prepared in large part by the Commu-

[18] Of relevance is the real magnitude of foreign claims to Hungarian resources. Under the armistice concluded on January 20, 1945, Hungary promised, in addition to reparations and occupation costs, to restore all legal rights and interests of the United Nations and their nationals as they existed before the war and also to return their property in complete good order. The $300 million indemnity was to be paid over a period of 6 years, with $33 million due to the Soviet Union during the first year. Other claims by the United Nations and their nationals were to be determined at a later date. The sum of $300 million did not include packaging, transportation, and insurance. These additional costs were estimated to add 15–20 percent to the total. Moreover, if Hungary were late in making deliveries, a 5 percent per month interest penalty was to be imposed. The real burden was greater than the nominal sum might suggest. According to the annex to article 12 of the armistice, products delivered for reparations were to be calculated in 1938 prices with an increase of 15 percent for industrial equipment and 10 percent for other goods, to reflect changes in world prices. In interpreting this annex, the Soviet Union determined what 1938 prices should be. Naturally, they were set quite low. Using prices relevant to Hungary, it was estimated that $300 million was, in fact, two or three times that amount. The national income of Hungary for 1946–47 was estimated to be approximately $1 billion (see Commercial Bank of Pest 1947, p. 3).

814

nist party.[19] The government undertook the program on its own initiative. It did not occur at the instigation of the United Nations or the Allied Control Commission, nor was it based on large foreign loans.[20]

Our discussion of the reform is to be organized in terms of its key elements:

1. proposals designed to increase the general acceptability of money;
2. the drastic reform of the fiscal system; and
3. the availability of foreign gifts and loans, the rescheduling of the reparations payments, and the fixing of Hungary's borders.

Measures to Increase the General Acceptability of Money

Apart from monetary and fiscal policies, three measures were designed to increase the general acceptability of the monetary unit.

1. A new unit of account was introduced to replace the badly depreciated pengö. This was the forint (Hungarian for florin, the old stable unit of account of the Hapsburg monarchy).[21] The regular pengö was exchanged for the forint at a rate of 400 octillion to one, while the conversion rate for the tax pengö was fixed at 200 million to one. The forint was given a gold content and the law provided that it was to be covered by gold to 25 percent of its face value. During the first 6 months after the reform the gold cover averaged in excess of 50 percent. However, the forint was not convertible into gold or foreign currencies.[22]

2. The Hungarian government recovered from the United States the $32 million in gold reserves of the central bank removed to Germany by the Nazi government. The gold was returned to Budapest on August 6, amid great press publicity.[23] Another $12 million in gold

[19] The architect of the reform was Professor Eugene Varga of the University of Rostov, a Hungarian who immigrated to the Soviet Union after World War I. It is a curious fact that a Marxist should have drawn up a stabilization program so much in agreement with modern monetary theory. Perhaps this supports the contention that monetary theory does not have an ideological basis.

[20] By contrast, the Hungarian stabilization effort in 1923 was prepared with the active aid of the League of Nations and based on a substantial foreign loan.

[21] Again by way of contrast, the pengö itself was not introduced until January 1, 1927, several years after the successful stabilization following Hungary's first hyperinflation.

[22] In the Hungarian stabilization program worked out with the assistance of the League of Nations in 1924, the Hungarian crown was pegged to the British pound, which did not then enjoy gold convertibility. When the pound was made convertible in 1925, the crown was returned to a gold base, although it was not itself convertible. This was also true of the pengö when it was introduced as the new unit of account. The practice of pegging the Hungarian unit of account to the British pound ended in September 1931 when Britain abandoned the gold standard.

[23] The gold weighed 22 tons and was brought to Budapest in the private train of Adolf Hitler (*New York Times*, August 7, 1946, p. 7).

and foreign exchange (largely in U.S. dollars) was produced from domestic sources during the grace period before laws went into force forbidding such holdings subject to draconian penalties. This combined sum of $44 million, equal in value to F517 million, provided a gold cover in excess of 100 percent for the notes of the central bank on the day the forint was introduced.

3. Article 50 of the statutes of the central bank was reimposed, forbidding the central bank directly or indirectly to lend to the government except on deposit of gold or foreign exchange in equivalent sums for the notes advanced (i.e., the practice of discounting treasury bills was ended). To give the treasury a breathing period before new taxes yielded sufficient revenue to cover expenditures, the law permitted an initial advance of F300 million.[24] The law also specified that prior to July 31, 1947, not more than 1 billion forints in notes could be issued by the central bank.

4. To control the supply of demand deposits, 100 percent reserve requirements were placed initially on commercial banks.

These changes in the nature of the currency unit were more than cosmetic. They accomplished a rather fundamental change. At the margin, the forint was backed by gold, foreign exchange, and commercial bills. The promises of the government did not enter as a factor determining the acceptability of money.[25]

The issue of forint notes proceeded at a faster pace than the formulators of the stabilization program envisioned. By December 1946, the issue of notes came close to exceeding the 1 billion forint limit. It was held below the ceiling only through rigid credit controls and deflation. In January 1947, the authorities waived the ceiling.[26] However, throughout 1947, the 25 percent gold cover was maintained. New notes were advanced only on discount of commercial paper, and the government lived within the limits of article 50 in that no new treasury borrowing was made.

---

[24] This extraordinary advance was not sufficient to cover the budget deficit during 1946 (see table 5). The government borrowed F60 million from the Postal Savings Bank and received F450 million from the profits of the revaluation of the gold reserves of the National Bank and the sale of goods obtained within the framework of UN relief and U.S. aid (see below).

[25] We do not claim that a successful stabilization program must rest on central bank adherence to the real-bills doctrine. Forcing a central bank to pursue such a discount policy remains controversial. We do suggest that the success of this stabilization program is in good measure due to the fact that the government was forced to place its interest-bearing debt with the private sector or with foreign parties whose acceptance depended on the government's fiscal policy.

[26] The original limit seems to have been imposed for psychological reasons. On December 31, 1946, F968 million in notes were outstanding of which 339 million were created in exchange for gold and foreign currencies and 495 million in exchange for commercial bills. The remainder represented notes advanced to the state.

816   JOURNAL OF POLITICAL ECONOMY

Reform of the Fiscal System

A comprehensive reform of the tax system was undertaken. Rates of
taxation were raised considerably over those in force prior to the war.
Income taxes were imposed at a rate of 2 percent on incomes exceeding F1,200 (about $100), rising to a maximum of 60 percent on in-
come from work and 80 percent on income from property. The maximum rates applied to incomes exceeding F84,000. The gross rent on
houses was subject to a tax ranging from 60 to 80 percent. The purchase tax was raised from the prewar rate of 2–5 percent to 3–10
percent. The company tax had to be paid according to turnover,
irrespective of profit. All taxes in arrears were subject to a monthly
penalty rate of 10 percent.

Expenditures were also subject to severe fiscal discipline. Just before stabilization, the number of civil servants was reduced in each
ministry to 90 percent of the number in the 1937–38 fiscal year. The
regular army was reduced to 20,000 and the members of the state
police to 5,000 (see National Bank of Hungary, *Monthly Bulletin,* January–June 1946, p. 21). Drastic economies were effected after stabilization. The civil service was reduced further and government salaries
and pensions were cut to less than 50 percent of those received in
1937–38. The magnitude of this reduction in administration costs can
be seen in the fact that the 1946–47 budget was approximately equal
to that for 1937–38, but with reparations and occupation costs not
found in the earlier budget accounting for some 40 percent of the
total (see Commercial Bank of Pest 1947, p. 7; Hungarian General
Credit Bank 1946, p. 7).

The results of the fiscal reform were dramatic. In August 1946,
only 21 percent of expenditures were covered by tax proceeds. This
rose to 33 percent in September and 96 percent in October. For the
fiscal year 1946–47, table 5 shows that tax revenue covered 78 percent of expenditures, and for fiscal year 1947–48 it covered 96 percent. The budget data also reveal that reparations and occupation
costs continued to be a heavy drain on state finances, amounting to 39
percent in 1946–47 and 27 percent in 1947–48.

These dramatic fiscal results could only have served to reinforce the
belief of market participants that a major regime change had taken
place.

Other Elements

The stabilization program contained or benefited from at least four
other provisions that furnished additional financial wherewithal, reduced uncertainty, or provided psychological support.

1. On May 2, 1946, the U.S. government provided Hungary with a
$10 million credit to purchase surplus American property. On June

TABLE 5

Public Finances of Hungary for Fiscal 1946–47 and 1947–48
(Millions of Forints)

	1946–47	1947–48
Expenditures:		
Goods and services	2,265	3,758
Reparations and occupation costs	1,436	1,707
Planned investment	...	833
Total	3,701	6,300
Revenue:		
Current tax receipts	2,891	6,047
Borrowing and extraordinary sources	812	359
Total	3,703	6,406

Source.—Kemény (1952, p. 138).

19, this sum was increased by an additional $5 million. The UN Relief Agency provided about $4 million in food supplies. These were sold by the Hungarian government and provided an extraordinary source of revenue.

2. On July 29, 1946, a peace conference was convened in Paris to deal with the lesser Axis powers. On that date, the text of the U.S. peace proposal was published together with comments by the USSR and the United Kingdom (see *New York Times*, July 31, 1946, pp. 15–18). The treaty left no ambiguity about the frontiers of Hungary. They were to be identical to those fixed by the Trianon treaty with the exception of several small villages opposite the Czech city of Bratislava, which Hungary was to give up. The text also provided for the continued occupation of Hungary by the Soviet army.

3. The amortization schedule for reparations was firmly fixed. The period of payment was, however, extended from 6 to 8 years. The annual payments to the USSR were fixed, in millions of U.S. dollars, at:

1945	1946	1947	1948	1949	1950	1951	1952
10.2	21.8	23.0	25.0	30.0	30.0	30.0	30.0

(the 1945 figure represents the amount actually delivered). Similar relief was granted by Czechoslovakia and Yugoslavia. Moreover, the $6 million interest penalty for nondelivery of goods in 1945 was canceled,[27] and the Soviet Union consented to take shares of the Petro-

---

[27] After the Communist takeover of Hungary, the Soviet Union suspended the remaining reparations payments. They were used from time to time to persuade a somewhat reluctant Hungary not to deviate too far from the Soviet line.

sani Colliery Company (the most important coal mining company in Rumania, a majority of whose share capital was Hungarian owned) as partial amortization of the 1946 and 1947 reparations payment. This transfer discharged a large fraction of the $21.8 million due in 1946.

4. The government selected August 1 as the date for stabilization because it corresponded to the time when the summer harvest would be brought to market. In addition, a purposeful effort was made to stock the stores of Budapest with imported merchandise to give the impression that goods were plentiful.[28]

IV. The Results

An effective stabilization should bring an abrupt end to inflation. An entirely successful stabilization should be accompanied by an abrupt reduction in expected inflation of equivalent magnitude. A reduction in inflation is easily documented. An accompanying reduction in expected inflation leaves two forms of indirect evidence. First, real money balances should abruptly rise as the public shifts away from foreign currency and barter. The magnitude of the increase should reflect the rate of inflation expected prior to stabilization. Second, unemployment should not rise as wage bargains are struck with the new (lower) rate of inflation in mind.

The results of the Hungarian stabilization effort were dramatic. From August 1 through December 31, 1946, the cost of living rose 6 percent. During 1947 the rise was approximately 19 percent. This modest rise in the price level was achieved in spite of a much more substantial increase in the money supply. The latter increased 221 percent between August 31 and December 31, 1946, and 132 percent during 1947.[29]

Inflation

The low poststabilization inflation rate is consistent with an effective regime change, although it is slightly higher than those reported by Sargent (1980). Before we take these inflation data at face value, we

[28] To obtain some of these goods, Hungary concluded a series of barter treaties during early 1946, with Rumania (April 13), Switzerland (April 27), Austria (May 13), and Poland (June 26). Ecker-Racz (interview, 1981) provided details of the actual barter transactions which involved a clever arbitrage of markets. Large quantities of Hungarian tobacco products, e.g., were sold in Vienna, where their price was high in dollars. The dollars were used to purchase cheap Polish sugar. The sugar was sold in Bucharest where its price was high in broken gold. The gold was taken to Budapest where it was struck by the Hungarian mint into gold Napoleons. These gold coins were then used to buy imported goods from Switzerland.

[29] Money is measured as the sum of National Bank of Hungary notes and all deposits at commercial banks and saving institutions (mainly the Postal Savings Bank).

should note a peculiarity of the Hungarian price system that raises a question about whether what the index reported was representative of price movements.

Prior to stabilization the Hungarian authorities concluded that inflation had distorted relative prices. They therefore set out to recast the entire structure of relative prices. The relative price structure of 1938 was largely accepted for farm prices. The price of wheat was then arbitrarily fixed at F40 per quintal, or 2.1 times the pengö price. On this basis the price of other farm products was determined. Because of the heavy loss of livestock during the war, a price multiplier exceeding that for grain (2.1 as noted above) was given to livestock. Finally, the relation between farm prices as a whole and industrial prices was set in favor of industry.[30]

The intention of the planners was that the forint price level should be on average (as measured by wholesale prices) fourfold the price level expressed in 1938 pengö.[31] As one might expect, these "scientifically" determined prices did not stand the test of time. From the outset they were on the whole quite contrary to those dictated by market forces; that is, agricultural prices were set too low. By July 1947, farm prices were some 70 percent above their December 1946 level, whereas industrial prices had risen on average less than 5 percent.

Not only were prices set artificially, but through the early months of stabilization they were subject to substantial state control, though cost passthroughs were allowed. The official price index soon after the stabilization may understate the true level of prices and, thus, lead to an overstatement of subsequent inflation as the controls were eased. The degree of understatement is difficult to assess. However, while we do know that a black market functioned, especially in foreign exchange, its extent was insignificant, which indicates that the official prices may roughly reflect the actual movement of prices.

Money Growth

Table 6 documents the dramatic increase in the notes outstanding, which, in the presence of relative price stability, represented an al-

---

[30] On the basis of 1938 = 100 for each respective price, the mandated price levels were: agricultural products, 270; animal products, 420; farm products (total), 330; industrial products, 460; all products, 400 (from Kemény 1952, p. 14).

[31] The fourfold increase was arrived at in the following way. Originally the pengö had been defined as 1/3,800 kg of fine gold. The devaluation following the international monetary crisis of 1931 reduced the pengö to 1/5,757 kg of fine gold. The monetary reform of 1946 set the forint equal to 1/13,210 kg of fine gold, producing a ratio of pengö to forint of 2.29 to 1. In setting the new price level, the planners assumed that world prices had risen 75 percent between 1938 and 1946 (2.29 × 1.75 = 4).

TABLE 6

NOTE ISSUE AFTER STABILIZATION
(Millions of Forints)

1946		1947	
August 7	114	January 31	1,017
August 15	227	February 28	1,093
August 23	294	March 31	1,173
August 31	356	April 30	1,258
September 7	416	May 31	1,408
September 15	460	June 30	1,468
September 23	526	July 31	1,592
September 30	607	August 31	1,754
October 7	656	September 30	1,834
October 15	719	October 31	1,869
October 23	745	November 30	1,829
October 31	843	December 31	1,992
November 7	821		
November 15	879		
November 23	852		
November 30	937		
December 7	926		
December 15	988		
December 23	956		
December 31	968		

SOURCE.—National Bank of Hungary, *Annual Report* (1946, p. 17; 1947, p. 28).

most equal increase in real balances.[32] The 17-fold increase in notes outstanding by the end of 1947 with little inflation certainly suggests a perceived regime change. Nevertheless, the data are not entirely consistent with an instantaneous change to expected price stability on August 1. As with other stabilizations the increase in the money supply was large but somewhat protracted.

One explanation is that the stabilization program was not entirely credible to all market participants. Only after they had been convinced by several months of stable prices did some individuals revert to holding the level of money balances commonly maintained in noninflationary times. Alternatively, there may be adjustment costs involved in adjusting one's payments practices and average money balances, leading to a gradual increase in money holding after a sudden change in expectations. Neither explanation seems entirely satisfactory.[33]

[32] Note issue is, of course, not the only measure of the money supply (see n. 29). However, it has the advantages of being available weekly for 1946 and of being more comparable across countries than other measures. Other measures of the Hungarian money supply do not show a significantly different monthly pattern.

[33] These explanations spring from the traditional analysis of the demand for money. Alternatively, one could view the postreform period as one of reintermediation, rather than remonetization of the economy, and explain matters in terms of the demand for

HUNGARIAN HYPERINFLATION

It is interesting that the poststabilization increase in money is larger in this case than in any of the four cases examined by Sargent, perhaps because of the much greater severity of prestabilization inflation. This explanation is made plausible by the fact that the positive relationship between the magnitude of prestabilization inflation and the rate of poststabilization money growth holds within Sargent's group as well.[34]

Unemployment and Output

Evidence on the effect of stabilization on output and employment is spotty and unclear. Stabilization was accompanied by a measurable rise in unemployment. Unemployment among trade union members stood at 10,498 in July 1946 (its monthly average in 1938 was 17,796). It rose to 40,698 in December 1946, reached 81,548 in June 1947, declined through August, and rose to a high of 103,687 in December 1947. For the first 6 months of 1948 (at which time the series ends) it averaged about 116,000 (with a very small deviation).[35] This increase in unemployment is substantial but in no way comparable to the amount of unemployment sometimes alleged to accompany each per-

---

credit. Sargent and Wallace (1982, pp. 1225–27) analyzed the behavior of an economy with private borrowing and lending facilitated by central bank intermediation. Note issue is generated by an accommodative discounting of private debt (consistent with a type of real-bills doctrine). They find that in such a model movements in the supply of money and the price level may not be closely related. One could take the Hungarian experience as evidence in favor of this prediction. As credit markets were reestablished, the central bank accommodated private borrowers by discounting their debt and issuing notes, while refusing to do the same for government. The resulting increase in the supply of money was not associated with comparable inflation, though the prereform increase in the supply of money to finance government deficits led to a different result. In such a model no stable demand for money (notes) exists, which is independent of the asset side of the central bank's balance sheet (see Sargent and Wallace 1982, esp. p. 1226, n. 11).

[34] If we take the month in which prices stabilized as the month of stabilization, we can use the note issue as of the end of that month as a base for calculating poststabilization money growth (weekly data are not available for most countries). For the post–World War II Hungarian case, the ratio of notes on August 31, 1947, to notes on August 31, 1946, is 4.93. Comparable ratios for the other cases are given below.

	Hungary	Austria	Poland	Germany
1-year money ratio	2.66	2.73	3.18	3.91
Inflation rate (percentage increase monthly prices)	46	47	81	322

The comparable inflation rate for post–World War II Hungary is 19,800 (Cagan 1956, p. 26).

[35] See *Monthly Bulletin* (Hungarian National Bank, October–December 1946, p. 132; May–December 1948, p. 165). It is doubtful whether these data are seasonally adjusted.

centage point drop in inflation in the United States. In addition, the highest unemployment seems to occur in late 1947 and 1948, by which time the most skeptical observer should have been convinced of the success of the stabilization program. The extent to which these data are representative of total unemployment is impossible to ascertain. In evaluating their significance, it should be remembered that in early 1947 some 250,000 prisoners of war and deported civilians were returned to Hungary.

Data on output provide an opposite indication, but they, too, are clouded by the extraordinary circumstances. From August 1, 1946, to July 31, 1947, real national income rose by 20 percent and continued to rise dramatically throughout 1947 and 1948 (the years for which data are available).[36] Since the country was recovering from the devastation of a major war, the rise in output is to be expected and the effects of the stabilization may be concealed in this more massive "supply" effect.[37]

The longer-run implications of the August 1 stabilization cannot be told, for Hungary soon moved from a market to a command economy. In June 1947, the Communists managed what was in retrospect a coup d'état.[38] Thereafter, the economy was progressively nationalized and subjected to central planning.

V. Conclusion

This paper has had two general purposes. The first was to discuss the role played by indexed money, the depressed state of national income, and the condition of public finances as factors influencing Hungary's hyperinflation. This discussion was made possible by the use of data and other information hitherto unavailable or unexploited. Its second purpose was to discuss the stabilization effort in order to isolate its key elements, to offer evidence that this is the type of regime change that will change the behavior of market participants, and to see if the severity of an inflation has any implications for the success of stabilization. We tentatively conclude that at least for

---

[36] This large rise in output was a minor but possibly significant factor in the ability of the Hungarian economy to absorb a large poststabilization increase in the money supply without substantial inflation.

[37] Sargent found incomplete and mixed results in this area too. Unemployment rose substantially after the Austrian stabilization, possibly because of dislocation effects following the war; output rose and unemployment fell after the German stabilization (1980, pp. 11, 22).

[38] In May 1947, while the Prime Minister of Hungary, Ferenc Nagy, was on vacation in Switzerland, he was accused by the Communists of complicity in a conspiracy to reestablish the Horthy regime. He was forced to resign and the government passed to the left-wing elements in his party. By 1948, these persons were replaced by Communists.

HUNGARIAN HYPERINFLATION 823

the Hungarian case it did not.[39] Price level stability was achieved rapidly, without a period of prolonged massive unemployment.

References

Ausch, Sandor. *Az 1945–1946 évi infláció és stabilizáció* [Inflation and stabilization during 1945–1946]. Budapest: Kossuth, 1958.

Berend, Ivan T., and Ranki, Gyorgy. *Hungary: A Century of Economic Development.* New York: Barnes & Noble, 1974.

Bomberger, William A., and Makinen, Gail E. "Indexation, Inflationary Finance, and Hyperinflation: The 1945–1946 Hungarian Experience." *J.P.E.* 88 (June 1980): 550–60.

Cagan, Phillip. "The Monetary Dynamics of Hyperinflation." In *Studies in the Quantity Theory of Money,* edited by Milton Friedman. Chicago: Univ. Chicago Press, 1956.

Commercial Bank of Pest. *Survey of the Economic Situation in Hungary.* Budapest, January 1947.

Donaldson-Rawlins, E. C. *Report on the Commercial and Industrial Situation in Hungary.* London: His Majesty's Stationery Office, 1925.

Ecker-Racz, L. László. "The Hungarian Thrift-Crown." *A.E.R.* 23 (September 1933): 471–74.

———. *Hungarian Currency Stabilization, 1946.* Budapest: U.S. Legation, 1946. (*a*)

———. *Hungarian Economic Developments January 1945–June 1946.* Budapest: U.S. Legation, 1946. (*b*)

———. *The Hungarian Economy, 1920–1954.* Washington: Council Econ. and Indus. Res., 1954.

Eckstein, Alexander. "National Income and Capital Formation in Hungary 1900–1950." In *Income and Wealth,* ser. 5, edited by Simon Kuznets. London: Bowes & Bowes, 1955.

Falush, Peter. "The Hungarian Hyper-inflation of 1945–46." *Nat. Westminster Bank Q. Rev.* (August 1976), pp. 46–56.

Helmreich, Ernst C., ed. *Hungary.* Westport, Conn.: Greenwood, 1973.

Humphrey, R. J. E. *Report on the Commercial and Industrial Situation in Hungary.* London: His Majesty's Stationery Office, 1924.

Hungarian General Credit Bank. *Report.* Budapest, August 1946.

Hungary. Central Statistical Office. *Rev. Hongroise Statis.,* nos. 10–12 (October–November 1946), pp. 154–56.

Kaldor, Nicholas. "A Study in Inflation." Pts. 1, 2. *Manchester Guardian Weekly* (November 29, 1946) and (December 6, 1946).

Kemény, György. *Economic Planning in Hungary, 1947–49.* London: Royal Inst. Internat. Affairs, 1952.

Makinen, Gail E. *Money, Banking, and Economic Activity.* New York: Academic Press, 1981.

Mitzakis, Michel G. *Le Relèvement financier de la Hongrie et la société des nations.* Paris: Presses Univ. France, 1926.

[39] Phillip Cagan offered the interesting observation that the more severe the hyperinflation, the fewer may be the obstacles to a successful stabilization. This is because of the effect of inflation on fixed-interest-rate contracts. When the inflation becomes severe, such contracts disappear, making the public much more accepting of the sudden transformation required for an abrupt stabilization (personal communication from Professor Cagan, January 4, 1981).

824   JOURNAL OF POLITICAL ECONOMY

National Bank of Hungary. *Annual Report*. Budapest, 1946, 1947.
————. *Monthly Bulletin*. Budapest, various issues, 1945–48.
Nogaro, Bertrand. "Hungary's Recent Monetary Crisis and Its Theoretical Meaning." *A.E.R.* 38 (September 1948): 526–42.
Sargent, Thomas J. "The Ends of Four Big Inflations." Conference Paper no. 90. Cambridge, Mass.: Nat. Bur. Econ. Res., 1980.
Sargent, Thomas J., and Wallace, Neil. "The Real-Bills Doctrine versus the Quantity Theory: A Reconsideration." *J.P.E.* 90 (December 1982): 1212–36.
Spulber, Nicolas. "National Income and Its Distribution." In *Hungary*, edited by Ernst Helmreich. Westport, Conn.: Greenwood, 1973.
United Nations Relief and Rehabilitation Agency. *Economic Rehabilitation in Hungary*. London: UNRRA European Regional Office, May 1947.
United Nations Statistical Office. *Monthly Bull. Statis.*, no. 6 (June 1947).

Name Index